# ADDENI

## to the
## Publisher's Preface

The Cook's Own Book, with its 13 editions before 1860, was widely distributed in both the South and the North by the beginning of the Civil War. Prior to 1861, most books were published in the North—particularly in Philadelphia and Boston. The commercial links between the two regions of the country ensured that books were widely disseminated, and the first edition from which this reprint was made was used by a distinguished—and divided—household in Tennessee.

As the Publisher's Preface states, Mary Middleton Rutledge Fogg was the granddaughter of two signers of the Declaration of Independence. Her husband, who was born in New England and whose family later gave the funds to build the Fogg Museum in Boston, took the oath of allegiance to the Union. Henry, one of the Fogg's sons, served in the Confederate Army as aide-de-camp to General Felix K. Zollicoffer. The general and Major Fogg were killed on January 19, 1862 at the Battle of Fishing Creek, Kentucky. (Zollicoffer was the first Confederate general to be killed in battle.) After a successful skirmish, Zollicoffer saw "friendly" troops some distance off, and rode toward them with his aide by his side. Unfortunately, his eyesight failed him and the Union troops he mistook for Confederates mortally wounded the two Tennesseeans. (Mary Fogg's brother, Lieutenant Colonel Arthur Middleton Rutledge, was also at Fishing Creek commanding an artillery unit the day his nephew was killed.)

There is no record that this conflict of loyalties within the Fogg family led to any major familial disintegration. Francis Fogg, in spite of his political sympathies, was considered one of the most able lawyers in Tennessee. (James K. Polk, 11th President of the United States, was a member of his law firm.) Fogg also served as a senator in the Tennessee Legislature.

The Cook's Own Book  was the cooking bible for families on both sides in a conflict which claimed the lives of more Americans than any war before or since. Many of the meals prepared by Civil War units were based on recipes from this book. Indeed, these recipes can be viewed as the foundation on which cookbooks of today are based. The Cook's Own Book is a valuable reference for Civil War reenactors and Living History cooks.


Edmund B. Stewart
Publisher

THE

# COOK'S OWN BOOK:

BEING A COMPLETE

## CULINARY ENCYCLOPEDIA:

COMPREHENDING ALL VALUABLE RECEIPTS

## FOR COOKING MEAT, FISH, AND FOWL,

AND COMPOSING EVERY KIND OF

### SOUP, GRAVY, PASTRY, PRESERVES, ESSENCES, &c.

THAT HAVE BEEN PUBLISHED OR INVENTED

### DURING THE LAST TWENTY YEARS.

PARTICULARLY THE VERY BEST OF THOSE IN THE

COOK'S ORACLE, COOK'S DICTIONARY, AND OTHER SYSTEMS OF

DOMESTIC ECONOMY.

WITH

## NUMEROUS ORIGINAL RECEIPTS,

AND A COMPLETE SYSTEM OF

## CONFECTIONERY.

---

### BY A BOSTON HOUSEKEEPER.

---

ALPHABETICALLY ARRANGED.

---

PUBLISHED

IN BOSTON, BY MUNROE AND FRANCIS;

NEW YORK, BY CHARLES S. FRANCIS, AND DAVID FELT; PHILADELPHIA
BY CAREY AND LEA, AND GRIGG AND ELLIOT.

1832.

*1*

THE

# COOK'S OWN BOOK

BEING A COMPLETE

## CULINARY ENCYCLOPEDIA:

COMPREHENDING ALL VALUABLE RECEIPTS

## FOR COOKING MEAT, FISH, AND FOWL,

AND COMPOSING EVERY KIND OF

## SOUP, GRAVY, PASTRY, PRESERVES, ESSENCES, &C.

THAT HAVE BEEN PUBLISHED OR INVENTED

## DURING THE LAST TWENTY YEARS.

PARTICULARLY THE VERY BEST OF THOSE IN THE

COOK'S ORACLE, COOK'S DICTIONARY, AND OTHER SYSTEMS OF

DOMESTIC ECONOMY.

WITH

## NUMEROUS ORIGINAL RECEIPTS,

AND A COMPLETE SYSTEM OF

## CONFECTIONERY.

———————

## BY A BOSTON HOUSEKEEPER.

———————

ALPHABETICALLY ARRANGED.

———◆———

PUBLISHED

IN BOSTON, BY MUNROE AND FRANCIS;

NEW YORK, BY CHARLES S. FRANCIS, AND DAVID FELT; PHILADEPHIA

BY CAREY AND LEA, AND GRIGG AND ELLIOT.

———————

1832

Library of Congress Catalogue Number  96-92400

Stewart, Edmund B. Sr.,  1933 -

The Cook's Own Book (1832).

Includes Publishers Preface on the historical significance of the book and its original owner,

and a Supplemental Glossary of Terms.


ISBN:  09652120-0-9    UPC 607019

1. Reference on Historic Cooking
2. Rare Books
3. History of Cooking
4. Cook Books

RARE BOOK REPUBLISHERS

P. O. Box 3202
Merrifield, Virginia. 22116-3202

# ACKNOWLEDGMENT

An undertaking such as this is not completed without the contributions of many people. The greatest contribution was, of course, made by the original author of *The Cook's Own Book*, A Boston housekeeper, who was in real life Mrs. N. K. M. Lee, of whom I know little, save her compilation of some 2,500 recipes in a volume which went through at least 13 editions before 1860.

Karen Hess, the foremost authority on culinary history in the United States, gave me enthusiastic encouragement and advice. Mrs. Hess was also a great help in clarifying many of the definitions for the Supplemental Glossary. I wish we could have made a facsimile copy of the original, but its condition made that impossible. However, the tedious effort we had to go through in making this reprint had its rewards: my familiarity with the full text of *The Cook's Own Book* was immeasurably enhanced by scanning, proofing, and reproofing of the reprint.

Barbara and Ben Smith, my cousins in Mt. Pleasant, SC, provided both encouragement and a photograph of the original owner of my copy of the book, Mary Middleton Rutledge Fogg. Barbara Doyle was kind enough to give me numerous articles about Mary Fogg and her contributions to the restoration of Mount Vernon, as well as a slide of Septima Sexta Middleton Rutledge from the collection at the Middleton Place Foundation. The Tennessee State Museum provided a photograph of the portrait of Francis Brinley Fogg, which hangs in the office of the Lieutenant Governor of Tennessee.

Paul Malone, a neighbor and friend, provided not only encouragement. but also wise counsel on publishing this book, since he has written two books and published them through his own Synergy Press.

I also want to thank Dan Poynter, for his very instructive book, The Self-Publishing Manual, which gave me clear sailing down the publishing path.

The greatest help and support has come from my wife of 39 years, Carolina Waring Stewart, who has filled the role of First Sergeant, Vice President for Operations, and Chief Editor for this undertaking. My thanks, and love, go to her.

# Publisher's Preface
## to
## The Cook's Own Book
## (1832)

It was almost like discovering that rare treasure in your grandmother's attic. Nine years after my mother's death, we finally stopped moving around the country long enough to unpack a large number of book cartons which had been in storage all those years. Some of the leather-bound books are very old; among them was an edition of Don Quixote, published in Paris in 1732. But the one which appealed to me most was _The Cook's Own Book_, written by "a Boston Housekeeper" (Mrs. N. K. M. Lee), printed in Boston in 1832, and inscribed with the name of the original owner, containing literally hundreds and hundreds of recipes. It also includes a long treatise on cooking— methods of cooking, the importance of the cook, healthy cooking, care of cooking utensils of the time, and how to judge the quality of meat, fish, fowl, fruits and vegetables. _The Cook's Own Book_ went through no less than 13 editions between 1832 and 1860, and was one of the most influential cooking encyclopedias ever published in this country.

Mary Middleton Rutledge Fogg
_Courtesy of the Rev. and Mrs. Benjamin Bosworth Smith_

Francis Brinley Fogg
_Courtesy ot the Tennessee State Museum, Historical Society Collection_

The book was owned by Mary Middleton Rutledge Fogg, my third great-aunt, and the granddaughter of two signers of the Declaration of Independence. Those familiar with the history of South Carolina, Tennessee, and Massachusetts will no doubt recognize one or more of her names, for Arthur Middleton and Edward Rutledge were two who signed the Declaration for South Carolina, and Fogg is a name well known in New England. The Fogg Museum in Boston is named for one of that family. It was to Tennessee that the Rutledges moved, and it was there Mary Rutledge met and married Francis Brinley Fogg, recently arrived from New England. Mary Middleton Rutledge Fogg left Charleston, SC in 1816 with her parents, two brothers, and two sisters. She was 15 at the time, and the long trek to Tennessee was made with 20 wagons, more than 50 slaves, and 12 cows. Her father, Henry Rutledge, had inherited 75,000 acres of frontier land along the Elk River at the base of the Cumberland Plateau from his father. The land was given to Edward Rutledge for his service to the country during the Revolution by a "grateful Congress." In 1821, after establishing their plantation called Chilhowee, or "place of the running deer," the Rutledges moved to Nashville and built their town house, Rose Hill. It was here that Mary Fogg, in partnership with her mother Septima Sexta, held classes for what was later to become the first public school in Nashville. The House of Industry as it was called, was for destitute and orphaned girls. Their success in establishing the school resulted in part from the seats on the Board of Trustees of the University of Nashville held by Mary's father and her husband, Francis Brinley Fogg. James K. Polk, serving in the Tennessee legislature at the time, was an ardent proponent of a system of public education in the state, and he and his wife supported the work of Mary Fogg and her mother.

She wrote seven books while living in Nashville. One was controversial at the time, and she did not show her authorship of <u>Barrington's Elements of Natural Science</u>. In it she rejected the politically prevalent theory that Blacks and Whites were different species. ". . . the human race is specifically one: there is no permanent or specific difference between one race and another. We would ask whether the black side of a cow or cat is of a different species from the white."

Mary R. Fogg was one of the first trustees in the program to restore Mount Vernon. She befriended Andrew Jackson and his wife Rachel in Nashville. Letters between them show her friendship was greatly valued by the President-elect at the time of his wife's sudden death. Mary and Francis Fogg endured the early deaths of all of their children. None lived beyond their thirty-first birthday; their eldest, Henry Middleton Fogg, aide to General Felix K. Zollicoffer, was killed with the General on January 19, 1862. General Zollicoffer was the first Confederate general killed in battle during the Civil War, and had been the editor of the Nashville Banner, as well as a Congressman from Tennessee for three terms.

Septima Sexta Middleton Rutledge
*Courtesy of Middleton Place Foundation, Charleston, SC*

Henry Middleton Rutledge, attributed to Rembrandt Peale.
*Portrait owned by Edmund B. Stewart*

While it cannot be proved, it is likely <u>The Cook's Own Book</u> was given by Mrs. Fogg to her niece, Emma Fredericka Rutledge, who came to live with her aunt after the untimely death of her mother, Henrietta, at thirty-five, when Emma was just one year old. Emma married another prominent Nashvillean, William B. Reese, who became the Dean of the Law School at Vanderbilt University.

<u>The Cook's Own Book</u> bears Mrs. Fogg's signature on the title page which is being republished with that intact. A cursory search shows no more than two or three cookbooks were printed in the United States prior to this one, and none which are considered encyclopedias on cooking, as is this one. The author — "A Boston Housekeeper" — begins her Preface: "The cook exercises a greater power over the public health and welfare than the physician. . . . After insanity the most grievous affliction of Providence, or rather improvidence and imprudence, is Dyspepsy: a malady that under different names has decimated the inhabitants of civilized countries, and of almost all countries, in which man is a 'cooking animal.' To the dyspeptic, the sun has no cheering ray, . . . the flowers are without fragrance, music is without melody. . . . This malady is beyond the science of the physician, but within the art of the cook." The Boston Housekeeper gives much instruction on the cook's role in the family. There are two pages devoted to the composition and care of cooking utensils of the 1830s. There follows a treatise on the diet, discussing in particular what is and is not pleasing to the stomach, . . . "But in our general practice of

eating, it cannot be said, 'we eat to live,' but are living passages through which we are constantly propelling solids and fluids, for the sake of pleasing our palate, at the severe cost often of our whole system. . . . As our food, therefore, is proper or improper, too much or too little, so will our blood and our juices be good or bad, overcharged or deficient, and our state of health accordingly good or diseased."

There follows a description of Boiling, Baking, Roasting, Frying, Broiling; observations about Butter ("good for dry constipated habits, but not for such as are bilious, asthmatic, or corpulent"); Honey, Sugar, Salt, Vinegar, and many other condiments and spices. The Preface of some 36 pages concludes with a

drawing of an ox, showing the 18 mentionable parts for eating. Included with the diagram are tables of weights and measurements, and the 1832 prices of various cuts of beef, (sirloin at ten cents a pound), pork, mutton, and fowl.

The next 298 pages begin with 19 recipes in which almonds are the main ingredient; eight for the use of anchovies; 32 for apples. Later, a full page is devoted to beef —cuts, storage, and corrections for tainting. Following are 68 recipes using beef. All in all, there are about 2,500 recipes in The Cook's Own Book. The original glossary has been expanded to include terms which may have fallen out of common use since 1832.

| Arthur Middleton, by Charles Fraser. *Miniature owned by Edmund B. Stewart* | Henrietta Middleton Rutledge, by Samuel S. Osgood. *Portrait owned by Edmund B. Stewart* |

What is so interesting about The Cook's Own Book is the large quantity of recipes which are as "inviting to the palate" today as they were 170 years ago. Through the description of preparing the enormous variety of dishes contained in the book, one gains a very rare glimpse of kitchen-work in American homes almost two centuries past. From that standpoint alone, The Cook's Own Book is of great reference value to those interested in the duties and responsibilities of the household cook in the years of our early history, as well as an encyclopedic collection of recipes which will keep our blood and our juices "good and overcharged!"

One last comment: there are errors in this book. We have intentionally left misspellings which appear in the 1832 edition, and have also given the punctuation as it originally appeared. Hopefully we have not added errors through our efforts to bring you an accurate reprint of this rare book.

*Edmund B. Stewart*
*Annandale, Virginia*
*August, 1996*

# PREFACE.

————

THE cook exercises a greater power over the public health and welfare than the physician, and if he should be a charlatan in his art, alas! for his employers.  Hitherto, or until of late years, the cook has had to educate himself, while the physician appropriates all the knowledge of antiquity, and of every succeeding age; his individual cases are all classed according to general principles, while the rules that have regulated the preparation of our food, have been discordant and unnatural.  In the present age, indeed, cookery has been raised to the dignity of an art, and sages have given their treatises to the world. Vèry has a monument in the cemetery of Père La Chaise, among the tombs of warriors, poets, and philosophers, recording of his life that it was 'consecrated to the useful arts.' Virgil however, writes that the best delights of Elysium were showered upon those who received wounds for their country, who lived unspotted priests, who uttered verses worthy of Apollo, or who, like Vèry, consecrated  their lives to the useful arts.  On the utilitarian principle the cook should be much elevated in public estimation, and were he to form  a strict alliance with the physician, the patriarchal ages would return, and men would die of nothing but sheer old age.

After insanity, the most grievous affliction of Providence, or rather  of improvidence and imprudence, is Dyspepsy; a malady that under different names has decimated the inhabitants of civilized countries, and of almost all countries, in which man is a 'cooking animal.' To the dyspeptic, the sun has no cheering ray, the air no elasticity or balm; the flowers are without fragrance, music is without melody, and beauty without charms. Life is a blank; affection has lost its power to soothe, and the blessings scattered by Providence, are converted into ministers of torment.  Food becomes a bane; the very  staff that supports life, gives the flagellation that renders life a curse.  All that can delight is lost,—but all that can depress and sting, has a  tenfold activity and power.

The dyspeptic's 'May of life, has fallen into the sear, the yellow leaf.'  Sleep that should visit every  pillow but  that of guilt, is to him no friend;   if he slumbers, it is to dream, like Clarence, of hideous forms of suffering, and to wake to their reality. This is but a faint picture of Dyspepsy

> 'Her gloomy presence saddens all the scene,
> Shades every flower and darkens every green,
> Deepens the murmur of the falling floods,
> And breathes a browner horror on the woods.'

This malady is beyond the science of the physician, but within the art of the cook; in the proverb, Doctor Diet is ranked above Doctor Quiet and Doctor Merryman; though all are good.

The late Mr. Abernethy referred almost all maladies to the stomach, and seldom prescribed any remedy but a proper diet. This it is the province of the cook to provide; and the design of this book to indicate. The work is not designed to spread a taste for pernicious luxuries: and every recipe has been sanctioned by custom. The responsibility of the cook is lightened, and his duty facilitated. He has here a dictionary of reference, an encyclopedia of his art. The details are full, and the authority is perfect. There were various works of merit that it was useful for the cook to study, but here are collected the best parts of all, with the convenience of alphabetical arrangement, and, in the compass of a moderate volume. If it is a sin to waste the best gifts of Providence, it should be little less than a felony to spoil them. When we have collected the materials for a house, we never trust the building to an unskilful architect: yet we are often obliged to commit the preparation of our feasts as well as of our common food, to agents without knowledge. This knowledge is now supplied.

More than health depends on the proper preparation of food: our very virtues are the creatures of circumstances, and many a man has hardened his heart, or given up a good resolution, under the operation of indigestion. Who that knows the world, ever solicits with confidence a friendly or charitable act of another before dinner.

The natural and moral world are reciprocally dependent; soul and body are so linked that when one loses its tone the other is deprived of its equanimity. The system of morals therefore becomes identified with that of cookery, and the great English moralist, who was learned in both systems, thus spoke of the connexion ; 'Some people' said Doctor Johnson, 'have a foolish way of not minding, or of pretending not to mind, what they eat. I for my part mind my belly very studiously, and very carefully, and I look upon it that he who does not mind his belly will hardly mind any thing else.'

It been the study of the author, to make every recipe plain, and the proportions certain; little is left to discretion, that could be reduced to measure. The system of confectionery is perfect; and if strictly followed every cook may become a first rate confectioner. Labor, care, and expense have been bestowed upon the work, and the publishers feel so secure of its merit, and of the public want of such a book, that they have caused it to be stereotyped. This would have been hazardous with a novel or almost any literary work; but the number of those who eat is far greater than of those who read. A good book few can estimate; all can enjoy a good dinner, and the publishers anticipate a proportionate encouragement.

Having devised this work for families, we hope that it may offend no one, that we give a word of counsel to domestics: our book may be every way good, yet will its usefulness be much impaired if domestics are not docile and faithful.

We have fortunately, in this country, but one class of people: all are free, and all are politically equal. Our domestics are in New England designated as *help,* to indicate that they are the equals, and assistants, rather than the inferiors of their employers. Yet the feeling of independence may be carried too far, and it may be ungraciously expressed. There is no disgrace, and there should be no shame in filling well a subordinate station; the hired ploughman, maid, or cook are not, in an offensive sense, any more the *servants* of their employers, than the merchant and the lawyer. All these engage to perform certain services for an equivalent, and it is the duty of all to do them faithfully.

The number of domestics is very large—perhaps the average is five to four families—and it may be even greater. Yet, unfortunately for their welfare, interest, or character, they are almost constantly shifting, and in few families do they remain long. In England, a good domestic is often provided for during life, and it is a desirable situation. It might be so here, if our domestics would strive to accommodate themselves to their situation. There is hardly a family, in which a kind, respectful, and faithful domestic might not be retained for years, and at the best wages. Here then is a home, comfort, and friends. Yet the greater number are contented to live a few months in a place, till the best years of life have slipped away, without provision for age, and without friends, or home. The proverb of the rolling stone contains the best lesson for domestics.

Service in any department is no sacrifice of independence. A domestic is in all things as free as any other class, but it is a bad kind of independence that would lead one, when desired to do a thing in the line of a common employment, to do it ungraciously, and rather as an irksome or unjust task, than as a duty.

Minor vexations, frequently repeated, are equal to greater individual calamities; as many small enjoyments constitute much of the pleasures of life. Around the social board every member of the family is collected thrice at least in twenty-four hours. Thither the head of the family returns from the labors or cares of his business to recruit his strength and to relax his mind. If he return to a table constantly and invariably ill spread; to a dinner to which he could invite no friend, and in which he can have no enjoyment; a cloud will gather on the calmest brow, and a feeling of dissatisfaction may be extended to other things. It is not beneath the solicitude of a good wife, who would not suffer any abatement in the affection of which she is the object, diligently to study this book, and constantly to provide a neat and well dressed repast.

BOSTON, March, 1832.

*\*\** *The articles which follow, on Roasting, Boiling, &c. are selected from the Cook's Oracle.*

# MANAGEMENT OF FAMILIES.

In domestic arrangement the table is entitled to no small share of attention, as a well conducted system of domestic management is the foundation of every comfort; and the respectability and welfare of families depend in a great measure on the prudent conduct of the female, whose province it is to manage the domestic concerns.

However the fortunes of individuals may support a large expenditure, it will be deficient in all that can benefit or grace society, and in every thing essential to moral order and rational happiness, if not conducted on a regular system, embracing all the objects of such a situation.

In domestic management, as in education, so much must depend on the particular circumstances of every case, that it is impossible to lay down a system which can be generally applicable.

The immediate plan of every family must be adapted to its own peculiar situation, and can only result from the good sense and early good habits of the parties, acting upon general rational principles.

What one family is to do, must never be measured by what another family does. Each one knows its own resources, and should consult them alone. What might be meanness in one, might be extravagance in another, and therefore there can be no standard of reference but that of individual prudence. The most fatal of all things to private families, is to indulge an ambition to make an appearance above their fortunes, professions, or business, whatever these may be.

The next point, both for comfort and respectability, is, that all the household economy should be uniform, not displaying a parade of show in one thing, and a total want of comfort in another. Besides the contemptible appearance that this must have to every person of good sense, it is productive of consequences, not only of present, but future injury to a family, that are too often irreparable.

In great cities in particular, how common is it that for the vanity of having a showy drawing-room to receive company, the family are confined to a close back room, where they have scarcely either air or light, the want of which must materially prejudice their health.

To keep rooms for show, where the fortune is equal to having a house that will accommodate the family properly, and admit of this also, belongs to the highest sphere of life; but in private families, to shut up the only room perhaps in the house which is really wholesome for the family to live in, is inflicting a kind of lingering murder upon the inmates; and yet how frequently this consideration escapes persons who mean well by their family, but who still have a grate, a carpet, and chairs, too fine for every day's use.

Another fruit of this evil is, seeing more company, and in a more expensive manner than is compatible with the general convenience of the family, introducing with it an expense in dress, and a dissipation of time, from which it suffers in various ways.

Social intercourse is not improved by parade, but quite the contrary; real friends, and the pleasantest kind of acquaintance, those who like to be sociable, are repulsed by it. It is a failure therefore every way — the loss of what is really valuable, and an abortive attempt to be fashionable.

A fundamental error in domestic life of very serious extent, involving no less the comfort than the health of the family, arises from the ignorance or mistaken notions of the mistress of the house upon the subjects of diet and cookery.

The subject of cookery is thought by too many women to be below their attention, or, when practically engaged in, it is with no other consideration about it than, in the good housewife's phrase, to make the most of every thing, whether good, bad, or indifferent; or to contrive a thousand mischievous compositions, both savory and sweet, to recommend their own ingenuity.

If cookery is worth studying, as a sensual gratification, it is surely much more so as a means of securing one of the greatest of human blessings—good health; and we cannot quit this part of the subject of domestic management without observing, that one cause of a great deal of injurious cookery originates in the same vanity of show that is productive of so many other evils. In order to set out a table with a greater number of dishes than the situation of the family requires, more cookery is often undertaken than there are servants to do it well, or conveniences in the kitchen for the purpose. Thus some viands are done before they are wanted for serving up, and stand by spoiling, to make room for others; these are again perhaps to be succeeded by something else; and too often are things served up that had better be thrown away, than to be used for food.

The leading consideration about food ought always to be its wholesomeness. Cookery may produce savory and pretty looking dishes without their possessing any of the qualities of food. It is at the same time both a serious and ludicrous reflection that it should be thought to do honor to our friends and ourselves to set out a table where indigestion and all its train of evils, such as fever, rheumatism, gout, and the whole catalogue of human diseases lie lurking in almost every dish. Yet this is both done, and taken as a compliment. We have indeed the "unbought grace of polished society, where gluttony loses half its vice by being stripped of its grossness." When a man at a public house dies of a surfeit of beef steak and porter, who does not exclaim, what a beast!

How infinitely preferable is a dinner of far less show where nobody need be afraid of what they are eating! and such a one will be genteel and respectable. If a person can give his friend only a leg of mutton, there is nothing to be ashamed of in it, provided it is a good one, and well dressed.

A house fitted up with plain good furniture, the kitchen furnished with clean wholesome-looking cooking utensils, good fires, in grates that give no anxiety lest a good fire should spoil them, clean good table linen, the furniture of the table and sideboard good of the kind, without ostentation, and a well-dressed plain dinner, bespeak a sound judgment and correct taste in a private family, that place it on a footing of respectability with the first characters in the country. It is only the conforming to our sphere, not the vainly attempting to be above it, that can command true respect.

## COOKING UTENSILS.

The various utensils used for the preparation and keeping of food are made either of metal, glass, pottery ware, or wood; each of which is better suited to some particular purposes than the others. Metallic utensils are quite unfit for many uses, and the knowledge of this is necessary to the preservation of health in general, and sometimes to the prevention of immediate dangerous consequences.

The metals commonly used in the construction of these vessels are silver, copper, brass, tin, iron, and lead. Silver is preferable to all the others, because it cannot be dissolved by any of the substances used as food. Brimstone unites with silver, and forms a thin brittle crust over it, that gives it the appearance of being tarnished, which may be accidentally taken with food; but this is not particularly unwholesome, nor is it liable to be taken often, nor in large quantities. The discoloring of silver spoons used with eggs arises from the brimstone contained in eggs.—Nitre or saltpetre has also a slight effect upon silver, but nitre and silver seldom remain long enough together in domestic uses to require any particular caution.

Copper and brass are both liable to be dissolved by vinegar, acid fruits, and pearl-ash. Such solutions are highly poisonous, and great caution should be used to prevent accidents of the kind. Vessels made of these metals are generally tinned, that is, lined with a thin coating of a mixed metal, containing both tin and lead. Neither acids, nor any thing containing pearl-ash, should ever be suffered to remain above an hour in vessels of this kind, as the tinning is dissolvable by acids, and the coating is seldom perfect over the surface of the copper or brass.

The utensils made of what is called block tin are constructed of iron plates coated with tin. This is equally to be dissolved as the tinning of copper or brass vessels, but iron is not an unwholesome substance, if even a portion of it should be dissolved and mixed in the food. Iron is therefore one of the safest metals for the construction of culinary utensils; and the objection to its more extensive use only rests upon its liability to rust, so that it requires more cleaning and soon decays. Some articles of food, such as quinces, orange peel, artichokes, &c. are blackened by remaining in iron vessels, which therefore must not be used for them.

Leaden vessels are very unwholesome, and should never be used for milk and cream, if it be ever likely to stand till it become sour. They are unsafe also for the purpose of keeping salted meats.

The best kind of pottery ware is oriental china, because the glazing is a perfect glass, which cannot be dissolved, and the whole substance is so compact that liquid cannot penetrate it. Many of the English pottery wares are badly glazed, and as the glazing is made principally of lead, it is necessary to avoid putting vinegar, and other acids into them. Acids and greasy substances penetrate into unglazed wares, excepting the strong stone ware; or into those of which the glazing is cracked, and hence give a bad flavor to any thing they are used for afterwards. They are quite unfit therefore for keeping pickles or salted meats. Glass vessels are infinitely preferable to any pottery ware but oriental china, and should be used whenever the occasion admits of it.

Wooden vessels are very proper for the keeping many articles of food, and should always be preferred to those lined with lead. If any substance has fermented or become putrid in a wooden cask or tub, it is sure to taint the vessel so as to make it liable to produce a similar effect upon any thing that may be put into it in future. It is useful to char the insides of these wooden vessels before they are used, by burning wood shavings in them, so as to coat the insides with a crust of charcoal.

As whatever contaminates food in any way must be sure, from the repetition of its baneful effects, to injure the health, a due precaution with respect to all culinary vessels is necessary for its more certain preservation. There is a kind of hollow iron ware lined with enamel, which is superior to every other utensil for sauces or preserves: indeed it is preferable for every purpose.

## DIET.

That we require food, as vegetables require water, to support our existence, is the primary consideration upon which we should take it. But in our general practice of eating, it cannot be said, " we eat to live," but are living passages or channels, through which we are constantly propelling both solids and fluids, for the sake of pleasing our palates, at the severe cost often of our whole system.

A reasonable indulgence in the abundant supplies of nature, converted by art to the purposes of wholesome food, is one of the comforts added to the maintenance of life. It is an indiscriminate gratification of our tastes, regardless of the consequences that may ensue from it, that is alone blamable. But so great is our general apathy in these respects, that even on the occurrence of diseases, from which we are all more or less sufferers, we scarcely ever reflect on our diet, as the principal, if not the sole cause of them. We assign them to weather, to infection, to hereditary descent, to spontaneous breeding, as if a disease could originate without a cause; or to any frivolous imaginary source, without suspecting, or being willing to own, mismanagement of ourselves.

We derive the renewal of our blood and juices, which are constantly exhausting, from the substances we take as food. As our food, therefore, is proper or improper, too much or too little, so will our blood and juices be good or bad, overcharged or deficient, and our state of health accordingly good or diseased.

By aliment, or food, is to be understood whatever we eat or drink, including seasonings; such as salt, sugar, spices, vinegar, &c. &c. Every thing, in short, which we receive into our stomachs. Our food, therefore, consists not only of such particles as are proper for the nourishment and support of the human body, but likewise contains certain active principles, viz. salts, oils, and spirits, which have the properties of stimulating the solids, quickening the circulation, and making the fluids thinner; thus rendering them more suited to undergo the necessary secretions of the body.

The art of preserving health, and obtaining long life, therefore consists in the use of a moderate quantity of such diet as shall neither increase the salts and oils, so as to produce disease, nor diminish them, so as to suffer the solids to become relaxed.

It is very difficult, almost impossible, to ascertain exactly what are the predominant qualities either in our bodies or in the food we eat. In practice, therefore, we can have no other rule but observing by experience what it is that hurts or does us good; and what it is our stomach can digest with facility, or the contrary. But then we must keep our judgment unbiased, and not suffer it to become a pander to the appetite, and thus betray the stomach and health, to indulge our sensuality.

The eating too little is hurtful, as well as eating too much. Neither excess, nor hunger, nor any thing else that passes the bounds of nature, can be good to man.

By loading the stomach, fermentation is checked, and of course digestion impeded; for the natural juice of the stomach has not room to exert itself, and it therefore nauseates its contents, is troubled with eructations, the spirits are oppressed, obstructions ensue, and fever is the consequence. Besides, that when thus overfilled, the stomach presses on the diaphragm, prevents the proper play of the lungs, and occasions uneasiness in our breathing. Hence arise various ill symptoms and depraved effects throughout the body, enervating the strength, decaying the senses, hastening old age, and shortening life. Though these effects are not immediately perceived, yet they are certain attendants of intemperance; for it has been generally observed in great eaters, that, though from custom, a state of youth, and a strong constitution, they have no present inconvenience, but have digested their food, suffered surfeit, and borne their immoderate diet well; if they have not been unexpectedly cut off, they have found the symptoms of old age come on early in life, attended with pains and innumerable disorders.

If we value our health, we must ever make it a rule not to eat to satiety or fulness, but desist while the stomach feels quite easy. Thus we shall be refreshed, light, and cheerful; not dull, heavy, or indisposed. Should we ever be tempted to eat too much at one time, we should eat the less at another. Thus, if our dinner has been larger than usual, let our supper be less, or rather quite omitted; for there is no man, however careful of his health, who does not occasionally transgress in this way.

With regard to the times of eating, they must to a certain degree be conformed to family convenience, but ought to be quite independent of the caprices of fashion. The great things to be guarded against are, either eating too soon after a former meal, or fasting too long.—The stomach should always have time to empty itself before it is filled again.

Some stomachs digest their contents sooner than others, and if long empty it may destroy the appetite, and greatly disturb both the head and animal spirits; for, from the great profusion of nerves spread upon the stomach, there is an immediate sympathy between that and the head. Hence the head is sure to be affected by whatever disorders the stomach, whether from any particular aliment that disagrees with it, or being overfilled, or too long empty. Such as feel a gnawing in the stomach, as it is called, should not wait till the stated time of the next meal, but take a small quantity of light, easily digested food, that the stomach may have something to work on.

Young persons in health, who use much exercise, may eat three times a day. But such as are in years, such as are weak, as do no work, use no exercise, or lead a sedentary life, eating twice in the day is sufficient; or, as in the present habits of society, it might be difficult to arrange the taking only two meals, let them take three very moderate ones. Old and weak persons may eat often, but then it should be very little at a time.

The quality of our food is a subject of greater difficulty than the quantity; moderation is an invariably safe guide in the latter instance; but though always favorable to prevent ill effects from any error in quality, it will not always be effectual.

To a person in good health, with a strong stomach, and whose constant beverage is water, cold or tepid, according to the season, or some aqueous liquor, the niceties of choice in food or cookery are less material than to persons with naturally weak stomachs, or to those in sickness, or for children. But all persons who would to a certainty preserve their health and faculties, and live out the natural term of life, should use plain food, as all high seasonings and compound mixtures have an injurious effect, sooner or later, on the strongest constitutions. If a few instances can be quoted to the contrary, these, like other anomalies in nature cannot constitute an exception to a well established fact.

No part of our aliment is more important than our beverage. It is essential to moisten and convey our more solid food into the stomach, and from thence to the respective parts of the body. To allay thirst, to dilute the blood, that it may circulate through the minutest vessels, to dissolve and carry off by the watery secretions the superfluous salts we take in our food; to answer these purposes no liquid is so effectual as pure water, with the exception of some few cases. No other liquid circulates so well, or mixes so immediately with our fluids. All other liquors are impregnated with particles which act strongly upon the solids or fluids, or both; but water being simple, operates only by diluting, moistening, and cooling, which are the great uses of drink pointed out to us by nature. Hence it is evident that water is in general the best and most wholesome drink; but some constitutions require something to warm and stimulate the stomach, and then fermented liquors taken in moderation are proper; such as beer, ale, cider, wine &c. the choice and quantity of which depend on the age, constitution, and manner of living of the drinker; and to have them pure is above all things essential; as otherwise, instead of being of any benefit, they will be highly detrimental.

Drams, or distilled spirituous liquors, the use of which is unhappily very prevalent, are of the most poisonous qualities; and from their direful effects are the destruction of thousands. From the degree of heat they have undergone in distillation they acquire a corrosive and burning quality, which makes them as certain to kill as laudanum or arsenic, though not so soon.

They contract the fibres and vessels of the body, especially where they are the tenderest, as in the brain, and thus destroy the intellectual faculties. They injure the coat of the stomach, and thus expose the nerves and weaken the fibres till the whole stomach becomes at last soft, flabby, and relaxed. From whence ensues loss of appetite, indigestion, and diseases that generally terminate in premature death. Spirituous liquors in any way, whether alone, mixed with water, in punch, shrub, noyau, or other liqueurs, are all slow poisons.

It would be endless to enter on an account of the different qualities of all sorts of wines, but it may be said in general, that all the light wines of a moderate strength, due age and maturity, are more wholesome for the constitution than the rich, hot, strong, heavy wines; for the light wines inflame the juices of the body less and go off the stomach with less difficulty.

The last thing to be said concerning liquors is, that wine and all other strong liquors, are as hard to digest as solid strong food This is not only evident with respect to persons of weak stomachs and digestion, but also from strong healthy people, who only drink either water or small beer at their meals, and are able to eat and digest almost double the quantity of what they could if they drank strong liquors. It appears very plain, therefore, that we should not drink strong liquors at our meals, as by their heat and activity they hurry the food undigested into the habit of the body, and by that means lay a foundation for various distempers. An abstinence, in short, from fermented liquors would preserve our mental faculties in vigor, and our bodies from many painful disorders that afflict mankind, as there is no doubt that we may principally ascribe to them the gout, rheumatism, stone, cancer, fevers, hysterics, lunacy, apoplexy, and palsy.

## BOILING.

This most simple of culinary processes is not often performed in perfection. It does not require quite so much nicety and attendance as roasting; to skim your pot well, and keep it really boiling (the slower the better) all the while, to know how long is required for doing the joint, &c., and to take it up at the critical moment when it is done enough, comprehends almost the whole art and mystery. This, however, demands a patient and perpetual vigilance, of which few persons are capable.

The cook must take especial care that the water really boils all the while she is cooking, or she will be deceived in the time; and make up a sufficient fire at first, to last all the time, without much mending or stirring. A frugal cook will manage with much less fire for boiling than she uses for roasting.

When the pot is coming to a boil there will always, from the cleanest meat and clearest water, rise a *scum* to the top of it, proceeding partly from the water; this must be carefully taken off as soon as it rises.

On this depends the good appearance of all boiled things. When you have skimmed well, put in some cold water, which will throw up the rest of the scum.

The oftener it is skimmed, and the cleaner the top of the water is kept, the sweeter and the cleaner will be the meat.

If let alone, it soon boils down and sticks to the meat, which, instead of looking delicately white and nice, will have that coarse and filthy appearance we have too often to complain of, and the butcher and poulterer be blamed for the carelessness of the cook in not skimming her pot.

Many put in *milk*, to make what they boil look white; but this does more harm than good: others wrap it up in a cloth; but these are needless precautions: if the scum be attentively removed, meat will have a much more delicate color and finer flavor than it has when muffled up. This may give rather more trouble, but those who wish to excel in their art must only consider how the processes of it can be most perfectly performed: a cook, who has a proper pride and pleasure in her business, will make this her maxim on all occasions.

It is desirable that meat for boiling be of an equal thickness, or, before thicker parts are done enough, the thinner will be done too much.

Put your meat into *cold* water, in the proportion of about a quart of water to a pound of meat: it should be covered with water during the whole of the process of boiling, but not drowned in it; the less water, provided the meat be covered with it, the more savory will be the meat, and the better will be the broth.

The water should be heated gradually, according to the thickness, &c. of the article boiled. For instance, a leg of mutton of ten pounds weight should be placed over a moderate fire, which will gradually make the water hot, without causing it to boil for about forty minutes; if the water boils much sooner, the meat will be hardened, and shrink up as if it was scorched: by keeping the water a certain time heating without boiling, the fibres of the meat are dilated, and it yields a quantity of scum, which must be taken off as soon as it rises

The editor placed a thermometer in water in that state which cooks call gentle simmering; the heat was 212°, i. e. the same degree as the strongest boiling.

Two mutton chops were covered with cold water; one boiled a gallop, while the other simmered very gently for three-quarters of an hour: the chop which was slowly simmered was decidedly superior to that which was boiled; it was much tenderer, more juicy, and much higher flavored. The liquor which boiled fast was in like proportion more savory, and when cold had much more fat on its surface. This explains why quick boiling renders meat hard, &c., because its juices are extracted in a greater degree.

Reckon the time from its first coming to a boil.

The old rule of 15 minutes to a pound of meat, we think rather too little: the slower it boils, the tenderer, the plumper, and whiter it will be.

For those who choose their food thoroughly cooked (which all will who have any regard for their stomachs), twenty minutes to a pound for fresh, and rather more for salted meat, will not be found too much for gentle simmering by the side of the fire, allowing more or less time, according to the thickness of the joint, and the coldness of the weather: to know the state of which, let a thermometer be placed in the pantry; and when it falls below 40 °, tell your cook to give rather more time in both roasting and boiling, always remembering, the slower it boils the better.

Without some practice it is difficult to teach any art; and cooks seem to suppose they must be right, if they put meat into a pot, and set it over the fire for a certain time, making no allowance whether it simmers without a bubble or boils a gallop.

Fresh-killed meat will take much longer time boiling than that which has been kept till it is what the butchers call *ripe*; and longer in *cold* than in *warm* weather: if it be *frozen*, it must be thawed before boiling as before roasting; if it be fresh-killed, it will be tough and hard, if you stew it ever so long, and ever so gently. In cold weather, the night before the day you dress it, bring it into a place of which the temperature is not less than 45 degrees of Fahrenheit's thermometer.

The size of the boiling-pots should be adapted to what they are to contain: the larger the saucepan the more room it takes upon the fire, and a larger quantity of water requires a proportionate increase of fire to boil it.

In small families we recommend block-tin saucepans, &c. as lightest and safest. If proper care is taken of them, and they are well dried after they are cleaned, they are by far the cheapest; the purchase of a new tin saucepan being little more than the expense of tinning a copper one.

Let the covers of your boiling-pots fit close, not only to prevent unnecessary evaporation of the water, but to prevent the escape of the nutritive matter, which must then remain either in the meat or in the broth; and the smoke is prevented from insinuating itself under the edge of the lid, and so giving the meat a bad taste.

If you let meat or poultry remain in the water after it is done enough, it will become sodden, and lose its flavor.

Beef and mutton a little *under*-done (especially very large joints, which will make the better hash or broil,) is not a great fault; by some people it is preferred: but lamb, pork, and veal are uneatable if not thoroughly boiled; but do not *over*-do them.

A trivet or fish-drainer put on the bottom of the boiling-pot, raising the contents about an inch and a half from the bottom, will prevent that side of the meat which comes next the bottom from being done too much, and the lower part of the meat will be as delicately done as the other part; and this will enable you to take out the contents of the pot, without sticking a fork, &c. into it. If you have not a trivet, use four skewers, or a soup-plate laid the wrong side upwards.

## BAKING.

Baking is one of the cheapest and most convenient ways of dressing a dinner in small families; and, I may say, that the oven is often the only kitchen a poor man has, if he wishes to enjoy a joint of meat.

I do not mean to deny the superior excellence of roasting to baking; but some joints, when baked, so nearly approach to the same when roasted, that I have known them to be carried to the table, and eaten as such with great satisfaction.

Legs and loins of pork, legs of mutton, fillets of veal, and many other joints, will bake to great advantage, if the meat be good; I mean well-fed, rather inclined to be fat: if the meat be poor, no baker can give satisfaction.

When baking a poor joint of meat, before it has been half baked I have seen it start from the bone, and shrivel up scarcely to be believed.

Besides those joints above mentioned, I shall enumerate a few baked dishes which I can particularly recommend.

A pig, when sent to the baker prepared for baking, should have its ears and tail covered with buttered paper properly fastened on, and a bit of butter tied up in a piece of linen to baste the back with, otherwise it will be apt to blister; with a proper share of attention from the baker, I consider this way equal to a roasted one.

A goose prepared the same as for roasting, taking care to have it on a stand, and when half done to turn the other side upwards. A duck the same.

A buttock of beef the following way is particularly fine. After it has been in salt about a week, to be well washed, and put into a brown earthen pan with a pint of water; cover the pan tight with two or three thicknesses of cap or foolscap paper: never cover anything that is to be baked with brown paper, the pitch and tar that is in brown paper will give the meat a smoky, bad taste: give it four or five hours in a moderately heated oven.

A ham (if not too old) put in soak for an hour, taken out and wiped, a crust made sufficient to cover it all over, and baked in a moderately heated oven, cuts fuller of gravy, and of a finer flavor, than a boiled one. I have been in the habit of baking small cod-fish, haddock, and mackerel, with a dust of flour, and some bits of butter put on them; eels, when large and stuffed;

herrings and sprats, in a brown pan, with vinegar and a little spice, and tied over with paper. A hare, prepared the same as for roasting, with a few pieces of butter, and a little drop of milk put into the dish, and basted several times, will be found nearly equal to roasting; or cut it up, season it properly, put it into a jar or pan, and cover it over and bake it in a moderate oven for about three hours. In the same manner, I have been in the habit of baking legs and shins of beef, ox cheeks, &c. prepared with a seasoning of onions, turnips, &c.: they will take about four hours: let them stand till cold, to skim off the fat; then warm it up all together, or part, as you may want it.

All these I have been in the habit of baking for the first families.

The time each of the above articles should take depends much upon the state of the oven, and I do consider the baker a sufficient judge; if they are sent to him in time, he must be very neglectful if they are not ready at the time they are ordered.


## ROASTING.


Let the young cook never forget that cleanliness is the chief cardinal virtue of the kitchen; the first preparation for roasting is to take care that the spit be properly cleaned with sand and water; nothing else. When it has been  well scoured with this, dry it with a clean cloth. If spits are wiped clean as soon as the meat is drawn from them, and while they are hot, a very little cleaning will be required. The less the spit is passed through the meat the better; and, before you spit it, joint it properly, especially necks and loins, that the carver may separate them easily and neatly, and take especial care it be evenly balanced on the spit, that its motion may be regular, and the fire operate equally on each part of it; therefore, be provided with balancing-skewers and cookholds, and see it is properly jointed.

Make up the fire in time; let it be proportioned to the dinner to be dressed, and about three or four inches longer at each end than the thing to be roasted, or the ends of the meat cannot be done nice and brown.

A cook must be as particular to proportion her fire to the business she has to do, as a chemist: the degree of heat most desirable for dressing the different sorts of food ought to be attended to with the utmost precision.

The fire that is but just sufficient to receive the noble sirloin will parch up a lighter joint.

Never put the meat down to a burned-up fire, if you can possibly avoid it; but should the fire become fierce, place the spit at a considerable distance, and allow a little more time.

Preserve the fat, by covering it with paper, for this purpose called "kitchen-paper," and tie it on with fine twine; pins and skewers can by no means be allowed; they are so many taps to let out the gravy: besides, the paper often starts from them and catches fire, to the great injury of the meat.

If the thing to be roasted be thin and tender, the fire should be little and brisk: when you have a large joint to roast, make up a sound, strong fire, equally good in every part, or your meat cannot be equally roasted, nor have that uniform color which constitutes the beauty of good roasting

Give the fire a good stirring before you lay the joint down; examine it from time to time while the spit is going round; keep it clear at the bottom, and take care there are no smoky coals in the front, which will spoil the look and taste of the meat, and hinder it from roasting evenly.

When the joint to be roasted is thicker at one end than the other, place the spit slanting, with the thickest part nearest the fire. Do not put meat too near the fire at first; the larger the joint, the farther it must be kept from the fire: if once it gets scorched, the outside will become hard, and acquire a disagreeable, empyreumatic taste; and the fire being prevented from penetrating into it, the meat will appear done before it is little more than half done, besides losing the pale brown color, which it is the beauty of roasted meat to have.

Be very careful to place the dripping-pan at such a distance from the fire as just to catch the drippings: if it is too near, the ashes will fall into it, and spoil the drippings.

If it is too far from the fire to catch them, you will not only lose your drippings, but the meat will be blackened and spoiled by the fœtid smoke, which will arise when the fat falls on the live cinders.

A large dripping-pan is convenient for several purposes. It should not be less than twenty-eight inches long and twenty inches wide, and have a covered well on the side from the fire, to collect the drippings; this will preserve them in the most delicate state: in a pan of the above size you may set fried fish, and various dishes, to keep hot.

The time meat will take roasting will vary according to the time it has been kept, and the temperature of the weather; the same weight will be twenty minutes or half an hour longer in cold weather, than it will be in warm; and if fresh killed, than if it has been kept till it is tender.

Everybody knows the advantage of *slow boiling*. *Slow roasting* is equally important.

It is difficult to give any specific rule for time; but if your fire is made as before directed, your meat-screen sufficiently large to guard what you are dressing from currents of air, and the meat is not frosted, you cannot do better than follow the old general rule of allowing rather more than a quarter of an hour to the pound; a little more or less, according to the temperature of the weather, in proportion as the piece is thick or thin, the strength of the fire, the nearness of the meat to it, and the frequency with which you baste it; the more it is basted the less time it will take, as it keeps the meat soft and mellow on the outside, and the fire acts with more force upon it.

Reckon the time, not to the hour when dinner is ordered, but to the moment the roasts will be wanted. Supposing there are a dozen people to sip soup and eat fish first, you may allow them ten or fifteen minutes for the former, and about as long for the latter, more or less, according to the temptations the "BON GOUT" of these preceding courses has to attract their attention.

When the joint is half done, remove the spit and dripping-pan back, and stir up your fire thoroughly, that it may burn clear and bright for the browning; when the steam from the meat draws towards the fire, it is a sign of its being done enough; but you will be the best judge of that, from the time it has been down, the strength of the fire you have used, and the distance your spit has been from it.

Half an hour before your meat is done, make some gravy, and just before you take it up, put it nearer the fire to brown it. If you wish to froth it, baste it, and dredge it with flour carefully: you cannot do this delicately nice without a very good light. The common fault seems to be using too much flour. The meat should have a fine light varnish of froth, not the appearance of being covered with a paste. Those who are particular about the froth use butter instead of drippings.

A good cook is as anxiously attentive to the appearance and color of her roasts, as a young beauty is to her complexion at a birthday ball. If your meat does not brown so much, or so evenly as you wish, take two ounces of glaze, *i. e.* portable soup, put four table-spoonfuls of water, and let it warm and dissolve gradually by the side of the fire. This will be done in about a quarter of an hour; put it on the meat equally all over with a paste-brush the last thing before it goes to table.

Though roasting is one of the most common, and is generally considered one of the most easy and simple processes of cookery, it requires more unremitting attention to perform it perfectly well than it does to make most made dishes.

That made dishes are the most difficult preparations deserves to be reckoned among the culinary vulgar errors; in plain roasting and boiling it is not easy to repair a mistake once made; and all the discretion and attention of a steady, careful cook, must be unremittingly upon the alert.

## FRYING.

Frying is often a convenient mode of cookery; it may be performed by a fire which will not do for roasting or boiling; and by the introduction of the pan between the meat and the fire, things get more equally dressed.

The Dutch oven or bonnet is a very convenient utensil for small things, and a very useful substitute for the jack, the gridiron, or frying-pan.

A frying-pan should be about four inches deep, with a perfectly flat and thick bottom, twelve inches long and nine broad, with perpendicular sides, and must be half filled with fat: good frying is, in fact, boiling in fat. To make sure that the pan is quite clean, rub a little fat over it, and then make it warm, and wipe it out with a clean cloth.

Be very particular in frying, never to use any oil, butter, lard, or drippings, but what is quite clean, fresh, and free from salt. Any thing dirty spoils the look; any thing bad-tasted or stale, spoils the flavor; and salt prevents its browning.

Fine olive oil is the most delicate for frying; but the best oil is expensive, and bad oil spoils every thing that is dressed with it.

For general purposes, and especially for fish, clean fresh lard is not near so expensive as oil or clarified butter, and does almost as well. Butter often burns before you are aware of it; and what you fry will get a dark and dirty appearance.

Dripping, if nicely clean and fresh, is almost as good as any thing; if not clean, it may be easily clarified. Whatever fat you use, after you have done frying, let it remain in the pan for a few minutes and then pour it through a sieve into a clean basin; it will do three or four times as well as it did at first, i. e. if it has not burned: but, the fat you have fried fish in must not be used for any other purpose.

To know when the fat is of a proper heat, according to what you are to fry, is the great secret in frying.

To fry fish, parsley, potatoes, or any thing that is watery, your fire must be very clear, and the fat quite hot; which you may be pretty sure of, when it has done hissing, and is still. We cannot insist too strongly on this point: if the fat is not very hot, you cannot fry fish either to a good color, or firm and crisp.

To be quite certain, throw a little bit of bread into the pan; if it fries crisp, the fat is ready; if it burns the bread, it is too hot.

The fire under the pan must be clear and sharp, otherwise the fat is so long before it becomes ready, and demands such attendance to prevent the accident of its catching fire, that the patience of cooks is exhausted, and they frequently, from ignorance or impatience, throw in what they are going to fry before the fat is half hot enough. Whatever is so fried will be pale and sodden, and offend the palate and stomach not less than the eye.

Have a good light to fry by, that you may see when you have got the right color: a lamp fixed on a stem, with a loaded foot, which has an arm that lengthens out, and slides up and down like a reading candlestick, is a most useful appendage to kitchen fireplaces, which are very seldom light enough for the nicer operations of cookery.

After all, if you do not thoroughly drain the fat from what you have fried, especially from those things that are full dressed in bread crumbs, or biscuit powder, &c, your cooking will do you no credit.

The dryness of fish depends much upon its having been fried in fat of a due degree of heat; it is then crisp and dry in a few minutes after it is taken out of the pan: when it is not, lay it on a soft cloth before the fire, turning it occasionally, till it is. This will sometimes take fifteen minutes: therefore, always fry fish as long as this before you want them, for fear you may find this necessary.

To fry fish, see receipt to fry soles, which is the only circumstantial account of the process that has yet been printed. If the cook will study it with a little attention, she must soon become an accomplished frier.

Frying, though one of the most common of culinary operations, is one that is least commonly performed perfectly well.

## BROILING

Cleanliness is extremely essential in this mode of cookery.

Keep your gridiron quite clean between the bars, and bright on the top: when it is hot, wipe it well with a linen cloth: just before you use it, rub the bars with clean mutton-suet, to prevent the meat from being marked by the gridiron.

Take care to prepare your fire in time, so that it may burn quite clear: a brisk and clear fire is indispensable, or you cannot give your meat that browning which constitutes the perfection of this mode of cookery, and gives a relish to food it cannot receive any other way.

The chops or slices should be from half to three-quarters of an inch in thickness; if thicker, they will be done too much on the outside before the inside is done enough.

Be diligently attentive to watch the moment that any thing is done: never hasten any thing that is broiling, lest you make smoke and spoil it.

Let the bars of the gridiron be all hot through, but yet not burning hot upon the surface: this is the perfect and fine condition of the gridiron.

As the bars keep away as much heat as their breadth covers, it is absolutely necessary they should be thoroughly hot before the thing to be cooked be laid on them.

The bars of gridirons should be made concave, and terminate in a trough to catch the gravy and keep the fat from dropping into the fire and making a smoke, which will spoil the broil.

Upright gridirons are the best, as they can be used at any fire without fear of smoke; and the gravy is preserved in the trough under them.

N. B. Broils must be brought to table as hot as possible; set a dish to heat when you put your chops on the gridiron, from whence to the mouth their progress must be as quick as possible.

When the fire is not clear, the business of the gridiron may be done by the Dutch oven or bonnet.

Take care to have a very clear, brisk fire; throw a little salt on it; make the gridiron hot, and set it slanting, to prevent the fat from dropping into the fire, and making a smoke. It requires more practice and care than is generally supposed to do steaks to a nicety; and for want of these little attentions, this very common dish, which every body is supposed capable of dressing, seldom comes to table in perfection.

Ask those you cook for, if they like it under, or thoroughly done; and what accompaniments they like best; it is usual to put a table-spoonful of ketchup, or a little minced eschalot, into a dish before the fire; while you are broiling, turn the steak, &c. with a pair of steak-tongs, it will be done in about ten or fifteen minutes; rub a bit of butter over it, and send it up garnished with pickles and finely-scraped horse-radish.

## BROTHS AND SOUPS.

The cook must pay continual attention to the condition of her stew-pans, soup-kettles, &c. which should be examined every time they are used. The prudent housewife will carefully examine the condition of them herself at least once a month. Their covers also must be kept perfectly clean and well tinned, and the stew-pans not only on the inside, but about a couple of inches on the outside: many mischiefs arise from their getting out of repair; and if not kept nicely tinned, all your good work will be in vain; the broths and soups will look green and dirty, taste bitter and poisonous, and will be spoiled both for the eye and palate, and your credit will be lost.

The health, and even life of the family, depends upon this, and the cook may be sure her employers had rather pay the tinman's bill than the doctor's; therefore, attention to this cannot fail to engage the regard of the mistress, between whom and the cook it will be my utmost endeavor to promote perfect harmony.

If she has the misfortune to scorch or blister the tinning of her pan, which will happen sometimes to the most careful cook, I advise her, by all means, immediately to acquaint her employers, who will thank her for candidly mentioning an accident; and censure her deservedly if she conceal it.

Take care to be properly provided with sieves and tammy cloths, spoons and ladles. Make it a rule without an exception, never to use them till they are well cleaned and thoroughly dried, nor any stew-pans, &c. without first washing them out with boiling water, and rubbing them well with a dry cloth and a little bran, to clean them from grease, sand, &c., or any bad smell they may have got since they were last used: never neglect this.

Though we do not suppose our cook to be such a naughty slut as to wilfully neglect her broth-pots, &c., yet we may recommend her to wash them immediately, and take care they are thoroughly dried at the fire, before they are put by, and to keep them in a dry place, for damp will rust and destroy them very soon: attend to this the first moment you can spare after the dinner is sent up.

Never put by any soup, gravy, &c. in metal utensils; in which never keep any thing longer than is absolutely necessary for the purposes of cookery; the acid, vegetables, fat, &c. employed in making soups, &c. are capable of dissolving such utensils: therefore stone or earthern vessels should be used for this purpose.

Stew-pans, soup-pots, and preserving pans, with thick and round bottoms (such as sauce-pans are made with), will wear twice as long, and are cleaned with half the trouble, as those whose sides are soldered to the bottom, for sand and grease get into the joined part, and cookeys say that it is next to an impossibility to dislodge it, even if their nails are as long as Nebuchadnezzar's.

Take care that the lids fit as close as possible, that the broth, soup, and sauces, &c. may not waste by evaporation. They are good for nothing, unless they fit tight enough to keep the steam in and the smoke out.

Stew-pans and saucepans should be always bright on the upper rim, where the fire does not burn them, but to scour them all over is not only giving the cook needless trouble, but wearing out the vessels.

Lean, juicy beef, mutton, or veal, form the basis of broth; procure those pieces which afford the richest succulence, and as fresh killed as possible.

Stale meat will make broth grouty and bad tasted, and fat meat is wasted. This only applies to those broths which are required to be perfectly clear: fat and clarified drippings may be so combined with vegetable mucilage, as to afford, at the small cost of one penny per quart, a nourishing and palatable soup, fully adequate to satisfy appetite and support strength: this will open a new source to those benevolent housekeepers, who are disposed to relieve the poor, will show the industrious classes how much they have it in their power to assist themselves, and rescue them from being objects of charity dependent on the precarious bounty of others, by teaching them how they may obtain a cheap, abundant, salubrious, and agreeable aliment for themselves and families.

This soup has the advantage of being very easily and very soon made, with no more fuel than is necessary to warm a room. Those who have not tasted it, cannot imagine what a salubrious, savory, and satisfying meal is produced by the judicious combination of cheap homely ingredients.

The general fault of our soups seems to be the employment of an excess of spice, and too small a portion of roots and herbs.

There is no French dinner without soup, which is regarded as an indispensable *overture*; and believe it an excellent plan to begin the banquet with a basin of good soup, which, by moderating the appetite for solid animal food, is certainly a salutiferous custom.

We again caution the cook to avoid over-seasoning, especially with predominant flavors, which, however agreeable they may be to some, are extremely disagreeable to others.

Zest, soy, cavice, coratch, anchovy, curry powder, savory ragout powder, soup herb powder, browning, ketchups, pickle liquor, beer, wine, and sweet herbs, and savory spice, are very convenient auxiliaries to finish soups, &c.

The proportion of wine should not exceed a large wine-glassful to a quart of soup. This is as much as can be admitted, without the vinous flavor becoming remarkably predominant; though not only much larger quantities of wine (of which claret is incomparably the best because it contains less spirit and more flavor, and English palates are less acquainted with it) but even *veritable eau de vie* is ordered in many books, and used by many (especially tavern cooks). So much are their soups overloaded with relish, that if you will eat enough of them they will certainly make you drunk, it they don't make you sick: all this frequently arises from an old cook measuring the excitability of the eaters' palates by his own, which may be so blunted by incessant tasting, that to awaken it, requires wine instead of water, and cayenne and garlic for black pepper and onion.

The art of composing a rich soup is so to proportion the several ingredients one to another, that no particular taste be stronger than the rest, but to produce such a fine harmonious relish that the whole is delightful. This requires that judicious combination of the materials which constitutes the *"chef d'oeuvre"* of culinary science.

In the first place, take care that the roots and herbs be perfectly well cleaned; proportion the water to the quantity of meat and other ingredients, generally a pound of meat to a quart of water for soups, and double that quantity for gravies. If they stew gently, little more water need be put in at first than is expected at the end; for when the pot is covered quite close, and the fire gentle, very little is wasted.

Gentle stewing is incomparably the best; the meat is more tender, and the soup better flavored.

It is of the first importance that the cover of a soup-kettle should fit very close, or the broth will evaporate before you are aware of it.

Place your soup-pot over a moderate fire, which will make the water hot without causing it to boil for at least half an hour; if the water boils immediately, it will not penetrate the meat, and cleanse it from the clotted blood, and other matters which ought to go off in scum; the meat will be hardened all over by violent heat; will shrink up as if it was scorched, and give hardly any gravy: on the contrary, by keeping the water a certain time heating without boiling, the meat swells, becomes tender, its fibres are dilated, and it yields a quantity of *scum*, which must be taken off as soon as it appears.

It is not till after a good half hour's hot infusion that we may mend the fire, and make the pot boil: still continue to remove *the scum;* and when no more appears, put in the vegetables &c. and a little salt. These will cause more *scum* to rise, which must be taken off immediately; then cover the pot very closely, and place it at a proper distance from the fire, where it will boil very gently and equally, and by no means fast.

By quick and strong boiling the volatile and finest parts of the ingredients are evaporated, and fly off with the steam, and the coarser parts are rendered soluble; so you lose the good, and get the bad.

Soups will generally take from *three* to *six* hours.

Prepare your broths and soups the evening before you want them. This will give you more time to attend to the rest of your dinner the next day; and when the soup is cold, the *fat* may be much more easily and completely removed from the surface of it. When you decant it, take care not to disturb the settlings at the bottom of the vessel, which are so fine that they will escape through a sieve, or even through a TAMIS, which is the best strainer, the soups appear smoother and finer, and it is much easier cleaned than any sieve. If you strain it while it is hot, pass it through clean tamis or napkin, previously soaked in cold water: the coldness of this will coagulate the fat, and only suffer the pure broth to pass through.

The full flavor of the ingredients can only be extracted by very long and slow simmering; during which take care to prevent evaporation, by covering the pot as close as possible: the best stew-pot is a digester.

Clear soups must be perfectly transparent; thickened soups, about the consistence of rich cream; and remember that thickened soups require nearly double the quantity of seasoning.

To thicken and give body to soups and sauces, the following materials are used: they must be gradually mixed with the soup till thoroughly incorporated with it; and it should have at least half an hour's gentle simmering after: if it is at all lumpy, pass it through a tamis or a fine sieve. Bread raspings, bread, isinglass, potato mucilage, flour, or fat skimmings and flour, or flour and butter, barley, rice, or oatmeal and water rubbed well together.

To their very rich gravies, &c. the French add the white meat of partridges, pigeons, or fowls, pounded to a pulp, and rubbed through a sieve. A piece of beef, which has been boiled to make broth, pounded in the like manner with a bit of butter and flour, and gradually incorporated with the gravy or soup, will be found a satisfactory substitute for these more expensive articles.

Meat from which broth has been made and all its juice has been extracted, is then excellently well prepared for POTTING, and is quite as good, or better, than that which has been baked till it is dry; indeed, if it be pounded, and seasoned in the usual manner, it will be an elegant and savory luncheon, or supper, and costs nothing but the trouble of preparing it, which is very little, and a relish is procured for sandwiches, &c. of what heretofore has been by the poorest housekeeper considered *the perquisite of the* CAT.

Keep some spare broth lest your soup-liquor waste in boiling, and get too thick, and for gravy for your made dishes, various sauces, &c.; for many of which it is a much better basis than melted butter.

The soup of mock turtle, and the other thickened soups, will supply you with a thick gravy sauce for *poultry, fish, ragouts,* &c.; and by a little management of this sort, you may generally contrive to have plenty of good gravies and good sauces with very little trouble or expense.

If soup is too thin or too weak, take off the cover of your soup-pot, and let it boil till some of the watery part of it has evaporated, or else add some of the thickening materials we have before mentioned; and have at hand some plain browning. This simple preparation is much better than any of the compounds bearing that name; as it colors sauce or soup without much interfering with its flavor, and is a much better way of coloring them than burning the surface of the meat.

When soups and gravies are kept from day to day, *in hot weather,* they should be warmed up every day, and put into fresh-scalded tureens or pans, and placed in a cool cellar; in temperate weather every other day may be enough.

We hope we have now put the common cook into possession of the whole *arcana* of soup-making, without much trouble to herself, or expense to her employers. It would greatly diminish the expense, and improve soups, if the agents employed to give them a zest were not put in above fifteen minutes before the finish, and half the quantity of spice, &c. would do. A strong heat soon dissipates the spirit of the wine, and evaporates the aroma and flavor of the spices and herbs, which are volatile in the heat of boiling water.

Warm fluids, in the form of soup, unite with our juices much sooner and better than those that are cold and raw: on this account, RESTORATIVE SOUP is the best food for those who are enfeebled by disease or dissipation, and for old people, whose teeth and digestive organs are impaired.

After catching cold, in nervous headaches, cholics, indigestions, and different kinds of cramp and spasms in the stomach, warm broth is of excellent service.

After intemperate feasting, to give the stomach a holyday for a day or two by a diet on mutton broth, or vegetable soup, &c. is the best way to restore its tone. "The stretching any power to its utmost extent weakens it. If the stomach be every day obliged to do as much as it can, it will every day be able to do less. A wise traveller will never force his horse to perform as much as he can in one day upon a long journey."

---

## OBSERVATIONS ON CERTAIN ARTICLES.

We shall conclude these Introductory Observations, with a few remarks on the qualities of certain Articles in common use.

### *Butter.*

Well made pure butter is lenient and nourishing, eaten cold, in moderation, with bread. But upon hot new bread, or hot toast, or used as sauce to animal food, it is not wholesome. In the two first instances it is very apt to turn acid in the stomach; and in the latter, to float uppermost in the stomach, and disturb the digestion. If melted thick and carefully, and eaten with vegetable food and bread only, it is not so liable to this objection.

Butter is good for dry, constipated habits, but not for such as are bilious, asthmatic, or corpulent.

## *Honey.*

Honey is nourishing and wholesome, particularly for persons with coughs, weak lungs, and short breath. It is balsamic, cleansing, and makes the body soluble.

Great care should be taken to get it fresh and pure; it is apt to turn sour by long keeping.

## *Sugar.*

Sugar used in moderation is nourishing and good, but much of it destroys the appetite, and injures the digestion. Moist sugar is the sweetest, and most opening; refined sugar, of a binding nature. The preparations made of sugar, such as barley sugar, sugar-candy, &c. are all indigestible and bad, as the good properties of the sugar are destroyed by the process it undergoes in the making them. They are particularly injurious to children, from cloying their delicate stomachs. Young children are in general better without sugar, as it is very apt to turn acid and disagree with weak stomachs; and the kind of food they take has natural sweetness enough in it not at all to require it.

## *Salt.*

Salt, moderately used, especially with flesh, fish, butter, and cheese, is very beneficial, as it naturally stimulates weak or disordered stomachs, and checks fermentations. But if it be immoderately used it has a contrary effect. Very little salt should be used with vegetable food of the grain or seed kind; for the less salt that is put to it the milder, cooler, pleasanter, and easier of digestion it will be. Salt excites the appetite, assists the stomach in digesting crude phlegmatic substances, is cleansing, and prevents putrefaction; but if too much used, it heats and dries the blood and natural moisture. It is best for phlegmatic, cold, and moist stomachs; and most injurious to hot, lean bodies.

Salt-petre is particularly bad for bilious persons.

## *Vinegar.*

Vinegar is cooling, opening, excites the appetite, assists digestion, is good for hot stomachs, resists putrefaction, and therefore very good against pestilential diseases. Too much use of it injures the nerves, emaciates some constitutions, is hurtful to the breast, and makes people look old and withered, with pale lips.

The best vinegar is that which is made of the best wines. Lemon-juice and verjuice have much the same qualities and effects as vinegar.

The commonest vinegar is least adulterated.

## *Mustard.*

Mustard quickens the appetite, warms the stomach, assists in digesting hard meats, and dries up surperfluous moisture. It seldom agrees with weak stomachs.

## Spices.

Cayenne pepper, black pepper, and ginger, may be esteemed the best of spices.

Nutmegs, cloves, mace, cinnamon, and allspice, are generally productive of indigestion and headache to weak persons.

## Garlic, &c.

Garlic, onions, rocambole, shallots, leeks, and horse-radish, are occasionally good for strong stomachs, but generally disagree with weak stomachs.

## Tea.

The frequent drinking of a quantity of strong tea, as is the general practice, relaxes and weakens the tone of the stomach, whence proceeds nausea and indigestion, with a weakness of the nerves, and flabbiness of the flesh, and very often a pale wan complexion. Milk, when mixed with it in some quantity, lessens its bad qualities, by rendering it softer, and nutritious; and, with a moderate quantity of sugar, it may then be a proper breakfast, as a diluent, to those who are strong, and live freely, in order to cleanse the alimentary passages, and wash off the salts from the kidneys and bladder. But persons of weak nerves ought to abstain from it as carefully as from drams and cordial drops; as it causes the same kind of irritation on the tender delicate fibres of the stomach, which ends in lowness, trembling and vapors.

It should never be drank hot by any body. Green tea is less wholesome than black or bohea.

## Coffee.

Coffee affords very little nourishment, and is apt to occasion heat, dryness, stimulation and tremors of the nerves; and for these reasons is thought to occasion palsies, watchfulness, and leanness. Hence it is very plain that it must be pernicious to hot, dry, and bilious constitutions. If moderately used it may be beneficial to phlegmatic persons, but, if drank very strong, or in great quantities, it will prove injurious even to them.

The following remarks on Coffee, were published in London, by a physician. 1st. The raw coffee should be round and small grained, free from dirt and of a light color. It should have no appearance of mouldiness, and be kept quite free from any strong smell. It should not be long kept in sacks with other provisions, as there is no substance more apt to obtain strong and disagreeable odors from the presence of its neighbors. Rum injures it; and Miller even goes so far as to state that a few bags of pepper on board a ship from India upon one occasion spoiled the whole cargo.

2nd. When the grains are large, flat, and of a green color, they should be kept on hand, in a dry situation, a long time before use. Every West India planter knows this fact, although his interest often induces him to send the article to market before it is old and dry enough.

3d. Roasting coffee is by far the most difficult operation of the housekeeper; when carried far enough, an aromatic oil is formed by the heat and forces itself out upon the surface of the grains, giving them a glossy appearance, and an odor which is considered their perfection; yet too little roasting prevents the aroma from appearing, and too much completely volatilizes it, leaving nothing but a flat bitter taste. The heat should be strong and the operation shortened as much as possible without burning the grains. The roaster should be close or well covered all the time, and in order to improve the looks and flavor, a small piece of butter may be added to the coffee, while parching.

4th. When thus prepared, coffee may be preserved for use in large quantities, without losing much of its freshness, provided the vessels containing it be well covered.

5th. An infusion of coffee is better than a decoction, simply because the heat, in the last case, being stronger and more lasting, drives off more of the aromatic oil. It is better, therefore to grind the coffee very fine, and then to expose it, by means of a bag or strainer, to the action of boiling water, than to boil it any length of time. Heat, though unavoidable, injures the flavor and the best coffee I remember to have tasted was made by exposing the powder to a pressure of *cold* water; a tea-spoonful of this extract, thrown into a cup of hot water, was sufficient. It is not a bad method to allow the ground coffee to lie in cold water between meals, and then prepare it by adding hot water. Just in proportion to the continuance of heat, in this and in the last operation, the fragrance disappears, and is replaced by a strong bitter taste, which, according to the experiments of Chenevix, depends upon the presence of tannin (resembling that in tan bark). Roasting, besides forming this bitter substance, deprives the coffee of its nutritious qualities.

## Chocolate.

Is rich, nutritious, and soothing saponaceous, and cleansing; from which quality it often helps digestion, and excites the appetite. It is only proper for some of the leaner and stronger sort of phlegmatic constitutions, and some old people who are healthy, and accustomed to bodily exercise.

## Cocoa.

Is of the same nature as chocolate, but not so rich; and therefore lighter upon the stomach.

## Fruit.

Fruits are of different degrees of digestibility. Those of a hard texture, as some kinds of apples, melons, apricots, several sorts of fleshy plums, and all immature fruits, are difficult of digestion.

Strawberries, raspberries, currants, gooseberries, cherries, green-gages, peaches, nectarines, melting pears, mulberries, figs, grapes, medlars, when all quite ripe, are more easily dissolved in the stomach.

Fruit, moderately eaten, is wholesome, particularly as correcting the grossness of animal food. But an excess of it, and especially of unripe fruit, is productive of many diseases; amongst children in particular, it often occasions such as the nettle rash and St. Anthony's fire.

Fruit invariably disagrees with bilious persons; but is a sovereign remedy for the sea scurvy, and for diseases arising from an excess of animal food.

## Nuts and Almonds.

Most kinds of nuts, and almonds, from their milky or oily nature, contain a good deal of nourishment; but they require to be well chewed, as they are difficult of digestion. Persons with weak stomachs should not eat them. The worst time at which they can be eaten is after a meal.

## *Olives.*

Olives that have been gathered immature or unripe, and put into a pickle to keep them sound, are apt, especially if frequently eaten, to obstruct the stomach and passages. The best way of eating them is with good bread, when the stomach is properly empty. To eat them upon a full stomach is very bad.

------

# NOTE.

Receipts for making all kinds of Bread, Biscuits, Blancmange, Buns, Broth, Cakes, Creams, Custards, Jams, Jellies, Paste, Pies, Puddings, Soups, Sauces, &c., will be found under these general heads; the method of cooking the several meats are arranged under the name of each meat Still there are interspersed throughout the book single receipts under the letter of the name, of which many of the above articles are composed. We will instance the following, viz:—

Cakes,—Almond, Crumpets, Echaudes, Fanchonettes, Flemish  wafers, Frangipane, Gateau, Gingerbread, Hedgehog, Jumbles, Kisses, Lemon Bonbons, Macaroons, Madelains, Meat, Muffins, Oat, Orange, Perlingo, Sally Lunns.

Bread,—Almond, Brentford, Filbert, French Rolls, Rusks.

Creams,—Under various fruits of which they are made.

Veal,—Friar's chicken, Gratin, and many articles under Calf.

Fowls,—See also Chickens, Capons.

Beef,—See also Ox.

The following Engraving represents the method of dividing an Ox for the table, in England, and in most of the southern cities of the United States. The method in Boston varies considerably, dividing into smaller pieces, and this plan we pursue in the following tables; but the manner of cooking each is nearly the same.

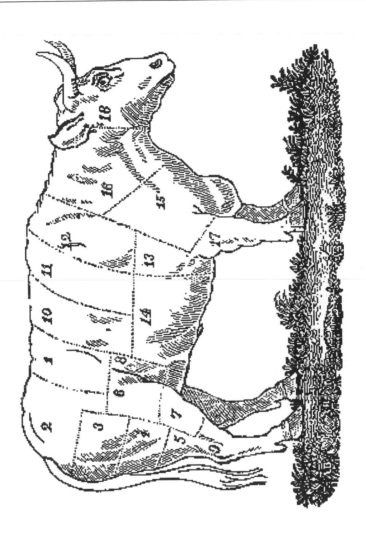

| | |
|---|---|
| 1. Sirloin. | 10. Fore rib: Five ribs. |
| 2. Rump. | 11. Middle rib: Four ribs. |
| 3. Edge Bone. | 12. Chuck: Three ribs. |
| 4. Buttock. | 13. Shoulder or leg-of-mutton piece. |
| 5. Mouse Buttock. | 14. Brisket. |
| 6. Veiny Piece. | 15. Clod. |
| 7. Thick Flank. | 16. Neck, or Sticking Piece. |
| 8. Thin Flank. | 17. Shin. |
| 9. Leg. | 18. Cheek. |

# MARKETING TABLES.

## BEEF.
## THE HIND QUARTER.

| | Price per lb. | | Method of cooking. |
|---|---|---|---|
| Sirloin | 10 to 12 | *cents* | Roasted. |
| Rump | 10 to 12 | ,, | Roasted, or Steak, or Stew. |
| Edge Bone | 6 to 8 | ,, | Boiled. |
| Round | 8 to 10 | ,, | {Alamode, Boiled, or savory salt-<br>{ ed Beef. |
| Veiny Piece | 6 to 8 | ,, | Steaks or Roast; or baked or salted. |
| Thick Flank | 6 to 8 | ,, | Steaks, or corned. |
| Thin Flank | 6 | ,, | do. |
| Leg Ran | 4 | ,, | Boil; Soup, or Stew. |
| Leg | 2 | ,, | Soup or Stew. |

## THE FORE QUARTER.

| | | | |
|---|---|---|---|
| First Cut, 2 Ribs | 10 | *cents* | Roast. |
| Second Cut, 2 Ribs | 10 | ,, | do. |
| Third Cut, 2 Ribs | 8 | ,, | do. |
| Fourth Cut, 2 Ribs | 6 | ,, | do. |
| Chuck Ribs | 5 | ,, | Boil or Stew, or for making gravy. |
| Shoulder of Mutton Piece | 5 | ,, | Steaks or Bouilli. |
| Shoulder Clod | 3 | ,, | Boil or Soup, or Beef Sausages. |
| Brisket | 6 | ,, | { Boil, or Bouilli; or stewing, or<br>{ Harricot, or Salted. |
| Rattleran | 6 | ,, | Boil. |
| Sticking Piece | 3 | ,, | Boil, or Soup. |
| Neck | 2 | ,, | Gravy. |
| Shin | 2 | ,, | { Soup; excellent Scotch barley.<br>{ Broth, Stewed. |
| Head (20 *cents*) | | | Soup, Stewed. |
| Tail (2 *cents*) | | | Soup, Stewed. |
| Heels, *given with the head* | | | Boiled, Jelly, Soup. |

## MUTTON.

| | | | |
|---|---|---|---|
| Leg | 8 to 10 | *cents* | Boil, Roast. |
| Loin | 6 to 8 | ,, | Chops—Roast, Boil, |

|                     |          |                                                    |
|---------------------|----------|----------------------------------------------------|
|                     |          | {  Boil, Roast, Irish Stew, Harricot,         |
| Rack, neck end      | 5 to 6 ,, | {    Stewed, Broth.                 |

|                |          |                    |
|----------------|----------|--------------------|
| Rack, best end | 6 to 8 ,, | Chops, or Broth.  |
| Shoulder       | 6 ,,      | Roast.            |
| Breast         | 6 ,,      | Broth,—Grilled.   |
| Head           | 4 ,,      | Broth.            |

The Chine or the Saddle, two
  Loins. The Haunch is a     }   Roasted, Venisonified.
  Leg and part of the Loin.

## VEAL

|                          |              |                                              |
|--------------------------|--------------|----------------------------------------------|
| Loin                     | 8 to 10 *cents* | Roast.                                    |
| Leg                      | ,,   ,, | Cutlets, Roast, Boil.                  |
| Fillet                   | ,,   ,, | {  Roasted, Veal Olives, Scotch<br>{    Collops |
| Knuckle,<br>or whole Leg | 8 ,,         | Broth, Ragout, Stew, Soup.                   |
| Breast                   | 8 to 10 ,,   | Roast,                                       |
| Breast and Neck          | 6 ,,         | Roast, Stew, Ragout, Curry.                  |
| Rack                     | 6 ,,         | Soup—Chops to fry.                           |
| Shoulder                 | 6 ,,         | Roast, or Bake.                              |
| Brisket                  | 8 ,,         | Stewed, Ragout.                              |
| Cutlets                  | 10 ,,        | Fried, Broiled.                              |
| Head, scalded, (50 to 60 *cts ea*) |    | Broiled plain, Hash.                         |

BEEF is *plentiest and cheapest from October to January; and best from January to May.*

VEAL *is best from April to July.*

MUTTON is *best from October to June.*

GRASS LAMB *is best from June to October.*

*The Quality of Butcher Meat varies quite as much as the price of it —according to its age—how it has been fed—and especially how it has been treated the week before it has been killed.*

## PORK

|                       | *Comes into Market.*           | *Plentiest.*   |
|-----------------------|--------------------------------|----------------|
| Roasting Pigs         | May                            | June.          |
| Quarter Pork          | July                           | August.        |
| Spare Ribs and Chine  | Aug.                           | Nov. & Dec.    |
| Middlings,            | salt, all the year.            |                |
| Bacon Hams            | November, and continue all the year. |          |

## POULTRY.

|  | Comes into Market. | Plentiest. |
|---|---|---|
| Chickens | July | Nov. |
| Fowls | All the year | do. |
| Ducks | July | October. |
| Geese | August | Nov. |
| Turkeys | September | Nov. & Dec. |
| Wild Ducks | do. | Oct. & Apr. |
| Brants | April | May. |
| Partridges | September | October. |
| Quails | do. | January. |
| Woodcocks | July | August. |

*Obs.*— POULTRY *is in greatest perfection, when in greatest plenty.*

*The price of it varies as much as the size and quality of it, and the supply at market, and the demand for it.*

*It is generally dearest from March to July, and cheapest about September, when the Game season commences, and the weather being colder, allows of its being brought from more distant parts.*

*The above information will, we trust, be very acceptable to Economical Families, who, from hearing the very high price Poultry sometimes costs, are deterred from ever inquiring about it. In the cheap seasons we have noted, it is sometimes as cheap as Butcher-meat.*

*Those who pay the highest, do not always pay the dearest, price. In fact, the Best Meat is the cheapest; and those who treat a tradesman liberally, have a much better chance of being well served, than those who are forever bargaining for the Market Penny. In dividing the Joints, there is always an opportunity of apportioning the Bones, Fat, Flaps, &c. so as to make up a variation of much more than a penny per pound in most pieces; and a Butcher will be happy to give the turn of his knife in favor of that Customer who cheerfully pays the fair price of the article he purchases; have those who are unwilling to do so any reason to complain? Have they not invited such conduct.*

### DIRECTIONS FOR CURING AND COOKING PICKLED FISH.[*]

The use of *Pickled Fish*, such as Mackerel, Salmon, Shad, &c. is becoming more general than formerly, and would be still more extensive if the proper mode of preparing them for the table was better understood. These fish constitute not only a salutary diet, but in many cases makes a very beneficial change in our food.

Whoever will give the following directions a fair trial will become sensible of their value:—

*First.* The fish should be kept covered by the pickle by means of a flat stone or slate, laid on them. The oil, or animal fat, which floats on the top of the cask, should not be removed, as it prevents the fish from rusting; but in taking the fish from the barrel or keg, this oil ought to be put aside, care being taken not to let the fish touch it. *Secondly*—The fish should be washed

---

[*] As the whole beauty of pickled Fish depends upon the right method of cooking it, we insert by itself the receipt of Capt. Henry Purkitt, Massachusetts Inspector of Fish, who obligingly handed it to the Editor.

clean, then put to soak in a large quantity of water for eight or ten hours, with the flesh side down. The time of soaking may be varied to suit the palate. It must again be washed clean, put it to soak six or eight hours in milk, (if you have it) then dry it by the fire. *Thirdly*—When dry lay it on the gridiron, with the flesh side downward, over pretty lively coals, for five minutes, or till it is moderately browned, then turn it with a plate, or some flat instrument that will not break the skin, and let it remain over the coals ten or fifteen minutes, or till it is cooked sufficiently. Slide it off the gridiron into the dish, and strip off the backbone with a broad knife: pat the fish, to cause the thick part of the fish to absorb the fat from the belly part; use no butter—then you will enjoy all the flavor and juices of the fish.

If a Mackerel or Shad so prepared does not relish, it must be more the fault of the palate, than of the food. How many articles, capable of being made into excellent dishes, are lost or spoiled from want of care and skill in dressing them.

# TABLE
# OF
# WEIGHTS AND MEASURES.

---

By which persons not having scales and weights at hand may readily  measure the articles wanted to form any receipt, without the trouble  of weighing. Allowance to be made for any extraordinary dryness or  moisture of the article weighed or measured.

—Ψ—

## WEIGHT AND MEASURE.

Eggs - - - - - - - - - ten eggs are - - - - - - one pound.
Brown sugar - - - - - - - one pound, two ounces, is - - one quart.
White sugar, powdered- - - - one pound, one ounce, is - - one quart.
Loaf-sugar, broken - - - - - one pound is- - - - - - one quart.
Butter—when soft - - - - - one pound is - - - - - - one quart.
Indian meal - - - - - - - one pound, two ounces, is- - one quart.
Wheat flour - - - - - - - one pound is - - - - - - one quart.

## LIQUIDS

Four large table-spoonfuls are - - - - - - - - - - - half a gill.
Eight large table-spoonfuls are - - - - - - - - - - one gill.
Sixteen large table-spoonfuls are - - - - - - - - - - half a pint.

---

A common-sized wine-glass - - - - - - - - - - - - - half a gill.
A common-sized tumbler holds - - - - - - - - - - - - half a pint.

# THE

# COOK'S OWN BOOK.

ABERDEEN CRULLA. (*See Cakes*.)

ALAMODE BEEF. *(See Beef.)*

ALAMODE VEAL. (*See Veal.*)

ALMOND CHEESECAKES. (1) Take half a pound of Jordan almonds, lay them in cold water all night; the next morning blanch them in cold water; then take them out and dry them in a clean cloth, beat them very fine in a little orange flower water; then take six eggs, leave out four whites, with a little beaten mace; beat them well in a marble mortar; take ten ounces of fresh butter, melt it, add a little grated lemon-peel, and put them in the mortar with the other ingredients; mix all well together and fill your patty-pans, having lined them with thin puff paste.

ALMOND CHEESECAKES. (2) Blanch and pound four ounces of almonds, and a few bitter with a spoonful of water; then add four ounces of sugar pounded, a spoonful of cream, and the whites of two eggs well beaten; mix all as quick as possible; put into very small patty-pans. and bake in a pretty warm oven twenty minutes.

ALMOND CHEESECAKES. (3) Blanch six ounces of sweet, and half an ounce of bitter almonds; let them lie half an hour in a drying stove, or before the fire; pound them very fine in a mortar, with two table-spoonfuls of rose water, to prevent them from oiling; set into a stew-pan half a pound of fresh butter; set it in a warm place, and

cream it very smooth with the hand, and add it to the almonds, with six ounces of sifted loaf sugar, a little grated lemon-peel, some good cream, and four eggs; rub all well together with the pestle; cover a patty-pan with puff paste; fill in the mixture; ornament it with slices of candied lemon-peel and almonds split, and bake it half an hour in a brisk oven.

ALMOND CONSERVE, BURNT. Blanch and cut six ounces of sweet almonds into small strips, lay them on paper and put them into an oven; when they are brown, take them out, and throw them into two pounds of sugar boiled to *petit casse*, stir the mixture well until it begins to blow, and then pour it into paper cases or moulds.

ALMONDS, ENGLISH FASHION. Mix almonds and filberts scalded in equal quantities; chop one half very fine, cut the rest each into two or three slices; put the whole in double their weight of sugar, prepared by boiling it with some lemon-peel rasped; stir the almonds very well in the sugar, taking it off the fire, and add one or two whites of eggs; pour it in paper large enough to contain the whole, and cut it in slices for use as you think proper, when baked as usual.

ALMOND FRAZE. Blanch a pound of Jordan almonds, and steep them in a pint of cream, ten yolks, and four whites of eggs; take out the almonds and pound them fine in a marble mortar; then mix them again in the cream and eggs, put in sugar and grated bread, and stir them all together; then put some fresh butter into the pan, let it be hot and pour it in, stirring it in the pan till they are of a sufficient consistence; and when enough, turn it into a dish, strew sugar over it, and serve it up.

ALMOND FRITTERS. Blanch three quarters of a pound of sweet almonds, pour over them three table-spoonfuls of rose water, and in a quarter of an hour a pint of cream; let them stand two or three hours, then pound them in a mortar till they become quite a paste; add the beaten yolks of six eggs, two or three pounded Naples biscuit; sweeten with pounded loaf sugar, and mix all well together; melt a quarter of a pound of fresh butter in a frying-pan, and when hot, pour in the mixture, and stir it constantly till thick, and of a light brown color. Serve it with sifted loaf sugar over the top.

ALMOND BROWN GINGERBREAD. Beat a quarter of a pound of blanched almonds with thin gum-water, a few drops of lemon-juice, a little powdered cinnamon, and some ginger finely grated and seered to give it a brown color; sweeten and smooth it well, roll it out thin, and cut it into squares; dry it in a stove or before the fire.

ALMOND ICEING, for BRIDE CAKE. The whites of six eggs, a pound and a half of double-refined sugar, a pound of Jordan almonds blanched and pounded with a little rose water, mix altogether and whisk it well for an hour or two, lay it over the cake and put it in the oven.

ALMOND MACAROONS, BITTER. Take a pound of bitter almonds, rub them well in a clean cloth, and beat them to a paste with the whites of three or four eggs; then put them into an earthen pan with three pounds of powder-sugar, mix them together well, and if the paste should be too dry, moisten it with white of egg. Drop it on sheets of paper in lumps about the size of a walnut, and bake them in a close, gentle oven.

ALMOND MACAROONS, SWEET, Are done in the same way. But two pounds of sugar are sufficient for a pound of almonds.

ALMOND MILK SOUP. Take half a pound of sweet almonds, put them on the fire with some water until near boiling, then blanch and throw them into fresh water; drain and pound them. Boil a pint of water, a little sugar, salt, cinnamon, coriander, and lemon-peel, for a quarter of an hour, and rub the almonds through a sieve to this. Lay some slices of toasted bread in a dish, and pour the milk of almonds on it, as hot as possible without boiling.

ALMOND PUFFS. Blanch two ounces of sweet almonds, and beat them fine with orange flower water, whisk the whites of three eggs to a high froth, strew in a little sifted sugar, mix the almonds with the sugar and eggs, and add more sugar till as thick as paste. Lay it in cakes, and bake it on paper in a cool oven.

ALMOND RICE. Blanch sweet almonds, and pound them in a marble mortar; mix them in a little boiling water; press them as long as there is milk in the almonds, adding fresh water every time; to every quart of almond-juice, put a quarter of a pound of rice and two teaspoonsful of orange flower water; mix them all together, and simmer it over a slow charcoal fire; stir it repeatedly, and when done, sweeten it at pleasure; serve it with beaten cinnamon strewed over.

ALMOND ROLLS, BITTER. Blanch and pound eight ounces of almonds five of sweet and three of bitter) to a very fine paste; then place eight ounces of flour on your slab; make a hole in the middle, and put into it eight ounces of powder-sugar, the yolks of four eggs, and a grain of salt; mix them all well together into a firm smooth paste, roll it out and cut it into four equal parts; roll each piece to the same length; cut them into pieces about the size of a walnut, and form them to the shape of a wild turnip, and as you do them put them on a baking-tin lightly buttered; *dorez* them and bake them of a proper color in a moderate oven. When they are taken from the oven, let them stand a little while to dry.

ALMOND PUDDING. *(See Pudding.)*

ALMOND TUMBLES. Blanch and pound three ounces of almonds very fine, when almost beaten enough, take the white of an egg beaten to froth, one pound of double-refined sugar well beaten, and put it in by degrees, working it into a paste with your hands, roll it out and bake it on buttered plates in a hot oven.

AMERICAN BLANCMANGE. *(See Blancmange.)*

AMERICAN GINGERBREAD. Take half a pound of fresh butter melted, one pound and a half of dried and sifted flour, the same quantity of brown sugar, a quarter of a pound of pounded ginger, nine eggs, the yolks and whites separately beaten, one glass of rose water, and one of white wine; mix all these well together, and beat it for an hour; then with a spoon spread it over flat tin pans, about the thickness of a penny-piece; bake it of a light brown, and while warm, cut it into oblong pieces, and place them on end till cool, when they will be very crisp.

AMERICAN VINEGAR. *(See Vinegar.)*

AMERICAN SNOW BALLS. Boil some rice in milk till it be swelled and soft; pare and carefully scoop out the core of five or six good-sized apples, put into each a little grated lemon-peel and cinnamon; place as much of the rice upon a bit of linen as will entirely cover an apple, and tie each closely.

Boil them two hours, and serve them with melted butter, sweetened with sugar.

ANCHOVIES. Wash half a dozen anchovies, and take the meat from the bones; cut them into four fillets, place them on a dish with some sweet herbs, cut small; and the yolks and whites of hard eggs, also cut small.

ANCHOVY BUTTER. Wash your anchovies carefully, take out the bones, and dry them; then pound them in a mortar until they are reduced to a paste; and mix this paste with double the quantity of fresh butter.

ANCHOVIES, BUTTER OF. Wash from the pickle some fine young anchovies, bone, and take off the heads, then pound them in a mortar with fresh butter till quite smooth, and rub it through a sieve.

ANCHOVY PASTE. Pound them in a mortar, then rub it through a fine sieve; pot it, cover it with clarified butter, and keep it in a cool place. If you have essence of anchovy, you may make anchovy paste extempore, by rubbing the essence with as much flour as will make a paste. *Mem.*—This is merely mentioned as the means of making it immediately; it will not keep.

ANCHOVY POWDER. Pound the fish in a mortar, rub them through a sieve, and make them into a paste with dried flour, roll it into thin cakes, and dry them in a Dutch oven before a slow fire; pounded to a fine powder, and put into a well-stopped bottle, it will keep for years; it is a very savoury relish, sprinkled on bread and butter for a sandwich, &c. See Oyster Powder.

ANCHOVY TOAST. (1) Cut some thin slices of bread about the length and breadth of a finger; fry them in oil. Place them on a dish, and pour on them a sauce made of oil, vinegar, whole pepper, parsley, scallion, and shallots, cut up together. Then cut the anchovies into thin slices, and lay them on the toast.

ANCHOVY TOAST. (2) Bone and wash the anchovies, pound them in a mortar with a little fresh butter; rub them through a sieve and spread them on a toast. You may add, while pounding the anchovies, a little made mustard and curry powder, or a few grains of Cayenne, or a little mace or other spice. It may be made still more savoury, by frying the toast in clarified butter—N. B. Keep your anchovies well covered; first tie down your jar with bladder moistened with vinegar, and then wiped dry; tie leather over that: when you open a jar, moisten the bladder, and it will come off easily; as soon as you have taken out the fish, replace the coverings; the air soon rusts and spoils anchovies.

ANCHOVY TOAST. (3) Bone and roll up two or three anchoivies, place them upon pieces of dry toast, and garnish with curled parsley.

ANGELICA TO CANDY. Cut the stalks when thick and tender, put them on in boiling water, and when very tender, drain it off and throw them into cold water; peel off the skin, and scald them in a thin sirup, made with the same proportion of sugar that there is of fruit; heat it twice a day till the sirup is almost dried in, and then dry them under garden glasses, or in a stove, and turn them twice a day.

APPLES. Cooks, in choosing apples for culinary purposes, should always be guided by the weight, the heaviest being always the best; and those are particularly to be taken, which, upon being pressed by the thumb, yield with a slight cracking noise. Large apples possessing these qualities should be taken in preference to small ones, as there is less waste in peeling and coring.

APPLE BLACK-CAP. (1) Divide twelve large apples in halves, core them, and place them on a thin patty-pan or mazerine, quite close to each other, with the flat side downwards; squeeze a lemon into two spoonfuls of orange flower water, which pour over them; shred fine some lemon-peel, throw it over them, and grate fine sugar all over. Set them in a quick oven, and bake them half an hour. When served, strew fine sugar all over the dish.

APPLE BLACK-CAP. (2) Pare the apples, lay them in your pan, strew a few cloves over them, a little lemon-peel cut very small, two or three blades of cinnamon, and some coarse sugar; cover the pan with brown paper, set it in an oven with the bread, and let it stand till the oven is cold.

APPLES, TO BAKE WHOLE. Put some sound and well chosen apples into a pan, with a small proportion of cloves, a little lemon-peel, some brown sugar, a glass or more of red wine, according to the quantity of fruit, put them into a quick oven, and bake them at least one hour. The sugar to be limited according to the quality of the apples.

APPLES, CHARLOTTE OF. (*See Charlotte.*)

APPLE CHEESECAKES. Pare, core, and boil twelve apples with sufficient water to mash them; beat them very smooth, add six yolks of eggs, the juice of two lemons, and some grated lemon-peel, half a pound of fresh butter beaten to a cream, and sweetened with powder sugar, beat it in with the apples. Bake in a puff crust and serve open.

APPLES CLEAR. Boil half a pound of loaf sugar in a pint of water; take off the scum and put in some large apples, pared, cored, and cut into quarters, with the peel and juice of a lemon; let them boil till clear, without a cover upon the sauce-pan.

APPLES COMPOTE. (1) Cut some apples in half, core them, prick the skins with a knife and throw them into cold water; then put them into a pan with some clarified sugar, and stew them gently till tender; place the apples in a dish, and pour the sirup through a sieve over them.

APPLES COMPOTE. (2) Pare and cut half a dozen fine apples in half, and put them into a pan with a little water and lemon-juice; then clarify half a pound of sugar, and when you have skimmed it put in your apples, and the juice of a lemon; turn the apples frequently. As soon as you find the fork will penetrate them, they are sufficiently done, and may be taken out; strain and reduce the syrup; strain it again, and then pour it over your apples, which may be served either hot or cold. Garnish with the peel of a very red apple, cut into various devices, and laid on the apples.

APPLES, WHOLE. The proceeding is the same as the last, except that the apples, when pared, are not divided, and the cores are taken out with a piercer.

APPLE DUMPLINGS. Pare and scoop out the core of six large baking apples, put part of a clove, and a little grated lemon-peel, inside of each, and enclose them in pieces of puff paste; boil them in nets for the purpose, or bits of linen, for an hour. Before serving, cut off a small bit from the top of each, and put in a tea-spoonful of sugar, and a bit of fresh butter; replace the bit of paste, and strew over them pounded loaf sugar.

APPLE DUMPLINGS, BAKED. Make them in the same way, but instead of tying them in cloths lay them in a buttered dish and bake them.

APPLES, DRIED OR BAKED. Always choose the clearest of baking apples, prick them rather deep with a pointed knife in several places, and put them in a moderate oven upon a baking plate; when half done squeeze them pretty flat with the hands, strew them on both sides with powder sugar, and put them again into a soaking oven, with some more sugar over them. Keep them in a dry place.

APPLES FESTOONED. Peel some golden pippins, core them whole, and stew them to three parts with sugar and a little water; make the sirup pretty rich to clog to the apples; wrap them round with a thin paste, cut with a paste cutter, and make knots or flowers with the same paste to put on the top of the apples; rasp some sugar over, and bake a very short time.

APPLE FLOATING ISLAND. Bake or scald eight or nine large apples; when cold pare and pulp them through a sieve, beat this up with fine sugar; put to it the whites of four or five eggs that have been beaten with a little rose water; mix it a little at a time, and beat it till it is light; heap it on a rich custard or on jelly.

APPLE FOOL. Pare, core, and cut into thin bits, some good stewing apples; stew them till tender, with a little water, two cloves, a bit of cinnamon, and the peel of half a lemon; pulp half a pound through a sieve, and add the same weight of brown sugar, the juice of a lemon, and the whites of two eggs; beat them all together for an hour. Serve it upon rich cream, or a boiled custard, in a glass dish. It may be made in the same way as the gooseberry fool, as may also stewed rhubarb.

APPLE FRAZE. Cut apples into thick slices, and fry them of a clear light brown; take them from the pan, and lay them to drain; they may be pared or not; then make a batter. Take five eggs, leaving out two whites, beat them up with cream or flour, and a little white wine, make it of the consistence of pancake batter; pour in a little melted butter, mixed with nutmeg and sugar. Let the batter be hot, and drop in the fritters, laying on every one a slice of apple, and then a spoonful of batter on each. Fry them of a pale brown, when taken up, strew double-refined sugar all over them.

APPLE FRITTERS. (1) Beat the yolks of eight eggs, the whites of four, well together, strain them into a pan; then take a quart of cream, make it moderately hot, and add two glasses of sack, three-quarters of a pint of ale, and mix them well together. When it is cool, put to it the eggs, beating it well together, then add nutmeg and ginger grated, salt and flour at pleasure. The batter should be pretty thick; then put in sliced apples, or scraped pippins, and fry them quick in butter.

APPLE FRITTERS. (2) Pare, core, and cut your apples into quarters, soak them for two or three hours in brandy, sugar, green lemon-peel, and orange flower water; when they have thoroughly imbibed the flavor of these ingredients, drain, and put them into a cloth well sprinkled with flour, and shake them so that the flour may adhere all over them; fry them of a good color, glaze with sugar and a hot salamander.

APPLE FRITTERS. (3) Stew some apples cut small, together with a little water, sugar, lemon-peel, and cinnamon; when soft, add a little white wine, the juice of half a lemon, and a bit of fresh butter; when cold, mix them with a batter, as for Tunbridge puffs, or enclose them in rounds of puff paste. Fry, and serve them with sifted loaf sugar over them.

APPLE FRITTERS. (4) Four well-beaten eggs, half a pint of cream, two table spoonfuls of yeast, three of white wine, and two of rose water; half a tea spoonful of grated nutmeg, and of salt; make it into a thick batter with flour, peel and core two or three apples, cut them into thin bits, and mix them with the batter; cover it over, let it stand, placed near the fire, about an hour; drop it into boiling lard, and serve them in a napkin with sugar strewed over them.

Gooseberries previously stewed may be done in the same way.

APPLES, GLAZED. Peel a dozen of apples and leave the tails; gore at the opposite side not quite through, and boil them with half a pint of red wine, some sugar, and a spoonful of brandy, simmer slowly that they may not break; when nearly done; take them out, reduce the sirup to a *caramel*, and put in the apples, rubbing them all over with it; or you may wrap them in a paste, rasp sugar over, bake a short time, and glaze with a white glaze.

APPLE MARMALADE. (1) Boil some pippins till they begin to get tender, then put them into cold water; pare and core them; squeeze the pulp through a sieve and put it over the fire, letting it remain till it becomes very thick; then weigh an equal quantity of fine sugar; boil it till the sugar arises in sparkles which cluster together; put the marmalade to it, and stir them well with a wooden spoon till the apple begins to boil; then take it off and when a little cool, put it into pots, but do not cover them till quite cold.

APPLE MARMALADE. (2) Pare, core, and cut your apples into small pieces, put them into water with a little lemon-juice to keep them white. Take them out after a short time and drain them. Weigh, and put them into a stew-pan; if for present use, half a pound of sugar will be sufficient for each pound of apples, but if for keeping, double that quantity will be necessary. Add to it a stick of cinnamon and the juice of a lemon. Put the stew-pan over a brisk fire and cover it; when the apples are pulped stir the mixture till of the proper consistence: then put the marmalade into pots.

APPLES IN PANCAKES. Cut some apples very small, stew them with a little white wine, grated lemon-peel, pounded cinnamon, and brown sugar; mash them, and spread it over pancakes; roll them up, and serve with sifted loaf sugar over them.

## APPLE POUPETON.

Pare some good baking apples, take out the cores, and put them into a skillet; to a pound and a half of apples, put a quarter of a pound of sugar, and a wine glass of water. Do them over a slow fire, add a little cinnamon, and keep them stirring. When of the consistence of a marmalade, let it stand till cool; beat up the yolks of four eggs, and stir in four table spoonfuls of grated bread, and a quarter of a pound of fresh butter; then form it into shape, bake it in a slow oven, turn it upside down on a plate, and serve.

## APPLE PRESERVE. (*See Preserves*.)

## APPLES AND RAISINS.

Pare and cut twelve apples into quarters, and each quarter into four pieces, put them into a pan with four ounces of good fresh butter, two of sugar, over which the *zeste* of an orange has been grated, and a quarter of a pound of currants well washed; toss up these ingredients over a moderate fire for a few minutes and then let them cool. Make a round under-crust seven inches in diameter, moisten the edge and put on it a band of puff paste three quarters of an inch high and half an inch thick; put your apples, &c. in this so as to form a sort of dome, cover them with the puff paste, taking care that it does not extend beyond the band, upon which it must be pressed down; wash it over with white of egg, and bake it in a gentle oven for about an hour. When a little cooled, take the whites of two eggs, whipped to a strong froth and mixed with two ounces of powder sugar, and mask with it your cake, sprinkling it with sifted sugar; then, having drained and dried some currants, mix them with sugar, and strew them over the dome; form a crown of small *meringues* with the remainder of the white of egg, and place it on the band; cover them with sifted sugar, and color the whole of a clear yellow in the oven, and then serve immediately.

## APPLES IN RICE. (1)

Scoop out the cores, and pare, very neatly, half a dozen good-sized apples; boil them in thin, clarified sugar; let them imbibe the sugar, and be careful to preserve their form. Make a marmalade with some other apples, adding to it apricot marmalade, and four ounces of rice previously boiled in milk, with sugar and butter, and the yolks of two or three eggs; put them into a dish for table, surround it with a border of rice, and place the whole apples in the rice, and marmalade and bake it. When done, put into each of the apples a tea-spoonful of any kind of sweetmeat you may think proper.

## APPLES IN RICE. (2)

Pare, core, and cut four or five good apples in quarters; boil some rice in a cloth, and when soft put in the apples, tie it up very loose, and boil gently till sufficiently done.

## APPLE SOUFFLET.

Prepare apples as for baking in a pudding, put them into a deep dish, and lay upon the top, about an inch and a half thick, rice boiled in new milk with sugar; beat to a stiff froth the whites of two or three eggs, with a little sifted loaf sugar, lay it upon the rice, and bake it in an oven a light brown. Serve it instantly when done.

## APPLE A LA TURQUE.

Neatly pare and pierce out the cores of eight or ten apples, put them on the fire with a thin sirup of clarified sugar, cover them close and let them simmer gently; turn them, that both sides may be done. When thoroughly done lay them on a dish, with a wet paper over them. Put a paste round the dish you serve them in, and bake in a gentle oven to harden it, then put in a layer of apple sauce, over which put the apples, and fill the holes where the cores were with dried cherries or apricot jam, then cover it with the apple sauce; beat up the whites of six eggs to a froth, and add powder sugar till they appear quite smooth; make the apples warm, and lay the white of egg over them, smooth it neatly over, and sift some powder sugar over it; color it in a gentle oven.

APPLE WATER. Cut three or four large apples into slices, put them into a jug, and pour a quart of boiling water over them; cover the jug. When quite cold, strain and sweeten it, and add a little lemon-juice.

APRICOTS IN BRANDY. Weigh equal quantities of loaf sugar and of apricots; scald them, and take off the skins. Clarify and boil the sugar, put the fruit into it, and let it remain for two or three days; put the apricots into glasses. Mix with the sirup the best pale brandy, half and half, and pour it over the apricots and keep them closely covered. Peaches and nectarines may be done in the same way.

APRICOTS, CHARLOTTE OF. Choose twenty-four fine, plump, but not too ripe, apricots, pare and divide them into eight parts, toss them up in a quarter of a pound of fine sugar, and two ounces of warm butter; in the meantime line a mould as directed (*see Charlotte*); pour in the apricots, and finish as usual. When turned on your dish, cover it lightly with apricot marmalade, and serve it immediately.

APRICOTS TO DRY. Pare the apricots, and carefully take out the stones; blanch the kernels, and put them into the apricots; strew over a pound of fruit the same quantity of finely-pounded loaf sugar, and let them stand till the sugar has extracted the juice, then boil all together gently; when the fruit is tender, take it out with care, and boil the sirup till very rich; pour it over the fruit, and in three days put it upon dishes, and dry them in the sun under garden glasses, turning them once or twice a-day, to keep the shape as round as possible. Any inferior apricots may be cut down and boiled in the sirup, for tarts.

APRICOT MARMALADE. Take some fine apricots, and choose from amongst them those which are of the deepest yellow and the ripest, (they must not be too ripe.) Peel them, take out the stones, and chop them up; weigh twelve pounds of them and put them into a preserving-pan, with nine pounds of powder sugar; place your pan over a quick fire, and keep your preparation constantly stirring with a long wooden spoon. To find out when the marmalade is sufficiently done, let a few drops fall into a glass of cold water, and if they do not spread in the water your marmalade is ready to put into pots. Another method of ascertaining when your marmalade is done is by taking some on the end of your finger and thumb, and just rub them together, and if on separating them you find the marmalade forms a thread, it is sufficiently done.

APRICOTS A LA PORTUGAISE. Take a dozen of ripe apricots, cut them in half, and take out the stones; place them on a silver plate, and pour over some clarifed sugar, with a little water; put them on a stove without covering them; when sufficiently done, take them from the fire, and strew sugar over; then put on the lid of the baking-pan under the fire, to make them of a good color.

APRICOTS, WHOLE. Choose the finest yellow, but not too ripe, apricots; take off the stalks, prick them on each side with a pin, make an incision with the point of a knife, through which extract the stone. Then put them on the fire with as much water as will cover them, until near boiling, when, if soft, the apricots should be thrown into cold water; take care they are all equally tender. Drain them on a hurdle, and in the meantime clarify and boil some suger to the degree you require; put in a little water, and when it boils remove it from the fire, and add to it the fruit, and having given than a few boilings together, let them cool, then drain and place them in your *compotiers*.

ARTICHOKES AND ALMONDS. Take

half a pound of sweet almonds blanched and beat fine, with two tea spoonfuls of orange-flower or rose water; then take a quart of cream, and boil it with a small quantity of cinnamon and mace; sweeten it with fine sugar, and mix it with the almonds; stir them together, and strain it through a sieve. Let the cream cool, and thicken it with the yolks of six eggs; then garnish a deep dish, and lay paste at the bottom; then put in shred artichoke bottoms, being first boiled; and upon these a little melted butter, shred citron, and candied orange; repeating the same until the dish is nearly full, then pour in the cream, and bake it without a lid. When it is baked, grate sugar over it, and serve it hot. Half an hour will serve to bake it.

ARTICHOKES BOILED. Soak them in cold water, wash them well, then put them into plenty of boiling water, with a handful of salt, and let them boil gently till they are tender, which will take an hour and a half, or two hours: the surest way to know when they are done enough, is to draw out a leaf; trim them and drain them on a sieve; and send up melted butter with them, which some put into small cups, so that each guest may have one.

ARTICHOKES TO BOIL. Cut off the stalks close to the bottom, wash them well, and let them lie for some hours in cold water; put them on in boiling water with a little salt in it, cover the pan closely, and boil them an hour and a half. If they are old, and have not been fresh gathered, they will take a longer time to boil. Melted butter is served with them in a sauce-tureen.

ARTICHOKE BOTTOMS, TO DRY AND PICKLE. Half boil the artichokes, strip off the leaves, and pull out the choke; put the bottoms into small jars, and cover them with a cold boiled brine of salt and water; put melted mutton suet on the top to exclude the air, and tie bladder over them. To dry them, they are boiled as for eating, the leaves and choke pulled out; and the bottoms dried upon dishes in an oven, and then kept in paper bags. When to be dressed, they must be laid into warm water, and soaked for two or three hours; they may then be plain boiled, and eaten with melted butter, or stewed in gravy with a little mushroom catsup, pepper, and salt, and thickened with a bit of butter rolled in flour. They are a great improvement to all made dishes and meat pies.

ARTICHOKE BOTTOMS, PICKLED. Boil the artichokes till the leaves can be pulled off without breaking the bottoms; leave on the part called the choke, set them aside till cold, then put them into wide-mouthed bottles. Boil, in vinegar, some salt, pepper, mace, and sliced nutmeg, and, when cold, pour it over the artichokes; tie bladder over the bottles.

ARTICHOKES, JERUSALEM. (1) Are boiled and dressed in the various ways directed for potatoes. N. B.—They should be covered with thick melted butter; or a nice white or brown sauce.

ARTICHOKES, JERUSALEM. (2) They must be neatly peeled, and boiled very gently by the side of the stove, with a little salt in the water; when done (but not too much, or they will not look well) place them on the dish, and serve with plain butter, or any other sauce you please.

ARTICHOKES, JERUSALEM, TO FRICASSEE. Wash and scrape or pare them; boil them in milk and water till they are soft, which will be from a quarter to half an hour. Take them out and stew them a few minutes in the following sauce:—Roll a bit of butter, the size of a walnut, in flour, mix it with half a pint of cream or milk; season it with pepper, salt, and grated nutmeg. They may be served plain boiled, with a little melted butter poured over them. Scorzonera is fricasseed in the same manner.

ARROW-ROOT. Mix with two or three

table-spoonfuls of arrow-root half a pint of cold water; let it stand for nearly a quarter of an hour, pour off the water, and stir in some pounded sugar; boil a pint of milk, and pour it gradually upon the arrow-root, stirring it one way all the time. Or it may be made with water in which lemon-peel has been boiled, and then a glass of Port or white wine and a little nutmeg stirred into it.

ASPARAGUS. Set a stew-pan with plenty of water in it on the fire; sprinkle a handful of salt in it; let it boil, and skim it; then put in your asparagus, prepared thus: scrape all the stalks till they are perfectly clean; throw them into a pan of cold water as you scrape them; when they are all done, tie them up in little bundles, of about a quarter of a hundred each, with bass, if you can get it, or tape (string cuts them to pieces;) cut off the stalks at the bottom that they may be all of a length, leaving only just enough to serve as a handle for the green part; when they are tender at the stalk, which will be in from twenty to thirty minutes, they are done enough. Great care must be taken to watch the exact time of their becoming tender; take them up just at that instant, and they will have their true flavor and color: a minute or two more boiling destroys both. While the asparagus is boiling, toast a round of a quartern loaf, about half an inch thick; brown it delicately on both sides; dip it lightly in the liquor the asparagus was boiled in, and lay it in the middle of a dish: melt some butter, then lay in the asparagus upon the toast, which must project beyond the asparagus, that the company may see there is a toast.

ASPARAGUS, BOILED. Scrape and tie them in small bundles; cut them even, boil them quick in salt and water; lay them on a toast dipped in the water the asparagus was boiled in; pour over them melted butter.

ASPARAGUS AND EGGS. Toast a slice of bread, butter it, and lay it on a dish; butter some eggs thus: take four eggs, beat them well, put them into a saucepan with two ounces of butter, and a little salt, until of a sufficient consistence, and lay them on the toast; meanwhile boil some asparagus tender, cut the ends small, and lay them on the eggs.

ASPARAGUS, FRENCH. Boil it, and chop small the heads and tender part of the stalks, together with a boiled onion; add a little salt and pepper, and the beaten yolk of an egg; beat it up. Serve it on sippets of toasted bread, and pour over it a little melted butter.

ASPARAGUS SOUP. *(See Soups.)*

ASPICK. Take a knuckle of veal, a knuckle of ham, a thick slice of beef, and if, they will not make your jelly stiff enough, add two calf's feet, or some swards of bacon rasped; put them into a sauce-pan with a pint of rich stock, and sweat it over a stove till reduced to a glaze, then moisten it with stock, boil and skim it well. Put to it two onions, two carrots, salt, parsley, scallions, four cloves, two bay leaves, and a clove of garlick; let the whole stew for seven hours, then strain off the liquor or *consomme*. Break four eggs into a stewpan, and put to them the *consomme* when cold, the juice of two lemons, and two spoonfuls of tarragon, and beat it with a whisk over the fire till near boiling, and when it does so, remove your stew-pan to a smaller fire, and place fire on the lid for half an hour; then pass it through a wet napkin doubled. If the jelly is not sufficiently clear, clarify it a second time. Put a layer of this jelly, about half an inch thick, at the bottom of an aspick mould, garnish it with truffles, whites of eggs, sprigs of parsley, &c. according to your taste, pour in another half inch of the jelly, while liquid, with great care, so as not to discompose your garnish, then put either calf's brains, breasts of fowl, veal sweetbreads, cocks' combs, kidneys, fat livers, or game. Be sure to lay whatever you may use, as equal and smooth as possible, then fill up your mould with jelly, and let it stand till set. When wanted, dip the mould in hot water an instant, place your dish on the top and turn it over.

ATTELETS, OYSTER.   *(See Oysters.)*

ATTELETS are silver skewers.

AUNT MARY'S PUDDING. *(See Puddings.)*

wwwwww

### B

BACCHIC CREAM.   *(See Cream.)*

BACCHIC SAUCE.   *(See Sauce.)*

BACON. Cover a pound of nice streaked bacon or salt pork with cold water, let it boil gently for three-quarters of an hour; take it up, scrape the under side well, and cut off the rind: grate a crust of bread not only on the top, but all over it, and put it before the fire for a few minutes: it must not be there too long, or it will dry it and spoil it. Two pounds will require about an hour and a half, according to its thickness; the hock or gammon being very thick, will take more. The boiling of bacon is a very simple subject to comment upon; but our main object is to teach common cooks the art of dressing common food in the best manner. Bacon is sometimes as salt as salt can make it, therefore before it is boiled it must be soaked in warm water for an hour or two, changing the water once; then pare off the rusty and smoked part, trim it nicely on the under side, and scrape the rind as clean as possible *Mem.*—Bacon is an extravagant article in housekeeping; there is often twice as much dressed as need be; when it is sent to table as an accompaniment to boiled poultry or veal, a pound and a half is plenty for a dozen people. A good German sausage is a very economical substitute for bacon; or fried pork sausages.

*Note.—Bacon in England and salt pork in America are the same thing. What we name bacon, the English call ham.*

BACON TO BROIL. Make up a sheet of paper into the form of a dripping-pan; cut your bacon into thin slices, cut off the rind, lay the bacon on the paper, put it upon the gridiron, set over a slow fire, and it will broil cleanly.

BACON AND EGGS. Cut a quarter of a pound of streaked bacon into thin slices, and put them into a stewpan over a slow fire, taking care to turn them frequently; when sufficiently done, pour the melted fat of the bacon into a dish, break over it seven or eight eggs, add two spoonfuls of gravy, a little salt and pepper, and stew the whole over a slow fire: pass a salamander over it, and serve.

BACON, GAMMON, TO BAKE. Lay it to steep all night in water, scrape it clean, and stuff it with all manner of sweet herbs, as thyme, sage, savory, sweet marjoram, penny-royal, strawberry leaves, violet leaves, and fennel; chop these small, and mix them with the yolks of hard eggs, pepper and nutmeg beaten, and boil it until tender. When it is cold pare off the under side, pull off the skin, season it with pepper and nutmeg, and put it in a pie or pasty, with whole cloves and slices of raw bacon laid over it, and butter; close it, and bake it.

BACON OR HAM SLICES. Ham, or bacon, may be fried, or broiled on a gridiron over a clear fire, or toasted with a fork: take care to slice it of the same thickness in every part. If you wish it curled, cut it in slices about two inches long (if longer, the outside will be done too much before the inside is done enough); roll it up, and put a little wooden skewer through it: put it in a cheese-toaster or Dutch oven, for eight or ten minutes, turning it as it gets crisp. This is considered the handsomest way of dressing bacon; but we like it best uncurled, because it is crisper, and more equally done. Slices of ham or bacon should not be more than half a quarter of an inch thick, and will eat much more mellow if soaked in hot water for a quarter of an hour, and then dried in a cloth before they are broiled, &c.

BACON RELISHING RASHERS. If you have any cold bacon you may make a very nice dish of it by cutting it into slices about a quarter of an inch thick; grate some crust of bread, as directed for ham and powder them well with it on both sides; lay the rashers in a cheese-toaster, they will be browned on one side in about three minutes, turn them and do the other. These are a delicious accompaniment to poached or fried eggs: the bacon having been boiled first, is tender and mellow. They are an excellent garnish round veal cutlets, or sweetbreads, or calf's head hash, or green peas or beans, &c.

BAIN MARIE. A flat vessel, containing boiling water, meant to hold other sauce-pans, either for purposes of cookery or to keep dishes hot. The advantages of preserving the heat of dishes by the *bain marie* is this, that no change is effected in the flavor of the ingredients.

BALM BEER. *(See Beer.)*

BANBURY CAKES. *(See Cakes.)*

BARLEY CREAM. *(See Cream.)*

BARLEY WATER. Take a couple of ounces of pearl barley, wash it clean with cold water, put it into half a pint of boiling water and let it boil for five minutes; pour off this water, and add to it two quarts of boiling water: boil it to two pints, and strain it. The above is simple barley water. To a quart of this is frequently added two ounces of figs, sliced; the same of raisins, stoned;

half an ounce of liquorice, sliced and bruised; and a pint of water. Boil it till it is reduced to a quart, and strain. *Obs.*—These drinks are intended to assuage thirst in ardent fevers and inflammatory disorders, for which plenty of mild diluting liquor is one of the principal remedies: and if not suggested by the medical attendant, is frequently demanded by honest instinct, in terms too plain to be misunderstood: the stomach sympathizes with every fibre of the human frame, and no part of it can be distressed without in some degree offending the stomach: therefore it is of the utmost importance to sooth this grand organ, by rendering everything we offer to it as elegant and agreeable as the nature of the case will admit of: the barley drink prepared according to the second receipt, will be received with pleasure by the most delicate palate.

BARLEY BROTH. *(See Broth.)*

BARLEY GRUEL. Take three ounces of pearl barley, of which make a quart of barley water; if it be not white, shift it once or twice; put in two ounces of currants clean picked and washed, and when they are plumped, pour out the gruel and let it cool a little; then put in the yolks of three eggs well beaten, half a pint of white wine, and of new thick cream half a pint; and lemon-peel; then sweeten with fine sugar to your taste; stir it gently over the fire, until it is thick as cream.

BARLEY PUDDING. *(See Pudding)*

BARBERRY JELLY. *(See Jelly.)*

BARBERRY CONSERVE. Put a pound of ripe barberries and half an ounce of powdered fennel seed into a silver vessel, with a glass of water; boil them three or four times, and press the juice through a sieve. Replace the vessel on the fire with the juice, and add to it a pound and a half of sugar, boiled *au casse*. Boil together a few times, and then pour the conserve into cases.

BARBERRY SIRUP. *(See Sirup.)*

BARBERRIES TO PICKLE. Boil the bruised berries of a few bunches in salt-and-water; strain, and put a gill of the liquor to a quart of vinegar, with an ounce of salt, a quarter of a pound of loaf sugar, a quarter of an ounce of pounded ginger, and a little sliced horse-radish; boil and strain it, then pour it hot over the barberries, the finest bunches having been previously selected and placed in jars; when cold, cover them closely with bladder. They may also be kept in a jar, with a strong brine of salt-and-water poured over them. When any scum is observed upon the surface, the brine must be poured off, and some fresh added. They are kept closely covered.

BARBERRY SIRUP. *(See Sirup.)*

BASIL VINEGAR. *(See Vinegar.)*

BATH BUNS. *(See Buns.)*

BATTER FOR FISH, MEAT, FRITTERS, &c. Prepare it with fine flour, salt, a little oil, beer, vinegar, or white wine and the whites of eggs beat up; when of a proper thickness it will drop out of the spoon about the size of a nutmeg at once. Fry in oil or hog's lard.

BATTER PUDDING. *(See Pudding.)*

BEANS. Cut, wash, and boil the beans, and then throw them into a cullender. Put a piece of butter into your table-dish, lay the beans on it, and garnish them with chopped parsley laid round like a cord; heat the dish and serve.

BECHAMELLE. Reduce some sauce *tournee* over a good fire, moisten with chicken broth or *consomme*, constantly stir-

ring to prevent its catching; when of the proper consistence, add two glasses of boiling cream, continue stirring; pass it through a hair sieve and serve.

BECHAMEL, OR WHITE SAUCE. Cut in square pieces, half an inch thick, two pounds of lean veal, half a pound of lean ham; melt in a stewpan two ounces of butter; when melted, let the whole simmer until it is ready to catch at the bottom (it requires great attention, as, if it happen to catch at the bottom of the stewpan, it will spoil the look of your sauce); then add to it three table-spoonfuls of flour; when well mixed, add to it three pints of broth or water (pour a little at a time, that the thickening be smooth); stir it until it boil; put the stewpan on the corner of the stove to boil gently for two hours; season it with four cloves, one onion, twelve pepper-corns, a blade of mace, a few mushrooms and a fagot made of parsley, a sprig of thyme, and a bay leaf. Let the sauce reduce to a quart, skim the fat off, and strain it through a tamis cloth. To make a bechamel sauce, add to a quart of the above a pint of good cream; stir it until it is reduced to a good thickness; a few mushrooms give a good flavor to that sauce; strain it through a tamis cloth.

BEEF. The names of the various pieces, according to the method of dividing the carcass, are as follows:---The hind quarter contains the Sirloin; Rump; Edge-bone; Buttock, or Round; Mouse Buttock; Veiny Piece; Thick Flank; Thin Flank; Leg Ran; Legs; Fore Rib; Five Ribs.—The fore quarter contains the Middle Rib of four ribs; Chuck of three ribs; Shoulder, or Leg-of-Mutton Piece, containing a part of the Blade-bone; Brisket; Clod; Neck End, or Sticking Piece; Shin; Cheek. Besides these are the Tongue and Palate. The Entrails consist of the Heart; Sweetbreads; Kidneys; Skirts; and three kinds of Tripe, the Double, the Roll, and the Red Tripe.

Ox beef is considered the best. The flesh should feel tender, be fine in the grain, and of a bright red color, nicely marbled or mixed with fat. The fat should be white, rather than of a yellow color.

Heifer beef is excellent when finely fed, and is most suitable for small families. The bone should be taken out of a round of beef before it is salted, and it must be washed, skewered, and bound round firmly before being boiled. Salt beef should be put on with plenty of cold water; and when it boils the scum removed. It is then kept simmering for some hours. A piece weighing fifteen pounds will require three hours and a half to boil. Carrots and turnips for garnishing should be put on to boil with the beef. If in the least tainted, a piece of charcoal may be boiled with it.

When beef is to be kept any length of time, it should be carefully wiped every day. In warm weather, wood vinegar is an excellent preservative: it is put all over the meat with a brush. To protect the meat from flies, it may be sprinkled over with pepper. Tainted meat may be restored by washing in cold water, afterwards, in strong, chamomile tea, after which it may be sprinkled with salt and used the following day, first washing it in cold water. Roughly pounded charcoal rubbed all over the meat also restores it when tainted. In Scotland meat is frequently kept a fortnight smothered in oatmeal, and carefully wiped every day; and if it should be a little tainted, it is soaked some hours before it is used, in oatmeal and water.

These directions equally apply to all sorts of meat. The sirloin is the prime joint for roasting. When to be used, it should be washed, then dried with a clean cloth, and the fat covered over with a piece of white paper tied on with thread. The spit should be kept at all times exceedingly clean: it must be wiped dry immediately after it is drawn from the meat, and washed and scoured every time it is used. Care should be taken to balance the roast properly upon the spit, but, if not exactly right, it is better to make it equal by fastening on a leaden-headed skewer than to pierce it again. The fire should be prepared by putting on plenty of coals at the back. When put down, it should be about ten inches from the fire, and gradually drawn nearer. It is first basted with a little butter or fresh dripping, and then well basted with its own fat all the time it is roasting. Ten minutes before serving, it should be sprinkled with a little salt, then dredged with flour, and basted till it is frothed. When it is drawn from the spit some gravy will run out, to which may be added a little boiling salt-and-water poured along the bone: the beef is then garnished with plenty of finely scraped horseradish. A sirloin, weighing about fifteen pounds, should be roasted for three hours and a half. A thinner piece of the same weight requires only three hours. In cold weather meat requires longer roasting than in warm, and if newly killed than if it has been kept.

BEEF ALAMODE. (1) Take about eleven pounds of the mouse buttock, or clod of beef, or a blade-bone, or the sticking-piece, or the like weight of the breast of veal; cut it into pieces of three or four ounces each; put three or four ounces of beef drippings, and mince a couple of large onions, and put them into a large deep stew-pan; as soon as it quite hot, flour the meat, put it into the stew-pan, keep stirring it with a wooden spoon; when it has been on about ten minutes, dredge it with flour, and keep doing so till you have stirred in as much as you think will thicken it; then cover it with boiling water (it will take about a gallon), adding it by degrees, and stirring it together; skim it when it boils, and then put in one drachm of ground black pepper, two of allspice, and two bay leaves; set the pan by the side of the fire, or at a distance over it and let it stew very slowly for about three hours; when you find the meat sufficiently tender, put it into a tureen, and it is ready for table.

BEEF ALAMODE. (2) Take the bone out of a small round of fine ox beef, cut some fat bacon in long strips, dip them into common and shallot vinegar mixed, and roll them in the following seasoning: Grated nutmeg, black and Jamaica pepper, one or two cloves, and some salt, parsley, chives, lemon-thyme, notted marjoram, and savoury, shred quite small. Lard the beef very thickly, bind it firmly with tape, and rub the outside with the seasoning. Put it into a saucepan, with the rind of a lemon, four large onions, the red part of three or four carrots, and two turnips cut into dice; add a tea-cupful of strong ale and one of vinegar; let it stew for six or eight hours, turning it two or three times. Half an hour before serving, take out the beef and vegetables, skim off the fat, strain the sauce, and thicken it with a little flour-and-water mixed smooth, add a tea-cupful of Port wine, return it all into the pot, and let it boil.

BEEF ALAMODE. (3) Take a rump or piece of beef, bone it, beat it well and lard it with fat bacon, then put it into a stewpan with some rind of bacon, a calf's foot, an onion, carrot, a bunch of sweet herbs, a bay leaf, thyme, a clove of garlic, some cloves, salt, and pepper, pour over the whole a glass of water, let it stew over a slow fire for six hours at least. A clean cloth should be placed over the stew pan before the lid is put on, which must be carefully closed. When it is done, strain the gravy through a sieve, clear off the fat, and serve.

BEEF ALADAUBE. Take a round, a rump, or a veiny piece of beef, lard it with bacon, half roast it, or fry it brown; put it into a stewpan or a pot that will just hold it; add some gravy, an onion stuck with cloves, half a pint of white wine, a gill of vinegar, a bunch of sweet herbs, pepper, cloves, mace, and salt; cover it down very close, let it but just simmer till it is tender; take two ox palates, two sweetbreads, truffles, morels, artichoke bottoms, stew them all together in some gravy, and pour over the beef; have ready some forced meat balls fried, make some long, others round, dip some sippets into batter, fry and cut them three corner ways, and stick them into the meat; lay the balls round the dish.

BEEF ALABRAISE. (1) Bone a rump of beef; lard it very thickly with salt pork seasoned with pepper, salt, cloves, mace, and allspice, and season the beef with pepper and salt; put some slices of bacon into the bottom of the pan, with some whole black pepper, a little allspice, one or two bay leaves, two onions, a clove of garlic, and a bunch of sweet herbs. Put in the beef, and lay over it some slices of bacon, two quarts of weak stock, and half a pint of white wine. Cover it closely, and let it stew between six and seven hours. Sauce for the beef is made of part of the liquor it has been stewed in, strained, and thickened with a little flour and butter, adding some green onions cut small, and pickled mushrooms. It is poured hot over the beef.

BEEF ALABRAISE. (2) After a rump of beef has hung for five or six days, bone, and lard it thickly, but so as not to appear upon the surface, with bits of salt pork or ham cut about half an inch square, and rolled in the following seasoning well mixed: —Finely minced onion, parsley, thyme, a little garlic, pepper, and salt. What is left over of the seasoning add to a pint of vinegar, one of Port wine, and a tea-cupful of salad oil; steep the beef in this for one night; the following day paper it, and roast it in a cradle spit. Baste it well, and serve it with a thick brown gravy. A little lemon-juice and sliced pickled cucumbers may be added. Garnish with slices of boiled carrot and scraped horseradish.

BEEF ALANGLAISE. Take a rump of beef, or any piece you like better of the same size; tie it up neatly with packthread, and put it into a stewpan with two or three carrots, a parsnip, three or four onions, a bunch of parsley and green onions, a clove of garlic, a bay leaf, thyme, and basil; moisten with some stock or water, season, and let the beef stew gently till half done, then put in a few small cabbages, prepared in the following manner; boil a large cabbage, and having squeezed it perfectly dry, take off the leaves one by one, and put within each leaf a little veal or other force-meat, surrounding it with three or four more of the leaves, in such a manner as to form little cabbages, something larger than an egg; tie these with packthread, and let them be stewed with the beef. When the whole is done, clean away the outside loose fat, and put your beef in a dish, cut the little cabbages in half, and place them round the dish, with the cut side outward. Take a little of the stew, strain it through a sieve, and having skimmed off the fat, add a little cullis to thicken it. Reduce this over the fire to the consistence of a sauce, serving it over the meat and cabbages.

BEEF BALLS. Mince very finely a piece of tender beef, fat and lean; mince an onion, with some boiled parsley; add grated bread crumbs, and season with pepper, salt, grated nutmeg, and lemon-peel; mix all together, and moisten it with an egg beaten; roll it into balls; flour and fry them in boiling fresh drippings. Serve them with fried bread crumbs, or with a thickened brown gravy.

BEEF BOUILLI. (1) In plain English, is understood to mean boiled beef; but its culinary acceptation, in the French kitchen, is fresh beef dressed without boiling, and only very gently simmered by a slow fire. Cooks have seldom any notion, that good soup can be made without destroying a great deal of meat; however, by a judicious regulation of the fire, and a vigilant attendance on the soup-kettle, this may be accomplished. You shall have a tureen of such soup as will satisfy the most fastidious palate, and the meat make its appearance at table, at the same time, in possession of a full portion of nutritious succulence. This requires nothing more than to stew the meat very slowly (instead of keeping the pot boiling a gallop, as common cooks too commonly do), and to take it up as soon as it is done enough. See "Soup and bouilli," "Beef Shin stewed,"

"Scotch barley broth." Meat cooked in this manner affords much more nourishment than it does dressed in the common way, is easy of digestion in proportion as it is tender, and an invigorating, substantial diet, especially valuable to the poor, whose laborious employments require support.

BEEF BOUILLI. (2) Take a rump of beef, or part of one; bone and tie it together in a neat form, and put it into a pot, with any odd bits of butcher's meat you may happen to have in the house, either beef, veal, or mutton; you may add, also, the bones, feet, and necks of poultry or game, the meat of which has been taken for other dishes; place your pot on a moderate fire, not quite full of water, and skim gently. When it has boiled a short time, put in some salt, turnips, six carrots, and six onions, into one of which you should stick three cloves; add a bunch of leeks. Let the whole boil gently, till the beef is perfectly done; then take it out, and serve it up either with fresh parsley, with a sauce, or with onions or other vegetables.

BEEF BROSE. After any large piece of beef has been taken out of the pot it was boiled in, skim off the fat with part of the liquor and boil it in a saucepan. Have ready in a bowl oatmeal that has been toasted brown before the fire, pour in the boiling liquor and stir it a little; if too thick, add more liquor and send it to table quite hot.

BEEF BAKED. Let a buttock of beef which has been in salt about a week, be well washed and put into an earthen pan, with a pint of water; cover the pan tight with two or three sheets of *foolscap* paper—let it bake four or five hours in a moderately heated oven.

BEEF BAKED WITH POTATOES. Boil some potatoes, peel, and pound them in mortar with one or two small onions; moisten them with milk and an egg beaten up; add a little salt and pepper. Season slices of beef, or mutton chops, with salt and pepper, and more onion, if the flavor is approved; rub the bottom of a pudding dish with butter, and put a layer of mashed potatoes, which should be as thick as a batter, and then a layer of meat, and so on alternately till the dish is filled, ending with potatoes. Bake it in an oven for one hour.

BEEF TO COLLAR. Cut off the end of a brisket of beef, and bone it; sprinkle it with salt and saltpetre, and let it lie a week; mix together some grated nutmeg, Jamaica and black pepper, some chopped lemon thyme, sweet marjoram, and parsley; strew it over the meat, roll it up hard, sew it in a cloth, put it into a large jar of water, tie it closely, and bake it in an oven; take it out of the jar and press it with a heavy weight. When it is quite cold, take off the cloth, and keep it dry.

BEEF BROTH. *(see Broth.)*

BEEF, COLD RUMP STEAKS TO WARM. Lay them in a stewpan, with one large onion cut in quarters, six berries of allspice, the same of black pepper, cover the steaks with boiling water, let them stew gently one hour, thicken the liquor with flour and butter rubbed together on a plate; if a pint of gravy, about one ounce of flour, and the like weight of butter, will do; put it into the stewpan, shake it well over the fire for five minutes, and it is ready; lay the steaks and onions on a dish and pour the gravy through a sieve over them.

BEEF CULLIS. *(See Cullis.)*

BEEF, COLD TENDERLOIN. (1) Cut off entire the inside of a large sirloin of beef, brown it all over in a stewpan, then add a quart of water, half a pint of Port wine, a tea-cupful of strong beer, two table-spoonfuls of vinegar, some pepper, salt, and a large onion finely minced; cover the pan closely, and let it stew till the beef be very tender. Garnish with pickles.

BEEF, COLD TENDERLOIN. (2) Cut off the meat with a little of the fat, into strips three inches long and half an inch thick; season with pepper and salt, dredge them with flour, and fry them brown in butter; then simmer them in a rich brown gravy; add of mushroom catchup, onion, and shallot vinegar, a table-spoonful each. Garnish with fried parsley.

BEEF FILLET IN MADERIA. Lard a good fillet of beef, the same as for roasting, join the ends together, and place it in this manner in a stewpan with some onions, carrots, and a *bouquet garni*, some *consomme* and Madeira, cover it with a buttered paper; let it boil for a moment, and afterwards let it boil slowly. Put fire upon the top of your stewpan. When it is done strain the broth through a silk sieve, reduce it, and serve it as a sauce to your meat.

BEEF FILLET ROASTED. This fillet lies only in the inside of the sirloin next to the chine, and is the tenderest part of the ox; spit this on a small spit, but do not run it through the best part of the meat: roast it gently, and baste it with butter; catch gravy in a dish while the beef is roasting; in the meantime make a sauce for it with sweet herbs and parsley shred fine, the yolks of four eggs, an onion, and some orange-peel chopped small; put these into sweet butter, gravy, a spoonful or two of strong broth and vinegar, stew them all together. Put your beef into this sauce, and serve it hot.

BEEF FRICANDEAU. Take a nice bit of lean beef, lard it with bacon, seasoned with pepper, salt, cloves, mace, and allspice. Put it into a stewpan with a pint of broth, a glass of white wine, a bundle of parsley, all sorts of sweet herbs, a clove of garlick, a shallot or two, four cloves, pepper and salt. When the meat is become tender, cover it close;

skim the sauce well, and strain it. Set it on the fire, and let it boil till it is reduced to a glaze. Glaze the larded side with this, and serve the meat on sorrel sauce.

BEEF GOBBETS. Take about six pounds of any piece of beef, except the leg or shin, cut it into pieces about the size of a hen's egg, put them into a stewpan, and just cover them with water, put them over the fire, and when the scum rises, skim it clear off, then put in some cloves, mace, allspice, and whole pepper, tied in a muslin, six heads of celery, cut an inch long, and well washed, a carrot or two cut in slices, two turnips cut in dice, a bundle of sweet herbs, some pepper and salt, and a crust of bread; stew it till the meat is tender, and then take out the spice, herbs, and bread; have some crusts of French roll crisped before the fire, put them in a dish, and put the meat, &c. over them. You put in two ounces of Scotch barley or rice when you put in the herbs.

BEEF GRAVY.  *(See Gravy.)*

BEEF H-BONE. Is to be managed in exactly the same manner as the round, but will be sooner boiled, as it is not so solid. An H-bone of 20lbs. will be done enough in about four hours; of 10lbs, in three hours, more or less, as the weather is hotter or colder. Be sure the boiler is big enough to allow it plenty of water-room: let it be well covered with water: set the pot on one side of the fire to boil gently: if it boils quick at first, no art can make it tender after. The slower it boils, the better it will look, and the tenderer it will be. The same accompanying vegetables as in "Beef Salt Round." Dress plenty of carrots, as cold carrots are a general favorite with cold beef. *Mem.*— Epicures say, that the *soft*, fat-like marrow, which lies on the back, is delicious when hot, and the *hard* fat about the upper corner is best when cold.

BEEF HASHED. (1)  Take three or four onions, chop them very fine, and put them into a stewpan with piece of butter and a little flour; stir it over the fire till nearly done and well browned; then moisten them with a little stock and half a glass of wine, adding some salt and coarse pepper; let them stew till they are thoroughly done, and very little sauce remains; then put in the cold beef, minced small, and let the whole simmer till it has taken the flavor of the onion. When you serve, add a spoonful of mustard and little vinegar.

BEEF HASHED. (2) Cut some of the underdone part of the beef, in slices, with some of the fat, put it into a small stewpan, with some onion or shallot, (a very little will do), a little water, pepper, and salt: boil it till the onion is quite soft, then put some of the gravy of the meat to it, and the hash. Do not let it boil; have a small hot dish with sippets of bread ready, and put the hash into it, but first mix a large spoonful of vinegar with it; if shallot vinegar is used there will be no need of the onion or raw shallot. You may add a spoonful of walnut liquor or catchup. Observe, that it is owing to *boiling* hashes or minces, that they get hard. All sorts of stews, or meat  dressed a second time, should be only simmered; and this last only hot through.

BEEF HAM.  Rub a little common salt over a piece of beef of about twenty pounds weight; take out the bone, and in one or two days, rub well into the beef the following ingredients, finely pounded and well mixed: —two ounces of sal-prunella, four ounces of brown sugar, six ounces of bay salt, one ounce of white pepper, and of cloves and nutmeg, a quarter of an ounce each; then strew over it half a pound of common salt. Let it lie fifteen days, turning it daily. It is then hung up; or when taken out of the pickle, it may be boiled, and allowed to stand till cold in the water in which it was boiled; or it may be baked in a deep dish, covered with a coarse paste.

BEEF HEART, TO ROAST. Wash it well, and clean all the blood carefully from the pipes: parboil it ten or fifteen minutes in boiling water; drip the water from it; put in a stuffing which has been made of bread crumbs, minced suet or butter, sweet marjoram, lemon thyme, and parsley, seasoned with salt, pepper, and nutmeg. Put it down to roast while hot, baste it well with butter, froth it up, and serve it with melted butter and vinegar; or with gravy in the dish, and current jelly in a sauce-tureen. To hash it, follow the directions given for hare.

BEEF HUNG, BURGESS'S METHOD OF BOILING. Hung beef for grating should be put on in boiling water, and, to preserve the color, kept boiling as fast as possible. Allow for six pounds of beef one hour and a half. It will keep good for a length of time.

BEEF, HUNTING. Rub well into a round of beef weighing about forty pounds, three ounces of saltpetre; let it stand five or six hours; pound three ounces of allspice, one of black pepper, and mix them with two pounds of salt, and seven ounces of brown sugar. Rub the beef all over with the salt and spices, let it remain fourteen days, and every other day turn and rub it with the pickle; then wash off the spices, and put it into a deep pan. Cut small nearly six pounds of beef suet, put some into the bottom of the pan, but the greater part upon the top of the beef. Cover it with a coarse paste, and bake it eight hours. When cold, take off the crust, and pour off the gravy. It will keep good for three months. Preserve the gravy, as a little of it improves the flavor of hashes, soups, or any made dishes.

BEEF KIDNEY. Take some kidneys, cut them into thin slices, and broil them with a piece of butter, some salt, pepper, parsley, and green onions, and a clove of garlick, the whole should be shred fine; when they are sufficiently done, take them off the fire (they should not broil too long, or they will become tough); add, when you serve them, a few drops of vinegar and a little cullis. Beef kidneys may likewise be served, with shallot sauce, or sauce *piquante*.

BEEF KIDNEY SAUCE  *(See Sauce.)*

BEEF MINCED. (1) Take some cold roasted fillet of beef, cut out all the fat and suet, then chop the meat as fine as possible, and put it into a reduced Spanish sauce made boiling hot; when ready to serve, add a bit of butter to it. Serve your mince with soft boiled eggs round it, or with pieces of toasted bread.

BEEF MINCED. (2) Mince your beef very small; put it into a saucepan with a little gravy and a little of the fat of fowl or any other fat, moisten it with some stock and a little white wine; season according to your taste, then let it simmer over a gentle fire till it is sufficiently done.

BEEF OLIVES. Cut the beef into long thin steaks; prepare a forcemeat made of bread-crumbs, minced beef suet, chopped parsley, a little grated lemon-peel, nutmeg, pepper, and salt; bind it with the yolks of eggs beaten; put a layer of it over each steak; roll and tie them with thread. Fry them lightly in beef dripping; put them in a stewpan with some good brown gravy, a glass of white wine, and a little Cayenne; thicken it with a little flour and butter; cover the pan closely, and let them stew gently an hour. Before serving, add a table-spoonful of mushroom catchup; garnish with cut pickles.

BEEF AND OYSTER SAUSAGES. Scald three-quarters of a pint of oysters in their own liquor; take them out and chop them finely; mince one pound of beef and mutton, and three-quarters of a pound of beef suet; add the oysters, and season with salt, pepper, mace, and two cloves pounded; beat up two eggs, and mix them well with the other ingredients, and pack it closely into a jar. When to be used, roll it into the form of small sausages; dip them into the yolk of an egg beaten up; strew grated bread crumbs over them, or dust with flour, and fry them in fresh dripping. Serve them upon fried bread hot.

BEEF PRESSED. Salt a piece of brisket (thin part of the flank) or the tops of the ribs, with salt and saltpetre, five days, then boil it gently till extremely tender; put it under a great weight, or in a cheese press, till perfectly cold. It eats excellently cold, and for sandwiches.

BEEF POTTED. Take three pounds of lean beef, salt it two or three days with half a pound of common salt, and half an ounce of saltpetre; divide it into pieces of a pound each, and put it into an earthen pan just sufficient to contain it; pour in half a pint of water; cover it close with paste, and set it in a very slow oven for four hours: when taken from the oven pour the gravy from it into a basin, shred the meat fine, moisten it with the gravy poured from the meat, and pound it thoroughly in a marble mortar with fresh butter, till it becomes a fine paste, season it with black pepper and allspice, or cloves pounded, or grated nutmeg; put it in pots, press it down as close as possible, put a weight on it, and let it stand all night; next day, when it is quite cold, cover it a quarter of an inch thick with clarified butter, and tie it over with paper.

BEEF SALT ROUND. As this is too large for a moderate family, we shall write directions for the dressing half a round. Get the tongue side. Skewer it up tight and round, and tie a fillet of broad tape round it, to keep the skewers in their places. Put it into plenty of cold water, and carefully catch the scum as soon as it rises: let it boil till all the scum is removed, and then put the boiler on one side of the fire, to keep *simmering* slowly till it is done. Half a round of 15lbs. will take about three hours: if it weighs more, give it more time. When you take it up, if any stray scum, &c sticks to it that has escaped the vigilance of your skimmer, wash it off with a paste-brush: garnish the dishes with carrots and turnips. Send up carrots, turnips, and parsnips, or greens &c. on separate dishes. Peas pudding, and MY PUDDING, are all very proper accompaniments. N. B.—The outside slices, which are generally too much salted and too much boiled, will make a very good relish as potted beef. For using up the remains of a joint of boiled beef, see also Bubble and Squeak.

BEEF RAGOUT. Take a rump of beef, cut the meat from the bone, flour and fry it, pour over it a little boiling water, about a pint of small beer; add a carrot or two, an onion stuck with cloves, some whole pepper, salt, a piece of lemon-peel, a bunch of sweet herbs; let it stew an hour, then add some good gravy; when the meat is tender take it out, strain the sauce, thicken it with a little flour; add a little celery ready boiled, a little catchup, put in the meat, just simmer it up. Or the celery may be omitted, and the ragout enriched by adding mushrooms fresh or pickled, artichoke-bottoms boiled and quartered, and hard yolks of eggs. A piece of flank, or any piece that can be cut free from bone, will do instead of the rump.

BEEF RISSOLES. Chop finely a pound of lean tender beef, and a quarter of a pound of beef suet; pound them in a marble mortar; mix with it a quarter of a pound of grated bread, a little onion, and a head of garlick bruised; season with salt and pepper; bind it with three eggs well beaten; make it up into small cakes, fry them of a light brown, then stew them in gravy for fifteen or twenty minutes.

BEEF RIBS BONED AND ROLLED. When you have kept two or three ribs of beef till quite tender, take out the bones, and skewer it as round as possible (like a fillet of veal): before they roll it, some cooks egg it, and sprinkle it with veal stuffing. As the meat is more in a solid mass, it will require more time at the fire; a piece of tenor twelve pounds weight will not be well and thoroughly roasted in less than four and a half hours. For the first half hour, it should not be less than twelve inches from the fire, that it may get gradually warm to the centre: the last half hour before it will be finished, sprinkle a little salt over it; and if you wish to froth it, flour it, &c.

BEEF RUMP BAKED. Take a rump of beef, what size you please, bone and lard it, season it with salt and fine spices put it into a stewpan just large enough to hold it, together with half a pint of white wine, some green onions, mushrooms, and shallots; some lean bacon is an improvement. Close the edges of the pan with a strong paste; let it stew in an oven for five or six hours according to the size of your meat, then serve it with its own sauce strained. You may dress a sirloin in the same way.

BEEF RUMP TO STEW. (1) Bind the beef tightly, stick in four cloves, and put it in a saucepan, with three quarts of water, a quarter of an ounce of black pepper half beaten, some salt, a bunch of sweet herbs, and three anchovies; turn it often, and when half done take it out, pour off the liquor; put in the beef again, with a pint of Port wine and half a pint of table beer made scalding hot, and some of the liquor strained; stew it till tender, clear off the fat, and if the sauce is not strong enough, add well-seasoned beef gravy; thicken it with flour rubbed down in a little cold water. Dish the beef, and pour the gravy round it.

BEEF RUMP TO STEW. (2) Tie up the beef, and put it on to stew with nearly as much cold water as will cover it; add three pounds of fat bacon cut into slices, a handful of thyme, eight onions, four small carrots, two turnips, two or three bay leaves, some black pepper, a little allspice, mace, and three cloves, a pint of Port wine and one of Sherry. Let it stew gently between seven and eight hours. Take out the beef, strain the liquor, and skim off all the fat; thicken it with a little flour rubbed down in cold water, boil it up, and pour it over the beef. Have ready carrots and turnips, cut according to fancy, and boiled tender in weak gravy, and put them round the beef before serving.

BEEF RUMP-STEAKS STEWED. The steaks must be a little thicker than for broiling: let them be all the same thickness, or some will be done too little, and others too much. Put an ounce of butter into a stew-pan, with two onions; when the butter is melted, lay in the rump-steaks, let them stand over a slow fire for five minutes, then turn them and let the other side of them fry for five minutes longer. Have ready boiled a pint of button onions; they will take from half an hour to an hour; put the liquor they were boiled in to the steaks; if there is not enough of it to cover them, add broth or boiling water, to make up enough for that purpose, with a dozen corns of black pepper, and a little salt, and let them simmer very gently for about an hour and a half, and then strain off as much of the liquor (about a pint and a half) as you think will make the sauce. Put two ounces of butter into a stewpan; when it is melted, stir in as much flour as will make it into a stiff paste; some add thereto a table-spoonful of claret, or Port wine, the same of mushroom catchup half a tea-spoonful of salt and a quarter of a tea-spoonful of ground black pepper: add the liquor by degrees; let it boil up for fifteen minutes; skim it, and strain it; serve up the steaks with the onions round the dish, and pour the gravy over. Veal cutlets or mutton chops may be done the same way, or as veal olives.

BEEF RUMP-STEAK BROILED WITH

ONION GRAVY. Peel and slice two large onions, put them into a quart stewpan, with two table-spoonfuls of water; cover the stewpan close, and set it on a slow fire till the water has boiled away, and the onions have got a little browned; then add half a pint of good broth, and boil the onions till they are tender; strain the broth from them, and chop them very fine, and season it with mushroom catchup, pepper, and salt: put the onion into it, and let it boil gently for five minutes; pour it into the dish, and lay over it a broiled rump steak. If instead of broth you use good beef gravy, it will be superlative.

BEEF SAUSAGES. Take two beef steaks about the size of two hands, and the thickness of a finger; beat them well to make them flat, and pare the edges of them; then mince the parings with beef suet, parsley, green onions, mushrooms, two shallots, and some basil leaves, the whole shred fine, and mixed into a forcemeat with the yolks of four eggs; spread this forcemeat on the slices of beef, and roll them up in the form of sausages; tie them up with packthread, and stew them with a little stock, a glass of wine, some salt, pepper, an onion stuck with two or three cloves, a carrot, and a parsnip; when they are done, strain the liquor; and, having skimmed off the fat, reduce it over the fire to the consistence of a sauce. Take care that the sauce is not too higly flavored, and serve it over your sausages; or they may be served with any ragout of vegetables you please. To serve the sausages cold, to make a dish for the second course, reduce the sauce by letting it boil with the sausages till almost all the fat is consumed; then let them stand to cool with what remains of the sauce adhering to them, and serve upon a napkin.

BEEF, SHORT OR SPICED. (To be eaten cold.) Hang up ten or twelve pounds of the middle part of a brisket of beef for three or four days, then rub well into it three ounces of finely powdered saltpetre, and, if spice is approved of, one ounce of allspice, and half an ounce of black pepper; let it stand all night, then salt it with three pounds of well-pounded bay salt, and half a pound of treacle, in which let it remain ten days, rubbing it daily. When it is to be boiled, sew it closely in a cloth, let the water only simmer, upon no account allowing it to boil, for nine hours over a slow fire, or upon a stove. When taken out of the water, place two sticks across the pot, and let the beef stand over the steam for half an hour, turning it from side to side, then press it with a heavy weight. It must not be taken out of the cloth till perfectly cold.

BEEF SOUP. *(See Soup.)*

BEEF, SPRING GARDEN. Cut a piece of lean beef into thin slices like *Scotch collops*, lard it thick with bacon, and put it into a pan with salt, pepper, mace, two or three bay leaves, and a bunch of sweet herbs; bake it; then clear out all the gravy, and fill it up with clarified butter.

BEEF TO SALT FOR IMMEDIATE USE. Salt a round of beef moderately upon the tops and sides, put it upon sticks, or the tongs of a cheese-tub, over a tub of cold water, and the salt will be drawn through it, so that it will be fit for boiling next day.

ANOTHER METHOD IS—To rub for half an hour into any piece of beef a good quantity of salt, and let it lie for three or four days without touching it, when it may be used.

BEEF SIRLOIN. The noble sirloin of about fifteen pounds (if much thicker, the outside will be done too much before the inside is enough), will require to be before the fire about three and a half or four hours; take care to spit it evenly, that it may not be heavier on one side than the other; put a little clean dripping into the drippingpan, (tie a sheet of paper over it to preserve the fat), baste it well as soon as it is put down, and every quarter of an hour all the time it is roasting, till the last half hour; then take off the paper, and make some gravy for it; stir the fire and make it clear: to brown and froth it, sprinkle a little salt over it, baste it with butter, and dredge it with flour; let it go a few minutes longer, till the froth rises, take it up, put it on the dish, &c. Garnish it with hillocks of horse-radish, scraped as fine as possible with a very sharp knife. A Yorkshire pudding is an excellent accompaniment.

BEEF SHIN STEWED. Desire the butcher to saw the bone into three or four pieces, put it into a stewpan, and just cover it with cold water; when it simmers, skim it clean; then put in a bundle of sweet herbs, a large onion, a head of celery, a dozen berries of black pepper, and the same of allspice: stew very gently over a slow fire till the meat is tender; this will take from about three hours and a half, to four and a half. Take three carrots, peel and cut them into small squares; peel and cut ready in small squares a couple of turnips, with a couple of dozen of small young round silver button onions; boil them, till tender; the turnips and onions will be enough in about fifteen minutes; the carrots will require about twice as long: drain them dry. When the beef is quite tender, take it it out carefully with a slice, and put it on a dish while you thicken a pint and a half of the gravy: to do this, mix three table-spoonfuls of flour with a tea-cupful of the beef liquor; stir this thoroughly together till it boils, skim off the fat, strain it through a sieve, and put your vegetables in to warm; season with pepper, salt, and a wine-glass of mushroom catchup, or Port wine, or both, and pour it over the beef. Dr. Kitchener commends this dish as one of the very best that can be carried to table, and advises it be called *Ragout Beef.* A LEG OF MUTTON is excellent dressed the same way.

BEEF STEAKS, BROILED. Cut the steaks off a rump or the ribs of a fore quarter; beat them well with a rolling-pin. Have the gridiron perfectly clean and heated over a clear quick fire; lay on the steaks, and, with meat tongs, keep turning them constantly, till they are done enough; throw a little salt over them a little before taking them off the fire. Serve them as hot as possible, plain, or with a made gravy and sliced onion, or rub a bit of butter upon the steaks the moment of serving. Mutton chops are broiled in the same manner.

BEEF STEAKS, STEWED. Fry the steaks in a little butter; take them out of the pan, and fry in it a minced onion; return the steaks, with a little boiling water or gravy, some pepper, salt, and a table-spoonful of vinegar; stew them gently for two or three hours; thicken the sauce with butter rolled in flour; and serve with or without pickles.

BEEF STEAK PIE. *(See Pie.)*

BEEF STEAK PUDDING. *(See Pudding.)*

BEEF STEAKS, DRESSED. Cut thin steaks, longer than they are broad, off a rump; beat them with a rolling-pin; season them with pepper, salt, and finely minced onion; roll and tie them with a thread; cut them even at the ends; fry them brown with a little butter; make a sauce with a piece of butter browned with flour, some gravy or water, a minced onion, pepper, and salt. Boil it, and add the steaks, and let them stew an hour. Before serving, add some mushroom catchup, and take off the threads.

BEEF, SCARLET. Mix a little mace, cloves, allspice, black pepper, and saltpetre together, rub it well into two pounds of tender lean beef; let it lie six days, turning it daily, and rubbing it with the pickle; then roll and tie it firmly with tape; put it and the pickle into a small jar, with a slice or two of beef suet under and over it; tie it closely, and bake it an hour. It is eaten cold, cut in thin slices, and garnish with parsley. If long kept, the color fades.

BEEF STEWED. (1) Stew in five quarts of water the middle part of a brisket of beef weighing ten pounds, add two onions stuck with two cloves, one head of celery, one large carrot, two turnips cut small, a handful of sorrel leaves, half an ounce of black pepper, and some salt. Stew it gently for six hours. Make a strong gravy with carrots and turnips, the turnips to be scraped and fried of a brown color in butter; add pepper, salt, a little Cayenne; thicken it with flour and butter, and pour it over the beef, with the carrots and turnips.

BEEF STEWED. (2) Take ten pounds of a brisket of beef, cut the short ribs, and put it into a well-buttered saucepan, with two large onions, stuck with three or four cloves, two or three carrots cut into quarters, a bunch of sweet herbs, a small lemon sliced, and five quarts of water; let it stew seven hours. Strain and clarify the gravy—thicken it with butter and flour. Chop the carrots with some capers, mushroom catchup, and Cayenne. Any other pickle that is liked may be added.

BEEF STOCK. *(See Stock.)*

BEEF, MUTTON, OR VEAL TEA. Cut a pound of lean gravy meat into thin slices; put it into a quart and half a pint of cold water; set it over a very gentle fire, where it will become gradually warm; when the scum rises, let it continue simmering gently for about an hour; then strain it through a fine sieve or a napkin; let it stand ten minutes to settle, and then pour off the clear tea. N. B.—An onion, and a few grains of black pepper, are sometimes added. If the meat is boiled till it is thoroughly tender, you may mince it and pound it and make potted beef.

BEEF TRIPE FRICASSEE. Let your tripe be very white, cut it into slips, put it into some boiled gravy, with a little cream and a bit of butter mixed with flour; stir it till the butter is melted; add a little white wine, lemon-peel grated, chopped parsley, pepper and salt, pickled mushrooms, or lemon-juice; shake all together; stew it a little.

BEER, SPRUCE. When ten gallons of water, six pounds of molasses, and three ounces of bruised ginger have boiled together for half an hour, two pounds of the outer sprigs of the spruce fir are to be added, and boiled for five minutes; the whole is then to be strained through a hair sieve, and when milk-warm, put into the cask, and a teacupful of good yeast stirred well into it. When it has fermented a day or two, it is to be bunged up, and the following day bottled. It will be fit for use in a week. The ginger is sometimes omitted, and instead of the spruce fir, three ounces of the essence may be used, which is to be well whisked, together with the molasses, and a gallon or two of warm water; then put into the cask, which is to be filled up with water, and the yeast added.

BEER, SPRUCE. (2) The proportions are ten gallons of water, three quarts of molasses, a tea-cupful of ginger, the same of allspice, three ounces of hops, three ounces and a half of the essence of spruce, and half a pint of good yeast. The hops, ginger, and allspice, must be boiled together till the hops fall to the bottom; the molasses and spruce are then to be dissolved in a bucket-full of the liquor, the whole strained into a cask, and the yeast well stirred in; when the fermentation ceases, the cask is to be bunged up.

BEER, BALM. Eleven gallons of water and ten pounds of brown sugar are to be clarified with the whites of twelve eggs, carefully skimmed and boiled till nearly reduced to ten gallons; two pounds and a half of the yellow flower of lemon balm being put into a cask, the liquor, when milk-warm, is to be poured over it, and four or five table-spoonfuls of thick yeast added. The cask must be filled up morning and evening with what works over it, and bunged up when the fermentation ceases. In a month the beer may be bottled, and in two or three months it will be fit for drinking. Half the quantity of the flower of lemon balm will probably be found to communicate a flavor sufficiently strong, if added when the fermentation is nearly over.

BEER, GINGER. For a ten-gallon cask, eleven gallons of water, fourteen pounds of sugar, the juice of eighteen lemons, and one pound of ginger are allowed; the sugar and water are boiled with the whites of eight eggs, and well skimmed; just before coming to the boiling point, the ginger, which must be bruised, is then added, and boiled for twenty minutes; when cold, the clear part is put into the cask, together with the lemon-juice and two spoonfuls of yeast; when it has fermented for three or four days, it is fined, bunged up, and in a fortnight bottled. It may be made without the fruit.

BEER, GINGER, QUICKLY MADE. A gallon of boiling water is poured over three-quarters of a pound of loaf sugar, one ounce and a quarter of ginger, and the peel of one lemon; when milk-warm, the juice of the lemon and a spoonful of yeast are added. It should be made in the evening, and bottled next morning, in half-pint stone bottles, and the cork tied down with twine.

B E E R TO BOTTLE. When the briskness and liveliness of malt liquors in the cask fail, and they become dead and vapid, which they generally do soon after they are tilted; let them be bottled. Be careful to use clean and dried bottles; leave them unstopped for twelve hours, and then cork them as closely as possible with good and sound new corks; put a bit of lump sugar as big as a nutmeg into each bottle: the beer will be ripe, *i. e.* fine and sparkling, in about four or five weeks: if the weather is cold, to put it up the day before it is drunk, place it in a room where there is a fire. Remember there is a sediment, &c. at the bottom of the bottles, which you must carefully avoid disturbing; so pour it off at once, leaving a wine-glassful at the bottom.

*₊* If beer becomes hard or stale, a few grains of carbonate of potash added to it at the time it is drunk will correct it, and make draught beer as brisk as bottled ale.

BEET ROOT, May be either baked or boiled; it will take from an hour and a half to three hours, according to the size of the root, to cook properly.

BEET ROOT PICKLED. Boil the roots tender, peel, and cut them in what shape you please. Put them into a jar, and pour over them a hot pickle of vinegar, pepper, ginger, and sliced horse-radish. You may add capsicums and Cayenne.

BENTON SAUCE. *(See Sauce.)*

BENTON CAKES. *(See Cakes.)*

BIRDS POTTED, HOW TO PRESERVE WHEN THEY BEGIN TO GROW BAD. When birds have come a great way they often smell so bad that they can scarcely be borne from the rankness of the butter, by managing them in the following manner they may be made as good as ever. Set a large saucepan of clean water on the fire; when it boils take off the butter at the top, then take the fowls out one by one, throw them into that saucepan of water half a minute, whip it out, and dry it in a cloth inside and out; continue till they are all done, scald the pot clean; when the birds are quite cold, season them with mace, pepper and salt, according to taste, put them down close in a pot, and pour clarified butter over them.

BISCUITS. (1) Weigh eight eggs, an equal weight of sugar, and the weight of four in flour; beat up the yolks of five, and put them in an earthen vessel with some rasped lemon-peel and the sugar, beat them together for a long time, then add the whites of eleven eggs also well beaten, then mix in the flour by degrees, pour this into paper cases of whatever form and size you please; strew powder sugar over them, and bake in a cool oven.

BISCUITS. (2) Make a pound of flour, the yolk of an egg, and some milk into a very stiff paste; beat it well, knead till quite smooth, roll very thin and cut into biscuits, prick and bake in a slow oven till dry and crisp.

BISCUITS, ALMOND. (1) Blanch and pound a quarter of a pound of sweet almonds, sprinkling them occasionally with fine sugar; then beat them up for a quarter of an hour with an ounce of flour, the yolks of three eggs, and four ounces of fine sugar, adding afterwards the whites of four eggs whipped to a froth: have ready some paper moulds made like boxes, about the length of two fingers square; butter them within, and put in the biscuits, throwing over them equal quantities of flour and powdered sugar: bake in a cool oven, and when the biscuits are done of a good color, take them out of the papers. Bitter almond biscuits are made in the same manner, with this difference, that to two ounces of bitter almonds must be added one ounce of sweet almonds.

BISCUITS, ALMOND. (2) Take eight ounces of sweet, and as many bitter almonds, fifteen whites, and eight yolks of eggs, two ounces of flour, and two pounds of powder sugar, pour boiling water on your almonds, and almost immediately after turn that away and pour cold water on them; rub off the skins one by one with a napkin, then pound them to a paste in a mortar, moistening them with the whites of two eggs. Beat the fifteen whites to a snow, and the eight yolks with half the quantity of the sugar, and then mix them with the almond paste; put

the remainder of the sugar into a basin; sift some flour over it; stir the mixture till all the ingredients are thoroughly incorporated, and pour it into small paper cases, glaze them with the sugar and flour sifted over them. Bake them in a pretty warm oven.

BISCUITS, ALMOND ( SMALL). Beat up the yolks of three eggs for ten minutes, with four ounces of powder sugar and one ounce of bitter almonds well pounded; then add a whole egg, and beat it up five minutes longer. Whip the whites to a strong froth; mix them and an ounce and half of fine sifted flour with the yolks; work this paste well, and then pour it into small well-buttered copper moulds melon-shaped; glaze them; sprinkle them with powder sugar, and bake for eighteen or twenty minutes in a moderate oven.

BISCUITS, ALMOND (SOUFFLES). Blanch half a pound of sweet almonds, cut them into dice and dry them in the oven. Make a glaze with the whites of two new-laid eggs; mix the almonds and a pinch of crisped orange-flowers into this, and put it into very small paper cases; do not fill them above half full, as they rise considerably in the oven, and would otherwise fall over and spoil their appearance; bake them in a moderately heated oven. As soon as they are pretty firm, they are done.

BISCUITS, ANISE (SMALL). Wash four drachms of starred anise, and dry it in the oven; work up the yolks of five eggs and a quarter of a pound of powder sugar for about ten minutes; whip the whites to a strong froth; and mix them lightly with the yolks: add a quarter of a pound of dry sifted flour and the anise; pour this paste into a paper case, eleven inches long by seven wide. Bake it in a slow oven for about forty or fifty minutes, when, if firm, take it out. As soon as it is cold remove the paper, and cut the biscuits into whatever forms you please: dry them in the oven until they become brittle.

BISCUIT, BREAD. Dry fine flour and powder sugar, of each half a pound, thoroughly: beat up four very fresh eggs for ten minutes, then add the sugar, beat them ten minutes longer, put the flour, and continue beating ten minutes more. Butter your baking plates and bake. Caraway or aniseed may be added, if you please.

BISCUITS, BUTTER. Make a paste as for sweet biscuits, and when you have put in the flour, pour over it eight ounces of melted butter, after it has cooled a little; mix them together a short time with a wooden spoon, and put into buttered moulds, which must only be filled three parts, as the paste puffs up considerably, and would rise from the moulds, without care.

BISCUIT CAKE. *(See Cake.)* .

BISCUITS, CHESTNUT. Take six ounces of roasted and skinned chestnuts, a little grated lemon-peel, a pound and a half of powder sugar, and ten whites of eggs. Pound the chestnuts to a paste, and then beat it up in an earthen pan with the other ingredients; when your paste is of a proper thickness, take it up with a knife, and lay it on paper, and form into biscuits whatever size you please. Bake them in a moderate oven, and when of a nice color take them out. Do not remove them from the paper till they are cold.

BISCUITS, DROP. (1) Pound and sift a pound of fine sugar, take the yolks of seven and the whites of ten eggs and beat well separately for an hour. Dry and sift a pound of fine flour, and when cold mix it with the eggs and sugar, beat all together for a quarter of an hour, drop upon paper, sift sugar over, and bake them.

BISCUITS, DROP. (2) Beat a pound of sugar, the yolks of four, and whites of two eggs, with a little white wine, then put in a pound of flour, and a few seeds, mix all well together. Butter a paper; lay your batter on in spoonfuls, ice them with fine sugar, and set them in a gentle oven.

BISCUITS EN CAPSULE. Put half a pound of fine sugar into an earthen pan, and pour over it the yolks of twelve eggs; put the whites into a preserving-pan, and whisk them for half an hour; in the meantime the sugar and yolks of eggs must be stirred with a wooden spoon, and pour them on the whites; stir them gently, add six ounces of fine flour and two of powder sugar sifted, and the grated rind of a lemon. Mix it all well together, but with great care, lest the snow of the whites should fall. With this fill some small buttered moulds, or paper cases, and bake them in a quick oven to a deep yellow, first sprinkling them with sugar. If they are in moulds, turn them out when baked; but they may remain in the paper cases, which need not be buttered.

BISCUITS, FILBERT. Take half a pound of filberts, an ounce of bitter almonds, the whites of six, and the yolks of three eggs, an ounce of flour, and half a pound of sugar; blanch and pound the filberts and almonds, adding, occasionally, a little white of egg to prevent their oiling. Beat the whites to a snow, then the yolks, mix the latter with half the sugar; beat them well, and having mixed the other ingredients together, put them into a sieve, and whilst you are beating, sift them into the whites; when all are thoroughly incorporated, pour the preparation into paper cases, and bake them in a moderate oven. A little grated lemon-peel, or any other aromatic ingredient added to the yolks, greatly improves these biscuits.

BISCUIT, FRENCH. Weigh five eggs, and their weight in dried and sifted flour, and in finely-pounded loaf sugar; beat the whites of the eggs to a stiff froth, and by degrees beat in the sugar and the flour, and then add the beaten yolks; with a spoon half fill yellow tea-cups, previously rubbed with butter, and sift loaf sugar over the top. Bake them in a quick oven. Or, drop the biscuit in a round form upon sheets of white paper buttered; sift sugar over them.

BISCUIT, KING'S. Put half a pound of butter into a basin, and work it about well with a wooden spoon; break six eggs and whisk them well, add a half pound of powder-sugar, and whisk ten minutes longer, and then mix them with the butter; stir in six ounces of currants, and the same of dried flour. When all is well mixed, drop it, the size of a shilling, on paper, and bake in a quick oven. Take them off while hot.

BISCUIT, LEMAN'S. Sift and dry a pound of fine flour; rub it into a quarter of a pound of butter, two ounces of pounded and sifted loaf sugar, and a bit of volatile salt about the size of a nut; mix in as much new milk warmed as will make it into a stiff paste; work it well together, and let it remain for two or three hours, and then roll it out, and make it into small square biscuits, and into round balls a little flattened; prick them with a fork, and bake them upon tins in a quick oven. Take care they do not become brown.

BISCUITS, NAPLES. Put three-quarters of a pound of fine flour to a pound of fine sifted sugar; sift both together three times, then add six eggs beaten well, and a spoonful of rose-water; when the oven is nearly hot, bake them, but not too wet.

BISCUIT, THE NUNS. Take the whites of twelve eggs, and beat them to a froth; a pound of almonds, blanch them, and beat them with the froth of the whites of eggs, as it rises; then take the yolks, and two pounds of fine sugar and beat them well together, then mix the almonds with the sugar and eggs; then add half a pound of flour, with the peel of four lemons grated, and some citron shred small; put the composition in little cakepans, and bake them in a quick oven, and when they are colored, turn them on tins to harden the bottoms: but before you set them in the oven again, sift on them some double-refined sugar. Let the pans be buttered, and fill them half way.

BISCUITS, POTATO. (1) Beat the yolks of fifteen eggs with a pound of sifted sugar, grate the rind of a lemon on a piece of lump sugar; scrape off the yellow sugar with a knife, and having dried it well, add it to the above, and continue to beat till it becomes quite white; in the meantime whip up an equal number of whites, and mix them lightly with the rest; then sift into it half a pound of potato flour; stir it in, and pour the preparation into paper cases, but not to fill them; glaze, and place the cases on paper laid on a clean baking-tin, and bake in a moderate oven.

BISCUIT, POTATO. (2) Beat separately the yolks and whites of fifteen eggs, and with the yolks beat a pound of pounded and sifted loaf sugar, and the grated peel of a lemon; when very light add the whites, and sift in through a silk sieve half a pound of flour of potatoes; mix all lightly together, half fill paper cases, and strew over them roughly pounded sugar, put a piece of paper upon a board, place the paper cases upon it, and bake them in a moderate oven. To ornament them, put here and there upon the top a little red-currant jelly, and serve them.

BISCUITS, THE QUEEN'S. Take a pound and a half of flour, a pound and a half of fine sugar, the whites of twenty-four, and the yolks of eighteen eggs, put in coriander seeds beaten small at discretion; mix these well together, and make them into a soft paste, add a little soft yeast or not. Lay this paste on paper, or in crusts about two inches broad, and four inches long, set them in a moderate oven, and when they begin to turn brown, take them out, and lay them on paper, in a dry place.

BISCUITS, RICE. Take the grated rind of a lemon, the whites of sixteen eggs, the yolks of six, half a pound of rice flour, ten ounces of powder sugar, two ounces of apple, and the same of apricot, marmalade, and two ounces of orange-flowers. Pound the marmalades and orange-flowers together, then add the whites of eggs, whipped to a snow; beat the yolks with the sugar for a quarter of an hour, put them to the rest, and when well mixed in, add the lemon-peel and rice-flour; work all together, pour the preparation into paper cases, bake them in a moderate oven, and glaze them.

BISCUITS, SMALL. Make a paste with a quarter of a pound of flour, three spoonfuls of fine powder sugar, and the same of marmalade; add whites of eggs to work it pretty soft; and make this paste to what shape and size you please.

BISCUITS, SPUNGE. Beat together, for half an hour, four well-beaten eggs, and half a pound of finely-pounded loaf sugar; then mix in lightly six ounces of dried and sifted flour, and the grated peel of a lemon, or a tea-spoonful of essence of lemon, with a table-spoonful of rose water. Flour the pans, fill them half full, and sift pounded sugar over them. Bake them in a quick oven.

BISCUITS, ST. CLOUD. Sift two ounces of rice-flour through a tammy into an earthen pan, with half a pound of powder sugar, the yolks of four eggs, and a little green lemon grated; beat them up together for a quarter of an hour: whisk the whites of eight eggs to a froth and mix them with the yolks. Put this into buttered moulds or paper cases, and bake in a moderate oven. When done take them from the mould while hot, and ice them in the following manner: beat up half the white of an egg and two spoonfuls of powder-sugar with a wooden spoon, add occasionally a few drops of lemon-juice; when it becomes quite white lay it over the biscuits; and place them in the oven a minute to dry.

BISCUIT, SUGAR. (1) The weight of eight eggs in finely-pounded loaf sugar, and of four in dried flour; beat separately the whites and yolks; with the yolks beat the sugar for half an hour, then add the whites and the flour, and a little grated nutmeg, lemon-peel, or pounded cinnamon. Bake them in yellow tea-cups, or drop them upon paper, as the French biscuits.

BISCUIT, SUGAR. (2) Mix together one pound of dried and sifted flour, the same quantity of pounded and sifted loaf sugar, ten well-beaten eggs, and a few pounded cloves. Drop this upon floured tins, and bake it.

BISCUIT, SWEET. One pound of flour, half a pound of butter, the same quantity of finely-pounded sugar, and two eggs, without being beaten; make it all into a very stiff paste with cool water, roll it out, and to form the biscuits, roll a bit of the paste into a ball about the size of the yolk of an egg, flatten it a little, and place them upon tins to bake.

BISCUITS, YARMOUTH. Pick and wash half a pound of currants, dry them well, rub a little flour with them, and put them with half a pound of powder-sugar, three-quarters of a pound of sifted flour, and half a pound of fresh butter; mix them into a paste with three eggs, roll it out to the thickness of the eighth of an inch, cut them into what shapes you please. Bake them of a light color in a hot oven.

BISHOP. Roast four good sized bitter oranges till they are of a pale brown color; lay them in a tureen, and put over them half a pound of pounded loaf sugar, and three glasses of claret; place the cover on the tureen, and let it stand till next day. When required for use, put the tureen into a pan of boiling water, press the oranges with a spoon, and run the juice through a sieve; then boil the remainder of the bottle of claret, taking care that it do not burn; add it to the strained juice, and serve it warm in glasses.

BLANC. A mixture of butter, salt, water, and a slice of lemon; also as follows: —Cut a pound of beef suet, and the same of fat bacon into dice, half a pound of butter, the juice of a lemon, salt and pepper, one or two onions, a bunch of parsley, a little thyme, a bay leaf and spice.

BLANCMANGE. (1) To one ounce of picked isinglass, put a pint of water, boil it till the isinglass is melted, with a bit of cinnamon; put to it three-quarters of a pint of cream, two ounces of sweet almonds, six bitter ones blanched and beaten, a bit of lemon-peel, sweeten it, stir it over the fire, let it boil, strain and let it cool, squeeze in the juice of a lemon, and put into moulds; garnish to your fancy. Blancmange may be colored green by adding spinach-juice; red, by a bit of cochineal in brandy, let it stand half an hour and strain it; yellow with saffron.

BLANCMANGE. (2) Boil for a few minutes a pint and a half of new milk, with an ounce of picked isinglass (if in summer, one ounce and a quarter), the rind of half a lemon peeled very thin, a little cinnamon, and a blade of mace, and two and a half ounces of lump sugar: blanch and pound eight or ten bitter, and half an ounce of sweet almonds very fine, with a spoonful of rose water, and mix them with the milk; strain it through a lawn sieve or napkin into a basin, with half a pint of good cream. Let it stand half an hour; pour it into another basin, leaving the sediment at the bottom, and when nearly cold fill it into moulds; when wanted, put your finger round the mould; pull out the blancmange; set it in the centre of a dish, and garnish with slices of orange. N. B.---About half a gill of noyeau may be substituted for the almonds.

BLANCMANGE. (3) Boil till dissolved, in a large tea-cupful of water, three-quarters of an ounce of isinglass; when milk-warm, add it to a quart of rich cream, with a stick of cinnamon, the peel of a lemon, two or three laurel leaves, or a few bitter almonds; sweeten with pounded loaf sugar; stir it over the fire, and let it boil for two or three minutes; strain it through a bit of muslin into a deep dish, and stir it till nearly cold, then pour it into an earthen-ware mould or shape; the following day, dip the mould into warm water for a minute or so, clap it with the hand to loosen the edge, place the glass or china dish over the mould, and turn it out quickly upon the dish. As much cow-heel stock as will half fill the shape may be substituted for the isinglass.

BLANCMANGE. (4) Blanch and pound with a little ratafia, or rose-water, two ounces of sweet, and six bitter almonds; dissolve three-quarters of an ounce of isinglass; add it, when milk-warm, to a quart of good cream; half milk half cream may be used; mix in the almonds the peel of a small lemon, and a bit of cinnamon; sweeten it with pounded loaf sugar, let it stand for two or three hours, put it into a saucepan, stir it constantly, and let it boil for six or eight minutes; strain it through a lawn sieve, and stir it till nearly cold, then pour it into a mould.

BLANCMANGE. (5) Blanch and pound one ounce of sweet almonds with a glass of sherry, and a table-spoonful of pounded loaf sugar; add it to three-quarters of an ounce of isinglass dissolved in half a pint of water, and boil it till the flavor of the almonds be extracted, stirring it all the time; strain it through a bit of thin muslin, and mix with it a quart of good cream; stir it till quite cold, and pour it into a shape.

BLANCMANGE, AMERICAN. Mix half a pint of cold water with two ounces of arrowroot, let it settle for fifteen minutes, pour off the water, and add a table-spoonful of laurel water, and a little sugar; sweeten a quart of new milk, boil it with a little cinnamon, and half the peel of a lemon; pick out the cinnamon and lemon, and pour the boiling milk upon the arrow-root, stirring it all the time. Put it into a mould, and turn it out the following day.

BLANCMANGE, DUTCH. Wash one ounce and a half of isinglass, pour a pint and a half of boiling water over it, let it stand for an hour, and then boil it for twenty minutes; strain, and when it is nearly cold, add the beaten yolks of six eggs, a pint of Lisbon wine, the peel of one and juice of two lemons, with a stick of cinnamon, and sweeten with pounded loaf sugar; stir it over the fire till it begin to simmer, but do not allow it to boil; pick out the peel and cinnamon, pour it into a basin, stir it till nearly cold, and put it into a shape.

BLANCMANGE EGGS. Make a small hole at the end of four or five large eggs, and let out all the egg carefully; wash the shell, drain, and fill them with blancmange, place them in a deep dish filled with rice or barley to keep them steady, and when quite cold, gently break and peel off the shell, Cut the peel of a lemon into delicately fine shreds, lay them into a glass dish, and put in the eggs; or serve them in a glass dish with a pink cream round them.

BLACK COCK, MOOR GAME, AND GROUSE, Are all to be dressed like partridges; the black cock will take as much as a pheasant, and moor game and grouse as the partridge. Send up with them currant-jelly and fried bread crumbs.

BOILING. See directions at beginning of the book.

BOLAR CAKE. *See Cake.*

BRANDY PUDDING. *See Pudding.*

BRAISING PAN. A deep well-tinned copper vessel, with two ears, the lid of which must close hermetically, and have a ledge round so that coals or hot ashes may be placed on the top when necessary.

BRAISING. This is a method of dressing meat, poultry, &c. &c. without its undergoing any evaporation. It is done by lining a braising-pan with thin slices of bacon, beef, or veal, upon which place whatever you may intend to *braise*, and also add carrots, onions, lemons, bay leaf, herbs, pepper and salt.

BRAWN, A COLLAR OF. Wash, scrape, and clean very thoroughly a large pig's head, feet, and ears; lay them into salt and water, with a little saltpetre, for three hours. To make the collar larger, boil two ox heels, with the head, feet, and ears, till all the bones can be taken out easily, then put the head round the mould, and the feet and small pieces into the middle; put it together while hot, and press it with a heavy weight till it becomes cold. Boil for half an hour, in as much of the liquor as will cover the brawn, one handful of salt, one ounce of pepper, and one or two bay leaves. When cold, pour it over the brawn.

BRAWN, MOCK. Take the blade bone out of the shoulder, and boil it gently two hours or more, according to the age of the boar. When it is cold, season it very highly with pepper, Cayenne, salt, a very little allspice, minced onion, and thyme. Let it lie a night in this seasoning; the following day, make a savoury forcemeat of pounded veal, ham, beef suet, minced parsley, thyme, and an onion, a little lemon-peel, salt, nutmeg, pepper, and Cayenne; bind it with an egg beaten, and stuff where the bone has been taken out. Put it into a deep pan with the brown side downwards, and lay under it twigs or small sticks, to keep it from sticking to the bottom; pour in a bottle of beer, and put it into the oven. When nearly done, take it out and clear off all the fat, add a bottle of Madeira and the juice of a large lemon, return it to the oven, and bake it till it become as tender as a jelly, so that a straw will pierce it easily. If the boar is an old one, it will require to be baked six or seven hours. This dish is eaten hot.

BRAWN, TO BAKE. Take raw lean brawn, and the same quantity of fat bacon, mince them small, then pound them in a stone mortar, with a handful of sage, seasoned with salt, pepper and ginger, add the yolks of eggs, and some vinegar, then put the brawn into a cold paste, lay on butter and bay leaves, make your pie round and bake it. To be eaten cold.

BREAKFAST CAKE. *See Cake.*

BREAD. ( 1) Put a quartern of flour into a large basin, with two tea-spoonfuls of salt; make a hole in the middle; then put in a basin four table-spoonfuls of good yeast; stir in a pint of milk, lukewarm; put it in the hole of the flour; stir it just to make it into a thin batter; then strew a little flour over the top; then put it on one side of the fire, and cover it over; let it stand till the next morning; then make it into dough; add half a pint more of warm milk; knead it for ten minutes, and then set it in a warm place by the fire for one hour and a half: then knead it again, and it is ready either for loaves or bricks: bake them from one hour and a half to two hours according to the size.

BREAD. (2) Mix into six pounds of sifted flour one ounce of salt, nearly half a pint of fresh sweet yeast as it comes from the brewery, and a sufficient quantity of warmed milk to make the whole into a stiff dough; work and knead it well upon a pasteboard, on which a little flour has been strewed, for fifteen or twenty minutes, then put it into a deep pan, cover it with a warmed towel, set it before the fire, and let it rise for an hour and a half, or perhaps two hours; cut off a piece of this sponge or dough; knead it well for eight or ten minutes, together with flour merely sufficient to keep it from adhering to the board; put it into small tins, filling them three-quarters full; dent the rolls all round with a knife, and let them stand a few minutes before putting them into the oven. The remainder of the dough must then be worked up for loaves, and baked either in or out of a shape.

BREAD, ALMOND. Take a pound of the best almonds, slice them the round way, beat and sift a pound of double-refined sugar, and strew it over the almonds as you cut them, stirring them frequently to prevent their sticking together; when all the sugar is used, put them into an earthen basin, with a few carraway seeds, a little gum dragon (dissolved in rose-water and strained), three grains of musk and ambergris dissolved in fine sugar, and the whites of two eggs beaten to a very light froth, and two spoonfuls of fine flour; when well mixed lay them on wafers the size of macaroons; open them with a knife or bodkin, lest two or three pieces stick together; the quicker you lay them, the better they will look; put them into a well-heated oven, taking care they do not scorch; when half baked, take them out, wash them with the white of an egg beaten to a froth, grate a little fine sugar over them, and bake them about half an hour longer.

BREAD AND BUTTER PUDDING, *See Pudding.*

BREAD, CHESTNUT. Roast a hundred fine chestnuts, being careful not to burn them; peel them well, and pound them with butter and double cream; pass them through a sieve; add two eggs, and then strain them again. Weigh your paste, and for every pound allow half a pound of powder, a little vanilla in powder, and two ounces of flour; mix these together, and form of the preparation as many chestnuts as it will make; Lay them on a sheet of wafer paper, butter and *dorez* them several times, and then bake them in a hot oven.

BREAD CHEESECAKES. Slice a large French roll very thin, pour on it some boiling cream; when cold, add six or eight eggs, half a pound of butter melted, some nutmeg, a spoonful of brandy, a little sugar, and half a pound of currants. Put them in puff paste as other cheesecakes.

BREAD, TO SERVE WITH COFFEE. Whip up the whites of ten eggs to a thick snow; add to them the yolks beaten with eight ounces of powder-sugar, place it over a charcoal fire, and whip it for half an hour, then take it from the fire, and whip again until cold. Mix in eight ounces of sifted flour. Have ready buttered two moulds lined with paper, pour the paste into them, and bake them in a moderate oven; when done, take them out of the moulds and remove the paper; when cold, cut them in slices about the size of a finger. Place them on a plate of copper, over a charcoal fire, and when one side is brown, turn them and brown the other side. These if kept dry will be good for a long time.

BREAD CRUMBS, FRIED. Rub bread that has been baked two days, through an iron sieve or cullender; put them into a stew-pan with two ounces of butter; place it over a moderate fire, and stir them with a wooden spoon till of a fine gold color; spread them on a sieve, and let them stand ten minutes to drain, turning them often.

BREAD, FRENCH. Take half a bushel (or six pounds) of flour, put it on the slab, make a hole in the centre, in which put two ounces of yeast; make your dough with warm water, to about the consistence of *brioche*; work it up well, adding two ounces of salt, dissolved in a little warm water; cover, and set it in a warm place to rise; on this part of the operation depends the quality of the bread. Having left the dough one or two hours, (according to the season), knead it again, and leave it as before, for two hours. In the meanwhile, heat the oven, divide the dough into eight equal parts, of which form

as many loaves, into any shape you please; put them into the oven as quickly as possible. As soon as they are done, rub the crusts with a little butter, which will give it a fine yellow color.

BREAD, FRENCH, OR ROLLS. Take half a bushel or six pounds of sifted flour, knead it into dough, with two quarts of milk, three-quarters of a pound of warm butter, half a pound of yeast, and two ounces of salt; when the whole is well worked up, cover, and leave it to rise. In two hours time, form it into rolls, and lay them on tinned plates. Place them in a slow oven. When they have been in an hour, put them into a very hot oven for twenty minutes. Rasp them as soon as they are baked.

BREAD FRITTERS. Boil half a pint of milk till reduced to half, with a little sugar, salt, half a spoonful of orange-flower water, and a little lemon-peel shred fine; have ready some pieces of crumb of bread, cut about the size of half-crowns, but thicker; put them into the milk to soak a little, then drain, flour, and fry them. Glaze them with sugar, and pass the salamander over them.

BREAD, LONDON. To make London bread, put a bushel of good flour which has been ground a month or six weeks, in one end of the trough, and make a hole in the middle of it. Take nine quarts of warm water, and mix it with one quart of good yeast; put it into the flour, and stir it well with your hands; let it remain until it rises as high as it will go, which will take about an hour and a quarter. Watch it carefully to its ultimate height, and do not suffer it to fall; then make up the dough with eight quarts more of warm water and one pound of salt; work it well with your hands, and then cover it over with a sack or other coarse cloth. Put the fire into the oven; heat it thoroughly, and by the time it is hot, the dough will be ready. Next make the dough into loaves, not exceeding four or five pounds each, sweep out the oven clean, and put in the loaves. Shut the oven close, and they will be baked in about two hours and a half; then open the oven, and draw the bread. In summer the water need not be more than blood warm, but in winter it must be a few degrees higher in heat. During a hard frost, however, the water should be as hot as the hand could bear it, though not sufficiently hot to scald the yeast, as that would spoil the whole batch of bread. Other quantities of bread are made in the same proportion.

BREAD, PLAIN SHORT. The same proportions of flour and butter must be used as in the receipt for short bread; this must be mixed together, rolled out, but not made quite so thick as in the rich kind; but in the same form, pricked with a fork, and pinched all round. A little sugar may be added.

BREAD, RICE. Take a pound of rice, and let it simmer in two quarts of water till it is quite tender; when it is of a proper warmth mix it thoroughly with four pounds of flour, adding yeast and salt, the same as for other bread; the proper quantity of yeast to be used, is about four spoonfuls; knead it well; then set it to rise before the fire. A portion of the flour should be reserved to make up the loaves. If the rice should require more water, it must be added, as some rice swells more than other.

BREAD, SPICED, COMMON. (1) Boil three pounds of honey in a gallon of water for a quarter of an hour; then pour it on the flour in the trough; mix them together well, until the flour will imbibe no more liquid; when a little cooled, add three ounces of potash, infused the night before in half a pint of milk, knead the whole well, putting to it some pounded anise. Roll out the paste, and with paste-cutters of various forms, cut it into little figures, lay them on a well-oiled tin, and bake them; when done, wash them over with milk. With this paste spiced nuts are made; when formed, lay them on tins, and leave in a warm place for two or three days before they are baked.

BREAD, SPICED, (2) FLEMISH. The evening before you wish to make your spiced bread, dissolve three ounces of white potash in half a pint of milk and set it aside. The next morning put a considerable quantity of sifted flour into a trough, make a hole in the heap, into which pour six pounds of clarified honey; whilst boiling, stir it well with a strong spatula, until the honey, reduced to a firm paste, will imbibe no more flour, then spread it all over the bottom of the trough, and leave it for about ten or fifteen minutes; at the end of that time, if the paste be sufficiently cool for you to bear your hand on it, rub its surface with the infusion of potash; then let a strong person knead it, in the same manner as the bakers knead bread. Have ready a number of different-sized moulds of pear tree wood, on which are cut (pretty deep) octagons of various dimensions; then cut your paste into as many pieces as you have moulds, in the following proportions:—for the mould containing a pound, take eighteen ounces of paste; for a half pound, fourteen ounces; a quarter of a pound seven ounces of paste, and so on; knead each piece separately on the slab, rub them with flour to prevent their adhering, and then put them into the respective moulds; press it down tight; in a minute or two turn them over, place them on a tin plate (previously rubbed with olive oil), and with a soft brush take off what flour may remain on the surface of the spiced bread, and bake them in a moderate oven. Whilst they are baking, dissolve some isinglass in a sufficient quantity of beer, with which, by means of a hair pencil, wash the outside of the spiced bread as soon as it is done; and then, while it is moist and warm, decorate it with blanched almonds, candied lemon and orange peel, cut into dice. You may, if you think proper, cut these sort of sweet meats into very small pieces, and knead them into your paste at first. When they are nearly cold, separate the pieces with a knife.

BREAD, SHORT. For two pounds of sifted flour allow one pound of butter, salt or fresh; a quarter of a pound of candied orange and lemon peel, of pounded loaf sugar, blanched sweet almonds, and carraway comfits, a quarter of a pound each; cut the lemon, the orange peel, and almonds into small thin bits, and mix them with a pound and a half of the flour, a few of the caraway comfits, and the sugar; melt the butter, and when cool, pour it clear from the sediment into the flour, at the same time mixing it quickly. With the hands, form it into a large round of nearly an inch thick, using the remainder of the flour to make it up with; cut it into four, and with the finger and thumb pinch each bit neatly all round the edge; prick them with a fork, and strew the rest of the carraway comfits over the top. Put the pieces upon white paper dusted with flour, and then upon tins. Bake them in a moderate oven.

BREAD, TIPSY. Pare off the crust, and cut into thin round slices of four or five inches, the crumb of a twopenny or threepenny roll; spread over each bit raspberry or strawberry jam, and place the slices one over the other pretty high in a glass dish, and pour over them as much sherry, sweetened with sugar, as the bread will soak in; stick round the sides, and over the top, blanched sweet almonds, cut like straws, and pour a custard round it. It may be made the day before, or two or three hours before dinner, and with the crumb of loaf bread.

BREAD SAUCE. *See Sauce.*

BRENTFORD ROLLS. Mix with two pounds of flour a little salt, two ounces of sifted sugar, four ounces of butter, and two eggs beaten with two spoonfuls of yeast, and about a pint of milk; knead the dough well, and set it to rise before the fire. Make twelve rolls, butter tin plates, and set them before the fire again to rise. When of a proper size, bake them for half an hour.

BRIOCHE. Divide half a quartern of flour into three parts, and knead into one of them half an ounce of yeast and a little warm water, wrap it in a cloth and set it by, in summer time for a quarter of an hour, and in winter for a whole hour. When it has risen, put it to the remainder of the flour, with a pound and a half of butter, ten eggs, half a glass of water, and nearly an ounce of salt; knead them together with your hand thoroughly, and then wrap it in a clean napkin and leave it nine or ten hours. Cut the paste into the size you wish to make the cakes, moisten, and roll them in the hand, flatten the top, and gild them with the yolk of an egg. Half an hour will be sufficient to bake the small ones; large cakes will require an hour and a half.

BROILING. See directions at beginning of the book.

BROCCOLI. Set a pan of clean cold water on the table, and a saucepan on the fire with plenty of water, and a handful of salt in it. Broccoli is prepared by stripping off all the side shoots, leaving the top; peel off the skin of the stalk with a knife; cut it close off at the bottom, and put it into the pan of cold water. When the water in the stewpan boils, and the broccoli is ready, put it in; let it boil briskly till the stalks feel tender, from ten to twenty minutes; take it up with a slice, that you may not break it; let it drain, and serve up. If some of the heads of broccoli are much bigger than the others, put them on to boil first, so that they may get all done together. *Obs.*—It makes a nice supper-dish served upon a toast, like asparagus. It is a very delicate vegetable, and you must take it up the moment it is done, and send it to table hot.

BROTH, BARLEY. Chop a leg of beef in pieces, boil it in three gallons of water, with a carrot and a crust of bread, till reduced to half; then strain it off and put it into the pot again with half a pound of barley, four or five heads of celery cut small, a bunch of sweet herbs, an onion, a little chopped parsley, and a few marigolds. Let it boil an hour. Take an old cock or large fowl and put it into the pot, boil till the broth is quite good. Season with salt, take out the onion and herbs, and serve it. The fowl may be omitted.

BROTH, OF BEEF. Wash a leg or shin of beef very clean, crack the bone in two or three places, add to it any trimmings you have of meat, game, or poultry (heads, necks, gizzards or feet) and cover them with cold water. Watch and stir it up well from the bottom, and the moment it begins to simmer, skim it carefully. Your broth must be perfectly clear and limpid—for on this depends the goodness of the soups, sauces, and gravies, of which it is the basis. Then add some cold water to make the remaining scum rise, and skim it again. When the scum has done rising, and the surface of the broth is quite clear, put in one carrot, a head of celery, two turnips, and two onions. It should not have any taste of sweet herbs, spice or garlic; either of these flavors may be added afterward, if desired. Cover it close, set it by the side of the fire, and let it simmer very gently, so as not to waste the broth, for four or five hours or more, according to the weight of the meat. Strain it through a sieve into a clean and dry stone pan, and set it in the coldest place you have.
☞ This is the foundation of all sorts of soups and sauces, brown and white.

BROTH, CHICKEN. Take the remaining parts of a chicken from which panada has been made, all but the rump; skin, and put them into the water it was first boiled in, with the addition of a little mace, onion, and a few pepper-corns, and simmer it. When of a good flavor, put to it a quarter of an ounce of sweet almonds beaten with a spoonful of water; boil it a little while, and when cold, take off the fat.

BROTH, CHICKEN PECTORAL. Pre-

pare a chicken in the usual way, and put it into a saucepan with two pints and a half of water, two ounces of pearl barley, the same of rice, and two ounces of the best honey; boil all together, skimming well for three hours, until it be reduced to two-thirds.

BROTH, JELLY. Take a joint of mutton, a capon, a fillet of veal, and three quarts of water; put these into an earthen pan, and boil them over a gentle fire till reduced to half; then squeeze all together, and strain the liquor through a napkin.

BROTH, MUTTON. Take two pounds of scrag of mutton; to take the blood out, put it into a stewpan, and cover it with cold water; when the water becomes milk-warm, pour it off; then put it in four or five pints of water, with a tea-spoonful of salt, a table-spoonful of best grits, and an onion; set it on a slow fire, and when you have taken all the scum off, put in two or three turnips; let it simmer very slowly for two hours, and strain it through a clean sieve.

BROTH, MUTTON, FOR THE SICK. Have a pound and a half of a neck or loin of mutton; take off the skin and the fat, and put it into a saucepan; cover it with cold water, (it will take about a quart to a pound of meat), let it simmer very gently, and skim it well; cover it up, and set it over a moderate fire, where it may stand gently stewing for about an hour; then strain it off. It should be allowed to become cold, when all the greasy particles will float on the surface, and becoming hard, can be easily taken off, and the settlings will remain at the bottom. N.B. —We direct the meat to be done no more than just sufficiently to be eaten; so a sick man may have plenty of good broth for nothing; as by this manner of producing it, the meat furnishes also a good family meal. This is an inoffensive nourishment for sick persons, and the only mutton broth that should be given to convalescents, whose constitutions require replenishing with re-storative aliment of easy digestion. The common way of making it with roots, onions, sweet herbs, &c. &c. is too strong for weak stomachs. Plain broth will agree with a delicate stomach, when the least addition of other ingredients would immediately offend it.

BROTH, MEAGRE, OR SOUP WITH HERBS. Set on a kettle of water, put in two or three crusts of bread, and all sorts of good herbs; season with salt; put in butter, and a bunch of sweet herbs; boil it for an hour and a half; then strain it through a sieve, or napkin. This will serve to make lettuce soup, asparagus soup, soup *de sante*, &c. with herbs.

BROTH, MULLAGATAWANY, OR CURRY. Make about two quarts of strong veal broth, seasoned with two onions, a bunch of parsley, salt and pepper; strain it, and have ready a chicken, cut in joints and skinned; put it into the broth, with a tablespoonful of curry-powder; boil the chicken till quite tender, and a little before serving, add the juice of a lemon, and stir in a teacupful of cream. Serve boiled rice to eat with this broth.

BROTH, RICE VEAL. Wash clean six pounds of a knuckle of veal, and cut it in two, put it in a saucepan with four quarts of boiling water, half a pound of rice well washed, a little mace, white pepper, and salt, and a handful of chopped parsley; let it boil for two hours. Serve part of the meat in the tureen with the broth. The thick part of the knuckle may be sent up as a separate dish, with parsley and butter poured over it.

BROTH, WHITE. Boil a fowl, and when it is enough, take it up, and put it into a dish; then boil your cream with a blade of mace, and thicken it with eggs; then put in the marrow of one beef bone, and take some of the broth, and mingle them together; put to it a spoonful of white wine, and let it thicken on the fire; then put the fowl hot out of the broth, set it on a chafing-dish of coals, and serve it.

BROWN ROUX, OR THICKENING Put into a nicely tinned saucepan about a pound of fresh butter, melt it slowly, and dredge in flour till it becomes like a paste, carefully stirring it all the time, put it for a few minutes upon a quick fire, and then return it to where there is less heat, and stir it till it assumes a light brown color, when it may be put into a jar. These thickenings keep for sometime.

BROWNING, Is a convenient article to color those soups or sauces of which it is supposed their deep brown complexion denotes the strength and savouriness of the composition. Burned sugar is also a favorite ingredient with the brewers, who use it under the name of " essentia bina" to color their beer: it is also employed by the brandy makers, in considerable quantity, to color brandy, to which, besides enriching its complexion, it gives that sweetish taste, and fulness in the mouth, which custom has taught brandy drinkers to admire, and prefer to the finest Cognac in its genuine state. When employed for culinary purposes, this is sometimes made with strong gravy, or walnut catchup. Those who like a *gout* of acid may add a little walnut pickle. Put half a pound of pounded lump sugar, and a tablespoonful of water, into a clean iron saucepan, set it over a slow fire, and keep stirring it with a wooden spoon till it becomes a bright brown color, and begins to smoke; then add to it an ounce of salt, and dilute it by degrees with water, till it is the thickness of soy; let it boil, take off the scum, and strain the liquor into bottles, which must be well stopped: if you have not any of this by you, and you wish to darken the color of your sauces, pound a tea-spoonful of lump sugar, and put it into an iron spoon, with as much water as will dissolve it; hold it over a quick fire till it becomes of a very dark brown color; mix it with the soup, &c. while it is hot.

BRUNSWICK TART. *See Tart.*

BRUSSELS SPROUTS TO BOIL. Trim and wash them perfectly clean, and let them lie an hour in cold water. Put them on in boiling water with a little salt, and boil them till tender. Drain off the water, and serve them hot.

BUBBLE AND SQUEAK. Chop small some boiled white cabbage; season it with pepper and salt, and fry it with a little butter; pepper and broil some slices of cold boiled salted beef; put the fried cabbage into a dish, and lay round it the slices of broiled beef, and serve it very hot. The beef does best when underdone.

BUNS, BATH. Rub together, with the hand, one pound of fine flour and a half a pound of butter; beat six eggs, and add them to the flour with table spoonful of good yeast. Mix them all together with half a tea-cup full of milk; set it in a warm place for an hour; mix in six ounces of sifted sugar, and a few caraway seeds. Mould them into buns with a table spoon on a baking plate; throw six or eight caraway comfits on each, and bake them in a hot oven about ten minutes. These quantities should make eighteen buns.

BUNS, COMMON. Rub four ounces of butter into two pounds of flour, four ounces of sugar, a few Jamaica peppers, and a few carraway seeds. Put a spoonful or two of cream into a cup of yeast, and as much good milk as will make the above into a light paste; set it by the fire to rise. They will bake quickly on tins; you may add nutmeg.

BUNS, CROSS. To the above mixture put one ounce and a half of ground all-spice, cinnamon and mace, mixed, and when half proved, press the form of a cross with a tin mould in the centre, and finish as above.

BUNS, PLUM. To two pounds of the plain bun paste, put half a pound of currants, a quarter of a pound of candied orange-peel, cut into small pieces, half a nutmeg grated, half an ounce of mixed spice, such as allspice, cinnamon, &c. Mould them into buns, jag them round the edges with a knife, and proceed as above.

BUNS, PLAIN. To four pounds of sifted flour put one pound of good moist sugar; make a cavity in the centre, and stir in a gill of good yeast, a pint of lukewarm milk, with enough of the flour to make it the thickness of cream; cover it over, and let it lie two hours; then melt to an oil (but not hot) one pound of butter, stir it into the other ingredients, with enough warm milk to make it a soft paste; throw a little flour over, and let them lie an hour; have ready a baking-platter rubbed over with butter; mould with the hand the dough into buns, about the size of a large egg; lay them in rows full three inches apart; set them in a warm place for half an hour, or till they have risen to double their size; bake them in a hot oven of a good color, and wash them over with a brush dipped into milk when drawn from the oven.

BUNS, RICHER. Put four pounds of fine flour into a wooden bowl; set a sponge of it with a gill of yeast and a pint of warm milk; then mix with it one pound of sifted sugar, one pound of oiled fresh butter, coriander seeds, cinnamon, and mace, a small quantity of each, pounded fine. Roll the paste into buns, set them on a baking-plate rubbed with butter, put them in a moderate oven to prove; then wash them with a paste-brush dipped in warm milk, and bake of a good color.

BUNS, SCOTS CHRISTMAS. Take four pounds of raisins stoned, two and a half of currants well cleaned and dried, half a pound of almonds blanched, of candied orange and lemon-peel a quarter of a pound each, cut small; of pounded cloves, pepper, and ginger, half an ounce each, four pounds of flour, and twenty-two ounces of butter.

Then rub the butter with the flour, till well mixed together; add a little warm water, and a quarter of a pint of fresh good yeast, and work it into a light smooth paste; cut off nearly one-third of the paste, to form the sheet or case, and lay it aside; with the rest work up the fruit, sweetmeats, and spices; make it into a round form like a thick cheese. Roll out the sheet of paste, lay the bun in the centre, and gather it all round, closing it at the bottom, by wetting the edges of the paste, and cutting it so as to lie quite flat. Turn it up, and run a wire or small skewer through from the top to the bottom every here and there, and prick the top with a fork. Double and flour a sheet of gray paper, and lay the bun upon it; bind a piece round the sides, also doubled and floured, to keep the bun in a proper shape. Bake it in a moderate oven.

BUNS, SEED. Take two pounds of plain bun dough, and mix in one ounce of caraway seeds, butter the insides of tart-pans, mould the dough into buns, and put one into each pan; set them to rise in a warm place, and when sufficiently proved, ice them with the white of an egg beat to a froth, lay some pounded sugar over that, and dissolve it with water splashed from the icing-brush. Bake ten minutes.

BURDWAN STEW. Cut into joints a cold fowl or duck, put it into a stewpan, with half a pint of gravy, a large wine-glass of ale, half a one of white wine, the juice of half a lemon, a tea-spoonful of soy and Cayenne; of mushroom catsup, lemon pickle, cucumber vinegar, corach escavecke, a dessert-spoonful each. Heat all thoroughly before serving.

BUTTER BURNT. Put two ounces of fresh butter into a small frying-pan; when it becomes a dark brown color, add to it a table-spoonful and a half of good vinegar, and a little pepper and salt. *Obs.*—This is used as sauce for boiled fish or poached eggs.

BURNET VINEGAR. *See Vinegar.*

BUTTER BISCUITS. *See Biscuits.*

BUTTER CAKES. *See Cakes.*

BUTTER, CLARIFIED. Put the butter in a nice, clean stewpan, over a very clear, slow fire; watch it, and when it is melted, carefully skim off the buttermilk, &c. which will swim on the top; let it stand a minute or two for the impurities to sink to the bottom; then pour the clear butter through a sieve into a clean basin, leaving the sediment at the bottom of the stewpan. *Obs.*—Butter thus purified will be as sweet as marrow, a very useful covering for otted meats, &c. and for frying fish equal to the finest Florence oil; for which purpose it is commonly used by Catholics, and those whose religious tenets will not allow them to eat viands fried in animal oil.

BUTTER, FRENCH MELTED. Mix, in a stewpan, with a quarter of a pound of fresh butter, a table-spoonful of flour, a little salt, half a gill of water, half a spoonful of white vinegar, and a little grated nutmeg. Put it on the fire, stir it, and let it thicken, but do not allow it to boil, lest it should taste of the flour.

BUTTER, MELTED. (1) Dust a little flour over a quarter of a pound of butter, put it into a saucepan, with about a wine-glass of water; stir it one way constantly till it be melted, and let it just boil: a round wooden stick, is the best thing to stir butter with in melting. If the butter is to be melted with cream, use the same proportion as of water, but no flour; stir it constantly, and heat it thoroughly, but do not let it boil. To oil butter, cut about a quarter of a pound into slices, put it into a small jar, and place it in a pan of boiling water. When oiled, pour it off clear from the sediment.

BUTTER, MELTED, (2) Is so simple and easy to prepare, that it is a matter of general surprise, that what is done so often, is so seldom done right. It is spoiled nine times out of ten, more from idleness than from ignorance, and rather because the cook won't than because she can't do it; which can only be the case when housekeepers will not allow butter to do it with. Good melted butter cannot be made with mere flour and water; there must be a full and proper proportion of butter. As it must be always on the table, and is the foundation of almost all our sauces, we have,

Melted butter and oysters,

----------------parsley,

----------------anchovies,

----------------eggs,

----------------shrimps,

----------------lobsters,

----------------capers, &c. &c. &c.

I have tried every way of making it; and I trust, that I have written a receipt, (3) which, if the cook will carefully observe, she will constantly succeed in giving satisfaction. In the quantities of the various sauces I have ordered, I have had in view the providing for a family of half a dozen moderate people. Never pour sauce over meat or even put it into the dish; however well made, some of the company may have an antipathy to it; tastes are as different as faces: moreover, if it is sent up separate in a boat; it will keep hot longer, and what is left may be put by for another time, or used for another purpose.

BUTTER, MELTED. (3) Keep a pint stewpan; for this purpose only. Cut two ounces of butter into little bits, that it may melt more easily, and mix more readily; put it into the stewpan with a large tea-spoonful (*i. e.* about three drachms) of flour, (some prefer arrow-root, or potato starch) and two table-spoonfuls of milk. When thoroughly mixed, add six table-spoonfuls of water; hold it over the fire, and shake it round every minute (all the while the same way), till it just begins to simmer; then let it stand quietly and boil up. It should be of the thickness of good cream. N. B.—

Two table-spoonfuls of mushroom catch-up instead of the milk, will make as good mushroom sauce as need be, and is a superlative accompaniment to either fish, flesh, or fowl. *Obs.*—This is the best way of preparing melted butter; milk mixes with the butter much more easily and more intimately than water alone can be made to do. This is of proper thickness to be mixed at table with flavouring essences, anchovy, mushroom, or cavice, &c. If made merely to pour over vegetables, add a little more milk to it. N. B.— If the butter oils, put a spoonful of cold water to it, and stir it with a spoon; if it is very much oiled, it must be poured backwards and forwards from the stewpan to the sauceboat till it is right again. MEM.— Melted butter made to be mixed with flavouring essences, catchups, &c. should be of the thickness of light batter, that it may adhere to the fish, &c.

BUTTER, OILED. Put two ounces of fresh butter into a saucepan; set it at a distance from the fire, so that it may melt gradually, till it comes to an oil; and pour it off quietly from the dregs. *Obs.*—This will supply the place of olive oil; and by some is preferred to it either for salads or frying.

BUTTER SAUCE. *See Sauce*

wwwww

## C.

CABBAGE AND CHEESE SOUP. *See Soup*.

CABBAGE, TO STEW. Wash a cabbage well, slice it as for pickling, and put it into a stewpan, with half a tea-cupful of Port wine, and a bit of butter kneaded in flour, a little salt and pepper; stir it till the butter is melted; cover the pan, and let it stew a little, but not to become too soft; as it eats better rather crisp; add a table-spoonful of vinegar, give it one boil, and serve it hot. The wine may be omitted.

CABBAGE, TO PICKLE. Choose two middling-sized well-colored, and firm red cabbages, shred them very finely, first pulling off the outside leaves; mix with them nearly half a pound of salt, tie it up in a thin cloth, and let it hang for twelve hours; then put it into small jars, and pour over it cold vinegar that has been boiled with a few barberries in it; tie the jar over closely with bladder; or boil, in a quart of vinegar, three bits of ginger, half an ounce of pepper and a quarter of an ounce of cloves. When cold, pour it over the red cabbage.

CAKES. Preparatory remarks. The currants and raisins should be prepared as directed under the article headed, Puddings and Pies, and the flour dried before the fire on a large sheet of white paper, then sifted and weighed. Almonds should be blanched by pouring hot water over them, and, after standing some minutes, taking off the skin, then throwing them into rose or cold water. When not pounded, they should be cut lengthwise into thin bits. Sugar should be roughly pounded, rolled with a bottle upon white paper, and then sifted. All spices, after being well dried at the fire, should be finely pounded and sifted. Lemon and orange-peel must be pared very thin, and pounded with a little sugar. The butter, after being weighed, should be laid into cold water, or washed in rose water, and if salt, be well washed in several waters. The yolks and whites of eggs should be separately and long beaten, then strained; two whisks should be kept exclusively for that purpose, as the whites especially require to be managed with the greatest care. A horn spoon should be used for mixing those cakes which are not directed to be beaten with the hand. To make cakes light, salvolatile, or smelling salts, may be added immediately before putting them into the oven, allowing, to a sponge cake, made of one pound of flour, one tea-spoonful; and two or three to a large plum cake. Cheese cakes, queen

cakes, sponge biscuits, and small sponge cakes, require a quick oven till they have risen; afterwards the heat should be more moderate. Plum, seed cakes, and all large kinds, must be well soaked; and therefore do not require a brisk oven. To preserve their color, a sheet of white paper is put over them, and after they have risen and become firm, they are turned round. To ascertain if a large cake be sufficiently done, a broad bladed knife is plunged into the centre of it, and if dry and clean when drawn out, the cake is baked; but if anything adheres to the blade, it must instantly be returned to the oven, and the door closed. When the oven is too hot, it is better to lessen the fire than to open the door.

CAKE. Take two pounds and a half of dried and sifted flour, the same of well cleaned and dried currants, two pounds of fresh butter, two of finely-pounded and sifted loaf sugar, a nutmeg grated, a tea-spoonful of pounded cinnamon, one ounce of citron and candied orange-peel, cut small, the yolks of sixteen, and the whites of ten eggs, beaten separately; then with the hand beat the butter to a cream, and add the sugar, then the eggs by degrees, and the flour in the same way, and then the currants, sweetmeats and spice, one glass of orange-flower water, and one of brandy. Butter a tin pan, line it with white paper buttered, put in the cake, and bake it in a moderate oven four hours.

CAKE, ALMOND. Blanch half a pound of sweet, and three ounces of bitter almonds; pound them to a paste in a mortar with orange-flower water; add half a pound of sifted loaf sugar, and a little brandy; whisk separately, for half an hour, the whites and yolks of twenty eggs, add the yolks to the almonds and sugar, and then stir in the whites, and beat them all well together. Butter a tin pan, sift bread raspings over it, put the cake into it, over the top of which strew sifted loaf sugar. Bake it in a quick oven for half or three-quarters of an hour.

CAKES, ALMOND SMALL. One pound of butter beaten to a cream, half a pound of finely-pounded and sifted loaf sugar, half a pound of dried and sifted flour, and the same quantity of blanched sweet almonds cut into thin small bits, one well-beaten egg, and a little rose water, must be mixed well together, and with a spoon dropped upon wafer paper or tins, and then baked.

CAKE, ALMOND. (1) Take eight ounces of Jordan and one ounce of bitter almonds, blanch and pound them very fine; then beat in with the almonds the yolks of eight eggs, and whisk up the whites to a solid froth. Then take eight table-spoonfuls of sifted sugar, five spoonfuls of fine flour, a small quantity of grated lemon-peel and pounded cinnamon, and mix all the ingredients. Rub the inside of a mould with fresh butter, fill it with the mixture and bake it of a light color.

CAKE, ALMOND. (2) Put a gill of flour upon a pie-board, and make a hole in the middle to receive a piece of butter the size of an egg, a little salt, a quarter of a pound of fine sugar, and six ounces of sweet almonds pounded very fine: knead the whole, and form it into a cake; bake and glaze it with sugar and a hot salamander.

CAKE, ALMOND. (3) Weigh three eggs in their shells, take the same weight of flour, of the finest fresh butter, and of grated loaf sugar. Pound with these ingredients three ounces of sweet almonds blanched; add a little grated lemon-peel or orange-flower water, and the whites and yolks of three eggs. Continue pounding till the whole forms a smooth paste. Butter the bottom of a baking-pan, and put in the cake with fire above and below. This cake may be served either hot or cold, with grated sugar over it.

CAKES, ANISEED. Put in an earthen pan eight ounces of sugar pounded, and the yolks of ten eggs; stir them together with a wooden spoon for half an hour. In the meantime have the whites of your eggs whipped to a thick snow, and then pour in the sugar and yolks. When thoroughly mixed, add an ounce of good aniseed, previously washed and dried, and ten ounces of flour; stir the whole gently, and then with a spoon lay it on white paper in cakes about the size of a crown-piece; sprinkle them with fine sugar and bake. Remove them from the paper while hot, with a knife.

CAKE, APPLE. Pare and core a dozen apples, and make them into marmalade with the *zeste* of a lemon and a little cinnamon, and pass them through a bolting; put them into a stewpan, with a spoonful of potato flour, half a pound of sugar, and two ounces of butter; dry it over the fire, and when cold add to it six eggs, stir them well in, and having buttered a mould, pour your preparation into it, and bake it in a slow oven; when done, turn it in a dish and serve it.

CAKE, ABERDEEN CRULLA. Beat to a cream a quarter of a pound of fresh butter and mix with it the same quantity of pounded and sifted loaf sugar, and four well-beaten eggs; add flour till thick enough to roll out; cut the paste into oblong pieces about four or five inches in length; with a paste cutter, divide the centre into three or four strips, wet the edges, and plait one bar over the other, so as to meet in the centre; throw them into boiling lard, or clarified suet; when fried of a light blown, drain them before the fire, and serve them in a napkin with or without grated loaf sugar stewn over them.

CAKE, BANBURY. Set a sponge with two table-spoonfuls of thick yeast, a gill of warm milk, and a pound of flour; when it has worked a little, mix with it half a pound of currants, washed and picked, half a pound of candied orange and lemon peel cut small, one ounce of spice, such as ground cinnamon, allspice, ginger, and grated nutmeg: mix the whole together with half a pound of honey; roll out puff paste a quarter of an inch thick, cut it into rounds with a cutter, about four inches over, lay on each with a spoon a small quantity of the mixture; close it round with the fingers in the form of an oval; place the join underneath; press it flat with the hand; sift sugar over it, and bake them on a plate a quarter of an hour.

CAKES, BATH BREAKFAST. Rub into two pounds of flour half a pound of butter, and mix with it one pint of milk a little warmed, a quarter of a pint of fresh yeast, four well-beaten eggs, and a tea-spoonful of salt; cover it, and let it stand before the fire to rise for three-quarters of an hour; make it into thick cakes about the size of the inside of a dinner plate; bake them in a quick oven, then cut them into three, that the middle slice, as also the top and bottom may be well buttered. Serve them very hot.

CAKE, BAIRN BRACK. To three pounds of dried flour allow one pound of fresh butter, one pound of good brown sugar, two ounces of caraway seeds, eight well-beaten eggs, three table-spoonfuls of fresh yeast, and some grated nutmeg; dissolve the butter in a pint of milk, so as to make the whole into a dough, not very stiff; work it well; cover it with a cloth, and set it before the fire to rise; when well risen, bake it in a buttered tin. When it becomes dry, it may be toasted and eaten with butter.

CAKES, BONNET. Boil in half a pint of water, for ten minutes, a bit of cinnamon and of lemon-peel; strain, and mix it with three table-spoonfuls of flour, and stir it over the fire for two or three minutes; add a bit of butter the size of a walnut; when cold, mix in the beaten yolks of two eggs, a little

salt and pepper; beat it well, drop a dessert-spoonful of the mixture into boiling lard, then drain them upon the back of a sieve, and when served, throw over pounded loaf sugar. Instead of the salt and pepper, a little preserve may be dropped upon each, before the sugar is thrown over.

CAKE, BABA. Take the fourth part of two pounds of flour, lay it on your pasteboard or slab, and having made a hole in the middle of it, put in half an ounce of yeast, work it up with one hand, whilst with the other you pour in warm water; make it into a rather soft paste, put into a wooden bowl, first pricking it in a few places, cover it with a cloth and let it stand. When it has risen well, take the remainder of the flour, and spread it on the first made paste; mix them well together, adding to them, half an ounce of salt, six eggs, a pound of fresh butter, half a pound of stoned raisins, two ounces of currants, half a glass of Malaga wine, and a little saffron in powder. Work them up together thoroughly, roll it out two or three times, and then let it stand for six hours; then having buttered a mould, pour in your preparation and bake it.

CAKE, BOLAR. One pound of flour dried in a slow oven, two spoonfuls of yeast, some almond milk, and water to mix for a sponge; when raised, beat up three-quarters of a pound of clarified butter, three eggs, and three-quarters of a pound of sugar, well-beaten till the spoon comes clean away; then add cinnamon powder, candied orange and lemon. Bake in earthen basins, well buttered; keep it before the fire till put in the oven.

CAKE, BOLAR. When the sponge is beat, as for the last, instead of mixing the sugar, it is rolled in the sugar and cinnamon.

CAKE, DUTCH BOLAR. Done, as above, without sugar; then prick holes with a sharp pointed knife, and while it is hot pour in three-quarters of a pound of clarified sugar, flavored with cinnamon or orange-flower. Almonds and sweetmeats are previously put in the cake. Ornament your cake with harlequin sugar-plums. This was a favorite cake of Queen Charlotte.

CAKE, BREAD. Take the quantity of a quartern loaf from the dough when making white bread, and knead well into it two ounces of butter, two of Lisbon sugar, and eight of currants. Warm the butter in a tea-cupful of good milk. By the addition of an ounce of butter, or sugar, or an egg or two, you may make the cake better. A tea-cupful of raw cream improves it much. It is best to bake it in a pan, rather than as a loaf, the outside being less hard.

CAKE, BRIDE. Take four pounds of fine flour well dried, four pounds of fresh butter, two pounds of loaf sugar, pounded and sifted fine, a quarter of an ounce of mace, and the same quantity of nutmegs; to every pound of flour put eight eggs; wash and pick four pounds of currants, and dry them before the fire; blanch a pound of sweet almonds, and cut them lengthways very thin, a pound of citron, a pound of candied orange, a pound of candied lemon and half a pint of brandy; first work the butter with your hand to a cream, then beat in your sugar a quarter of an hour; beat the whites of your eggs to a very strong froth; mix them with your sugar and butter; beat the yolks half an hour, at least, and mix them with your cake; then put in your flour, mace, and nutmeg; keep beating it till the oven is ready; put in your brandy, and beat the currants and almonds lightly in, tie three sheets of paper round the bottom of your hoops to keep it from running out; rub it well with butter, put in your cake, and the sweetmeats in three lays, with cake between every lay; after it is risen and colored, cover it with paper before your oven is stopped up; it will take three hours baking.

CAKE, BRIE. Take some rich cheese, knead it with a pint and half of flour, three quarters of a pound of butter, and a little salt; moisten it with five or six eggs beaten up; when it is well kneaded, let it stand for an hour; then form your cake and bake as usual.

CAKES, BENTON-TEA. Rub into a pound of flour, six ounces of butter, and three spoonfuls of yeast, and make into a paste with new milk; make into biscuits, and prick them with a clean fork.

CAKES, BUTTER. Beat a dish of butter with your hands to a cream, add two pounds of sifted sugar, three pounds of dried flour, and twenty-four eggs, leave out half the whites, and then beat all together for an hour; when you are going to put it in the oven add a quarter of an ounce of mace and a nutmeg, a little sack and brandy, seeds and currants, if you think proper.

CAKE, WITHOUT BUTTER. Take the weight of three eggs in sugar, and the weight of two in flour; when the five eggs are well beaten, gradually add the sugar, and then the flour, with a little grated lemon-peel, or a few caraway seeds. Bake it in a tin mould, in rather a quick oven.

CAKES, CHESHIRE. Beat for half an hour the yolks of eight, and the whites of five eggs; add half a pound of pounded and sifted loaf sugar, a quarter of a pound of dried and sifted flour, and the grated peel of a small lemon; beat all well together, and bake it in a floured tin.

CAKES, CARAWAY (1) Three quarters of a pound of flour, half a pound of butter well rubbed into it, a quarter of a pound of sifted loaf sugar, and some caraway seeds; make these into a stiff paste with a little cold water, roll it out two or three times, cut it into round cakes, prick them, and bake them upon floured tins. For a change, currants may be substituted for the caraway seeds.

CAKES, CARAWAY. (2) Mix half a pound of sifted loaf sugar with a pound of flour and a quarter of a pound of butter, add some caraway seeds; make it into a stiff paste, with three well-beaten eggs, and a little rose water; roll it out thin, cut it into round cakes, prick them with a fork, and bake them upon floured tins in a quick oven.

CAKES, CURD CHEESE. Boil, in two quarts of cream, the well-beaten yolks of four, and the whites of five eggs; drain off the whey gently, and mix with the curd grated nutmeg, pounded cinnamon, three table-spoonfuls of best rose water, as much white wine, four ounces of pounded loaf sugar, the same quantity of butter beaten to a cream, and of pounded biscuit. Mix all these ingredients well together, and stir in a quarter of a pound of currants. Bake it in a large tin, or in patty-pans lined with paste; or it may be baked in a dish previously buttered.

CAKES, CURRANT. (1) Take two pounds of fine flour, one pound and a half of butter, the yolks of five or six eggs, one pound and a half of sugar, six spoonfuls of white wine, three spoonfuls of caraway seeds, two nutmegs, and one pound of currants; beat up the butter with your hand till it is very thin; dry the flour well; put in the caraway seeds, and nutmegs, finely grated; afterwards put them all into your batter, with the eggs, white wine, and rose water; mingle them well together; put in the currants; let your oven be pretty hot, and as soon as they are colored they will be sufficiently done.

CAKES, CURRANT. (2) Take half a pound of cleaned and dried currants, the same quantity of dried and sifted flour, a quarter of a pound of pounded sugar, a quarter of a pound of fresh butter, four yolks, and three whites of eggs, both well beaten, and a little grated nutmeg or pounded cinnamon; then beat the butter to a cream; add the sugar, and then the eggs and the flour, beat these well for twenty minutes, mix in the currants and the grated nutmeg. Drop the cakes in a round form upon buttered paper, or bake them in small tins in a quick oven.

CAKES, CURRANT. (3) Take six ounces of currants, the same quantity of pounded loaf sugar, a little grated nutmeg, half a pound of butter, and three-quarters of a pound of dried and sifted flour; rub the butter with the flour till they be well mixed, then add the other ingredients, and bind them with three beaten yolks of eggs, and two or three spoonfuls of rose or orange-flower water; roll it out, and cut it into round cakes with the top of a wine glass or a tin.

CAKE, COMMON. (1) Take two quarts of flour, mix with it three-quarters of a pound of butter, a tea-cupful of fresh yeast, one pint of milk, nine well-beaten eggs, two pounds of well-cleaned currants, one pound and a half of good brown sugar, the grated peel of a lemon, and one nutmeg; a glass of brandy must be stirred in just before it be put into a buttered tin. Bake it for two hours or more.

CAKE, COMMON. (2) Rub into one pound of flour a quarter of a pound of good butter; mix, with two well-beaten eggs, and a table-spoonful of fresh yeast, as much warm milk as will make the flour into a very thick batter. Let this remain near the fire, covered with a cloth for an hour, then mix into it six ounces of good brown sugar, and nine ounces of well-cleaned and dried currants; let it stand again for half an hour, and bake it in a buttered tin for an hour.

CAKE, COMMON. (3) One pound and a

half of flour, one pound of good brown sugar, eight well-beaten eggs, and one ounce of caraway seeds, are to be mixed together; then add of fresh yeast, milk, and of water, one table-spoonful each. Let it stand a little time, and bake it in a floured tin.

CAKES, COLD HARBOR. Dissolve one ounce of butter in as much milk warmed as will make four pounds of flour into a stiff paste; about two pints may be required; add half a tea-spoonful of salt, one egg beaten together with a table-spoonful of yeast; mix it all well, cover it with a cloth, and let it remain before the fire for half an hour; then make it into small round balls, and bake them upon tins in a quick oven.

CAKES, CREAM. (1) Put a pound of flour upon a pie-board; make a hole in the middle, put in half a pint of clotted cream, and a little salt; mix the paste lightly, let it stand for half an hour, then add half a pound of butter; roll it out, five times, the same as puff paste, and form it into small cakes, gild them with the yolk of egg, and bake in an oven.

CAKES, CREAM. (2) Sift some double-refined sugar; beat the whites of seven or eight eggs; shake in as many spoonfuls of the sugar; grate in the rind of a large lemon; drop the froth on a paper, laid on tin, in lumps at a distance; sift a good deal of sugar over them; set them in a moderate oven; the froth will rise; just color them; you may put raspberry jam, and stick two bottoms together; put them in a cool oven to dry.

CAKES CREAM. (3) Put into a stew-pan, two glasses of cream, a quarter of a pound of butter, the rind of a lemon, cut small, a quarter of a pound of powder-sugar, and a pinch of salt. Set it on the fire, and when it begins to boil, put it by the side of the stove; take out the lemon-peel, and add, by degrees, as much flour as the liquid will bear; keep stirring it constantly, and place it on the fire again, for five minutes, then pour it into a basin; add to it, one by one, as many eggs as will make the paste stick to the fingers; put the paste on a slab, and make your cakes of a round form.

CAKES, CANAPES. Roll out three-quarters of a pound of puff paste, keeping it long and narrow; do not let it be more than a quarter of an inch thick, and about three inches wide. Cut the paste across with a sharp knife, in slips three-eights of an inch in width, and place them on the cut side, on a baking-plate, each two inches apart; bake them in hot oven, and when nicely colored, sprinkle them with sugar, and glaze them. When done, remove them from the plate; and just before they are served, mask them with apricot marmalade, or any other you may like better, and arrange them on your dish *en couronne*.

CAKES, CURD. Take a quart of curds, eight eggs, leaving out four whites; put in sugar, grated nutmeg, and a little flour; mix these well together, heat butter, in a frying-pan, drop them in, and fry like fritters.

CAKES, DERBY OR SHORT. Rub in with the hand one pound of butter into two pounds of sifted flour; put one pound of currants, one pound of good moist sugar, and one egg; mix all together with half a pint of milk: roll it out thin, and cut them into round cakes with a cutter; lay them on a clean baking-plate, and put them into a middling-heated oven for about five minutes.

CAKE, DIET BREAD. Boil, in half a pint of water, one pound and a half of lump sugar; have ready one pint of eggs, three parts yolks, in a pan; pour in the sugar, and whisk it quick till cold, or about a quarter of an hour; then stir in two pounds of sifted flour; case the inside of square tins with white paper; fill them three parts full; sift a little sugar over, and bake it in a warm oven, and while hot remove them from the moulds.

CAKE, DAUPHINE. Beat separately the whites and yolks of twenty eggs; to the yolks add a pound of pounded and sifted loaf sugar the grated peel of one lemon, and two or three table-spoonfuls of orange-flower water; then stir in the whites, and lightly mix in half a pound of dried and sifted flour. Bake it in a moderate oven.

CAKE, FASHION. Mix a handful of flour with a pint of good cream, half a pound of beef suet, melted and sifted, a quarter of a pound of powder-sugar, half a pound of raisins, stoned and chopped, dried flowers of orange, a glass of brandy, a little coriander, and salt; bake it as all other cakes, about an hour, and glaze or garnish it.

CAKE, FOURRES. Make a puff paste, form it into two equal parts the size of the dish in which you mean to place your cake, and the thickness of two crowns each; then take one of the cakes and put upon it some sweetmeats, leaving about an inch, as a border, all round; wet it with water and place the other cake upon it, draw up the edges carefully with your fingers; gild them with the yolk of egg, and bake them in an oven.

CAKE, FRENCH: Twelve eggs, the yolks and whites beaten well and separately, one pound of pounded and sifted loaf sugar, the grated peel of a large lemon, half a pound of sifted and dried flour, the same weight of sifted and dried ground rice, four ounces of sweet, and one of bitter almonds, pounded in a mortar together, with a table-spoonful of orange-flower water. Mix all these ingredients gradually, and beat them well. Paper the pan, and bake the cake for one hour.

CAKE, FAMILY. Take rice and flour, of each six ounces, the yolks and whites of nine eggs, half a pound of lump sugar, pounded and sifted, and half an ounce of caraway seeds. Having beaten this one hour, bake it for the same time in a quick oven. This is a very light cake, and is very proper for young people and delicate stomachs.

CAKES, RICH GINGERBREAD. To one pound of dried and sifted flour, allow half a pound of pounded loaf sugar, three-quarters of a pound of fresh butter washed in rose water, one pound of treacle, one nutmeg grated, the weight of a nutmeg of pounded mace, and as much of pounded cinnamon, one ounce of pounded ginger, one and a half of candied orange and lemon-peel, cut small, half an ounce of blanched sweet almonds, cut it into long thin bits, and two well-beaten eggs. Melt the butter with the treacle, and when nearly cold, stir in the eggs and the rest of the ingredients; mix all well together, make it into round cakes, and bake them upon tins.

CAKE, GINGERBREAD. Take two pounds of treacle, two and a quarter of flour, of brown sugar and fresh butter three-quarters of a pound each, four ounces of caraway seeds, the same quantity of candied orange-peel cut small, four well-beaten eggs, and half an ounce of pearl ashes; beat the butter to a cream, and mix it with the rest of the ingredients. The next day work it well up, and bake it in a buttered tin.

CAKE, GLOVE. With flour make into a paste thick enough to roll out, the beaten yolks of ten eggs, five table-spoonfuls of rich sweet cream, a little sugar, and some cardamons; cut it into fanciful forms with small tins, and throw them into fresh boiling lard or butter; when of a light brown color, drain them before the fire. If fried in butter, add a little water to the butter, and make it boiling hot.

CAKES, GIRDLE. Rub three ounces of fresh butter into one pound of flour, with half a tea-spoonful of salt; moisten with a sufficiency of sweet butter-milk to make it into a paste; roll it out, and cut it into cakes with a cup or tumbler, and bake them upon a girdle.

CAKES, HONEY. One pound and a half of dried and sifted flour, three-quarters of a pound of honey, half a pound of finely pounded loaf sugar, a quarter of a pound of citron, and half an ounce of orange-peel cut small, of pounded ginger and cinnamon, three quarters of an ounce. Melt the sugar with the honey, and mix in the other ingredients; roll out the paste, and cut it into small cakes of any form.

CAKES, HEART. With your hand work a pound of butter to a cream, then put to it twelve eggs, with only six of the whites well-beaten, a pound of dried flour, a pound of sifted sugar, four spoonfuls of good brandy, and a pound of currants washed and dried before the fire. As the pans are filled, put in two ounces of candied orange and citron, and continue beating the cake till you put it into the oven. This quantity will be sufficient to fill three dozen of middling sized pans.

CAKES, IRISH SEED. Beat to a cream eight ounces of fresh butter, and a quarter of a pint of rose water, putting in a table-spoonful of rose water at a time; by degrees, mix into it a pound of sifted loaf sugar, and then nine well-beaten eggs; add twelve ounces of flour, and three of flour of rice dried and sifted, a quarter of a pound of blanched and pounded sweet or bitter almonds, a tea-spoonful of essence of lemon; and one ounce of caraway seeds; beat all these well together; bake it in a cake tin, which must be buttered and lined with paper, also buttered. It will require about one hour and a half to bake in a quick oven. It may be made without the almonds or the essence of lemon.

CAKES, LITTLE. To a pound of flour dried, add a pound of lump sugar rolled very fine, the peel of two lemons chopped small, and five ounces of butter; mix them thoroughly; let it stand sometime before the fire, then add three eggs well beaten, the whites separately, pick them with a fork into small lumps, and bake them on a tin: this quantity will make about eighty cakes. Instead of lemon-peel you may, if you please, add sixty bitter almonds blanched and beaten with white of egg until they are quite fine.

CAKES, MANON. Form some puff paste into an under-crust and cover some baking-plates with it; then spread all over them some *frangipane*, or marmalade, of whatever sort you please; add some sweet-meat, and then cover with a very thin crust; gild and ornament them, then put them in the oven; when they are three parts done, sprinkle them with sugar, and glaze. When they are glazed put them to finish baking in a more gentle oven, and when done take them out of the tins, and serve them either hot or cold.

CAKES, MONTROSE. Of dried and sifted flour, pounded and sifted loaf sugar, and of fresh butter, one pound each will be required, also twelve well-beaten eggs, three quarters of a pound of cleaned and dried currants; beat the butter to a cream with the sugar; add the eggs by degrees, and then the flour and currants, with two table-spoonfuls of brandy, one of rose water, and half a grated nutmeg; beat all well together for twenty or thirty minutes, when it is to be put into small buttered tins, half filling them, and baking them in a quick oven. The currants may be omitted.

CAKES, MEAT. *See Meat.*

CAKES, NUNS. Take four pounds of very fine flour, and mix with it three pounds of double-refined sugar, finely beat and sifted; dry them by the fire till your other materials are prepared; take four pounds of butter, beat it in your hands till it is very soft like cream; beat thirty-four eggs, leave out sixteen whites and take out the treads from all; beat the eggs and butter together till it appears like butter, pour in four or five spoonfuls of rose or orange-flower water, and beat it again; then take your flour and sugar with six ounces of caraway seeds, strew it in by degrees, beating it up all the while, for two hours together; put in as much tincture of cinnamon, or ambergris, as you please; butter your hoop, and let it stand three hours in a moderate oven.

CAKES, NUNS' BEADS. Pound in a mortar four ounces of good cheese, with a little salt, the beaten yolks of three eggs, and some crumbs of bread; roll them as large as walnuts, cover them with puff paste, and fry them in butter a light brown color. Serve them in a napkin.

CAKES, OATMEAL. One only should be made at a time, as the mixture dries quickly. Put two or three handfuls of meal into a bowl, and moisten it with water merely sufficient to form it into a cake; knead it out round and round with the hands upon the paste-board, strewing meal under and over it; it may be made as thin as a wafer, or thicker, according to taste, and put it on a hot iron plate, called a girdle. Bake it till it be a light brown on the under side, then take it off, and toast that side before the fire which was uppermost on the girdle. The toaster is such as is commonly used for heating smoothing irons having a back to support the cake. To make these cakes soft, they must not be toasted before the fire, but both sides done quickly on the girdle.

CAKE, PLUM . Three pounds of flour, three pounds of currants, three-quarters of a pound of almonds, blanched and beat grossly, about half an ounce of them bitter, four ounces of sugar, seven yolks and six whites of eggs, one pint of cream, two pounds of butter, half a pint of good ale yeast; mix the eggs and the yeast together, strain them; set the cream on the fire, melt the butter in it; stir in the almonds, and half a pint of sack, part of which should be put into the almonds while beating; mix together the flour, currants and sugar, what

nutmegs, cloves and mace are liked: stir these to the cream: put in the yeast.

CAKES, POTATO CHEESE. (1) Boil and peel half a pound of good potatoes, bruise them in a mortar, and when nearly cold drop in the yolk and white of an egg at intervals, until four have been added, beating the potatoes well all the time; then add a quarter of a pound of sifted bread crumbs, and put in two more eggs. Beat to a cream six ounces of fresh butter, with the same quantity of pounded loaf sugar; put it into the mortar, with the grated peel of one lemon, and mix all thoroughly. Line the patty-pans with paste; fill them three parts full, and bake them in a moderate oven.

CAKES, POTATO CHEESE. (2) Pound in a mortar five ounces of potatoes with four of fresh butter, and the same quantity of pounded loaf sugar, the grated peel and juice of half a lemon, three well-beaten eggs, and a table-spoonful of brandy; mix all well together, and bake as before directed.

CAKES, PARLIAMENT. Put into a sauce pan two pounds of treacle, and when it boils, add a quarter of a pound of butter, and pour it upon two pounds of flour; add a little alum, and a bit of pearlash about the size of a nut, and an ounce of ginger. Work it well with the hand till quite smooth; let it stand a day and a night, then roll it out very thin, and cut it into oblong cakes.

CAKE, POUND. (1) Take one pound of dried and sifted flour, the same quantity of sifted loaf sugar, and of fresh butter washed in rose water; the well-beaten  yolks of twelve, and the whites of six eggs; then with the hand beat the butter to a cream, by degrees add the sugar, then the eggs and the flour; beat it all well together for an hour. Bake it in a tin pan buttered, or in small ones in a quick oven.

CAKE, POUND. (2) Take of dried and

sifted flour, sifted loaf sugar, fresh butter, cleaned and dried currants, one pound each, and twelve eggs; then whisk the yolks and whites of the eggs separately, while another with the hand beats the butter to a cream; and as the froth rises upon the eggs add it to the butter, and continue so doing till it is all beaten in; mix the flour and sugar together, and add them by degrees; the last thing, mix in the currants together with a glass of brandy; It will require to be beaten during a whole hour. Bake it in a buttered tin.

CAKE, POUND. (3) To a pound of sifted sugar, add a pound of fresh butter, and mix them with the hand ten minutes; put to them nine yolks and five whites of eggs well-beaten; whisk all well, and add a pound of sifted flour, a few caraway seeds, a quarter of a pound of candied orange-peel cut into slices, a few currants washed and picked, and mix all together as light as possible.

CAKE, QUEEN. Beat one pound of butter to a cream, with some rose water, one pound of flour dried, one pound of sifted sugar, twelve eggs; beat all well together; add a few currants washed and dried; butter small pans of a size for the purpose, grate sugar over them; they are soon baked. They may be done in a Dutch oven.

CAKE, ROYAL. Put a very little lemon-peel, shred fine, into a stewpan, with two ounces of sugar, a small pinch of salt, a piece of butter half the size of an egg, a glass of water, and four or five spoonfuls of flour; stir over the fire till the paste becomes thick, and begins to adhere to the stewpan; then take it off, put in an egg, and stir it in the paste till it is well mixed, continue to add one egg at a time, till the paste softens without becoming liquid; then put in some dried orange flowers, and two bitter almond biscuits, the whole shred fine; make the paste into little cakes, about the size round of a half-crown; put them on buttered paper, gild them with the yolk of an egg beat up, and bake half an hour in an oven moderately hot.

CAKE, RICH. To two pounds and a half of dried and sifted flour allow the same quantity of fresh butter washed with rose water, two pounds of finely-pounded loaf sugar, three pounds of cleaned and dried currants, one nutmeg grated, half a pound of sweetmeats cut small, a quarter of a pound of blanched almonds pounded with a little rose-water, and twenty eggs, the yolks and whites separately beaten. The butter must be beaten with the hand till it become like cream; then add the sugar, and by degrees the eggs, after these the rest of the ingredients, mixing in at last the currants, with a tea-cupful of brandy, and nearly as much orange-flower water. This mixture must be beaten together rather more than an hour, then put into a cakepan, which has previously been buttered and lined with buttered paper; fill it rather more than three-quarters full. It should be baked in a moderate oven for three hours, and then cooled gradually, by at first letting it stand sometime at the mouth of the oven.

CAKE, RICE. (1) Whisk ten eggs for half an hour, add to them half a pound of flour of rice, half a pound of pounded and sifted loaf sugar, and the grated peel of two lemons; mix this into half a pound of fresh butter, previously beaten to a cream. Bake the cake in a buttered tin.

CAKE, RICE. (2) Take six ounces of ground rice, six ounces of flour, three-quarters of a pound of fine sugar sifted, nine eggs, the yolks and whites beaten separately; mix all well together, grate in the rind of a lemon, and beat it well half an hour.

CAKES, LITTLE RICE. Whisk well six yolks and two whites of eggs; then with a horn spoon beat in six ounces of finely-pounded loaf sugar, add eight ounces of sifted ground rice, and two table-spoonfuls of orange-flower or rose water, or the grated peel of a lemon, and just before the mixture is to be put into the tins, stir into it six ounces of fresh butter melted; dust the patty pans with flour, or rub them with butter; let them be half filled, and bake the cakes in a quick oven.

CAKES, SMALL ROUT. Rub into one pound of dried and sifted flour, half a pound of butter, six ounces of pounded and sifted loaf sugar, and the yolks of two well-beaten eggs; mix them all into a paste with a little rosewater; divide the quantity, put a few dried currants or caraway seeds into one half; roll out the paste, cut it into small round cakes, and bake them upon buttered tins.

CAKE RICE, A SWEET DISH. Wash well and drain a quarter of a pound of rice. Boil with a quart of fresh cream the peel of one lemon, and when nearly cold take it out and put in the rice; place the sauce pan over a slow fire, and when the rice has swollen, add a little salt, and sweeten with pounded loaf sugar; when the rice is quite tender, add the yolks of eight eggs, and mix in gradually the beaten whites, with a good bit of fresh butter, and pour it into a mould; turn this round, that the butter may equally cover every part of it, then pour out the butter, and strew over the inside a layer of grated bread; with a paste brush or a slip of paper, sprinkle all over it some of the clarified butter, add more grated bread, pour in the rice, and bake it in a moderate oven for an hour. Turn it out upon a dish, and serve it with or without a garnishing of preserved raspberries, cherries, or currants.

CAKES, SPANISH. Rub, till quite fine and smooth, one pound of butter with two pounds of flour, then add a pound of good brown sugar, rolled fine; mix all together with four well-beaten eggs; break the paste into small bits or knobs, and bake them upon floured tins.

CAKES, SHREWSBURY. Take a pound of butter, and put it in a little flat pan, rub it till it is as fine as cream, then take one pound of powdered sugar, a little cinnamon and mace pounded, and four eggs, yolks and whites together; beat them with your hand till it is very light; then take one pound and a half of sifted flour, work it together, and roll it on your dresser, to what size you like, only very flat, let your oven be rather slow, and let them change their color, then take them out.

CAKE, SPONGE. (1) Weigh ten eggs, and their weight in very fine sugar, and that of six in flour; beat the yolks with the flour, and the whites alone, to a very stiff froth: then by degrees mix the whites and the flour with the other ingredients, and beat them well half an hour. Bake in a quick oven an hour.

CAKE, SPONGE. (2) Take the juice and grated rind of a lemon, twelve eggs, twelve ounces of finely-pounded loaf sugar, the same of dried and sifted flour; then with a horn spoon beat the yolks of ten eggs, add the sugar by degrees, and beat it till it will stand when dropped from the spoon; put in at separate times the two other eggs, yolks and whites; whisk the ten whites for eight minutes, and mix in the lemon-juice, and when quite stiff, take as much as the whisk will lift, and put it upon the yolks and sugar, which must be beaten all the time; mix in lightly the flour and grated peel, and pour it all gradually over the whites; stir it together, and bake it in a buttered tin, or in small tins; do not more than half fill them.

CAKES, SHORT. Dissolve half a pound of fresh butter in as much milk as will make a pound and a half of flour into a paste, roll it out about a quarter of an inch thick, and cut it into large round cakes. Do them in a frying-pan, and serve them hot. They are eaten with butter.

CAKES, SALLY LUNN. Take one pint

of milk quite warm, a quarter of a pint of thick small-beer yeast; put them into a pan with flour sufficient to make it as thick as batter,—cover it over, and let it stand till it has risen as high as it will, *i. e.* about two hours: add two ounces of lump sugar, dissolved in a quarter of a pint of warm milk, a quarter of a pound of butter rubbed into your flour very fine; then make your dough the same as for French rolls, &c.; and let it stand half an hour; then make up your cakes, and put them on tins: when they have stood to rise, bake them in a quick oven. Care should be taken never to put your yeast to water or milk too hot, or too cold, as either extreme will destroy the fermentation. In summer it should be lukewarm, in winter a little warmer, and in very cold weather, warmer still. When it has first risen, if you are not prepared, it will not hurt to stand an hour.

CAKES, SUGAR. Take half a pound of dried flour, the same quantity of fresh butter washed in rose water, and a quarter of a pound of sifted loaf sugar; then mix together the flour and sugar: rub in the butter and add the yolk of an egg beaten with a table-spoonful of cream; make it into a paste, roll, and cut it into small round cakes, which bake upon a floured tin.

CAKES, TEA. With a pound of flour rub half a pound of butter; add the beaten yolks of two, and the white of one egg, a quarter of a pound of pounded loaf sugar, and a few caraway seeds; mix it to a paste with a little warm milk, cover it with a cloth, and let it stand before the fire for nearly an hour; roll out the paste, and cut it into round cakes with the top of a glass, and bake them upon floured tins.

CAKE, TWELFTH. Two pounds of sifted flour, two pounds of sifted loaf sugar, two pounds of butter, eighteen eggs, four pounds of currants, one half pound of almonds blanched and chopped, one half

pound of citron, one pound of candied orange and lemon peel cut into thin slices, a large nutmeg grated, half an ounce of ground allspice; ground cinnamon, mace, ginger, and corianders, a quarter of an ounce of each, and a gill of brandy. Put the butter into a stewpan, in a warm place, and work it into a smooth cream with the hand, and mix it with the sugar and spice in a pan, (or on your paste board) for sometime; then break in the eggs by degrees, and beat it at least twenty minutes; stir in the brandy, and then the flour, and work it a little; add the fruit, sweetmeats, and almonds, and mix all together lightly; have ready a hoop cased with paper, on a baking-plate; put in the mixture, smooth it on the top with your hand, dipped in milk; put the plate on another, with saw dust between, to prevent the bottom from coloring too much: bake it in a slow oven four hours or more, and when nearly cold, ice it with icing. This mixture would make a handsome cake, full twelve or fourteen inches over.

CAKE, WHITE. Take of dried and sifted flour, of fresh butter and of finely-pounded loaf sugar, one pound each; five well-beaten eggs, a quarter of a pint of cream, of candied orange and lemon peel, cut small, three quarters of an ounce each; one ounce of caraway seeds, half a grated nutmeg, a glass of brandy, and a little rose water; then beat the butter to a cream, and add all the other ingredients to it, and at the last mix in one table-spoonful of fresh yeast; let the cake rise before the fire for half an hour. Bake it in a buttered tin. Instantly upon taking it out of the oven, with a feather, brush the top all over with the beaten white of an egg, and then sift loaf sugar upon it. Let it stand at the mouth of the oven to harden.

CAKES, YEAST. Take a pound of flour, two pounds of currants, washed and picked, a quarter of a pound of fresh butter, a quarter of a pound of Lisbon sugar, a quarter of a pound of citron and candied orange-peel cut into slices, cinnamon and mace, a small quantity of each pounded and sifted. Make a hole in the centre of the ingredients, put in a gill of sweet wine, a little warm milk, mix all together, fill a hoop with it, let it remain till it rises, and bake it.

CAKES, YORKSHIRE. Take two pounds of flour, and mix with it four ounces of butter, melted in a pint of good milk, three spoonfuls of yeast, and two eggs; beat all well together, and let it rise; then knead it, and make it into cakes; let them rise on tins before you bake, which do in a slow oven. Another sort is made as above, leaving out the butter. The first is shorter, the last lighter.

CAKE, BISCUIT. One pound of flour, five eggs well-beaten and strained, eight ounces of sugar, a little rose or orange-flower water, beat the whole thoroughly, and bake it for one hour.

CALF'S BRAINS, WITH OYSTERS. Blanch and clean the brains, then wipe them dry, dip them into yolks of eggs, and roll them in bread crumbs; fry them in boiling lard till of a good color, drain them very dry, and serve with oysters, stewed either white or brown. Garnish with broiled ham cut in small round pieces.

CALF'S BRAINS. Cleanse two calves' brains, and stew them in stock with two or three spoonfuls of vinegar, a bunch of parsley, scallions, a clove of garlic, three cloves, thyme, laurel, and basil; when sufficiently stewed, cut each piece of the brain in two, dip them in a batter made of two handfuls of flour, diluted with a little oil, half a pint of white wine, and salt. Fry them in lard until the batter is crisp and the brains of a gold color.

CALF'S BRAINS, WITH FRIED PARSLEY. Blanch three or four brains of nearly an equal size; parboil them, and take off the skin; then boil them in water, with a little salt, vinegar and butter. Serve them with a sauce made of a little browned butter, a table-spoonful of vinegar, some salt and pepper, and some parsley fried very green.

CALF'S CHITTERLINGS. Cut them open with scissors, wash and cleanse them thoroughly, lay them for a night into salt-and-water, then wash them well, parboil, and cut them into small pieces, dip them into a thick batter, seasoned with pepper, salt, and a little white wine. Fry them of a light brown color in beef dripping; serve with a fringe of fried parsley. Or, After being parboiled, they may be roasted, when they must be constantly basted with butter, dredged with flour to froth them nicely; then served with melted butter, and lemon pickle poured over them. Or, They may be baked—when, after being parboiled, they are rubbed over with butter, and put into the oven on an iron frame, which is placed in a deep dish. This oblong frame of white iron, about two inches high, will be found useful in baking every kind of meat.

CALF'S CHAUDRON, FRICASSEE. Parboil a calf's chaudron, and when cold, cut it in pieces about as big as walnuts; season them with salt, pepper, nutmeg, cloves, mace, an onion, tarragon, and parsley, shred fine; fry them in a ladleful of good broth and fresh butter; make a sauce of mutton gravy, orange and lemon juice, eggs' yolks, and grated nutmeg; toss up these ingredients with the chaudron, then dish it and serve.

CALF'S-FEET PUDDING. *See Puddings*.

CALF'S FEET JELLY. *See Jelly*.

CALF'S FEET, POTTED. Boil the feet as for jelly, pick all the meat from the bones, add to it half a pint of gravy, a little salt, pepper, and nutmeg, garlic, a shallot and some shred ham; simmer it for half an hour, dip a mould into water, put in a layer of the meat, then some neatly-cut pickled beet root, and some boiled minced parsley, then a layer of meat, and so on, till the mould be filled; when cold, turn it out. Garnish with pickled eggs, beet root, and parsley.

CALF'S FEET, PLAIN. Scald, clean, and blanch some calves' feet, boil them till the bones will come out, then stew them in a blane. See Calf's Head, plain. When done, drain and serve them with parsley and butter.

CALF'S HEAD, HASHED. Boil the head almost enough, and take the meat of the best side neatly from the bone, and lay it in a small dish; wash it over with the yolks of two eggs, and cover it with crumbs, a few herbs, nicely shred, a little pepper, salt, and nutmeg, all mixed together previously. Set the dish before the fire, and keep turning it now and then, that all parts may be equally brown. In the meantime slice the remainder of the head, and the tongue, (peeled); put a pint of good gravy into a pan with an onion, a small bunch of herbs, (consisting of parsley, basil, savory, tarragon, knotted marjoram, and a little thyme), a little salt and Cayenne, a shallot, a glass of Sherry, and a little oyster liquor: boil this for a few minutes, and strain it upon the meat, which must be sprinkled with flour. Add some fresh or pickled mushrooms, a few truffles and morels, and two spoonfuls of catchup; beat up half the brains, and put them to the rest, with a bit of butter and flour. Simmer the whole. Beat the other part of the brains with shred lemon-peel, a little nutmeg and mace, some parsley shred, and an egg; fry this in little cakes of a fine gold color; dip some oysters into the yolk of an egg, and fry the same way, also some good forcemeat balls, and garnish the dish with them.

CALF'S HEAD SOUP, OR MOCK TURTLE. *See Soups.*

CALF'S HEAD. With a sharp knife cut all the meat entire from the bone, cut out the tongue, and carefully take out the brains; lay them all in cold water for two or three hours. Mince very small two pounds of lean veal, and one pound of beef suet, with the grated crumb of a penny loaf, some sweet herbs, grated lemon-peel, nutmeg, pepper, and salt; mix them well together, and bind it with the yolks of four eggs beaten up; reserve as much of the forcemeat as will make twenty small balls: wash the head clean, wipe it dry, and put the forcemeat into the inside; close it, and tie it firmly with tape; put it into a stewpan with two quarts of gravy, half a pint of white wine, and a bunch of sweet herbs; cover it closely, and let it stew gently; boil the tongue, cut it into thin slices, mince the brains with a little parsley and a table-spoonful of flour, add some pepper, salt, grated lemon-peel, and nutmeg; beat two eggs and mix with the brains, drop it with a spoon in small cakes into a pan of boiling dripping, and fry them of a light brown color. Fry the forcemeat balls, and drain them, with the cakes, upon the back of a sieve before the fire; when the head has stewed till it be sufficiently tender, put it into a dish and take off the tape, strain the gravy, and thicken it with a table-spoonful of flour of rice, and a little bit of butter; if not well seasoned, add more salt and pepper, put in the tongue, make it all hot, and pour it over the head. Garnish with the brain-cakes, forcemeat balls, and cut lemon.

CALF'S HEAD, ROASTED. Wash and clean it well, parboil it, take out the bones, brains, and tongue; make forcemeat sufficient for the head, and some balls with bread crumbs, minced suet, parsley, grated ham, and a little pounded veal, or cold fowl; season with pepper, salt, grated nutmeg, and lemon-peel; bind it with an egg, beaten up, fill the head with it, which must then be sewed up, or fastened with skewers and tied. While roasting, baste it well with butter; beat up the brains with a little cream, the yolk of an egg, some minced parsley, a little pepper and salt; blanch the tongue, cut it into slices, and fry it with the brains, forcemeat balls, and thin slices of bacon. Serve the head with white or brown thickened gravy, and place the tongue, forcemeat balls, and brains round it. Garnish with cut lemon. It will require one hour and a half to roast.

CALF'S HEAD, PLAIN. Clean a calf's head nicely, and cut out the bone of the lower jaw, and of the nose, taking out the nose bone as close to the eyes as possible; wash the head well in warm water, and let it blanch in some clean water. Prepare a blane, or sauce, as follows:—One pound of beef suet, and one pound of fat bacon, cut small, half a pound of butter, a bunch of parsley, a little thyme, two or three bay leaves, one or two onions, and the juice of a lemon; season with salt, pepper, mace, cloves, and allspice; boil all this an hour in six pints of water, then tie up the head in a cloth, boil it in the sauce about three hours, and drain it; take out the tongue, skin and replace it; serve quite hot, with the following sauce—minced shallots, parsley, the brains minced, some vinegar, salt, and pepper.

CALF'S HEAD, SOUSED. Scald and bone a calf's head, and soak it for seven or eight hours, changing the water twice; dry it well. Season with salt and bruised garlic; roll it up, bind it very tight, and boil it in white wine, salt and water; when done, put it, with the liquor, in a pan, and keep it for use. Serve up either whole, or in slices, with oil, vinegar, and pepper.

CALF'S HEAD, BIGAREE. Clean and blanch a calf's head, boil it till the bones will come out easily, then bone and press it between two dishes, so as to give it an oblong form; beat with the yolks of four eggs a little melted butter, pepper, and salt. Divide the head when cold, and brush it all over with the beaten eggs, and strew over it grated bread; repeat this twice. With the grated bread, which is put over one half, a good quantity of finely-minced parsley should be mixed; place the head upon a dish, and bake it of a nice brown color.

Serve it with a sauce of parsley and butter, and with one of good gravy, mixed with the brains which have been previously boiled, and chopped, and seasoned with a little Cayenne and salt.

CALF'S HEART, ROASTED. Fill the heart with the following forcemeat: a quarter of a pound of beet suet, chopped small, grated bread, parsley, marjoram, lemon-peel, pepper, salt, nutmeg, and the yolk of an egg. Lay a veal caul, or a sheet of paper on the stuffing to keep it in its place. Put the heart into a Dutch oven, before a clear fire, and turn it frequently, till thoroughly roasted all round. Garnish with slices of lemon, and pour melted butter over it.

CALF LIVER, BROILED. Slice it, season with pepper and salt, and broil nicely: rub a bit of cold butter on it, and serve hot and hot.

CALF'S LIVER, LARDED AND ROASTED. Lard a fine calf's liver the same as a fricandeau, and let it lie for twenty-four hours in vinegar, with a sliced onion, some parsley, a little thyme, a bay leaf, some salt and pepper. Roast, and baste it well with butter, then glaze it with a light glaze, and serve it with a poivrade, or any other sauce.

CALF'S LIVER, ROASTED. (1) Wash and wipe it; then cut a long hole in it, and stuff it with crumbs of bread, chopped anchovy, a good deal of fat bacon, onion, salt, pepper, a bit of butter, and an egg; sew the liver up; lard it, wrap it in a veal caul, and roast it. Serve with good brown gravy and currant jelly.

CALF'S LIVER, ROASTED. (2) Lard a calf's liver with streaky bacon; roast and baste it frequently with its own gravy.

CALF'S LIVER, ROASTED. (3) Lard a fine calf's liver, and pickle it in vinegar, with an onion, cut into slices, parsley, salt, pepper, thyme, and a bay leaf. When it has been soaked for twenty-four hours, fasten it on a spit, roast and baste it frequently. Glaze it with a light glaze, as it is naturally of a black color. Serve under it a brown *poivrade*.

CALF'S LIVER, SCOLLOPS. Parboil and cut into slices a very nice calf's liver, and shape them into hearts. Stew some fine herbs, parsley, shallots, and mushrooms; then add the calf's liver, and let it stew over a slow fire; when done on one side, turn and season it with pepper and salt; take out the liver, dredge in a little flour over the herbs, and add some more gravy; let this boil for ten minutes, then heat the liver in the sauce before serving it. This may be eaten at breakfast.

CALF'S PLUCK. Wash it very clean, and, if liked, stuff the heart with a force-meat, made of crumbs of bread, butter, and parsley, and seasoned with pepper, salt, and grated nutmeg. Fasten it firmly with the liver and lights, tying them to the skewers while roasting; baste it well with butter, and froth it the same way in which veal is done, and serve it with melted butter, mixed with a table-spoonful of lemon pickle, or vinegar poured over it.

CAPER SAUCE. *See Sauce.*

CAPILLAIRE. Take fourteen pounds of sugar, three pounds of coarse sugar, six eggs beat in with the shells, three quarts of water; boil it up twice; skim it well, then add to it a quarter of a pint of orange-flower water; strain it through a jelly-bag, and put it into bottles; when cold, mix a spoonful or two of this sirup, as it is liked for sweetness in a draught of warm or cold water.

CAPILOTADE ITALIAN. Cut up a cold roast fowl; then take a good slice of butter, and some shred mushrooms and potherbs; fry these till they are about to turn brown, with a tea-spoonful of flour: then add to them a large glass of white wine. Let the whole simmer together for a quarter of an hour; next put in the pieces of fowl, and heat them up for a few minutes. Garnish your dish with fried slices of bread; and just before you serve, pour into the saucepan two table-spoonfuls of oil, taking care that it does not boil, and stir it up well with the sauce.

CAPONS OR FOWLS, Must be killed a couple of days in moderate, and more in cold weather, before they are dressed, or they will eat tough: a good criterion of the ripeness of poultry for the spit, is the ease with which you can then pull out the feathers; when a fowl is plucked, leave a few to help you to ascertain this. They are managed exactly in the same manner, and sent up with the same sauces as a turkey, only they require proportionately less time at the fire. A full-grown five-toed fowl, about an hour and a quarter. A moderate-sized one, an hour  A chicken from thirty to forty minutes. Here, also, pork sausages fried are in general a favorite accompaniment, or turkey stuffing; see forcemeats; put in plenty of it, so as to plump out the fowl, which must be tied closely (both at the neck and rump), to keep in the stuffing. Some cooks put the liver of the fowl into this forcemeat, and others mince it and pound it, and rub it up with flour and melted butter. When the bird is stuffed and trussed, score the gizzard nicely, dip it into melted butter, let it drain, and then season it with Cayenne and salt; put it under one pinion, and the liver under the other; to prevent their getting hardened or scorched, cover them with double paper buttered. Take care that your roasted poultry be well browned; it is as indispensable that roasted poultry should have a rich brown complexion, as boiled poultry should have a delicate white one.

CAPON, TO CHOOSE. If it is young, his spurs are short and his legs smooth; if a true capon, a fat vein on the side of his breast, the comb pale, and a thick belly and rump; if fresh, he will have a close hard vent; if stale, a loose open vent.

CAPON, THE FRENCH WAY. Take a quart of white wine, season the capon with salt, cloves, and whole pepper, a few shallots; and then put the capon in an earthen pan; you must take care it has not room to shake; it must be covered close, and done over a slow charcoal fire.

CAPON PASTY. Roast a capon, let it be cold, take the flesh from the bones and slice it, but keep the thighs and pinions whole. Add to the flesh of the capon, four sweetbreads and half a pint of oysters, season them with salt, cloves, nutmeg, and mace, sweet majoram, pennyroyal, and thyme, minced; lay a sheet of paper or paste in your pasty-pan, and lay the thighs and pinions on the bottom, and strew them over with sliced onions, then put in the flesh of the capon, the sweetbreads, and the oysters, cut in halves; over these strew a handful of chesnuts, boiled and blanched, then put butter over them, close up your pan and bake it; when done, add gravy, good stock, drawn butter, anchovies, and grated nutmeg; Garnish with slices of lemon, and serve. Turkey may be done in the same manner.

CAPONS A LA TURQUE. Pick, and clean very nicely, two fine capons; wash the inside perfectly clean with warm water, and let them soak in warm water for a quarter of an hour; dry them well, and put into them some rice which has been boiled till soft in some rich well-seasoned stock, truss and cover them with layers of bacon, wrap them in paper, and roast them for an hour by a hanging-jack; serve them, putting all round the dish a part of the rice which was prepared for the stuffing, and pour over the fowls a veloute sauce. One fine large fowl may be dressed in this manner.

CAPSICUMS, TO PICKLE. Gather the pods, with the stalks on, before they turn red; cut a slit down the side with a penknife, and take out all the seeds, but as little of the meat as possible; lay them in a strong brine for three days, changing it evey day; then take them out, lay them on a cloth, and lay another over them till they are quite dry; boil vinegar enough to cover them, put in some mace and nutmeg beat small; put the pods into a glass or jar, and when the liquor is cold, pour it over, then tie a bladder and leather over them.

CARDOONS, WITH CHEESE. String and cut them an inch long, put them into a saucepan with red wine, seasoned with pepper and salt, stew them till they are tender, put in a piece of butter rolled in flour, and when of a proper thickness pour them into a dish, squeeze the juice of an orange into the sauce, and scrape over them some Parmesan or Cheshire cheese, and then brown them with a cheese-iron, but not of too high a color.

CARDOONS, TO DRESS. Cut them in pieces six inches long, and put them on a string; boil till tender, have ready a piece of butter in a pan, flour and fry them. They may also be tied in bundles, and served as asparagus boiled on a toast, and pour butter over.

CARDOONS, SPANISH. Cut them into lengths of three inches, be careful not to use those which are hollow and green; boil them for half an hour, then put them into lukewarm water to cleanse them from their slime; then dress them in some stock, with a spoonful of flour, some salt, onions, roots, a bunch of sweet herbs, a little verjuice, and a little butter; when done, put them into a cullis with some stock; cook them for an hour in this sauce, and serve.

CARROTS. Let them be well washed and brushed, not scraped. An hour is enough for young spring carrots; grown carrots must be cut in half, and will take from an hour and a half to two hours and a half. When done, rub off the peels with a clean coarse cloth, and slice them in two or four, according to their size. The best way to try if they are done enough, is to pierce them with a fork. Many people are fond of cold carrot with cold beef; ask if you shall cook enough for some to be left to send up with the cold meat.

CARAMEL, OR BOILED SUGAR. Break into a small copper or brass pan, one pound of refined sugar,—put in a gill of spring water;—set it on a fire, and when it boils, skim it quite clean, and let it boil quick, till it comes to the degree called Crack, which may be known by dipping a teaspoon or skewer into the sugar, and let it drop to the bottom of a pan of cold water; and if it remains hard, it has attained that degree; squeeze in the juice of half a lemon, and let it remain one minute longer on the fire, then set the pan into another of cold water:—have ready moulds of any shape, — rub them over with sweet oil, dip a spoon or fork into the sugar, and throw it over the mould in fine threads, till it is quite covered: —make a small handle of caramel, or stick on two or three small gum paste rings, by way of ornament, and place it over small pastry of any description.

CARP, BOILED. Scale and clean a brace of carp, reserving the liver and roe; take half a pint of vinegar, or a quart of sharp cider, add as much water as will cover the fish, a piece of horse-radish, an onion cut into slices, a little salt, and a faggot of sweet herbs; boil the fish in this liquor, and make a sauce as follows:—strain some of the liquor the fish has been boiled in, and put to it the liver minced, a pint of Port wine, two anchovies, two or three heads of shallots chopped, some salt and black pepper, a little Cayenne, a table-spoonful of soy; boil and strain it, thicken it with flour and butter, pour it over the carp hot, garnish with the roe fried, cut lemon and parsley.

CARP, STEWED. Scale and clean a brace of carp, reserving the liver and roe; pour over the fish in a deep pan a pint of vinegar, which may be elder vinegar, if the flavor is preferred, with a little mace, three cloves, some salt and Jamaica pepper, two onions sliced, a faggot of parsley, basil, thyme, and majoram; let them soak an hour, then put them in a stewpan with the vinegar, and other things, the liver chopped, a pint of Madeira, and three pints of veal stock; stew them an hour or two according to their size; take out the fish and put them over a pan of hot water to keep warm while the following sauce is made:—Strain the liquor, and add the yolks of three eggs beaten, half a pint of cream, a large spoonful of flour, and a quarter of a pound of butter, stir it constantly, and just before putting it over the carp, squeeze in the juice of a lemon. Boil or fry the roe. Plain boiled carp may be served with this sauce, and is dished in a napkin.

CARP, FRIED. Clean and scale a carp; split it up the back; flatten the backbone, sprinkle your fish with flour, then sprinkle the roes which have been put aside, put the whole into a frying-pan made very hot, fry to a rich color, and serve it with lemon-juice.

CARROT FRITTERS. Beat two or three boiled carrots to a pulp with a spoon; add to them six eggs and a handful of flour; moisten them with either cream, milk, or white wine, and sweeten them. Beat all together well, and fry in boiling lard. When of a good color, take them off and squeeze on them the juice of a Seville orange, and strew over fine sugar.

CARROT PUDDING. *See Pudding.*

CASSILE. Mix two table-spoonfuls of potato-flour with two or three of cream or good milk; boil for a few minutes with a quart of cream or milk, the peel of a lemon and a bit of cinnamon; stir it with the flour and cream; sweeten, and stir it again over the fire for three or four minutes; pour it into a mould; turn it out when cold.

CAULIFLOWER. Choose those that are close and white, and of the middle size; trim off the outside leaves; cut the stalk off flat at the bottom, let them lie in salt and water an hour before you boil them. Put them into boiling water with a handful of salt in it; skim it well, and let it boil slowly till done, which a small one will be in fifteen, a large one in about twenty minutes; take it up the moment it is enough, a minute or two longer boiling will spoil it.

CAULIFLOWERS OR BROCCOLI, PICKLED. Choose those that are hard, yet sufficiently ripe, cut away the leaves and stalks. Set on a stewpan half full of water, salted in proportion of a quarter of a pound of salt to a quart of water; throw in the cauliflower, and let it heat gradually; when it boils take it up with a spoon full of holes, and spread them on a cloth to dry before the fire, for twenty-four hours at least; when quite dry, put them, piece by piece, into jars or glass tie-overs, and cover them with the pickle we have directed for beet roots, or make a pickle by infusing three ounces of the curry powder for three days in a quart of vinegar by the side of the fire. Nasturtiums are excellent prepared as above.

CAULIFLOWERS, PICKLED. Cut the cauliflowers in pieces, and throw them into boiling water for a quarter of an hour; then lay them on cloths to drain. Put them in a jar with cloves and salt, and cover them with the best vinegar.

CAULIFLOWER SALAD. When you have prepared and boiled the cauliflowers, drain and let them cool; cut them in pieces; season them with salt, pepper, oil and vinegar, and eat them as any other salad.

CAUDLE. (1) Boil up half a pint of fine gruel, with a bit of butter the size of a large nutmeg, a large spoonful of brandy, the same of white wine, one of capillaire, a piece of lemon-peel, and nutmeg.

CAUDLE. (2) Make a fine smooth gruel of half-grits; when boiled, strain it, stir it at times till cold. When wanted for use, add sugar, wine, and lemon-peel, with some nutmeg. According to taste, you may add, if you please, besides the wine, a spoonful of brandy, or lemon-juice.

CAUDLE, BROWN. Boil the gruel the same as for white caudle, with six spoonfuls of oatmeal, and strain it; then add a quart of good ale, not bitter; boil it, then sweeten it according to your taste, and add half a pint of white wine. When you do not put in the white wine, let it be half ale.

CAUDLE, COLD. Boil a quart of spring water; when cold, add the yolk of an egg, the juice of a small lemon, six spoonfuls of sweet wine, sugar to your taste, and one ounce of sirup of lemons.

CECILS. Mix over the fire for a few minutes the following ingredients: minced meat of whatever kind you please, bread crumbs, plenty of onion, lemon-peel, nutmeg, parsley chopped, pepper, salt, a little butter, and some anchovies. When nearly cold, roll them up into balls about the size of an egg; moisten them with egg, strew bread crumbs over them, and fry them of a good clear color: serve them with made gravy.

CELERY, TO STEW. Wash and clean some heads of celery, cut them into pieces of two or three inches long, boil them in veal stock till tender. To half a pint of cream add the well-beaten yolks of two eggs, a bit of lemon-peel, grated nutmeg, and salt, also a bit of butter; make it hot, stirring it constantly; strain it upon the celery; heat it thoroughly, but do not let it boil.

CHARLOTTE. (1) Cut a sufficient number of thin slices of white bread to cover the bottom and line the sides of a baking-dish, first rubbing it thickly with butter. Put thin slices of apples into the dish in layers, till the dish is full, strewing sugar and bits of butter between. In the meantime soak as many thin slices of bread as will cover the whole, in warm milk; over which place a plate, and a weight, to keep the bread close upon the apples; let it bake slowly for three hours. For a middling-sized dish, you should use half a pound of butter for the whole.

CHARLOTTE. (2) This second course may be made of any kind of fruit you please, and is eaten hot. If apples are used, pare, core, and cut about twenty of them into small pieces, and put them into a stew-pan with some water, a good piece of fresh butter, powder-sugar, pounded cinnamon, and grated lemon-peel, and stew till the water is dried up; then set them to cool in an earthen ware vessel. Cut some very thin slices of crumb of bread, dip them in melted fresh butter, and lay them neatly all over the bottom and round the sides of the stewpan; then pour in the apples, leaving a hole in the middle, in which put apricot marmalade. Cover the whole with bread, sliced thin, and buttered as above. Place it in a hot oven, bake it an hour, and turn it out.

CHARLOTTE DES POMMES. Pare, core, and mince fourteen or fifteen French rennet apples; put them into a frying-pan, with some pounded loaf sugar, a little pounded cinnamon, grated lemon-peel, and two ounces and a half of fresh butter; fry them a quarter of an hour over a quick fire, stirring them constantly. Butter a shape of the size the charlotte is intended to be; cut strips of bread about the width of two fingers, and long enough to reach from the bottom to the rim of the shape, so that the whole be lined with bread; dip each bit into melted butter, and then put a layer of the fried apples, and one of apricot jam or marmalade, and then one of bread dipped into butter; begin and finish with it. Bake it

in an oven for nearly an hour; turn it out to serve it. It may be boiled, and served with a sweet sauce.

CHEESE, BOILED. Grate a quarter of a pound of good cheese, put it into a sauce pan, with a bit of butter the size of a nut-meg, and half a tea-cupful of milk, stir it over the fire till it boil, and then add a well-beaten egg; mix it all together, put it into a small dish, and brown it before the fire.

CHEESE, CAKE OF. Take about the fourth part of a close, fat Brie cheese, pound and rub it through a sieve; mix with it a pint and a half of flour; lay it on the board, make a hole in the middle, into which put three quarters of a pound of butter, and work it in well; add to it a little Gruyere cheese grated, and six eggs. Knead these all together well; mould it up, and let it stand for half an hour; then roll it out, and make it into a cake of about three inches; mark it with a knife on one side in chequers, and on the other in rays; *dorez*, and bake it in a moderate oven.

CHEESE CREAM. Warm three half pints of cream with one half pint of milk, or according to the same proportion, and put a little rennet to it; keep it covered in a warm place till it is curdled; have a proper mould with holes, either of China or any other; put the curds into it to drain, about an hour, or less: serve with a good plain cream, and pounded sugar over it.

CHEESECAKES. (1) Put two quarts of new milk into a stewpan, set it near the fire, and stir in two table-spoonfuls of rennet: let it stand till it is set (this will take about an hour), break it well with your hand, and let it remain half an hour longer; then pour off the whey, and put the curd into a colander to drain; when quite dry, put it in a mortar, and pound it quite smooth; then add four ounces of sugar, pounded and sifted, and three ounces of fresh butter; oil it first by putting it in a little potting-pot, and setting it near the fire; stir it all well together: beat the yolks of four eggs in a basin, with a little nutmeg, grated, lemon-peel, and a glass of brandy; add this to the curd, with two ounces of currants, washed and picked; stir it all well together, have your tins ready lined with puff paste about a quarter of an inch thick, notch them all round the edge, and fill each with the curd. Bake them twenty minutes. When you have company, and want a variety, you can make a mould of curd and cream, by putting the curd in a mould full of holes, instead of the colander: let it stand for six hours, then turn it out very carefully on a dish, and pour over it half a pint of good cream sweetened with loaf sugar, and a little nutmeg. What there is left, if set in a cool place, will make excellent cheesecakes the next day.

CHEESECAKES. (2) Put a spoonful of rennet into a quart of milk; when turned, drain the curd through a coarse sieve, gently break the curd, and rub in a quarter of a pound of butter, a quarter of a pound of sugar, nutmeg, and two Naples biscuits grated, the yolks of four eggs, and the white of one, half an ounce of almonds, half bitter and half sweet, well beaten in a mortar, with two spoonfuls of rose water, four ounces of currants; put in the curd, and mix all together. One quart of milk, and three dessert spoonfuls of rice-flour, six eggs, leave out three of the whites, and currants to your taste.

CHEESECAKES. (3) Beat eight eggs well, while a quart of milk is on the fire, and when it boils, put in the eggs, and stir them till they come to a curd; then pour it out, and when it is cold, put in a little salt, two spoonfuls of rose water, and three-quarters of a pound of currants well washed; put it into puff paste, and bake it. If you use tin patties to bake in, butter them, or you will not be able to take them out; but if you bake them in glass or china, only an upper crust will be necessary, as you will not want to take them out when you send them to table.

CHEESECAKES. (4) Take one pound of loaf sugar pounded, six yolks, and four whites of eggs beaten, the juice of three fine lemons, the grated rind of two, and a quarter of a pound of fresh butter; put these ingredients into a saucepan, and stir the mixture gently over a slow fire till it be of the consistence of honey; pour it into small jars, and when cold put paper dipped in brandy over them. It will keep good for a year.

CHEESE, POUNDED. Cut a pound of good mellow cheese into thin bits; add to it two, and if the cheese is dry, three ounces of fresh butter; pound, and rub them well together in a mortar till it is quite smooth. When cheese is dry, and for those whose digestion is feeble, this is the best way of eating it; and spread on bread, it makes an excellent luncheon or supper. The *piquance* of this is sometimes increased by pounding with it curry powder, ground spice, black pepper, Cayenne, and a little made mustard; and some moisten it with a glass of Sherry. If pressed down hard in a jar, and covered with clarified butter, it will keep for several days in cool weather.

CHEESE, ROASTED. Grate three ounces of fat cheese, mix it with the yolks of two eggs, four ounces of grated bread, and three ounces of butter; beat the whole well in a mortar, with a dessert spoonful of mustard, and a little salt and pepper. Toast some bread, cut it into proper pieces; lay the paste, as above, thick upon them, put them into a Dutch oven covered with a dish, till hot through, remove the dish, and let the cheese brown a little. Serve as hot as possible.

CHEESE, STEWED. Melt three-quarters of an ounce of butter in a tea-cupful of cream, mix with it a quarter of a pound of good cheese finely grated, beat it well together; put a slice of toasted bread into a dish, and pour the mixture over it; and brown it with a salamander.

CHEESE TOASTED, OR RABBIT. Cut a slice of bread, toast it, and soak it in red wine, put it before the fire; cut some cheese in very thin slices, and rub some butter over the bottom of a plate, lay the cheese upon it, and pour in two or three spoonfuls of white wine, and a little mustard; cover it with another plate, and set it on a chafing-dish of coals two or three minutes, then stir it till it is well mixed; when it is mixed enough, lay it upon the bread, and brown it with a salamander.

CHEESE TOASTED. Cut a slice of bread about half an inch thick; pare off the crust, and toast it very slightly on one side so as just to brown it, without making it hard or burning it. Cut a slice of good fat mellow cheese, a quarter of an inch thick, not so big as the bread by half an inch on each side: pare off the rind, cut out all the specks and rotten parts, and lay it on the toasted bread in a cheese-toaster; carefully watch it that it does not burn and stir it with a spoon to prevent a pellicle forming on the surface. Have ready good mustard, pepper and salt. If you observe the directions here given, the cheese will eat mellow, and will be uniformly done, and the bread crisp and soft, and will well deserve its ancient appellation of a "rare bit." This Receipt, as well as every other worth extracting, is from the Cook's Oracle. The Editor goes on to say. We have nothing to add to the directions given for toasting the cheese in the last receipt, except that in sending it up, it will save much time in portioning it out at table, if you have half a dozen small silver or tin pans to fit into the cheese-toaster, and do the cheese in these: each person may then be helped to a separate pan, and it will keep the cheese much hotter than the usual way of eating it on a cold plate. *Obs.*—Ceremony seldom triumphs more completely over comfort than in the serving out of this dish; which, to be presented to the palate in perfection, it is imperatively indispensable that it be introduced to the mouth as soon as it appears on the table.

CHERRY BRANDY. (1) Pick and bruise eight pounds of black maroons, and the same quantity of small black cherries; let them stand for two months in a cask with six gallons of brandy, two pounds of crushed sugar, and a quart of sack well stirred together. At the end of that time it may be drawn off and bottled.

CHERRY BRANDY. (2) Choose fine sound morella cherries, and having taken off the stalks, place them in layers in glass jars; strew powder-sugar between each layer, and cover them with brandy. As soon as the cherries have imbibed the brandy, pour in more, so as to keep them constantly covered.

CHERRIES, DRIED. Take large cherries, not too ripe; pick off the stalks, and take out the stones with a quill cut nearly as for a pen: to three pounds of which take three pounds or pints of clarified sugar; boil it to the degree of blown; put in the cherries, give them a boil, and set them by in an earthen pan till the next day; then strain the sirup, add more sugar, and boil it of a good consistence; put the cherries in, and boil them five minutes, and set them by another day: repeat the boiling two more days, and when wanted, drain them sometime, and lay them on wire sieves to dry in a stove, or nearly cold oven.

CHERRY PUDDING. *See Puddings.*

CHERVIL, Is principally used in soups and stuffing, and is generally preserved with other herbs as follows: take of sorrel, chervil, beet, purslain, and cucumbers, if in season, quantities according to your liking; wash them well; mince and press them in your hand, to squeeze out all the water. Put them into a kettle with water, some butter, add salt, and boil them until the water is entirely consumed. Then take them out, and when cold, put them into pots; cover them with warmed butter. When you want to use these herbs, put them into some stock that has very little salt in it. If they are required for a farce or garnish, boil them a minute or two in some butter; thicken with the yolks of eggs and milk; when so prepared, they may be served under hard eggs or broiled fish. For sauce, it must be chopped small, boiled in salt and water, and mixed with melted butter.

CHESTNUTS, Should be placed on the fire in a pan with holes to roast; first slitting or cutting a notch in the skins, to prevent their flying off. When done, serve them in dessert on a napkin, as hot as possible. Some boil the chestnuts instead of roasting them, as the skins are then cleaner, but the nuts not quite so mealy; the better way is to boil them in plenty of water, and when nearly done, take them out and roast them.

CHICKENS. Having picked the chickens, singe them well to remove all the hairs, &c, which may remain on the skin; then bruise the bone close to the foot, and draw the strings from the thigh; take out the crop by a slit cut in the back of the neck; then cut off the neck, leaving skin enough to turn over the back. Cut off the vent, and take out the inside, being careful not to break the gall; break the back-bone and the two bones leading to the pinions; wipe the chicken with a cloth, and put in a little pepper and salt. If the chicken is to be trussed for roasting, proceed as follows:—Turn the legs close down to the apron and run a skewer through; run another skewer in the joint of one wing through the body to the other wing; and having washed the liver and gizzard, place them in the pinions. For boiling, the under part of the thigh must be cut, and the legs placed under the apron, only letting the ends be seen. Be sure to preserve the breast very full.

CHICKEN BROTH. *See Broth.*

CHICKENS, BROILED OR GRILLED.

Pick and singe them nicely, wash them clean, and dry them in a cloth; cut them down the back, truss the legs and wings, as for boiling, flatten them, and put them upon a cold gridiron; when they become a little dry, put them upon a plate, baste them with butter, and strew a little salt and pepper over the inside, which part is laid first upon the gridiron; baste them frequently, and let them broil slowly for about half an hour. Serve them very hot; with melted butter poured over them, or plenty of stewed mushrooms. The livers and gizzards may be broiled with them, fastened into the wings, or well seasoned, broiled, and served with the chickens.

CHICKEN BAKED IN RICE. Cut a chicken into joints as for a fricassee, season it well with pepper and salt, lay it into a pudding dish lined with slices of ham or bacon, add a pint of veal gravy, and an onion finely minced; fill up the dish with boiled rice well pressed and piled as high as the dish will hold, cover it with a paste of flour and water; bake it one hour, and before serving take off the paste.

CHICKENS BOILED. (1) Put the chickens into a saucepan by themselves, and boil a small one for fifteen, a larger one twenty minutes.

CHICKENS BOILED. (2) When they are drawn and trussed, lay the chickens in skim milk for about two hours; then put them into cold water, cover them close, and set them over a slow fire, and skim them well. As soon as they have boiled slowly, take them from the fire and let them remain in the water close covered for half an hour; then drain and serve with white sauce.

CHICKEN, BROILED. Split a couple of chickens, take out the inside and backbones, beat them with a wooden spoon, dip them in clarified butter, and broil them, the inside next the fire (which should be of charcoal), and only turn them to color them. When done, pour on them a sauce made as follows:—Boil some stewed mushrooms with beef stock and plain sauce, an equal quantity of each, until of a proper consistence; flavor it with lemon-juice and Cayenne pepper.

CHICKENS CHIRINGATE. Having taken off the feet, beat the breast bones of your chickens flat without breaking the skin, flour and fry them in butter; when of a nice brown take all the fat from the pan, leaving in the chickens, over which lay a pound of gravy beef cut in thin slices, another piece of beef also cut thin, some mace, cloves, pepper, an onion, a carrot, and a bunch of sweet herbs: pour a quart of boiling water over the whole, cover it quite close, and let it stew; in a quarter of an hour take out the chickens, but let the gravy continue boiling, and when very rich strain it; then put it again into the pan with a little red wine and a few mushrooms; then put in the chickens, and when they are hot, dish them up, and pour the sauce over them; garnish with slices of lemon and broiled ham.

CHICKENS CREME. (1) Parboil a couple of young chickens, cut them in pieces, and throw into warm water for half an hour; then do them over the fire in a little fresh butter, with salt, parsley, pepper, morels, &c. sprinkle with flour, and dilute with a glass of boiling water; cover the stew pan close, and let it stand on hot ashes until the water has soaked into the chicken, then add half a pint of cream and a little butter. The yolks of three eggs may be put in also, but in that case, a small quantity of verjuice should be put in before the cream.

CHICKENS CREME. (2) Stuff and roast your chickens, and when you take them from the spit, rub them with butter, cover them with bread-crumbs, wrap them in slices of bacon, and bake them a short time; serve with well thickened cream-sauce.

CHICKEN CROQUETTES. (1) Reduce two spoonfuls of *veloute* or sauce *tournee*, and add to it the yolks of four eggs; put to this the white meat of a chicken minced very small, and well mixed with the sauce, take it out and roll it into balls about the size of a walnut; roll them in bread-crumbs, giving them an elongated form, then dip them in some well-beaten egg, bread them again, and fry them of a light brown.

CHICKEN CROQUETTES. (2) Mix well into some very thick *bechamelle* and some glaze the breast of a chicken, some tongue, truffles and mushrooms all minced very small; when quite cold roll them into little balls about the size of a nut, and having beaten up three eggs throw the balls into them. Take them out quickly and roll them in bread-crumbs; dip them a second time into the eggs, and cover them again with bread-crumbs; fry them as other *croquettes*. Lay fried parsley on a napkin in a dish, place the *croquettes* on, and round it, and serve.

CHICKEN CURRY. Take the skin off, cut up a chicken, and roll each piece in curry-powder and flour (mixed together a spoonful of flour to half an ounce of curry) fry two or three sliced onions in butter; when of a light brown, put in the meat and fry them together till the meat becomes brown; then stew them together with a little water for two or three hours. More water may be added if too thick.

CHICKEN CAPILOTADE. Put into a stewpan a little butter and flour: add mushrooms, parsley, and shallots cut small, dilute these with equal quantites of stock, and red or white wine. When the sauce is well boiled, skim it; cut a roasted fowl in pieces, and put it into this sauce, stew it gently for a quarter of an hour. Add some gherkins cut in thin slices.

CHICKEN, COLD FRIED. Cut the chicken in quarters, and take off the skin, rub it with an egg beaten up, and cover it with grated bread seasoned with pepper, salt, grated lemon-peel, and chopped parsley, fry it in butter, thicken a little brown gravy with flour and butter, add a little Cayenne, lemon pickle, and mushroom catchup.

CHICKENS FRICASSEED. Prepare and cut up two chickens; put them in a stewpan with some butter, parsley, a bay leaf, thyme, basil, two cloves, mushrooms, and a slice of ham; let them stew till scarcely any sauce remains, then add a little flour, warm water, salt and pepper; stew it again and reduce the sauce. When nearly done put in the yolks of three eggs beaten up with a little cream or milk; thicken it over the fire, but do not let it boil; a small quantity of lemon-juice or vinegar may be added. Place the breasts and bones of the chickens on a dish, lay the legs and wings over them, and then pour the sauce over the whole; garnish with the mushrooms. Take off the skins before you cut up the chickens if you wish the fricassee very white.

CHICKEN FRITTERS. Make a batter with four eggs, some new milk, and rice-flour; to this, add a pint of cream, powder-sugar, candied lemon-peel cut small, fresh lemon-peel grated, and the white parts of a roasted chicken shred small, set all these together on a stove, and stir well for some-time; when done, take it off, roll out the mixture, cut it into fritters, and fry them; strew sugar over a dish, lay in the fritters, strew sugar on a dish, lay in the fritters, strew sugar over, and serve them hot.

CHICKENS IN A MINUTE. Cut a chicken in pieces, and put it in a stewpan with a little butter, add to it some mushrooms, parsley, sprinkle flour over, and shake them; moisten it with stock or water, and white wine; when it has boiled once, take it from the fire and put in the yolks of one or two eggs, and a little vinegar or lemon-juice.

CHICKENS AND OYSTERS. Fill your chickens with young oysters cut small, truffles, parsley, and spices, and roast them. Blanch about two dozen young oysters, and toss them up in some melted butter, with chopped herbs and olive oil. When they have been on the fire a quarter of an hour, add a little white wine and half a glass of good stock, thicken it over the fire for another quarter of an hour, and when the chickens are ready to serve, pour the sauce on them, and garnish the dish with oysters and some lemon.

CHICKEN PANADA. Boil a chicken in a quart of water until nearly done; then skin it, cut off the white meat, and pound it with a little of the liquor it was boiled in to a thick paste; season it with salt, nutmeg, and lemon-peel; boil it up all together for a few minutes.

CHICKEN AND HAM POTTED. Season some pieces of chicken, with mace, cloves, and pepper, and bake them for about three hours in a close covered pan with some water; then pound them quite small, moistening either with melted butter, or the liquor they were baked in. Pound also some ham, and put this with the chicken in alternate layers, in potting pans, press them down tight, and cover them with butter.

CHICKEN PULLED. (1) Half roast a chicken or fowl, skin and pull off in small flakes all the white meat and the meat of the legs, break the bones, and boil them in a little water till the strength be drawn out, strain it, and when it becomes cold skim and put it into a sauce pan with a little mace, white pepper, and salt; add a bit of butter mixed with flour, and rather more than a quarter of a pint of cream, then put in the meat, and a little mushroom powder; before serving, add the squeeze of a lemon.

CHICKEN PULLED. (2) Pick all the white meat from the bones of a cold roasted fowl, cut off the legs, and keep the back and sidesmen in one. Score, and season the legs and back with pepper and salt, and broil them; warm up the white meat in some water, and which has been strained and thickened with a piece of butter, mixed with flour, a little milk, and the yolk of an egg beaten up and seasoned with white pepper and salt; serve the broiled back upon the mince, and the legs at each end.

CHICKEN PIE. *See Pie.*

CHICKEN ROASTED. *See Fowls.*

CHICKENS, SCOTCH WAY. Cut your chickens into quarters, put them into a saucepan, with only just water enough to cover them, a bunch of parsley, some chopped parsley, and a little mace, cover them close down, when it boils, add six eggs well-beaten; when the chickens are done, take out the parsley, and serve them in a deep dish with the sauce.

CHICKENS AND TOMATA SAUCE. Mix together, in a stewpan, a little butter, salt, pepper, lemon-juice, and grated nutmeg, a sufficient quantity to put in two chickens; tie it in, and lay thin slices of lemon on the breast of the chickens, and lay them in a stewpan lined with thin rashers of bacon; cover them with the same, and stew them with fire above and below for three quarters of an hour; when done, drain them in a cloth; untie them, and serve with tomata sauce.

CHINA CHILO. Mince a pint basin of undressed neck of mutton, or leg, and some of the fat; put two onions, a lettuce, a pint of green peas, a tea-spoonful of pepper, four spoonfuls of water, and two or three ounces of clarified butter, into a stewpan closely covered; simmer two hours, and serve in the middle of a dish of boiled dry rice. If Cayenne is approved, add a little.

CHILI, OR CAYENNE WINE. Pound and steep fifty fresh red Chilies, or a quarter of an ounce of Cayenne pepper in half a pint of brandy, white wine, or claret, for fourteen days. This is a *"bonne bouche"* for the lovers of Cayenne, of which it takes up a larger proportion of its favor than of its fire: which being instantly diffused, it is a very useful auxiliary to warm and finish soups, sauces, &c.

CHOCOLATE. According as you wish to make this beverage, either with milk or water, put a cup of one or other of these liquids into a chocolate-pot, with one ounce of cake chocolate. Some persons dissolve the chocolate in a little water before they put it into the milk. As soon as the milk or water begins to boil, mill it. When the chocolate is dissolved, and begins to bubble, take it off the fire, letting it stand near it for a quarter of an hour; then mill it again to make it frothy; afterwards serve it out in cups. The chocolate must not be milled, unless it is prepared with cream.

CHOCOLATE CREAM. *See Creams.*

CHOCOLATE FROTHED OR WHIPPED. Put half a pound of chocolate to a glass of water over a small fire, stirring it with a wooden spoon until perfectly dissolved; then take it off and add six yokes of eggs, a pint of double cream, and three quarters of a pound of powder-sugar. Pour the whole into a pan, and when cold, whip it up as directed. SEE *Cream Frothed.*

CHOCOLATE WINE. Take a pint of Sherry, or a pint and a half of Port, four ounces and a half of chocolate, six ounces of fine sugar, and half an ounce of white starch, or fine flour; mix, dissolve, and boil all these together for about ten or twelve minutes. But if your chocolate is made with sugar, take double the quantity of chocolate, and half the quantity of sugar.

CHOPS OR STEAKS. Those who are nice about steaks, never attempt to have them, except in weather which permits the meat to be hung till it is tender, and give the butcher some days' notice of their wish for them. If, friendly reader, you wish to entertain your mouth with a superlative beef-steak, you must have the inside of the sirloin cut into steaks. The next best steaks are those cut from the middle of a rump, that has been killed at least four days in moderate weather, and much longer in cold weather, when they can be cut about six inches long, four inches wide, and half an inch thick: do not beat them, which vulgar trick beats the cells in which the gravy of the meat is contained, and it becomes dry and tasteless. N. B.— If your butcher sends steaks which are not tender, we do not insist that you should object to let him be beaten. Desire the butcher to cut them of even thickness; if he does not, divide the thicker from the thinner pieces, and give them time accordingly.

CHOWDER. Lay some slices cut from the fat part of a belly-piece of pork, in a deep stewpan, mix sliced onions with a variety of sweet herbs, and lay them on the pork. Bone and cut a fresh cod into thin slices, and place them on the pork; then put a layer of pork, on that a layer of biscuit, then alternately the other materials until the pan is nearly full, season with pepper and salt, put in about a pint and a half of water, lay a paste over the whole, cover the stewpan very close, and let it stand, with fire above as well as below, for four hours; then skim it well, and put it in a dish, pour a glass of Madeira made hot over it, also some Jamaica pepper, stewed mushrooms, truffles, and oysters; brown the paste slightly, and lay it over the whole.

CHOWDER FOR TEN OR TWELVE. Take of salt pork cut in thin slices, as much as will make half a pint of fat, when tried, which will do for two good sized cod or haddock. Be careful not to burn the fat. First, put your fat in the pot. Secondly, cut your fish in as large pieces as will go into the pot; then put a layer of fish on the fat; pepper, salt and a few cloves, then a layer of the slices of pork, strewed over with onions cut fine; then a layer of shipbread or hard crackers

dipped in water; then your thickening. Go on again with fish, &c. &c. as above, till your pot is nearly full, then put in water until you can just see it, and let it stew slowly, so as not to break the fish. After coming to a boil, it will be done in twenty-five or thirty minutes. N. B.—Some like potatoes cut in slices, which may be introduced between each layer. Likewise wine or cider, as you fancy. ☞ This Receipt is according to the most approved method, practiced by fishing parties in Boston harbor.

CHOWDER, CLAM, May be made in the same way, substituting a sufficient quantity of clams instead of cod, the heads or hard leathery parts being first cut off. Many prefer clam chowder, nicely cooked, to chowder made of cod, haddock, &c. The pilgrims to Plymouth, it is said, could cook this shell fish and lobsters in nearly fifty different ways and even as puddings, pancakes, &c.

CHOUX. Put a pint of water into a stewpan, with half a pound of fresh butter, the rinds of two lemons grated, a quarter of pound of sugar, and a very little salt; as soon as the water begins to boil, add as much flour as the liquor will imbibe; when the paste becomes very thick, keep stirring with a spoon until quite done, then let it cool. After that, break into it a sufficient number of eggs to make the paste soft; taking care that it be firm enough to allow you to work it up with the hand; when it may be formed according to fancy. This paste may be glazed and garnished either with almonds or pistachio nuts; when baking the *choux,* be careful to keep the oven tightly closed.

CITRON CHEESECAKES. Boil a pint of cream, and when cold, mix with it two eggs well-beaten; then boil them together until they become a curd. Beat a few blanched almonds in a mortar, with a little orange-flower water; put them to the curd, and add some Naples biscuits and green citron, chopped very small. Sweeten, and bake in tins.

CITRON PUDDING. *See Puddings.*

CLARET PUFFS. Mix together, and sweeten with pounded loaf sugar, a pint of claret, and rather more than one of rich cream; let it stand a night, and then whisk it to a froth, which take off as it rises, and put upon the back of a sieve to drain; heap it upon a dish, sweeten some rich cream, and pour it round the froth, to make it float.

CLOVE, ESSENCE OF. Infuse a drachm of oil of cloves in two ounces of the strongest spirits of wine, apothecary's measure.

CLOVE WATER. Mix a little cinnamon with the cloves, or the scent will be too strong; allow half a score of cloves to a quart of water; put in a good piece of sugar; let them infuse some time over hot embers, or in a warm place; then strain it for use.

COBBLER. Name given to bread toasted on one side only.

COCHINEAL PREPARED. Pound an ounce of cochineal to a very fine powder, pound also an ounce of cream of tartar and two drachms of alum; put these ingredients into a saucepan with half a pint of water; when it boils take it from the fire, and let it cool; pour it off into a bottle, as free from sediment as possible, and set it by for use.

COCOA. Put into a saucepan one ounce of good cocoa and one quart of water; cover it, and when it boils, set it by the side of the fire to simmer for two hours. It is sometimes made in a larger quantity, poured from the sediment, and boiled up as it is required.

COCOA-NUT SWEETMEAT. (1) Cut the nut out of the shell, pare it carefully, and throw it into cold water; then grate it, and boil it in clarified sugar, (a pound to each pound of the cocoa-nut) until quite thick;

stir it frequently to prevent its burning. Then pour it on a well buttered dish or marble slab, and cut it into whatever forms you think proper.

COCOA-NUT SWEETMEAT. (2) Proceed as above, but do not boil the sugar so thick by a great deal, then stir into it whilst hot the yolks of six eggs; this must be served in jelly glasses.

COD. A cod-fish should be firm and white, the gills red, and the eye lively, a fine fish is very thick about the neck; if the flesh is at all flabby it is not good. Cod is in its prime during the months of October and November, if the weather be cold; from the latter end of March to May, cod is also very fine. The length of time it requires for boiling depends on the size of the fish, which varies from one pound to twenty; a small fish, about two or three pounds weight will be sufficiently boiled in a quarter of an hour or twenty minutes after the water boils. Prepare a cod for dressing in the following manner:—empty and wash it thoroughly, scrape off all the scales, cut open the belly, and wash and dry it well, rub a little salt inside, or lay it for an hour in strong brine. The simple way of dressing it is as follows:—Tie up the head, and put it into a fish-kettle with plenty of water and salt in it; boil it gently, and serve it with oyster sauce. Lay a napkin under the fish, and garnish with slices of lemon, horse-radish, &c.

COD BAKED. (1) Soak a fine piece of the middle of fresh cod in melted butter, with parsley and sweet herbs shred very fine; let it stand over the fire for sometime, and then bake it. Let it be of a good color.

COD BAKED. (2) Choose a fine large cod, clean it well, and open the under part to the bone and put in stuffing made with beef suet, parsley, sweet herbs shred fine, an egg, and seasoned with salt, pepper, nutmeg, mace and grated lemon-peel; put this inside the cod, sew it up, wrap it in a buttered paper, and bake it; baste it well with melted butter.

COD, TO CRIMP. Cut a fresh cod into slices or steaks; lay them for three hours in salt-and-water, and a glass of vinegar; when they may be boiled, fried, or broiled.

COD PIE. *See Pie.*

COD SOUNDS. This is the white skin of the belly, and is reckoned a great delicacy, and may be either boiled, broiled, or fried. Previous to dressing either way, they should be well soaked, washed, and boiled a little.

COD SOUNDS, BOILED WITH GRAVY. Scald them in hot water, and rub them well with salt; blanch them, that is, take off the blacked dirty skin, then set them on in cold water, and let them simmer till they begin to be tender; take them out, flour, and broil them on the gridiron. In the meantime, take a little good gravy, a little mustard, a little bit of butter rolled in flour, give it a boil, season it with pepper and salt. Lay the sounds in your dish, and pour the sauce over them.

COD SOUNDS, BROILED. Let them lie in boiling water till it is nearly cold, rub them with salt, and pull off the black and dirty skin, boil them in hot water, drain, and dust them with flour, rub them over with butter, season with white pepper and salt, and broil them. Put a table-spoonful of catchup, half a one of soy, and a little Cayenne, into melted butter, heat and pour it over them.

COD SOUNDS, ROASTED OR BAKED. Wash and clean four or five cod sounds, and boil them till nearly done in milk-and-water; when cold, make a forcemeat of bread crumbs; a piece of butter, salt, nutmeg, white pepper, and some chopped oysters; beat up the yolks of two eggs to bind it, lay it over the sounds, roll them up, and fasten with a small skewer, baste them with melted butter, and roll them in finely grated bread crumbs seasoned with pepper and salt; put them on a tin in a Dutch oven, turn and baste them with a feather dipped in melted butter, and strew over bread crumbs as before; when done; and of a nice brown, serve them with oyster sauce in the dish.

COD'S HEAD AND SHOULDERS, TO BOIL. Wash it clean; tie it up, and dry it with a cloth. Allow in the proportion of every three measures of water, one of salt; when it boils take off the scum; put in the fish, and keep it boiling very fast for twenty-five or thirty minutes. Serve with the roe and milt parboiled, cut into slices, and fried, and garnish with curled parsley and horse-radish. Sauces; —oyster, melted butter, or anchovy butter.

COFFEE. The coffee-pot should be three parts full of boiling water; the coffee is to be added a spoonful at a time, and well stirred between each; then boil gently, still stirring to prevent the mixture from boiling over as the coffee swells, and to force it into combination with the water, this will be effected in a few minutes, after which, the most gentle boiling must be kept up during an hour. The coffee must then be removed from the fire to settle, one or two spoonfuls of cold water thrown in assists the clarification, and precipitates the grounds. In about an hour, or as soon as the liquor has become clear, it is to be poured into another vessel, taking care not to disturb the sediment. Coffee made in this manner will be of the finest flavor, and may be kept three days in summer, and four or five in winter; when ordered for use, it only requires heating in the coffee-pot, and may be served up at two minutes' notice. Coffee should never be roasted but at the precise time of its being used, and then it should be watched with the greatest care, and made of a gold color rather than a brown one; above all, take care not to burn it, for a very few grains burnt will be sufficient to communicate a bitter and rancid taste to several pounds of coffee. It is the best way to roast it in a roaster, (over a charcoal fire), which turns with the hand, as by that means it is not forgot, which often is the case when on a spit before the fire.

COFFEE, FRENCH METHOD OF PREPARING. 1st. Let your coffee be dry, not in the least mouldy or damaged.—2d. Divide the quantity that is to be roasted into two parts.—3d. Roast the first part in a coffee-roaster, the handle of which must be kept constantly turning until the coffee becomes the color of dried almonds or bread raspings, and has lost one eighth of its weight — 4th. Roast the second part until it assumes the fine brown color of chestnuts, and has lost one fifth of its weight.—5th. Mix the two parts together, and grind them in a coffee mill.—6th. Do not roast or make your coffee until the day it is wanted.—7th. To two ounces of ground coffee, put four cups of cold water. Draw off this infusion, and put it aside.—8th. Put to the coffee which remains in the *biggin*, three cups of boiling water, then drain it off and add this infusion to that which has been put aside. By this method you obtain three cups more. When your coffee is wanted, heat it quickly in a silver coffee-pot, taking care not to let it boil, that the perfume may not be lost by undergoing any evaporation. Then pour it into cups, which each person may sweeten according to his taste. Particular care should be taken not to make coffee in a tin vessel; it should be made either in a China vessel, or one of Delft ware or in one of silver. For a long time, tin biggins, invented by Monsieur de Belloy, were made use of; but some person has since improved upon his plan, by making them of silver or porcelain, which are found to be much better.

COFFEE CREAM. (1) Mix three cups of good coffee with one pint of cream, and sugar according to taste; boil them together, and reduce them about one-third; observe that the coffee must be done as if it was for drinking alone, and settled very clear, before you mix it with the cream.

COFFEE CREAM. (2) Boil a calf's foot in water till it wastes to a pint of jelly; clear off the sediment and fat. Make a teacup of *very strong* coffee; clear it with a bit of isinglass, to be perfectly bright; pour it to the jelly, and add a pint of *very* good cream, and as much fine Lisbon sugar as is pleasant; give one boil up, and pour into the dish. It should jelly, but not be stiff. Observe that your coffee be fresh.

COLLOPS. Cut some veal cutlets; fry them a good brown, but not too much; take some good gravy, thicken it with a little flour, boil it a few minutes; add Cayenne, catchup, truffles, morels, salt, mushrooms pickled, grated lemon-peel; simmer this up, just heat the collops through, add what gravy came from them, but do not let them boil, or they will be hard; add forcemeat balls, hard yolk of eggs; lay round little slices of bacon, notched and toasted, and sliced lemon.

COLLOPS, MINCED. Cut two pounds of lean tender beef into thin slices—it is best taken from off the rump, or round; mince it very finely; brown two ounces of butter in a frying-pan, dredging it with a little flour, then add the minced meat, and keep beating it with a beater till of a nice brown color. Have ready some highly-seasoned beef gravy, which, with the minced collops, put into a saucepan, and let it stew half an hour; and just before serving, put a table-spoonful of mushroom catchup, and, if liked, some green pickles. Beef suet is as often used as butter to fry the collops in.

COLLOPS, RUSSIAN. Break four eggs into a stewpan, and mix with them two spoonfuls of flour, then half a glass of good cream, a spoonful of warm butter, and a grain of salt; when these are well mixed together, pour some of it into a large frying-pan, and fry it of a light color on both sides; then take it out, and fry more in the same way, like pancakes, until you have a dozen very thin, cut each in half, and trim them into oblong pieces all the same size: lay on each some *quenelle*, minced fowl or game, as if for *croquettes*; wrap the fried batter round it, wetting the edges, that they may adhere properly, with a little of the batter, having reserved some for the purpose; then have ready beaten, six eggs and a little salt, mask them with bread-crumbs, fry them of a good color, and serve them quickly.

COLLOPS, SCOTCH. Cut veal cutlets (taken from the fillet) into small thin pieces, and fry them in a little boiling lard till of a light brown color. Drain then dry, put them into a stewpan, add cullis, stewed mushrooms, some blanched truffles, morels, pieces of artichoke bottoms, some slices of throat sweetbreads, and egg balls. Let them simmer over a slow fire till tender, season to the palate, and serve them with rashers of broiled bacon round them.

COLD MEAT BROILED, WITH POACHED EGGS. The inside of a sirloin of ·beef is best for this dish, or a leg of mutton. Cut the slices of even and equal thickness, and broil and brown them carefully and slightly over a clear smart fire, or in a Dutch oven; give those slices most fire that are least done; lay them in a dish before the fire to keep hot, while you poach the eggs, and mash potatoes.

COLORING FOR JELLIES, CAKES, &c. For a beautiful *red*, boil fifteen grains of cochineal in the finest powder, with a drachm and a half of cream of tartar, in half a pint of water very slowly, half an hour. Add, in boiling, a bit of alum the size of a pea. Or use beet-root sliced, and some liquor poured over. For *white*, use almonds finely powdered with a little drop of water; or use cream. For *yellow*, yolks of eggs, or a bit of saffron steeped in the liquor, and squeezed. For *green*, pound spinach-leaves, or beet-leaves, express the juice, and boil a tea-cupful in a saucepan of water, to take off the rawness.

CONSOMME. Take eight or ten pounds of beef-steaks, eight old hens, two young ones, and four knuckles of veal; put these into a large pot, and fill it with strong broth; skim it well, cooling it three or four times to make the scum rise, after which let it boil gently; put into the pot carrots, turnips, onions, and three cloves. When your meat is sufficiently done, pass the liquor through a fine napkin or silk sieve, that it may be very clear. No salt need be put in if strong broth be used.

COUGLAUFFLE, GERMAN. Take three pounds of flour, an ounce and a half of yeast, an ounce of fine salt, a quarter of a pound of sugar, twelve eggs, the yolks of twelve more, two pounds of fresh butter, three glasses of milk, and a quarter of a pound of sweet almonds. Proceed with these materials in the following manner: — put the butter (having slightly warmed half a pound of it), into a glazed pan, and with a large wooden spoon work it up for six or seven minutes; then put in two whole eggs, and stir it two minutes; then add three yolks, and stir again two minutes; in this manner put in the whole number of eggs and yolks; which will produce a kind of smooth cream. Then by degrees mix in two pounds of the flour, dissolve the yeast in a glass of warm milk, strain it through a napkin, stir this in well, with another half pound of flour; make a hollow in the paste, in which put the salt and sugar in powder; afterwards pour on it a glass of hot milk, and mix the whole together with the remainder of the flour; continue to work it up for some minutes after the whole ingredients are put in, adding, a small quantity of warm milk, which will render it smooth. Have a mould ready, butter it, and lay the sweet almonds, each cut in half, over the bottom of the mould, in forms, on which pour the paste carefully, and in small quantities, so as not to derange the almonds. Place your mould in a warm, but not a hot place, that the cake may rise properly; and when that operation has taken place, put it into a moderate oven, which should be kept closed; in an hour's time look at the *Couglauffle*, and if it be flexible, and of a light color, let it remain thirty or forty minutes longer; but if it be firm and red it is sufficiently done; when taken from the mould put it into the oven again for a few minutes.

COUGLAUFFLES, SMALL. To make a dozen small *couglauffles*, take three quarters of a pound of flour, three drachms of yeast, two of salt, two whole eggs, three yolks, two ounces of sugar, a little cream, and half a pound of butter. The preparation is made the same as the German *Couglauffle*. When the paste is made, divide it into twelve equal parts; butter a dozen small biscuit moulds, and fill each with your preparation, and let them stand: when risen so as to fill the moulds, put them into a brisk oven, and take them out as soon as they are of a light color.

COUQUES. Put into a saucepan the yolks of sixteen eggs, the rinds of two lemons, half an ounce of salt, and two ounces of sugar; on these pour a pint of boiling cream, stirring it quick; set it on the fire, but do not let it boil, strain it through a bolting, and then let it cool; take two pounds of flour, and make a quarter of it into leaven with half an ounce of yeast and a little warm water, keep it rather moist, and put it into a warm place to rise: in the meantime, make the remainder of the flour into a paste, with the cream and a quarter of a pound of butter, knead it up five or six times; then put in the leaven, and knead it again twice; tie it up in a floured cloth, and set it in a warm place. In about two hours take it out, and cut the paste in pieces the size of an egg, form them to that shape, and lay them on a baking tin, and leave them for half an hour to rise, then gild and bake them in a hot oven; when done, open each on one side, take out a little of the crumb, in the place of which put a bit of butter worked up with a little salt, and serve them.

COURT BOUILLON. Cut a proper quantity of carrots, onions, celery, and turnips, and put them into a saucepan with butter, parsley, garlic, thyme, basil, salt, a *mignonette* and cloves; sweat them over a gentle fire; add white wine, vinegar or verjuice; boil, and then strain it, and serve it with whatever you may require it for. It is generally used for fish.

COURT BOUILLON FOR ALL SORTS OF FRESH WATER FISH. Put some water into a fish-kettle, with a quart of white wine, a slice of butter, salt, pepper, a large bunch of parsley and young onions, a clove of garlic, thyme, bay-leaves, and basil all tied together, some sliced onions and some carrots; boil the fish in this *court bouillon*, (which will serve for several times) and do not scale it; when the fish will admit of it, take care to boil it wrapped in a napkin, which makes it more easy to take out without danger of breaking.

COW-HEEL, In the hands of a skilful cook, will furnish several good meals; when boiled tender, cut it into handsome pieces, egg and bread-crumb them, and fry them a light brown; lay them round a dish, and put in the middle of it sliced onions fried, or the accompaniments ordered for tripe. The liquor they were boiled in will make soups.

CRACKNELS. Mix a quart of flour, half a nutmeg grated, the yolks of four eggs beaten, with four spoonfuls of rosewater, into a stiff paste, with cold water; then rub in a pound of butter, and make into a cracknel shape; put them into a kettle of boiling water and boil them till they swim; then take them out, and put them into cold water; when hardened, lay them out to dry, and bake them on tin plates.

CRACKNELS, SMALL SOFT. Blanch half a pound of sweet almonds, and pound them to a fine paste, adding to them by degrees six eggs; when thoroughly pounded, pour on them a pound of powder-sugar, the same of butter, and the rinds of two lemons grated; beat up these ingredients in the mortar: put a pound of flour on a slab, and having poured the almond paste on it, knead them together until they are well incorporated; roll it out, and cut the cracknels into such forms as you may think proper, rub them with yolk of egg, and strew over them powder-sugar or cinnamon: then lay them on a buttered tin, and bake them in a moderate oven, taking great care that they do not burn. When done, put them into glasses, and if preserved in a dry place they are the better for keeping.

CRANBERRIES, DIFFERENT WAYS OF DRESSING. For pies and puddings, with a good deal of sugar. Stewed in a jar, with the same; this way they eat well with bread, and are very wholesome. Thus done, pressed, and strained, the juice makes a fine drink for people in fevers.

CREAM, ALMOND. Blanch and pound to a paste, with rose water, six ounces of almonds, mix them with a pint and a half of cream which has been boiled with the peel of a small lemon; add two well-beaten eggs, and stir the whole over the fire till it be thick, taking care not to allow it to boil; sweeten it, and when nearly cold, stir in a table-spoonful of orange-flower or rose water.

CREAM, APPLE. (1). Boil twelve large apples in water till soft, take off the peel, and press the pulp through a hair sieve upon half a pound of pounded loaf sugar; whip the whites of two eggs, add them to the apples, and beat all together till it becomes very stiff, and looks quite white. Serve it heaped up on a dish.

CREAM, APPLE. (2). Peel and core five large apples; boil them in a little water, till soft enough to press through a sieve; sweet-

en, and beat with them the whisked whites of five eggs. Serve it with cream poured round it.

CREAM, ARROW-ROOT. Mix a table-spoonful of arrow-root with a tea-cupful of cold water; let it settle, and pour the water off. Sweeten and boil a quart of milk with the peel of a lemon and some cinnamon; pick them out, and pour it boiling upon the arrow-root, stirring it well and frequently till it be cold. Serve it in a glass or china dish, with or without grated nutmeg on the top. It may be eaten with any preserved fruit, or fruit tarts.

CREAM, BACCHIC. Put a pint and a half of white wine, with some lemon-peel, coriander seed, a bit of cinnamon, and three ounces of sugar, into a stewpan, and let them boil a quarter of an hour; then mix half a tea-spoonful of flour with the yolks of six eggs in another stewpan, and stir in by degrees the other previously boiled ingredients. When about half cold, strain the whole through a sieve and put it in a dish in hot water, over the fire, till the cream is set; lastly, take it out, and put it in a cool place till ready to serve.

CREAM, BARLEY. Boil a small quantity of pearl barley in milk and water, till tender, strain off the liquor, and put the barley into a quart of cream, to boil a little. Then take the whites of five eggs and the yolk of one, beat them with one spoonful of flour, and two of orange-flower water. Take the cream from the fire, mix the eggs in by degrees, and set it over the fire again to thicken. Sweeten it, and pour into cups or glasses for use.

CREAM, BURNT. Boil a pint of cream with the peel of a lemon, sweeten it with pounded loaf sugar; beat, with the yolks of six, and whites of four eggs, one table-spoonful of flour, the same of orange-flower water and of ratafia; strain the cream, and when nearly cold, mix it with the eggs and other things; stir it over the fire till it becomes as thick as a custard; put it into the dish it is to be served in. Boil with a little water some pounded loaf sugar, till it turn brown, but do not stir it till taken off the fire; by degrees pour it in figures over the top of the cream. It may be eaten hot or cold.

CREAM CAKES. *See Cakes.*

CREAM, CHOCOLATE. (1) Take a pint of milk, a gill of cream, the yolks of three eggs, and five ounces of powder sugar, mix these ingredients together, set them on the fire, stir it constantly, and let it boil till reduced to a quarter; then add two ounces of grated chocolate; and having boiled a little longer, strain it, and let it cool. Serve it cold.

CREAM, CHOCOLATE. (2) Take about half a cake of chocolate, bruise it to pieces, put it in a stewpan with a little milk, and stir it over a gentle fire till it looks smooth and thick; then add a little more milk, and stir it again over the fire; continue this till it takes the thickness of cream; sweeten it to your palate with clarified sugar; stir in a little thick cream with a very little isinglass, rub it through the tammy, and set it in the mould.

CREAM CUSTARD. *See Custard.*

CREAM FRITTERS. Mix a handful of flour, with three whole eggs, and the yolks of six, four pounded macaroons, some dried orange-flowers, browned in sugar, a little candied lemon-peel chopped very fine, half a pint of cream, half a pint of milk, and lump of sugar; boil the whole over a gentle fire for a quarter of an hour, till the cream turns to a thick paste; then let it cool in a dish well floured, shaking flour all over it. When cold, cut the paste into small pieces, roll them in your hands till they become round; and fry them of a good color; when you serve them, powder them all over with sugar.

CREAM FROTH. Put a pint of fresh double cream into a stone pan, with half a pound of powder sugar, a pinch of gum dragon, a little crisped orange-flower, and three drops of cedrat essence; when the sugar is dissolved, place the pan in another, in which is three pounds of ice beaten up with saltpetre; whip the cream in the usual manner, taking off the froth as it rises with a skimmer, lay it gently on a sieve over a pan; if the cream does not froth properly, add the whites of two eggs. This cream is usually served in large silver or gilt goblets, and should be prepared two or three hours before it is wanted .

CREAM FOR FRUIT TARTS. Boil a stick of cinnamon, two or three peach leaves, or a few bruised bitter almonds, in a quart of milk; strain, sweeten, and mix it, when cool, with three or four well-beaten eggs; stir it constantly over the fire till it thickens. It may be eaten with stewed apples, prunes, damsons, or any other fruit.

CREAM, IMPERIAL. Boil a quart of cream with the thin rind of a lemon; then stir it till nearly cold, have ready in a dish or bowl that you are to serve in, the juice of three lemons strained, with as much sugar as will sweeten the cream, which pour into the dish from a large teapot, holding it high, and moving it about to mix with the juice. It should be made at least six hours before it is served, and will be still better if a day.

CREAM ITALIAN. (1) Boil a pint and a half of milk in a stewpan, then add to it the peel of a young lemon, some coriander seed, a bit of cinnamon, rather more than half a quarter of a pound of sugar, and two or three grains of salt; let it boil till half is consumed; then let it stand to cool, and have ready in another stewpan a little flour, beat up with the yolks of six eggs; stir it by degrees into the cream; strain it through a sieve, and put it in the dish for table, placing the dish in some hot water over the fire till the cream is set. Before serving, brown with a salamander.

CREAM ITALIAN. (2) Put a gill of good fresh cream, two eggs, three spoonfuls of powder-sugar, and a little orange-flower water, into a pan, and whip them up together; and when the cream is sufficiently thick, put it into a deep dish, with plenty of powder-sugar; set it on hot ashes, cover it, and lay hot ashes on the top; which must be renewed until the cream is done enough; then let it cool, and serve it.

CREAM, LEMON. Steep the thinly-pared rinds of four large lemons in a pint of water for twelve hours; strain, and dissolve in it three-quarters of a pound of fine loaf sugar, add the juice of the lemons strained, and the well-beaten whites of seven, and the yolk of one egg. Boil it over a slow fire, stirring it constantly one way, till it is like a thick cream; pour it into a glass or china dish.

CREAM, ORANGE. (1) Squeeze and strain the juice of eleven oranges, sweeten it well with pounded loaf sugar, stir it over a slow fire till the sugar be dissolved, and take off the scum as it rises; when cold, mix it with the well-beaten yolks of twelve eggs, to which a pint of cream has been added; stir it again over the fire till thick. Serve in a glass dish or custard-cups.

CREAM, ORANGE. (2) Sweeten, with pounded loaf sugar, a quart of good cream; mix with it a small wine-glass of orange-flower water, the grated rind and the juice of a Seville orange; whisk it till quite thick; soak some macaroons in white wine, and pile them in the middle of a glass or china dish, and heap the whipped cream over them as high as possible. Some hours after, ornament it with slices of green citron cut into straws, and stuck into the cream.

CREAM, RATAFIA. In a tea-cupful of

thin cream boil two or three large laurel, or young peach leaves; when it has boiled three or four minutes, strain, and mix with it a pint of rich sweet cream; add three well-beaten whites of eggs, and sweeten it with pounded loaf sugar. Put it into a saucepan, and stir it gently one way over a slow fire till it be thick; pour it into a china dish, and when quite cold, ornament it with sweet-meats cut out like flowers; or strew over the top harlequin comfits.

CREAM, RASPBERRY. (1) Mix a little pounded loaf sugar with a pint and a half of good cream, about a tea-cupful of raspberry jelly, the grated rind of one, and the juice of half a lemon; beat it well together, and, with a syllabub mill, mill it slowly for half an hour, or till it be thick and solid. Put it into a glass dish, or serve it in custard glasses.

CREAM, RASPBERRY. (2) Put six ounces of raspberry jam to a quart of cream, pulp it through a lawn sieve, mix it with the juice of a lemon and a little sugar, and whisk it till thick. Serve it in a dish or glasses. Strawberry cream may be made in the same way. For common use, substitute good milk for the cream.

CREAM, RED CURRANT. (1) Pick the currants from the stalks, put them into a jar closely covered, and stand it in a pan of cold water; let it boil for two hours, strain the juice through a sieve, and sweeten it well with pounded loaf sugar. When cold, add a quart of cream to a pint of juice, and beat it with a whisk till thick. Serve in a deep glass dish.

CREAM, RED CURRANT. (2) Squeeze three-quarters of a pint of juice from red currants when full ripe, add to it rather more than a quarter of a pound of pounded loaf sugar, and the juice of one lemon; stir it into a pint and a half of cream, and whisk it till quite thick.

CREAM ROSEAT. Beat to a stiff froth

the whites of four eggs; sweeten and boil a pint of good milk, drop about three table-spoonfuls of the froth into it, turn it over once or twice with the spoon, take it out, and put it upon the back of a lawn sieve placed over a large plate; repeat this till it is all done; add to the milk another half pint, with a little more sugar, and mix it with the beaten yolks of the eggs; stir it over the fire till thick; put it into a basin, and stir now and then till nearly cold; add a table-spoonful of rose water, and one of brandy. Serve it in a glass dish, and lay the whites of the eggs over the top at equal distances. Cut citron and candied orange-peel into straws, and put them over the whites of the eggs, or strew over them colored comfits.

CREAM OF RICE SOUP. Mix one or two table-spoonfuls of sifted flour of rice with a little good stock, rather cold than hot; add this to some boiling stock, and keep stirring till it boils; and let it boil till suffi-ciently thick. The flour of rice may be made as follows:—Wash in several waters a pound of rice; wipe it in a clean towel, and when perfectly dry pound and sift it through a sieve.

CREAM, SNOW. Take a pint of fresh cream, and mix with it eight spoonfuls of powder-sugar, the whites of two eggs, and a spoonful of orange-flower water, or any other aromatic ingredient you like better; whip it, and remove the froth or snow in the usual way. This cream may be colored ac-cording to your fancy, with saffron, car-mine, or indigo.

CREAM, SOLID. Squeeze the juice of a large lemon upon three or four table-spoonfuls of pounded loaf sugar, add two table-spoonfuls of brandy, and one pint of cream; pour it from one cup into another, till it be sufficiently thick.

CREAM, SPANISH. Boil, in half a pint of water, half an ounce of isinglass, till dis-solved; strain, and mix it with a quart of cream or good milk; if cream, not so much isinglass; stir it over the fire till it come to a boil; when a little cooled, add gradually the beaten yolks of six eggs, and a glass of white wine. Pour it into a deep dish, sweeten with pounded loaf sugar, stir it till cold, and then put it into a shape.

CREAM, STONE. Put three table-spoon-fuls of lemon-juice, and the grated peel of one, some preserved apricots, or any other sweetmeat, into a glass or China dish. Boil a quarter of an ounce of isinglass in a little water, till dissolved; add it to a pint of cream, sweetened well with pounded loaf sugar; boil it, and stir it all the time; pour it into a jug, stir it now and then till milk-warm, then pour it over the sweetmeat round and round. It may be made the day before being served.

CREAM, SWISS. (1) Boil the grated peel of a large lemon, and three-quarters of a pound of pounded loaf sugar, in a pint of cream; squeeze the juice of the lemon upon a table-spoonful of flour, work it well to-gether, and gradually add to it the boiling cream, and heat it all over the fire; pour it into a basin, and when nearly cold, put it into a glass or China dish, and garnish it with candied orange-peel, and citron cut into straws. This cream requires to be con-stantly stirred till it is put into the dish in which it is to be served.

CREAM, SWISS. (2) Whisk upon a hot plate, the yolks of eight eggs, half a pound of finely-pounded sugar, the grated rind of a lemon, and half a pint of light French or Rhenish white wine, and send it warm to table.

CREAM TART. *See Tart.*

CREAM, WHIPPED. Sweeten, with pounded loaf sugar, a quart of cream, and add to it a lump of sugar which has been rubbed upon the peel of two fine lemons or bitter oranges; or flavor it with orange-flower water, a little essence of roses, the juice of ripe strawberries, or of any other fruit. Whisk the cream well in a large pan, and as the froth rises, take it off, and lay it upon a sieve placed over another pan, and return the cream which drains from the froth, till all is whisked, then heap it upon a dish, or put it into glasses. Garnish with thinly pared citron, or cedrat cut into small leaves, or into any fanciful shape. To color the rose cream, or to heighten that of strawberry, a little carmine or lake may be mixed with the cream, which may be iced when made.

CREAM, WHITE LEMON. (1) Rub, with some lumps of loaf sugar, the rinds of six lemons, and grate off the remainder; squeeze and strain the juice, and add the grated peel and sugar, with three-quarters of a pound of pounded loaf sugar; put to this a quart of rich cream, and whisk it till very thick. The following day, soak five or six sponge buscuits in white wine, and put over them the cream.

CREAM, WHITE LEMON. (2) Boil the thin peel of two lemons in a pint of cream; strain, and thicken it with the well-beaten yolks of three, and whites of four, eggs; sweeten it with pounded loaf sugar, stir it till nearly cold, and put it into glasses.

CROQUANTE OF PASTE. Roll out paste, about the eighth of an inch thick; rub over a plain mould with a little fresh butter; lay on the paste very even, and equally thin on both sides; pare it round the rim; then with a small penknife cut out small pieces, as fancy may direct, such as diamonds, stars, circles, sprigs, &c.; or use a small tin cutter of any shape: let it lie to dry sometime, and bake it a few minutes in a slack oven, of a light color: remove it from the mould, and place it over a tart, or any other dish of small pastry.

CROQUE. These are large pieces of ornamental confectionary formed of various materials, as *gimblettes, croquignoles, genoises, &c.*, or of oranges, cut into quarters, chestnuts, green nuts, &c., arranged within moulds according to fancy, and cemented together with boiled sugar.

CROQUETS. Pound, in a marble mortar, cold veal and fowl, with a little suet, some chopped lemon-peel, lemon thyme, chives, and parsley. Season with nutmeg, pepper, and salt; mix all well together, and add the yolk of an egg well-beaten; roll it into balls, and dip them into an egg beaten up, then sift bread crumbs over them, and fry them in butter.

CROQUETTES OF BOILED MEAT. Mince some boiled meat very small; add to it some sausage-meat, mashed potatoes, crumbs of bread, soaked in milk, and sweet herbs; make them into a paste, and form it into little balls; roll them in very fine raspings, and fry them of a nice color. Serve them with sauce *piquante*.

CROQUETS OF SWEETBREADS. Mince some cold sweetbreads, which have been dressed, and boil them in a sauce veloute; when quite cold, form them into balls, or into rolls, about two inches long; fry and serve them with fried parsley in the middle. Or, make the croquet meat into a rissole. Roll out a piece of thin puff paste, enclose the meat in it, brush it over with a beaten egg, and strew over it grated bread; fry it of a light brown color.

CRUMPETS. (1) Make a pint of warm milk, a quarter of a pint of yeast broth, strained into a strong batter, with a sufficient quantity of flour; cover, and set it in a warm place to rise; then add a quarter of a pint of warm milk, an ounce of butter worked up in a little flour, but only flour enough to prevent the batter from being too thin; in a quarter of an hour have the iron rings ready on a plate of iron over a stove; pour the batter into these rings, and bake them.

CRUMPETS, OR PIKELETS. (2) Set a sponge as for bread, excepting that half milk and half water must be used; and to every half-quartern of flour, two eggs must be added; beat the eggs thoroughly. Bake them in rings as usual.

CRUST, FOR VENISON PASTY. Work into a paste with warm water, two pounds and a half of butter, a peck of fine flour, and four eggs; work it smooth, and to a good consistence. The paste should be put round the inside, but not at the bottom of the dish; let the cover be tolerably thick, to bear the long continuance in the oven.

CRUST, RAISED. (1) Melt, in one pint of water, one pound of fresh lard; weigh four pounds of flour, put it into a basin, and when the water and lard is hot, with a horn spoon stir it by degrees amongst the flour. When well mixed, work it with the hands till it is a stiff paste, when it is fit for use.

CRUST, RAISED. (2) Put into a saucepan one pint and a half of water, four pounds of flour, and four ounces and a half of butter; stir it till it is a thick paste, take it out, and add the yolks of three or four beaten eggs; work it well together, roll it out rather more than half an inch thick; cut out the top and bottom, and a long piece of proper depth for the sides. Brush round the bottom with well-beaten whites of eggs; set on the sides, keeping the paste rather within the edge of the bottom; pinch it all round, to make the pieces adhere, then fill the pie, and brush round the upper sides of the crust and the outer edges of the cover with egg; lay on the cover, pinch it round neatly, and ornament it according to fancy with leaves, festoons, or chains of rings made of the paste.

CRUST SHORT. (1) Pound, sift, and dry two ounces of white sugar; then mix it with a pound of well dried flour, rubbing into it, so fine as not to be seen, three ounces of butter; then put the yolks of two eggs into some cream, and mix the whole into a smooth paste; roll it out thin, and bake it in a moderate oven.

CRUST SHORT, NOT SWEET, BUT RICH. (2) Mix into a stiffish paste, using as little water as possible, six ounces of butter, with eight ounces of fine flour, (rubbing the butter well into the flour, before mixing it with the water) beat it well, and roll it thin. This crust is proper as well as the above, for tarts of fresh or preserved fruits. Let it bake in a moderate oven.

CUCUMBERS STEWED. Peel and cut cucumbers in quarters, take out the seeds, and lay them on a cloth to drain off the water: when they are dry, flour and fry them in fresh butter; let the butter be quite hot before you put in the cucumbers; fry them till they are brown, then take them out with an egg-slice, and lay them on a sieve to drain the fat from them (some cooks fry sliced onions, or some small button onions, with them, till they are a delicate light brown color, drain them from the fat, and then put them into a stewpan with as much gravy as will cover them): stew slowly till they are tender; take out the cucumbers with a slice, thicken the gravy with flour and butter, give it a boil up, season it with pepper and salt and put in the cucumbers; as soon as they are warm, they are ready. The above, rubbed through a tamis, or fine sieve, will be entitled to be called "cucumber sauce." See Cucumber Vinegar. This is a very favorite sauce with lamb or mutton-cutlets, stewed rump-steaks, &c. &c.: when made for the latter, a third part of sliced onion is sometimes fried with the cucumber.

CUCUMBERS AND ONIONS SLICED. Cut full-grown cucumbers into slices about a quarter of an inch thick, and slice some onions thin; then lay them in a dish together, and strew salt over them; cover them with another dish, and let them remain for twenty-four hours. Put them into a cullender to drain, then into a large jar, and pour over them boiled vinegar, three successive days;

the last time of boiling the vinegar add pepper and ginger, pour it over them hot, and closely cover them when cold.

CUCUMBER MANGOES. Cut a long narrow piece out of the sides of large Turkey cucumbers, scoop out the seeds, and with a part of them mix some mustard seed, shred garlic, and grated horse-radish; stuff space as full as it will admit of, and replace the piece which was cut off; bind them with a thread; put over them hot vinegar three successive days, and boil with it the last time pepper, flour of mustard, and some salt; put them into jars, and pour over them the boiling vinegar, and when cold, cover them closely.

CULLIS. (1) To a quart of gravy, put a table-spoonful of thickening, or from one to two table-spoonfuls of flour, according to the thickness you wish the gravy to be, into a basin, with a ladleful of the gravy; stir it quick; add the rest by degrees, till it is all well mixed; then pour it back into a stewpan, and leave it by the side of the fire to simmer for half an hour longer, that the thickening may thoroughly incorporate with the gravy, the stewpan being only half covered, stirring it every now and then; a sort of scum will gather on the top, which it is best not to take off till you are ready to strain it through a tamis. Take care it is neither of too pale nor too dark a color; if it is not thick enough, let it stew longer, till it is reduced to the desired thickness; or add a bit of glaze, or portable soup to it, if it is too thick, you can easily thin it with a spoonful or two of warm broth, or water. When your sauce is done, stir it in the basin you put it into once or twice, while it is cooling.

CULLIS. (2) Lay over the bottom of a stewpan as much lean veal as will cover it an inch thick; then cover the veal with some slices of undressed bacon (gammon is the best), three onions, three bay leaves, some sweet herbs, two blades of mace, and three cloves. Put on the lid of the stewpan, and set it over a slow fire; but when the juices come out, let the fire be a little quicker. When the meat is of a nice brown color, fill the stewpan with good beef broth, boil and skim it, then let it simmer for an hour; add a little water mixed with as much flour as will make it properly thick; boil it half an hour, and strain it. You may keep this cullis a week.

CULLIS, A FAMILY ONE. Roll a piece of butter in flour, and stir it in a stewpan till the flour is of a fine yellow color. Then put in some thin broth: a little gravy, a glass of white wine, a bundle of sweet herbs, two cloves, a little nutmeg or mace, a few mushrooms, pepper and salt. Let it stew an hour over a slow fire, then skim all the fat clean off, and strain it through a sieve.

CULLIS, WHITE. Take a piece of veal, cut it into small bits, with some thin slices of ham, and two onions, each cut into four; moisten it with broth, seasoned with mushrooms, a bunch of parsley, green onions, three cloves, and so let it stew. Being stewed, take out the meat and roots with a skimmer, put in a few crumbs of bread and let it stew softly; take the white of a fowl, or two chickens, and put it into a mortar; being well pounded, mix it in the cullis, but it must not boil, and the cullis must be very white; but if not white enough, pound two dozen of sweet almonds blanched, and put it into the cullis; then boil a glass of milk, and add it to the cullis; let it be of a good flavor, and strain it off; then put it into a small kettle, and keep it warm. It may be used for white loaves, crust of white bread, and biscuits.

CURACOA. Put five ounces of thin-cut Seville orange-peel, that has been dried and pounded, or, which is still better, of the fresh peel of a fresh shaddock, which may be bought at the orange and lemon shops in the beginning of March, into a quart of the finest and cleanest rectified spirit; after it has been infused a fortnight, strain it, and add a quart of sirup and filter. See the following receipt.

CURACOA; HOW TO MAKE A QUART. To a pint of the cleanest and strongest rectified spirit, add two drachms and a half of the sweet oil of orange-peel; shake it up: dissolve a pound of good lump sugar in a pint of cold water; make this into a clarified sirup, which add to the spirit: shake it up, and let it stand till the following day: then line a funnel with a piece of muslin, and that with filtering-paper, and filter it two or three times till it is quite bright. This liquor is an admirable cordial; and a tea-spoonful in a tumbler of water is a very refreshing summer drink, and a great improvement to punch.

CURDS AND CREAM. (1) With about half a table-spoonful of rennet, turn two quarts of milk just from the cow; drain off the whey, and fill a mould with the curd; when it has stood an hour or two, turn it out. Strew colored comfits over it, sweeten some cream, mix grated nutmeg with it, and pour it round the curd.

CURDS AND CREAM. (2) Put two quarts of new milk into the dish in which it is to be served, and turn it with a tea-spoonful of rennet; when the curd has come, serve it with cream in a separate dish.

CURRANTS, AND OTHER FRUIT, TO CANDY. Boil the fruit in clarified sugar as for preserving; take it out of the sirup and drain it upon sieves; sift over it through a lawn sieve, till quite white, pounded loaf sugar. Place them in a cool oven, and turn and dust them with sugar till dry.

CURRANT FRITTERS WITHOUT EGGS. Stir into half a pint of mild ale, as much flour as will make it into a thick batter; add a little sugar and a few currants; beat it up quickly, and with a spoon drop it into boiling lard.

CURRANT MARMALADE. Take some ripe red currants, pick them, and squeeze out the juice from some of them; put to it some juice of raspberries; then put to this the whole currants, boil them gently; and when they begin to break, put in an equal weight of sugar boiled to candy height; boil them together, mash them as they boil; skim them, put in some rose water, and when it becomes as thick as marmalade, put it into pots.

CURRANT PUDDING. *See Pudding.*

CURRANTS FOR TARTS. Gather the fruit perfectly dry, and before it be too ripe, pick it from the stalks, and put it into clean, dry, wide mouthed bottles; if the flavor of raspberries is approved, some may be added with the currants; tie tightly over each bottle a piece of sound bladder previously soaked in water; set them into a pan of cold water with a little straw at the bottom, and a little between the bottles; put them on the fire, and when they begin to simmer, keep them in that state about three-quarters of an hour, but they must not be allowed to boil; take the pan off the fire; the bladders will be raised, but will fall soon after, and sink into the mouth of the bottles; in an hour, take them out, and tie strong paper over each, and set them in a dry cool place. The bottles may be placed in a bottle rack with the neck downwards. Damsons, cherries, and gooseberries, may be done in this way; any sort will keep for a year. Cut off the stalks of the cherries, and top and tail the gooseberries.

CURRANT TART. *See Tarts.*

CURRIES. Cut fowls or rabbits into joints, and wash them clean; put two ounces of butter into a stewpan: when it is melted, put in the meat, and two middling-sized onions sliced, let them be over a smart fire till they are of a light brown, then put in half a pint of broth; let it simmer twenty minutes. Put in a basin one or two table-spoonfuls of curry powder, a tea-spoonful of flour, and a tea-spoonful of salt; mix it smooth with a little cold water, put it into the stewpan, and shake it well about till it boils: let it simmer twenty minutes longer; then take out the meat, and rub the sauce through a tamis or sieve: add to it two table-spoonfuls of cream or milk; give it a boil up; then pour it into a dish, lay the meat over it: send up the rice in a separate dish.

CURRY. Cut a fowl into small pieces, skin it, and let it blanch in cold water for two hours; mince an onion very small, and put it into a saucepan, with two ounces of butter, and a large table-spoonful of flour of rice stirred in by degrees; brown it well, and when just boiling, add a quart of cold water, with the pieces of fowl and a large table-spoonful of curry powder mixed in it. Let it boil till the fowl be quite tender, and just before serving, squeeze the juice of half a lemon over the blade of a knife into it. Vinegar will answer instead of the juice; and if it be required very fine, in place of rice, thicken it with an ounce of sweet almonds blanched and pounded.

CURRY BALLS *for Mock Turtle, Veal, Poultry, Made Dishes, &c.* Are made with bread-crumbs, the yolk of an egg boiled hard, and a bit of fresh butter about half as big, beaten together in a mortar, and seasoned with curry powder.

CURRY, DRY. Skin and cut a fowl into joints, or take off small cutlets from the best end of a neck of veal; fry in butter three or four minced onions, and drain them; then fry the fowl or veal, and dust it with three tea-spoonfuls of curry powder, and a quarter of a tea-spoonful of Cayenne. Put the fried meat and onions into a stewpan, with a little salt, half a pint of milk, and the same quantity of water; keep the pan closely covered, and let it stew till perfectly tender, and ten minutes before serving, add two tea-spoonfuls of lemon-juice.

CURRY, FISH. After a cod-fish, had-dock, or mackerel has lain some hours in salt, cut it into pieces, and stew it in water sufficient to cover it, into which a large table spoonful of curry powder has been mixed. Fry in a quarter of a pound of butter, a shallot and two or three onions minced, a little pepper and salt. When well browned, add it to the fish, and stew all together till it be quite tender. Sprats make a good curry, but should be stewed in less water.

CURRY, INDIAN. Stew in two ounces of butter, for ten minutes, a teaspoonful of Cayenne, and one of pepper, a dessert-spoonful of pounded coriander seed, six small onions, and two heads of garlic minced. Cut the fowl or rabbit into small pieces, and cover it over with the curd of sweet milk. Put the whole into a stewpan, with as much boiling water as may be desired for sauce, and let it simmer till very tender.

CURRY POWDER. (1) Put the following ingredients in a cool oven all night, and the next morning pound them in a marble mortar, and rub them through a fine sieve. Coriander-seed, three ounces, turmeric, three ounces, black pepper, mustard, and ginger, one ounce of each, allspice and less cardamons, half an ounce of each, cumin seed, a quarter of an ounce. Thoroughly pound and mix together, and keep them in a well-stopped bottle. Those who are fond of curry sauces, may steep three ounces of the powder in a quart of vinegar or white wine for ten days, and will get a liquor impregnated with all the flavor of the powder.

CURRY POWDER. (2) Pound extremely fine, in a mortar, six ounces of coriander seed, three ounces of pepper, one ounce and a half of fennigreck seed, one ounce of cumin seed, three ounces of turmeric, and three-quarters of an ounce of Cayenne; sift it through muslin, and put it before the fire for four or five hours, stirring it every now and then. Keep it in a bottle with a glass stopper.

CURRY OF VEAL, FOWL, &c. Fry sliced veal, rabbit, fowl, or sweetbreads, in a good deal of butter, dusting it with flour. Dust one side with curry powder; then turn and dust the other, strewing over it finely minced onions, taking care not to burn them. When the meat is of a light brown, add some white stock, with a little salt; stew it till tender. Before serving, skim off the fat, and add a tea-spoonful of lemon-juice or vinegar. Rabbit, fowl, and sweetbreads should be parboiled.

CUSTARD. (1) Sweeten a quart of thin cream, or good milk, with pounded loaf sugar; boil it with a bit of cinnamon, and half the peel of a lemon; strain it, and when a little cooled, mix it gradually with the well-beaten yolks of ten eggs; stir it over a slow fire till it be pretty thick, pour it into a basin, and add a table-spoonful of rose water, and one of brandy; keep stirring it every now and then till cold, and then put it into glasses, cups, or a dish. It may be made the day before it is used.

CUSTARD. (2) Boil a pint of milk with lemon-peel and cinnamon; mix a pint of cream, and the yolks of five eggs, well beaten; when the milk tastes of the seasoning, sweeten it enough for the whole; pour it into the cream, stirring it well; then give the custard a simmer till of a proper thickness. Do not let it boil; stir the whole time one way; then season with a large spoonful of peach water, and two tea-spoonfuls of brandy, or a little ratafia. If you wish your custards to be extremely rich, put no milk, but a quart of cream.

CUSTARDS. (3) Take six eggs, leave out the whites; mix your eggs and sugar together with some rose water; then boil a pint of cream, and put in the eggs (the cream must not boil after the eggs have been put in). Stir them to prevent them from curdling.

CUSTARDS, ALMOND. Blanch and pound fine, with half a gill of rose water, six ounces of sweet, and half an ounce of bitter almonds; boil a pint of milk, as in Baked Custard sweeten it with two ounces and a half of sugar; rub the almonds through a fine sieve, with a pint of cream; strain the milk to the yolks of eight eggs, and the whites of three well-beaten; stir it over a fire till it is of a good thickness; take it off the fire, and stir it till nearly cold, to prevent its curdling. N. B.—The above may be baked in cups, or in a dish, with a rim of puff paste put round.

CUSTARD, APPLE. Take thirty fine apples, and pierce out the cores of ten of them which are of an equal size; pare and trim them neatly, and boil them in six ounces of sugar till pretty firm. Peel and cut the remaining apples very small, and put them into the above sirup; shred the rind of an orange, and mix with them; stir the whole constantly to prevent their sticking to the pan; when sufficiently done rub the marmalade through a horse-hair sieve. Prepare the crust as before mentioned, but dress the sides a little higher; mix two spoonfuls of apricot marmalade with that of your apples, and then put four spoonfuls of it into the custard; place the whole apples, (having put apricot marmalade in the place of the cores), and then add the remainder of the apple marmalade, taking care not to cover the apples with it. Finish as above. At the instant of serving it mask it with apple jelly, apricot or quince marmalade, cherry juice or verjuice. Garnish the top of each apple with a cherry or verjuice-berry. Serve this hot or cold.

CUSTARD, APRICOT GLAZED. Cut twenty fine apricots in half, take out the stones; toss up twelve apricots in four ounces of powder-sugar, and place them in a cream according to the directions for apple custard; bake and glaze as therein directed. Put a glass of water and a quarter of a pound of powder-sugar with the rest of the fruit into a preserving-pan; when the sirup is properly reduced, take the skin from the apricots and arrange them in the custard; garnish each half apricot with a kernel, and when ready to serve, pour the sirup on it. Serve hot or cold.

CUSTARD, BAKED. (1) Boil a pint of cream with mace and cinnamon; when cold, take four eggs, leaving out two of the whites, a little rose and orange-flower water, a little white wine, nutmeg, and sugar to your taste; mix them well together, and bake them in china cups.

CUSTARD, BAKED. (2) Boil in a pint of milk, a few coriander seeds, a little cinnamon and lemon-peel; sweeten with four ounces of loaf sugar, and mix with it a pint of cold milk; beat well eight eggs for ten minutes, and add the other ingredients; pour it from one pan into another six or eight times, strain it through a sieve, and let it stand some time; skim off the froth from the top, fill it in earthen cups; and bake them immediately in a hot oven, give them a good color; about ten minutes will do them.

CUSTARD, BOILED. (1) Boil in a pint of milk, five minutes, lemon-peel, corianders, and cinnamon, a small quantity of each, half a dozen of bitter almonds, blanched and pounded, and four ounces of loaf sugar: mix it with a pint of cream, the yolks of ten eggs, and the whites of six, well-beaten; pass it through a hair sieve, stir it with a whisk over a slow fire till it begins to thicken, remove it from the fire, and continue to stir it till nearly cold; add two table-spoonfuls of brandy, fill the cups or glasses, and grate nutmeg over.

CUSTARDS, BOILED. (2) Put a quart of new milk into a stewpan, with the peel of a lemon cut very thin, a little grated nutmeg, a bay or laurel leaf, and a small stick of cinnamon; set it over a quick fire, but be careful it does not boil over: when it boils, set it beside the fire, and simmer ten minutes; break the yolks of eight, and the whites of four eggs into a basin; beat them well; then pour in the milk a little at a time, stirring it

as quick as possible to prevent the eggs curdling; set it on the fire again, and stir it well with a wooden spoon; let it have just one boil; pass it through a tamis, or fine sieve: when cold add a little brandy, or white wine, as may be most agreeable to the eater's palate. Serve up in glasses, or cups. Custards for baking are prepared as above, passed through a fine sieve; put them into cups; grate a little nutmeg over each: bake them about fifteen or twenty minutes.

CUSTARD, COMMON. Boil a pint of milk with a bit of cinnamon and two or three laurel leaves; mix with a table-spoonful of flour, or potato flour, two and a half of cold milk, put it into a lawn sieve, and pour the boiling milk upon it; let it run into a basin, mix in by degrees the well-beaten yolks of three eggs; sweeten, and stir it over the fire for a few minutes to thicken.

CUSTARDS OR CREAMS, TO ORNAMENT. Whisk for one hour the whites of two eggs together with two table-spoonfuls of raspberry, or red currant sirup or jelly; lay it in any form upon a custard or cream, piled up to imitate rock. It may be served in a dish with cream round it.

CUSTARD, DURHAM. To a pint of cream add the well-beaten yolks of two eggs, and about a third of a pint of mild strong ale; sweeten, and stir it over the fire till it nearly boils, then pour it into a dish, in the bottom of which is laid thin toasted bread, cut into square bits.

CUSTARD OF FRESH FRUIT. Have ready a tin or copper mould, and line it completely with paste, taking care that it takes all the form of the mould. Then take a sufficient quantity of apricots, peaches, plums, or any other fruit you please; and having taken out the stones, seeds, and stalks, mix the fruit up with powder-sugar; put it into the crust, and bake it in a hot oven. When ready for table, mask it with the sirup and kernels, blanched and cut in halves.

CUSTARD, LEMON. (1) Boil two glasses of white wine, half a pint of water, and two table-spoonfuls of brandy; when nearly cold, add the grated peel and juice of two lemons, with half a pound of pounded loaf sugar, and the well-beaten yolks of six eggs; stir it over a slow fire till it thickens, pour it into a basin, and stir now and then till cold; put it into a dish, or cups, with sifted loaf sugar over the top.

CUSTARD, LEMON. (2) Put the juice of four lemons, with three ounces of pounded loaf sugar, into a deep dish. Boil the grated peel of one lemon and two ounces of pounded loaf sugar in a quart of cream, and pour it over the juice and sugar. It will keep for four days.

CUSTARD, ORANGE. Sweeten the strained juice of ten oranges with pounded loaf sugar, stir it over the fire till hot, take off the scum, and when nearly cold add to it the beaten yolks of twelve eggs, and a pint of cream; put it into a saucepan, and stir it over a slow fire till it thickens. Serve in cups or a dish.

CUSTARD, RICE. Mix a pint of milk, half a pint of cream, one ounce of sifted ground rice, five or six bitter almonds, blanched and pounded with two table-spoonfuls of rose water; sweeten with loaf sugar, and stir it all together till it nearly boils; add the well-beaten yolks of three eggs; stir, and let it simmer for about a minute; pour it into a dish, or serve it in cups, with sifted loaf sugar over the top.

CUSTARD, TURKEY. Put a pound and a half of good rice into cold water over the fire, and when it boils, take it off and drain it well; then put it into a large saucepan, with twelve glasses of good milk, a pound of butter, the same of sugar, on which have been rasped the peels of four oranges or ce-

drats, and a grain of salt. Put the saucepan over a moderate fire to swell the rice, taking care that none of the grains burst; stir it a little, and when done, add to it two pounds of dry currants, the yolks of twelve eggs, and some spoonfuls of *Chantilly* cream; after which mix in the twelve whites whipped firm. Prepare the crust in the usual way; bake it in a moderate oven two hours and a half; when ready for table, brown it with a salamander.

CUSTARD, TURNING OUT. Mix with the well-beaten yolks of four eggs a pint of new milk, half an ounce of isinglass dissolved, or enough of calf's-feet stock to stiffen it, and two laurel leaves; sweeten with pounded loaf sugar, and stir it over a slow fire till it thickens; pour it into a basin, and stir it till a little cooled, then pour it into cups to turn out when quite cold. Beat the yolks of two eggs with a little cream; add it to nearly half a pound of brown sugar burnt; strain it through a sieve, and when cold pour it round the custards.

wwwwww

## D

DAMSONS BOTTLED. Gather them on a dry day before they are ripe, when they have just turned their color. Put them in wide-mouthed bottles, cork them close, and let them stand a fortnight; then carefully examine them, and if any of them are mouldy or spotted, take them out of the bottles, and cork the rest close. Put the bottles in sand, and they will keep good till the spring.

DAMSON DUMPLINGS. Make a good hot paste crust, roll it pretty thin, lay it in a basin, and put in as many damsons as you please: Wet the edge of the paste and close it up; boil it in a cloth for an hour; pour melted butter over it, grate sugar round the edge of the dish, and serve.

DAMSON JELLY. *See Jelly.*

DAMSON, OR OTHER PLUM CHEESE. Take damsons that have been preserved without sugar; pass them through a sieve, to take out the skins and stones. To every pound of pulp of fruit put half a pound of loaf sugar, broke small; boil them together till it becomes quite stiff; pour it into four common-sized dinner plates, rubbed with a little sweet oil; put it into a warm place to dry, and when quite firm, take it from the plate, and cut it into any shape you choose. N. B.—Damson cheese is generally used in desserts.

DAMSONS FOR WINTER USE. Gather the damsons when just ripe, and perfectly sound; fill a two-gallon brandy keg, and pour over two pounds of molasses; close the keg firmly, and turn it every day.

DEER HORNS. Beat one white, and six yolks of eggs; mix them with five table-spoonfuls of pounded and sifted loaf sugar, the same quantity of sweet cream, ten sweet almonds, blanched and pounded, the grated peel of one lemon, and as much flour as will make the whole into a paste sufficiently thick to roll out. Then cut it with tins for the purpose, into the form of horns, branches, or any other shape, and throw them into boiling lard.

DEVIL. (1) Score the leg of a roasted turkey, goose, or fowl; pepper and salt it well, broil it, and pour over it the following sauce made quite hot: three table-spoonfuls of gravy, one of melted butter, and one of lemon juice, a large wine-glass of Port wine, of mustard, Chili vinegar, Harvey sauce, and mushroom catchup, a tea-spoonful each; a little Cayenne and pepper. The devil may be served without a sauce, and be more highly seasoned. When this dish is to be served cold; the fat being carefully removed from the goose, it may be ornamented or covered with cold jelly made as follows:—Boil for five hours in four quarts of water the bones of the goose, with three nicely cleaned calf's feet, strain it, and when cold take off all the fat, and boil the jelly with some whole pepper, ginger, and salt; add two ounces of dissolved isinglass, the juice of two lemons, and the beaten whites of three or four eggs; stir it while it is upon the fire, and allow it to boil about ten minutes; then run it through a jelly-bag, and repeat this till it becomes quite clear.

DEVIL. (2) The gizzard and rump, or legs, &c. of a dressed turkey, capon, or goose, or mutton or veal kidney, scored, peppered, salted, and broiled, sent up for a relish, being made very hot, has obtained the name of a "devil."

DEVONSHIRE JUNKET. (1) Turn some new milk from the cow with a little rennet; sweeten some thick cream, add a little pounded cinnamon, make it scalding hot, and when cold pour it over the curd, and put a little wine and sugar into the bottom of the dish.

DEVONSHIRE JUNKET. (2) Turn some new milk, as for cheese cakes, in a wide shallow dish; when cold, pour over the top a pint of rich cream mixed with pounded loaf sugar, six dessert-spoonfuls of brandy, and some grated nutmeg.

DEVONSHIRE WHITE POT. Beat up a pint of cream with four eggs, a little salt, some sliced nutmeg, and a good deal of sugar; then slice very thin, almost the whole of the crum of a penny loaf; put it into a dish; pour the eggs and cream to it; a handful of Smyrna raisins boiled, and a little sweet butter: bake it.

DIGESTER. An iron boiler, with a top to screw on, to prevent the steam from escaping.

DRIPPINGS, TO CLARIFY. Put your dripping into a clean saucepan over a stove or slow fire; when it is just going to boil, skim it well, let it boil, and let it stand till it is a little cooled; then pour it through a sieve into a pan. *Obs.*—Well-cleansed drippings, and the fat skimmings of the broth-pot, when fresh and sweet, will baste everything as well as butter except game and poultry, and should supply the place of butter for common fries, &c.; for which they are equal to lard, especially if you repeat the clarifying twice over. N. B.—If you keep it in a cool place, you may preserve it a fortnight in summer, and longer in winter. When you have done frying, let the dripping stand a few minutes to settle, and then pour it through a sieve into a clean basin or stone pan, and it will do a second and a third time as well as it did the first; only the fat you have fried fish in must not be used for any other purpose.

DRINK, COOLING. A palatable and cooling drink may be made by pouring hot water over slices of lemon; when cold, to be strained and sweetened.

DUCK. Mind your duck is well cleaned, and wiped out with a clean cloth: for the stuffing, take an ounce of onion and half an ounce of green sage; chop them very fine, and mix them with two ounces, *i. e.* about a breakfast-cupful, of bread crumbs, a bit of butter about as big as a walnut, a very little black pepper and salt, and the yolk of an egg to bind it; mix these thoroughly together, and put into the duck. From half to three-quarters of an hour will be enough to roast it, according to the size: contrive to have the feet delicately crisp, as some people are very fond of them; to do this nicely you must have a sharp fire.

DUCK, TO BOIL. Make a paste, allowing half a pound of butter to a pound of flour. Truss a duck as for boiling; put into the inside a little pepper and salt, one or two sage leaves, and a little onion finely minced; enclose the duck in the paste, with a little jellied gravy. Boil it in a cloth, and serve it with brown gravy poured round it.

DUCKS, TO CHOOSE. Their feet should be supple, and they should be hard and thick on the breast and belly. The feet of a tame duck are thick, and inclining to a dusky yellow. The feet of a wild duck are reddish, and smaller than the tame; they should be picked dry. Ducklings should be scalded.

DUCK, DRESSED IN DIFFERENT WAYS. Take either a large duck, or two ducklings, which truss like a fowl for boiling; put it into a pot (just about large enough to hold the duck) with thin slices of bacon, a little stock, a glass of wine, pepper, salt, onions, carrots, a head of celery sliced, a bunch of sweet herbs, two cloves, and a bay-leaf; when done, take out the duck, wipe the fat off very clean, and serve with sauce or ragout you choose, such as sweetbreads, green-peas, turnips, chestnuts, olives, cucumbers, or any sort of stewed greens, according to the season.

DUCKS, GEESE, DRESSED, OR HASHED. Cut an onion into small dice; put it into a stewpan with a bit of butter; fry it, but do not let it get any color; put as much boiling water into the stewpan as will make sauce for the hash; thicken it with a little flour; cut up the duck, and put it into the sauce to warm; do not let it boil; season it with pepper and salt, and catchup. Divide the duck into joints; lay it by ready; put the trimmings and stuffing into a stewpan, with a pint and a half of broth or water; let it boil half an hour, and then rub it through a sieve; put half an ounce of butter into a stewpan; as it melts, mix a table-spoonful of flour with it; stir it over the fire a few minutes, then mix the gravy with it by degrees; as soon as it boils, take off the scum, and strain through a sieve into a stewpan; put in the duck, and let it stew very gently for ten or fifteen minutes, if the duck is rather under-roasted: if there is any fat, skim it off: line the dish you serve it up in with sippets of bread either fried or toasted.

DUCK OR GOOSE FORCED. Cut the goose open at the back, and carefully take out the bones, excepting those of the legs and wings. Take out all the meat from the body, leaving the skin perfectly whole. With the meat pound three-quarters of a pound of lean and tender beef, add three handfuls of grated bread, four well-beaten eggs, and half a pint of rich sweet cream; season with pepper, mace, and salt; mix it all well together; let it stand for half an hour, and then put it into the goose, which sew up, and make it of as natural a form as possible; but take care that it be not too much stuffed. Boil it for half an hour in some good stock, and then put it into a flat tin baking-pan, with some fresh butter over and under it. Bake it in an oven another half hour, and serve it with the following sauce: Brown a table-spoonful of butter with flour, add about a pint of the stock in which the goose has been boiled, three grated onions, two table-spoonfuls of capers cut fine, a little lemon pickle, and a few small pickled onions; boil it about a quarter of an hour, and just before pouring it over the goose, stir in gradually half a pint of rich cream.

DUCK, HASHED, Cut a duck in pieces, and flour it; put in a stewpan some gravy, a little Port wine, shallots chopped fine, salt, pepper, and a bit of lemon; boil this; then put in the duck, toss it up, take out the lemon, and serve with toasted sippets.

DUCKS ROASTED. Season them with sage and onion shred, pepper and salt; half an hour will roast them. Gravy-sauce or onion sauce. Always stew the sage and onion in a little water, as it prevents its eating strong, and takes off the rawness of them.

DUCK, TO STEW. (1) Cut one or two ducks into quarters; fry them a light brown in butter; put them into a saucepan, with a pint of gravy, a tea-cupful of Port wine, four onions whole, pepper and some salt, a bunch of parsley, two sage leaves, a sprig of winter savory, and sweet marjoram. Cover the pan closely, and stew them till tender; take out the herbs and pepper; skim it; if the sauce be not sufficiently thick, mix with two table-spoonfuls of it a little flour, and stir it into the saucepan; boil it up, and garnish the dish with the four onions.

DUCK, TO STEW. (2) Put into a duck some pepper, salt, a minced onion, and one leaf of sage also minced; half roast it; brown with two ounces of butter, a table-spoonful of flour; add as much weak stock as will cover the duck, and some pepper and salt; put in the duck, and a quart of green peas; let it stew for half an hour, stirring it now and then. For a variety, a dozen of middling-sized onions may be substituted for the peas, and stewed the same length of time. Cold roasted duck may be dressed exactly in the same manner; and to hash it, cut it into joints, and heat it thoroughly in gravy, adding a little soy, and a glass of Port wine.

DUCK, WILD. These birds should be fat, the claws small, reddish and supple; if not fresh, on opening the beak they will smell disagreeable; the breast and rump should be firm and heavy; the flesh of the hen-bird is the most delicate, though the cock generally fetches the highest price. Pick them dry, cut the wings very close to the body, take off the necks, draw and singe them, truss up the legs and skewer them; and having rubbed them with their livers, spit, and roast them; take them up with the gravy in, and serve with lemons.

DUCK, WILD, SALMIS OF. Cut off the best parts of a couple of roasted wild ducks, and put the rest of the meat into a mortar, with six shallots, a little parsley, some pepper, and a bay-leaf, pound all these ingredients together well, and then put them into a saucepan with four ladlesful of stock, half a glass of white wine, the same of broth, and a little grated nutmeg; reduce these to half, strain them, and having laid the pieces on a dish, cover them with the above: keep the whole hot, not boiling, until wanted for table.

DUMPLINGS, HARD. Mix as for a paste, some flour with small beer or water, and a little salt; roll them in balls rather larger than an egg; when the water boils put them in: half an hour will boil them; currants may be added; they are good boiled with beef. They are eaten either with cold or melted butter.

DUMPLINGS, HALF-HOUR. Mince finely half a pound of suet, mix it with the same proportion of grated bread, and a table-spoonful of flour, a quarter of a pound of currants, some sugar, a little grated lemon-peel, nutmeg, and three well-beaten eggs; roll the mixture into round balls, tie them in bits of linen, and boil them for half an hour. Serve with melted butter and sugar poured over them.

DUMPLINGS, NORFOLK. With a pint of milk, two eggs, a little salt, and some flour, make a batter; drop this in small quantities into a pot of boiling water; they will be boiled in three minutes; throw them into a sieve or cullender to drain.

DUMPLING PASTE. Make a paste with flour, milk, salt and yeast; let it stand sometime in a warm place to ferment; then cut the paste into pieces of what size you please, and boil them a good while; let them cool; then cut each into two, and soak them in milk, sugar, and lemon-peel, about an hour, and drain and flour them fit for frying; or, you may dip them in oil or melted butter to broil, basting with the same as they were dipped in.

DUTCH CREAM CHEESE. Beat the yolks of eight, and the whites of three eggs, and mix them with a pint of butter milk; add this to three quarts of boiling milk just from the cow; let it boil up once, take it off the fire, cover it, and let it stand a little that the curd may form; then put it into a small hair sieve, and press it with a weight for twenty-four hours, when it may be turned out. It is eaten with cream and sugar.

DUTCH FLUMMERY. (1) Boil, with a pint of white wine, some sugar, the juice of two, and the peel of one lemon, a stick of cinnamon, and half an ounce of dissolved isinglass; strain, and mix it with the well-beaten yolks of seven eggs, stir it over the fire till it simmer, but do not allow it to boil; stir it till quite cold, and put it into a shape.

DUTCH FLUMMERY. (2) Boil for ten minutes, in half a pint of white wine, and the same proportion of water, the juice of three, and the peel of two lemons, rather more than a quarter of a pound of loaf sugar, and an ounce of isinglass dissolved; strain, and mix it gradually with the beaten yolks of five eggs; put it again over the fire, and stir it for five minutes; stir it till cold, and put it into a shape.

~~~~~~~~~

E.

ECHAUDE'S. Lay a quartern of flour on a pasteboard or slab, make a hole in the centre, in which put an ounce of salt, and a little water to dissolve it, a pound of butter, twenty eggs; mix the two latter well together, then the flour; work it thoroughly with your hands, if it be very firm add more eggs. When perfectly smooth, sprinkle a cloth with flour, lay the paste on it, and set it in a cool place for ten or twelve hours. The next day heat about three quarts of water, and having cut your paste into small pieces, about an inch square, and having floured each, put them into hot but not boiling water, shake the kettle the instant after you have thrown them in, and as they rise, if they are firm to the touch, they are sufficiently done, and must be taken out of the saucepan, and thrown into cold water; let them remain two or three hours; then drain, and leave them again for three hours or more, and then bake them for about twenty minutes.

EELS AND SOLES, STEWED WIGGY'S WAY. Take two pounds of fine silver eels: the best are those that are rather more than a half-crown piece in circumference, quite fresh, full of life, and "as brisk as an eel": wash them in several different waters, and divide them into pieces about four inches long. Some cooks, dredge them with a little flour, wipe them dry, and then egg and crumb them, and fry them in drippings till they are brown, and lay them to dry on a hair sieve. Have ready a quart of good beef gravy; it must be cold when you put the eels into it: set them on a slow fire to simmer very gently for about a quarter of an hour, according to the size of the eels; watch them, that they are not done too much; take them carefully out of the stewpan with a fish-slice, so as not to tear their coats, and lay them on a dish about two inches deep.

EELS BAKED. Skin and clean some eels; take a shallow pan, and cut the eels in lengths according to the depth of the pan; put them in, letting them stand up-right in it; the pan should be filled; put in a little water, some salt, pepper, shallots cut small, some sweet herbs, and a little parsley cut small; set them in the oven to bake; when they are done take the liquor that comes from them, put it into a sauce-pan, and thicken it with a piece of butter rolled in flour, and a little white wine.

EELS BOILED. Small ones are prefer-able. Curl and put them on in boiling salt-and-water, with a little vinegar. Garnish with parsley. Sauce;—parsley and butter.

EELS COLLARED. Take an eel, and cut it open; take out the bones; cut off the head and tail; lay the eel flat, and shred sage as fine as possible; mix with black pepper pounded, nutmeg grated, and salt; lay it all over the eel; roll it up hard in a cloth; tie it up tight at each end; then set over the fire some water, with pepper and salt, five or six cloves, three or four blades of mace, a bay-leaf or two; boil these with the bones, head, and tail, well; then put in the eel, and boil it till it is tender; then take it out, and boil the liquor, and when it is cold, put it to the eel; do not take off the cloth till you use them.

EELS FRIED. Cut them into pieces of three or four inches long, and then score across in two or three places; season them with pepper and salt, and dust them with flour, or dip them into an egg beat up, and sprinkle them with finely-grated bread crumbs; fry them in fresh lard or dripping. Let them drain and dry upon the back of a sieve before the fire. Garnish with parsley. Sauce;—melted butter, and lemon pickle. If small, they may be curled and fried whole.

EEL PIE. Take eels about half a pound each; cut them into pieces three inches long, season them with pepper and salt, and fill your dish. Add a gill of water or veal broth, cover it with paste, rub it over with a paste-brush dipped in yolk of egg, ornament it with some of the same paste, bake it an hour; and when done, make a hole in the centre, and pour in the following sauce through a funnel: the trimmings boiled in half a pint of veal stock, seasoned with pep-per and salt, a table-spoonful of lemon-juice, and thickened with flour and water strained through a fine sieve: add it boiling hot.

EELS POTTED. Bone them; season them well upon both sides with pepper, salt, a little mace, and Jamaica pepper; let them lie for six hours, then cut them into small pieces, and pack them close into a dish; cover them with a coarse paste and bake them. When quite cold, take off the paste, and pour over them clarified butter.

EEL SOUP. *See Soups.*

EELS STEWED.(1) Cut the eels into pieces about four inches long; take two onions, two shallots, a bunch of parsley, thyme, two bay leaves, a little mace, black and Jamaica pepper, a pint of good gravy, the same of Port wine, and the same of vinegar, six anchovies bruised; let all boil together for ten minutes; take out the eels; boil the sauce till reduced to a quart; strain and thicken it with a table-spoonful of flour, mixed smooth in a little cold water. Put in the eels, and boil them till they are tender. Eels may also be roasted with a common stuffing.

EELS STEWED. (2) Cut the eels into pieces, season well two pounds and a half with salt and black pepper, put an ounce of butter into a stewpan with a large handful of sorrel, three or four sage leaves, half an onion cut small, a little grated lemon-peel, and one anchovy chopped; put in the eels and pour over half a pint of water, stew them gently for half an hour, shaking them occasionally; before serving, add a little grated nutmeg, and the juice of half a lemon.

EELS SPITCHCOCKED. This the French cooks call the English way of dressing eels. Take two middling-sized silver eels, scour them with salt, slit them on the belly side, and take out the bones and wash and wipe them nicely; then cut them into pieces about three inches long, and wipe them quite dry; put two ounces of butter into a stewpan with a little minced parsley, thyme, sage, pepper, and salt, and a very little chopped eschalot; set the stewpan over the fire; when the butter is melted, stir the ingredients together, and take it off the fire, mix the yolks of two eggs with them, and dip the eel in, a piece at a time, and then roll them in bread-crumbs, making as much stick to them as you can; then rub the gridiron with a bit of suet, set it high over a very clear fire and broil your eels of a fine crisp brown. Dish them with crisp parsley, and send up with plain butter in a boat, and anchovy and butter.

EGGS. (1) Eggs may be preserved for twelve months, in a sweet and palatable state for eating in the shell, or using for sal-ads, by boiling them for one minute; and when wanted for use let them be boiled in the usual manner: the white may be a little tougher than a new-laid egg, but the yolk will show no difference.

EGGS. (2) Pour a gallon of water over a pound of unslacked lime, stir it well; the following day, poor off the clear water into a jar, and put in the eggs as they are laid. In this manner they will continue perfectly good for six months or more.

There are so many different ways of dressing eggs, that the recipes would almost fill a volume; we have, therefore, given such as we esteem the best, and the most adapted to the English taste.

EGGS AND BACON RAGOUT. Boil half a dozen eggs for ten minutes; throw them into cold water; peel them and cut them into halves; pound the yolks in a marble mortar, with about an equal quantity of the white meat of dressed fowl, or veal, a little chopped parsley, an anchovy, an eschalot, a quarter of an ounce of butter, a table-spoonful of mushroom catchup, a little Cayenne, some bread-crumbs, and a very little beaten mace, or allspice; incorporate them well together, and fill the halves of the whites with this mixture; do them over with the yolk of an egg, and brown them in a Dutch oven, and serve them on relishing rashers of bacon or ham.

EGGS AND BREAD. Put half a handful of bread crumbs into a saucepan, with a small quantity of cream, salt, pepper, and nutmeg, and let it stand till the bread has imbibed all the cream; then break ten eggs into it, and having beaten them up together, fry it like an omelet.

EGGS AND CREAM. Boil half a pint of cream till reduced to half the quantity; then add eight eggs, season them with salt and pepper, boil them together, till the eggs are partly hard; pass a salamander over the top, and serve.

EGGS A LA TRIPE. Cut into thick round slices a dozen of hard-boiled eggs, and put them into the following sauce: cut three large white onions into dice, fry them white in butter, and when nearly done, dust them with flour, and moisten them with some milk and a few spoonfuls of cream; keep stirring with a wooden spoon, to prevent their burning. When the sauce is done, grate in a little nutmeg, season with a little salt and pepper, and put in the eggs.

EGG BALLS. Boil four eggs for ten minutes, and put them into cold water; when they are quite cold, put the yolks into a mortar with the yolk of a raw egg, a tea-spoonful of flour, same of chopped parsley, as much salt as will lie on a shilling, and a little black pepper, or Cayenne; rub them well together, roll them into small balls (as they swell in boiling); boil them a couple of minutes.

EGGS BOILED, TO EAT IN THE SHELL, OR FOR SALADS. The fresher laid the better: put them into boiling water; if you like the white just set, about two minutes boiling is enough; a new-laid egg will take a little more; if you wish the yolk to be set, it will take three, and to boil it hard for a salad, ten minutes. A new-laid egg will require boiling longer than a stale one, by half a minute.

EGGS BOURGEOISE. Spread some butter over the bottom of a dish, cover it entirely with thin slices of crumb of bread, on that lay thin slices of cheese, then eight or ten eggs, season them with salt, pepper and nutmeg, set the dish over a stove to cook gently till done.

EGGS, BUTTERED. Beat and strain ten or twelve eggs; put a piece of butter into a saucepan and keep turning it one way till melted; put in the beaten eggs, and stir them round with a silver spoon till they become quite thick. Serve them in a dish upon buttered toast. They may be eaten with fish, fowl, or sausages.

EGGS EN SURPRISE. Take a dozen eggs, and make a small hole at each end of every egg, through which pass a straw and break the yolk; then blow out the yolk carefully. Wash the shells, and having drained, dry them in the open air; mix the yolk of an egg with a little flour to close one of the holes of the shells, and when dry, fill half the number by means of a small funnel, with chocolate cream, and the remaining six with coffee or orange-cream. Close the other end of your eggs, and put them into a saucepan of hot water; set them on the fire, taking care they do not boil; when done, remove the cement from the ends; dry, and serve them on a folded napkin.

EGGS, FRIED. Eggs boiled hard, cut into slices, and fried, may be served as a second course dish, to eat with roasted chickens.

EGGS FRIED WITH BACON. Lay some slices of fine streaked bacon (not more than a quarter of an inch thick) in a clean dish, and toast then before the fire in a cheese-toaster, turning them when the upper side is browned; first ask those who are to eat the bacon, if they wish it much or little done, i. e. curled and crisped, or mellow and soft: if the latter, parboil it first. Well-cleansed dripping, or lard, or fresh butter, are the best fats for frying eggs. Be sure the frying-pan is quite clean; when the fat is hot, break two or three eggs into it; do not turn them, but, while they are frying, keep pouring some of the fat over them with a spoon; when the yolk just begins to look white, which it will in about a couple of minutes, they are done enough; the white must not lose its transparency, but the yolk be seen blushing through it: if they are done nicely, they will look as white and delicate as if they had been poached; take them up with a tin slice, drain the fat from them, trim them neatly, and send them up with the bacon round them.

EGGS FRIED, AND MINCED HAM OR BACON. Choose some fine salt pork, streaked with a good deal of lean; cut this into very thin slices, and afterward into small square pieces; throw them into a stewpan, and set it over a gentle fire, that they may lose some of their fat. When as much as will freely come is thus melted from them, lay them on a warm dish. Put into a stewpan a ladle-full of melted bacon or lard; set it on a stove; put in about a dozen of the small pieces of bacon, then stoop the stewpan and break in an egg. Manage this carefully, and the egg will presently be done: it will be very round, and the little dice of bacon will stick to it all over, so that it will make a very pretty appearance. Take care the yolks do not harden; when the egg is thus done, lay it carefully in a warm dish, and do the others.

EGG FRITTERS. Pound a dozen hard boiled eggs with a little cream, and a quarter of a pound of beef marrow; then pound half a dozen macaroons, some bitter almonds, a little sugar, and lemon-peel; mix these with the pounded eggs, and form them into fritters, dip them into a batter made with flour, butter, salt, and lemon-peel; fry them in very hot lard, sprinkle sugar over, and serve.

EGGS FROTHED. Beat up the yolks of eight eggs and the whites of four (set aside the remaining whites) with a spoonful of water, some salt, sugar, and the juice of a lemon; fry this, and then put it on a dish; whip the four whites (which were set aside) to a froth with sugar, and place it over the fried eggs; bake it in a Dutch oven, or with a high cover fitted for the purpose.

EGGS, GLASS. Butter a dish, and break into it a piece of butter nearly as large as an egg: add a tea-cupful of cream, and drop in four or five eggs; put upon each a little pepper and salt, set the dish upon a stove and serve it when the eggs are firm, which may be in ten or fifteen minutes.

EGG MARMALADE.(1) Blanch and pound with a little rose water, two ounces of sweet almonds, the same of orange marmalade, and four of citron; add two spoonfuls of brandy, and when quite smooth, the beaten yolks of six and the whites of two eggs, with a little pounded loaf sugar; put it into a saucepan, and stir it till it becomes thick, then pour it into a shape. When quite cold, serve it, turned out and garnished with flowers.

EGG MARMALADE. (2) Clarifiy a pound of sugar, keeping it rather thick; when cool, add to it the yolks of twenty eggs, which should be perfectly free from the whites, and well stirred, but not beaten; set these on the fire, stirring continually until it boils, and then continue to stir until sufficiently thick; if any scum should arise, it need not be taken off as the boiling and stirring will effectually remove it. Orange-flower water may be added, if approved.

EGGS, TO POACH. The cook who wishes to display her skill in poaching, must endeavour to procure eggs that have been laid a couple of days—those that are quite new-laid are so milky that, take all the care you can, your cooking of them will seldom procure you the praise of being a prime poacher; you must have fresh eggs, or it is equally impossible. The beauty of a poached egg is for the yolk to be seen blushing through the white, which should only be just sufficiently hardened, to form a transparent veil for the egg. Have some boiling water in a tea-kettle; pass as much of it through a clean cloth as will half fill a stewpan; break the egg into a cup, and when the water boils, remove the stewpan from the stove, and gently slip the egg into it; it must stand till the white is set; then put it over a very moderate fire, and as soon as the water boils, the egg is ready; take it up with a slice, and neatly round off the ragged edges of the white; send them up on bread toasted on one side only, with or without butter; or without a toast garnished with streaked bacon nicely fried, or slices of broiled beef or mutton, anchovies, pork sausages, or spinage. The bread should be a little larger than the egg, and about a quarter of an inch thick; only just give it a yellow color: if you toast it brown, it will get a bitter flavour; or moisten it by pouring a little hot water upon it: some sprinkle it with a few drops of vinegar, or of essence of anchovy.

EGGS POACHED, WITH SAUCE OF MINCED HAM. Poach the eggs as before directed, and take two or three slices of boiled ham; mince it fine with a gherkin, a morsel of onion, a little parsley, and pepper and salt; stew all together a quarter of an hour; serve up your sauce about half boiling; put the eggs in a dish, squeeze over the juice of half a Seville orange, or lemon, and pour the sauce over them.

EGG PUNCH. Take a punch-glass, and put into it a wine-glass of sirup of punch (see that article), and the yolk of an egg; beat them together with a spoon, and then fill up the glass with boiling water, stirring a little as you pour it in.

EGG TOAST. Put a glass of thick cream, some sugar, two or three macaroons pounded, with a few almonds, a little grated lemon, give them a boil; then add the yolks of eight and whites of three eggs, beat the whole up over a slow fire; and lay on very thin slices of fried bread; sprinkle sugar over, and serve.

EGG WINE. Beat up an egg, mix with it a spoonful of cold water; set on the fire a glass of white wine, half a glass of water, sugar, and nutmeg. When it boils, pour a little of it to the egg by degrees, till the whole is in, stirring it well; then return the whole into the saucepan, set it over a gentle fire, stir it one way for a minute, not longer, for if it boil, or the egg is stale, it will curdle; serve with toast. You may make it as above, without warming the egg, and it will be lighter on the stomach, though not so agreeable to the palate.

ELDER FLOWER FRITTERS. They are made whilst the elder flowers are in bloom; and they should marinate three or four hours in brandy, sugar, orange-flower water, and lemon-peel; when drained, dip them in a good thick batter to fry, and serve with rasped sugar, as in general.

ELDER ROB. Gather the elderberries when quite ripe, put them into a stone jar, tie a bladder or paper over the top, and place the jar in a pan of water; let it boil till the berries are very soft, strain them through a coarse cloth, and to every pint of juice allow half a pound of good brown sugar; put it into a preserving-pan, stir it, and when it boils, take off the scum, and let it boil for one hour.

ELDER VINEGAR. Choose the elder-flowers when just blown, take away all the stalks, and when the flowers are about half dry, put them into a jar, and fill the jar with vinegar, close it tight, and let it stand in the sun for twenty days; then draw it off, press the flowers, and having filtered the whole, bottle it; take care to keep the bottles closely corked.

ELDERBERRIES. Can be made to produce excellent wine, allowing to a ten gallon cask forty pounds of fruit, forty pounds of sugar, and a quarter of a pound of tartar. When elderberry wine is desired for a warm cordial, it is made in the following manner:—Twenty-five pounds of fruit are to be boiled for an hour, in eleven gallons of water, and along with it, tied in a piece of linen, one ounce of allspice, and two of ginger; forty pounds of sugar being put into a tub, the boiling liquor is strained over it, pressing the fruit quite dry; a quarter of a pound of crude tartar, or cream of tartar, is then added to the liquid. When it has stood two days in the tub, it may be removed to the cask, treated, as for sweet wine, in the usual manner, and bottled in March following. When to be drank, a portion of it is heated with some sugar, two or three cloves, and a little nutmeg.

EMPOTAGE. Put into a large saucepan, three or four pounds of beef-steaks, a knuckle of veal, and four old hens; moisten this quantity of meat with two ladlesful of broth; set it on a stove, and let it boil till properly reduced, taking care that none of the meat burns, which would make the *empotage* of too high a color; fill up your saucepan with broth, adding carrots, turnips, and onions; let all these ingredients stand over the fire for three hours and a half; then strain the whole through a silk sieve, that it may be perfectly clear.

ENDIVE IN VELOUTE. Take off all the outer leaves of your endive, and having opened the hearts, put them into cold water to wash them. In the meanwhile heat a kettle of water, put in it a handful of salt, then throw in the endive; keep it constantly under the water, to prevent their turning black. As soon as the endive is tender, drain, and then put it into cold water, and when quite cold, drain it again; press the water out with your hands; then chop it small, and put it into a saucepan, with some butter, salt, and pepper, stir it well, and then add five spoonfuls of *veloute*, the same of *consomme*; reduce it till pretty thick, and then put it in a dish, with fried bread round it. Endive may also be dressed with cream, in which case, put two spoonfuls of flour into it, and moisten it with cream.

ENDIVE IN GRAVY OF VEAL. Wash and clean thoroughly ten or twelve heads of fine endive, take off the outer leaves, and blanch the heads in hot water; throw them into cold water, and then squeeze them as dry as possible. Stew them in as much gravy as will cover them; add a tea-spoonful of pounded sugar, and a little salt. When perfectly tender, put in a little veloute sauce, and serve quite hot.

ENTREE. There is no word precisely equivalent to this in English. Any dish of butcher's meat, fowl, game, or fish, dressed for the *first* course, is called an *entree*.

ENTREMET. There is no word equivalent to this in English. All dishes of vegetables, jellies, pastries, salad, prawns, lobsters, and, in general, everything that appears in the second course, except the roast, is called an *entremet*.

ESCHALOT WINE. Peel, mince, and pound in a mortar, three ounces of eschalots, and infuse them in a pint of Sherry for ten days; then pour off the clear liquor on three ounces more eschalots, and let the wine stand on them ten days longer. This is rather the most expensive, but infinitely the most elegant preparation of eschalot, and imparts the onion flavour to soups and sauces, for chops, steaks, or broiled meats, hashes, &c. more agreeably than any: it does not leave any unpleasant taste in the mouth, or to the breath; nor repeat, as almost all other preparations of garlic, onion, &c. do. N. B.—An ounce of scraped horseradish may be added to the above, and little thin-cut lemon-peel.

ESPAGNOLE. Take an old fowl, and about fourteen pounds of leg or shoulder of veal; chop the latter into pieces, and put it, with very little water, into a large saucepan, with two carrots, three onions, a pound of ham, a few peppercorns, a small quantity of spice, and a clove of garlic; let this stew over a moderate fire, shaking it frequently, till it becomes of a brown color, when you may add to it a sufficient quantity of hot water, to come about four inches above the meat. Set it by the side of the stove to boil gently, skimming when necessary, till the meat comes from the bones; then strain it through a silk sieve, and set it by for use.

ESSENCE. Take half a bottle of white wine, half a glass of the best vinegar, the juice of two lemons, three ounces of salt, half an ounce of whole pepper, a little nutmeg and mace, four cloves, four bay-leaves, thyme, parsley, one small clove of garlic, ten shallots, pounded, and an ounce of dry mushrooms; put all these ingredients into an earthen pan, over a brisk fire; when near boiling, lessen the fire, and let it stand on hot ashes for six or seven hours; then strain it through a coarse sieve, and afterwards filter it. Keep it in closely corked bottles: a small quantity is sufficient to flavour a dish.

wwwwww

# F

FANCHONETTES. Put into a saucepan, two ounces of flour, three of sugar, one of butter, two of pounded almonds, some green lemon-peel, two yolks, and one whole egg, a little salt, and half a pint of milk; put these ingredients on the fire, and let them set like a cream; line some tartlet-tins, or moulds, with puff paste, fill them with the preparation; place the moulds on a tin, and bake the *fanchonettes* in a brisk oven; when about three parts done, take them out, put frothed eggs on, sprinkle sugar over, and replace them in the oven to finish the baking.

FAWN, Like a sucking pig, should be dressed almost as soon as killed. When very young, it is trussed, stuffed, and spitted the same way as a hare: but they are better eating when of the size of a house lamb, and are then roasted in quarters; the hind-quarter is most esteemed.

They must be put down to a very quick fire, and either basted all the time they are roasting, or be covered with sheets of fat bacon; when done, baste it with butter, and dredge it with a little salt and flour, till you make a nice froth on it.

N. B.—We advise our friends to half roast a fawn as soon as they receive it, and then make a hash of it.

Send up venison sauce with it.

FILBERT ROLLS. Having peeled half a pound of filberts, put them into a preserving pan over a moderate fire, and stir them constantly with a spatula until they become equally colored of a light yellow: then set them to cool. When cold, pound them with a little white of egg to a paste; then mix them with half a pound of flour, the same of powder sugar, and the yolks of four or five eggs, and then finish the operation as directed for *almond rolls*. Froth, and trace on the surface an ear of wheat, or anything else, with the point of a knife: take care to dry them well in the baking, that they may be crisp. Course powder sugar may also be strewed over, before they are put in the oven.

FISH. *We insert all the best remarks that various culinary authors have made on* FISH.

There is a general rule in choosing most kinds of fish; if their gills are red, their eyes plump, and the whole fish stiff, they are good; if, on the contrary, the gills are pale, the eyes sunk, and the fish flabby, they are stale. The greatest care should be taken that the fish is properly cleansed before being dressed, but not washed beyond what is absolutely necessary for cleaning, as by perpetual watering, the flavour is diminished. When clean, if the fish is to be boiled, some salt, and a little vinegar should be put into the water, to give it firmness. Care should be taken to boil the fish well, but not to let it break. Cod, whiting, and haddock are much better for being a little salted, and kept for a day.

There is often a muddy smell and taste attached to fresh-water fish, which may be got rid of by soaking it, after it has been thoroughly cleaned in strong salt and water; or, if the fish is not too large, scald it in the same; then dry and dress it.

Care should be taken that the fish is put into cold water, and allowed to do very gently, otherwise the outside will break before the inside is done.

Crimp fish must be put into boiling water; and as soon as it boils up, a little cold water should be put in, to check the excessive heat, and simmer it for a few minutes.

If the fish is not taken out of the water the instant it is done, it will become woolly; to ascertain when it is ready, the fish plate on which it is dressed may be drawn up, and if sufficiently done, it will leave the bone. To keep hot for serving, and to preserve it from losing its color, the fish plate should be placed crossways over the fish-kettle, and a clean cloth put over the fish.

Small fish may be either nicely fried plain, or done over with egg and bread crumbs, and then fried. Upon the dish on which the fish is to be served, should be placed a folded damask napkin, and upon this put the fish, with the liver and roe; then garnish the dish with horse-radish, parsley, and lemon. Fish is a dish which is almost more attended to than any other.

To fry or broil fish properly, after it is well cleaned and washed, it should be wrapped in a nice soft cloth, and when perfectly dry, wetted with egg, and sprinkled all over with very fine bread crumbs; it will look still better to be done over with egg and crumbs a second time. Then having on the fire a thick-bottomed frying-pan, with plenty of lard or dripping, boiling hot; put the fish into it, and let it fry tolerably quick till it is done, and of a nice brown yellow. If it is done before it has obtained a nice brown color, the pan should be drawn to the side of the fire, the fish carefully taken up, and placed either upon a sieve turned upwards, or on the under side of a dish, and placed before the fire to drain, and finish browning; if wanted particularly nice, a sheet of cap paper must be put to receive the fish. Fish fried in oil obtains a much finer color than when done in lard or dripping. Butter should never be used, as it gives a bad color. Garnish your dish with a fringe of curled raw parsley, or with fried parsley.

When fish is to be broiled, it must be seasoned, floured, and done on a very clean gridiron; which, when hot, should be rubbed over with suet, to hinder the fish from sticking. It should be broiled over a very clear fire, to prevent its tasting smoky, and great care must be taken not to scorch it.

FISH. This department of the business of the kitchen requires considerable experience, and depends more upon practice than any other. A very few moments, more or less, will thoroughly spoil fish; which, to be eaten in perfection, must never be put on the table till the soup is taken off.

So many circumstances operate on this occasion, that it is almost impossible to write general rules.

There are decidedly different opinions whether fish should be put into cold, tepid, or boiling water.

Fish must by no means be allowed to remain in the water after it is boiled; if therefore it should be ready before it can be sent to table, it must be dished, the cover put on, and a cloth put over it. The dish is then to be set across the fish-kettle.

Fish should be fried over a clear quick fire; and with dripping, or hog's lard in preference to butter. The pan should be deep; and to ascertain that it is clean, a little fat is first fried in it, poured out, and the pan wiped with a clean cloth; as much dripping or lard is then put in as will entirely cover the fish. When it is boiling hot, and begins to smoke, the fish is put in; if small, they may be turned in three or four minutes, by sticking in a fork near the head with one hand, and with the other supporting the tail with a fish-slice. When they are done, they should be laid before the fire upon an old soft towel, and turned now and then till they are dry upon both sides; or they may be put upon a large sieve, turned upwards, and which is kept for the purpose, or put on the under side of a dish.

The fire for broiling fish must be very clear, and the gridiron perfectly clean, which, when hot, should be rubbed with a bit of suet. The fish, while broiling, must be often turned.

Several respectable fishmongers and experienced cooks have assured the editor, that they are often in danger of losing their credit by fish too fresh, and especially turbot and cod, which, like meat, require a certain time before they are in the best condtion to be dressed. They recommend them to be put into cold water, salted in proportion of about a quarter of a pound of salt to a gallon of water. Sea-water is best to boil sea-fish in. It not only saves the expense of salt, but the flavor is better. Let them boil slowly till done; the sign of which is, that the skin of the fish rises up, and the eyes turn white.

It is the business of the fishmonger to clean them, &c. but the careful cook will always wash them again.

Garnish with slices of lemon, finely scraped horseradish, fried oysters, smelts, whitings or strips of soles.

The liver, roe, and chitterlings should be placed so that the carver may observe them, and invite the guest to partake of them.

Fish, like meat, requires more cooking in cold than in warm weather. If it becomes FROZEN, it must be thawed by the means we have directed for meat.

Fish are plenty and good, and in great variety, in all the towns and cities on the extensive coast of the United States. Some of the interior towns are also supplied with fish peculiar to the lakes and rivers of this country.

All kinds of fish are best sometime before they begin to spawn; and are unfit for food for sometime after they have spawned.

Fish, like animals, are fittest for the table when they are just full grown; and what has been said respecting vegetables, applies equally well to fish.

The most convenient utensil to boil fish in, is a turbot-kettle. This should be twenty-four inches long, twenty-two wide, and nine deep. It is an excellent vessel to boil a ham in, &c. &c.

N. B.—The liver of the fish pounded and mixed with butter, with a little lemon-juice &c. is an elegant and inoffensive relish to fish. Mushroom sauce extempore or the soup of mock turtle, will make an excellent fish sauce.

For liquids, you have meat gravy, lemon-juice, sirup of lemons, essence of anchovy, the various vegetable essences; mushroom catchup, and the whites and yolks of eggs, wines, and the essence of spices.

FISH, NEW METHOD OF DRESSING. Take any sort of fish you think proper, being very careful that it is quite fresh; clean it thoroughly, dry, and season it to your taste; then put it (without any moisture), into a pan, which may be closely covered; with the exception of a small hole, to allow of evaporation. Put it into an oven as soon as the bread is drawn, and let it stand until the whole is so completely dissolved, that the bones are not perceptible. When cold, this makes a very transparent, well-flavored jelly.

FISH CONSOMME. Take carp, tench, perch, eels, pike, and other fresh-water fish of the same kind; clean them well, and cut them into pieces, as near of a size as may be; lay them in a stewpan, on a layer of sliced onions and carrots; as soon as they begin to sweat, put in a bit of butter, and leave them for a quarter of an hour; moisten them with fish broth, and let them boil gently for an hour; keep the pan closely covered; this will afford a very nourishing broth.

FISH KETCHUP. Take rather more than a pint of vinegar, three pints of red Port, two table-spoonfuls of pepper, pounded very fine, plenty of shallots and horseradish, the peel of half a lemon, and two or three bay-leaves, and a pound of anchovies; let the whole boil together until the anchovies are dissolved, then strain, and when cold, put it into bottles. Two or three spoonfuls are sufficient for a pound of butter.

FISH FORCEMEAT. Take two ounces of either turbot, sole, lobster, shrimps, or oysters; free from skin, put it in a mortar with two ounces of fresh butter, one ounce of bread-crumbs, the yolk of two eggs boiled hard, and a little eschalot, grated lemon-peel, and parsley, minced very fine; then pound it well till it is thoroughly mixed and quite smooth; season it with salt and Cayenne to your taste; break in the yolk and white of one egg, rub it well together, and it is ready for use. Oysters parboiled and minced fine, and an anchovy, may be added.

FISH GRAVY. (1) Cut two or three little fish of any kind into small pieces; put them into a saucepan, with rather more water than will cover them, a bit of toasted bread, a blade of mace, some lemon-peel, whole pepper, and a bunch of sweet-herbs; let it simmer gently till it is rich and good; brown a little bit of butter in a stewpan, and when it is browned, strain the gravy into it; and let it boil for a few minutes.

FISH GRAVY. (2) Put some slices of onion into a stewpan, and heat them on the fire; when they are completely dissolved, add a piece of butter, and some small fish, or pieces of carp, tench, perch or any other you find convenient. As soon as they begin to dissolve, and give out their moisture; put a glassful of root broth to them, and boil them for half an hour; then add a glass of white wine, and a little lemon-juice, and boil it another half hour, when it may be pressed through a sieve, with great force.

FISH RECHAUFFE. (1) After pike, cod, skate, turbot, soles, or any other white fish has been dressed, pick it from the bones into small bits; add to a pound of fish, or in the same proportion, half a pint of good cream, one table-spoonful of mustard, the same of anchovy essence, the same of ketchup, and of Harvey sauce, a little flour, some salt, pepper, and butter; make it all hot in the saucepan, then put it into a dish in which it is to be served up, strew crumbs of bread over it, and baste it with butter till it is a little moist, then brown it with a salamander, or in a Dutch oven. A wall of mashed potatoes round the dish is an improvement.

FISH RECHAUFFE. (2) Pick from the bone in large flakes about two pounds of cold salmon, cod fish, or soles; melt a quarter of a pound of butter in half a pint of cream, with a little flour and salt; add the fish and heat it thoroughly.

FISH SAUCE. *See Sauces*.

FLEMISH WAFERS. Put into a deep pan half a pound of flour; strain and mix with it half a pint of warmed milk, and two table-spoonfuls of fresh yeast; work the paste till it be soft and smooth, and place it in a stove, or close to the fire, to rise; then add the beaten yolks of six eggs, half a pound of fresh butter beaten to a cream, and a lump of sugar which has been rubbed upon the peel of a lemon, and then pounded; last of all, beat in lightly the well-whisked whites of the eggs; again place the pan in a warm place, and it will rise to nearly double its bulk. Heat and rub the irons, which should be square, with a little butter; fill one side with the mixture, and close them; when one side is done turn the other, and when of a fine color, take out the wafers; put them upon a plate, and whilst hot, sift over this quantity a quarter of a pound of grated loaf sugar.

FLIP. To make a quart of flip:—Put the ale on the fire to warm, and beat up three or four eggs, with four ounces of moist sugar, a tea-spoonful of grated nutmeg or ginger, and a quartern of good old rum or brandy. When the ale nearly boils put it into one pitcher, and the rum, eggs, &c. into another; turn it from one to another till it is as smooth as cream. This is called a *Yard of Flannel*.

FLOATING ISLAND. Boil; with a pint of milk, a bit of cinnamon, and half the peel of a lemon; when almost cold, strain it, and mix with it the beaten white of one, and the yolks of three eggs; stir it over the fire till thick, pour it into a dish, and stir it now and then till cold. Whisk the whites of two eggs, and half a pint of Guava, quince, or red currant jelly, till it be very stiff.

FLOUNDERS BOILED. (1) Put on a stewpan with a sufficient quantity of water to cover the flounders which are to be dressed; put in some vinegar and horse-radish; when the water boils put in the fish, having been first well cleaned, and their fins cut off; they must not boil too fast for fear they should break; when they are sufficiently done, lay them on a fish plate, the tails in the middle. Serve them with parsley and butter.

FLOUNDERS BOILED. (2) Wash and clean them well, cut the black side of them the same as you do turbot, then put them into a fish-kettle, with plenty of cold water and a handful of salt; when they come to a boil, skim them clean, and let them stand by the side of the fire for five minutes, and they are ready. *Obs.*—Eaten with plain melted butter and a little salt, you have the sweet delicate flavor of the flounder, which is overpowered by any sauce.

FLOUNDERS OR PLAICE, FRIED OR BOILED. Flounders are perhaps the most difficult fish to fry very nicely. Clean them well, flour them, and wipe them with a dry cloth to absorb all the water from them; flour or egg and bread-crumb them.

FLUMMERY. Steep three large handfuls of very small white oatmeal a day and night in cold water; then pour it off clear; then add as much more water, and let it stand another day and night. Then strain it through a fine hair sieve, and boil it till it is of the consistence of hasty pudding, keeping it well stirred all the time it is boiling. When first strained, put to it one large spoonful of white sugar, and two of orange-flower water. Pour it into shallow dishes, and serve to eat with wine, cider, milk or cream, and sugar.

FLUMMERY DUTCH. Boil very gently for half an hour, two ounces of isinglass in three half pints of water; add a pint of white wine, the juice of three lemons and the thin rind of one, and rub a few lumps of sugar on another to obtain the essence, and with them add as much more sugar as will make it sufficiently sweet; and having beaten up the yolks of seven eggs, give them and the above, well mixed, one scald; stir all the time, and pour the whole into a basin; stir it till it is half cold; then let it settle, and put into a melon shape.

FLUMMERY FRENCH. Beat an ounce of isinglass fine, put it into a quart of cream, and boil it gently for a quarter of an hour, keeping it stirring all the time. Then take it off, sweeten it with fine powder sugar, put in a spoonful of rose and another of orange-flower water, strain it through a sieve, and stir it till half cold. Put it into a mould or basin, and when cold, turn it into a dish and garnish with currant jelly.

FONDUS. Put some grated cheese into a basin, with pepper and a little melted butter; and the yolks of eggs; stir them together; whip the whites of the eggs to a firm froth, and add them, a little at a time, to the cheese, stirring lightly with a wooden spoon; half fill as many paper cases as you can, and bake them, like biscuits, in a moderate oven. Serve them as quickly as possible after they are done.

FORCEMEAT STUFFING. Forcemeat is now considered an indispensable accompaniment to most made dishes, and when composed with good taste, gives additional spirit and relish to even that "sovereign of savouriness," turtle soup.

It is also sent up in patties, and for stuffing of veal, game, poultry, &c.

The ingredients should be so proportioned, that no one flavor predominates.

To give the same stuffing for veal, hare, &c. argues a poverty of invention; with a little contrivance, you may make as great a variety as you have dishes.

The poignancy of forcemeat should be proportioned to the savouriness of the viands to which it is intended to give an additional zest. Some dishes require a very delicately flavored forcemeat, for others, it must be full and high seasoned. What would be piquante in a turkey, would be insipid with turtle.

Most people have an acquired and peculiar taste in stuffings, &c. and what exactly pleases one, seldom is precisely what another considers the most agreeable.

Custom is all in matters of taste: it is not that one person is naturally fond of this or that, and another naturally averse to it; but that one is used to it, and another is not.

The consistency of forcemeats is rather a difficult thing to manage; they are almost always either too light or too heavy.

Take care to pound it till perfectly smooth, and that all the ingredients are thoroughly incorporated.

Forcemeat-balls must not be larger than a small nutmeg. If they are for brown sauce, flour and fry them; if for white, put them into boiling water, and boil them for three minutes: the latter are by far the most delicate.

If not of sufficient stiffness, it falls to pieces, and makes soup, &c. grouty and very unsightly.

Sweetbreads and tongues are the favorite materials for forcemeat. Forcemeat should be made sufficiently consistent to cut with a knife, but not dry or heavy. No one flavor should predominate greatly; according to what it is wanted for, a selection may be made from the following list, being careful to use the least of those articles which are the most pungent:

Cold fowl, or veal, scraped ham, fat bacon, beef suet, crumbs of bread, parsley, white pepper, salt, nutmeg, yolks and whites of eggs, well beaten, to bind the mixture.

The forcemeat may be made with any of these articles without any striking flavor; therefore any of the following different ingredients may be made use of to vary the taste.

Oysters, anchovies, tarragon, savory, penny-royal, knotted-marjoram, thyme, basil, yolks of hard eggs, cayenne, garlic, shallots, chives, Jamaica pepper in fine powder, or two or three cloves.

To force or stuff turkeys, geese, ducks, &c., see under the heads of the different ways of dressing turkeys, geese, &c.

FORCEMEAT. Take an equal quantity of lean veal scraped, and beef suet shred; beat them in a marble morter; add pepper, salt, cloves, pounded lemon-peel, and nutmeg grated, parsley and sweet herbs, chopped fine, a little shallot and young onion, a few bread-crumbs grated fine, and yolk of egg sufficient to work it light; roll this into balls with a little flour; if for white sauce, boil them; if for brown sauce, fry them.

FORCEMEAT BALLS FOR FISH SOUPS, OR FISH STEWED. Beat the flesh and soft parts of a middling sized lobster, half an anchovy, a large piece of boiled celery, the yolk of a hard egg, a little Cayenne, mace, salt, and white pepper, with two tablespoonfuls of bread-crumbs, one spoonful of oyster liquor, two ounces of butter warmed, two eggs beaten for a long time; make into balls, and fry them of a nice brown color in butter.

FORCEMEAT-BALLS FOR TURTLE, MOCK TURTLE, OR MADE DISHES. Pound some veal in a marble mortar; rub it through a sieve with as much of the udder as you have veal, or about a third of the quantity of butter: put some bread crumbs into a stewpan, moisten them with milk, add a little chopped parsley and eschalot, rub them well together in a mortar till they form a smooth paste; put it through a sieve; and, when cold, pound, and mix all together, with the yolks of three eggs boiled hard; season it with salt, pepper, and curry powder, or Cayenne; add to it the yolks of two raw eggs; rub it well together, and make small balls: ten minutes before your soup is ready, put them in.

FOWLS. When a cock is young, his

spurs are short; take care that you are not deceived by their having been cut or pared, a trick that is often practised. If fresh their vent will be close and dark. Hens are best, just before they begin to lay, and yet are full of egg; if they are old, their combs and legs are rough.

All poultry should be very carefully picked, every plug removed, and the hair nicely singed with paper.

The cook should be careful in drawing poultry of all sorts, not to break the gallbag, for no washing will take off the bitter where it has touched.

If for roasting, black-legged fowls are the most moist. A good-sized fowl will take from three-quarters of an hour to an hour in roasting, a middling-sized one about half an hour, and a very small one, or chicken, twenty minutes.

Tame fowls require more roasting, and are longer in heating through than others. All sorts should be continually basted, that they may be served with a froth, and appear of a fine color. The fire must be very quick and clear before any fowls are put down. Serve with egg sauce, bread sauce, or garnished with sausages or scalded parsley.

A large barn-door fowl, well hung, should be stuffed in the crop with sausage-meat, and served with gravy in the dish, and with bread sauce.

The head should be turned under the wing, like a turkey.

For boiling, choose those that are not black legged; pick them carefully, singe, wash, and truss them. Flour them, and put them in boiling water; a good-sized one will be done in half an hour.

Serve with parsley and butter; oyster, lemon, liver, or celery sauce. If for dinner, ham, tongue, or bacon, is commonly served with them.

Fowls are trussed in the same manner as chickens. (See *Chickens*).

Chickens or fowls should be killed at least one or two days before they are to be dressed.

Turkeys (especially large ones) should not be dressed till they have been killed three or four days at least, in cold weather six or eight, or they will neither look white or eat tender.

Turkeys, and large fowls, should have the strings or sinews of the thighs drawn out.

Truss them with the legs outward, they are much easier carved.

FOWL A LA HOLANDAISE. Make a forcemeat of grated bread, half its quantity of minced suet, an onion, or few oysters, and some boiled parsley, season with pepper, salt, and grated lemon-peel, and an egg beaten up to bind it. Bone the breast of a good-sized young fowl, put in the force-meat, cover the fowl with a piece of white paper buttered, and roast it rather more than half an hour; have ready a thick batter made of flour, milk, and eggs, take off the paper, and pour some of the batter over the fowl; as soon as it becomes dry add more, and do this till it is all crusted over, and of a nice brown color; serve it with melted butter and lemon pickle, or a thickened brown gravy.

FOWL BOILED WITH RICE. Stew a fowl in some well-skimmed clear mutton broth, and seasoned with onion, mace, pepper, and salt. About half an hour before it is ready, put in quarter of a pint of rice well washed and soaked. Simmer till tender; then strain it from the broth, and put the rice on a sieve before the fire. Keep the fowl hot, lay it in the middle of a dish, and the rice round it without the broth. The less liquor the fowl is done with, the better. Serve with gravy, or parsley and butter for sauce.

FOWL BROILED. Split them down the back, well salt and pepper them; then broil them. Serve with mushroom sauce.

FOWL CAPILOTADE. Take the remains of a ready dressed fowl, and put them into a stewpan; then do up some parsley, shallots, and four mushrooms, all shred small, in a little butter; as soon as the latter becomes liquid, add four ladlefuls of *espagnole*, and two of *consomme*, reduce, and skim it; pour it on your fowl, set it on the fire to simmer for a quarter of an hour, before you send it to table.

FOWL CURRY. *See Curry.*

FOWLS DRESSED TO DRESS AGAIN. Cut them in quarters, beat up an egg or two (according to the quantity you dress) with a little grated nutmeg, and pepper and salt, some parsley minced fine, and a few crumbs of bread; mix these well together, and cover the fowl, &c. with this batter, broil them, or put them in a Dutch oven, or have ready some dripping hot in a pan, in which fry them a light brown color; thicken a little gravy with some flour, put a large spoonful of catchup to it, lay the fry in a dish, and pour the sauce round it. You may garnish with slices of lemon and toasted bread.

☞ *Turkey, Goose, Duck, Rabbit, Pigeon, are all dressed same way.*

FOWL, GAME, OR RABBIT HASHED. Cut them into joints, put the trimmings into a stewpan with a quart of the broth they were boiled in, and a large onion cut in four; let it boil half an hour; strain it through a sieve: then put two table-spoonfuls of flour in a basin, and mix it well by degrees with the hot broth; set it on the fire to boil up, then strain it through a fine sieve: wash out the stewpan, lay the poultry in it, and pour the gravy on it (through a sieve); set it by the side of the fire to simmer very gently (it must not boil) for fifteen minutes; five minutes before you serve it up, cut the stuffing in slices, and put it in to warm, then take it out, and lay it round the edge of the dish, and put the poultry in the middle; carefully skim the fat off the gravy, then shake it round well in the stewpan, and pour it to the hash. N. B.— You may garnish the dish with bread sippets lightly toasted.

FOWL HASHED. Cut a cold roasted fowl into pieces as for a fricassee, put the trimmings into a saucepan with two or three shallots, a little lemon-peel, a blade of mace, a quarter of a pound of lean ham, and a pint of stock; simmer it for half an hour, strain it, put a bit of butter into a saucepan, and when melted, dredge in as much flour as will dry it up, stirring it all the time; then add the gravy, let it boil a minute, and put in the fowl, also a little pepper, salt, and a dust of sugar. Before serving, squeeze in a little lemon-juice.

FOWL MINCED WITH VEAL. Mince the white part of a cold roasted or boiled fowl; put it, and some thin slices of veal, into a saucepan, also some white stock, a squeeze of a lemon, a few drops of shallot vinegar, and a dust of sugar; simmer it for a short time, and serve it upon bread sippets, with the slices of veal laid on the mince.

FOWL PULLED. Skin a cold chicken, fowl or turkey; take off the fillets from the breasts, and put them into a stewpan with the rest of the white meat and wings, sidebones, and merry-thought, with a pint of broth, a large blade of mace pounded, an eschalot minced fine, the juice of half a lemon, and a roll of the peel, some salt, and a few grains of cayenne; thicken it with flour and butter, and let it simmer for two or three minutes, till the meat is warm. In the meantime, score the eggs and rump, powder them with pepper and salt, broil them nicely brown, and lay them on, or round your pulled chicken. Three table-spoonfuls of good cream, or the yolks of as many eggs, will be a great improvement to it.

FOWL OR RABBIT. We can only recommend this method of dressing when the fire is not good enough for roasting. Pick and truss it the same as for boiling, cut it open down the back, wipe the inside clean with a cloth, season it with a little pepper and salt, have a clear fire, and set the gridiron at a good distance over it, lay the chicken on with the inside towards the fire (you may egg it and strew some grated bread over it), and broil it till it is a fine brown: take care the fleshy side is not burned. Lay it on a hot dish; pickled mushrooms, or mushroom sauce thrown over it, or parsley and butter, or melted butter flavored with mushroom ketchup. Garnish it with slices of lemon; and the liver and gizzard slit and notched, seasoned with pepper and salt, and broiled nicely brown, with some slices of lemon.

FOWLS WITH RICE, CALLED PIL-LACE. Boil a pint of rice in as much water as will cover it, with black pepper, a few blades of mace, and half a dozen cloves tied up in a bit of cloth; when the rice is tender, take out the spice; stir in a piece of butter; boil a fowl and a piece of bacon; lay them in the dish, cover them with the rice: lay round the dish, and upon the rice, hard eggs, cut in halves, quarters, and lengthways, with onions, first boiled, and then fried.

FOWLS ROASTED. Well pepper and salt the fowls before you split them; roast them before a clear fire; froth them up when nearly done by sprinkling them over with flour and salt, and basting them with butter. When done, be careful in taking out the skewers. Serve them with very good clear gravy in the dish, and bread or egg sauce in a boat.

FOWL ROASTED WITH CHEST-NUTS. Roast some chestnuts very carefully, so that they may not be burnt, then take off the skins, and peel them. Take about a dozen of them, cut them small and bruise them in a mortar. Parboil the liver of a fowl; bruise it, and cut about a quarter of a pound of ham or bacon, and pound it. Then mix them all together, with a good quantity of chopped parsley, sweet herbs, some mace, pepper, salt, and nutmeg. When these are are all well mixed together, put it into your fowl, and roast it. The best way of doing this is to tie the neck, and hang it up by the legs to roast, with a string, and then baste it with butter. For sauce, take the rest of the chestnuts, peel and skin them, put them into some good gravy with a little white wine; and thicken it with a piece of butter rolled in flour. Then place your fowl in the dish; pour in the sauce; garnish with lemon, and serve.

FOWL WITH ITS OWN GRAVY. Truss a fowl the same as for boiling, lard it quite through with bacon, ham, and parsley; put it in a pan with a little butter, two or three slices of peeled lemon, a bundle of sweet herbs, three cloves, sliced onions, carrots, pepper, salt, a little stock, and a glass of white wine; stew them gently till they are done; skim and strain the sauce, and serve it with the fowl.

FOWL, WILD. The flavor of wild fowl is preserved better by not stuffing them; put into each, pepper, salt, and a bit of butter. Wild fowl do not require so much dressing as tame; they should be done of a fine color, and nicely frothed. A rich brown gravy should be served in the dish, and when the breast is cut into slices, before it is taken from the bone, it will be much improved by a squeeze of lemon, some salt and pepper. If you wish to take off the fishy smell which these birds frequently have, put an onion, salt, and hot water into the dripping pan, and for the first ten minutes baste them with this; then remove the pan, and keep constantly basting with batter.

FRAISE. *See Calf's Chitterlings*.

FRANGIPANE. Take a saucepan, and put into it five spoonfuls of flour, five eggs, a pint of milk, an ounce of butter and a little salt; set it on the fire, stirring constantly until it has boiled ten minutes, taking great care that it does not burn; then pour it into a basin, and let it cool. Take a few almonds, (to every six sweet put one bitter), bruise them, and some macaroons, and when reduced to powder, mix them with a little crisped orange-flour (also in powder), and a sufficient quantity of powder-sugar to sweeten it: add these to the above preparation, and stir them in well with a wooden spoon. If your frangipane be too thick, add another egg or two, and then make whatever use of it you may desire. You may, if you think proper, substitute pistachios for the sweet almonds, in which case a little spinach essence must be added to color it, the macaroons and orange-flowers omitted, and three bitter almonds only used.

FRENCH BEANS. Cut off the stalk end first, and then turn to the point and strip off the strings. If not quite fresh, have a bowl of spring-water, with a little salt dissolved in it, standing before you, and as the beans are cleaned and stringed, throw them in. When all are done, put them on the fire in boiling water, with some salt in it; after they have boiled fifteen or twenty minutes, take one out and taste it; as soon as they are tender take them up; throw them into a colander or sieve to drain. To send up the beans whole is much the best method when they are thus young, and their delicate flavor and color are much better preserved. When a little more grown, they must be cut across in two after stringing; and for common tables they are split, and divided across; cut them all the same length, but those who are nice never have them at such a growth as to require splitting. When they are very large they look pretty cut into lozenges.

FRENCH BEANS, NASTURTIUMS, &c. When young, and most other small green vegetables, may be pickled the same way as gherkins.

FRENCH BEANS FOR WINTER USE. Gather them when young, and on a dry day, put a layer of salt into a jar, and then one of about two inches thick of beans; do this till the jar be nearly full; place a small plate upon the top of them, and tie a bladder closely over the jar; keep it in a cool dry place. When to be used, soak them a night in cold water, and change it on them repeatedly in the course of the day they are to be dressed. Cut them, and put them on in boiling water.

FRENCH BEANS TO DRESS DRIED. Boil for more than two hours, in two quarts of water, a pound of the seeds or beans of scarlet runners; fill a pint basin with onions peeled or sliced, brown them in a saucepan, with rather more than a quarter of a pound of fresh butter; stir them constantly; strain the water from the beans, and mix them with the onions; add a teaspoonful of pepper, some salt, and a little gravy. Let them stew for ten minutes, and stir in the beaten yolks of two eggs, and a table-spoonful of vinegar. Serve them hot.

FRENCH SUPPER DISH. Pare off the crust, and cut one or two slices of bread into bits of two or three inches square; fry them in butter; put them upon a hot dish, and lay upon each bit some warmed preserve, or stew for a few minutes, in sweet wine and a little sugar, some stoned bloom raisins, and put them upon and round the toast. The preserves may be heated by placing the jars in hot water by the side of the fire.

FRIARS' CHICKEN. Put four pounds of a knuckle of veal into four quarts of water; boil it gently for two hours; strain it off; cut three chickens, or two young fowls into joints; skin them, and when the broth boils put them in; season with white pepper and salt; let them boil a short time, and add a handful of parsley chopped small; when the chickens are boiled tender, have ready six or seven well-beaten eggs; stir them quickly into the broth one way, immediately before taking it off the fire. This broth may be made entirely of veal instead of chickens.

FRICANDELLANS. Mince about two pounds of tender lean beef, and three-quarters of a pound of fresh suet, then pound it till it be as smooth as a paste, and carefully pick out all the threads and sinews, add four well-beaten eggs, half a pint of rich cream, and as much grated and sifted bread as will make it sufficiently consistent to form into rolls resembling corks, and season it with salt, and pepper. Boil the corks in some good stock, or in boiling water.

FRICASSEE BROWN. Take two or three young rabbits, cut them in pieces, and stew them in gravy made of beef, some whole pepper, two shallots, one or two anchovies, a bit of horse-radish, and a little sweet marjoram powdered small. Stew the rabbits about a quarter of an hour, then take them out of the gravy, strain the liquor, fry your rabbits in lard or butter; add a glass of claret; you may fry some forcemeat balls, made with the livers of the rabbits parboiled, and a little parsley  shred small, some nutmeg grated, pepper, salt, a few bread crumbs, and two buttered eggs; mix these all together, make them up into balls, dip them in the yolk of egg, roll them in flour, then fry them, and garnish your dish with them, with fried parsley, and sliced lemon.

FRICASSEE WHITE.  Cut a couple of rabbits into pieces, and let them soak in warm water to cleanse them from the blood; then lay them in a cloth to dry; put them into a stewpan with milk and water, and let them stew till they are tender, and then take a clean pan, and put into it half a pint of cream, and a quarter of a pound of butter; stir them well together till the butter is melted; be careful to keep it constantly stirring, or it will be greasy; put in the rabbits, take a little dried mace, a little pounded nutmeg, and a few mushrooms; shake them together for a few minutes, and then  put it to the rabbits. You may add white wine if you choose.

FRIED TOASTS. Cut the crumb of a twopenny loaf into round or oblong pieces, nearly an inch thick, and soak them for four or five hours in a pint of cream, mixed with three well-beaten eggs, half a pint of white wine, a little grated nutmeg, and sweetened with pounded loaf sugar. Fry them  in butter, till of a light brown color, and serve with wine and sugar sauce.

FRITTERS. (1) Make them of any of the batters directed for pancakes, by dropping a small quantity into the pan, or make the plainer sort, and put pared apples sliced and cored in the batter, and fry some of it with each slice. Currants or sliced lemon, as thin as possible, are very nice.

FRITTERS. (2) Fritters should be sent to table served upon a folded napkin in the dish.  Any sort of  sweetmeat or ripe fruit, may be made into fritters.

FRITTERS,  ENGLISH-AND-FRENCH. Take a marrow pudding, and when nearly cold, cut it into thin slices, and then cut them again into pieces two inches long, by three-quarters of an inch wide, dip them into batter, then fry them in the usual manner; when drained, glaze them with fine sugar, and serve  them very hot.  The batter for the fritters is made as follows:—Put a glass and a half of water, a  grain of salt, and two ounces of fresh butter into a saucepan; when it boils stir in a sufficient quantity of flour to make it a rather firm batter, keep it stirring three minutes, then pour it into  another vessel.

FRITTERS A LA DAUPHINE. Take a pound of *brioche* paste, and roll it out as thin as possible, to  the form of a long square, on part of this lay  small quantities of apricot marmalade at intervals,  slightly wet the paste round each piece of preserve, and lay over the plain part of the paste so as to  cover the other completely, press it down lightly that the  marmalade may not escape in the cooking, and cut out your fritters with a circular paste-cutter of  two inches in diameter; flour them a little, and then lay them in rather a hot friture, when the paste will swell them into little balls; as soon as they are of a proper color take them out, drain them on a napkin, sprinkle them with fine sugar, and serve them.

FRITTERS A LA COTE. Soak in brandy some leaves and the young and tender shoots of the vine, dip them in a batter made of milk, yolks of eggs, and flour, fry them in boiling oil, sprinkle them with sugar. Elder flowers are made into fritters in the same manner.

FRITTERS AU BLANC. Mix together a handful of rice-flour and some milk, set them on the fire, stirring constantly, add a little cream, sugar, lemon-peel, and orange-flowers; when it has become of a proper consistence, take it from the fire; as soon as it is cold, roll it into balls about the size of a nut, dip them in batter and fry them.

FRITTERS BLONDIN. Put some butter into a saucepan, and when it is melted add to it a glass of milk, and a pinch of salt, keep it on the fire till it boils; then mix in a sufficient quantity of flour to make it into a consistent paste, which will not stick to the fingers; spread it on a table, roll it out to the thickness you may require, cut it into round, oval, or any other formed pieces you may think proper, and fry them of a nice color, in the best oil; sprinkle sugar over, and serve them.

FRITTERS, FRENCH, OF BRANDY FRUITS. Take a dozen apricots (or other fruits) preserved in brandy, drain, and cut them in half: then wrap them in wafers cut round and previously moistened, dip them in the same kind of batter as that used for fritters *English-and-French*, and fry them; sprinkle them with sugar, and serve.

FRITTERS EN SURPRISE. Take eight middling-sized apples, pare, and leave on the stalks; cut off about a fourth part of the stalk end of each apple, and scoop out the inside of each piece, so as to form a sort of cup with a lid; put them to soak for two hours in a glass of brandy with a little lemon-peel and cinnamon; at the end of that time take them out, drain, and fill each apple with apricot marmalade, or frangipane; mix up a little flour and white of egg to cement the tops of the apples to the other parts; dip them in batter and fry them. When they are of a proper color, glaze and serve them.

FRITTERS MIGNON. Put two good spoonfuls of flour into a stewpan, and mix it with the whites and yolks of two eggs, a little salt, two ounces of sugar, some lemon-peel grated, half a tea-spoonful of milk, and half a tea-spoonful of cream; stir it over a slow fire, and, when done and well thickened, spread the cream upon a floured dish, shake flour over it, and, when cold, cut it into bits with a paste-cutter, dip each bit into a paste made with two spoonfuls of flour, a spoonful of brandy, and a little salt, mixed with two eggs; fry the fritters, and serve, glazed with sugar and a salamander.

FRITTERS, ROYAL. Put a quart of new milk into a saucepan, and as soon as it begins to boil, pour in a pint of white wine; then take it off and let it stand five or six minutes, skim off the curd, and put it into a basin; beat it up well with six eggs, and season it with nutmeg; then beat it with a whisk, and add flour sufficient to give it the proper consistence of batter. Put in some sugar and fry them quick.

FRITTERS, SOUFFLES. Make some flour and beer into a batter that will flow a little; take a little of it out with a spoon, throw it into a frying-pan with boiling oil; the moment it rises, take it out, and proceed in the same way till all the batter is used; then sprinkle them with salt, and serve.

FROMAGE CUIT. Cut half a pound of Cheshire cheese into thin bits, and pound it in a mortar; add by degrees the well-beaten yolks of two, and the white of one egg, and half a pint of cream; mix it well together and bake it for ten or fifteen minutes.

FROST OR ICING FOR CAKES. Beat till very light the whites of four eggs, and add gradually three-quarters of a pound of double-refined sugar, pounded and sifted through a lawn sieve; mix in the juice of half a lemon, beat it till very light and white; place the cake before the fire, pour over it the icing, and smooth over the top and sides with the back of a spoon.

FROTH TO PUT ON CREAM, CUSTARD, OR TRIFLE. Sweeten half a pound of the pulp of damsons, or any other sort of scalded fruit; put to it the whites of four eggs beaten, and beat the pulp with them till it will stand as high as you wish, and being put on the cream, &c, with a spoon, it will take any form; it should be rough, to imitate a rock.

FRUIT, CANDIED. (1) It must first be preserved, then dipped in warm water, dried with a cloth, and strewed all over with sifted sugar, and dried in a stove or oven, turning as occasion requires.

FRUIT, CANDIED. (2) When the fruit is preserved, dry it in a stove till the sirup is quite out, dip it into sirup boiled to candy height, and dry it again. All dried and candied fruit must be kept in a very dry place.

FRUIT IN JELLY. Have in readiness a plain mould, either long or round, about three inches deep; then have ready some mould jelly, and spread it at the bottom of the mould, about a quarter of an inch thick; let it be cold; then put in ripe peaches, grapes, or any sort of ripe fruit you please, preserved fruit, or China oranges cut into quarters, or whatever shape you choose; put in a little warm jelly, and let it stand till it is cold, to fasten the fruit in its place, otherwise it will rise up; then fill the mould up with warm jelly, let it stand till it is quite cold, then turn it into a dish, and garnish it according to your own taste.

FRUIT, PRESERVED, REMARKS ON USING. Preserved fruits should not be baked long; those that have been presented with their full proportion of sugar, require no baking; the crust should be baked in a tin shape, and the fruit be afterwards added; or it may be put into a small dish or tartpans, and the covers be baked on a tin cut out according to your taste.

FRUIT, TO PREPARE FOR BRANDY. Take the proposed quantity of fruit, gathered before they are perfectly ripe; dry them carefully, prick and put them into cold water; when all in, set the vessel over a moderate fire, keeping the water, however, constantly nearly boiling, until the fruit will give to the touch; then throw them, with great care, into cold water again; drain away this water, and add fresh; change the water twice more within a quarter of an hour, after which, drain them for the last time, and put them in bottles; if any of the fruit is the least broken or bruised, it must be put aside, as it would spoil the rest. In the meanwhile, take a proper quantity of sugar (as a pound and a half for twenty-five peaches); clarify and boil it to *la nappe*; measure, and put double its quantity of good brandy; mix and pour them into a glazed pan; let them stand awhile, and then pour the mixture on the fruit.

FRUIT TO PREPARE FOR CHILDREN. Put apples sliced, or plums, currants, gooseberries, &c. into a stone jar, and sprinkle as much Lisbon sugar as necessary among them; place the jar on a hot hearth, or in a saucepan of water, and let it remain till the fruit is perfectly done. Slices of bread or rice may be stewed with the fruit, or the fruit may be eaten with slices of dry bread, or with rice, plain boiled.

G.

GAME. In choosing venison, the fat of that which is good is thick, clear, and bright; the clift part smooth and close. When the venison is perfectly fresh, it is hung in a cool place, and carefully wiped dry every day. When extreme tenderness is required from long keeping, but without its having a high flavor, it is well rubbed over with powdered charcoal.

The haunch is the prime joint, and when it is required to be roasted, it is first well washed in lukewarm milk-and-water, and then made quite dry before it is spitted. It is then covered with a sheet of well-buttered white paper, over which is laid a coarse paste of flour-and-water, about a quarter of an inch thick; this is again covered with buttered white paper, and tied on with pack-thread. A substantial fire being made, the haunch is put down, and constantly basted with fresh beef dripping, till nearly done, when the paste is taken off, the meat well basted with butter, and lightly dredged with flour, till it froths and becomes of a fine light brown color. It is served with its own gravy in the dish, if there be enough of it; also a sauce tureen of good brown gravy, and one of currant jelly sauce beat up, and melted with a little Port wine and sugar.

A large haunch takes about four hours to roast.

A neck and shoulder, when roasted, is managed in the same way as the haunch, omitting the paste; but it is more frequently used for soups, pasties, and collops.

Hare.—When fresh the body is stiff; and if young, the claws are smooth and sharp, the ears tender and easily torn. Hares are kept from a week to a fortnight for roasting; but for soup, they cannot have been too recently killed.

Rabbits are chosen by the same rules as hares.

Wild fowl, in general, is chosen by the same rules as tame poultry. The birds should be plump and fat, and hard in the vent. If the skin comes off when rubbed hard with the finger, they are stale. Old birds improve by keeping for sometime; young birds are best if dressed soon; and small birds, of all descriptions, should be immediately dressed. In warm weather, a stopper of charcoal should be put into the vent of all game, and a string tied tightly round the neck.

To roast pheasants and partridges, they are picked, cleaned, and nicely singed; a slit is made in the back part of the neck, and the craw taken out, leaving on the head, the feet twisted closely to the body, the claws cut off, and the head turned under the wing. Both sorts are roasted by the directions for roasting a turkey or a fowl. A pheasant is served with gravy in the dish; partridges with a gravy, or laid upon buttered toast, and melted butter poured round them. Bread sauce is served with both. A pheasant will require nearly an hour to roast; partridges half an hour. Guinea, and pea-fowl are roasted in the same way as pheasants.

To roast black-cock, follow the directions for roasting pheasants and partridges; it will require an hour, and is served with gravy in the dish, and bread sauce in a sauce tureen.

Moorfowl are roasted in the same manner, and require three-quarters of an hour. They may be served upon buttered toast, or with gravy in the dish, and bread sauce in a sauce tureen.

To restore tainted game or poultry, pick it carefully, clean, and wash it, then put into each bird a little newly-made pounded charcoal, tied in a bit of muslin. Before serving, take out the bag, which will have a most offensive smell, while the bird will be left perfectly sweet.

To roast wild duck.—It should be roasted by a quick fire, well basted with butter, and browned. It will require nearly three-quarters of an hour, and when to be served, some beef gravy is poured through the duck into the dish, and in a sauce tureen some hot Port wine is served. The carver makes four cuts along the breast, it is then sprinkled with salt and a little Cayenne, the juice of half a lemon is squeezed over it, and the Port wine is then poured all over.

To roast a wild goose, the same directions are followed as for wild duck, allowing more time to roast it, according to the size of the bird.

Widgeons and teal are dressed in the same manner as the wild duck, and are roasted in ten minutes, and may be served upon fried bread crumbs.

Woodcocks and snipes are roasted without being drawn; a piece of toasted bread buttered is put under each bird, to catch the trail; they are well basted with butter, and served upon the hot toast over which they were roasted; a rich brown gravy, or melted butter, is poured round them. Woodcocks will require half an hour, snipes and quails fifteen or twenty minutes to roast.

Ortolans and green plovers are not drawn, and are roasted and served in the manner as woodcocks.

To roast larks, wheatears, and other small birds, they are nicely picked, gutted, cleaned, and trussed; brushed over with melted butter, and rolled in grated bread, then spitted on a bird spit which is fastened upon a larger one. They are basted with butter, and sprinkled with some bread crumbs. They will require nearly fifteen minutes to roast, and are served upon fried bread crumbs, and brown gravy in a sauce tureen.

Wild pigeons may be roasted, or made into a pie.

Plover's eggs are boiled hard, and served in a napkin, or with green moss put round each in the dish.

GAME, ESSENCE OF. Take four rabbits, four partridges, two pounds of veal, two pounds of steaks; put them into a stewpan, with a bottle of white wine; boil them until the whole is entirely re- ducd to a jelly; then add to it broth, and *consomme*, (equal quanties of each), eight carrots, ten onions, three cloves, a little thyme and basil; let the whole boil very gently, until the meat is quite done; then strain it through a napkin. No salt need be put into it, as the broth and *consomme* are sufficiently seasoned to flavor the *es- sence of game.*

GAME FRITTERS. Take any of those parts of cold roasted game, which can be cut into thin slices, dip them into good batter, and fry them in olive oil, or lard. Sprinkle the fritters when done, with salt and spices, pounded very fine.

GAME HASHED. *See Fowl.*

GARLIC BUTTER SAUCE. Pound half a dozen cloves of garlic; rub them through a silk sieve, with a wooden spoon; put this into a mortar with some butter, and beat it until thoroughly incor- porated; then put this butter into any sauce you please.

GARLIC, ESSENCE OF. Take an earthen skillet, place it on the fire, and put into it a bottle of white wine, half a glass of vinegar, the juice of two lemons, six cloves of garlic, the same number of cloves, the quarter of a nutmeg, and two bay-leaves: when near boiling, reduce the fire, and let it stand on hot ashes for seven or eight hours; strain it through a coarse sieve, and then filter it. Keep it in very closely corked bot- tles. A very small quantity of this essence is requisite to impart its flavor to a dish.

GARLIC GRAVY. Slice a pound and a half of veal, or beef; season it with pepper and salt; put it into a stewpan, with two car- rots split, and four cloves of garlic sliced, a quarter of a pound of sliced ham and a large spoonful of water; put the stewpan over a gentle fire, and watch when the meat begins to stick to the pan; when it does, turn it, and let it be very well browned, (but take care that it is not in the least burnt); then dredge it with flour, and pour in a quart of broth, a bunch of sweet herbs, a couple of cloves bruised, and slice in a lemon; set it on the fire again, then let it simmer gently for an hour and a half longer; then skim off the fat, and strain off the gravy, by pouring it through a napkin, straining and pressing it very hard.

GATEAU DE COMPIEGNE. Take three

pounds of flour, two pounds of butter, an ounce and four drachms of yeast, an ounce of salt, a quarter of a pound of sugar, a glass of cream, twelve yolks and twelve whole eggs, and five or six spoonfuls of whipped cream.

With these ingredients proceed as follows: sift the flour, of which put a fourth part on the slab, make a hole in the middle, put into it a glass of warm water and the yeast; mix them together as lightly, and with as much despatch as possible, adding more warm water if necessary; when well worked up for some minutes, gather it together, (it ought to leave the slab and the hand freely), put it into a saucepan; cover it and place it, in a tolerably warm situation to rise. Take the rest of the flour, lay it on the slab, make a hole in the middle of it, in which put the salt, sugar, and cream; stir these together well, and then put in the eggs, one at a time, (break them into a basin, in case all should not be good); the eggs being put in, add by degrees the butter, stirring them well; then mix the flour, a little at a time, with the above, until the whole is formed into a smooth paste; more eggs must be added if it be too stiff; work it up a little, and then add the leaven; work that in; and lastly, put in the whipped cream. The whole operation being thus performed, have ready a cylindrical fluted mould, (about eight inches in diameter, and nine in height); butter it by means of a sponge, being careful that it is done in all parts, otherwise the *gateau* will adhere to it; place the mould in a moderately warm place, but where there is a free current of air. When the *gateau* has risen so as to fill the mould, and the surface is a little inflated, it should be put into the oven instantly, if not, it falls and becomes heavy. The oven must be of a moderate heat, and kept closed while the *gateau* is baking; take it out in about an hour, if it be flexible and light colored, replace it for thirty or forty minutes; but if, on the contrary, it is red, and firm to the touch, place a tin plate on the top, and put it in the oven till done; remove the mould with care, and the *gateau* is finished. If the mould does not come away quite so well as it ought, strike it gently with a spatula. When taken out, put it in the oven for a few minutes to dry.

This *gateau* is sometimes varied by the addition of six ounces of sugared anise, and the same quantity of dry currants.

GATEAU DE POMMES. Boil in a pint of water one pound and a half of loaf sugar till it become a rich sirup; weigh two pounds of apples after they have been peeled, cored, and cut small; boil them in the sirup with the grated peel and juice of a large lemon till they are reduced to a pulp; put it into a mould. The following day, serve it, turned out in a glass dish, with a rich custard.

GERMAN PUFFS. (1) Mix very well with two large table-spoonfuls of flour, a quarter of a pint of cream, two well-beaten eggs, and a tea-spoonful of grated nutmeg, a very little salt, and one ounce of butter beaten to a cream; bake it in buttered cups for twenty or thirty minutes; turn them out upon a dish, and serve them instantly; pour a sweet sauce round them.

GERMAN PUFFS. (2) Beat to a cream a quarter of a pound of fresh butter, blanch and pound one ounce of sweet almonds with a little rose water, beat five yolks and three whites of eggs; mix all together with two large table-spoonfuls of flour, and sweeten it with pounded loaf sugar; bake it in buttered cups, and serve them with a sweet sauce.

GHERKINS OR CUCUMBERS PICKLED. Choose gherkins very green and straight, brush, and place a layer in a pan, sprinkle them with fine salt, then another layer of gherkins, which sprinkle with salt also, and continue this operation until you have used nearly a bushel of gherkins, leave them in the salt for twenty-four hours, which will draw all the water from them; at the end of that time drain and place them in a jar, with a handful of allspice, the same of tarragon, a little balm, ten shallots, six cloves of garlic, two or three long peppers, twenty cloves, a lemon cut in quarters, and two small handfuls of salt. Boil two gallons of the best vinegar, pour it over the gherkins, and let them stand till the next day, when boil the vinegar a second time, and pour it on again; the following day boil the vinegar for the third and last time, pour it over the gherkins, and when quite cold, cover the jar with a wet parchment.

GIBLET PIE. *See Pies.*

GIBLETS STEWED. Clean two sets of giblets, put them into a saucepan, just cover them with cold water, and set them on the fire; when they boil, take off the scum, and put in an onion, three cloves, or two blades of mace, a few berries of black pepper, the same of allspice, and half a tea-spoonful of salt; cover the stewpan close, and let it simmer very gently till the giblets are quite tender: this will take from one hour and a half to two and a half, according to the age of the giblets; the pinions will be done first and must then be taken out, and put in again to warm when the gizzards are done: watch them that they do not get too much done: take them out and thicken the sauce with flour and butter; let it boil half an hour, or till there is just enough to eat with the giblets, and then strain it through a tamis into a clean stewpan; cut the giblets into mouthfuls; put them into the sauce with the juice of half a lemon, a table-spoonful of mushroom ketchup; pour the whole into a soup-dish, with sippets of bread at the bottom. Ox-tails prepared in the same way are excellent eating.

GINGERBREAD. Rub one pound of butter well into three pounds of flour; then add one pound of powder-sugar, one pound of treacle, and two ounces of ginger pounded and sifted very fine; one nutmeg grated very fine; then warm a quarter of a pint of cream and mix all together; you may add carraways and sweetmeats if you choose; make it into a stiff paste, and bake it in a slow oven. If cake or biscuits are kept in paper or a drawer, they will acquire a disagreeable taste. A pan and cover, or tureen, will preserve them long and moist; or if to be crisp, laying them before the fire will make them so.

GINGERBREAD, AMERICAN. *See American.*

GINGERBREAD WITHOUT BUTTER. Mix two pounds of treacle; of orange, lemon, citron, and candied ginger, each four ounces, all thinly sliced; one ounce of coriander-seeds, one ounce of caraways, and one ounce of beaten ginger, in as much paste as will make a soft paste; lay it in cakes or tin plates, and bake it in a quick oven. Keep it dry in a covered earthen vessel, and it will be good for some months.

GINGERBREAD INDIAN. Take twelve ounces of pounded loaf sugar, a quarter of a pound of fresh butter, one pound of dried flour, two ounces of pounded ginger, and of cloves and cinnamon a quarter of an ounce each. Mix the ginger and the spice with the flour; put the sugar and a small tea-cupful of water into a saucepan; when it is dissolved, add the butter, and as soon it is melted, mix it with the flour and other things; work it up, and form the paste into cakes or nuts, and bake them upon tins.

GINGERBREAD, LAFAYETTE. Five eggs; half a pound of brown sugar; half a pound of fresh butter, a pint of sugar-house molasses; a pound and a half of flour; four table-spoonfuls of ginger; two large sticks of cinnamon; three dozen grains of allspice; three dozen of cloves; the juice and grated peel of two lemons. Stir the butter and sugar to a cream; beat the eggs very well; pour the molasses at once, into the butter and sugar. Add the ginger and other spice, and stir all well together. Put in the egg and flour alternately, stirring all the time. Stir the whole very hard, and put in the lemon at the last. When the whole is mixed, stir it till very light. Butter an earthen pan, or a thick tin or iron one, and put the gingerbread in it. Bake it in a moderate oven, an hour or more, according to its thickness. Take care that it do not burn. Or you may bake it in small cakes, or little tins. Its lightness will be much improved by a small tea-spoonful of pearlash dissolved in a tea-spoonful of vinegar, and stirred lightly in at the last. Too much pearlash will give it an unpleasant taste. If you use pearlash, you must omit the lemon, as its taste will be entirely destroyed by the pearlash. You may substitute for the lemon some raisins and currants, well floured to prevent their sinking.

GINGERBREAD NUTS. (1) Take four pounds of flour, half a pound of sifted sugar, an ounce of caraway-seeds, half an ounce of ginger pounded and sifted, six ounces of fresh butter, and two ounces of candied orange-peel cut into small slices; then take a pound of treacle or honey, and a gill of cream, make them warm together; mix it, with all the ingredients, into a paste, and let it lay six hours; then roll it out, make it into nuts, and bake them in a moderate oven.

GINGERBREAD NUTS. (2) Take one pound of dried and sifted flour, one pound of treacle, three ounces of brown sugar, four ounces of fresh butter, one ounce and a half of pounded and sifted ginger, of candied orange-peel and citron, cut small, three-quarters of an ounce each; melt the butter with the treacle, and when it is about milk-warm, add it to the flour and other ingredients, and then mix all well together; with a spoon drop the nuts upon buttered tins, and bake them.

GINGERBREAD NUTS. (3) Dissolve a quarter of a pound of butter in three-quarters of a pound of treacle, put it into a pan large enough to contain the rest of the ingredients, and when almost cold, stir in one pound of dried and sifted flour, half a pound of coarse brown sugar, half an ounce of caraway seeds, three-quarters of an ounce of pounded ginger, and the grated peel of a lemon; mix all these well together, and let it stand till it be stiff, or till the following day, then make it into nuts, by pinching it into pieces with the finger and thumb. Bake them upon buttered tins in a quick oven. Half an ounce of coriander seed may be added.

GINGERBREAD NUTS. (4) Rub half a pound of butter into two pounds of flour; add one pound of coarse sugar, and one ounce of pounded ginger; mix all well together with one pound and two ounces of treacle; form it into nuts, or roll it out, and cut it into round cakes; bake them upon tins.

GINGERBREAD, OATMEAL. Sift four pounds of oatmeal, and mix with it four pounds of treacle, half a pound of brown sugar, the same quantity of melted butter, and three-quarters of an ounce of powdered ginger. Work it all well together, let it remain for twenty-four hours, and then make it into cakes.

GINGER BEER. *See Beer.*

GINGER CAKES. Put four pounds of flour upon the dresser; then take a copper saucepan, and break into it six eggs, and mix them well with a spoon; add one pint of cream to them, and beat them well; put the saucepan over the fire, stir till your mixture is warm; put two pounds of butter into the cream and eggs, and one pound of sugar, and keep stirring it over a very slow fire, just to melt all the butter; put in four ounces of pounded ginger, and as soon as all the butter is melted, pour it all into the middle of the flour; mix it as well as you possibly can, till it becomes a fine paste; then roll it out with flour under it on your dresser; cut them to the size of the top of a tea-cup, a quarter of an inch in thickness; and before you put them into the oven (which should be very hot), place three papers under them.

GINGER IMITATION. Peel off the outer coat of the tender stems of lettuce that is short, cut it into bits one or two inches long, and throw it into cold water; to each pound put in a tea-spoonful of Cayenne, and a little salt; let it stand one or two days; allow an equal proportion of fine loaf sugar, which clarify. Soak some good ginger in hot water, slice it, and add it to the sugar, allowing one ounce and a half to the pound, and boil it for fifteen minutes; strain off the water from the lettuce, and pour over it the sirup, keeping back the ginger, with which the sirup must be boiled three times, and poured over the lettuce, two or three days intervening between each boiling; and at last add the strained juice of one or two lemons.

GLACE, ROYAL. Put the white of a new-laid egg into a pan, and mix with it a sufficient quantity of white powder-sugar to make a *glace* or icing, neither too dry nor too liquid; beat it well, and add a little lemon-juice to whiten it. By mixing with this *glace*, carmine, saffron, indigo, spinach-juice, &c.; it will be either rose-colored, yellow, blue, green, &c. according to your taste.

GLAZE. (1) Take the remains of any liquor in which meat has been cooked, and strain it through a silk sieve until quite clear; then put it into a saucepan and reduce it over a brisk fire: as soon as it is sufficiently done, that is, when it sticks to the spoon, put it into a smaller saucepan, and set it in the *bain-marie*; when wanted, add a small piece of fresh butter to it, to correct its saltiness.

GLAZE. (2) Make a *consomme* with whatever remnants of fowls or meat that may be in the house; strain it, and then put it on the fire with two or three whites of eggs beaten to a snow; stir till it boils, and then set on the side of the stove, and place fire on the saucepan lid; as soon as the eggs are set, pass the glaze through a wet cloth; reduce this over a large fire, stirring it constantly with a wooden spoon to prevent its sticking; then pour it into a pot for use. When wanted, put a small quantity of it into a saucepan, and make it hot over a slow fire; and, in this state, lay it gently over such articles as may require glazing, by means of a feather.

GLAZE. (3) Desire the butcher to break the bones of a leg or a shin of beef, of ten pounds weight (the fresher killed the better); put it into a soup-pot (a digester is the best utensil for this purpose) that will well hold it; just cover it with cold water, and set it on the fire to heat gradually till it nearly boils (this should be at least an hour); skim it attentively while any scum rises; pour in a little cold water to throw up the scum that may remain; let it come to a boil again, and again skim it carefully: when no more scum rises, and the broth appears clear (put in neither roots, nor herbs, nor salt), let it boil for eight or ten hours, and then strain it through a hair sieve into a brown stone pan; set the broth where it will cool quickly; put the meat into a sieve, let it drain, make potted beef, or it will be very acceptable to many poor families. Next day remove every particle of fat from the top of it, and pour it through a tamis, or fine sieve, as quietly as possible, into a stewpan, taking care not to let any of the settlings at the bottom of the stone pan go into the stewpan, which should be of thick copper, perfectly well tinned; add a quarter of an ounce of whole black pepper to it; let it boil briskly, with the stewpan uncovered, on a quick fire; if any scum rises, take it off with a skimmer: when it begins to thicken, and is reduced to about a quart, put it into a smaller stewpan; set it over a gentler fire, till it is reduced.

GODIVEAU. Take fillet of veal or breasts of fowl or game, fresh pork or sausage meat, beef-marrow or suet, equal quantities of each, veal sweetbreads, truffles, and mushrooms; season these articles with pepper, cloves, and nutmeg, all in powder; pound them all together, put in (one at a time) the yolks of eggs; pour in also a little water, pounding continually, until it is reduced to a sort of paste. Make a small ball of it, which boil in a little water to ascertain whether it be sufficiently salt; sweet herbs may be added when you are about to use it. The *godiveau* is used as a *farce* for *tourtes* and hot pies.

GOOSE, TO CHOOSE. Be careful in choosing a goose, that the bill and feet are yellow, as it will be young: when old the feet and bill are red. When they are fresh the feet are pliable; if stale they are dry and stiff. Green geese, are in season from May or June, till they are three months old; they should be scalded. A stubble goose is good till it is five or six months old, and should be picked dry.

GOOSE ROASTED. A stubble goose should be stuffed with sage and onion, chopped small, and mixed with pepper and salt; boil the sage and onion in a little water before they are chopped, or mix a few bread crumbs with them when chopped; either will render them less strong. Put it first at a distance from the fire, and by degrees draw it nearer. A slip of paper should be skewered on the breast bone. Baste it very well. When the breast is rising, take off the paper, and be careful to serve it before the breast falls, it will be spoiled by coming to table flattened. Serve it with good gravy and apple sauce, in boats. It will take about an hour and a half to roast.

GOOSE TO TRUSS. The goose must be first well picked and stubbed, then cut off the pinions at the first joint, and the feet also. Make a slit in the back of the neck, and take out the throat, cut off the neck close to the back and the skin, but leave enough to turn over the back; make a slit between the vent and the rump, through which draw out the entrails, then wipe it clean. Draw the legs up, keeping them close to the side, then put a skewer into the wing, through the middle of the leg, body, and the leg and wing on the other side; put another skewer through the small of the leg, which keep close to the sidesmen; run it through, and do the same on the other side. Cut through the end of the vent, through which put the rump, to prevent the stuffing from falling out.

GOOSEBERRY CREAM. Boil one quart of gooseberries very quick, in as much water as will cover them: stir in about half an ounce of good butter; when they are soft, pulp them through a sieve; sweeten the pulp while it is hot, with sugar, then beat it up with the yolks of four eggs; serve in a dish, cups, or glasses.

GOOSEBERRY FOOL. Put gooseberries into a stone jar, with some fine sugar; put the jar either in a stove, or in a saucepan of water, over the fire; if in a stove, a large spoonful of water should be added to the fruit. When it is done to pulp, press it through a colander; have ready a sufficient quantity of new milk, and a teacupful of raw cream, boiled together, or you may use an egg instead of the cream; leave it to get cold, then sweeten well with fine sugar, and mix the pulp by degrees with it.

GOOSEBERRY MARMALADE. Boil them a moment, or only scald them in boiling water, sift them through a sieve; reduce them over the fire to half, then mix them with sugar prepared to the ninth degree (*a la grande plume*), half a pound of sugar to a pound of fruit.

GOOSEBERRY JAM. *See Jam.*

GOOSEBERRY PASTE. Gather, when quite ripe, the rough red gooseberries; top and tail them; put them into a jar, tie it over with bladder, and boil it in a pot of water till the fruit be perfectly soft; pour off the thin juice, and with a wooden spoon rub the gooseberries through a fine hair sieve; allow rather more than half the weight of the pulp of pounded loaf sugar, mix it together, and boil it till it will jelly, which will take almost two hours; stir, and skim it, then put it into a dish, and serve when cold, to be eaten with cream. The thin juice may be boiled with its weight of good brown sugar, and used as gooseberry jelly.

GOURDS FRIED. (1)   Cut five or six gourds in quarters; take off the skin and pulp; stew them in the same manner as for table: when done, drain them quite dry; beat up an egg, and dip the gourds in it, and cover them well over with bread crumbs; make some hog's-lard hot, and fry them a nice light color; throw a little salt and pepper over them, and serve up quite dry.

GOURDS FRIED. (2) Take six or eight small gourds, as near of a size as possible; slice them  with a cucumber-slice; dry them in a cloth, and then fry them in very hot lard;  throw over a little pepper and salt, and serve  up on a napkin. Great attention is requisite to do these well; if the fat is quite hot they are done in a  minute, and will soon spoil; if not hot enough, they will eat greasy and tough.

GOURDS STEWED.   Take off all the skin of six or eight gourds, put them into a stewpan, with water, salt, lemon-juice, and a bit of butter, or fat bacon, and let them stew gently till quite tender, and serve up with a rich Dutch sauce, or any other sauce you please that is *piquante*.

GRAPES, COMPOTE.  Boil a quarter of a pound of sugar with half a glass of water, till it is reduced to a strong sirup; skim, and then put into it a pound of grapes, picked from the stalks, and the seeds taken out; give them a boil two or three times, and then place them in a dessert dish: if there is any scum upon them, carefully wipe it off with white paper.

GRAPES, PICKLED.  The grapes must be at their full growth, but not ripe, cut them in small bunches; put them in a stone jar, with vine leaves between each layer of grapes, till the jar is full; then take as much spring-water as will cover the grapes and the leaves; as it heats put in as much salt as will make a brine  sufficiently strong to bear an egg; you must use half bay salt and half common salt; when it boils, skim it; strain it through a flannel bag, and let it stand to settle; by the time it is cold it will be quite settled; strain it a second time through a flannel bag; then pour it into the jar, upon the grapes, which must be well covered; fill the jar with vine leaves; then tie it over with a double cloth, and set a plate upon it; let  it stand for two days, then take off the cloth, pour away the brine, and take out the leaves and the grapes, and lay them between two cloths to dry; then take two quarts of vinegar, one quart of spring-water, and  one pound of coarse sugar, boil it for a short time, and skim it very clean as it boils; let it stand till it is quite cold; wipe the jar very clean and dry, lay some fresh vine leaves at the bottom, between every bunch of grapes, and on the top; then pour and strain the pickle on the grapes; fill the jar; let the pickle be above the grapes; tie up a thin piece of board in a flannel, lay it on the grapes to keep them under the pickle; tie them down with a bladder, and over that a leather. Always keep the grapes under the pickle.

GRATIN.  Cut half a pound of fillet of veal into dice, and put it into a stewpan with a piece of butter, a few  mushrooms, parsley, shallots chopped small, salt, pepper, and spices; stir them up with a wooden spoon; and when the meat has been on the fire about a quarter of an hour, take the drain off the butter, mince it  very small, and put it into a mortar, with fifteen fowl or game livers, well washed, dried, and parboiled, all the bitter parts taken out, pound them, adding at times as much panada as you have meat; boil some calf's udder, trim, and remove all the skin when cold, and put about a third of the quantity of meat, and pound them together, adding, one at a time, three yolks, and three whole eggs; season with salt, pepper, and spices; when well pounded, set it by in an earthen pan for use.

GRAVY. *See also Cullis and Sauces.*

GRAVIES, DIRECTIONS RESPECT-ING.—The skirts of beef and the kidney, will make quite as good gravy as any other meat, if prepared in the same manner.

The kidney of an ox, or the milt, makes excellent gravy, cut all to pieces, and pre-pared as other meat; and so will the shank end of mutton that has been dressed, if much gravy is not required.

The shank-bones of mutton add greatly to the richness of gravy; but they should be first well soaked, and scoured clean.

To obtain the flavor of French cookery, and to improve the taste of the gravies, tar-ragon should be used; but it must not be added till a short time before serving.

GRAVY. (1) Take three pounds of beef steaks, two rabbits, (excepting the heads and breasts), a knuckle of veal, five carrots, six onions, two cloves, two bay leaves, a bunch of parsley and scallions; put all these into a stewpan, with two ladlesful of broth, and set them over a good fire to reduce; then cover the stove, and let the stewpan stand over it, until the meat begins to give out the gravy, and adheres slightly; the jelly at the bottom of the stewpan ought to be nearly black, and when that is the case, take it from the stove, and let it stand for ten minutes; then fill up the stewpan with good broth, or water, (if the latter, not so large a quantity); let this simmer for three hours; skim and season it well. If water is used instead of broth, the gravy must be strained before it is used. Gravy may also be made of any pieces of ready dressed meat, in the follow-ing manner: cut some onions into slices, lay them at the bottom of the stewpan, and the meat on them, with the same ingredients as above, and two or three glasses of water, then proceed in the same manner as the other, until the bottom of the stewpan is nearly black, when add water according to the quantity of meat; put salt if necessary, and simmer the whole for two hours; then strain it through a sieve.

GRAVY. (2) Cut down into slices four pounds of lean beef, rub the bottom of the pot with butter, and put in the meat; turn it frequently till it be well browned, and do it slowly, then add four quarts of cold water; when it has boiled two hours, put in two dessert-spoonfuls of whole pepper, one car-rot, and three onions; let it stew gently for four hours longer, strain it, and when it is required for use, take off the fat. This gravy answers for all made dishes when brown gravy sauce is used.

GRAVY AND STUFFING FOR DUCKS. Boil all the giblets excepting the liver for an hour in a pint of water with a chopped onion, some salt and pepper; strain, and add a very little browning, with a tea-spoonful of coratch, and one of mushroom ketchup; for the stuffing, mince the raw liver with two sage leaves, a small onion, some pepper and salt, a bit of butter, and grated bread crumbs.

Send your sauces to table as hot as pos-sible.

Nothing can be more unsightly than the surface of a sauce in a frozen state, or gar-nished with grease on the top. The best way to get rid of this is to pass it through a tamis or napkin previously soaked in cold water; the coldness of the napkin will coagulate the fat, and only suffer the pure gravy to pass through: if any particles of fat remain, take them off by applying filtering paper, as blotting paper is applied to writing.

Let your sauces boil up after you put in wine, anchovy, or thickening, that their fla-vors may be well blended with the other ingredients; and keep in mind that the *top-knot* of COOKERY is, to entertain the mouth without offending the stomach.

GRAVIES AND SAUCES. It is of as much importance that the cook should know how to make a boat of good gravy for poultry, &c. as that it should be sent up of proper complexion, and nicely frothed.

We shall endeavor to introduce to her all the materials which give flavor in *sauce* which is the *essence of soup*, and intended to contain more relish in a *tea-spoonful* than the former does in a *table-spoonful*.

We hope to deserve as much praise from the *economist* as we do from the *bon vivant*; as we have taken great pains to introduce to him the methods of making substitutes for those ingredients, which are always expensive, and often not to be had at all. Many of these cheap articles are as savory and as salutary as the dearer ones, and those who have large families and limited incomes, will, no doubt, be glad to avail themselves of them.

The reader may rest assured, that whether he consults this book to diminish the expense or increase the pleasures of hospitality, he will find all the information that was to be obtained up to 1832, communicated in the most unreserved and intelligible manner.

A great deal of the elegance of cookery depends upon the accompaniments to each dish being appropriate and well adapted to it.

We can assure our readers, no attention has been wanting on our part to render this department of the work worthy of their perusal; each receipt is the faithful narrative of actual and repeated experiments, and has received the most deliberate consideration before it was here presented to them. It is given in the most circumstantial manner, and not in the technical and mysterious language former writers on these subjects seem to have preferred; by which their directions are useless and unintelligible to all who have not regularly served an apprenticeship at the stove.

It will be to very little purpose that I have taken so much pains to teach how to manage roasts and boils, if a cook cannot or will not make the several sauces that are usually sent up with them.

We have, therefore, endeavored to give the plainest directions how to produce, with the least trouble and expense possible, all the various compositions the English kitchen affords; and hope to present such a wholesome and palatable variety as will suit all tastes and all pockets, so that a cook may give satisfaction in all families. The more combinations of this sort she is acquainted with, the better she will comprehend the management of every one of them.

Let your sauces each display a decided character; send up your plain sauces (oyster, lobster, &c.) as pure as possible: they should only taste of the materials from which they take their name.

The imagination of most cooks is so incessantly on the hunt for a relish, that they seem to think they cannot make sauce sufficiently savory without putting into it everything that ever was eaten; and supposing every addition must be an improvement, they frequently overpower the natural flavor of their PLAIN SAUCES, by overloading them with salt and spices, &c.: but, remember, these will be deteriorated by any addition, save only just salt enough to awaken the palate.

On the contrary, of COMPOUND SAUCES; the ingredients should be so nicely proportioned, that no one be predominant; so that from the equal union of the combined flavors such a fine mellow mixture is produced, whose very novelty cannot fail of being acceptable to the preserving *gourmand*, if it has not pretensions to a permanent place at his table.

An ingenious *cook* will form as endless a variety of these compositions as a *musician* with his seven notes, or a *painter* with his colors; no part of her business offers so fair and frequent an opportunity to display her abilities: SPICES, HERBS, &c. are often very absurdly and injudiciously jumbled together.

Why have clove and allspice, or mace and nutmeg, in the same sauce; or marjoram, thyme, and savory; or onions, leeks, eschalots, and garlic? one will very well supply the place of the other, and the frugal cook

cook may save something considerable by attending to this, to the advantage of her employers, and her own time and trouble.

☞ *See* SAUCES *and* CULLIS *for other important particulars.*

GRAVIES, ESSENCE OF HAM FOR. Pick off all the bits of meat from a ham-bone, pound them, break the bone, and put all into a saucepan, together with nearly half a pint of water, and a bunch of sweet herbs; simmer gently for sometime, stirring it occasionally; then add a pint of good beef gravy, and some pepper, and continue to simmer it till it be well flavored with the herbs; strain, and keep it for improving rich gravies and sauces of all descriptions.

GRAVY FOR BOILED MEAT, May be made with parings and trimmings; or pour from a quarter to half a pint of the liquor in which the meat was boiled, into the dish with it, and pierce the inferior part of the joint with a sharp skewer.

GRAVY FOR ROAST MEAT.   (1) Most joints will afford sufficient trimmings, &c. to make half a pint of plain gravy, which you may color with a few drops of browning: for those that do not, about half an hour before you think the meat will be done, mix a salt-spoonful of salt, with a full quarter-pint of boiling water; drop this by degrees on the brown parts of the joint; set a dish under to catch it (the meat will soon brown again); set it by; as it cools, the fat will float on the surface; when the meat is ready, carefully remove the fat, and warm up the gravy, and pour it into the dish.

The common method is, when the meat is in the dish you intend to send it up in, to mix half a tea-spoonful of salt in a quarter pint of boiling water, and to drop some of this over the corners and underside of the meat, and to pour the rest through the hole the spit came out of: some pierce the inferior parts of the joints with a sharp skewer.

The following receipt was given us by a very good cook:—You may make good browning for roast meat and poultry, by saving the brown bits of roast meat or broiled; cut them small, put them into a basin, cover them with boiling water, and put them away till next day; then put it into a saucepan, let it boil two or three minutes, strain it through a sieve into a basin, and put it away for use. When you want gravy for roast meat, put two table-spoonfuls into half a pint of boiling water with a little salt: if for roasted veal, put three table-spoonfuls into half a pint of thin melted butter.

The gravy which comes down in the dish, the cook (if she is a good housewife) will preserve to enrich hashes or little made dishes, &c.

GRAVY FOR ROAST MEAT. (2) About a quarter of an hour before the meat is taken from the fire, put a common dish with a tea-spoonful of salt in it under the meat; when it has all run into the dish, remove it, baste and froth the meat, and pour the gravy into the dish on which the roast is to be served.

GRAVY MADE FROM BONES.  Break into small pieces a pound of beef, mutton, or veal bones, if mixed together so much the better; boil them in two quarts of water, and after it boils, let it simmer for nearly three hours:  boil with it a couple of onions, a bunch of sweet herbs, some salt and pepper; strain, and keep it for making gravy or sauces. The bones of broiled and roasted meat being scraped, washed clean, and boiled in less water, answer equally well for this purpose.

GRAVY MADE WITHOUT MEAT. (1) Slice three onions, and fry them brown in a little butter; add them to half a pint of water, and the same of beer, put in some pepper-corns, salt, a little lemon-peel, three cloves, a little mace or pepper, a spoonful of walnut pickle, and one of mushroom ketchup, of soy and essence of anchovy a dessert-spoonful each, a small bunch of sweet herbs, and a quarter of a slice of bread toasted brown on both sides; simmer all together in a closely covered saucepan for twenty minutes, then strain it for use, and when cold take off the fat. It will taste exactly like a gravy made with meat.

GRAVY MADE WITHOUT MEAT. (2) Knead a good deal of flour into a piece of butter the size of an egg, fry it in a frying-pan over a clear fire, stir it constantly with a wooden spoon till it become a nice brown color, taking particular care that it be made perfectly smooth; pour in some boiling water, add a little finely-minced onion, some whole pepper and a little salt, put it into a small saucepan, cover it closely, and simmer it for a short time; strain, and mix with it a little mushroom ketchup, and Port wine.

GRAVY OR RICH CULLIS. Cut into slices some lean beef, veal, and mutton, cover the bottom of the saucepan with the veal, then put in a few slices of salt pork, next a layer of beef, add a few onions sliced, and the red part of one or two carrots, a little mace, two or three cloves, some whole pepper, and two or three bay-leaves, above that the mutton; cover the pan closely, set it on a slow fire; and when the meat is a fine brown, mix quite smooth a small quantity of flour in water, stir it in, and then add as much boiling water as will cover the meat well, and a little salt; cover the pan closely, and let it stew an hour and a half; strain, and keep it for use; it will continue good for eight or ten days.

GRAVY DRAWN. Put a few pounds of gravy-beef sliced, and a little whole pepper, into a jar with a cover to fit closely; set the jar into a pot of cold water, and when it boils, add as it wastes more hot water, and keep it boiling gently for six or seven hours, when the richest gravy imaginable will be obtained. It may be used in that state, or reduced with water.

GRAVY, TO MAKE A PINT OF RICH. Brown a quarter of a pound of but-ter, dredging in two table-spoonfuls of flour, and stirring it constantly; add a pound of gravy-beef cut into small bits, and two or three onions chopped. When it becomes brown, add some whole pepper, one carrot, a bunch of sweet herbs, and three pints of water; let it boil gently till reduced to one, then strain it. This gravy may be served with roasted turkey or fowl.

GRAVY, TO CLARIFY. Clarify gravy, drawn from beef or veal, with the beaten whites of eggs, allowing one white to a quart. Gravies and soups which are to be clarified should be made very strong, and be highly seasoned.

GRAVY AND SAUCE INGREDIENTS. Browning for made dishes.—Put into a saucepan one pound of good brown sugar, stir it constantly over a slow fire, boil it till it is as thick as treacle, and resembles it in color; take the pan off the fire, stir it for a minute or two, and pour in very slowly a quart of boiling water, stirring constantly; put it again on the fire, and boil it for a little; pour it into a bowl, and when cold, bottle it. This browning will keep good for a year, and very little of it serves for coloring soups, gravies, or sauces.

To clarify butter.—Put the butter cut into slices into a nicely-cleaned brass pan, stir it gently till dissolved: when it boils, draw the pan to the side of the fire, skim it, and let it boil gently a second time, and if any scum again rises, take it off; let it settle for two or three minutes, and strain it gently through a sieve which has a piece of muslin laid into it.

Fresh beef suet, picked free from skin and sinews, is dissolved in the same way; it is then strained through muslin into small jars, and when cold, covered with bladder, or it may be strained into cold water; and the cake when cold, wiped dry, folded in white paper, and kept in a linen bag.

Beef suet will keep fresh for some time if finely chopped and dredged with flour, and kept in white paper bags in a cool place.

Beef and mutton drippings are clarified exactly in the manner butter is done, and each kept in a separate jar.

To melt hog's-lard, put it into a jar placed in a pot of water or water bath, strain it into clean bladders or small jars, and cover them with paper. Thus prepared, it will keep good a length of time, and is the best thing for frying fish in.

To fry parsley, wash it, pick it clean, and put it into fresh cold water; take it out and then throw it into boiling lard or dripping, when it will instantly become crisp; it is then taken out with a slice.

GRUEL. DR. KITCHENER'S. Ask those who are to eat it, if they like it thick or thin; if the latter, mix well together by degrees, in a pint basin, one table-spoonful of oatmeal, with three of cold water; if the former, use two spoonfuls.

Have ready in a stewpan, a pint of boiling water or milk; pour this by de-grees to the oatmeal you have mixed; re-turn it into the stewpan; set it on the fire, and let it boil for five minutes; stirring it all the time to prevent the oatmeal from burning at the bottom of the stewpan; skim and strain it through a hair sieve.

2d. To convert this into caudle, add a little ale, wine, or brandy, with sugar; and if the bowels are disordered, a little nut-meg or ginger, grated.

*Obs.*—Gruel may be made with broth in-stead of water; and may be flavored with sweet herbs, soup roots, and savory spices, by boiling them for a few minutes in the water you are going to make the gruel with.

## H.

HAM. If it is a very dry Westphalia ham, it must be soaked, according to its age and thickness, from twelve to twenty-four hours; for a green ham, from four to eight hours will be sufficient. Lukewarm water will soften it much sooner than cold, when sufficiently soaked, trim it nicely on the un-derside, and pare off all the rusty and smoked parts till it looks delicately clean.

Give it plenty of water-room, and put it in while the water is cold; let it heat very gradually, and let it be on the fire an hour and a half before it comes to a boil; let it be well skimmed, and keep it simmering very gently: a middling-sized ham of fifteen pounds will be done enough in about four or five hours, according to its thickness.

If not to be cut till cold, it will cut the shorter and tenderer for being boiled about half an hour longer. In a very small family, where a ham will last a week or ten days, it is best economy not to cut it till it is cold, it will be infinitely more juicy.

Pull off the skin carefully, and preserve it as whole as possible; it will form an excel-lent covering to keep the ham moist; when you have removed the skin, rub some bread raspings through a hair sieve, or grate a crust of bread; put it into the perforated cover of the dredging-box, and shake it over it, or glaze it; trim the knuckle with a fringe of cut writing-paper. You may garnish with spinage or turnips, &c.

To pot ham is a much more useful and economical way of disposing of the remains of the joint, than making essence of it.

HAM AND EGGS. Cut some ham into thin slices, and broil them on a gridiron. Fry some eggs in butter. Serve it, laying an egg on each slice of ham.

HAM, ESSENCE OF. Take three or four pounds of lean ham, cut it into pieces about an inch thick, and lay them in a stew-pan, with slices of carrots, parsnips, and three or four onions; let them stew till they stick to the pan, but take care they do not burn; then by degrees pour in some good veal gravy, a few fresh mushrooms cut in pieces, (or mushroom-powder), truffles, mo-rels, cloves, parsley, leek, basil, and a crust of bread; cover it close, and simmer till pretty thick, then strain it off for use.

HAM GRAVY. Take a deep sauce pan, put into it a piece of fresh butter, several slices of ham, about six pieces of veal the size of a walnut, and two or three carrots cut in small pieces; set these over a slow fire, and let them stand till they give out their juices, and the ham and veal become crisp and stick; then put in a little stock, and let it boil; in an hour's time add a glass of white wine, leave it a quarter of an hour, when it will be sufficiently done; take off every particle of fat; strain it into a pan, and set it by for use.

HAM LOAF. Soak a fine ham in cold water for one or two days, according to its age; then put it into a saucepan just big enough to hold it, with no more water than will cover it, and a pint of white wine; let it boil, skimming it carefully, till done. When cold, take out the hock and under bones, and the skin; pare away some of the fat, and trim it to an oval form as much as possible. Make a farce with the parings of the fat, some veal or game, and sweet herbs minced and pounded. Take a pan the size you wish to have your loaf, lay all over the inside a pretty firm paste, and then (having cut your ham into thin slices) place alternate layers of it and the farce in the pan, until it be quite full. Put a crust over the top, which must unite with that in which the ham is; turn it over on a baking plate, flour it, and put it into a very hot oven for an hour and a half or two hours, according to its size. Serve it cold.

HAM, MINCED, WITH FRIED EGGS. *See Eggs.*

HAM OMELET. Take a slice of boiled ham, mince it as small as possible, and mix it with a dozen eggs beaten with a little veal gravy; fry it (keeping it of an equal thickness) in the usual manner.

HAM, OR TONGUE POTTED. Cut a pound of the lean of cold boiled ham or tongue, and pound it in a mortar with a quarter of a pound of the fat, or with fresh butter (in the proportion of about two ounces to a pound), till it is a fine paste (some season it by degrees with a little pounded mace or allspice): put it close down in pots for that purpose, and cover it with clarified butter, a quarter of an inch thick; let it stand one night in a cool place. Send it up in the pot, or cut out in thin slices.

HAM ROASTED WITH MADEIRA. Take a fine Westphalia or Bayonne ham, pare and trim it of as round a form as poss- ble, take off the end bone, and remove the rind from the knuckle; then lay the ham on a gridiron over the fire, till you can take it up with ease; soak it, if necessary, and put it in a pan, with slices of carrots and onions, thyme, bay-leaf, and coriander; pour a bottle of Madeira upon it, cover it with a clean cloth, and close the pan as tight as possible, and let it remain twenty-four hours; then wrap the ham in very thick paper, fasten it with paste, so that it may be completely en- closed, tie it on a spit, and put it to roast for three hours; then make a small hole in the paper, and pour in, by means of a funnel, the Madeira wine, paste paper over the hole, and let it roast another hour. When done, take off the paper carefully, so that none of the gravy may escape, mix it with some re- duced *espagnole*, glaze the ham, and serve it.

HAM TOAST. Cut some crumb of bread into thin slices; then take an equal number of thin slices of ham, beat them well with a rolling pin, and then soak them in warm water for about two hours; take them out, dry them well, and put them into a saucepan with a little bacon, a slice of veal, and half a glass of stock; let them boil for half an hour, and then add half a glass of veal *blond*. Fry your bread to a nice color in some lard; lay it on a dish, and on each piece lay a slice of the ham; pour the sauce over them. Take particular care to cut the ham as nearly as possible the size and shape of the bread.

HAM TO STEW. Soak the ham in luke-warm water for twelve hours, drain it, and scrape the rind; put it into a stewpan with some slices of fat bacon round the sides, four quarts of weak stock, a good deal of parsley, a bunch of sweet herbs, six large onions, four carrots, a little allspice and pepper, a pint of Madeira, and one of Port wine. Cover the ham with slices of fat bacon, and put over it a sheet of white paper; stew it eight hours, or ten if it be a very large ham. Before serving, take off the rind, strain the sauce, skim it well, and boil it till reduced to a glaze, and pour it round the ham, or serve it with any other sauce that may be preferred.

HAM WITH MADEIRA. Soak in water for two hours a Bayonne, or any other fine ham, boil it for two hours, trim it quickly; and then put it into a stewpan, with thin slices of veal at the bottom; add some carrots and parsley, and season with spices. Pour over the ham a pint of rich stock and a bottle of Madeira; let it boil for two hours, strain and skim the fat off the sauce, which, with the ham, must be served quite hot.

HARE. As soon as the cook receives a hare, she should take out the liver, &c., wipe it well, put in a little pepper, and hang it up. When wanted for dressing, cut off the four legs at the first joint, raise the skin of the back, and draw it over the hind legs; leave the tail whole, then draw the skin over the back, and slip out the four legs; cut it from the neck and head; skin the ears, and leave them on. Clean the vent. Cut the sinews under the hind legs; bring them forward; run a skewer through one hind leg, the body, and another hind leg; do the same with the fore legs; lay the head rather back; put a skewer in at the mouth, through the back of the head and between the shoulders; put in the stuffing, and tie it round with a string, passing it over the legs to keep them in their

places: the hare is then ready for roasting. See *Hare Roasted*.

HARE, JUGGED. Having skinned a hare, cut off the shoulders and legs, and divide the back into three pieces; rub them well with fat bacon, and put them into a stewpan with the trimmings, allspice, mace, whole pepper, a small clove of garlic, two bay-leaves, three onions, parsley, thyme, sweet marjoram, a quart of veal stock, and three gills of Port wine; simmer the whole till three parts done; then take out the shoulders, legs, and back; put them into another stewpan, strain the liquor to them, add a little flour and butter, stew them till quite done; take off the fat, season with cayenne, salt, and lemon-juice, and serve the whole in a deep dish.

HARE ROASTED, Cut the skin from a hare that has been well soaked; put it on the spit and rub it well with Madeira, pricking it in various places that it may imbibe plenty of wine; cover it entirely with a paste, and roast it. When done, take away the paste, rub it quickly over with egg, sprinkle bread-crumbs, and baste it gently with butter (still keeping it turning before the fire) until a crust is formed over it and it is of a nice brown color; dish it over some *espagnole* with Madeira wine boiled in it; two or three cloves may be stuck into the knuckles if you think proper.

HASHED HARE. Cut up the hare into pieces fit to help at table, and divide the jotnts of the legs and shoulders, and set them by ready. Put the trimmings and gravy you have left, with half a pint of water (there should be a pint of liquor), and a ta-ble-spoonful of currant jelly, into a clean stewpan, and let it boil gently for a quarter of an hour: then strain it through a sieve into a basin, and pour it back into the stewpan; now flour the hare, put it into the gravy, and let it simmer very gently till the hare is warm (about twenty minutes); cut the stuff-ing into slices, and put it into the hash to get warm, about five minutes before you serve it; divide the head, and lay one half on each side the dish.

HARICOT BY WAY OF SOUP. Cut a large neck of mutton into two pieces, put the scrag into a stewpan with a quart of water, four large carrots, and turnips; boil it gently over a slow fire till all the goodness be out of the meat; then bruise the vegetables into the soup to thicken it. Fry six onions (sliced) in butter, and put the other part of the meat to the soup, and stew till the latter is tender; season with pepper and salt, and serve it very hot in a tureen.

HARICOT MUTTON. Cut the best end of a neck or loin of mutton, that has been kept till tender, into chops of equal thickness, one rib to each; trim off some of the fat, and the lower end of the chine bone, and scrape it clean, and lay them in a stewpan, with an ounce of butter; set it over a smart fire; if your fire is not sharp, the chops will be done before they are colored; the intention of frying them is merely to give them a very light browning.

While the chops are browning, peel and boil a couple of dozen of young button onions in about three pints of water for about fifteen or twenty minutes, set them by, and pour off the liquor they were boiled in into the stewpan with the chops: if that is not sufficient to cover them, add as much boiling water as will remove the scum as it rises, and be careful they are not stewed too fast or too much; so take out one of them with a fish-slice, and try it: when they are tender, which will be in about an hour and a half, then pass the gravy through a sieve into a basin, set it in the open air that it may get cold, you may then easily and completely skim off the fat; in the meantime set the meat and vegetables by the fire to keep hot, and pour some boiling water over the button onions to warm them. Have about six ounces of carrots, and eight ounces of turnips, peeled and cut into slices, or shaped into balls about as big as a nutmeg; boil the

carrots about half an hour, the turnips about a quarter of an hour, and put them in a sieve to drain, and then put them round the dish, the last thing.

Thicken the gravy by putting an ounce of butter into a stewpan; when it is melted, stir in as much flour as will stiffen it; pour the gravy to it by degrees, stir together till it boils; strain it through a fine sieve or tamis into a stewpan, put in the carrots and turnips to get warm, and let it simmer gently while you dish up the meat; lay the chops round a dish, put the vegetables in the middle, and pour the thickened gravy over. Some put in capers, &c. minced gherkins, &c.

Rump-steaks, veal cutlets, and beef-tails, make excellent dishes dressed in the like manner.

HASH, COLD. Mince a nice white piece of veal, wash and core some anchovies; take some pickled oysters, pickled cucumbers, and a lemon; shred and mix them with the veal, and place it in a dish; lay round it slices of veal, fillets of anchovies, pickled cucumbers sliced, whole pickled oysters, mushrooms and capers; lettuces shred small; pour in oil and vinegar, salt and pepper, and serve.

HASHES, MADE DISHES, STEWS, RAGOUTS, SOUPS, TO WARM. Put what you have left into a deep hash-dish or tureen; when you want it, set this in a stewpan of boiling water: let it stand till the contents are quite warm.

HATTERED KIT. (1) Make two quarts of new milk scalding hot, and pour it quickly upon four quarts of fresh-made butter milk, after which it must not be stirred; let it remain till cold and firm, then take off the top part, drain it in a hair sieve, and put it into a shape for half an hour. It is eaten with cream, served in a separate dish.

HATTERED KIT. (2) Put into the dish it is to be served in, one-third of cream with two-thirds of butter-milk, add a little pounded loaf sugar, and beat it well together. Strew over it a little pounded cinnamon, and let it stand for three or four hours.

HAWTHORN LIQUOR. The full blossoms of the white thorn are to be picked dry and clean from the leaves and stalks, and as much put into a large bottle as it will hold lightly without pressing down; it is then to be filled up with French brandy, and allowed to stand two or three months, when it must be decanted off, and sweetened with clarified sugar, or with capillaire. Without the sweetening, it is an excellent seasoning for puddings and custards.

HEDGEHOG TO MAKE. Blanch two pounds of sweet almonds, beat them to a paste in a mortar, moistening occasionally with Canary and orange-flower water; beat the yolks of twelve, and the whites of seven eggs with a pint of cream and some powder sugar; put this with the almond paste and half a pound of fresh butter into a saucepan, set it over a stove and keep it constantly stirring till sufficiently firm to be moulded into the shape of a hedgehog: stick it full of blanched almonds, cut lengthwise, into slips, and place it in a dish; beat up the yolks of four eggs, put them to a pint of cream (sweetened to the taste); stir them over a slow fire till hot, then pour it round the hedgehog and let it stand: when cold, serve it. A good calf's-foot jelly may be poured round, instead of the cream, if preferred.

HERBS, A BUNCH OF SWEET, Is made up of parsley, sweet marjoram, winter savory, orange and lemon thyme; the greatest proportion of parsley.

HERBS, SWEET. These in cookery, are parsley, chibbol, rocambole, winter savory, thyme, bay-leaf, basil, mint, borage, rosemary, cress, marigold, majoram, &c. The relishing herbs or *Ravigotte* are tarragon, garden-cress, chervil, burnet, civet, and green mustard.

HERBS TO DRY, SWEET AND SAVORY. It is very important to those who are not in the constant habit of attending the markets to know when the various seasons commence for purchasing sweet herbs.

All vegetables are in the highest state of perfection, and fullest of juice and flavor, just before they begin to flower: the first and last crop have neither the fine flavor, nor the perfume of those which are gathered in the height of the season; that is, when the greater part of the crop of each species is ripe.

Take care they are gathered on a dry day, by which means they will have a better color when dried. Cleanse your herbs well from dirt and dust; cut off the roots; separate the bunches into smaller ones, and dry them by the heat of a stove, or in a Dutch oven before a common fire, in such quantities at a time, that the process may be speedily finished; *i. e.* 'Kill 'em quick,' says a great botanist; by this means their flavor will be best preserved: there can be no doubt of the propriety of drying herbs, &c. hastily by the aid of artificial heat, rather than by the heat of the sun. In the application of artificial heat, the only caution requisite is to avoid burning; and of this a sufficient test is afforded by the preservation of the color. The common custom is, when they are perfectly dried to put them in bags, and lay them in a dry place; but the best way to preserve the flavor of aromatic plants is take off the leaves as soon as they are dried and to pound them, and put them through a hair sieve, and keep them in well-stopped bottles. The common custom is to put them into paper bags, and lay them on a shelf in the kitchen, exposed to all the fumes, steam, and smoke, &c.: thus they soon lose their flavor.

N. B.—Herbs nicely dried are a very acceptable substitute when fresh ones cannot be got; but, however carefully dried, the flavor and fragrance of the fresh herbs are incomparably finer.

HERRINGS. There are three sorts of

herrings, fresh, salted, and dried or red herrings. They are emptied and cleaned like any other fish; when fresh, they are broiled, and served with melted butter, white sauce, &c.

The salted herring should be soaked in cold water before it is cooked; this is also broiled; sometimes, however, it is cut in pieces, and eaten raw.

The red herring is split down the back, the head and tail are cut off, and the fish broiled like the others.

They may also be dressed as follows: when they have lain in cold water a sufficient time, soak them for two hours in milk, then split them down the back; then have ready some melted butter, in which has been mixed basil and bay-leaf, minced small, the yolks of two eggs, pepper and nutmeg; rub the herrings well with this, bread them; broil them over a gentle fire, and serve with lemon-juice.

The best red herrings are full of roe, are firm and large, and have a yellow cast.

Of the fresh herring the scales are bright if good, the eyes are full, and the gills red, the fish also should be stiff.

HERRINGS, BOILED. Scale, and otherwise prepare the herrings in the usual way; dry them well, and rub them over with a little salt and vinegar; skewer their tails in their mouths, lay them on a fish-plate, and put them into boiling water; in ten or twelve minutes take them out, drain them, lay them on the dish, the heads towards the middle; serve them with melted butter and parsley, and garnish with horseradish.

HERRINGS, RED. Plain broil them, or pour over some beer made hot, and when it is cold drain and wipe them dry, heat them thoroughly, and rub over a little butter, and sprinkle them with pepper.

HERRINGS TO BAKE. They must be perfectly fresh, and well cleaned, but not washed; the heads and fins cut off, and the bones cut out; strew over them pepper, salt,

and a slice of onion minced very finely, to each; roll them up tight; pack them into a jar, and pour over in the proportion of a pint of vinegar to two of water, with half an ounce of whole black pepper; tie over the jar a piece of bladder or paper, and bake them in an oven for an hour. Take off the cover when they are cold, and pour over a little cold vinegar, and tie them up.

HERRINGS TO FRY. Scrape off the scales; cut off the fins; draw out the gut, keeping in the roes and melts; wipe them in a clean cloth; dredge them with flour, and fry them in boiling dripping; put them before the fire to drain and keep hot. Sauces;—melted butter, and parsley and butter. When herrings are to be broiled, they are prepared in the same manner, and done upon the gridiron. They must not be washed.

HIPPOCRAS. Take one ounce of cinnamon, two drachms of ginger, two pennyweights of cloves, nutmeg, and galangal a penny-weight of each. Pound these together well, and infuse them in a pint of red or white wine, and a pint of malmsey; to this, add a pound of the best loaf sugar. These proportions will make a quart of the liquor.

HOG'S HEAD. Put a head into some pickle, and when it has lain sufficiently long, take it out and boil it till the bones will come out with ease; then skin, bone, and chop the meat, whilst hot; season it with pepper (black and white), nutmeg, and salt, if necessary; lay part of the skin at the bottom of a potting pan, press in the meat, cover it with the remainder of the skin, put on a weight, and let it stand till quite cold. Then turn it out. Boil the liquor it was dressed in with some vinegar, skim it well, and when cold put the head into it.

HONEY TO CLARIFY.—M. FOUQUE'S METHOD. Take six pounds of honey, a pound and three-quarters of water, two ounces and a quarter of pounded chalk, five ounces of coal, (pulverised, washed,

## Page 126

and well-dried), the whites of three eggs beaten in three ounces of water, for each pound of honey.

Put the honey, water, chalk, and eggs, into a copper vessel, capable of holding about one-third more than the above quantities; let them boil for two minutes, throw in the coal, mixing it with a spoon, and continue the boiling two minutes longer; then take the saucepan from the fire, and let it stand nearly a quarter of an hour, that the liquor may cool; then take a new sieve (which must be well washed, or it will impart a disagreeable taste), pass the honey through it, taking care to filter the first drops twice, as they generally carry with them some portion of the coal.

The sirup which still adheres to the coal, and other materials, may be separated as follows: pour boiling water on them until they no longer retain any sweetness; then put these different waters together, set them over a large fire to evaporate, till the sirup only remains. This sirup contracts the favor of barley sugar, and must not be added to the clarified honey.

HORSERADISH POWDER. The time to make this is during November and December; slice it the thickness of a shilling, and lay it to dry very gradually in a Dutch oven (a strong heat soon evaporates its flavor); when dry enough, pound it and bottle it.

HOT PICKLE. Boil, in two quarts of vinegar, a quarter of a pound of salt, two ounces of shallots or garlic, and two of ginger, one ounce of pepper, one of yellow mustard seed, and a quarter of an ounce of cayenne; put into a jar that will hold four quarts, two ounces of allspice, and pour on it the hot pickle. When cold, put in any fresh-gathered vegetables or fruit, such as asparagus, cauliflower, French beans, radish pods, unripe apples, gooseberries, currants, which may be added as the opportunity offers, and, as the pickle wastes, it should be replenished with the same

mixture.

H-BONE OF BEEF. *See Beef.*

HUNG BEEF. *See Beef*

HUNTING BEEF. *See Beef.*

HUNTER'S PIE. *See Irish Stew*

I.

ICE. Sorbetieres or moulds for cream or fruit-ices, are made of two sorts of materials, block-tin and pewter; of these, the latter is the best, the substance to be iced congealing more gradually in it than in the former; an object much to be desired, as when the ice is formed too quickly, it is very apt to be rough, and full of lumps like hail, especially if it be not well worked with the spatula; the other utensils necessary for this operation, are, a deep pail, with a cork at the bottom, and a wooden spatula about nine inches long; being so far provided, fill the pail with pounded ice, over which spread four handfuls of salt; then having filled the sorbetiere, or mould, with cream, &c.; put on the cover, and immerse it in the centre of the ice-pail; taking care the ice touches the mould in all parts; throw in two more handfuls of salt, and leave it a quarter of an hour; then take the cover from the mould, and with the spatula stir the contents up together, so that those parts which touch the sides of the mould, and consequently congeal first, may be mixed with the liquid in the middle; work this about for seven or eight minutes, cover the mould, take the pail by the ears, and shake it round and round for a quarter of an hour; open the mould a second time, and stir as before; continue these operations alternately, until the cream, or whatever it may be, is entirely congealed, and perfectly smooth, and free from lumps. Take care to let out the water, which will collect at the bottom of the pail, by means of the cork, and press the ice close to the sorbetiere with the spatula.

When the cream is iced, take it from the pail, dip the mould in warm water, but not to let it remain an instant; dry it quickly, turn it out, and serve it as soon as possible.

All sorts of ices are finished in this manner; the preparation of the articles of which they are composed, constitutes the only difference between them.

ICE, A VERY LARGE CAKE. Beat the whites of twenty fresh eggs; then, by degrees, beat a pound of double-refined sugar, sifted through a lawn sieve, mix these well in a deep earthen pan; add orange-flower water, and a piece of fresh lemon-peel; do not use more of the orange-flower water than is just sufficient to flavor it. Whisk it for three hours till the mixture is thick and white; then, with a thin broad bit of board, spread it all over the top and sides, and set it in a cool oven, and an hour will harden it.

ICE FOR ICING (HOW TO PREPARE). Take a few pounds of ice, break it almost to powder, and throw in among it a large handful and a half of salt; you must prepare in the coolest part of the house, that as little of the warm air as possible may come. The ice and salt being in a bucket, put your cream into an ice-pot, and cover it; immerse it in the ice, and draw that round the pot, so that it may touch every part. In a few minutes put a spatula or spoon in, and stir it well, removing the parts that ice round the edges to the centre. If the ice-cream or water, be in a form, shut the bottom close, and move the whole in the ice, as you cannot use a spoon to that without danger of waste. There should be holes in the bucket, to let the ice off as it thaws.

ICING FOR CAKES. For a large cake, beat and sift eight ounces of fine sugar, put it into a mortar, with four spoonfuls of rose water, and the whites of two eggs, beaten and strained, whisk it well, and when the cake is almost cold, dip a feather in the icing, and cover the cake well; set it in the oven to harden, but do not let it remain long enough to discolor. Keep the cake in a dry place.

ICING FOR TARTS. Beat the yolk of an egg and some melted butter well together; wash the tarts with a feather, and sift sugar over as you put them into the oven; or beat white of egg, wash the paste, and sift white sugar.

ICING, FOR TWELFTH OR BRIDE CAKE. Take one pound of double-refined sugar, pounded and sifted through a lawn sieve; put into a pan quite free from grease; break in the whites of six eggs, and as much powder blue as will lie on a sixpence; beat it well with a spattle for ten minutes; then squeeze in the juice of a lemon, and beat it till it becomes thick and transparent. Set the cake you intend to ice in an oven or warm place five minutes; then spread over the top and sides with the mixture as smooth as possible. If for a wedding cake only, plain ice it; if for a twelfth cake, ornament it with gum paste, or fancy articles of any description. A good twelfth cake, not baked too much, and kept in a cool dry place, will retain its moisture and eat well, if twelve months old.

ICING FOR FRUIT TARTS, PUFFS, OR PASTRY. Beat up in a half-pint mug the white of two eggs to a solid froth; lay some on the middle of the pie with a paste-brush; sift over plenty of pounded sugar, and press it down with the hand, wash out the brush, and splash by degrees with water till the sugar is dissolved, and put it in the oven for ten minutes, and serve it up cold.

IMPERIAL. Put two ounces of cream of tartar, and the juice and peel of two lemons, into a stone jar, pour on them seven quarts of boiling water, stir, and cover close. When cold, sweeten it with loaf sugar, strain it, bottle and cork it tight. Add in bottling, half a pint to the whole quantity.

INDIA PICKLE. (1) Take one pound of ginger, put it into a pan with salt and water, and let it lay all night, then scrape it, and cut it into thin slices; put it into a pan with half a pound of bay salt, and let it lay till all the following ingredients are prepared; a pound of garlic peeled, and laid in salt for three days, then take it out, wash it, then let it lay in salt for another three days, then take it out and let it lay in the sun for another, till half dry; an ounce of long pepper, an ounce of capsicum, salted and laid in the sun for three days, a pint of black mustard-seed bruised, half an ounce of turmeric, beat very small; put all these ingredients together in a jar, then put in as much vinegar, as, when the cabbage, or whatever you intend to pickle, is put into it, the vinegar will rise to the top of the jar. Then take cabbage, cauliflower, or whatever you choose to pickle, and cut them into small pieces, throw a good handful of salt over them, and set them in the sun (when it is very hot) for three days, drain the water from them every day, and fresh salt them again, turning the leaves till they are dry, then put them into the pickle, being particular that they are completely covered with the vinegar; tie it up close, let it stand a fortnight, fill it again with more vinegar, carefully watch it from time to time, to fill it up with vinegar, as it will waste very fast.

INDIA PICKLE. (2) One gallon of vinegar, one pound of garlic, a quarter of a pound of long pepper split, half a pound of flour of mustard, one pound of ginger scraped, and split, and two ounces of turmeric. When you have prepared the spice, and put it into the jar, pour the vinegar boiling hot over it, and stir it every day for a week. Then put in your cabbage, cauliflower, or whatever you intend to pickle.

INDIAN CURRY. *See Curry.*

IRISH PUFFS. Add to five well-beaten yolks and two whites of eggs, a large table-spoonful of flour, not quite an ounce of melted butter, and half a tea-spoonful of salt; beat it all well for ten minutes, and add half a pint of cream; bake it in buttered tea-cups; turn them out, and serve them with a sweet sauce.

IRISH ROCK. Blanch a pound of sweet and an ounce of bitter almonds, pick out a few of the sweet almonds, and cut them like straws, and blanch them in rose water; pound the rest in a mortar with a table-spoonful of brandy, four ounces of pounded and sifted loaf sugar, and half a pound of salt butter well washed; pound them till the mass looks very white, and set it in a cool place to stiffen; then dip two table-spoons into cold water, and with them form the paste, as much like an egg as possible; place in the bottom of a glass dish, a small plate or saucer turned, and lay the rock high up; stick over it the cut almonds with green sweetmeats, and ornament with a sprig of myrtle.

IRISH STEW, OR HUNTER'S Pie. Take part of a neck of mutton, cut it into chops, season it well, put it into a stew-pan, let it brase for half an hour, take two dozen of potatoes, boil them, mash them, and season them, butter your mould, and line it with the potatoes, put in the mutton, bake it for half an hour, then it will be done, cut a hole in the top, and add some good gravy to it.

IRISH STEW. Take five thick mutton chops, or two pounds off the neck or loins; two pounds of potatoes; peel them, and cut them in halves; six onions, or half a pound of onions; peel and slice them also: first put a layer of potatoes at the bottom of your stewpan, then a couple of chops and some of the onions; then again potatoes, and so on, till the pan is quite full; a small spoonful of white pepper, and about one and a half of salt, and three gills of broth or gravy, and two tea-spoonfuls of mushroom ketchup; cover all very close in, so as to prevent the steam from getting out, and let them stew for an hour and a half on a very slow fire. A small slice of ham is a great addition to this dish. The cook will be the best judge when it is done, as a great deal depends on the fire you have. Great care must be taken not to let it burn, and that it does not do too fast.

ISINGLASS, TO CLARIFY. Take an ounce and quarter of the best isinglass, cut it into small pieces, and wash them several times in warm water. Put the isinglass into a preserving pan, with five glasses of filtered water, set it on the fire, and, as soon as it boils, place it at the side of the stove, so as to keep up the boiling; take off the scum directly it rises; and when the whole is reduced to three-quarters, strain it through a cloth into a basin for use. Some add, in clarifying isinglass, lemon-peel, to remove its disagreeable taste; but as good isinglass ought to have no flavor, and as the lemon-peel is certain to give a yellow tinge to that, it is much better left out.

ITALIAN CHEESE. Mix with nearly half a pound of pounded loaf sugar, the juice of three lemons, two table-spoonfuls of white wine, and a quart of cream; beat it with a whisk till quite thick, which may be in half an hour; put a bit of muslin into a hair sieve, and pour in the cream. In twelve hours turn it out, and garnish with flowers. It may be put into a tin shape, with holes in it.

ITALIAN MACAROONS. Take one pound of Valentia or Jordan almonds, blanched, pound them quite fine with the whites of four eggs; add two pounds and a half of sifted loaf sugar, and rub them well together with the pestle; put in by degrees about ten or eleven more whites, working them well as you put them in; but the best criterion to go by in trying their lightness is to bake one or two, and if you find them heavy, put one or two more whites; put the mixture into a biscuit-funnel, and lay them out on wafer-paper, in pieces about the size of a small walnut, having ready about two ounces of blanched and dry almonds cut into slips, put three or four pieces on each, and bake them on wires, or a baking-plate, in a slow oven. *Obs.*—Almonds should be blanched and dried gradually two or three days before they are used, by which means they will work much better, and where large quantities are used, it is advised to grind them in a mill provided for that purpose.

J.

JAM, APRICOT. (1) Weigh equal quantities of pounded loaf sugar and of apricots; pare and cut them quite small; as they are done, strew over half of the sugar. The following day boil the remainder, and add the apricots; stir it till it boils, take off the scum, and when perfectly clear, add part of the kernels blanched, and boil it two or three minutes.

JAM, APRICOT. (2) Allow equal proportions of pounded loaf sugar and of apricots; pare, and cut them small; as they are done, strew part of the sugar over them, and put the parings into cold water. Break the stones, blanch and pound the kernels, which, with the shells and parings, boil till half the quantity of water is reduced, and there is a sufficiency of the liquor, when strained, to allow three or four table-spoonfuls to a pound of apricots; put it, with the sugar and fruit, into a preserving pan; mash, and take off the scum; boil it quickly, till transparent.

JAM, APRICOT, OR ANY PLUM. After taking away the stones from the apricots, and cutting out any blemishes they may have; put them over a slow fire, in a clean stewpan, with half a pint of water; when scalded, rub them through a hair sieve: to every pound of pulp put one pound of sifted loaf sugar; put it into a preserving-pan over a brisk fire, and when it boils skim it well, and throw in the kernels of the apricots, and half an ounce of bitter almonds, blanched; boil it a quarter of an hour fast, and stirring it all the time; remove it from the fire, and fill it into pots, and cover them as directed in Raspberry Jam. N. B.—Green gages or plums may be done in the same way, omitting the kernels or almonds.

JAM, BLACK CURRANT. Gather your currants on a dry day, when they are full ripe, pick them from the stalks, wash them well in a basin, and to every pound of currants, put a pound of double refined sugar, beaten and sifted; put them into a preserving pan, boil them half an hour, skim, and keep them stirring all the time: then put them into pots: when cold, put brandy paper over, and tie white paper over all.

JAM, CHERRY. Having stoned and boiled three pounds of fine cherries, bruise them, and let the juice run from them, then boil together half a pound of red currant juice, and half a pound of loaf sugar, put the cherries into these whilst they are boiling, and strew on them three-quarters of a pound of sifted sugar. Boil all together very fast for half an hour, and then put it into pots. When cold put on brandy papers.

JAM, GOOSEBERRY. Take what quantity you please of red, rough, ripe gooseberries; take half their quantity of lump sugar; break them well, and boil them together for half an hour, or more if necessary. Put it into pots, and cover with paper.

JAM, GOOSEBERRY, FOR PUDDINGS. Allow equal weight of the red rough gooseberries, and of good brown sugar; gather the fruit upon a dry day; top and tail them, and put a layer alternately of gooseberries and of sugar into a preserving pan; shake it frequently, skim it well, and boil it till the sirup

jellies, which may be ascertained by cooling a little in a saucer. Black and red currants may be done in this way for common use.

JAM, PEACH. Gather the peaches when quite ripe, peel and stone them, put them into a preserving-pan, and mash them over the fire till hot; rub them through a sieve, and add to a pound of pulp the same weight of pounded loaf sugar, and half an ounce of bitter almonds, blanched and pounded; let it boil ten or twelve minutes, stir and skim it well.

JAM, RASPBERRY. Weigh equal proportions of pounded loaf sugar and of raspberries; put the fruit into a preserving-pan, and with a silver spoon bruise and mash it well; let boil six minutes; add the sugar, and stir it well with the fruit; when it boils, skim it, and boil it for fifteen minutes.

JAM, STRAWBERRY. Gather the scarlet strawberries when perfectly ripe, bruise them well, and add the juice of other strawberries; take an equal weight of lump sugar, pound and sift it, stir it thoroughly into the fruit, and set it on a slow fire; boil it twenty minutes, taking off the scum as it rises; pour it into glasses, or jars, and when cold, tie them down.

JAM, WHITE OR RED CURRANT. Pick the fruit very nicely, and allow an equal quantity of finely-pounded loaf sugar; put a layer of each alternately into a preserving pan, and boil for ten minutes; or they may be boiled the same length of time in sugar previously clarified and boiled candy high.

JAUNE MANGE. Boil an ounce of isinglass in three-quarters of a pint of water till melted; strain it, then add the juice of two Seville oranges, a quarter of a pint of white wine, the yolks of four eggs, beaten and strained; sugar according to taste; stir it over a gentle fire till it just boils up: when cold, put it into a mould, taking care, if there should happen to be any sediment, not to pour it in.

JELLY. To a quart of the stock jelly put half a pound of loaf sugar pounded, a stick or two of cinnamon broken into small bits, the peel of a lemon, a pint of currant wine, and one of Sherry or Teneriffe, and the beaten whites of five eggs; put it all into a nicely-cleaned saucepan, stir it gently till it boils, and boil it for three or four minutes. Pour it into a jelly-bag, with a basin or mug placed underneath; run it immediately through the bag again into another basin, and repeat this till it begins to drop. It will then be as transparent as possible, and may be put into moulds or glasses. When all has apparently dripped, pour about a pint of boiling water into the bag, which will produce a little thin jelly fit to drink; the stand with the jelly-bag should be placed near to the fire; Sherry alone, or Teneriffe, may be used. The jelly may be put into quart bottles corked tightly, which will make it keep good for some weeks; place the bottle in warm water when it is required for use.

JELLY, ALE OR PORTER. For a large shape, put to the prepared stock or jelly, more than half a bottle of strong ale or porter, a pound of loaf sugar, the peel of one, and the juice of four large lemons, a stick of cinnamon, and the beaten whites of eight eggs; put it all into a saucepan, stir it gently; let it boil for fifteen minutes, and pour it into a jelly-bag till it runs perfectly clear.

JELLY, APPLE. (1) Pare, core, and cut thirteen good apples into small bits; as they are cut, throw them into two quarts of cold water; boil them in this, with the peel of a lemon, till the substance is extracted, and nearly half the liquor wasted; drain them through a hair sieve, and to a pint of the liquid add one pound of loaf sugar pounded, the juice of one lemon, and the beaten whites of one or two eggs; put it into a saucepan, stir it till it boils, take off the scum, and let it boil till clear, and then pour it into a mould.

JELLY, APPLE. (2) Pare and mince three dozen of juicy acid apples, put them into a pan, cover them with water, and boil them till very soft; strain them through a thin cloth or flannel bag; allow a pound of loaf sugar to a pint of juice; clarify and boil it; add the apple juice, with the grated peel and juice of six lemons; boil it for twenty minutes; take off the scum as it rises.

JELLY, APPLE. (3) Pare and cut into slices eighteen large acid apples; boil them in as much water as will cover them; when quite soft, dip a coarse cloth into hot water, wring it dry, and strain the apples through it; to each pint of juice allow fourteen ounces of fine loaf sugar, clarify it, and add, with the apple juice, the peel of a large lemon; boil it till it jellies, which may be in twenty minutes; pick out the lemon peel, and immediately put it into jars.

JELLY, APRICOT. Take eighteen fine apricots, let them be of a nice red color, stone them, and cut them in pieces into some sirup, (usually made with twelve ounces of sugar, but for apricot jelly it should be rather more liquid than for other jellies.) When the fruit is done put it into a napkin, to express out all the juice you possibly can; which you must add to the sirup in which the apricots have been done, and which has been previously strained through a silk sieve, and after having mixed with it a proper quantity of isinglass to thicken it, finish the same as all other jellies.

JELLY, ARROW-ROOT. Steep for some hours, in two table-spoonfuls of water, the peel of a lemon, and three or four bitter almonds pounded; strain, and mix it with three table-spoonfuls of arrow-root, the same quantity of lemon-juice, and one of brandy; sweeten, and stir it over the fire till quite thick, and when quite cold, put it into jelly glasses.

JELLY, BARBERRY. (1) Pick a pint of barberries, and put them into a stew-pan with boiling water, cover it close and let it stand till nearly cold. Set on the fire some clarified sugar with a little water, (making a quart together;) when it begins to boil, skim it well, put in the barberries, let them boil an hour; squeeze the juice of three lemons through a sieve into a basin, to this, pass the liquor from the barberries, and then the isinglass.

JELLY, BARBERRY. (2) Take some very ripe barberries (what quantity you please) and before you seed them take two thirds of their weight in sugar. Boil your sugar; then put your barberries into it, and, give the whole a few boilings, then pass it through a silk sieve into a pan, pressing the barberries with a spoon to extract as much juice as possible from them; this done, put it again over the fire, and when you perceive it begins to form the scum, take it off and pour it into pots.

JELLY, BREAD FOR AN INVALID. Cut the crum of a penny roll into thin slices, and toast them equally of a pale brown; boil them gently in a quart of water till it will jelly, which may be known by putting a little in a spoon to cool; strain it upon a bit of lemon-peel, and sweeten it with sugar. A little wine may be added.

JELLY BROTH *See Broth.*

JELLY, CALF'S FEET. (1) Take four feet, slit them in two, take away the fat from between the claws, wash them well in luke-warm water; then put them in a large stew-pan, and cover them with water: when the liquor boils, skim it well, and let boil gently six or seven hours, that it may be reduced to about two quarts; then strain it through a sieve, and skim off all the oily substance which is on the surface of the liquor.

If you are not in a hurry, it is better to boil the calf's feet the day before you make the jelly; as when the liquor is cold, the oily part being at the top, and the other being firm, with pieces of kitchen paper applied to it, you may remove every particle of the oily substance, without wasting any of the liquor.

Put the liquor in a stewpan to melt, with a pound of lump sugar, the peel of two lemons, the juice of six, six whites and shells of eggs beat together, and a bottle of Sherry or Madeira; whisk the whole together until it is on the boil; then put it by the side of the stove, and let it simmer a quarter of an hour; strain it through a jelly-bag: what is strained first must be poured into the bag again, until it is as bright and as clear as rock-water; then put the jelly in moulds, to be cold and firm: if the weather is too warm, it requires some ice.

When it is wished to be very stiff, half an ounce of isinglass may be added when the wine is put in.

It may be flavored by the juice of various fruits, spices, &c. and colored with saffron, cochineal, red beet juice, spinage juice, claret, &c. and it is sometimes made with cherry brandy, or noyeau rouge, or Curacoa, or essence of punch, instead of wine.

JELLY, CALF'S FEET. (2) Take the fat and bones from eight feet, and soak them in water for three or four hours; then boil them in six quarts of water, skimming often; when reduced to a third, strain and set it by to cool; when cold, take every particle of fat from the top, and remove whatever may have settled at the bottom. Dissolve it in an earthen pan, adding to it two quarts of white wine, mace, cinnamon, and ginger, or not, as you please. Beat up the whites of twelve eggs with three pounds of fine sugar, mix these with the jelly, boil it gently, adding the juice of two lemons, and then strain it for use.

JELLY, CHERRY. Take the stones and stalks from two pounds of fine clear ripe cherries; mix them with a quarter of a pound of red currants, from which the seeds have been extracted; express the juice from these fruits, filter and mix it with three-quarters of a pound of clarified sugar, and one ounce of isinglass. Finish the same as *Barberry jelly*.

JELLY OF CURRANTS, GRAPE, RASPBERRY, Are all made precisely in the same manner. When the fruit is full ripe, gather it on a dry day: as soon as it is nicely picked, put it into a jar, and cover it down very close.

Set the jar in a saucepan about three parts filled with cold water; put it on a gentle fire, and let it simmer for about half an hour. Take the pan from the fire, and pour the contents of the jar into a jelly-bag: pass the juice through a second time; do not squeeze the bag.

To each pint of juice add a pound and a half of very good lump sugar pounded; when it is dissolved, put it into a preserving-pan; set it on the fire, and boil gently; stirring and skimming it the whole time (about thirty or forty minutes), *i. e.* till no more scum rises, and it is perfectly clear and fine: pour it while warm into pots; and when cold, cover them with paper wetted in brandy.

Half a pint of this jelly, dissolved in a pint of brandy or vinegar, will give you excellent currant or raspberry brandy or vinegar.

*Obs.*—Jellies from other fruits are made in the same way, and cannot be preserved in perfection without plenty of good sugar.

Those who wish jelly to turn out very stiff, dissolve isinglass in a little water, strain through a sieve, and add it in the proportion of half an ounce to a pint of juice, and put it in with the sugar.

The best way is the cheapest. Jellies made with two small a proportion of sugar, require boiling so long; there is much more waste of juice and flavor by evaporation than the due quantity of sugar costs; and they neither look nor taste half so well.

JELLY, DAMSON. To eight pounds of damsons, put eight pounds of fine sugar, and half a pint of water; boil them for half an hour over a gentle fire, till the skins break; then take them off, and set them by for an hour; set them on the fire again, for half an hour more; set them by again for the same time; do so the third time; while they stand off the fire, put a weight upon them to keep them under the sirup. The last time, you must boil them till you perceive they are of a very high color in the part where the skin is broken; then take them off, set them by to cool, and when they are cold, drain off the sirup, and make the jelly in the following manner:—Boil a quantity of green apples, green gooseberries, and quince cores, to a mash; then strain them through a hair sieve. Take an equal quantity of this jelly and the former sirup, and boil them over a gentle fire together till they jelly; skim it well, and while it is hot, put it into glasses or pots.

JELLY FOR ENTREMETS. Hartshorn, calf's feet, and isinglass, are the usual materials used to coagulate sweet jellies; of these three, the latter is the best, as, when properly clarified, (for which see isinglass), it is the clearest, and has no unpleasant flavor.

JELLY FRUIT. Clarify half a pound of sugar, but the instant before it is quite clear, put in a small quantity of cochineal; then strain, and mix with it an ounce of clarified isinglass, and the juice of two lemons; add to this the fruit of which your jelly is to be composed; stir them together lightly, pour the jelly into a mould quickly, and put the mould on ice. Observe that the sugar and isinglass should be no more than lukewarm when mixed together. These jellies may be made of any kind of fruit, or the grated rinds of lemon, orange, or cedrats.

JELLY, GLOUCESTER. Take an ounce of rice, the same of sago, pearl-barley, hartshorn-shavings, and eringo root; simmer with three pints of water, till reduced to one pint, strain it. When cold it will be a jelly; when you use it, serve dissolved in wine, milk, or broth.

JELLY, GRAPE. Take out the stones, then mash the grapes with your hands, (they must be ripe) then squeeze them through a cloth to extract all the juice from them, and boil and finish the same as currant jelly. Use half a pound of sugar to each pound of fruit.

JELLY, HARTSHORN. Boil half a pound of hartshorn shavings for three hours and a half in four pints and a half of water; strain it through a bit of muslin, and stir into it three ounces of dissolved isinglass; if large, the peel of one, if small, of two lemons, and their juice, half the peel of an orange, three parts of a tea-cupful of brandy, and one of white wine; sweeten with pounded loaf sugar, and when lukewarm put it into a saucepan with the beaten whites of six eggs; stir it, and let it boil for two minutes; strain it through a jelly-bag two or three times till perfectly clear.

JELLY, ORANGE. (1) Squeeze the juice of eight oranges and six lemons, grate the peel of half the fruit, and steep it in a pint of cold water; mix it with the juice, three-quarters of a pound of loaf sugar, one ounce and a quarter of isinglass, and the beaten whites of seven eggs; put it into a saucepan, and stir till it boils; let it boil a few minutes, and strain it through a jelly-bag till clear; put it into a mould or glasses.

JELLY, ORANGE. (2) Boil in a pint of water one ounce and a quarter of picked isinglass, the rind of an orange cut thin, a stick of cinnamon, a few corianders, and three ounces of loaf sugar, till the isinglass is dissolved; then squeeze two Seville oranges or lemons, and enough oranges to make a pint of juice: mix all together, and strain it through a tamis or lawn sieve into a basin; set it in a cold place for half an hour; pour it into another basin free from sediment; and when it begins to congeal, fill your

mould: when wanted, dip the mould into lukewarm water; turn it out on a dish, and garnish with orange or lemon cut in slices, and placed round. N. B.—A few grains of saffron put in the water will add much to its appearance.

JELLY, OX-HEEL. Slit them in two, and take away the fat between the claws. The proportion of water to each heel is about a quart: let it simmer gently for eight hours (keeping it clean skimmed); it will make a pint and a half of strong jelly, which is frequently used to make calf's feet jelly, or to add to mock turtle and other soups.

JELLY, PEACH. Cut ten or twelve peaches in halves, take out the stones and peel them; set a pint of smooth clarified sugar, diluted with water, on the fire; when it has boiled and been skimmed, put in the peaches, the kernels should be broken and put in with them; let them boil, very gently for ten minutes, then take out four or five of the halves, and lay them on a plate to be in readiness for garnishing the jelly; let the remainder of the peaches boil for ten minutes longer; while they are boiling take three lemons, cut off the rind, squeeze the juice through a silk sieve in a basin, pass the liquor of the peaches into it, and then the isinglass, running it through the sieve two or three times, in order to mix it well; fill the mould half full of jelly, and when set, put in the peaches and a little more jelly, and when that is set, fill up the mould. The reason why the lemons are peeled before they are squeezed for this jelly is, that the oil in the rind would rather spoil the favor of the jelly, than be any addition.

JELLY, QUINCE. Quinces for jelly ought not to be quite ripe, they should, however, be of a fine yellow color; take off the down which covers them, quarter, core, put them into a saucepan, with water enough to cover them; set them on the fire, and when soft, lay the pieces on a sieve to drain, pressing them very slightly; strain the liquor, and measure it; clarify, and boil to *casse* an equal quantity of sugar; then take it off, add the liquor to it, stirring it well; when mixed, put it on the fire, still stirring; as soon as the jelly spreads over the spoon, and falls from it like treacle; take it from the fire, and when cold, pour it into pots.

JELLY, RASPBERRY. Take two thirds of rasberries, and one third red currants; pick them, press the juice through a sieve into a pan, cover, and place it in a cellar, or any other cool place for three days; at the end of that time raise the thick skin formed at the top, and pour the juice into another vessel: weigh it, and put it, with half the quantity of sugar, into a preserving pan, set it on the fire; a great deal of scum will rise at first, which must all be taken off; leave it on the fire for an hour; then pour a few drops on a cold plate, if it cools of the proper consistence for jellies, take it from the fire and whilst hot pour it into pots; Let the jelly be quite cold before the pots are covered.

JELLY, RUM. Clarify, and boil to a sirup, a pound of loaf sugar; dissolve one ounce of isinglass in half a pint of water, strain it through a sieve into the sirup when it is half warm, and when nearly cold, stir in a quart of white wine; mix it well, and add one or two table-spoonfuls of old Jamaica rum, stir it for a few minutes, and pour it into a mould, or into glasses.

JELLY, STRAWBERRY. Put some fresh-gathered strawberries into an earthen pan, bruise them with a wooden spoon, add a little cold water, and some finely-pounded loaf sugar. In an hour or two, strain it through a jelly-bag, and to a quart of the juice add one ounce of isinglass, which has been dissolved in half a pint of water, well-skimmed, strained, and allowed to cool; mix all well, and pour it into an earthen mould.

Raspberry jelly, red currant jelly, and red currants mixed with raspberries, may be made exactly in the same manner; and the bright red color may be improved by mixing in a little carmine or lake. When this kind of jelly is to be made with cherries, the fruit should be boiled a few minutes in clarified sugar, and when cold, the juice of one or two lemons may be added with the isinglass.

A little lemon juice may be added to any of the other jellies, in proportion to the acidity of the fruit.

They may be iced by covering and surrounding the mould with ice, without any salt.

JUICE. The proportion of oranges should be double that of lemons; the fruit being selected free from decay, and wiped dry, they are to be squeezed, and the juice strained through a sieve into an earthen pan; to each pint, according to the acidity of the fruit, a pound and a half, or a pound and three-quarters, of double-refined sugar, broken small, is to be added. It must be stirred and skimmed daily, till the sugar is well incorporated, or as long as the scum rises; and when it has been a month in the pan, it may be boiled.

JUICE OF FRESH FRUIT ICED. Press through a sieve the juice of a pint of pickled currants or raspberries, add to it four or five ounces of pounded loaf sugar, a little lemon juice, and a pint of cream. It may be whisked previous to freezing, and a mixture of the juice may be used.

JULIENNE. This soup is composed of carrots, turnips, leeks, onions, celery, lettuce, sorrel and chervil; the roots are cut in thin slips about an inch long, the onions are halved and then sliced; the lettuce and sorrel chopped small; toss up the roots in a little butter, when they are done, add the lettuces, &c. moisten them with broth, and boil the whole over a slow fire for an hour or more, if necessary; prepare some bread in the usual way, and pour the julienne over it.

JUMBLES. Mix one pound of fine flour with one pound of fine powder sugar, make them into a light paste with whites of eggs well beaten; add half a pint of cream, half a pound of fresh butter, melted, and a pound of blanched almonds, pounded; knead them all together, thoroughly, with a little rose water, and cut out the jumbles into whatever forms you think proper; and either bake them in a gentle oven, or fry them in fresh butter; serve them in a dish, melt fresh butter with a spoonful of mountain, and strew fine sugar over the dish.

JUSTICE'S ORANGE SIRUP FOR PUNCH OR PUDDINGS. Squeeze the oranges, and strain the juice from the pulp into a large pot; boil it up with a pound and a half of fine sugar to each pint of juice; skim it well; let it stand till cold; then bottle it, and cork it well. *Obs.*—This makes a fine, soft, mellow-flavored punch; and, added to melted butter, is a good relish to puddings.

wwwwww

## K.

KAVIA. Take the hard roes of several sturgeon, and lay them in a tub of water; take away all the fibres as you would from a calf's brains, then, with a whisk, beat the roes in the water, shaking off from the whisk whatever fibres may be adhering to it; then lay the roes on sieves for a short time; after which put them into fresh water again; and continue to whip them, and change the water, until the roes are perfectly cleansed and free from fibre; lay them on sieves to drain, season them well with salt and pepper; wrap them in a coarse cloth, tying them up like a ball, and let them drain thus till the next day, when serve them with fried bread, and shallots chopped small. If they are to be kept for sometime, put more salt to them.

KEBOBBED VEAL. *See Veal.*

KELLY'S SAUCE. *See Sauce.*

KERRY BUTTER MILK. Put six quarts of butter-milk into a cheese cloth, hang it in a cool place, and let the whey drip from it for two or three days; when it is rather thick, put it into a basin, sweeten it with pounded loaf sugar, and add a glass of brandy, or of sweet wine, and as much raspberry jam, or sirup, as will color and give it an agreeable flavor. Whisk it well together, and serve it in a glass dish.

KETCHUP, ENGLISH. Peel ten cloves of garlic, bruise them, and put them into a quart of white wine vinegar; take a quart of white Port, put it on the fire, and when it boils, put in twelve or fourteen anchovies, washed and cut in pieces; let them simmer in the wine till they are dissolved; when cold, put them to the vinegar; then take half a pint of white wine, and put into it some mace, some ginger sliced, a few cloves, a spoonful of whole pepper bruised; let them boil a little; when almost cold, slice in a whole nutmeg, and some lemon-peel, with two or three spoonfuls of horse-radish; add it to the rest, stop it close, and stir it once or twice a day. Keep it close stopped up. See *Mushroom Ketchup.*

KEW MINCE. Cut a pound of meat from a leg of cold roasted mutton, and mince it very finely, together with six ounces of suet, mix with it three or four table-spoonfuls of crumbs of bread, the beaten yolks of four eggs, one anchovy chopped, some pepper and salt, and half a pint of Port wine; put it into a caul of veal, and bake it in a quick oven; turn it out into a dish, and pour some brown gravy over it; serve with it venison sauce. When a veal caul is not to be had, the mince may be done in a saucepan.

KID. Kid is good eating when it is but three or four months old, its flesh is then delicate and tender, but is not used after it has done sucking. To be good, it ought to be fat and white. It is dressed in the same manner as lamb or fawn.

KIDNEYS. Cut them through the long

way, score them, and sprinkle them over with a little pepper and salt; in order to broil all over alike, and to keep them from curling on the gridiron, run a wire skewer right through them. They must be broiled over a clear fire, being careful to turn them frequently till they are done; they will take about ten or twelve minutes broiling, provided they are done over a brisk fire; or, if you choose, you may fry them in butter, and make gravy for them in the pan (after the kidneys are taken out), by putting in a tea-spoonful of flour; as soon as it looks brown, put in a sufficient quantity of water as will make gravy; they will take five minutes longer frying than broiling. Garnish with fried parsley: you may improve them if you think proper, by chopping a few parsley leaves very fine, mix them with a bit of fresh butter, and a little pepper and salt, and then put some of this mixture over each kidney.

KISSES. (1) Put the whites of eight eggs, and two spoonfuls of orange-flower water, into a China basin, and whisk till they become a firm froth, then add half a pound of sifted sugar, stir it in with great care by means of a spatula: that done, lay small pieces of this mixture on white paper; make each drop about the size of a ratafia, rather conical than flat; place the paper which contains them on a piece of wood about an inch thick, and put them in a very hot oven: watch them, and as soon as you perceive they begin to look yellowish, take them out, and detach them from the paper with a knife as cautiously as possible, for they are very tender. Take a small spoon, and with the end of it remove the moist part, which is at the bottom, so as to make them a little hollow, and as you do them, lay each on the paper, the hollow side upwards; put them on the wood into the oven again for a few minutes to dry; when done, lay them in boxes, and keep them in a dry and warm place. If they are for table, fill the hollow of each with a little whipped cream or raspberry jam; put them together by couples, the cream or jam

inside; place them in a dish, and serve them as soon as possible.

KISSES. (2) One pound of the best loaf sugar, powdered and sifted. The whites of four eggs. Twelve drops of essence of lemon. A tea-cup of currant jelly. Beat the whites of four eggs till they stand alone. Then beat in, gradually, the sugar, a tea-spoonful at a time. Add the essence of lemon, and beat the whole very hard. Lay a wet sheet of paper on the bottom of a square tin pan. Drop on it, at equal distances, a small tea-spoonful of stiff currant jelly. With a large spoon, pile some of the beaten white of egg and sugar, on each lump of jelly, so as to cover it entirely. Drop on the mixture as evenly as possible, so as to make the kisses of a round smooth shape. Set them in a cool oven, and as soon as they are colored, they are done. Then take them out and place them two bottoms together. Lay them lightly on a sieve, and dry them in a cool oven, till the two bottoms stick fast together, so as to form one ball or oval.

KNUCKLES. *See the several meats to which they belong.*

L.

LAMB. The fore quarter of lamb consists of the shoulder, the neck, and the breast together; the hind quarter is the leg and loin. There are also the head and pluck, the fry or sweetbreads, skirts, lambstones, and liver. In choosing the fore quarter, the vein in the neck should be ruddy, or of a bluish color. In the hind quarter, the knuckle should feel stiff, the kidney small, and perfectly fresh. To keep it, the joints should be carefully wiped every day, and in warm weather, sprinkled with a little pepper. The fore quarter is the prime joint, and should be roasted and basted with butter; the gravy is made as for beef or mutton. Mint sauce is served in a sauce tureen, and half a lemon is sent to table with it, the juice of which is squeezed upon the ribs after the shoulder is cut off, and they have been sprinkled with salt. If the joint weighs five pounds, it will require to be roasted one hour; if ten pounds, one hour and three-quarters. The hind quarter may be roasted, or the leg of it boiled. The loin is then cut into steaks, fried, and served round it; the outside bones being covered with a fringe of fried parsley. A dish of spinach is generally served with the lamb.

LAMB, Is a delicate, and commonly considered tender meat; but those who talk of tender lamb, while they are thinking of the age of the animal, forget that even a chicken must be kept a proper time after it has been killed, or it will be tough picking. To the usual accompaniments of roasted meat, green mint sauce, and a salad, is commonly added; and some cooks, about five minutes before it is done, sprinkle it with a little fresh gathered and finely minced parsley. Lamb, and all young meats, ought to be thoroughly done; therefore do not take either lamb or veal off the spit till you see it drop white gravy. When green mint cannot be got, mint vinegar is an acceptable substitute for it; and crisp parsley on a side plate, is an admirable accompaniment.

*Hind-Quarter*, Of eight pounds, will take from an hour and three-quarters to two hours: baste and froth it. The leg and the loin of lamb, when little, should be roasted together; the former being lean, the latter fat, and the gravy is better preserved.

*Fore-Quarter*, Of ten pounds, about two hours. It is a pretty general custom, when you take off the shoulder from the ribs, to squeeze a Seville orange over them, and sprinkle them with a little pepper and salt. This may as well be done by the cook before it comes to table; some people are not remarkably expert at dividing these joints nicely.

*Leg*, Of five pounds, from an hour to an hour and a half.

*Shoulder*, With a quick fire, an hour.

*Ribs*, About an hour to an hour and a quarter: joint it nicely, crack the ribs across, and divide them from the brisket after it is roasted.

*Loin*, An hour and a quarter.

*Neck*, An hour.

*Breast*, Three-quarters of an hour.

LAMB BREAST. Cut it into pieces, and stew it in a weak stock, with a glass of Port wine; add pepper and salt. When it is perfectly tender, thicken the sauce with butter and flour. Have ready cucumbers stewed in gravy, put them over the lamb before serving. A breast of mutton may be served in the same way.

LAMB CHOPS BROILED. Cut a loin or best end of the neck into chops, flatten them, and cut off the fat and skin; rub the gridiron with a little fat, and broil them on a clear fire. Turn them with steak tongs, till quite done. Serve them hot.

LAMB CHOPS. Cut a neck or loin of lamb into chops; rub them over with the beaten yolk of an egg; dip them into grated bread, mixed with plenty of chopped parsley, and season with lemon-peel, pepper, and salt; fry them a light brown in good dripping; make a sauce with the trimmings, and thicken the sauce with butter rolled in flour; add a little lemon pickle and mushroom ketchup. Garnish with fried parsley. They may be served with or without the gravy.

LAMB CUTLETS. Cut the cutlets off the loin, into round bits; trim off the fat and skin; dip them into the beaten yolk of an egg, and then into bread crumbs, mixed with minced parsley, grated nutmeg, and lemon-peel, pepper, and salt. Fry them a light brown in clarified beef suet; drain them on the back of a sieve before the fire. Serve them with melted butter with a little lemon pickle in it, or a brown sauce thickened. Garnish with cut lemon.

LAMB DRESSED WITH RICE. Half roast a small fore quarter of lamb; cut it into steaks, season them with a little salt and pepper; lay them into a dish, and pour in a little water. Boil a pound of rice with a blade or two of mace; strain it, and stir in a good piece of fresh butter, and a little salt, add also the greater part of the yolks of four eggs beaten; cover the lamb with the rice, and with a feather put over it the remainder of the beaten eggs. Bake it in an oven till it has acquired a light brown color.

LAMB FEET. Clean, well wash, and blanch six lamb's feet; stew them, till they become tender, in some white stock, with a slice of lean ham, one onion, some parsley, thyme, two blades of mace, a little whole pepper, and a few mushrooms. Before serving, strain the sauce; thicken it with flour and butter, and half a pint of cream; boil it a quarter of an hour, add the feet and the juice of half a small lemon. Garnish with sippets of thin toasted bread, cut into a three-cornered shape.

LAMB FRY. Fry it plain, or dip it in an egg well beaten on a plate, and strew some fine stale bread-crumbs over it; garnish with crisp parsley.

LAMB, LEG OF, BOILED. It should be boiled in a cloth, that it may look as white as possible. Cut the loin in steaks, dip them in egg, strew them over with bread-crumbs, and fry them a nice brown, serve them round the dish, and garnish with dried or fried parsley; serve with spinach to eat with it.

LAMB PIE, THE GERMAN WAY. Cut a quarter of lamb into pieces, and lard them with small lardons of bacon, seasoned with salt, pepper, cloves, nutmeg, and a bay-leaf; add fat bacon pounded, small onions, nutmeg, and sweet herbs; put these into the pie, and let it bake for three hours; when baked, cut it open, skim off all the fat, pour in a ragout of oysters,

and serve hot.

LAMB PIE, A SAVORY ONE. Cut the meat into pieces, and season it with pepper, salt, mace, cloves, and nutmeg, finely beaten. Make a good puff paste crust, put the meat into it, with a few lamb stones and sweetbreads, seasoned the same as the meat. Then put in some oysters and forcemeat balls, the yolks of hard eggs, and the tops of asparagus, about two inches long, first boiled green. Put butter all over the pie, put on the lid, and let it bake for an hour and a half in a quick oven. In the meantime, take a pint of gravy, the oyster liquor, a gill of red wine, and a little grated nutmeg. Mix all together with the yolks of two or three eggs, finely beaten, and keep stirring it the same way all the time. When it boils, pour it into the pie, put on the lid again, and serve it to table.

LAMB, TO ROAST OR BOIL. A quarter of an hour is generally allowed to each pound of meat; a leg of lamb of five pounds will therefore take an hour and a quarter to roast or boil, the other joints in the same proportion; serve either with salad, pickles, brocoli, cauliflowers, string beans, pease, potatoes, or cucumbers, raw or stewed.

LAMB SHOULDER, GRILLED. Boil it; score it in chequers about an inch square, rub it over with the yolk of an egg, pepper and salt it, strew it with bread-crumbs and dried parsley, or sweet herbs, and *carbonado*, i. e. grill, i. e. broil it over a clear fire, or put it in a Dutch oven till it is a nice light brown; send up some gravy with it, or make a sauce for it of flour and water well mixed together with an ounce of fresh butter, a table-spoonful of mushroom or walnut ketchup, and the juice of half a lemon. See Grill sauce. Breasts of lamb are often done in the same way, and with mushroom or mutton sauce.

LAMB STEAKS FRIED. Fry them of

the nicest brown; when served, throw over them a good quantity of crumbs of bread fried, and crisped parsley. Or you may season them and broil them in buttered papers, either with crumbs and herbs, or without, according to taste.

LARD, HOG'S. The lard should be carefully melted in a jar, put into a kettle of water, and boiled; run it into bladders that have been particularly well cleaned. It is best to have the bladders small, as the lard will keep better, for, after the air reaches it, it becomes rank. Whilst it is melting, put in a sprig of rosemary. This being a very useful article in frying fish, it should be prepared with great care. Mixed with batter; it makes a fine crust.

LARKS. These delicate little birds are in high season in November. When they are thoroughly picked, gutted, and cleansed, truss them; do them over with the yolk of egg, and then roll them in bread-crumbs; spit them on a lark spit, and fasten that on to a larger spit, ten or fifteen minutes will be sufficient time to roast them in before a quick fire; whilst they are roasting, baste them with fresh butter, and sprinkle them with bread-crumbs till they are well covered with them. Fry some grated bread in butter, set it to drain before the fire, that it may harden. Serve the crumbs in the dish under the larks, and garnish with slices of lemon.

LAVENDER DROPS. Fill a quart bottle with the blossoms of lavender, and pour on it as much brandy as it will contain; let it stand ten days, then strain it, and add of nutmeg bruised, cloves, mace, and cochineal, a quarter of an ounce each, and bottle it for use. In nervous cases, a little may be taken dropped on a bit of sugar; and in the beginning of a bowel complaint, a teaspoonful, taken in half a glass of peppermint water will often prove efficacious.

LAVENDER WATER. Put into a large bottle, eight ounces of the best rectified spirits of wine, three drachms of oil of lavender, one drachm of essence of ambergris, and threepence-worth of musk; cork it tightly, and shake it well every day, for a fortnight or three weeks.

LEAVES, TO GREEN, FOR ORNAMENTING FRUIT. Take small leaves of a pear-tree, keep them close stopped in a pan of verjuice and water, give them a boil in some sirup of apricots; put them between two pieces of glass to dry; smooth and cut them into the shape of apricot-leaves (the leaves should be procured with stalks); stick them about the apricots or any other preserved fruit; but the leaves must be cut in the shape of the leaf which belongs to the fruit you ornament.

LEEKS. Leeks are most generally used for soups, ragouts, and other made dishes, they are very rarely brought to table; in which case dress them as follows:—Put them into the stock-pot till about three parts done; then take them out, drain, and soak them in vinegar seasoned with pepper, salt, and cloves; drain them again, stuff the hearts with a *farce*, dip them in batter, and fry them.

LEIPZEGER PANCAKES. Beat well the whites of four, and the yolks of eight fresh eggs, and add, by degrees, half a pound of pounded loaf sugar, a pint and a half of sweet cream just warmed, half a pound of clarified fresh butter, two tablesspoonfuls of fresh yeast, and a wine-glass full of spirits of wine; then mix in as much sifted flour as will make it into a thick batter; let it rise for half an hour, roll it out thin; cut it into rounds or oblong pieces, and lay on them jam or marmalade; double them, and let them stand again to rise, and fry them in boiling fresh lard or butter.

LEMONADE. To a gallon of spring water add some cinnamon and cloves, plenty of orange and plenty of lemon-juice, and a bit of the peel of each; sweeten well with loaf sugar, and whisk it with the whites of six eggs, and the yolk of one; give it a boil, and then let it simmer for ten minutes; then run it through a jelly-bag, and let it stand till cold, before it is drank.

LEMONADE TRANSPARENT. The peel of fourteen lemons having been soaked in two quarts of water for two hours, their juice, one pound and a half of sugar, and a quart of white wine, are to be added; a quart of new milk, made boiling hot, is then to be mixed with it, and when it has stood an hour, it is to be strained through a jelly-bag till it runs clear.

LEMON BONBONS. Take two pounds of the best lump sugar, clarify and boil it to *caramel*; but just before it reaches that point, grate the rind of a lemon and put in it; in the meanwhile melt a little butter; skim, and pour it off clear; take a spoonful of this butter, and rub it with your hand over a copperplate or marble slab, on which pour the *caramel* sugar: then have a sword blade, take an end in each hand, and impress lines in the sugar about an inch apart; then impress similar lines across the first, so as to form small cakes; this operation should be performed as quickly as possible, lest the sugar should cool before the whole is marked; when however all is done, pass the blade carefully between the sugar and the slab, lay it on sheets of white paper, and when perfectly cold, separate the *bonbons*, and wrap each in paper; keep them in a dry place.

LEMON BRANDY. Three quarts of brandy being put into an earthen jar that is fitted with a cover, a pound and three-quarters of fine loaf sugar, the thin parings of six lemons, and the juice of twelve, are to be added; one quart of boiling milk is to be poured over the mixture, which must be stirred daily for eight days; it is then to be run through a jelly-bag and bottled.

LEMON CHEESECAKES. Boil the peel of two large lemons till they are quite tender, and then pound it well in a mortar, with four or five ounces of loaf sugar, the yolks of six eggs, half a pound of fresh butter, and a little curd beaten fine: pound and mix altogether, lay a rich puff paste in some patty-pans, fill them half full, and bake them carefully.

LEMON CHEESECAKES. Mix four ounces of sifted lump sugar, and four ounces of butter together, and gently melt it; then add the yolks of two, and the white of one egg, the rind of three lemons shred fine, and the juice of one lemon and a half, one savory biscuit, some blanched almonds, pounded, three spoonfuls of brandy; mix the whole well together, and put it to paste made with the following ingredients: eight ounces of flour, six ounces of butter, two-thirds of which must be mixed with the flour first; then wet it with six spoonfuls of water, and roll in the remainder of the butter.

LEMON CHIPS. Take large smooth-rinded Malaga lemons; race or cut off their peel into chips with a small knife (this will require some practice to do it properly); throw them into salt and water till next day; have ready a pan of boiling water, throw them in and boil them tender. Drain them well: after having lain sometime in water to cool, put them in an earthen pan, pour over enough boiling clarified sugar to cover them, and then let them lie two days; then strain the sirup, put more sugar, and reduce it by boiling till the sirup is quite thick; put in the chips, and simmer them a few minutes, and set them by for two days: repeat it once more; let them be two days longer, and they will be fit to candy, which must be done as follows: take four pints of clarified sugar, which will be sufficient for six pounds of chips, boil it to the degree of *blown* (which may be known by dipping the skimmer into the sugar, and blowing strongly through the holes of it; if little bladders appear, it has attained that degree); and when the chips are thoroughly drained and wiped on a clean cloth, put them into the sirup, stirring them about with the skimmer till you see the sugar become white; then take them out with two forks; shake them lightly into a wire sieve, and set them into a stove, or in a warm place to dry. Orange chips are done in the same way.

LEMON ESSENCE. Rasp your lemons all round, very thin, and for every quarter of a pound of rind, allow one pound of sugar; mix it well with a large spaddle till you find it is all of the same color, and that the rind is well mixed; put it into a stone jar, and press it down as hard as you can; put a bladder over the paper you cover with, and tie it over quite tight; put it by, and in a month's time it will be fit for use.

LEMON JUICE TO PRESERVE. Squeeze, and strain a pint of lemon-juice; put into a China basin one pound of double-refined sugar finely pounded and sifted, add the lemon-juice, and stir it with a silver spoon till the sugar be perfectly dissolved. Bottle it, and cork it tightly; seal the cork, or tie bladder over it, and keep it in a dry cool place.

LEMON MARMALADE. Allow to a pound of lemons eighteen ounces of fine loaf sugar; grate the rind of a few; cut them into half; squeeze and strain the juice; boil the skins in the same way as those of the orange skins are done; scoop out the pulp and white part; cut half into thin chips or parings, and pound the other half in a mortar; pound the sugar, and pour over it the juice; stir, and let it boil for five minutes; skim it; take it off the fire; put in the parings and the pounded skins; boil it for five minutes, then add the grated peel, and let it boil for five minutes more; take it off, and stir it till half cold, before putting it into jars.

LEMON MINCE PIES. Squeeze out the juice from a large lemon; boil the outside till sufficiently tender to beat to a mash, add to it three large apples chopped, and four ounces of suet, half a pound of currants, four ounces of sugar; put the juice of the lemon, and add candied fruit, the same as for other pies. Make a short crust, and fill the patty-pans in the usual manner.

LEMON-PEEL ESSENCE. Wash and brush clean the lemons; let them get perfectly dry: take a lump of loaf sugar, and rub them till all the yellow rind is taken up by the sugar: scrape off the surface of the sugar into a preserving pot, and press it hard down; cover it very close, and it will keep for sometime.

LEMON-PEEL QUINTESSENCE. Best oil of lemon, one drachm, strongest rectified spirit, two ounces, introduced by degrees till the spirit kills, and completely mixes with the oil. This elegant preparation possesses all the delightful fragrance and flavor of the freshest lemon-peel. *Obs.*—A few drops on the sugar you make punch with will instantly impregnate it with as much flavor as the troublesome and tedious method of grating the rind, or rubbing the sugar on it. It will be found a superlative substitute for fresh lemon-peel for every purpose that it is used for: blancmange, jellies, custards, ice, negus, lemonade, and pies and puddings, stuffings, soups, sauces, ragouts; &c.

LEMON-PEEL TINCTURE. A very easy and economical way of obtaining, and preserving the flavor of lemon-peel, is to fill a wide-mouthed pint bottle half full of brandy, or proof spirit; and when you use a lemon, pare the rind off very thin, and put it into the brandy, &c.: in a fortnight it will impregnate the spirit with the flavor very strongly.

LEMON PICKLE. (1) Grate off a little of the outer rind of two dozen of lemons, divide them into four rather more than half way down, leaving the bottom part whole;

rub on them equally half a pound of finely-beaten salt, spread them upon a large dish, and put them into a cool oven. When the juice has dried up, put them into a stone jar, with an ounce of cloves and one of mace finely beaten, one ounce of nutmeg cut into thin slices, a quarter of an ounce of cayenne, and four ounces of garlic peeled, also half a pint of white mustard-seed bruised and tied in a bit of muslin. Pour over the whole two quarts of boiling vinegar, stop the jar closely, and let it stand for three months; then strain it through a hair sieve, pressing it well through; let it stand till the next day, pour off the clear, and put it into small bottles. Let the dregs stand covered some days, when it will become fine. It will keep good for years. When the lemons are to be used as pickle, no straining is necessary.

LEMON PICKLE. (2) Cut into quarters, and pick out all the seeds of six middling sized lemons; put them into a jar, strew over them two ounces of well beaten salt; cover the jar with a cloth and plate, and let it stand three days; then put to them cloves and a quarter of an ounce of mace beaten fine, one ounce of garlic or shallot, two of mustard-seed bruised, and one nutmeg sliced. Make a quart of vinegar boiling hot, and pour it over the ingredients; cover the jar, and in three or four days close it with a bung, and tie leather over it. It will be fit for use in a week, and is an improvement to most sauces, and particularly to fish sauce.

LEMON POSSET. Squeeze the juice of two lemons into a China bowl, or small deep dish, that will hold a quart; sweeten it like sirup, add a little brandy; boil one pint of cream with a bit of orange-peel; take out the peel; when cold, put the cream into a teapot, pour it to the sirup, holding it high. Make it the day before it is wanted.

LEMON PUDDING. *See Pudding.*

LEMON RINDS MARMALADE. Hav-ing squeezed the juice from your lemons, cut out all the white part, and put the rinds into boiling water; as soon as they begin to soften, take them from the fire, and throw them into cold water; then lay them on a sieve to drain, and make them into marmalade, in the same manner as apricots. Orange rinds are done this way.

LEMON SPONGE. Boil half an ounce of isinglass in a pint of water till dissolved; strain it, and the following day add the juice of two lemons, and the grated peel of one; rub through a hair sieve, into the isinglass a good quantity of raspberry jam, that has stood before the fire some time, and whisk it all together till like a sponge; put it into an earthen mould, set it in a cold place for some hours, and turn it out. Any other sort of preserve may be used, and if made with only orange or lemon-juice, sweeten it with sugar, or make it with orange jelly which may have been left the day before.

LEMON SYLLABUBS. Take a pint of cream, a pint of white wine, the peel of two lemons grated, and the juice; sugar according to taste; let it stand some time; mill or whip it, lay the froth on a sieve; put the remainder into glasses, and lay on the froth. They should be made the day before they are wanted. If you should wish them to taste very strong of the lemon, you must make use of the juice of six lemons, and nearly a pound of sugar; they will keep four or five days.

LEMONS, SIRUP OF. Put a pint of fresh lemon-juice to a pound and three-quarters of lump sugar; dissolve it by a gentle heat; skim it till the surface is quite clear; add an ounce of thin-cut lemon-peel; let them simmer (very gently) together for a few minutes, and run it through a flannel. When cold, bottle and cork it closely, and keep it in a cool place. *Or,* dissolve a quarter of an ounce (avoirdupois) of citric, *i.e.* crystallized lemon acid, in a pint of clarified sirup; flavor it with the peel, or dissolve the acid in equal parts of simple sirup, and sirup of lemon-peel.

LEMON WATER. Put two slices of thinly pared lemon into a teapot, a little bit of the peel, and a bit of sugar, or a large spoonful of capillaire; pour in a pint of boiling water, and stop it close for two hours.

LEMON CONSERVE, WHITE. Boil a pound of the finest sugar, take it off the fire, and squeeze into it the juice of one lemon at different times, stirring continually; it will make the sugar as white as milk if properly done; take care not to drop any of the seeds into it; work it well together, and when it is of an equal substance (which prove in the same manner as any other jelly), pour it into a mould. Lemon conserve is made in the same manner, only that the sugar must be boiled to a greater height than for white lemon conserve.

LOBSTER. Buy these alive; the lobster merchants sometimes keep them till they are starved, before they boil them; they are then watery, have not half their flavor, and like other persons that die of a consumption, have lost the calf of their legs. Choose those that (as an old cook says, are "heavy and lively," and) are full of motion, which is the index of their freshness. Those of the middle size are the best. Never take them when the shell is incrusted, which is a sign they are old. The male lobster is preferred to eat, and the female (on account of the eggs) to make sauce of. The hen lobster is distinguished by having a broader tail than the male, and less claws. Set on a pot, with water salted in proportion of a table-spoonful of salt to a quart of water; when the water boils, put it in, and keep it boiling briskly from half an hour to an hour, according to its size; wipe all the scum off it, and rub the shell with a very little butter or sweet oil; break off the great claws, crack them carefully in each joint, so that they may not be shattered, and yet come to pieces easily; cut the tail down the middle, and send up the body whole.

LOBSTERS, *to choose*. The heaviest are considered the best. When alive, if they are quite fresh, the claws will have a strong motion when you put your finger on the eyes and press them. When you buy them ready boiled, try whether their tails are stiff and pull up with a spring, otherwise that part will be flabby. The cock-lobster may be distinguished from the hen by the narrow back part of the tail, and the two uppermost fins within it are stiff and hard; but those of the hen are soft, and the tail broader. The male, though generally the smallest, has the highest flavor, the flesh is firmer, and the color when boiled is a deeper red. They come in about April, and remain in season till the oysters return. Hen lobsters are preferred for sauces, on account of their coral.

☞ *Lobsters are sold in Boston, already boiled, and are always fresh and good.*

LOBSTER A LA BRAISE. Pound the meat of a large lobster very fine with two ounces of butter, and season it with grated nutmeg, salt, and white pepper; add a little grated bread, beat up two eggs, reserve part to put over the meat, and with the rest make it up into the form of a lobster. Pound the spawn and red part, and spread it over it; bake it a quarter of an hour, and just before serving, lay over it the tail and body shell, with the small claws put underneath to resemble a lobster.

LOBSTERS OR CRABS, BUTTERED. Pick all the meat from the bodies of either, mince it small, put it into a saucepan with two or three table-spoonfuls of white wine, one of lemon-pickle, and three or four of rich gravy, a bit of butter, some salt, pepper, and grated nutmeg; thicken it with the yolks of two eggs beat up, and when quite hot, put it into the large shells; garnish them with an edging of bread toasted.

LOBSTER FRICASSEE. Break the shells, and take out the meat carefully, cut it and the red part, or coral, into pieces, adding the spawn; thicken with flour and butter some white stock, with which the shells have been boiled; season it with white pepper, mace, and salt, put in the lobster and heat it up; just before serving, add a little lemon-juice, or lemon pickle. The stock may be made with the shells, only boiled in a pint of water, with some white pepper, salt, and a little mace, thickened with cream, flour, and butter.

LOBSTER KETCHUP. Choose a lobster that is full of spawn, and weighing as nearly as possible three pounds; pick out all the meat, and pound the red part or coral in a marble mortar; when completely bruised, add the meat, pound, and moisten it with a little sherry wine, mix with it a tea-spoonful of cayenne, add the rest of the bottle of sherry, and mix it thoroughly; put it into two wide-mouthed bottles, and on the top put a small table-spoonful of whole pepper, cork the bottles tightly, and tie them over with leather. It will keep good a twelve-month, and exactly resembles fresh lobster sauce. Four table-spoonfuls heated in melted butter are sufficient for a large sauce-tureen.

LOBSTER PATTIES. (1) Pick the meat and red berries out of a lobster, mince them finely, add grated bread, chopped parsley, and butter; season with grated nutmeg, white pepper, and salt; add a little white stock, cream, and a table-spoonful of white wine, with a few chopped oysters; heat it all together. Line the patty-pans with puff paste; put into each a bit of crumb of bread, about an inch square, wet the edge of the paste, and cover it with another bit; with the paste-cutter mark it all round the rim, and pare off the paste round the edge of the patty-pan. When baked, take off the top, and with a knife take out the bread and a little of the inside paste, put in the prepared lobster, lay on the top paste, and serve them in a napkin. An-other way to prepare the paste.—Roll it out nearly half an inch thick, and cut it into rounds with a tin cutter, and, with one or two sizes less, mark it in the middle about half through. When they are baked, carefully cut out the inner top of the paste, and scoop out the inside, so as to make room for the mince, which put in, and place on the top.

LOBSTER PATTIES. (2) Prepare the patties as in the last receipt. Take a hen lobster already boiled; pick the meat from the tail and claws, and chop it fine; put it into a stewpan, with a little of the inside spawn pounded in a mortar till quite smooth, an ounce of fresh butter, half a gill of cream, and half a gill of veal consomme, cayenne pepper, and salt, a tea-spoonful of essence of anchovy, the same of lemon-juice, and a table-spoonful of flour and water; stew it five minutes.

LOBSTER PIE. (1) Boil the lobsters, and cut the meat of the tail into four bits; take out the meat from the claws and bodies, pound it in a mortar, add the soft part of one lobster, and season with pepper, salt, and nutmeg, add three table-spoonfuls of vinegar; melt half a pound of butter, and mix it with the pounded meat and the crumb of a slice of grated bread. Put puff paste round the edge and side of the dish; put in the tail of the lobster, then a layer of oysters with their liquor, and next the pounded meat; cover it with a puff paste, and bake it till the paste be done. Before serving, pour in some rich gravy, made of a little weak stock in which the lobster shells have been boiled, with an onion, pepper, and salt, and which has been strained and thickened with a bit of butter rolled in flour.

LOBSTER PIE. (2) Take out, as whole as possible, the meat from the tail and claws of two or three boiled lobsters; cut them into slices, and season them with nutmeg, pepper, and salt. Make a forcemeat of the soft part of the bodies, together with grated bread, some parsley, and one anchovy minced, grated lemon-peel, mace, salt, and pepper, the yolks of two hardboiled eggs bruised, and a bit of butter; mix it all together with the well-beaten yolk of an egg, and make it up into small balls. Put the lobster into the pie-dish, and cover it with the forcemeat balls, and hard-boiled yolks of eggs; add more than half a pint of rich white stock, a glass of white wine, and a tablespoonful of lemon-juice or vinegar. Cover it with puff paste, and bake it only till the paste be done.

LOBSTER SAUCE. Choose a fine spawny hen lobster; be sure it is fresh, pick out the spawn and the red coral into a mortar, add to it half an ounce of butter, pound it quite smooth, and rub it through a hair-sieve with the back of a wooden spoon; cut the meat of the lobster into small squares, or pull it to pieces with a fork; put the pounded spawn into as much melted butter as you think will do, and stir it together till it is thoroughly mixed; now put to it the meat of the lobster, and warm it on the fire; take care it does not boil, which will spoil its complexion, and its brilliant red color will immediately fade. The above is a very easy and excellent manner of making this sauce. Some use strong beef or veal gravy instead of melted butter, adding anchovy, cayenne, ketchup, cavice, lemon-juice, or pickle, or wine, &c.

LUNCHEON FOR AN INVALID. Put bread crumbs and red currant, or any other jelly, alternately into a tumbler, and when nearly half full, fill it up with milk.

wwwwwww

## M.

MACARONI, TO MAKE. Beat four eggs for eight or ten minutes, strain them, and stir in flour till stiff enough to work into a paste upon a marble, or stone slab; add flour till it be a stiff paste, and work it well;

cut off a small bit at a time, roll it out as thin as paper, and cut it with a paste-cutter or knife into very narrow strips; twist and lay them upon a clean cloth, in a dry, warm place; in a few hours it will be perfectly hard; put it into a box, with white paper under and over it. It may be cut into small stars, or circles, to be used for soup, and does not require so much boiling as the Italian Macaroni.

MACARONI. The usual mode of dressing it in England is by adding a white sauce, and Parmesan or Cheshire cheese, and burning it; but this makes a dish which is proverbially unwholesome: its bad qualities arise from the oiled and burnt cheese, and the half-dressed flour and butter put into the white sauce. Macaroni plain boiled, and some rich stock or portable soup added to it quite hot, will be found a delicious dish and very wholesome. Or, boil macaroni as directed in the receipt for the pudding, and serve it quite hot in a deep tureen, and let each guest add grated Parmesan and cold butter, or oiled butter served hot, and it is excellent; this is the most common Italian mode of dressing it. Macaroni with cream, sugar, and cinnamon, or a little varicelli added to the cream, makes a very nice sweet dish. *See Macaroni Pudding for the Boiling of it.*

MACARONI DRESSED SWEET. Boil two ounces of macaroni in a pint of milk, with a bit of lemon-peel, and a good bit of cinnamon, till the pipes are swelled to their utmost size without breaking. Lay them on a custard-dish, and pour a custard over them hot. Serve cold.

MACARONI GRATIN. Lay fried bread pretty closely round a dish, boil your macaroni in the usual way, and pour it into the dish; smooth it all over, and strew breadcrumbs on it, then a pretty thick layer of grated Parmesan cheese; drop a little melted butter on it, and color it with a salamander.

MACARONI NAPOLITAINE. Boil two pounds of macaroni for half an hour, in salt and water; then put it into a cullender to drain. Take three-quarters of a pound of cheese grated; put a layer of macaroni, in a deep dish or tureen, and on it a layer of macaroni, the cheese, and so on, alternately, till both are used up, making the cheese the top; pour over it some gravy, melt half a pound of fresh butter, and put on the whole. Serve it very hot.

MACARONI TO SERVE. (1) Simmer it in a little stock, with pounded mace and salt. When quite tender, take it out of the liquor, lay it in a dish, grate over it a good deal of cheese, then over that put bread grated very fine. Warm some butter without oiling, and pour it from a boat through a little earthen cullender all over the crums, then put the dish in a Dutch oven to roast the cheese, and brown the bread of a fine color. The bread should be in separate crums, and look light.

MACARONI TO SERVE. (2) Wash it well, and simmer it in half milk, and half of veal or mutton stock, till the macaroni is tender; then take a spoonful of the liquor, put to it the yolk of an egg, beaten in a spoonful of cream; just make it hot to thicken, but do not let it boil; pour it over the macaroni, and then grate fine old cheese all over it, and add bits of butter; brown it nicely with the salamander.

MACARONI STEWED. Boil a quarter of a pound of macaroni in beef stock, till nearly done; then strain it, and add a gill of cream, two ounces of butter, a table-spoonful of the essence of ham, three ounces of grated Parmesan cheese, and a little cayenne pepper and salt; mix them over a fire for five minutes, then put it on a dish, strew grated Parmesan cheese over it, smooth it over with a knife, and color it with a very hot salamander.

MACARONI TIMBALE. Take some puff paste, roll it thin, and cut it into narrow bands; twist each into a kind of cord, which place round the insides of buttered moulds, snail fashion; fill each mould with macaroni, cover the tops with grated bread, and Parmesan cheese (equal quantities of each); put the *Timbales* into a warm oven, and bake them three-quarters of an hour; then turn them on a dish, and serve.

MACAROONS. Take a pound of sweet almonds blanched, and nicely pounded, add a little rose-water to prevent their oiling; add a pound of sifted sugar, then whisk the whites of ten eggs to a solid froth, and add to the above; beat all together for some time. Have ready wafer paper on tin plates, drop the mixture over it separately, the size of a shilling, or smaller; sift over them a little sugar, and bake them.

MACAROONS, SWEET. Blanch a pound of sweet almonds, throw them into cold water for a few minutes, lay them in a napkin to dry, and leave them for twenty-four hours; at the end of that time, pound them, a handful at a time, adding occasionally some white of egg, till the whole is reduced to a fine paste; then take two pounds of the best lump sugar, pound and sift it, then put it to the almonds, with the grated rinds of two lemons; beat these ingredients together in the mortar, adding one at a time, as many eggs as you find necessary to moisten the paste, which should be thin, but not too much so, as in that case it would run; your paste being ready, take out a little in a spoon, and lay the macaroons on sheets of white paper either round or oval, as you please; lay them at least an inch apart, because they spread in baking, and if put nearer would touch. The whole of your paste being used, place the sheets of paper on tins in a moderate oven for three-quarters of an hour.

This kind of cake requires great care and attention; it will be well therefore to take notice of the following rules: 1. To mind that the almonds are perfectly dry before you begin to pound them. 2. Take great care that not a particle of the yolk is mixed with the white of egg, which would entirely spoil the color of the macaroons, and prevent their rising in the oven; to avoid this, open each separately, and if perfectly fresh, divide the yolk and white with great care. 3. The oven must be no more than moderately heated, nothing being more liable to burn than almonds and sugar; by the least negligence in this respect, the surface would be burned, whilst the inside would remain unbaked. The best method to obviate any mischief of this sort:—put two or three macaroons into the oven to try it; leave them in the usual time; and if, when you take them out, they are of a clear yellow, the oven is properly heated, and the whole of the macaroons may then be put in.

MACKEREL, TO CHOOSE. Their gills should be of a fine red, their eyes full, and the whole fish stiff and bright; if the gills are of a faint color, the fish limber and wrinkled, they are not fresh.

MACKEREL BAKED. Cut off their heads, open them, and take out the roes and clean them thoroughly; rub them on the inside with a little pepper and salt, put the roes in again, season them (with mixture of powdered allspice, black pepper, and salt, well rubbed together), and lay them close in a baking-pan, cover them with equal quantities of cold vinegar and water, tie them down with strong white paper doubled, and bake them for an hour in a slow oven. They will keep for a fortnight.

MACKEREL BOILED. This fish loses its life as soon as it leaves the sea, and the fresher it is the better. Wash and clean them thoroughly (the fishmongers seldom do this sufficiently), put them into cold water with a handful of salt in it; let them rather simmer than boil; a small mackerel will be done enough in about a quarter of an hour; when the eye starts and the tail splits, they are done; do not let them stand in the water a moment after; they are so delicate that the heat of the water will break them.

MACKEREL BROILED. Clean a fine large mackerel, wipe it on a dry cloth, and cut a long slit down the back; lay it on a clean gridiron, over a very clear, slow fire; when it is done on one side, turn it; be careful that it does not burn; send it up with fennel sauce; mix well together a little finely minced fennel and parsley, seasoned with a little pepper and salt, a bit of fresh butter, and when the mackerel are ready for the table, put some of this into each fish.

MACKEREL, THE GERMAN WAY. Split them down the back, and season them with pepper and salt; broil them, and serve with the following sauce; pick and wash some fennel, parsley, mint, thyme, and green onions; but use only a small quantity of each. Boil them tender in a little veal stock; then chop them up, and add to them some fresh butter, the liquor they were boiled in, some grated nutmeg, the juice of half a lemon, a little cayenne pepper, and salt. Let it boil, thicken it with flour, and serve in a sauce boat.

MADE DISHES. Be careful to trim off all the skin, gristle, &c. that will not be eaten; and shape handsomely, and of even thickness, the various articles which compose your made dishes; this is sadly neglected by common cooks. Only stew them till they are just tender, and do not stew them to rags; therefore, what you prepare the day before it is to be eaten, do not dress quite enough the first day. We have given receipts for the most easy and simple way to make HASHES, &c. Those who are well skilled in culinary arts can dress up things in this way, so as to be as agreeable as they were the first time they were cooked.

MADELAINES. Take nine ounces of powder-sugar, eight of flour, the yolks of four and six whole eggs, two spoonfuls of brandy, and a grain of salt; put these into a saucepan, stirring continually, until the paste thickens; after which, stir only one minute; clarify ten ounces of good fresh butter, with which, butter about two and thirty madelaine moulds, pour the remainder of the butter into your preparation; set it on a gentle stove, stir till it begins to become liquid, take it off before it has time to get too hot, put a little of this into each mould, and bake them in a moderate oven.

MADELAINES IN SURPRISE. Make them in the usual way; when cold, cut a thin slice from the bottom, take out nearly all the inside; pound four ounces of blanched filberts, mix them with eight spoonfuls of apricot marmalade, which mixture put into the madelaines, and place the slice taken from the bottom, and serve them.

MAITRE D'HOTEL, COLD. Put a quarter of a pound of butter into a saucepan, with some parsley and shallots, minced small, salt, whole pepper, and lemon-juice; mix the whole together with a wooden spoon. Pour the *Maitre d'Hotel* either over, under, or into whatever meat or fish you intend to serve.

MAITRE D'HOTEL MAIGRE. Put into some nicely melted butter a little chopped parsley, salt, and lemon-juice; one or two minced shallots may be added, and heat it all together.

MARCHPANE ROYAL. Take a pound of sweet almonds, blanch and throw them into cold water, drain and pound them, moistening with orange-flower and plain water, but take care not to put too much at once. The almonds being reduced to a paste, put them into a preserving pan with half a pound of powder sugar, set the pan on a moderate fire to dry the paste, which will be sufficiently so if, when you touch it, it no longer sticks to your finger, then take it out and place it on a plate or wafer paper, previously sprinkled with sugar: as soon as it is cold cut it in pieces, which roll in your hand

to the size of your little finger; form them into rings, and lay them on iron gratings, glaze and put them into a brisk oven to color. The above paste may also be employed as follows: roll it out and cut it in half, spread over one piece apricot marmalade, or any other preserve you please, cover it with the other piece, cut it into lozenges, crescents, &c., according to your fancy, lay them on the grating as above, glaze and color them in a quick oven.

MARJORAM, SWEET, TO PRESERVE. Beat up very well the white of an egg, then beat very fine and sift some double-refined sugar; take some marjoram and rub it on a glass that is quite clean, and lay it in the form of the glass; so do it with the egg, then sear it with the sugar on it, and lay it on paper to dry.

MARMALADE. Marmalade may be composed of almost any fruits; the best, however, for this purpose are, apricots, peaches, oranges, quinces, egg-plums, apples, &c. They are usually made by boiling the fruit and sugar together to a kind of pulp, stirring them constantly whilst on the fire; it is kept in pots, which must not be covered till the marmalade is quite cold. The proportion of sugar is half a pound to each pound of fruit.

☞ *See Names of Articles, of which it is made.*

MARROW BONES. Chop the bones at each end so as to stand steady, then wash them clean, saw them in halves, cover the top with a floured cloth: boil them, and serve with dry toast.

MATELOTE MEAT. Take beef, veal, mutton, and pork, a large slice of each, and a small one of leg of lamb; cut them in small pieces, which put into a saucepan with equal quantities of stock and champaign, salt and spices, cover them very close, and set them on hot ashes for six hours, then serve it.

MEAD. (1) To every gallon of water put four pounds of honey, boil it an hour. Then put it into a tub with some yeast on a toast; cover it over. If it ferments well after three or four days, draw it off clear, and put it into a cask, with one lemon sliced to every gallon; add a bottle of brandy to every ten gallons. The rind of Seville oranges cut very thin, suspended in the barrel, is a great improvement to the flavor. It is best to wash the cask round with part of the brandy, before the liquor is put in.

MEAD. (2) One part of honey is dissolved in three parts of water, and boiled over a moderate fire till it is reduced to two-thirds of the quantity. It is then skimmed, and put into a barrel, which must be quite full; it is allowed to subside for three or four days, and then drawn off for use. To make it from the combs from which honey has been drained, they are to be beaten in warm water, and after the liquor has subsided, it is to be strained. The cottagers in Scotland make an excellent beer by adding a little yeast to the strained liquor, and allowing it to ferment, for a few days, in a cask, and then bottling it.

MEAT CAKES. Take whatever meat, game, or poultry, you may chance to have, (it is the better for being under-done); mince it fine, adding a little fat bacon or ham, or anchovy; season with a little pepper and salt; mix the whole well together, and make it into small cakes, about three inches in length, an inch and a half in width, and half an inch thick; fry them of a light brown, and serve them with good gravy; or put it into a mould, and boil or bake it.

MEAT, TO KEEP HOT. If your meat is done before you are ready to serve, take it up, set the dish over a pan of boiling water, put a deep cover over it, so as not to touch the meat, and then put a cloth over that. This way will not dry up the gravy.

MILK COFFEE FOR BREAKFAST. *See Coffee.*

MILK PUNCH. (1) Beat up two eggs well, mix them in a quart of milk, sugar, nutmeg, and lemon-peel to your taste; boil it gently, stirring it all the time till thick enough; take it off the fire a very few minutes, then add to it a full quarter of a pint of rum. It must be stirred all the time the rum is pouring in, or it will not be good.

MILK PUNCH. (2) Eight pounds of refined sugar are to be dissolved in the strained juice of three dozen lemons, and, when quite settled, two gallons of brandy, and two gallons and a half of cold water, are to be added, and also the lemon-peel; one gallon of boiling milk being then poured over the ingredients, they are to stand closely covered for twenty-four hours; when, being skimmed and run through a very thick jelly-bag, it may be quickly bottled, and will be fit for immediate use; but it improves by keeping.

MINCED COLLOPS. This is a favorite Scotch dish; few families are without it: it keeps well, and is always ready to make an extra dish. Take beef, and chop and mince it very small; to which add some salt and pepper. Put this, in its raw state, into small jars, and pour on the top some clarified butter. When intended for use, put the clarified butter into a frying-pan, and slice some onions into the pan, and fry them. Add a little water to it, and then put in the minced meat. Stew it well, and in a few minutes it will be fit to serve up. *See Collops.*

MINCE MEAT. Two pounds of beef suet, picked and chopped fine; two pounds of apple, pared, cored, and minced; three pounds of currants, washed and picked; one pound of raisins, stoned and chopped fine; one pound of good moist sugar; half a pound of citron, and one pound of candied lemon and orange-peel, cut into thin slices; two pounds of ready-dressed roast beef, free from skin and gristle, and chopped fine; two nutmegs, grated; one ounce of salt, one of ground ginger, half an ounce of coriander seeds, half an ounce of allspice, half an ounce of cloves, all ground fine; the juice of six lemons, and their rinds grated; half a pint of brandy, and a pint of sweet wine. Mix the suet, apples, currants, meat-plums, and sweetmeats, well together in a large pan, and strew in the spice by degrees; mix the sugar, lemon-juice, wine, and brandy, and pour it to the other ingredients, and stir it well together; set it by in close-covered pans in a cold place: when wanted, stir it up from the bottom, and add half a glass of brandy to the quantity you require. N. B.— The same weight of tripe is frequently substituted for the meat, and sometimes the yolks of eggs boiled hard. *Obs.*—The lean side of a buttock, thoroughly roasted, is generally chosen for mince meat.

MINUTEN FLEISH. Cut from off a leg of veal some slices as thin as the blade of a knife, and about four inches long; season them with pepper and salt, lay them into a deep dish, pour over them nearly half a pint of white wine, let it stand for three hours. Cover the bottom of a stewpan with butter, dredge each slice of the veal on both sides with flour; add a little more wine, and as much good white stock as will cover it, and the juice of a lemon. Cover the pan closely, and let it simmer five minutes, and serve it instantly, otherwise it will become hard.

MOCK ARRACK. Dissolve two scruples of flowers of benjamin in a quart of good rum, and it will immediately impart to it the inviting fragrance of "Vauxhall nectar."

MOCK BRAWN. *See Brawn.*

MOCK CAPER SAUCE. *See Sauce Caper.*

MOCK GOOSE, OR LEG OF PORK ROASTED WITHOUT THE SKIN. Parboil it; take

off the skin, and then put it down to roast; baste it with butter, and make a savory powder of finely minced, or dried and powdered sage, ground black pepper, salt, and some bread-crumbs, rubbed together through a colander; you may add to this a little very finely minced onion: sprinkle it with this when it is almost roasted. Put half a pint of made gravy into the dish, and goose stuffing under the knuckle skin; or garnish the dish with balls of it fried or boiled.

MOCK ICE. Of preserved strawberries, raspberries, and red currant jelly, a tablespoonful each; rub it through a sieve, with as much cream as will fill a shape; dissolve three-quarters of an ounce of isinglass in half a pint of water; when almost cold, mix it well with the cream, put it into a shape, set it in a cool place, and turn it out the following day.

MOCK TURTLE. *See Soup Calf's Head.*

MOORFOWL, TO STEW. Truss them, keeping on their heads, but draw the legs within the body; mix well some salt and pepper with flour and a piece of butter, and put a small bit into each bird; fry them all over of a nice brown in butter. Brown some butter and flour, and add to it some good gravy, seasoned with pepper, salt, mace, and two cloves pounded; boil up the sauce, put in the moorfowl, and let them stew very slowly till tender. A little before taking them off the fire, add a table-spoonful of mushroom ketchup. If the birds are old, stew them for two hours; if young ones, half that time. Cold roasted moorfowl are dressed exactly in the same way only cut into joints, and stewed very gently nearly as long. Half an hour before serving, a small tea-cupful of Port wine should be added.

MUFFINS. (1) Take one pint of milk quite warm, and a quarter of a pint of thick small-beer yeast; strain them into a pan, and add sufficient flour to make it like a batter; cover it over, and let it stand in a warm place until it has risen; then add a quarter of a pint of warm milk, and one ounce of butter rubbed in some flour quite fine; mix them well together: then add sufficient flour to make it into dough, cover it over, and let it stand half an hour; then work it up again, and break it into small pieces: roll them up quite round, and cover them over for a quarter of an hour; then bake them.

MUFFINS. (2) Mix two pounds of flour with a couple of eggs, two ounces of butter melted in a pint of milk, and four or five spoonfuls of yeast; beat it thoroughly, and set it to rise two or three hours. Bake it on a hot hearth in flat cakes, and turn them, when done, on one side.

MUFFINS. (3) Take two quarts of warm water, two spoonfuls of yeast, three pounds of flour; beat it well for half an hour, and let it stand an hour or two; bake them on an iron baking-stove (rub it well over with mutton-suet as often as they are laid on); as soon as they begin to color, turn them; they will be sufficiently baked when colored on both sides.

MULLAGATAWNY. Boil slowly in two quarts of water one pound of split peas, half an ounce of butter, two onions sliced, a little salt, cayenne, and two blades of mace. When the peas are tender, put in a large fowl, cut in joints and skinned, two quarts of boiling water, or stock, if the soup be required very rich; twenty minutes before serving, add a large table spoonful of curry-powder, and the same of ground rice.

☞ *For Mullagatawny Soup, see Soups.*

MULLED WINE. Put into a pint of Port wine two or three cloves and a bit of cinnamon; boil it for a few moments; take out the spice, sweeten it with loaf sugar, and grate in a little nutmeg. Serve with a slice of toasted bread, the crust pared off, and cut into oblong pieces. The Port wine is sometimes boiled with a third of its quantity of water.

MUSHROOMS, TO CHOOSE. The mushrooms proper to be used in cookery grow in the open pasture land, for those that grow near or under trees, are poisonous. The eatable mushrooms first appear very small, and of a round form, on a little stalk. They grow very rapidly, and the upper part and stalk are white. As they increase in size, the under part gradually opens, and shows a fringed fur of a very fine salmon color, which continues more or less till the mushroom has gained some size, and then turns to a dark brown. These marks should be attended to, and likewise whether the skin can be easily parted from the edge and middle, and whether they have a pleasant smell. Those which are poisonous have a yellow skin, and the under part has not the clear flesh color of the real mushroom; besides which, they smell rank and disagreeable, and the fur is white or yellow.

MUSHROOM KETCHUP. If you love good ketchup, gentle reader, make it yourself, after the following directions, and you will have a delicious relish for made dishes, ragouts, soups, sauces, or hashes.

Mushroom gravy approaches the nature and flavor of meat gravy, more than any vegetable juice, and is the superlative substitute for it: in meagre soups and extempore gravies, the chemistry of the kitchen has yet contrived to agreeably awaken the palate, and encourage the appetite. A couple of quarts of double ketchup, made according to the following receipt, will save you some score pounds of meat, besides a vast deal of time and trouble; as it will furnish, in a few minutes, as good sauce as can be made for either fish, flesh, or fowl.

I believe the following is the best way of extracting and preparing the essence of mushrooms, so as to procure and preserve their flavor for a considerable length of time.

Look out for mushrooms from the beginning of September.

Take care they are the right sort, and fresh gathered. Full-grown flaps are to be preferred: put a layer of these at the bottom of a deep earthen pan, and sprinkle them with salt; then another layer of mushrooms, and some more salt on them; and so on alternately, salt and mushrooms: let them remain two or three hours, by which time the salt will have penetrated the mushrooms, and rendered them easy to break; then pound them in a mortar, or mash them well with your hands, and let them remain for a couple of days, not longer, stirring them up, and mashing them well each day; then pour them into a stone jar, and to each quart add an ounce and a half of whole black pepper, and half an ounce of allspice; stop the jar very close, and set it in a stewpan of boiling water, and keep it boiling for two hours at least. Take out the jar, and pour the juice clear from the settlings through a hair sieve (without squeezing the mushrooms) into a clean stewpan; let it boil very gently for half an hour: those who are for superlative ketchup, will continue the boiling till the mushroom-juice is reduced to half the quantity; it may then be called double catsup or dog-sup.

There are several advantages attending this concentration; it will keep much better, and only half the quantity be required; so you can flavor sauce, &c. without thinning it: neither is this an extravagant way of making it, for merely the aqueous part is evaporated; skim it well, and pour it into a clean dry jar, or jug; cover it close, and let it stand in a cool place till next day; then pour it off as gently as possible (so as not to disturb the settlings at the bottom of the jug,) through a tamis, or thick flannel bag, till it is perfectly clear; add a table-spoonful of good brandy to each pint of ketchup, and let it stand as before; a fresh sediment will be deposited, from which the ketchup is to be quietly poured off, and bottled in pints or half pints (which have been washed with brandy or spirit): it is best to keep it in such quantities as are soon used.

Take especial care that it is closely corked, and sealed down, or dipped in bottle cement.

If kept in a cool, dry place, it may be preserved for a long time; but if it be badly corked, and kept in a damp place, it will soon spoil.

Examine it from time to time, by placing a strong light behind the neck of the bottle, and if any pellicle appears about it, boil it up again with a few peppercorns.

MUSHROOMS TO PICKLE. Cut off the stalks, and wash clean, in cold water, some small button mushrooms; rub them with a bit of flannel, then throw them into fresh water, and when perfectly clean, put them into a saucepan with fresh cold water, and let them boil eight or ten minutes; strain off the water, lay them into the folds of a cloth. Boil, in a quart of vinegar, a quarter of an ounce of pepper, the same of allspice, and two or three blades of mace, and a teaspoonful of salt; put the mushrooms into a jar, and when the vinegar is cold, pour it, with the spices, over them.

MUSHROOMS TO STEW. For a good-sized dish, take a pint of white stock, season it with salt, pepper, and a little lemon pickle, thicken it with a bit of butter rolled in flour; cleanse and peel the mushrooms, sprinkle them with a very little salt, boil them for three or four minutes, put them into the gravy when it is hot, and stew them for fifteen minutes.

MUSTARD. Mix (by degrees, by rubbing together in a mortar) the best flour of mustard, with vinegar, white wine, or cold water, in which scraped horseradish has been boiled; rub it well together for at least ten minutes, till it is perfectly smooth; it will keep in a stone jar closely stopped, for a fortnight: only put as much into the mustard-pot as will be used in a day or two. *Obs.*— Mustard is the best of all the stimulants that are employed to give energy to the digestive organs. Some opulent epicures mix it with Sherry or Madeira wine, or distilled or flavored vinegar, instead of horseradish water. The French flavor their mustard with Champaigne and other wines, or with vinegar flavored with capers, anchovies, tarragon, elder, basil, burnet, garlic, eschalot, or celery, warming it with cayenne, or the various spices; sweet, savory, fine herbs, truffles, ketchup, &c. &c., and seem to consider mustard merely as a vehicle of flavors.

MUSTARD IN A MINUTE. Mix very gradually, and rub together in a mortar, an ounce of flour of mustard, with three table-spoonfuls of milk (cream is better), half a tea-spoonful of salt, and the same of sugar; rub them well together till quite smooth. *Obs.*—Mustard made in this manner is not at all bitter, and is therefore instantly ready for the table.

MUTTON. (1) The pipe that runs along the bone of the inside of a chine of mutton ought to be taken away; and if it is to be kept any length of time, the part close round the tail should be rubbed with salt, previously cutting out the kernel.

It is best for the butcher to take out the kernel in the fat on the thick part of the leg, as that is the part most likely to become tainted. The chine and rib-bones should be wiped every day; and the bloody part of the neck be cut off, in order to preserve it. The brisket changes first in the breast; therefore, if it is to be kept, it is best, should the weather be hot, to rub it with a little salt.

When intended for roasting, it should hang as long as it will keep, the hind quarter particularly; but not so long as to become tainted.

Mutton for boiling ought not to hang long, as it will prevent its looking of a good color. The greatest care should be taken to preserve, by paper, the fat of what is roasted.

MUTTON. (2) As beef requires a large,

sound fire, mutton must have a brisk and sharp one. If you wish to have mutton tender, it should be hung almost as long as it will keep; and then good eight-tooth, *i. e.* four years old mutton, is as good eating as venison.

The leg, haunch, and saddle will be the better for being hung up in a cool airy place for four or five days at least; in temperate weather, a week; in cold weather, ten days.

*A Leg*, of eight pounds, will take about two hours: let it be well basted, and frothed.

*A Chine or Saddle, (i. e.* the two loins) of ten or eleven pounds, two hours and a half: it is the business of the butcher to take off the skin and skewer it on again, to defend the meat from extreme heat, and preserve its succulence; if this is neglected, tie a sheet of paper over it (baste the strings you tie it on with directly, or they will burn): about a quarter of an hour before you think it will be done, take off the skin or paper, that it may get a pale brown color, then baste it and flour it lightly to froth it. N. B. Desire the butcher to cut off the flaps and the tail and chump end, and trim away every part that has not indisputable pretensions to be eaten. This will reduce a saddle of eleven pounds weight to about six or seven pounds.

*A Shoulder*, of seven pounds, an hour and a half. Put the spit in close to the shank-bone, and run it along the blade-bone. N. B. The blade-bone is a favorite luncheon or supper relish, scored, peppered and salted, and broiled, or done in a Dutch oven.

*A Loin*, of mutton, from an hour and a half to an hour and three-quarters. The most elegant way of carving this, is to cut it lengthwise, as you do a saddle. N. B. Spit it on a skewer or lark spit, and tie that on the common spit, and do not spoil the meat by running the spit through the prime part of it.

*A Neck*, about the same time as a loin. It must be carefully jointed, or it is very difficult to carve. The neck and breast are, in small families, commonly roasted together; the cook will then crack the bones across the middle before they are put down to roast: if this is not done carefully, they are very troublesome to carve. Tell the cook, when she takes it from the spit, to separate them before she sends them to table. N. B. The best way to spit this is to run iron skewers across it, and put the spit between them.

*A Breast*, an hour and a quarter.

MUTTON, BAKED WITH POTATOES. *See Beef.*

MUTTON BREAST COLLARED. Bone it and take out all the gristles, make a forcemeat with crumbs of bread, chopped parsley, a little lemon thyme, and one anchovy minced; season with salt and white pepper, rub the mutton over with an egg beaten up, cover it with the forcemeat, roll it firmly; tie it with tape, and put it on in boiling water. Make a good gravy of the bones, two onions, a bunch of parsley and lemon thyme, pepper and salt; strain and thicken it with a piece of butter mixed with flour. A little before serving, add a table-spoonful of vinegar and two of mushroom ketchup. Garnish with cut lemon or pickles.

MUTTON, BREAST, ROASTED WITH WINE. Skin and bone a breast of mutton, then roll it up in a collar like a breast of veal. Roast it, and baste it with half a pint of red wine; when you have used up all the wine, finish basting with butter. Have a little good gravy in readiness, and when the mutton is done, set it upright in a dish, pour in the gravy, prepare sweet sauce the same as for venison, and send it up to table without any garnish.

MUTTON BROTH. Cut a neck of mutton into pieces, preserving a handsome piece to be served up in the tureen; put all into a stewpan with three quarts of cold beef stock, or water, with a little oatmeal mixed in it; some turnips, onions, leeks, celery cut in pieces, and a small bunch of thyme and parsley. When it boils, skim it clean, and when nearly done, take out the piece you intend to serve in the tureen, and let the other pieces stew till tender; then have ready turnips cut into dice, some leeks, celery, half a cabbage, some parsley, all cut small, and some marigolds; wash them, strain the liquor off the meat, skim it free from the fat, add it to the ingredients with the piece of mutton intended for the tureen, adding a little pearl barley. Season with salt, simmer all together till done, and serve with toasted bread on a plate.

MUTTON CHOPS. Cut the chops off a loin or the best end of a neck of mutton, pare off the fat, dip them into a beaten egg, and strew over them grated bread, seasoned with pepper, salt, and some finely minced parsley; fry them in a little butter, and lay them upon the back of a sieve to drain before the fire. Thicken about half a pint of gravy, add a table-spoonful of ketchup, and one of Port wine; put the gravy into the dish, and lay in the chops; garnish with fried parsley or cut lemon.

MUTTON CHOPS, BAKED. Cut a neck of mutton into neat chops, season them with salt and pepper, butter a dish, lay in the chops and pour over them a batter made of a quart of milk, four eggs beaten up, four table-spoonfuls of flour, and a little salt. An hour will bake them.

MUTTON CHOPS MAINTENON. Cut a neck of mutton into chops; beat them flat with a rolling-pin. Bruise the yolk of a hard-boiled egg, and mix with it chopped sweet herbs, grated bread, nutmeg, salt, and pepper. Cover the steaks with it, and put each into a piece of well-buttered paper; broil them over a clear fire, turning them often. Serve them in the paper, or with a browned gravy.

MUTTON CUTLETS. Cut into cutlets a pound and a half of the thick part of a leg of mutton, and beat them; mix with grated bread crumbs, some pepper, salt, and finely chopped parsley, lemon thyme, and sweet marjoram. Rub the cutlets with melted butter, and cover them thickly with the prepared bread; fry them for ten minutes in butter, then put them into a saucepan with some good gravy thickened with flour and butter, and simmer them for ten or fifteen minutes.

MUTTON FILLET, STEWED. Put a fillet of mutton or a piece of beef, weighing about seven pounds, into a stewpan, with a carrot, a turnip, an onion stuck with two or three cloves, and a pint of water. Put round the edge of the stewpan, a rim of coarse paste, that the cover may be kept very close, and let it stew gently, three hours and a half; take out the meat, skim off the fat, strain and thicken the gravy, have ready some boiled carrots and turnips cut to fancy, add them to the gravy, make all hot, and serve with a garnish of sliced gherkins.

MUTTON CUTLETS BREADED AND BROILED. Trim and season your cutlets with pepper and salt, put them into some melted butter, and when they have imbibed a sufficient quantity of it, take them out, and cover them completely with bread crumbs; give the cutlets a good shape, and broil them over a clear fire; take care not to do the cutlets too much, to burn the bread.

MUTTON GRAVY FOR VENISON OR HARE. The best gravy for venison is that made with the trimmings of the joint: if this is all used, and you have no undressed venison, cut a scrag of mutton in pieces; broil it a little brown; then put it into a clean stewpan, with a quart of boiling water; cover it close, and let it simmer gently for an hour: now uncover the stewpan, and let it reduce to three-quarters of a pint; pour it through a hair sieve; take the fat off, and send it up in a boat. It is only to be seasoned with a little salt, that it may not overpower the natural flavor of the meat.

MUTTON, TO HASH. Cut the meat into thin slices, trim off all the sinews, skin, gristle, &c.; put in nothing but what is to be eaten, lay them on a plate, ready; prepare your sauce to warm it in, put in the meat, and let it simmer gently till it is thoroughly warm: do not let it boil, as that will make the meat tough and hard, and it will be a harsh, instead of a hash. Select for your hash those parts of the joint that are least done. Hashing is a mode of cookery by no means suited to delicate stomachs: unless the meat, be considerably under-done the first time, a second dressing must spoil it, for what is done enough the first time, must be done too much the second.

MUTTON HAM, TO CURE. Cut a hind quarter of good mutton into the shape of a ham, pound one ounce of salt-petre, with one pound of coarse salt and a quarter of a pound of brown sugar, rub the ham well with this mixture, taking care to stuff the hole of the shank well with salt and sugar, and let it lie a fortnight, rubbing it well with the pickle every two or three days; then take it out and press it with a weight for one day; smoke it with saw-dust for ten or fifteen days, or hang it to dry in the kitchen. If the ham is to be boiled soon after it has been smoked, soak it one hour, and if it has been smoked any length of time it will require to be soaked several hours. Put it on in cold water, and boil it gently two hours. It is eaten cold at breakfast, luncheon, or supper. A mutton ham is sometimes cured with the above quantity of salt and sugar, with the addition of half an ounce of pepper, a quarter of an ounce of cloves, and one nutmeg.

MUTTON HAUNCH, LIKE VENISON. Take a fat haunch of large fine mutton, let it hang a week, then pound one ounce of black, and one ounce of Jamaica pepper, and rub them over the mutton, pour a bottle of Port wine over it, and let it remain in this five days, basting it frequently every day with the liquor, take it out and hang it up four or five days more, or as long as the weather favors its keeping; wipe it three or four times a day with a clean cloth.

While it is roasting baste it with the liquor it was steeped in, adding a little more Port wine; a quarter of an hour before taking it from the fire, baste it well with butter, and dredge flour over it to froth it up. Serve it with sauces as for venison.

MUTTON HAUNCH. It should be kept as long as you can possibly keep it sweet by the different modes; and if necessary, wash it with warm milk and water, or vinegar, and when going to be dressed, be careful to wash it well, to prevent the outside from having a bad flavor from keeping; before you put the haunch to the fire, fold it in a paste of coarse flour, or strong paper; then set it a good distance from the fire, and allow proportionable time for the paste; do not take it off, till about thirty-five or forty minutes before serving the mutton, and then baste continually; bring the haunch nearer before taking off the paste, and froth it up in the same manner as venison. For gravy, take a pound and a half of a loin of mutton, and simmer it in a pint of water till reduced to half, use no seasoning but salt: brown it with a little burnt sugar, and serve it up in the dish; but there should be a good deal of gravy in the meat, for though long at the fire, the covering and distance will prevent its roasting out. Serve with currant-jelly sauce.

MUTTON LEG. (1) If your leg of mutton is roasted, serve with onion or currant-jelly sauce, if it is boiled, serve with caper-sauce and vegetables. In roasting or boiling, a quarter of an hour is usually allowed for each pound of meat.

MUTTON LEG. (2) Cut off the shank bone, and trim the knuckle, put it into luke-warm water for ten minutes, wash it clean, cover it with cold water, and let it simmer *very gently*, and skim it carefully. A leg of nine pounds will take two and a half or three hours, if you like it thoroughly done, especially in very cold weather.

The *tit-bits* with an epicure are the "knuckle," the kernel, called the *"pope's eye,"* and the *" gentleman's"* or *" cramp bone."*

When mutton is very large, you may divide it, and *roast the fillet*, i. e. the large end, and *boil the knuckle end*; you may also cut some fine cutlets off the thick end of the leg, *and so have two or three good hot dinners.*

*The liquor the mutton is boiled in*, you may convert into good soup in five minutes, and Scotch barley broth. Thus managed, a leg of mutton is a most economical joint.

MUTTON LEG STUFFED. Make a stuffing with a little beef-suet chopped, some parsley, thyme, marjoram, a little grated lemon, nutmeg grated, pepper, salt, and a few bread crumbs, mix all together with the yolk of an egg, put this under the skin in the thickest part of a leg of mutton under the flap; then roast it, and serve it to table with some good gravy in the dish.

MUTTON LEG STUFFED WITH OYSTERS. Make a forcemeat of beef-suet, chopped small, the yolks of hard boiled eggs, with three anchovies, a little onion, thyme, savory, and some oysters, a dozen or fourteen, all cut fine, some salt, pepper, grated nutmeg, and crumbs of bread, mixed up with raw eggs; put this forcemeat under the skin in the thickest part of the leg of mutton, under the flap, and at the knuckle. For sauce, some oyster-liquor, a little red wine, an anchovy, and some more oysters stewed, and served under the mutton.

MUTTON LOIN. Roast it; some people think it eats much better if cut lengthways like a saddle. It may also be used for steaks, pies, or broth, only taking care to cut off as much fat as possible

MUTTON LOIN, STEWED. Bone and skin the loin; stew it in a pint of water, turning it frequently; when the liquor is half wasted, take out the loin and strain it, and when cold take off the fat; make a rich highly-seasoned gravy of the bones; strain and mix it with the liquor the loin was stewed in; add a tea-cupful of Port wine, and some small mushrooms; thicken the sauce with butter rolled in flour; put in the mutton, and heat it thoroughly; garnish with pickles.

MUTTON NECK. (1) This joint is particularly useful, as so many dishes may be made of it. The bone ought to be cut short.

The best end of the neck may be boiled, and served with turnips; or if you think proper, it may be roasted, or dressed in steaks, or made into pies, or used for harrico.

You may stew the scrags in broth; or in a little water, with small onions, some peppercorns, and a small quantity of rice, all served together.

When you wish that a neck which is to be boiled should look particularly well, saw down the chine bone, strip the ribs half way down, and chop off the ends of the bones, about four inches.

To make the fat look particularly white, the skin should not be taken off till it is boiled.

The fat belonging to the neck or loin of mutton, if chopped very fine, makes a most excellent suet-pudding, or crust for a meat pie.

MUTTON NECK. (2) Put four or five pounds of the best end of a neck (that has been kept a few days) into as much cold soft water as will cover it, and about two inches over; let it simmer very slowly for two hours: it will look most delicate if you do not take off the skin till it has been boiled.

MUTTON PASTY, TO EAT AS NICE AS VENISON. Take a fat loin of mutton, and let it hang for several days, then bone it. Beat it well with a rolling pin; then rub ten pounds of meat with a quarter of a pound of sugar, and pour over it one glass of Port, and one glass of vinegar. Let it lie for five days and five nights; after which, wash and wipe the meat very dry, and season it highly with Jamaica pepper, nutmeg, and salt. Lay it in your dish, and to ten pounds put one pound of butter, spreading it over the meat. Put a crust round the edge of the dish, and cover with a thick crust, otherwise it will be over-done before the meat is soaked; it must be baked in a slow oven.

Put the bones in a pan in the oven, with just sufficient water to cover them, and one glass of Port, a small quantity of pepper and salt; by this means you will have a little rich gravy to add to the pasty when drawn.

Sugar gives a greater shortness to meat, and a better flavor than salt, too great a quantity of which hardens the meat. Sugar is quite as great a preservative.

MUTTON POLPETTES. Take the lean of any joint of cold roasted mutton, pare off the skin, and mince the meat with a little grated bacon and calf's udder; season with salt, pepper, nutmeg, a few mushrooms and parsley, shred small; unite them together with the yolks of three eggs, and make twelve or fifteen balls of it, dip them in beaten egg, and bread them twice. Flatten these balls a little, and fry them in clarified butter; when done, drain and place them on the dish. Serve them with tomato sauce or glaze.

MUTTON, ROLLED. Bone a shoulder of mutton carefully, so as not to injure the skin, cut all the meat from the skin, mince it small, and season it highly with pepper, nutmeg, and a clove, some parsley, lemon thyme, sweet marjoram chopped, and a pounded onion, all well mixed, together with a well-beaten yolk of an egg; roll it up very tightly in the skin, tie it round, and bake it in an oven two or three hours, according to the size of the mutton. Make a gravy of the bones and parings, season with an onion, pepper and salt, strain and thicken it with flour and butter; add vinegar, mushroom ketchup, soy, and lemon pickle, a ta-ble-spoonful of each, and a tea-cupful of Port wine; garnish with forcemeat balls, made of grated bread, and part of the mince.

MUTTON, COLD SHOULDER BROILED. A cold shoulder of roast mutton having only a little meat upon the blade bone, may be scored, sprinkled with pepper and salt, then broiled and served with caper sauce poured over it, or melted butter, in which should be mixed of mushroom ketchup, lemon pickle, and Harvey sauce, a table-spoonful each.

MUTTON SHOULDER, BAKED. Lard a shoulder of mutton with streaked bacon, put it into an earthen stewpan proportioned to the size of the joint of meat, with two or three sliced onions, a parsnip and carrot sliced, one clove of garlic, two cloves, half a bay-leaf and some basil; add about a quarter of a pint of water or stock (stock is the best), some salt and pepper; put the meat into the sauce, and set it in an oven. When the meat is done, strain the sauce through a sieve, and skim it, squeezing the vegetables so as to make a thickening for your sauce: serve the sauce with the meat.

MUTTON SHOULDER, STEWED. (1) Bone a shoulder of mutton with a sharp knife, and fill the space with the following stuffing:—grated bread, minced suet, parsley, pepper, salt, and nutmeg; bind with the yolks of two eggs well beaten. Sew or fasten it with small skewers; brown it in a frying-pan with a bit of butter. Break the bone, put it into a saucepan, with some water, an onion, pepper, salt, and a bunch of parsley; let it stew till the strength be extracted; strain, and thicken it with butter rolled in flour; put it, with the mutton, and a glass of Port wine, into the saucepan; cover it closely, and let it stew gently for two hours. Before serving, add two table-spoonfuls of mushroom ketchup. Garnish with pickles.

MUTTON SHOULDER, STEWED. (2) Bone and flatten a shoulder of mutton, sprinkle over it pepper and salt, roll it up tightly, bind it with tape, and put it into a stewpan that will just hold it, pour over it a well-seasoned gravy made with the bones, cover the pan closely, and let it stew till tender; before serving, take off the tape, thicken the gravy, and garnish with cut pickles.

MUTTON STEAKS, BROILED. Cut some mutton steaks from the loin, about half an inch thick, take off the skin, and part of the fat. As soon as the gridiron is hot, rub it with a little suet, lay on the steaks (place the gridiron over the fire aslant), turn the steaks frequently; when they are done, put them into a hot dish, rub them with a little butter; slice a shallot very thin into a spoonful of water, and pour it on them; add a little ketchup; garnish with scraped horse-radish, and pickles, and send them up hot to table.

~~~~~~~~~

## N.

NAPLES CURD. Put into a quart of new milk a stick of cinnamon, boil it a few minutes, take out the cinnamon, and stir in eight well-beaten eggs, and a table-spoonful of white wine; when it boils again, strain it through a sieve; beat the curd in a basin, together with about half an ounce of butter, two table-spoonfuls of orange-flower water, and pounded sugar sufficient to sweeten it. Put it into a mould for two hours before it is sent to table. White wine, sugar, and cream, may be mixed together, and poured round the curd; or it may be served in a sauce tureen.

NASTURTIUMS PICKLED. As soon as the blossoms are off, gather the little knobs; put them into cold water with some salt; shift them once a day for three successive days; make a cold pickle of white wine vinegar, a little white wine, shallot, pepper, cloves, mace, nutmeg, cut in quarters, and horse-radish; and put your nasturtium buds into this pickle.

NEAT'S TONGUE FRESH, IN A PLAIN WAY. Lard a tongue with tolerable-sized lardons, and boil it in broth, or in water, with a few onions and roots; when it is done, peel it, and serve it with broth, sprinkling it over with a little pepper and salt; it is also used without larding, and being boiled fresh in this manner, is considered very good for mince-pie meat.

NEAT'S TONGUE, ROASTED, A LA FRANCAISE. Boil a neat's tongue, and blanch it; set it by till it is cold, then cut a hole in the under part, and take out the meat, mince it with two or three hard eggs, an apple, beef-suet, and bacon; season with salt, beaten ginger, and sweet herbs, shred very fine; stuff the tongue with this forcemeat; then cover the end with a veal caul, lard it with bacon, and roast it; serve with a sauce made of gravy, butter, and the juice of oranges, garnish the dish with sliced lemon-peel and barberries.

NOUGAT. Blanch and wash a pound of sweet almonds, and having drained them well, cut each into five slips, which place in a gentle oven to dry; let them be all equally colored of a clear yellow; in the meantime, put three-quarters of a pound of fine sugar into a preserving pan, set it on a stove, stirring with a wooden spoon until completely dissolved; then take the almonds out of the oven, and whilst hot throw them into the liquid sugar; mix them together well. Have ready a mould well oiled, of any shape you think proper, in the interior of which place the slips of almonds, by means of lemon-juice, when the whole is covered, remove the mould carefully, and serve the *Nougat*.

NOYAU. (1) Peaches and nectarines, in equal quantities, are to be bruised, the stones broken, and the kernels blanched and bruised; they are then to be put into a jar in layers, one of fruit, one of kernels, and one of pounded loaf sugar, and so on until the jar is full; as much white brandy is then to be added as the jar will hold; and when it has stood for five or six months, it is to be filtered and bottled for use.

NOYAU. (2) One pound of bitter almonds, blanched, is to be steeped three months in four quarts of large-still proof whisky, or pale brandy, four pounds of loaf sugar are then to be clarified and added to the strained or filtered spirits, together with half a pint of pure honey. It is sometimes colored with a little cochineal; and may also be made, allowing three parts of sweet, and one of bitter almonds.

NOYAU. (3) The rinds of three large lemons, half a pound of pounded loaf sugar, one ounce of bitter almonds, blanched and pounded, are to be mixed into a quart of the best Hollands gin, three table-spoonfuls of boiling milk being added. It is to be put into a bottle or jar, and shaken every day for three weeks, and then filtered through chamois leather or blotting paper, when it will be fit for use.

O.

OAT CAKES—are made in the same manner as muffins, using sifted oatmeal instead of flour, and three gallons of water instead of two: pull the dough into pieces, roll and finish the cakes as directed for muffins. When wanted, pull the edges apart, toast them nicely on both sides, and then open them completely; lay in small pieces of butter, until you have as much as you may want; close them again, set them before the fire, and cut each in halves or quarters.

OATMEAL PORRIDGE. Boil some water in a saucepan with a little salt, and stir oatmeal into it with a thevil; when of a proper thickness, let it boil for four or five minutes, stirring it all the time; then pour it into a dish, and serve with it cream or milk. It is sometimes eaten with porter and sugar, or ale and sugar. If made with milk instead of water, less meal is requisite, and it is then eaten with cold milk.

OLIVE ROYALS. Boil one pound of potatoes, and when nearly cold rub them perfectly smooth with four ounces of flour and one ounce of butter, and knead it together till it become a paste; roll it out about a quarter of an inch thick, cut it into rounds, and lay upon one side any sort of cold roasted meat cut into thin small bits, and seasoned with pepper and salt; put a very small bit of butter over it, wet the edges, and close the paste in the form of a half circle. Fry them in boiling fresh dripping of a light brown color; lay them before the fire, on the back of a sieve, to drain. Serve them with or without gravy in the dish. For a change, mince the meat, and season it as before directed. The potatoes should be very mealy.

OLIVES. There are three sorts, the Italian, Spanish, and French; they may be had of various sizes and flavors, some prefer one sort, and some another.

The fine salad oil is made from this fruit, for which purpose they are gathered ripe; for pickling they are gathered when only half ripe, at the latter end of June; they are put into fresh water to soak for a couple of days; after this they are thrown into limewater, in which some pearl-ashes have been dissolved; in this liquor they lie for six and thirty hours; they are then put into water which has had bay-salt dissolved in it; this is the last preparation, and they are sent over to us in this liquor; they are naturally, as they grow on the tree, extremely bitter, and therefore all these preparations are necessary to bring them to their fine flavor. To some olives they add a small quantity of essence of spices, which is an oil drawn from cloves, nutmeg, cinnamon, coriander, and sweet fennel-seed distilled together for that purpose; twelve drops are sufficient for a bushel of olives; some prefer them flavored with this essence.

OMELETS AND VARIOUS WAYS OF DRESSING EGGS. There is no dish which may be considered as coming under the denomination of a made dish of the second order, which is so generally eaten, if good, as an omelet; and no one is so often badly dressed: it is a very faithful assistant in the construction of a dinner.

When you are taken by surprise, and wish to make an appearance beyond what is provided for the every-day dinner, a little portable soup melted down, and some zest and a few vegetables, will make a good broth; a pot of stewed veal warmed up; an omelet; and some apple or lemon fritters, can all be got ready at ten minutes notice, and with the original foundation of a leg of mutton, or a piece of beef, will make up a very good dinner when company unexpectedly arrives, in the country.

The great merit of an omelet is, that it should not be greasy, burnt, nor too much done: if too much of the white of the eggs left in, no art can prevent it being hard, if it is done: to dress the omelet, the fire should not be too hot, as it is an object to have the whole substance heated, without much browning the outside.

One of the great errors in cooking an omelet is, that it is too thin; consequently, instead of feeling full and moist in the mouth, the substance presented is little better than a piece of fried leather: to get the omelet thick is one of the great objects. With respect to the flavors to be introduced, these are infinite; that which is most common, however, is the best, viz. finely chopped parsley, and chives or onions, or eschalots: however, one made of a mixture of tarragon, chervil, and parsley, is a very delicate variety, omitting or adding the onion or chives. Of the meat flavors, the veal kidney is the most delicate, and is the most admired by the French: this should be cut in dice, and should be dressed (boiled) before it is added; in the same manner, ham and anchovies, shred small, or tongue, will make a very delicately flavored dish.

The objection to an omelet is, that it is too rich, which makes it advisable to eat but a small quantity. An addition of some finely mashed potatoes, about two table-spoonfuls, to an omelet of six eggs, will much lighten it.

Omelets are often served with rich gravy; but, as a general principle, no substance which has been fried should be served in gravy, but accompanied by it, or what ought to eat dry and crisp, becomes soddened and flat.

In the compounding the gravy, great care should be taken that the flavor does not overcome that of the omelet, a thing too little attended to: a fine gravy, with a flavoring of sweet herbs and onions, we think the best; some add a few drops of tarragon vinegar; but this is to be done only with great care: gravies to omelets are in general thickened: this should never be done with flour; potato starch, or arrow-root, is the best.

Omelets should be fried in a small frying-pan made for that purpose, with a small quantity of butter. The omelet's great merit is to be thick, so as not to taste of the outside; therefore use only half the number of whites that you do yolks of eggs: every care must be taken in frying, even at the risk of not having it quite set in the middle: an omelet, which has so much vogue abroad, is here, in general, a thin doubled-up piece of leather, and harder than soft leather sometimes. The fact is, that as much care must be bestowed on the frying, as should be taken in poaching an egg. A salamander is necessary to those who will have the top brown; but the kitchen shovel may be substituted for it.

The following receipt is the basis of all omelets, of which you may make an endless variety, by taking, instead of the parsley and eschalot, a portion of sweet herbs, or any of the articles used for making forcemeats, or any of the forcemeats.

Omelets are called by the name of what is added to flavor them: a ham or tongue omelet; an anchovy, or veal kidney omelet, &c.: these are prepared exactly in the same way as in the first receipt, leaving out the parsley and eschalot, and mincing the ham or kidney very fine, &c., and adding that in the place of them, and then pour over them all sorts of thickened gravies, sauces, &c.

OMELET. (1) Five or six eggs will make a good-sized omelet; break them into a basin, and beat them well with a fork; and add a salt-spoonful of salt; have ready chopped two drachms of onion, or three drachms of parsley, a good clove of eschalot minced very fine; beat it well up with the eggs; then take four ounces of fresh butter, and break half of it into large bits, and put it into the omelet, and the other half into a very clean frying-pan; when it is melted, pour in the omelet, and stir it with a spoon till it begins to set, then turn it up all round the edges, and when it is of a nice brown it is done: the safest way to take it out is to put a plate on the omelet, and turn the pan upside-down: serve it on a hot dish; it should never be done till just wanted. If maigre, grated cheese, shrimps, or oysters. If oysters, boil them four minutes, and take away the beard and gristly part; they may either be put in whole, or cut in bits.

OMELET. (2) Beard and parboil twelve or sixteen oysters, seasoning them with a few peppercorns, strain and chop them; beat well six eggs; parboil and mince a little parsley; mix all together, and season with a little nutmeg, salt, and a table-spoonful of mushroom ketchup; fry it lightly in three ounces of butter, and hold it for a minute or two before the fire.

OMELET. (3) Beat well and strain six eggs; add them to three ounces of butter made hot; mix in some grated ham, pepper, salt, and nutmeg, some chopped chives and parsley. Fry it of a light bown color.

OMELET. (4) Take as many eggs as you think proper (according to the size of your omelet) break them into a basin with some salt and chopped parsley; then beat them well, and season them according to taste, then have ready some onion chopped small; put some butter into a frying-pan, and when it is hot (but not to burn) put in your chopped onion, giving them two or three turns; then add your eggs to it, and fry the whole of a nice brown, you must only fry one side. When done, turn it into a dish, the fried side uppermost, and serve.

OMELET FRITTERS. Make two or three thin omelets, adding a little sweet basil to the usual ingredients; cut them into small pieces and roll them into the form of olives; when cold, dip them into batter, or enclose them in puff paste, fry, and serve them with fried parsley.

OMELET WITH KIDNEY OF VEAL. To eight well-beaten eggs, add a little salt, and part of a cold roasted kidney of veal, finely minced; season with pepper, and a little more salt; melt in a frying-pan one ounce and a half of butter, and pour in the omelet; fry it gently, and keep the middle part moist; when done, roll it equally upon a knife, and serve it very hot.

OMELET AU NATUREL. Break eight or ten eggs into a pan, add pepper, salt, and a spoonful of cold water, beat them up with a whisk; in the meantime put some fresh butter into a frying-pan, when it is quite melted and nearly boiling, put in the eggs, &c. with a skimmer; as it is frying take up the edges, that they may be properly done; when cooked, double it; serve very hot.

ONIONS. The small round silver button onions, about as big as a nutmeg, make a very nice pickle. Take off their top coats, have ready a stewpan, three parts filled with boiling water, into which put as many onions as will cover the top: as soon as they look clear, immediately take them up with a spoon full of holes, and lay them on a cloth three times folded, and cover them with another till you have ready as many as you wish: when they are quite dry, put them into jars, and cover them with hot pickle, made by infusing an ounce of horseradish, same of allspice, and same of black pepper, and same of salt, in a quart of best white-wine vinegar, in a stone jar, on a trivet by the side of the fire for three days, keeping it well closed; when cold, bung them down tight, and cover them with bladder wetted with the pickle and leather.

ONIONS STEWED. The large Portugal onions are the best: take off the top-coats of half a dozen of these (taking care not to cut off the tops or tails too near, or the onions will go to pieces), and put them into a stewpan broad enough to hold them without laying them atop of one another, and just cover them with good broth. Put them over a slow fire, and let them simmer about two hours; when you dish them, turn them upside down, and pour the sauce over.

ONIONS TO PICKLE. Peel the onions till they look white; boil some strong salt and water, and pour it over them; let them stand in this twenty-four hours, keep the vessel closely covered to retain the steam: after that time wipe the onions quite dry, and when they are cold, pour boiling vinegar, with ginger and white pepper over them. Take care the vinegar always covers the onions.

ONION SAUCE, YOUNG. Peel a pint of button onions, and put them in water till you want to put them on to boil; put them into a stewpan, with a quart of cold water; let them boil till tender; they will take (according to their size and age) from half an hour to an hour.

ONION SAUCE. Those who like the full flavor of onions only cut off the strings and tops (without peeling off any of the skins), put them into salt and water, and let them lie an hour; then wash them, put them into a kettle with plenty of water, and boil them till they are tender: now skin them, pass them through a colander, and mix a little melted butter with them. N. B. Some mix the pulp of apples, or turnips, with the onions, others add mustard to them.

ONIONS, TO PREPARE FOR SEASONING. Peel and mince three or four onions, put them into a saucepan with a little cold water. Let them boil till quite tender, and then pulp them with the liquor through a hair sieve, when it may be mixed with any made dishes or sauces.

ONIONS YOUNG, TO PICKLE. Choose some of the small silver onions, put them on in cold water, and when it is scalding hot, take them out with an egg slice; peel off the skins till they look white and clear; lay them into the folds of a cloth. Boil, in a quart of vinegar, half an ounce of pepper, a quarter of an ounce of allspice, the same of garlic, and one sliced nutmeg; put the onions into a jar, and pour over them the boiling vinegar and spices. When cold, tie leather over the jar.

ONIONS, PLAIN BOILED. Peel them, and let them lie an hour in cold water, put them on in boiling milk and water; boil them till tender, and serve them with melted butter poured over them.

ONIONS, ROAST. Roast them with the skins on in a Dutch oven, that they may brown equally. They are eaten with cold fresh butter, pepper, and salt.

ONIONS STEWED. (1) Take a dozen of good-sized onions, peel and put them on in the following sauce:—A pint of veal stock, a bit of butter rolled in flour, a little pepper, and salt. Stew them gently for an hour, and, just before serving, mix in three table-spoonfuls of cream. To stew them in a brown sauce, take the same quantity of good gravy. In a stewpan brown, of a light color, a little butter and flour, add the gravy and onions, with a little pepper and salt, and stew them gently one hour.

ONIONS STEWED. (2) Peel five or six large onions, put them into a Dutch oven or cheese-toaster to roast, turn them frequently, and when they are well browned, put them into a saucepan, with a bone of dressed or undressed meat, a slice of bacon, a little water, and some pepper. Cover the pan closely, and stew them till tender. Take out the bone and the bacon; thicken the sauce with a bit of butter rolled in flour.

ORANGE BISCUITS. Take the grated rind of an orange, six fresh eggs, a quarter of a pound of flour, and three-quarters of a pound of powder sugar; put these into a mortar, beat them to a paste, which put into cases, and bake like other biscuits.

ORANGE CHEESECAKES. To be made in the same way, as lemon cheesecakes.

ORANGE CREAM, FROTHED. Make a pint of cream very sweet, put it over the fire, let it just boil, put the juice of a large orange into a small deep glass, having previously steeped a bit of orange-peel for a short time in the juice, when the cream is almost cold, pour it out of a tea-pot upon the juice, holding it as high as possible.

ORANGE CUSTARD. Having boiled the rind of a Seville orange very tender, beat it in a mortar to a fine paste; put to it the juice of a Seville orange, a spoonful of the best brandy, four ounces of loaf-sugar, and the yolks of four eggs; beat them all well together ten minutes, then pour in by degrees a pint of boiling cream; keep beating it till cold; put it into custard glasses. Set them in an earthen dish of hot water; let them stand till they are set, then stick preserved orange, or orange chips, on the top. It may be served hot or cold.

ORANGE FOOL. Take the juice of six oranges, six eggs well beaten, a pint of cream, a quarter of a pound of sugar, a little cinnamon and nutmeg. Mix all well together; stir it over a slow fire till thick, then put in a small piece of butter, and keep stirring it till cold.

ORANGE GINGERBREAD. Sift two pounds and a quarter of fine flour, and add to it a pound and three-quarters of treacle, six ounces of candied orange-peel cut small, three-quarters of a pound of moist sugar, one ounce of ground ginger, and one ounce of allspice: melt to an oil three-quarters of a pound of butter; mix the whole well together, and lay it by for twelve hours; roll it out with as little flour as possible, about half an inch thick; cut it into pieces three inches long and two wide; mark them in the form of checkers with the back of a knife; put them on a baking-plate about a quarter of an inch apart; rub them over with a brush dipped in the yolk of an egg beat up with a tea-cupful of milk; bake it in a cool oven about a quarter of an hour: when done, wash them slightly over again, divide the pieces with a knife (as in baking they will run together).

ORANGE LIQUOR. To each orange, one quart of strong spirits, and one pound and a quarter of loaf sugar are allowed; six or eight cloves are to be stuck into each orange, which, with the spirits and sugar, is to be put into a jar. It must be closely covered, and stirred occasionally in the course of two months; it is then to be filtered through blotting paper, and bottled for use.

Lemon liquor is made in the same way, substituting lemons for oranges. Instead of mixing the sugar with the other materials in the jar, it may be made into a sirup, and added to the strained or filtered spirits. This, though more troublesome, will be found a better method.

ORANGE OR LEMON-PEEL, TO MIX, WITH STUFFING. Peel a Seville orange, or lemon, very thin, taking off only the fine yellow rind (without any of the white); pound it in a mortar with a bit of lump sugar; rub it well with the peel; by degrees add a little of the forcemeat it is to be mixed with: when it is well ground and blended with this, mix it with the whole: there is no other way of incorporating it so well. Forcemeats, &c. are frequently spoiled by the insufficient mixing of the ingredients.

ORANGE SIRUP, FOR PUNCH OR PUDDING. *See Justice.*

ORANGEADE. (1) Squeeze the juice; pour some boiling water on the peel, and cover it closely, boil water and sugar to a thin sirup, and skim it; when all are cold, mix the juice, the infusion, and the sirup, with as much water as will make a rich sherbet; strain it through a jelly-bag.

ORANGEADE. (2) This refreshing beverage is made precisely in the same manner as lemonade, only substituting oranges for lemons.

ORANGE PEEL RATAFIA. Put the peel of a dozen thick-skinned oranges into a gallon of brandy; dissolve two pounds of sugar in the juice of the oranges, add to it the brandy, and having stirred them together well, close the vessel tightly; and leave it for a month; then strain it off, and bottle it.

ORGEAT. (1) Pound very fine one pound of Jordan, and one ounce of bitter, almonds, in a marble mortar, with half a gill of orange-flower water to keep them from oiling; then mix with them one pint of rose and one pint of spring-water; rub it through a tamis cloth or lawn sieve, till the almonds are quite dry, which will reduce the quantity to about a quart: have ready three pints of clarified sugar or water, and boil it to a crack (which may be known by dipping your fingers into the sugar, and then into cold water; and if you find the sugar to crack in moving your finger, it has boiled enough); put in the almonds; boil it one minute, and when cold put it into small bottles close corked; a table-spoonful of which will be sufficient for a tumbler of water: shake the bottle before using. If the orgeat is for present use, the almonds may be pounded as above, and mixed with one quart of water, one quart of milk, a pint of capillaire or clarified sugar, rubbed through a tamis or fine sieve, and put into decanters for use.

ORGEAT. (2) A quarter of a pound of sweet, and one ounce and a half of bitter almonds, are to be blanched, and thrown into cold water, then beaten in a marble mortar, and moistened occasionally with a spoonful of milk, to prevent their oiling; three pints of milk are then to be mixed gradually with them, and after being sweetened, boiled, stirred till cold, and strained, a glass of wine or brandy is to be added.

OVEN, DIRECTIONS FOR THE. Be very careful to keep your oven clean, and that there are no remains of sugar or fat that may have run over from any thing that has been baking. Puff-pastes require a moderately hot oven, but not too hot, or it will spoil the shape and turn it over; tart-paste, or short crust, requires a slower oven; petits-bhoux, one still slower; but for raised pies, let it be as hot as for puff-paste at first, and well closed, so that the pies may not fall.

Therefore, when you give a dinner where paste is necessary, endeavor to make it in the morning; heat your oven first for the puff-paste, which must be baked the first; then let the oven go gradually down, and bake your pastes in rotation, as the heat falls. Savoy biscuits require a cool oven, and, by degrees, raise the heat as the biscuits are baking. For souffles or light puddings, have a gentle oven, and contrive so as to have them ready by the time they are wanted, or they will fall. The greatest attention should also be paid in heating the oven for baking cakes, particularly for those that are large. If not pretty quick, the batter will not rise. Should you fear its catching by being too quick, put paper over the cake to prevent its being burnt. If not long enough lighted to have a body of heat, or if it has become slack, the cake will be heavy. To know when it is soaked, take a broad bladed knife that is very bright, and plunge it into the centre; draw it instantly out, and if the least stickiness adheres, put the cake immediately in, and shut up the oven. If the heat was sufficient to raise, but not to soak, fresh fuel must be quickly put in, and the cakes kept hot until the oven is fit to finish the soaking, but this must only be done in a case of great emergency; for those who are employed ought to be particularly careful that no mistake occur from negligence.

OX-CHEEK STEWED. Prepare this the day before it is to be eaten; clean it, and put it into soft water just warm; let it lie three or four hours, then put it into cold water, and let it soak all night; next day wipe it clean, put it into a stewpan, and just cover it with water; skim it well when it is coming to a boil, then put two whole onions, stick two or three cloves into each, three turnips quartered, a couple of carrots sliced, two bay-leaves, and twenty-four corns of all-spice, a head of celery, and a bundle of sweet-herbs, pepper, and salt; to these, those who are for a "haut gout" may add cayenne and garlic, in such proportions as the palate that requires them may desire. Let it stew gently till perfectly tender, *i. e.* about three hours; then take out the cheek, divide it into handsome pieces, fit to help at table; skim, and drain the gravy; melt an ounce and a half of butter in a stewpan; stir into it as much flour as it will take up; mix with it by degrees a pint and a half of the gravy; add to it a table-spoonful of basil, tarragon, or elder vinegar, or the like quantity of mushroom or walnut ketchup, or cavice, or Port wine, and give it a boil.

OX CHEEK, TO BOIL. Wash very

clean, half a head; let it lie in cold water all night; break the bone in two, taking care not to break the flesh. Put it on in a pot of boiling water, and let it boil from two to three hours; take out the bone. Serve it with boiled carrots and turnips, or savoys. The liquor the head has been boiled in may be strained and made into Scots barley broth, or Scots kale.

OX FEET JELLY. Put a little hot water over the top of the stock, pour it off, and wipe it dry with a clean cloth; put a quart of it into a saucepan with the beaten whites of five or six eggs, the juice of five lemons made very sweet with good brown sugar, a clove or two, and a little cinnamon pounded; let it boil twenty minutes, stirring it all the time; take it off the fire, and add a pint, or half a pint of white wine, and run it through a jelly-bag till clear.

OX-TAILS STEWED. Divide them into joints; wash them; parboil them; set them on to stew in just water enough to cover them, —and dress them in the same manner as we have directed in Stewed Giblets, for which they are an excellent substitute.

OYSTERS. Some piscivorous gourmands think that oysters are not best when quite fresh from their beds, and that their flavor is too brackish and harsh, and is much ameliorated by giving them a feed.

To FEED oysters.—Cover them with clean water, with a pint of salt to about two gallons (nothing else, no oatmeal, flour, nor any other trumpery); this will cleanse them from the mud and sand, &c. of the bed; after they have lain in it twelve hours, change it for fresh salt and water, and in twelve hours more they will be in prime order for the mouth, and remain so two or three days: at the time of high water you may see them open their shells; in expectation of receiving their usual food. This process of feeding oysters is only employed when a great many come up together.

Common people are indifferent about the manner of opening oysters, and the time of eating them after they are opened; nothing, however, is more important in the enlightened eyes of the experienced oyster-eater.

Those who wish to enjoy this delicious restorative in its utmost perfection, must eat it the moment it is opened, with its own gravy in the under shell; if not eaten while absolutely alive its flavor and spirit are lost.

Shell-fish have long held a high rank in the catalogue of easily digestible and speedily restorative foods; of these the oyster certainly deserves the best character, but we think it has acquired not a little more reputation for these qualities than it deserves; a well-dressed chop or steak, will invigorate the heart in a much higher ratio; to recruit the animal spirits, and support strength, there is nothing equal to animal food; when kept till properly tender, none will give so little trouble to the digestive organs, and so much substantial excitement to the constitution.

OYSTER ATTELETS. Cut into small pieces a sweetbread and a slice or two of bacon, beard some large oysters, and season all highly with chopped parsley, shallot, a little thyme, pepper and salt. Then fasten them alternately upon wire skewers; put sifted bread crumbs over them, and broil or fry them of a light brown color. Take them off the skewers, and serve them with some rich gravy, to which add a little ketchup and lemon pickle.

OYSTERS, BAKED. Grate a small loaf of stale bread. Butter a deep dish well, and cover the sides and bottom with bread crumbs. Put in half the oysters with a little mace and pepper. Cover them with crumbs and small bits of butter strewed over them. Then put in the remainder of the oysters. Season them. Cover them as before with crumbs and butter. If the oysters are fresh pour in the liquor. If they are salt, substitute a little water. Bake it a very short time.

OYSTERS, FRIED. (1) Make a batter as for pancakes, seasoned with grated nutmeg, white pepper, and salt, and add some finely grated bread crumbs; dip in the oysters; and fry them of a light brown in beef dripping.

Another way is, to dip them into the white of an egg beat up, and roll them in finely grated bread crumbs, seasoned with grated nutmeg, pepper and salt, and fry them as directed.

OYSTERS, FRIED. (2) The largest and finest oysters are to be chosen for this purpose; simmer them in their own liquor for a couple of minutes, take them out and lay them on a cloth to drain, beard them and then flour them, egg and bread-crumb them, put them into boiling fat, and fry them a delicate brown. *Obs.*—An elegant garnish for made dishes, stewed rump-steaks, boiled or fried fish, &c.; but they are too hard and dry to be eaten.

OYSTERS, FRIED. (3) For frying, choose the largest and finest oysters. Beat some yolks of eggs, and mix with them grated bread, and a small quantity of beaten nutmeg and mace, and a little salt. Having stirred this batter well, dip your oysters into it, and fry them in lard, till they are of a light brown color. Take care not to do them too much. Serve them up hot. For grated bread, some substitute crackers pounded to a powder, and mixed with yolk of egg and spice.

OYSTERS, TO KEEP AND FATTEN. Put them into water, and wash and clean them with a birch broom; laying them with the deep shell downwards into a tub or broad platter, and then sprinkle them over with salt. The following day pour over them and fill the vessel with clean cold water, in which they must remain an hour, then pour it off again; sprinkle them with salt, and let this be repeated every day. This method will keep them good for a fortnight.

OYSTER KETCHUP. (1) Take fine fresh oysters; wash them in their own liquor; skim it; pound them in a marble mortar; to a pint of oysters add a pint of Sherry; boil them up, and add an ounce of salt, two drachms of pounded mace, and one of cayenne; let it just boil up again; skim it, and rub it through a sieve, and when cold, bottle it, cork it well, and seal it down.

N. B. It is the best way to pound the salt and spices, &c. with the oysters.

*Obs.*—This composition very agreeably heightens the flavor of white sauces, and white made-dishes; and if you add a glass of brandy to it, it will keep good for a considerable time longer than oysters are out of season.

OYSTER KETCHUP. (2) Boil one hundred oysters with their liquor, till the strength be extracted from them; strain them well, and add to the liquor an equal quantity of wine, one half Port and the other Sherry, also a quarter of an ounce of mace, the same of white pepper and of allspice, a drachm or tea-spoonful of ginger, and six anchovies; boil all together about fifteen minutes. Put into a jar twelve shallots, the peel of a lemon, and a piece of horse-radish cut small; pour upon them the boiling liquor, and when cold, bottle it, together with the spices.

OYSTER LOAVES. Cut off the top of some small French rolls, take out the crumb, and fry them brown and crisp with clarified butter, then fry some bread crumbs; stew the requisite quantity of oysters, bearded and cut in two, in their liquor, with a little white wine, some gravy, and seasoned with grated lemon-peel, pounded mace, pepper, and salt and a bit of butter; fill the rolls with the oysters, and serve them with the fried bread crumbs in the dish.

OYSTER PATTIES. (1) Roll out puff paste a quarter of an inch thick, cut it into squares with a knife, sheet eight or ten patty pans, put upon each a bit of bread the size of half a walnut; roll out another layer of paste of the same thickness, cut it as above, wet the edge of the bottom paste, and put on the top, pare them round to the pan, and notch them about a dozen times with the back of the knife, rub them lightly with yolk of egg, bake them in a hot oven about a quarter of an hour: when done, take a thin slice off the top, then, with a small knife or spoon, take out the bread and the inside paste, leaving the outside quite entire; then parboil two dozen of large oysters, strain them from their liquor, wash, beard, and cut them into four, put them into a stewpan with an ounce of butter rolled in flour, half a gill of good cream, a little grated lemon-peel, the oyster liquor, free from sediment, reduced by boiling to one half, some cayenne pepper, salt, and a teaspoonful of lemon-juice; stir it over a fire five minutes, and fill the patties.

OYSTER PATTIES. (2) Make some rich puff paste, and bake it in very small tin patty-pans. When cool, turn them out upon a large dish. Stew some large fresh oysters with a few cloves, a little mace and nutmeg, some yolk of egg boiled hard and grated, a little butter, and as much of the oyster liquor as will cover them. When they have stewed a little while, take them out of the pan, and set them away to cool. When quite cold, lay two or three oysters in each shell of puff-paste.

OYSTER PIE. Beard a quart of fine oysters, strain the liquor, and add them to it. Cut into thin slices the kidney fat of a loin of veal; season them with white pepper, salt, mace, and grated lemon-peel; lay them on the bottom of a pie dish, put in the oysters and liquor, with a little more seasoning put over them the marrow of two bones. Lay a border of puff paste round the edge of the dish; cover it with paste, and bake it nearly three-quarters of an hour.

OYSTERS, PRESERVED. Open the oysters carefully, so as not to cut them except in dividing the gristle which attaches the shells; put them into a mortar, and when you have got as many as you can conveniently pound at once, add about two drachms of salt to a dozen oysters; pound them, and rub them through the back of a hair sieve, and put them into a mortar again, with as much flour (which has been previously thoroughly dried) as will make them into a paste; roll it out several times, and, lastly, flour it, and roll it out the thickness of a half-crown, and divide it into pieces about an inch square; lay them in a Dutch oven, where they will dry so gently as not to get burnt: turn them every half hour, and when they begin to dry, crumble them; they will take about four hours to dry; then pound them fine, sift them, and put them into bottles and seal them over.

N. B. Three dozen required seven and a half ounces of dried flour to make them into a paste which then weighed eleven ounces; when dried and powdered, six and a quarter ounces.

To make half a pint of sauce, put one ounce of butter into a stewpan with three drachms of oyster powder, and six tablespoonfuls of milk; set it on a slow fire; stir it till it boils, and season it with salt.

This powder, if made with plump, juicy, oysters, will abound with the flavor of the fish; and if closely corked, and kept in a dry place, will remain good for sometime.

This extract is a welcome succedaneum while oysters are out of season, and in such inland parts as seldom have any, is a valuable addition to the list of fish sauces: it is equally good with boiled fowl, or rump steak, and sprinkled on bread and butter makes a very good sandwich, and is especially worthy the notice of country housekeepers, and as a store sauce for the army and navy.

OYSTERS, TO PICKLE. Open them carefully, preserving all their liquor; put them into a saucepan over the fire, stirring them now and then, and when the liquor boils take them off, skim the surface, and put the oysters into a bowl; let the liquor settle, pour off the clear part, and put it on to boil, with, to three hundred oysters, half an ounce of whole black pepper, a little mace and allspice; boil it ten minutes, then add the oysters, and let them boil two minutes; put them into a jar, and when they are cold, tie a paper over it.

OYSTER SAUCE. When your oysters are opened, take care of all the liquor and give them one boil in it. Then take the oysters out, and put to the liquor three or four blades of mace. Add to it some melted butter, and some thick cream or rich milk. Put in your oysters and give them a boil.

OYSTER SOUP. (1) Three pints of large fresh oysters. Two table-spoonfuls of butter, rolled in flour. A bunch of sweet herbs. A quart of rich milk. Pepper to your taste. Take the liquor of three pints of oysters. Strain it, and set it on the fire. Put into it, pepper to your taste, two table-spoonfuls of butter rolled in flour, and a bunch of sweet marjoram and other pot-herbs. When it boils add a quart of rich milk—and as soon as it boils again take out the herbs, and put in the oysters just before you send it to table.

OYSTER SOUP. (2) Boil in water the crumb of two twopenny rolls, with a few blades of mace, a tea-spoonful of whole white pepper, and four onions cut small. Pick out the spice, and rub the bread and onions through a hair sieve, then add it to three quarts of well-seasoned strong veal stock. Rub down three ounces of butter, with a table-spoonful of flour, and mix it gradually with half a pint of the soup, and then stir all well together. When it has boiled a short time, add with the liquor half a hundred or more of fine oysters, and let the whole simmer for ten or fifteen minutes. If the soup is not quite salt enough with the liquor of the oysters, a little salt may be added.

OYSTERS SCALLOPED. (1) Put them, with their liquor strained, two or three blades of mace, a few peppercorns, a little cayenne, and a piece of butter the size of a walnut, kneaded with flour, into a stewpan. Simmer them very gently for half an hour, by no means letting them boil; pick out the mace and pepper; have ready, finely grated bread-crumbs, seasoned with pepper and salt; put into the scallop-shells, or into a dish, alternately a layer of bread-crumbs, then one of oysters and part of their liquor; and stick over the last layer of bread-crumbs a few bits of butter, and brown them in a Dutch oven for fifteen or twenty minutes.

OYSTERS SCALLOPED. (2) Take off the beards, stew them in their liquor strained, with a little mace, white pepper, and salt. Fry in a stewpan, with a bit of butter, some grated bread-crumbs, till of a nice brown; put them alternately with the oysters into a dish.

OYSTERS SCALLOPED. (3) *A good way to warm up any cold fish.* Stew the oysters slowly in their own liquor for two or three minutes, take them out with a spoon, beard them, and skim the liquor, put a bit of butter into a stewpan; when it is melted, add as much fine bread-crumbs as will dry it up, then put to it the oyster liquor, and give it a boil up, put the oysters into scallop-shells that you have buttered, and strewed with bread-crumbs, then a layer of oysters, then of bread-crumbs, and then some more oysters; moisten it with the oyster liquor, cover them with bread-crumbs, put about half a dozen little bits of butter on the top of each, and brown them in a Dutch oven. Essence of anchovy, ketchup, cayenne, grated lemon-peel, mace, and other spices, &c. are added by those who prefer piquance to the genuine flavor of the oyster.

Cold fish may be re-dressed the same way. N. B. Small scallop-shells, or saucers that hold about half a dozen oysters, are the most convenient.

OYSTERS STEWED. (1) Stew with a quart of oysters, and their liquor strained, a glass of white wine, one anchovy bruised, seasoned with white pepper, salt, a little mace, and a bunch of sweet herbs; let all stew gently a quarter of an hour. Pick out the bunch of herbs, and add a quarter of a pound of fresh butter kneaded in a large table-spoonful of flour, and stew them ten or twelve minutes. Serve them garnished with bread-sippets and cut lemon. They may be stewed simply in their own liquor, seasoned with salt, pepper, and grated nutmeg, and thickened with cream, flour, and butter.

OYSTERS STEWED. (2) Open the oysters and strain the liquor. Put to them some grated stale bread, and a little pepper and nutmeg. Throw them into the liquor, and add a glass of white wine. Let them stew but a very short time, or they will be hard. Have ready some slices of buttered toast with the crust off. When the oysters are done, dip the toast in the liquor, and lay the pieces round the sides and in the bottom of a deep dish. Pour the oysters and liquor upon the toast and send them to table hot.

OYSTERS STEWED. (3) Large oysters will do for stewing, and by some are preferred. Stew a couple of dozen of these in their own liquor; when they are coming to a boil, skim well, take them up and beard them; strain the liquor through a tamis-sieve, and lay the oysters on a dish. Put an ounce of butter into a stewpan; when it is melted, put to it as much flour as will dry it up, the liquor of the oysters, and three table-spoonfuls of milk or cream, and a little white pepper and salt; to this some cooks add a little ketchup, or finely-chopped parsley, grated lemon-peel, and juice; let it boil up for a couple of minutes, till it is smooth, then take it off the fire, put in the oysters, and let them get warm (they must not themselves be boiled, or they will become hard); line the bottom and sides of a hash-dish with bread-sippets, and pour your oysters and sauce into it.

## P.

PALATES AND SWEETBREADS. Boil the palates till the black skin can be easily peeled off; parboil the sweetbreads with them; skin and cut the palates into pieces, and if the sweetbreads are large, cut them in two the long way; dust them with flour, and fry them of a light brown, in butter; then stew them in rather more than a pint of the liquor in which they were boiled. Brown a piece of butter with flour; add it, with a little cayenne, salt, pepper, grated lemon-peel, and nutmeg, and a glass of white wine. A little before serving stir in a spoonful of vinegar, or the squeeze of a lemon.

PANADA. (1) Boil some pieces of stale bread in a sufficient quantity of cold water to cover them, with a little cinnamon, lemon-peel, and caraways; when the bread is quite soft, press out all the water, and beat up the bread with a small piece of butter, a little milk, and sugar to the taste; a little spice may be added.

PANADA. (2) Set a little water on the fire with a glass of white wine, some sugar, a very little nutmeg, and lemon-peel; meanwhile grate some crumbs of bread: the moment the water boils up, put in the bread-crumbs (without taking it off the fire), and let it boil as fast as it can. When of a proper consistence, that is, when just of a sufficient thickness to drink, take it off the fire.

PANCAKES AND FRITTERS. Break three eggs in a basin; beat them up with a little nutmeg and salt; then put to them four ounces and a half of flour, and a little milk; beat it of a smooth batter; then add by degrees as much milk as will make it of the thickness of good cream: the frying-pan must be about the size of a pudding plate, and very clean, or they will stick; make it hot, and to each pancake put in a bit of butter about as big as a walnut: when it is melted, pour in the batter to cover the bottom of the pan; make them the thickness of half a crown; fry them of a light brown on both sides. The above will do for apple fritters, by adding one spoonful more of flour; peel your apples, and cut them in thick slices; take out the core, dip them in the batter, and fry them in hot lard; put them on a sieve to drain; dish them neatly, and grate some loaf-sugar over them.

PANCAKES IN APPLES. Cut some apples very small, stew them with a little white wine, grated lemon-peel, pounded cinnamon, and brown sugar; mash them, and spread it over pancakes; roll them up, and serve with sifted loaf sugar over them.

PANCAKES COMMON. With nearly half a pound of flour, mix five well-beaten eggs, and then add, by degrees, a quart of good milk; fry them in fresh lard, and serve them with pounded loaf-sugar strewed between each.

PANCAKES FINE. To three table-spoonfuls of flour add six well-beaten eggs, three table-spoonfuls of white wine, four ounces of melted butter nearly cold, the same quantity of pounded loaf-sugar, half a grated nutmeg, and a pint of cream; mix it well, beating the batter for sometime, and pour it thin over the pan.

PANCAKE, RICE. Add to three well-beaten eggs a pint of new milk, three table-spoonfuls of boiled rice, some sugar, and a little pounded cinnamon; mix it all well together, and fry it in butter; brown the upper side for a minute before the fire; serve it, cut into four, with pounded sugar strewed over it.

PANCAKE RISSOLES. Mince finely some cold veal, season it with grated lemon-peel, nutmeg, pepper, salt, and a little lemon pickle; warm it up with some good gravy, and a small bit of butter rolled in flour. Have ready a batter as for pancakes, seasoned with a little salt and grated nutmeg. Fry a thin pancake, turn it, and put into the middle two table-spoonfuls of the minced veal; fold it in at each side and at the ends in an oblong form, and fry them of a light brown color; lay them upon the back of a sieve to drain before the fire. Four or six will make a dish. They are served as a corner or top dish.

PANCAKES, SCOTCH. Mix with six table-spoonfuls of flour a little cream, add the beaten yolks of six eggs, and then mix in a pint of cream, the grated peel of a small lemon, a table-spoonful of pounded sugar, and a little ratafia; when the batter is very well beaten, and just before using, mix in the whites of the eggs beaten with a knife, to a stiff froth. Put a little butter or lard into the frying-pan, make it hot, pour it out, and wipe the pan with a clean cloth; put in some butter or lard, and when hot, pour in a tea-cupful of the batter; shake it, and when firm, prick it a little with a fork, but do not turn it; hold it before the fire a minute to brown. Serve them with pounded loaf-sugar strewed over them.

PANCAKES, THICK. Beat separately the yolks and whites of two eggs; mix with the yolks a table-spoonful and a half of flour, a little sugar and white wine, half a pint of cream or good milk; add the whites, and fry it in a broad saucepan, with butter or clarified suet; brown the upper side before the fire; warm any sort of preserve, spread it upon one half, and turn the other over it, and strew upon it pounded loaf sugar.

PANNEQUETS. Put into a pan, two ounces of sifted flour, four of powder-sugar, the same of bitter macaroons, and a spoonful of dried orange-flowers; break up all these articles, and mix with them the yolks of ten eggs, four large glasses of double cream, and a pinch of salt. Wash the bottom of a frying-pan lightly with some warm clarified butter, then put in it a spoonful of the above preparation, spread it over the pan, to make the paste as thin as possible; when the *pannequet* becomes lightly colored, turn it over carefully, and do the other side; then put it on a tin plate, spread a little apricot marmalade over, and having strewed crushed macaroons on that, roll up the *pannequet* till about an inch in diameter; in the meantime put a second spoonful of your preparation into the pan, and proceed in the above manner, garnishing one *pannequet* whilst another is cooking; taking care, however, to set the pan over a gentle fire. When all are done, cut the *pannequets* three inches in length, glaze, and dish them.

PARSLEY. To preserve parsley through the winter:—in May, June, or July, take fine fresh-gathered sprigs; pick, and wash them clean; set on a stewpan half full of water; put a little salt in it; boil, and skim it clean, and then put in the parsley, and let it boil for a couple of minutes; take it out, and lay it on a sieve before the fire, that it may be dried as quick as possible; put it by in a tin box, and keep it in a dry place: when you want it, lay it in a basin, and cover it with warm water a few minutes before you use it.

PARSLEY BUTTER. Wash some parsley very clean, and pick it carefully leaf by leaf; put a tea-spoonful of salt into half a pint of boiling water: boil the parsley about ten minutes; drain it on a sieve; mince it quite fine, and then bruise it to a pulp. The delicacy and excellence of this elegant and innocent relish depends upon the parsley being minced very fine: put it into a sauce-boat, and mix with it, by degrees, about half a pint of good melted butter, only do not put so much flour to it, as the parsley will add to its thickness: never pour parsley and butter over boiled things, but send it up in a boat.

PARSLEY, CRISP. Pick and wash young parsley, shake it in a dry cloth to drain the water from it; spread it on a sheet of clean paper in a Dutch oven before the fire, and turn it frequently until it is quite crisp. This is a much more easy way of preparing it than frying it, which is not seldom ill done.

PARSNIPS, TO BOIL. Scrape and wash them nicely; when large, divide them; boil them in milk and water till quite tender; they will take nearly as long to boil as carrots. They may also be mashed like turnips.

PARTRIDGES TO CHOOSE. When they are young the bill is of a dark color, and their legs are of a yellowish color; and when fresh, the vent is firm, but this part will look greenish when stale. The plumage on the breast of the hen is light, that on the cock is tinged with red.

PARTRIDGES BROILED. Take five partridges, cut them in halves, trim and dip them in melted butter, and bread them twice; a quarter of an hour before dinner broil them.

PARTRIDGES MINCED. Take the fillets from eight roasted partridges, mince, and put them into a saucepan; make a light *roux*, in which put the livers and lights of the birds, a bay-leaf, a clove, three shallots, and a little sage, give them a few turns, and then add two large glasses of stock, reduce the sauce to half, strain and put it to the mince, stirring till it is thick and smooth; make it hot, but not boiling; serve it over fried bread, and garnish your dish, with either poached or hard eggs.

PARTRIDGE IN BREAD. Take a nice shaped loaf, of about a pound weight; make a hole at one end, through which take out all the crumbs, rub the crust over with a little butter or lard, and set it in the oven for a few minutes to dry: fill this with minced partridge (see that article), and put the loaf, bottom upwards, into a stewpan; add two spoonfuls of veal blond, with any other garnish you please; let it remain on the fire till the bread is soft enough to allow a straw to penetrate it, then take it out and dish it with the sauce round.

PARTRIDGE PIE IN A DISH. Take four partridges, pick and singe them; cut off their legs at the knee; season with pepper, salt, chopped parsley, thyme, and mushrooms. Put a veal steak and a slice of ham at the bottom of the dish; put in the partridges with half a pint of good *consomme*. Line the edges of the dish with puff paste, and cover with the same; do it over with egg, and let it bake for an hour.

PARTRIDGE TO ROAST. Take out the entrails, and singe the partridge over the stove, then roll a bit of butter in pepper and salt, and put it into the inside of the bird; truss it neatly with the head turned on one side, keeping the breast as full as possible; over which should be laid slices of fat bacon tied on with pack-thread; before it is put on the spit, break the back-bone, that it may lay the better on the dish. A good sized partridge will take half an hour; when nearly done, take away the bacon, brown the partridge well; sprinkle it with flour and salt, and froth it with butter; serve it with water-cresses, a good gravy under it, and bread sauce in a boat.

PARTRIDGE TO TRUSS. Let it be well picked and singed, then cut a slit in the back of the neck, and carefully take the crop out without breaking it; then cut off the vent, and draw out the inside; after this, well wipe the inside, and then put in a little pepper and salt, mixed with a bit of butter. Having cleansed it, proceed to truss the bird, by first cutting off the pinion at the first joint, so that the feathers need not be picked off that part; break the back-bone, and truss it in the same manner as a fowl, by pressing the legs close to the apron, then turn the bird on the breast, and run a skewer through the end of the pinion, the leg, the body, and the leg and pinion on the other side, with the head fixed on the end of the skewer, and over the breast lay a slice of fat bacon, and tie it on with pack-thread. If for boiling or stewing, truss them the same as a fowl for boiling.

PARTRIDGES TO STEW. Truss the partridges as fowls are done for boiling; pound the livers with double the quantity of fat bacon and bread-crumbs boiled in milk; and some chopped parsley, thyme, shallots, and mushrooms; season with pepper, salt, grated lemon-peel, and mace. Stuff the inside of the birds, tie them at both ends, and put them into a stewpan lined with slices of bacon; add a quart of good stock, half a pint of white wine, two onions, a bunch of sweet herbs, and a few blades of mace; let them stew gently till tender; take them out, strain and thicken the sauce with flour and butter, make it hot, and pour it over the partridges.

PASTE. Be very particular that your slab or paste table, rolling-pin and cutters are clean, and free from all old paste, and be very careful that both the flour and butter are extremely good. Have a dry sieve always in readiness, in or by the flour tub, so as to use none without sifting it; for, though it may appear pure and fine, bran, or small particles of old paste may have fallen into it; sifting is, therefore, always necessary. Weigh one pound of flour, lay it in a circle on the slab: break one egg in the centre, put a small quantity of salt, and a little bit of butter; mix all these together lightly, add a little water, mix them again, then add more water, and so proceed until it binds into paste; but take care that you do not make it too stiff, nor squeeze it much together, till you find there is sufficient water; then work it well together, and roll it out on the slab, but do not roll it too thin; work a pound of butter on the slab, spread it out to the size of the paste, with a knife cut it off altogether, and lay it on the paste; then double the ends of the paste together, to inclose the butter; then give it one turn, thus: roll it out till you just perceive the butter through the paste; turn the end which is next to you half way over, and the other end over that, roll it once or twice with the rolling-pin; then let it stand, this is called one turn; then, in three minutes time, turn it again, and so proceed until you have given it six turns; then roll it out, and cut it for patties or any shape you please; but observe not to put over them too much egg, as that will prevent their rising; as soon as they are baked, take them off the sheet, lay them on paper, and when cold, scrape the bottoms, neatly cut out the insides ready for whatever you mean to put into them. For baking, see directions for the oven.

**PASTE, BEEF DRIPPING.** Rub into one pound of flour half a pound of clarified beef dripping, till it all looks like flour; work it to a stiff paste with cold water, and roll it out two or three times. This paste answers very well for common pies, but must be used when hot and fresh baked.

**PASTE FOR BOILED PUDDINGS.** Pick and chop very fine half a pound of beef suet, add to it one pound and a quarter of flour, and a little salt: mix it with half a pint of milk or water, and beat it well with the rolling-pin, to incorporate the suet with the flour.

**PASTE FOR CHEESECAKES.** Rub equal quantities of flour and butter, together with a little pounded and sifted loaf sugar, make it into a paste, with warm milk, roll it out, and line the pans with it.

**PASTE, CRISP.** Rub a quarter of a pound of flour, add two table-spoonfuls of pounded loaf-sugar, and the well-beaten yolks of two or three eggs, work it well with a horn-spoon, and roll it out very thin, touching it as little as possible with the hands; the moment before putting into a quick oven rub it over with the well-beaten white of an egg, and sift all over the tart finely-pounded sugar. This crust may be used for any fruit tarts.

**PASTE FOR CROQUANTS OR Cut Pastry.** To half a pound of fine flour put a quarter of a pound of sifted loaf-sugar; mix it well together with yolks of eggs till of a good stiffness.

**PASTE FOR A COMMON DUMPLING.** Rub into a pound of flour six ounces of butter, then work it into a paste with two well-beaten eggs and a little water. This paste may be baked, a large table-spoonful of pounded loaf-sugar being added to it.

**PASTE FOR FAMILY PIES.** Rub into one pound and a half of flour half a pound of butter, wet it with cold water sufficient to make it into a stiff paste; work it well, and roll it out two or three times.

**PASTE, POTATO.** Mash sixteen ounces of boiled potatoes, while they are warm, then rub them between the hands, together with twelve ounces of flour; when it is well mixed, and all looks like flour, add half a tea-spoonful of salt, and, with a little cold water, make it into a stiff paste; beat and roll it out three or four times, making it very thin the last time. Lay it over black currant jam, raspberries, or any sort of preserve, rub the edges with water, roll it up like a bolster pudding, and boil it in a buttered and floured cloth for three or four hours. Serve it with a sweet sauce.

**PASTE, PUFF.** Weigh an equal quantity of flour and butter, rub rather more than the half of the flour into one third of the butter, then add as much cold water as will make it into a stiff paste; work it until the butter be completely mixed with the four, make it round, beat it with the rolling-pin, dust it, as also the rolling-pin, with flour, and roll it out towards the opposite side of the slab, or paste-board, making it of an equal thickness; then with the point of a knife put little bits of butter all over it, dust flour over and under it, fold in the sides and roll it up, dust it again with flour, beat it a little, and roll it out, always rubbing the rolling-pin with flour, and throwing some underneath the paste, to prevent its sticking to the board. If the butter is not all easily put in at the second time of rolling out the paste, the remainder may be put in at the third; it should be touched as little as possible with the hands.

PASTE, PYRAMID. Make a rich puff paste, roll it out a quarter of an inch thick, and cut it into five or seven pieces with scalloped tin paste cutters, which go one within another; leave the bottom and top piece entire, and cut a bit out of the centre of the others; bake them of a light brown upon buttered paper placed upon tins. When served, build them into a pyramid, laying a different preserved fruit upon each piece of paste, and on the top a whole apricot, with a sprig of myrtle stuck into it, or green-gages, ornamented with a bunch of barberries.

PASTE FOR MEAT OR SAVORY PIES. Sift two pounds of fine flour to one and a half of good salt butter, break it into small pieces, and wash it well in cold water; rub gently together the butter and flour, and mix it up with the yolk of three eggs, beat together with a spoon; and nearly a pint of spring-water; roll it out, and double it in folds three times, and it is ready.

PASTE FOR RAISED PIES. Take four pounds of flour, one pound of butter, and a little salt, mix these together, adding water, a little at a time, taking care not to put too much, as this paste must be made as stiff as possible; when thoroughly mixed, give it two or three turns, roll it and cut it out to the shape you want for your pie. Sometimes the butter is melted in warm water, and so mixed with the flour; then it will not require so much water, and the paste will stand better; but as you work your paste, when you find it get too cold, warm it a little; the first method of doing it is the best, if intended to be eaten.

PASTE, RICE. (1) Mix together half a pound of sifted ground rice and a quarter of a pound of fresh butter, work it into a paste with cold water, dredge flour over the paste-board and rolling-pin, roll out the paste, and put over it, in little bits, another quarter of a pound of butter; fold and roll it out three times, strewing each time a little flour over and under it, as also over the rolling-pin. Cover the tart, and glaze it before being baked. This paste must be eaten the day it is baked.

PASTE, RICE. (2) Boil, in a pint of water, half a pound of good rice; drain off the water, and pound the rice in a mortar, with a small bit of butter, and an egg beaten; then roll it out to cover any fruit tart.

PASTE, RICH SHORT. Weigh equal quantities of flour, of butter, and of pounded and sifted loaf-sugar; rub the butter with the flour, then mix in the sugar, and rub it together till it will roll out; put it about half an inch thick over the tart, which may be of cherries, raspberries, or currants.

PASTE, SHORT, FOR TARTS. Take one pound of flour, lay it on the slab, and in the centre put half a pound of butter, two eggs, a very little salt, and a little water, mix them lightly together, and continue adding more water, till you find it bind; mix it on the slab a little, and give it two turns, it is then ready for use.

PASTE, SUET. Rub well with half a pound of fresh beef suet, chopped as finely as possible, three-quarters of a pound of flour, and half a tea-spoonful of salt; make it into a stiff paste with cold water, work it well, beat it with the rolling-pin, and roll it out two or three times. This paste answers for any kind of boiled fruit pudding.

PASTE, SWEET. Rub into half a pound of flour three ounces of butter and the same of pounded loaf-sugar, add one beaten egg, and as much warm water as will make it into a paste; roll it thin for any kind of fruit tart, rub it over with the beaten white of an egg, and sift sugar over it.

PASTE FOR STRINGING TARTLETS. Mix with your hands a quarter of a pound of flour, an ounce of fresh butter, and a little cold water; rub it well between the board and your hand till it begins to string; cut it into small pieces, roll it out, and draw it into fine strings, lay them across your tartlets in any device you please, and bake them immediately.

PATTIES FOR FRIED BREAD. Cut the crumb of a loaf of bread into square or round pieces nearly three inches high, and cut bits the same width for tops; mark them neatly with a knife; fry the bread of a light brown color in clarified beef-dripping or fine lard. Scoop out the inside crumb, take care not to go too near to the bottom; fill them with mince meat, prepared as for patties, with stewed oysters, or with sausage meat; put on the tops, and serve them upon a napkin.

PATTIES, LOBSTER. *See Lobsters.*

PEACHES, CHARLOTTE OF. Take twenty tolerably ripe peaches, cut them in halves, and scald them in a light sirup; then drain and cut each half into three pieces (lengthwise) of equal thickness; put these into a pan with a quarter of a pound of powder-sugar, and half the quantity of warm butter; fry them lightly, and having prepared your *Charlotte* in the usual way, pour in the peaches and finish it (see *Charlotte*). When in the dish for table, cover it completely with the sirup, and serve immediately.

PEARS BAKED. (1) Take twelve large baking pears; pare and cut them into halves, leaving the stem about half an inch long; take out the core with the point of a knife, and place them close together in a block-tin saucepan, the inside of which is quite bright, with the cover to fit quite close; put to them the rind of a lemon cut thin, with half its juice, a small stick of cinnamon, and twenty grains of allspice; cover them with spring-water, and allow one pound of loaf-sugar to a pint and a half of water: cover them up close, and bake them

for six hours in a very slow oven: they will be quite tender, and of a bright color. *Obs.*—Prepared cochineal is generally used for coloring the pears; but if the above is strictly attended to, it will be found to answer best.

PEARS BAKED. (2) Take half a dozen fine pears, peel, cut them in halves, and take out the cores; put them into a pan with a little red wine, a few cloves, half a pound of sugar, and some water. Set them in a moderate oven till tender, then put them on a slow fire to stew gently; add grated lemon-peel, and more sugar if necessary. They will be sufficiently red.

PEARS COMPOTE. Choose your fruit carefully, take off the tops, and trim the tails, wash and drain them well; then put them into a skillet with sugar, cinnamon, two or three cloves, a little red wine, and some water. Set them on a slow fire, taking care to skin them. When sufficiently done, they will look wrinkled. Peel your fruit, and put it into a well glazed pipkin, with a glass of wine, a little cinnamon, sugar to the taste, and a little water; put in also a pewter spoon; cover the pipkin close, and set it on hot ashes. When done, the pears will be of a fine red color.

PEARS TO COMPOUND. Take a dozen large pears, coddle them; when tender, take them out and lay them in cold water, pare and cut them in halves; take out the cores, put them in sirup made thus:— Two pounds and a half of sugar to three pints of water, a little lemon-peel pared very thin, boiled in them, and a little cochineal bruised and put into a muslin bag: cover them, boil them quick till they are tender and of a good color; when cold, squeeze in the juice of two or three lemons.

PEARS PRESERVED. Take care in making this preserve that the fruit be not too ripe; they are in a fit state as soon as the pips are black. Set the pears on the fire in a sufficient quantity of water to cover them; take them off when quite soft, and throw them into cold water; pare them lightly, cut off the stalks, prick each with a pin sufficiently long to reach the core, and put them again into cold water, with a handful of alum; set them on the fire to boil uutil the pears are tender, then take them out, and put them into cold water for the third time. Clarify and boil some sugar, put some water to it, and when it boils, add the pears, cover the pan, and give the whole a boil; skim and pour it into an earthen pan and leave it. The next day, drain the sirup from the pears, add a little more clarified sugar to it, and boil it again; pour it over the fruit, and leave it as before; the next and two successive days, proceed in the same way, each time increasing the degree of boiling, then add the pears, give the preserve a boil (covered), skim and pour it into a pan, and place it in a stove for two days, then drain the fruit, and put it by for use.

PEARS STEWED. (1) Wash and prick some large stewing pears, and set them on the fire in a large stewing-pan of water to scald; when scalded, take them out, and put them on the fire in a pan with a sufficient quantity of thin clarified sugar to cover them, a stick of cinnamon, a little mace, and two or three cloves; let them stew gently till they begin to soften and look rather red, then put in a bottle of Port wine, and let them continue stewing until perfectly done, and look very rich and red; then put them in a basin or jar, with the liquor over them; they will be all the better for keeping four or five days.

PEARS STEWED. (2) Pare, cut into quarters, and take out the core of six good baking pears; throw them as they are done into water. To a pound of fruit allow a quarter of a pound of brown sugar, and three cloves; put them into a saucepan, cover them with cold water, keep the pan closely covered, and stew them gently, till red and tender; add, just before serving, a glass of Port wine. They may be eaten hot or cold, with cream, after dinner or at supper.

PEAS, GREEN. Young green peas, well dressed, are among the most delicious delicacies of the vegetable kingdom. They must be young; it is equally indispensable that they be fresh gathered, and cooked as soon as they are shelled for they soon lose both their color and sweetness. After being shelled, wash them, drain them in a cullender, put them on in plenty of boiling water, with a tea-spoonful of salt, and one of pounded loaf sugar; boil them till they become tender, which, if young, will be in less than half an hour; if old, they will require more than an hour; drain them in a cullender, and put them immediately into a dish with a slice of fresh butter in it; some people think it an improvement to boil a small bunch of mint with the peas; it is then minced finely, and laid in small heaps at the end or sides of the dish. If peas are allowed to stand in the water after being boiled they lose their color.

PEAS FOR A SECOND COURSE. Put a quart of fine green peas, together with a bit of butter the size of a walnut, into as much warm water as will cover them, in which let them stand for eight or ten minutes. Strain off the water, put them into a saucepan, cover it, stir them frequently, and when a little tender, add a bunch of parsley, and a young onion, nearly a dessert-spoonful of loaf-sugar, and an ounce of butter mixed with a tea-spoonful of flour; keep stirring them now and then till the peas be tender, and add, if they become too thick, a table-spoonful of hot water. Before serving, take out the onion and parsley.

PEAS PUDDING. Take a pint of good split peas, and having washed, soak them well in warm water; then tie them in a cloth, put the pudding into a saucepan of hot water, and boil it until quite soft. When done, beat it up with a little butter and salt; serve it with boiled pork or beef.

PEAS POWDER. Pound together in a marble mortar half an ounce each of dried mint and sage, a drachm of celery-seed, and a quarter of a drachm of cayenne pepper; rub them through a fine sieve. This gives a very savory relish to peas soup, and to water gruel, which, by its help, if the eater of it has not the most lively imagination, he may fancy he is sipping good peas soup. *Obs.*— A drachm of allspice, or black pepper, may be pounded with the above as an addition, or instead of the cayenne.

PEPPER POT. Take as much spinach as will fill a good sized dish, put it in a saucepan without any water, set it on the fire, and let it boil; then drain off all the liquor, chop the spinach very fine, and return it to the saucepan, with the water just drained from it, more water, onions, three or four potatoes, a lettuce or head of endive cut small, the bones of any cold roast meat, if you have them, and half a pound of bacon; put the whole on the fire, and when it has boiled for about an hour, put in a few suet dumplings; leave it twenty or thirty minutes longer; season it well with cayenne, and serve.

PEPPER POT IN A TUREEN. Stew gently in four quarts of water, till reduced to three, three pounds of beef, half a pound of lean ham, a bunch of dried thyme, two onions, two large potatoes pared and sliced; then strain it through a cullender, and add a large fowl, cut into joints and skinned, half a pound of pickled pork sliced, the meat of one lobster minced, and some small suet dumplings, the size of a walnut. When the fowl is well boiled, add half a peck of spinach, that has been boiled and rubbed through a cullender; season with salt and cayenne. It is very good without the lean ham and fowl.

PERCH BOILED. Put them into cold water, and let them boil carefully; serve with melted butter and soy.

PERCH BROILED. Scrape, gut, and wash them; dry them in a cloth, dust them with flour, and broil them. Sauce;—melted butter. Or they may be broiled without gutting them. They may also be stewed as carp are done.

PERCH WITH WINE. Having scaled and taken out the gills, put the perch into a stewpan, with equal quantities of stock and white wine, a bay-leaf, a clove of garlic, a bunch of parsley and scallions, two cloves, and some salt. When done, take out the fish, strain off the liquor, the dregs of which mix with some butter and a little flour; beat these up, set them on the fire, stirring till quite done, adding pepper, grated nutmeg, and a ball of anchovy butter. Drain the perch well, and dish them with the above sauce.

PERLINGO. Take a pound and a half of sifted flour, and having placed it on your slab, make a hole in the middle of it, into which put three-quarters of a pound of brown sugar, half a pound of fresh butter, the rind of two lemons grated, and ten eggs; knead all these ingredients together well, until you have a pretty firm paste; if it should be too thin, add a handful more flour. Then cut the paste into small pieces, each of which roll in the palms of your hands, till they are the length and thickness of your finger; take a round stick (about half the diameter of your paste), press this down on each of the pieces, so that they may be their original thickness on one side, and thin on the other; when all are thus pressed, form them into little crowns (the flat side inwards, and the thin end uppermost), lay them on white paper, and bake them in a moderate oven; in the meanwhile, make some white sugar varnish or icing, and when the perlingos are sufficiently done, dip them carefully in the varnish, one by one; then replace them in the oven, a minute or two, to dry.

PERRY. Perry is a pleasant and wholesome liquor, made from the juice of pears, by means of fermentation, somewhat in the same manner as cider is made from apples.

PETTITOES. Boil the feet, the liver, and the heart, of a sucking pig, in a little water, very gently, then split the feet, and cut the meat very small, and simmer it with a little of the water till the feet are perfectly tender; thicken with a bit of butter, a little flour, a spoonful of cream, and a little pepper and salt; give it a boil up, pour it over a few sippets of bread, put the feet on the mince.

PICKLE FOR MEAT. Six pounds of salt, one pound of sugar, and four ounces of saltpetre, boiled with four gallons of water, skimmed, and allowed to cool, forms a very strong pickle, which will preserve any meat completely immersed in it. To effect this, which is essential, either a heavy board or a flat stone must be laid upon the meat. The same pickle may be used repeatedly, provided it be boiled up occasionally with additional salt to restore its strength, diminished by the combination of part of the salt with the meat, and by the dilution of the pickle by the juices of the meat extracted. By boiling, the albumen, which would cause the pickle to spoil, is coagulated, and rises in the form of scum, which must be carefully removed.

An H-bone, of ten or twelve pounds, weight will require about three-quarters of a pound of salt, and an ounce of moist sugar, to be well rubbed into it. It will be ready in four or five days, if turned and rubbed every day.

The time meat requires salting depends upon the weight of it, and how much salt is used: and if it be rubbed in with a heavy hand, it will be ready much sooner than if only lightly rubbed.

N. B. Dry the salt, and rub it with the sugar in a mortar.

PORK requires a longer time to cure (in proportion to its weight) than beef. A leg of pork should be in salt eight or ten days; turn it and rub it every day.

Salt meat should be well washed before it is boiled, especially if it has been in salt long, that the liquor in which the meat is boiled, may not be too salt to make soup of. If it has been in salt a long time, and you fear that it will be too salt, wash it well in cold water, and soak it in luke-warm water for a couple of hours. If it *very salt*, lay it in water the night before you intend to dress it.

PICKLE FOR TONGUES. To four gallons of water, add two pounds and a half of treacle, eight pounds of salt, two ounces of saltpetre; boil it, and skim it until clear, sprinkle salt over the tongue, and let it stand two days, wipe it clean before you put it into the pickle, which must be quite cold; boil the pickle every two or three months, adding two or three handfuls of salt, skimming it well. Half the quantity is sufficient for two tongues.

PICKLE FOR BEEF. Allow to four gallons of water two pounds of brown sugar and six pounds of salt, boil it about twenty minutes, taking off the scum as it rises; the following day pour it over the meat which has been packed into the pickling-tub. Boil it every two months, adding three ounces of brown sugar and half a pound of common salt. By this means it will keep good a year. The meat must be sprinkled with salt, and the next day wiped dry, before pouring the pickle over it, with which it should always be completely covered. With the addition of two ounces of saltpetre and one pound of salt, this pickle answers for pickled pork, hams, and tongues. The tongues should be rubbed with common salt, to cleanse them, and afterwards with a little saltpetre, and allowed to lie four or five days before they are put into the pickle. The meat will be ready for use in eight or ten days, and will keep for three months.

PICKLES. Pickles ought to be stored in a dry place and the vessels most approved of for keeping them in, are wide-mouthed glass bottles, or strong stone-ware jars, having corks or bungs, which must be fitted in with linen, and covered with bladder or leather; and for taking the pickles out and returning them to the jar, a small wooden spoon is kept. The strongest vinegar is used for pickling; that of cider more particularly recommeded, but sugar vinegar will generally be found sufficiently strong. It is essential to the excellence and beauty of pickles, that they be always completely covered with vinegar.

*See Hot Pickles, India Pickles, Onions, Cucumbers, &c. &c.*

PIE, ANGLO-FRANCAIS. Take a deep dish, line the edge with puff paste like a common pie: stew a quarter of a pound of rice with some sugar until quite soft and sweet; take a pound of ripe juicy cherries, which pick and roll in a quarter of a pound of powder-sugar, and lay about a quarter of them at the bottom of the dish; cover these with a fourth part of the rice, then the cherries again, and so on till your materials are used, taking care to keep the pie high in the middle; cover it with a layer of puff paste, which wash over lightly with some white of egg, and strew a little powder-sugar over; put it in a moderate oven for an hour and a quarter; then take it out, mask the crust with apricot marmalade, and a few macaroons crushed. Serve it either hot or cold.

PIE, APPLE. (1) Take eight russetings, or lemon pippin apples; pare, core, and cut not smaller than quarters; place them as close as possible together into a pie-dish, with four cloves; rub together in a mortar some lemon-peel, with four ounces of good moist sugar, and, if agreeable, add some quince jam; cover it with puff paste; bake it an hour and a quarter. (Generally eaten warm).

PIE, APPLE. (2) Pare, quarter, and core the apples; cut them into thin bits. Put into the bottom of a pie-dish a table-spoonful of brown sugar, with a teaspoonful of grated ginger and lemon-peel, then a layer of apples, and so on alternately, till the dish is piled as full as it will hold. The next day wet the rim of the dish, line it with puff or tart paste, brush it with water, and cover it with paste; press the edge all round, notch it with a paste-cutter, and make a small hole with the point of a knife in the middle. It may be seasoned with two tablespoonfuls of lemon or orange marmalade, pounded cinnamon, mace, and cloves, in addition to the ginger and lemon-peel.

PIE, APPLE WITH MUSCADEL RAISINS. Peel twenty renneting apples, cut them in quarters, and then cut each quarter irto five or six pieces; toss them in a pan with four ounces of sugar in powder, (over which should be grated the peel of a lemon), four ounces of butter lukewarm, and four ounces of fine muscadel plums. Line the edge of a deep dish with good puff paste, then put in your fruit, and cover your dish with a good puff paste a quarter of an inch in thickness, glaze with the white of an egg, and strew sugar over it. Let it bake an hour in a moderate oven, and serve it hot.

PIE, APRICOT. Line a dish with puff paste and then put in eighteen fine apricots, (cut in halves and the stones taken out,) with four ounces of sugar in powder, and four ounces of butter lukewarm. Then lay on the upper crust, glaze with the white of egg, and strew sifted sugar all over. Let it bake in a moderate oven to a nice light color. Serve it hot. When you wish to serve it cold, you must leave out the butter.

PIE, BEEF KIDNEY. Cut some kidneys into thin slices, and place them in the bottom of your pie-dish, then sweet herbs chopped, such as parsley, thyme, shallots, mushrooms, pepper, and salt; continue this till the dish is full, then cover the whole with slices of bacon, then finish your pie; bake it in the oven; when done, take out the bacon, and skim off the fat; make a sauce with a glass of while wine, a tolerable quantity of cullis, and reduce it to the consistence of a good sauce, then squeeze an orange in it. Serve your pie hot.

PIE, BEEF-STEAK. Cut the steaks off a rump, or any nice piece of beef, fat and lean together, about half an inch thick; beat them a little with a rolling-pin, put over them some pepper, salt, and parboiled onion minced; roll them up, and pack them neatly into the dish, or lay the beef in slices; add some spoonfuls of gravy, and a tea-spoonful of vinegar. Cover the pie with a puff paste, and bake it for an hour. It is a common but mistaken opinion, that it is necessary to put stock or water into meat pies. Beet, mutton, veal, and pork, if not previously dressed, will be found to yield a sufficiency of gravy, and the pie will be better without any additional liquid. N. B.—Large oysters, parboiled, bearded, and laid alternately with the steaks, their liquor reduced and substituted instead of the ketchup and wine, will be a variety.

PIE, CHICKEN. Parboil, and then cut up neatly two young chickens; dry them; set them over a slow fire for a few minutes; have ready some veal stuffing or forcemeat, lay it at the bottom of the dish, and place in the chickens upon it, and with it some pieces of dressed ham; cover it with paste. Bake it from an hour and a half to two hours; when sent to table, add some good gravy, well seasoned, and not too thick. Duck pie is made in like manner, only substituting the duck stuffing instead of the veal. N. B.—The above may be put into a raised French crust and baked; when done, take off the top, and put a ragout of sweetbread to the chicken.

PIE, COD. Lay a fine piece of fresh cod in salt for several hours, then wash it well, season it with pepper; salt, nutmeg and mace; place it in a dish, with a little butter and some good stock. Lay a crust over, and bake it; when done, pour in a sauce, made as follows:—a spoonful of stock, a quarter of a pint of cream, flour and butter, grate in a little nutmeg and lemon-peel, and a few oysters, boil the whole once.

PIE, COLD BEEF, VEAL, OR MUTTON. Pound in a mortar some boiled potatoes; boil a cupful of milk, and while hot, mix it with the potatoes, and beat them till they become like a light paste; roll it out, cut it with a flat dish, the size of a pie dish, so as it may be laid from off it upon the pie; cut the meat into slices, season it with pepper and salt, put half a pint of gravy, wet the edges of the dish, and put over it the paste, and bake it till the paste be sufficiently done.

PIE, DEVIZES. Cut into very thin slices, after being dressed, cold calf's head, with some of the brains, pickled tongue, sweetbreads, lamb, veal, a few slices of bacon, and hard-boiled eggs; put them in layers into a pie-dish, with plenty of seasoning between each, of cayenne, white pepper, allspice, and salt; fill up the dish with rich gravy; cover it with a flour and water paste; bake it in a slow oven, and when perfectly cold, take off the crust, and turn the pie out upon a dish; garnish it with parsley and pickled eggs cut into slices.

PIE, DUCK. Scald a couple of ducks, and make them very clean; cut off the feet, pinions, necks, and heads. Take out the gizzards, livers, and hearts; pick all clean, and scald them. Pick out the fat of the inside, lay a good puff-paste crust all over the dish, season the ducks both inside and out, with pepper and salt, and lay them in the dish, with the giblets at each end, properly seasoned. Put in as much water as will nearly fill the pie, lay on the crust, and let it be well baked.

PIES, EGG MINCE. Boil six eggs until they are hard, shred them small; shred double the quantity of suet; then add one pound of currants picked and washed, (if the eggs were large you must use more currants) the peel of one lemon shred very fine, and the juice, six spoonfuls of sweet wine, mace, nutmeg, sugar, a very small quantity of salt, orange, lemon, and citron candies. Make a light paste for them.

PIE, FRENCH. Mince some cold roast veal together with a little ham, season it highly with pepper, salt, mace, and lemon peel; add a large table-spoonful of mushroom ketchup, and a quarter of a hundred of oysters, with their liquor, and three or four table-spoonfuls of rich gravy. Line a dish with puff paste, put in the ingredients, cover the pie, and let it remain in the oven long enough to bake the paste.

PIE, GIBLET. Stew the giblets in a little water, with an onion stuck with two or three cloves, a bunch of sweet herbs, some salt, and whole pepper; cut a fowl into joints, skin and wash it, season it with pepper, salt, and half an onion finely minced. Take out the onion, herbs, and whole pepper; put the fowl, giblets, and gravy into a dish, add a glass of white wine, and two table-spoonfuls of mushroom ketchup; cover the dish with puff paste, and bake it for an hour.

PIE, GOOSE. Prepare a very strong raised crust, and make the sides thick and stiff. Take the bones out of a goose, turkey, and fowl, cutting each down the back; season them highly with pepper, salt, mace, cloves, and nutmeg, all finely pounded and well mixed. Lay the goose upon a dish, with the breast skin next the dish; lay in the turkey, put some slices of boiled ham and tongue, and then the fowl; cover it with little bits of ham or bacon. Put it all into the pie, made of an oval form, and the sides to stand an inch and a half above the meat; put on the top, and make a hole in the centre of it. Brush the outside of the pie all over with the beaten whites of eggs, and bind it round with three folds of buttered paper; paste the top over in the same way, and when it comes out of the oven, take off the paper, and pour in at the top, through a funnel, a pound and a half of melted butter.

PIES, LOBSTER. *See Lobster.*

PIE, ITALIAN. Mix together some chopped thyme, parsley, and one or two sage leaves, some salt, white and cayenne pepper; lay into the bottom of a dish some thin slices of lean veal, sprinkle them with the seasoning, and add slices of ham, and a few forcemeat balls; put a layer of seasoned veal, and of ham and forcemeat balls, till the dish is full, and then add the yolks of five hard-boiled eggs, and some good white stock; cover the dish with a puff paste, and bake it for an hour. Before serving, pour in, through a funnel at the centre of the crust, a tea-cupful of rich cream.

PIES, MAIGRE FISH. Salt-fish pie. The thickest part must be chosen, and put in cold water to soak the night before wanted; then boil it well, take it up, take away the bones and skin, and if it is good fish it will be in fine layers; set it on a fish-drainer to get cold: in the meantime, boil four eggs hard, peel and slice them very thin, the same quantity of onion sliced thin; line the bottom of a pie-dish with fish forcemeat, or a layer of potatoes sliced thin, then a layer of onions, then of fish, and of eggs, and so on till the dish is full; season each layer with a little pepper, then mix a tea-spoonful of made mustard, the same of essence of anchovy, a little mushroom ketchup, in a gill of water, put it in the dish, then put on the top an ounce of fresh butter broke in bits; cover it with puff paste, and bake it one hour. Fresh cod may be done in the same way, by adding a little salt. All fish for making pies, whether soles, flounders, herrings, salmon, lobster, eels, trout, tench, &c. should be dressed first; this is the most economical way for Catholic families.

PIES, MINCE. (1) Carefully stone and

cut, but not too small, one pound and a half of bloom raisins; cut small half a pound of orange-peel, mince finely half a dozen of middling-sized good apples, a quarter of a pound of sweet almonds, pounded to a paste with a little white wine, half a nutmeg grated, a quarter of an ounce of pepper, one head of clove, and a little cinnamon pounded; one pound and half of fresh beef suet, finely minced, one pound of good brown sugar; mix all these ingredients extremely well, and add half a pint of white wine, and one glass of brandy. Pack it closely into small stone jars, and tie them over with paper. When it is to be used, add a little more wine.

PIES, MINCE. (2) Cut the root off a neat's tongue, rub the tongue well with salt, let it lie four days, wash it perfectly clean, and boil it till it becomes tender; skin, and when cold, chop it very finely. Mince as small as possible two pounds of fresh beef suet from the sirloin, stone and cut small two pounds of bloom raisins, clean nicely two pounds of currants, pound and sift half an ounce of mace and a quarter of an ounce of cloves, grate a large nutmeg; mix all these ingredients thoroughly, together with one pound and a half of good brown sugar. Pack it in jars. When it is to be used, allow, for the quantity sufficient to make twelve small mince pies, five finely-minced apples, the grated rind and juice of a large lemon, and a wine-glass and a half of brandy; put into each a few bits of citron and preserved orange-peel. Three or four whole green lemons, preserved in good brown sugar, and cut into thin slices, may be added to the mince meat.

PIES, BRANDY, MINCE. Clean a pound of currants, mince a pound of nonpareil apples, and one of fresh beef suet; pound a pound of loaf sugar; weigh each article after being prepared; the peel of two lemons grated, and the juice of one; a quarter of a pound of citron, the same of orange-peel minced. Mix all these ingredients well with a quart of brandy.

PIES, LEMON MINCE. Weigh one pound of fine large lemons, cut them in half, squeeze out the juice, and pick the pulp from the skins; boil them in water till tender, and pound them in a mortar; add half a pound of pounded loaf sugar, the same of nicely cleaned currants, and of fresh beef suet minced, a little grated nutmeg, and citron cut small. Mix all these ingredients well, and fill the patty-pans with rather more of the mince than is usually put.

PIE, MUTTON OR VEAL. Cut into chops, and trim neatly, and cut away, the greatest part of the fat of a loin, or best end of a neck of mutton (the former the best), season them, and lay them in a pie-dish, with a little water and half a gill of mushroom ketchup (chopped onion and potatoes, if approved); cover it with paste, bake it two hours; when done, lift up the crust from the dish with a knife, pour out all the gravy, let it stand, and skim it clean; add, if wanted, some more seasoning; make it boil, and pour it into the pie. Veal pie may be made of the brisket part of the breast; but must be parboiled first.

PIE, PIGEON OR LARK. Truss half a dozen fine large pigeons as for stewing, season them with pepper and salt; lay at the bottom of the dish a rump-steak of about a pound weight, cut into pieces and trimmed neatly, seasoned, and beat out with a chopper: on it lay the pigeons, the yolks of three eggs boiled hard, and a gill of broth or water, and over these a layer of steaks; wet the edge of the dish, and cover it over with puff paste, or the paste as directed for seasoned pies; wash it over with yolk of egg, and ornament it with leaves of paste and the feet of the pigeons; bake it an hour and a half in a moderate-heated oven: before it is sent to table make an aperture in the top, and pour in some good gravy quite hot.

PIE, RAISED PORK. Make a raised

185

crust, of a good size, about four inches high; take the rind and chine bone from a loin of pork, cut it into chops, beat them with a chopper, season them with pepper and salt, and fill your pie; put on the top and close it, and pinch it round the edge; rub it over with yolk of egg, and bake it two hours with a paper over it, to prevent the crust from burning. When done, pour in some good gravy, with a little ready-mixed mustard (if approved). N. B.—As the above is generally eaten cold, it is an excellent repast for a journey, and will keep for several days.

PIE, POTATO. Peel and slice your potatoes very thin into a pie-dish; between each layer of potatoes put a little chopped onion (three-quarters of an ounce of onion is sufficient for a pound of potatoes); between each layer sprinkle a little pepper and salt; put in a little water, and cut about two ounces of fresh butter into little bits, and lay them on the top: cover it close with puff paste. It will take about an hour and a half to bake it. N. B. The yolks of four eggs (boiled hard) may be added; and when baked, a table-spoonful of good mushroom ketchup poured in through a funnel. *Obs.*—Cauliflowers divided into mouthfuls, and button onions, seasoned with curry-powder, &c. make a favorite vegetable pie.

PIES, RAISED, MUTTON OR PORK. Put two pounds and a half of flour on the paste-board; and put on the fire, in a saucepan, three-quarters of a pint of water, and half a pound of good lard; when the water boils, make a hole in the middle of the flour, pour in the water and lard by degrees, gently mixing the flour with it with a spoon; and when it is well mixed, then knead it with your hands till it becomes stiff: dredge a little flour to prevent its sticking to the board, or you cannot make it look smooth: do not roll it with the rolling-pin, but roll it with your hands, about the thickness of a quart pot; cut it into six pieces, leaving a little for the covers; put one hand in the middle, and keep the other close on the out-

side till you have worked it either in an oval or a round shape: have your meat ready cut, and seasoned with pepper and salt: if pork, cut in small slices; the griskin is the best for pasties: if you use mutton, cut it in very neat cutlets, and put them in the pies as you make them; roll out the covers with the rolling-pin just the size of the pie, wet it round the edge, put it on the pie, and press it together with your thumb and finger, and then cut it all round with a pair of scissors quite even, and pinch them inside and out, and bake them an hour and a half.

PIE, RAISED FRENCH. Make about two pounds of flour into a paste; knead it well, and into the shape of a ball; press your thumb into the centre, and work it by degrees into any shape (oval or round is the most general), till about five inches high; put it on a sheet of paper, and fill it with coarse flour or bran; roll out a covering for it about the same thickness as the sides; cement its sides with the yolk of egg; cut the edges quite even, and pinch it round with the finger and thumb, rub yolk of egg over it with a paste-brush, and ornament it in any way fancy may direct, with the same kind of paste. Bake it of a fine brown color, in a slow oven; and when done, cut out the top, remove the flour or bran, brush it quite clean, and fill it up with a fricassee of chicken, rabbit, or any other *entree* most convenient. Send it to table with a napkin under.

PIE, HAM RAISED. Soak a small ham four or five hours; wash and scrape it well; cut off the knuckle, and boil it for half an hour; then take it up and trim it very neatly; take off the rind and put it into an oval stewpan, with a pint of Madeira or Sherry, and enough veal stock to cover it. Let it stew for two hours, or till three parts done; take it out and set it in a cold place; then raise a crust as in the foregoing receipt, large enough to receive it; put in the ham, and round it the veal forcemeat; cover and ornament; it will take about an hour and a half to bake in a slow oven: when done, take off the cover, glaze the top, and pour round the following sauce, viz. take the liquor the ham was stewed in; skim it free from fat; thicken with a little flour and butter mixed together; a few drops of browning, and some cayenne pepper.

PIE, SEA. Skin and cut into joints a large fowl; wash and lay it into cold water for an hour; cut some salt beef into thin slices, and if it is very salt, soak it a short time in water; make a paste of flour and butter in the proportion of half a pound of butter to one of flour, cut it into round pieces according to the size of the bottom of the pot in which the pie is to be stewed; rub with butter the bottom of a round iron pot, and lay in a layer of the beef, seasoned with pepper, and finely-minced onion; then put a layer of the paste, and then the fowl, highly seasoned with pepper, onion, and a little salt; add another layer of paste, and pour in three pints of cold water; cover the pot closely, and let it stew gently for nearly four hours, taking care it does not burn, which, if neglected, it is apt to do. It is served in a pudding dish, and answers well for a family dinner.

PIE, SQUAB, OR DEVONSHIRE. Take a few good baking-apples, pare, core, and slice them; chop some onions very small; line a deep dish with paste, put in a layer of the apples, strew a little sugar, and some of the chopped onions over them; season them, and lay lean mutton chops, also seasoned, more onions, then the apples, &c. as before, and so on till the dish is quite full; cover, and bake the pie.

PIE, SQUASH. One pint of squash, stewed and strained; one pint of milk, and one of cream; ten eggs; half teacup of rose-water; quarter pound of sugar, and one grated nutmeg. Bake in plates lined with puff paste.

PIE, SWEETBREAD. Parboil five or six sweetbreads; cut them into two or three pieces, stew them ten or fifteen minutes in a little white stock, with some chopped shallot, a bit of butter rolled in flour, some salt, and white pepper, and a good many mushrooms. Put them into a pie-dish, with some asparagus tops, forcemeat balls, and hard-boiled yolks of eggs, and slices of fat bacon on the top; cover it, and bake it till the paste be done enough; or it may be put into a vol-au-vent, and served upon a napkin; or baked in a plate.

PIE, VEGETABLE. Of a variety of vegetables, such as carrots, turnips, potatoes, artichoke bottoms, cauliflower, French beans, peas, and small button onions, equal quantities of each; half boil them in good broth for a short time, put them into a pie dish, cover it with puff paste, and bake it in a slow oven; make a gravy of a bit of veal, a slice of ham, pepper, salt, a bay leaf, mushrooms, shallots, parsley, and an onion; when it has boiled thick, strain the liquor, and mix in three or four table-spoonfuls of cream, and pour it into the pie before being served. The cream may be omitted.

PIG, Is in prime order for the spit when about three weeks old.

It loses part of its goodness every hour after it is killed; if not quite fresh, no art can make the crackling crisp.

To be in perfection, it should be killed in the morning to be eaten at dinner: it requires very careful roasting. A sucking-pig, like a young child, must not be left for an instant.

The ends must have much more fire than the middle: for this purpose is contrived an iron to hang before the middle part, called a pig-iron. If you have not this, use a common flat iron, or keep the fire fiercest at the two ends.

For the stuffing, take of the crumb of a stale loaf about five ounces; rub it through a colander; mince fine a handful of sage (i. e. about two ounces), and a large onion (about an ounce and a half). Mix these together with an egg, some pepper and salt, and a bit of butter as big as an egg. Fill the belly of the pig with this, and sew it up: lay it to the fire, and baste it with salad oil till it is quite done. Do not leave it a moment: it requires the most vigilant attendance.

Roast it at a clear, brisk fire at some distance. To gain the praise of epicurean pig-eaters, the crackling must be nicely crisped and delicately lightly browned, without being either blistered or burnt.

A small, three weeks old pig will be done enough in about an hour and a half.

Before you take it from the fire, cut off the head, and part that and the body down the middle: chop the brains very fine, with some boiled sage leaves, and mix them with good veal gravy, or beef gravy, or what runs from the pig when you cut its head off. Send up a tureenful of gravy besides. Currant sauce is still a favorite with some of the old school.

Lay your pig back to back in the dish with one half of the head on each side, and the ears one at each end, which you must take care to make nice and crisp; or you will get scolded, and deservedly, as the silly fellow was who bought his wife a pig with only one ear.

When you cut off the pettitoes, leave the skin long round the ends of the legs. When you first lay the pig before the fire, rub it all over with fresh butter or salad oil: ten minutes after, and the skin looks dry; dredge it well with flour all over, let it remain on an hour, then rub it off with a soft cloth.

N. B. A pig is a very troublesome subject to roast; most persons have them baked. Send a quarter of a pound of butter, and beg the baker to baste it well.

PIG, BAKED. Lay your pig in a dish, flour it well all over, then rub it over with butter; butter the dish you lay it in, and put it into the oven. When done enough, take it out, and rub it over with a butter cloth; then put it again into the oven till it is dry, then take it out and lay it in a dish; cut it up, take a little veal gravy, and take off the fat in the dish it was baked in, and there will be some good gravy at the bottom; put that to the veal gravy, with a little bit of butter, rolled in flour; boil it up, and put it in a dish in which the pig has been laid, and put the brains with some sage into the belly. Some persons like a pig to be brought to table whole, in which case you are only to put what sauce you like into the dish.

PIG, BARBICUED. Scald, &c., a pig, of about nine or ten weeks old, the same as for roasting; make a stuffing with a few sage-leaves, the liver of the pig, and two anchovies boned, washed, and cut extremely small; put them into a mortar, with some bread-crumbs, a quarter of a pound of butter, a very little cayenne pepper, and half a pint of Madeira wine; beat them to a paste, and sew it up in the pig; lay it at a good distance before a large brisk fire; singe it well; put two bottles of Madeira wine into the dripping-pan, and keep basting it all the time it is roasting; when half done, put two French rolls into the dripping-pan; and if there is not wine enough in the dripping-pan, add more: when the pig is nearly done, take the rolls and sauce, and put them into a saucepan, with an anchovy cut small, a bunch of sweet herbs, and the juice of a lemon; take up the pig, send it to table with an apple in its mouth, and a roll on each side; then strain the sauce over it.

Some barbicue a pig of six or seven weeks old, and stick it all over with blanched almonds, and baste it in the same manner with Madeira wine.

PIG, TO COLLAR. Cut off the feet, head, and tail; bone and wash it well, and dry it in a cloth. Season it highly with a quantity of pepper and salt; roll it up firmly, and bind it with a piece of linen; sew it tightly. Put it on in boiling water, with the bones, let it boil for an hour, then put it under a weight to press till it be cold, and take off the cloth.

PIG'S CHEEK, TO COLLAR. Strew

over a pig's face, and a neat's or pig's tongue, a little salt and saltpetre; let it stand eight or nine days, then boil them with two cow-heels, till all be sufficiently tender to admit of the bones being taken out; lay upon a dish a piece of strong cloth, put the cheek upon it with the rind downwards; season it highly with pepper, cloves, and a little salt; add the tongue and cow-heels, with more seasoning; roll and sew it up firmly, put it into a jar and boil it for two hours, then press it with a heavy weight, and when cold take off the cloth. The cow-heel may be omitted, and both cheeks used.

PIG'S CHEEK, TO CURE. Strew salt over it, and let it lie two or three days, then pour over it the following mixture when it is cold; half a pound of bay salt, half an ounce of saltpetre, a quarter of a pound of coarse brown sugar, one handful of common salt, and a penny-worth of cochineal, boiled in a pint of strong beer or porter; let it lie in the pickle a fortnight, turning it daily, then hang it to smoke for a week. When to be dressed, put it into lukewarm water to soak for a night, and in dressing it, follow the directions given for boiling hams.

PIG'S FEET AND EARS PICKLED. Wash the feet and ears very clean, and between every foot put a bay-leaf; when they are well soaked, add some cloves, mace, coriander-seed, and ginger; put a bottle of white wine to three pair of feet and ears, some bay-leaves, a bunch of sweet herbs; let them boil gently till they are tender, then take them out of the liquor, lay them in an earthen pan; when cold, take off the fat, and strain the liquor over them. They eat well cold, or warmed in the jelly, thickened with butter rolled in flour; or take the feet and ears out of the jelly, dip them in yolk of egg, and then in crumbs of bread, and broil them, or fry them in butter; lay the ears in the middle, and the feet round: or ragout them.

PIG'S FEET AND EARS SOUSED.

Clean them, and boil them till they are tender; then split the feet, and put them and the ears in salt and water. When you use them, dry them well in a cloth, dip them in batter, fry them, and send them to table with melted butter in a boat. They may be eaten cold, and will keep a considerable time.

PIG'S FEET, TO STEW. Clean them well, and boil them till they are tender. Brown some butter with flour, and add it to a quantity of gravy or water sufficient to stew the feet in. Season with a minced onion, three sage leaves, salt, and black pepper. Cut the feet in two, add them, and cover the pan closely; let them stew half an hour. A little before serving, mix in half a tablespoonful of lemon pickle or vinegar, and pick out the sage leaves.

PIG'S HARSLET. (1) Parboil the liver and lights, slice and fry them along with thin bits of bacon. Garnish with fried parsley.

PIG'S HARSLET. (2) Wash and dry some livers, sweetbreads, and some fat and lean pieces of pork, beating the latter with a rolling-pin to make them tender; season with pepper, salt, and sage, and a little onion shedded fine; when mixed, put all into a cawl and fasten it tight with a needle and thread, and roast it by a jack, or by a string. Or, serve in slices, with parsley, for a fry. Serve with a sauce of Port wine and water, and mustard, just boiled up, and put it into a dish.

PIG'S HEAD COLLARED. Very nicely scour the head and ears; take off the hair and snout, and take out the eyes and brain; let it lay for one night in water; then drain it; salt it extremely well, with common salt and saltpetre, and let it lie for five days. Boil it sufficiently to take out the bones; then lay it on a dresser, turning the thick end of one side of the head towards the thick end of the other, to make the roll of an equal size; sprinkle it well with salt and white pepper, and roll it with the ears; and, if you think proper, put the pig's feet round the outside, when boned, or the thin parts of a couple of cow-heels. Put it into a cloth, bind with a broad tape, and boil it till quite tender; then put it under a weight, and do not take off the covering until it is quite cold. If you wish it to be more like brawn, salt it longer; and let the proportion of saltpetre be greater, and put in also some pieces of lean pork, and then cover it with cow-heel, to look like the horn. This may be kept either in or out of pickle of salt and water, boiled with vinegar. If likely to spoil, slice and fry it, either with or without batter.

PIG'S HEAD, TO POT. Split the head of a small pig, take out the brains, cut off the ears, and let it lie in cold water for one day, then boil it till all the bones come out, take off the skin, keeping it as whole as possible. Chop the tongue and all the meat while it is hot; season it highly with pepper, salt, and nutmeg; place part of the skin at the bottom of a potting-pan or bowl, lay in the chopped meat, and put the rest of the skin over the top; press it down hard, place a small plate upon it, put on that a heavy weight, which must not be taken off till it be perfectly cold. Boil up part of the liquor with some vinegar and salt, and keep the head in this pickle. It may be served for breakfast or luncheon, and is eaten with vinegar and mustard.

PIG'S HEAD AND FEET, SOUSED. Clean them extremely well and boil them; take for sauce part of the liquor, and add vinegar, lime or lemon juice, salt, cayenne, and pepper, put in, either cut down or whole, the head and feet; boil all together for an hour, and pour it into a deep dish. It is eaten cold with mustard and vinegar.

PIG'S KIDNEYS, AND SKIRTS. Clean and wash them very nicely, cut the kidneys across, and the skirts into small square bits; fry them a light brown in beef dripping, brown a bit of butter the size of a walnut, with a little flour, and add as much

boiling water as may be required of gravy, and an onion minced small. Add the meat, a little pepper, salt, and mushroom ketchup, and let it stew till tender.

PIGEONS. Pigeons should be extremely fresh; when so, and in good order, they are plump and fat at the vent, and their feet pliable; but when they are stale, the vent is open, green, and withered. Tame pigeons are considered preferable to the wild.

PIGEONS WHOLE, TO BROIL. Clean them well, cut off the wings and neck, leaving skin enough at the neck to tie; make a forcemeat with bread crumbs, three or four of the livers, one anchovy, some parsley minced, and a quarter of a pound of butter; season with salt, pepper, and grated nutmeg, bind it with the yolk of an egg beaten up, and put into each pigeon a piece the size of a large walnut; tie the neck and rump, rub them with butter, and dust them with pepper, salt, and nutmeg mixed; broil them over a slow fire; to baste them, put them upon a plate, and with a feather brush them over with butter; broil them of a nice brown color; serve them with melted butter and parsley, or a thickened brown gravy.

PIGEON PIE. Chop some parsley and lemon thyme, with a few mushrooms; stew these in a little butter, into which put half a dozen young pigeons, with pepper and salt in their insides, and their legs turned in; stew them for a few minutes and turn them; when they begin to fry, put in sufficient *consomme* to cover them, in which let them stew till they are well done; take them from the fire to cool; in the meantime make a good puff paste, part of which roll out, and place round the edge of a dish; lay the pigeons in with the yolks of four eggs, boiled hard; and pour over them half of the liquor they were stewed in; add a little pepper and salt, then lay on the top paste, trimming it neatly round, the same as you would any other pie; on the top form a star of leaves, with a hole in the centre; egg it lightly over, and put it to bake in a moderate oven, taking care that it has not too much color; when done, add to the liquor that remained from the pigeons, a little butter sauce, make it very hot, and pour it on the pie. Serve it hot, either for a remove or side dish.

PIGEONS WITH RICE AND PARMESAN CHEESE. Pick and wash clean half a dozen nice pigeons, cut them into quarters; brown some butter with flour, add to it a pint of good stock, with three grated onions, some pepper and salt, stew the pigeons in this till tender, take them out and mix in the juice of one lemon, boil and strain the sauce over the pigeons. Boil about three-quarters of a pound of whole rice in a pint and a half of stock, with half a pound of fresh butter, some grated nutmeg and salt; when it is tender, add two handfuls of grated Parmesan cheese. Put more than half of the rice equally round the dish in which the pigeons are placed, and cover them with what remains, brush it over with a well-beaten egg, and then strew it thickly with more Parmesan; cover a flat baking-tin with salt, place the dish upon this, and bake it for nearly three-quarters of an hour in a slow oven; it should be of a fine gold color.

PIGEONS, TO ROAST. Pick, clean, singe, and wash them well; truss them with three feet on, and put into them some pepper and salt. While roasting, baste them with butter. A little before serving, dust them with flour, and froth them with butter. Roast them for half an hour. Serve them with parsley and butter in the dish, or make a gravy of the giblets, some minced parsley, seasoned with pepper and salt. Thicken with a little flour and butter; pour it with the giblets into the dish, and then put in the pigeons.

PIGEONS, STEW. (1) Clean them nicely, truss them as for boiling, put into their inside some pepper and salt; brown in a sauce-pan three ounces of butter with a table-spoonful of flour, add as much

gravy or water as will nearly cover the pigeons, put them in with the livers, gizzards, and pinions, salt, and some minced parsley, spinach may also be added; let them stew for three-quarters of an hour; add, a few minutes before serving, the yolks of four or six hard-boiled eggs.

PIGEONS, STEW. (2) Wash and clean six pigeons, cut them into quarters, and put all their giblets with them into a stewpan, a piece of butter, a little water, a bit of lemon-peel, two blades of mace, some chopped parsley, salt, and pepper; cover the pan closely, and stew them till they be tender; thicken the sauce with the yolk of an egg beaten up with three table-spoonfuls of cream and a bit of butter dusted with flour; let them stew ten minutes longer before serving.

PIKE, BAKED. Scrape the scales off a large pike, take out the gills, and clean it, without breaking the skin; stuff the fish with a forcemeat made of two handfuls of grated bread, one of finely-minced suet, some chopped parsley, and a little fresh butter, seasoned with pepper, salt, mace, grated lemon-peel and a nutmeg, pounded all together in a mortar, with two whole eggs. Fasten the tail of the pike into its mouth with a skewer, then dip it, first into a well-beaten egg, and then into grated bread, which repeat twice; baste it over with butter, and bake it in an oven.

If two of them are to be served, make one of them of a green color, by mixing a quantity of finely-minced parsley with the grated bread. When the fish is of a fine brown color, cover it with paper until it is done. Serve with a Dutch sauce in a sauce-tureen.

PIKE, BOILED. Wash clean, and take out the gills; stuff them with the following forcemeat: equal parts of chopped oysters, grated bread crumbs, beef suet, or butter, two anchovies, a little onion, pepper, salt, nutmeg, minced parsley, sweet marjoram, thyme and savory; an egg to bind it. Stuff the insides, and sew them up; put them on in boiling salt-and-water, with a glass of vinegar, and let them boil half an hour. Sauces; —oyster, and melted butter. They may also be broiled.

PILLAU, TO MAKE. Wash very clean two pounds of rice, stew it till perfectly tender with a little water, half a pound of butter, some salt, whole pepper, cloves and mace, and keep the stewpan closely covered; boil two fowls and one pound and a half of bacon, put the bacon in the middle, and the fowls on each side, cover them all over with the rice, and garnish with hard-boiled eggs and fried whole onions.

PLOVERS, TO CHOOSE. Choose them by the hardness of the vent, which shows that they are fat; and when new, they are limber-footed. In other respects, choose them by the same marks as other fowls. There are three sorts; the gray, green, and bastard plover or lapwing.

PLOVERS, TO DRESS. Green plovers should be dressed the same as woodcocks, without drawing, and served on a toast. Gray plovers should be stewed.—Make a forcemeat with the yolks of two hard eggs bruised, some marrow cut fine, artichoke bottoms cut small, and sweet herbs, seasoned with pepper, salt, and nutmeg: stuff the birds, and put them into a saucepan, with just a sufficient quantity of good gravy to cover them, one glass of white wine, and a blade of mace; cover them close, and let them stew very gently till they are tender; then take up the plovers, lay them in a dish, keep them hot; put a piece of butter rolled in flour, to thicken the sauce, let it boil till smooth; squeeze into it a little lemon; skim it, and pour it over the plovers.

POINT DE JOUR FRITTERS. Mix with two handfuls of flour a glass of sweet wine, a table-spoonful of brandy, and warm milk, sufficient to make it into a paste; add the well-beaten whites of four eggs, a little minced citron, candied orange-peel or currants; beat it well together, and drop it through a wide tin funnel, into boiling lard. Serve with pounded loaf sugar strewed over them.

POIVRADE. Put into a stewpan a large bunch of parsley-leaves, some scallions, two bay-leaves, a little thyme, a dessert-spoonful of fine white pepper, a glass of vinegar, and a small quantity of butter; set the pan on the fire, and reduce the whole till nearly all gone, when add two ladlefuls of *espagnole*, and one of stock; reduce these again to the proper consistence, and strain it for use.

PORK. DAIRY-FED pork is the best; the flesh should look white and smooth, and the fat be white and fine. In preparing a hog for bacon, the ribs are cut, with a very little flesh on them, from the side, which has the fore and hind leg attached to it; the hind leg is then called a gammon of bacon, but it is generally reserved for a ham. On each side there is a large spare rib, which is usually divided into two, one called the sweet bone, the other the blade bone. There are also griskins, chine, or back bone.

Hog's lard is the inner fat of the bacon hog.

Porkers are not so old as hogs; they make excellent pickled pork, but are chosen more particularly for roasting.

To roast a leg, a small onion is minced together with three sage leaves, seasoned with pepper and salt, and put under the skin at the knuckle bone; the skin is cut into strips nearly half an inch apart, and rubbed over with a bit of butter. If weighing seven or eight pounds, it will require nearly three hours to roast.

A spare rib should be roasted, is basted with butter, and has sage leaves dried, rubbed to a powder, and mixed with salt and pepper, sprinkled over it.

Both a loin and neck are jointed, the skin scored in narrow strips, and rubbed with butter. If weighing six or seven pounds, it will require rather more than two hours to roast.

A griskin may be either broiled or roasted.

A chine is stuffed here and there with bread crumbs, mixed with a little butter, and seasoned with some finely shred sage, parsley, and thyme, some pepper and salt. The skin is cut into strips and rubbed with butter; it is then roasted, and served with apple sauce, as are also the preceding roasts.

A porker's head is stuffed like a sucking pig, sewed firmly, and hung on a string to roast.

The shoulder may be roasted, but, being very fat, it is generally preferred pickled.

The breast may be made into a pie, or broiled.

To boil hams, they should be put on in water, the chill taken off, and simmered for four or five hours, taking care not to allow them to boil.

The prime season for pork is from November to March.

Take particular care it be done enough: other meats under-done are unpleasant, but pork is absolutely uneatable; the sight of it is enough to appal the sharpest appetite, if its gravy has the least tint of redness.

Be careful of the crackling; if this be not crisp, or if it be burned, you will be scolded. Pickled Pork, takes more time than any other meat. If you buy your pork ready salted, ask how many days it has been in salt; if many, it will require to be soaked in water for six hours before you dress it. When you cook it, wash and scrape it as clean as possible; when delicately dressed, it is a favorite dish with almost everybody. Take care it does not boil fast; if it does, the knuckle will break to pieces, before the thick part of the meat is warm through; a leg of seven pounds takes three hours and a half very slow simmering. Skim your pot very carefully, and when you take the meat out of the boiler, scrape it clean.

A leg of nice pork, nicely salted, and nicely boiled, is as fine a cold relish as cold ham; especially if, instead of cutting into the middle when hot, and so letting out its juices, you cut it at the knuckle: slices broiled are a good luncheon, or supper.

*Mem.*—Some persons who sell pork ready salted have a silly trick of cutting the knuckle in two; we suppose that this is done to save their salt; but it lets all the gravy out of the leg; and unless you boil your pork merely for the sake of the pot-liquor, which in this case receives all the goodness and strength of the meat, friendly reader, your oracle cautions you to buy no leg of pork which is slit at the knuckle.

If pork is not done enough, nothing is more disagreeable; if too much, it not only loses its color and flavor, but its substance becomes soft like a jelly.

It must never appear at table without parsnips; they are an excellent vegetable, and deserve to be much more popular; or carrots, turnips, and greens, or mashed potatoes, &c.

*Obs.*—Remember not to forget the mustard-pot.


PORK, LEG, Of eight pounds, will require about three hours: score the skins across in narrow stripes (some score it in diamonds), about a quarter of an inch apart; stuff the knuckle with sage and onion, minced fine, and a little grated bread, seasoned with pepper, salt, and the yolk of an egg.

Do not put it too near the fire: rub a little sweet oil on the skin with a paste-brush, or a goose-feather: this makes the crackling crisper and browner than basting it with dripping; and it will be a better color than all the art of cookery can make it in any other way; and this is the best way of preventing the skin from blistering, which is principally occasioned by its being put too near the fire.


PORK Spare Rib, Usually weighs about

eight or nine pounds, and will take from two to three hours to roast it thoroughly; not exactly according to its weight, but the thickness of the meat upon it which varies very much. Lay the thick end nearest to the fire.

A proper bald spare rib of eight pounds weight (so called because almost all the meat is pared off), with a steady fire, will be done in an hour and a quarter. There is so little meat on a bald spare rib, that if you have a large, fierce fire, it will be burned before it is warm through. Joint it nicely, and crack the ribs across as you do ribs of lamb.

When you put it down to roast, dust on some flour, and baste it with a little butter; dry a dozen sage leaves, and rub them through a hair-sieve, and put them into the top of a dredging box; and about a quarter of an hour before the meat is done, baste it with butter; dust with the pulverized sage.

*Obs.*—Make it a general rule never to pour gravy over any thing that is roasted; by so doing, the dredging, &c.is washed off, and it eats insipid.

Some people carve a spare rib by cutting out in slices the thick part at the bottom of the bones. When this meat is cut away, the bones may be easily separated, and are esteemed very sweet picking.

Apple sauce, mashed potatoes, and good mustard are indispensable.


PORK CHEESE. Choose the head of a small pig which may weigh about twelve pounds the quarter. Sprinkle over it and the tongues of four pigs, a little common salt and a very little saltpetre. Let them lie four days, wash them, and tie them in a clean cloth; boil them until the bones will come easily out of the head, take off the skin as whole as possible, place a bowl in hot water and put in the head, cutting it into small pieces. In the bottom of a round tin, shaped like a small cheese, lay two strips of cloth across each other, they must be long enough to fold over the top when the shape is full, place the skin round the tin, and nearly half

fill it with the meat, which has been highly seasoned with pepper, cayenne and salt; put in some tongue cut into slices, then the rest of the meat and the remainder of the tongue, draw the cloth tightly across the top; put on it a board or a plate that will fit into the shape, and place on it a heavy weight, which must not be taken off till it be quite cold. It is eaten with vinegar and mustard, and served for luncheon or supper.


POTATOES. The vegetable kingdom affords no food more wholesome, more easily procured, easily prepared, or less expensive, than the potato: yet, although this most useful vegetable is dressed almost every day, in almost every family, for one plate of potatoes that comes to table as it should come, ten are spoiled.

Wash them, but do not pare or cut them, unless they are very large. Fill a saucepan half full of potatoes of equal size (or make them so by dividing the larger ones), put to them as much cold water as will cover them about an inch: they are sooner boiled, and more savory, than when drowned in water. Most boiled things are spoiled by having too little water, but potatoes are often spoiled by too much: they must merely be covered, and a little allowed for waste in boiling, so that they may be just covered at the finish.

Set them on a moderate fire till they boil; then take them off, and put them by the side of the fire to simmer slowly till they are soft enough to admit a fork (place no dependence on the usual test of their skins' cracking, which, if they are boiled fast, will happen to some potatoes when they are not half done, and the insides quite hard). Then pour the water off (if you let the potatoes remain in the water a moment after they are done enough, they will become waxy and watery), uncover the saucepan, and set it at such a distance from the fire as will secure it from burning; their superfluous moisture will evaporate, and the potatoes will be perfectly dry and mealy.

You may afterward place a napkin,

folded up to the size of the saucepan's diameter, over the potatoes, to keep them hot and mealy till wanted.

This method of managing potatoes is in every respect equal to steaming them; and they are dressed in half the time.

There is such an infinite variety of sorts and sizes of potatoes, that it is impossible to say how long they will take doing: the best way is to try them with a fork. Moderate-sized potatoes will generally be done enough in fifteen or twenty minutes.

POTATOES, NEW. The best way to clean new potatoes is to rub them with a coarse cloth or flannel, or scrubbing-brush.

New potatoes are poor, watery, and insipid, till they are full two inches in diameter: they are not worth the trouble of boiling before midsummer day.

*Obs.* Some cooks prepare sauces to pour over potatoes, made with butter, salt, and pepper, or gravy, or melted butter and ketchup; or stew the potatoes in ale, or water seasoned with pepper and salt; or bake them with herrings or sprats, mixed with layers of potatoes, seasoned with pepper, salt, sweet herbs, vinegar, and water; or cut mutton or beef into slices, and lay them in a stewpan, and on them potatoes and spices, then another layer of the meat alternately, pouring in a little water covering it up very close, and boiling it slowly.

POTATO BALLS. Mix mashed potatoes with the yolk of an egg; roll them into balls; flour them, or egg and bread-crumb them; and fry them in clean drippings, or brown them in a Dutch oven.

POTATO BALLS RAGOUT, Are made by adding to a pound of potatoes a quarter of a pound of grated ham, or some sweet herbs, or chopped parsley, an onion or eschalot, salt, pepper, and a little grated nutmeg, or other spice, with the yolk of a couple of eggs: they are then to be dressed as Potato Balls.

*Obs.* An agreeable vegetable relish, and a good supper-dish.

POTATOES BOILED, TO BROIL. After boiling potatoes not quite sufficiently to send to table, put them on a gridiron over a clear fire, and turn them frequently till they are of a nice brown color all over; serve them hot; take care they do not become too hard, as that spoils the flavor.

POTATOES CASSEROLE. Boil and peel some good mealy potatoes, pound them, and mix with them some butter, cream, and a little salt, put them about an inch and a half high upon a flat dish, and leave an opening in the centre; bake them of a light brown color, and take out as much from the centre as will admit of a ragout, fricassee, or macaroni, being put into it.

POTATOES, COLCANNON. Boil potatoes and greens, or spinage, separately; mash the potatoes; squeeze the greens dry; chop them quite fine and mix them with the potatoes, with a little butter, pepper, and salt; put it into a mould, buttering it well first; let it stand in a hot oven for ten minutes.

POTATO CROQUETTES. When boiled and peeled, allow four large mealy potatoes, half their weight of butter and of pounded loaf sugar, two eggs beaten, half the grated peel of a lemon, and a little salt; pound the potatoes in a mortar with the other ingredients; beat the yolks of four eggs; roll up the croquettes; dip them in the beaten eggs, and roll them in sifted bread crumbs; in an hour, roll them again as before, and fry them in butter; put them upon the back of a sieve before the fire to drain.

POTATO EGGS. Mash perfectly smooth six or seven boiled potatoes, add a piece of butter the size of a walnut, the beaten yolk of an egg, half an onion pounded, a little boiled minced parsley, some pepper and salt; make it into the form of small eggs or pears, roll them into a well-beaten egg, and then into grated bread seasoned, with pepper and salt; fry them in plenty of lard or dripping till they are of a fine brown color, lay them before the fire to drain; serve them with a fringe of fried parsley.

POTATOES FRIED IN SLICES OR RIBBONS. Peel large potatoes; slice them about a quarter of an inch thick, or cut them in shavings round and round, as you would peel a lemon; dry them well in a clean cloth, and fry them in lard or dripping. Take care that your fat and frying-pan are quite clean; put it on a quick fire, watch it, and as soon as the lard boils, and is still, put in the slices of potato, and keep moving them till they are crisp. Take them up, and lay them to drain on a sieve: send them up with a very little salt sprinkled over them.

POTATOES FRIED WHOLE. When nearly boiled enough, put them into a stew-pan with a bit of butter, or some nice clean beef-drippings; shake them about often (for fear of burning them), till they are brown and crisp; drain them from the fat.

*Obs.*—It will be an elegant improvement previous to frying or broiling the potatoes, to flour them and dip them in the yolk of an egg, and then roll them in fine-sifted bread-crumbs; they will then deserve to be called POTATOES FULL DRESSED.

POTATOES RAW OR COLD, TO FRY. Wash, peel, and put them into cold water for one or two hours, cut them into slices about half an inch thick, and fry them a light brown in boiling clarified beef suet. Cold boiled potatoes, cut in slices, may be done in the same manner.

POTATO FRITTERS. Peel, and pound in a mortar, six mealy potatoes, with a little salt, a glass of white wine, some pounded sugar, cinnamon, and an ounce of butter; roll it out with a little flour, cut them the size of a wine glass, and fry them in boiling clarified dripping. Serve them with sifted loaf sugar over them.

POTATOES, MASHED. (1) When your potatoes are thoroughly boiled, drain them quite dry, pick out every speck, &c. and while hot, rub them through a colander into a clean stewpan. To a pound of potatoes put about half an ounce of butter, and a ta-ble-spoonful of milk: do not make them too moist; mix them well together. *Obs.*— When the potatoes are getting old and specky, and in frosty weather, this is the best way of dressing them. You may put them into shapes or small tea-cups; egg them with yolk of egg; and brown them very slightly before a slow fire.

POTATOES, MASHED. (2) Boil the potatoes, peel and mash them very smoothly; put for a large dish four ounces of butter, two eggs beat up in half a pint of good milk, and some salt; mix them well together, heap it upon a dish with a table-spoon to give it a rough and rocky appearance, or put it on a dish and score it with a knife, dip a brush or feather into melted butter, and brush over the top lightly; put it into a Dutch oven, and let it brown gradually for an hour or more. To mash potatoes in a plain way, mix with them two ounces of butter, half a pint of milk, and a little salt. When mashed potatoes are not browned, it is a great improvement to add pepper, salt, and one onion minced as finely as possi-ble; heat the potatoes in a saucepan, and serve them hot.

POTATOES, ROASTED. Wash and dry your potatoes, (all of a size), and put them in a tin Dutch oven, or cheese-toaster: take care not to put them too near the fire, or they will get burned on the outside before they are warmed through. Large potatoes will require two hours to roast them. N. B. To save time and trouble, some cooks half boil them first. This is one of the best oppor-tunities the BAKER has to rival the cook.

POTATOES ROASTED UNDER MEAT. Half boil large potatoes, drain the water from them, and put them into an earthen dish, or small tin pan, under meat that is roasting, and baste them with some of the dripping: when they are browned on one side, turn them and brown the other; send them up round the meat, or in a small dish.

POTATOES SCALLOPED. Mash potatoes as directed, then butter some nice clean scallop-shells, patty-pans, or tea-cups or saucers; put in your potatoes; make them smooth at the top; cross a knife over them; strew a few fine bread-crumbs on them: sprinkle them with a paste-brush with a few drops of melted butter, and then set them in a Dutch oven; when they are browned on the top, take them carefully out of the shells, and brown the other side.

POTATO SNOW. The potatoes must be free from spots, and the whitest you can pick out; put them on in cold water; when they begin to crack, strain the water from them, and put them into a clean stewpan by the side of the fire till they are quite dry, and fall to pieces; rub them through a wire sieve on the dish they are to be sent up in, and do not disturb them afterward.

POT POURRI. Gather, when perfectly dry, a peck of roses; pick off the leaves, and strew over them three-quarters of a pound of common salt; let them remain two or three days, and if any fresh flowers are added, some more salt should be sprinkled over them. Mix with the roses half a pound of finely-pounded bay salt, the same quantity of allspice, of cloves, and of brown sugar, a quarter of a pound of gum-benjamin, and two ounces of orris-root; add a glass of brandy, and any sort of fragrant flower, such as orange and lemon flowers, rosemary, and a great quantity of lavender flowers—also white lilies: a green orange stuck with cloves may be added. All the flowers must be gathered perfectly dry.

POTTING BEEF, VEAL, GAME, or POULTRY. Take three pounds of lean gravy beef, rub it well with an ounce of saltpetre, and then a handful of common salt; let it lie in salt for a couple of days, rubbing it well each day; then put it into an earthen pan or stone jar that will just hold it; cover it with the skin and fat that you cut off, and pour in half a pint of water; cover it close with paste, and set it in a very slow oven for about four hours.

When it comes from the oven, drain the gravy from it into a basin; pick out the gristles and the skins; mince it fine; moisten it with a little of the gravy you poured from the meat, which is a very strong consomme (but rather salt), and it will make excellent pease soup, or browning; pound the meat patiently and thoroughly in a mortar with some fresh butter, till it is a fine paste (to make potted meat smooth there is nothing equal to plenty of elbow-grease); seasoning it by degrees, as you are beating it, with a little black pepper and allspice, or cloves pounded, or mace, or grated nutmeg.

Put it in pots, press it down as close as possible, and cover it a quarter of an inch thick with clarified butter; and if you wish to preserve it a long time, over that tie a bladder. Keep it in a dry place.

You may mince a little ham or bacon, or an anchovy, sweet or savory herbs, or an eschalot, and a little tarragon, chervil, or burnet, &c., and pound them with the meat, with a glass of wine, or some mustard, or forcemeat.

It is a very agreeable and economical way of using the remains of game or poultry, or a large joint of either roasted or boiled beef, veal, ham, or tongue, &c. to mince it with some of the fat, or moisten it with a little butter, and beat it in a mortar with the seasoning, &c.

Meat that has been boiled down for gravies, &c. (which has heretofore been considered the perquisite of the cat) and is completely drained of all its succulence, beat in a mortar with salt and a little ground black pepper and allspice, as directed in the foregoing receipt, and it will make as good potted beef as meat that has been baked till its moisture is entirely extracted, which it must be, or it will not keep two days.

MEM.—Meat that has not been previously salted, will not keep so long as that which has.

POULTRY. In choosing a turkey, the young cock bird is to be preferred; the best have black legs, and if young, the toes and bill are pliable and feel soft. A hen turkey is chosen by the same rules.

Fowls with black legs are the best; if fresh, the vent is close and dark; if young, the combs are bright in the color, and the legs smooth—the spurs of a young cock are short.

A goose, if young and fine, is plump in the breast, the fat white and soft, the feet yellow, and but few hairs upon them.

Ducks may be chosen by the same rules, and are hard and thick on the breast and belly.

Pigeons should be quite fresh, the breast plump and fat, the feet elastic, and neither flabby nor discolored at the vent.

To prepare a turkey for dressing, every plug is carefully picked out; and in drawing turkeys and fowls, care must be taken not to break the gall bag, nor the gut which joins the gizzard, as it is impossible to remove the bitterness of the one, or the grittiness of the other. The hairs are singed off with white paper; the leg-bone is broken close to the foot, and the sinews drawn out;—a cloth is then put over the breast, and the bone flattened with a rolling-pin, the liver and gizzard, made delicately clean, are fastened into each pinion. A stuffing made with sausage meat, adding some grated bread, and mixing it with the beaten yolks of two eggs, or a stuffing as for a fillet of veal, is then put into the breast, and the turkey, well rubbed over with flour, is put down to roast. It is basted constantly with butter, and when the steam draws towards the fire, it is nearly done;—it is then dredged with flour,

and basted with more butter, served with gravy in the dish, and garnished with sausages, or with forcement balls if veal stuffing is used, and bread sauce in a sauce tureen.

*To boil a turkey.* After being nicely cleaned, it is trussed with the legs drawn in under the skin, stuffed with a forcemeat, as for veal, adding a few chopped oysters; then boiled in a well-floured cloth, and served with oyster, white or celery sauce, poured over it, and also some in a sauce tureen. Boiled ham, tongue, or pickled pork, is eaten with it. A large-sized turkey will require more than two hours to boil. Turkey, with celery sauce, is stuffed and trussed neatly, laid all over with slices of bacon, tied in a cloth, and boiled in water, with a little salt, butter, and lemon-juice added. It is served thickly covered with celery sauce.

Turkey poults are stuffed and roasted in the same manner as a full-grown turkey. They will require rather more than an hour to roast. They are dressed with the heads twisted under the wing, as are also turkeys sometimes, but it seems an injudicious custom, as the side on which the head is cannot be nicely browned, and in carving, the blood from the neck is apt to mingle with the gravy.

*To roast a fowl.* It is picked, nicely cleaned, and singed; the neck is cut off close by the back, the fowl is then washed, and if a large one, stuffed with forcemeat. It is trussed and dredged with flour; and when put down to roast, basted well with butter, and frothed up. When the steam is observed to draw towards the fire, it is sufficiently done; served with gravy in the dish, and bread sauce in a butter tureen. A good-sized fowl will require above an hour to roast.

Chickens are roasted as the above, and served with gravy in the dish, which is garnished with fried eggs, and bread sauce in a sauce tureen; they will require from half an hour to three-quarters to roast.

*To boil a fowl.* When nicely singed, washed, and trussed, it is well dredged with flour, and put on in boiling water, and if a large one, boiled nearly an hour. It is served with parsley and butter, white, or liver sauce.

Two boiled fowl, served with a tongue between them, make a handsome top dish.

Boiled chickens are improved by being stuffed, and will require nearly half an hour to boil.

*To roast a goose.* After being well cleaned, picked, and singed, it is washed, made perfectly dry, and stuffed with about four table-spoonfuls of grated bread, an onion finely minced, together with three sage-leaves, seasoned with salt and pepper, and mixed with a well-beaten egg; or, the stuffing is made of boiled mashed potatoes, seasoned in the same way as the other, and mixed with a beaten egg. If roasted on a spit, each end is tied on tightly; it is basted at first with a little bit of butter, after which the fat that drops from it is used. It is served with gravy in the dish, and apple sauce in a sauce tureen. A large goose will require an hour and a half to roast. At table, an opening is cut in the apron, and a glass of Port wine with which is mixed a large tea-spoonful of made mustard, is poured into the body of the goose. This is also an improvement to ducks.

A green goose, about two or three months old, is seasoned with pepper and salt only, and requires to be basted with butter. It requires about an hour to roast.

*To roast ducks.* They are nicely picked, cleaned, singed, and washed, seasoned with pepper and salt; or stuffed, and served with gravy, as directed in pp. 116, 117. A duck may be boiled for nearly an hour, and served with onion sauce poured over it.

PRESERVES, SWEETMEATS. &c. All sweet-meats should be preserved in a brass pan, which must be well scoured with sand and vinegar, washed with hot water, and wiped perfectly dry before it is used.

An iron plate or stove is preferable to a fire for preserving on; and by boiling the fruit quickly, the form, color, and flavor, will be better preserved, and there will be less waste than in slow boiling. A round wooden stick, smaller at one end than at the other, in Scotland called a thevil, is better adapted for stirring sugar or preserves with than a silver spoon, which last is only used for skimming. That there may be no waste in taking off the scum, it is put through a fine silk sieve, or through a hair sieve, with a bit of muslin laid into it; the clear part will run into the vessel placed below, and may be returned to the preserving-pan.

A silver soup ladle is used for putting preserves into the jars, which should be of brown stone, or of white wedgewood ware. After the jellies or preserves are put in, they must not be moved till quite cold, when they are covered with a piece of white paper, cut so as to fit into the jar, and dipped into brandy or rum. They are then stored in a cool dry place, and should be looked at occasionally. If in a few weeks they be observed to ferment, the sirup should be first strained from the fruit, then boiled till it is thick, and again poured over the fruit, previously put into clean jars.

Sugar, low in price, and consequently coarse in quality, is far from being cheapest in the end; while that which is most refined is always the best. White sugars should be chosen as shining and as close in texture as possible.

The best sort of brown sugar has a bright and gravelly appearance.

A jelly-bag is made of half a square of flannel folded by the corners, and one side sewed up; the top bound with tape, and four loops also of tape sewed on, so as to hang upon a stand made of four bars of wood, each thirty-six inches in height, fastened with four bars at the top, each measuring ten inches, with hooks upon the corners. Twelve inches from the bottom four more bars are placed. A pan or basin is put underneath to receive the juice or jelly as it drops through the bag.

*To save Sugar in Preserving Cherries, Green Gages, Damsons, Currants, and Raspberries.* Gather the fruit perfectly dry, and to a pound allow five ounces of finely pounded loaf sugar; put a layer of fruit into a wide-mouthed bottle or jar, and then one of sugar, till the vessel is full; tie over it tightly two folds of sound bladder, and put them into a copper or pan, with straw in the bottom, and water as high as the necks, and let them simmer for three hours. When the water cools, take out the bottles, and keep them in a cool dry place.

—— FRUIT, WITHOUT SUGAR. Take damsons when not too ripe; pick off the stalks, and put them into wide-mouthed glass bottles, taking care not to put in any but what are whole, and without blemish; shake them well down (otherwise the bottles will not be half full when done); stop the bottles with new soft corks, not too tight; set them into a very slow oven (nearly cold) four or five hours; the slower they are done the better; when they begin to shrink in the bottles, it is a sure sign that the fruit is thoroughly warm: take them out, and before they are cold, drive in the corks quite tight; set them in a bottle-rack or basket, with the mouth downwards, and they will keep good several years.

Green gooseberries, morello cherries, currants, green gages, or bullace, may be done the same way.

*Obs.*—If the corks are good, and fit well, there will be no occasion for cementing them; but should bungs be used, it will be necessary.

—— APPLES. (1) Pare, core, and quarter six pounds of good hard baking apples; finely pound four pounds of loaf sugar; put a layer of each alternately, with half a pound of the best white ginger, into a jar; let it remain eight-and-forty hours; infuse, for half that time, in a little boiling water, half a quarter of a pound of bruised white ginger; strain and boil the liquor with the apples till they look clear, and the sirup rich and thick, which may be in about an hour. Take off the scum as it rises. When to be eaten, pick out the whole ginger.

—— PRESERVED APPLES. (2) Weigh equal quantities of good brown sugar and of apples; peel, core, and mince them small. Boil the sugar, allowing to every three pounds a pint of water; skim it well, and boil it pretty thick; then add the apples, the grated peel of one or two lemons, and two or three pieces of white ginger; boil till the apples fall, and look clear and yellow. This preserve will keep for years.

—— APPLES, GREEN CODLINGS. Gather the codlings when not bigger than French walnuts with the stalks and a leaf or two on each. Put a handful of vine leaves into a preserving-pan, then a layer of codlings, then vine leaves, and then codlings and vine leaves alternately, until it is full, with vine leaves pretty thickly strewed on the top, and fill the pan with spring water; cover it close to keep in the steam, and set it on a slow fire till the apples become soft. Take them out, and pare off the rinds with a penknife, and then put them into the same water again with the vine leaves; but taking care that the water is become quite cold, or it will cause them to crack; put in a little alum and set them over a slow fire till they are green, when, take them out and lay them on a sieve to drain. Make a good sirup and give them a gentle boil three successive days; then put them in small jars with brandy paper over them, and tie them down tight.

—— APPLES, GOLDEN PIPPINS. Take the rind of an orange and boil it very tender; lay it in cold water for three days; take two dozen golden pippins, pare, core, and quarter them, and boil them to a strong jelly, and run it through a jelly-bag till it is clear; take the same quantity of pippins, pare and core them, and put three pounds of loaf sugar in a preserving-pan with a pint and a half of spring water; let it boil; skim it well and put in your pippins, with the orange rind cut into long thin slips; then let them boil fast till the sugar becomes thick and will almost candy; then put in a pint and half of pippin jelly, and boil fast till the jelly is clear; then squeeze in the juice of a fine lemon; give the whole another boil, and put the pippins in pots or glasses with the orange-peel.

Lemon-peel may be used instead of orange, but then it must only be boiled, and not soaked.

—— APRICOTS. Pare your apricots, and stone what you can whole, then give them a light boiling in water proportioned to the quantity of fruit, only just enough; then take the weight of the apricots in sugar, and take the liquor in which they have boiled, and the sugar, and boil it till it comes to a sirup, and give them a light boiling, taking off the scum as it rises. When the sirup jellies it is enough; then take up the apricots and cover them with the jelly; put cut paper over them, and lay them down when cold.

—— BLACK CURRANTS. Gather the currants upon a dry day; to every pound allow half a pint of red currant juice, and a pound and a half of finely-pounded loaf sugar. With scissors clip off the heads and stalks; put the juice, sugar, and currants into a preserving pan; shake it frequently till it boils; carefully remove the fruit from the sides of the pan, and take off the scum as it rises; let it boil for ten or fifteen minutes. This preserve may be eaten with cream, and made into tarts.

—— CHERRIES. To a pound of cherries allow three-quarters of a pound of pounded loaf sugar; carefully stone them, and as they are done, strew part of the sugar over them; boil them fast, with the remainder of the sugar, till the fruit is clear and the sirup thick; take off the scum as it rises. Or they may be boiled ten minutes in an equal quantity of sugar, which has been previously clarified and boiled candy high. Part of the kernels may be added.

—— CUCUMBERS. Take large and fresh-gathered cucumbers; split them down and take out all the seeds; lay them in salt and water that will bear an egg three days; set them on a fire with cold water, and a small lump of alum, and boil them a few minutes, or till tender; drain them, and pour on them a thin sirup; let them lie two days; boil the sirup again, and put it over the cucumbers; repeat it twice more; then have ready some fresh clarified sugar, boiled to a blow; put in the cucumbers, simmer it five minutes; set it by till next day; boil the sirup and cucumbers again and set them in glasses for use.

—— CUCUMBERS, SMALL. Weigh equal proportions of small green cucumbers and of fine loaf sugar, clarify it; rub the cucumbers with a cloth, scald them in hot water, and, when cold, put them into the sirup, with some white ginger and the peel of a lemon; boil them gently for ten minutes. The following day just let them boil, and repeat this three times, and the last, boil them till tender and clear.

—— DAMSONS. (1) To every pound of damsons allow three-quarters of a pound of pounded loaf sugar; put into jars alternately a layer of damsons, and one of sugar; tie them over with bladder or strong paper, and put them into an oven after the bread is withdrawn, and let them remain till the oven is cold. The following day strain off the sirup, and boil it till thick. When cold, put the damsons one by one into small jars, and pour over them the sirup, which must cover them. Tie them over with wet bladder.

—— DAMSONS. (2) Prick them with a needle, and boil them with sugar the same proportion as in the receipt to preserve damsons, till the sirup will jelly. Carefully take off all the scum.

—— GREEN GAGES. Put the plums into boiling water, pare off the skin, and divide them; take an equal quantity of pounded loaf sugar, strew half of it over the fruit; let it remain some hours, and, with the remainder of the sugar, put it into a preserving pan; boil till the plums look quite clear, take off the scum as it rises, and a few minutes before taking them off the fire, add the kernels.

—— LARGE SWEET GREEN Goose-BERRIES. (1) Weigh equal proportions of sugar and of fruit; with a penknife slit the gooseberries on one side, and take out all the seeds; put them into a preserving pan with cold water, scald them; pour off the water when cold; put over and under them vine leaves, with more cold water; set them over the fire to green. Clarify the sugar; put the gooseberries into a deep jar, and pour the boiling sirup over them; in two days pour it off, boil, and put it over the fruit; repeat this till the sirup becomes thick, then put them into small jars.

—— LARGE SWEET GREEN Goose-BERRIES. (2) Gather the largest-sized gooseberries, and allow an equal quantity of pounded loaf sugar; cut the gooseberries in half, and take out the seeds; wet the sugar with a little water, and put all together into a preserving pan; carefully stir and scum them, and boil them till the sirup is clear and the fruit soft.

—— GOOSEBERRIES. The tops and tails being removed from the gooseberries, allow an equal quantity of finely-pounded loaf sugar and put a layer of each alternately into a large deep jar; pour into it as much dripped currant juice, either red or white, as will dissolve the sugar, adding its weight in sugar; the following day put all into a preserving pan and boil it.

—— GREEN PEAS. Put into a saucepan of boiling water fresh gathered and fresh-shelled peas, but not very young; as soon as they boil up, pour off the water, and put them upon a large dry cloth folded, and then upon another, that they may be perfectly dry without being bruised; let them lie some time before the fire, and then put them into small paper bags, each containing about a pint, and hang them up in the kitchen. Before using, soak them for two or three hours in water, and then boil them as directed for green peas, adding a little bit of butter, when they are put on to boil.

PRESERVED JARGONELLE PEARS. Gather pears with stalks before they are quite ripe; allow equal quantities of fine loaf sugar and of fruit. Pare the pears as thinly as possible, keeping on the stalks; carefully cut out the black top; as they are peeled put them into cold water. Put cabbage leaves into the bottom of a preserving-pan; lay in the pears, cover them with cold water and one or two cabbage leaves upon the top; boil them thirty minutes, and lay them upon a dish. To six pounds of sugar, allow a pound of water, boil and skim it; then add one ounce of white ginger, previously soaked in hot water, and scraped clean, add the juice and thinly pared rinds of two lemons. Boil the sirup ten minutes, put in the pears, and let them boil twenty minutes; take them out, put them into a bowl or deep dish, boil the sirup eight minutes, and when cold pour it over the pears; cover them with paper; in four days pour off the sirup, boil it eight minutes, and pour it over the pears when cold. In four days repeat this process, and do it a third time; then stick a clove in each pear, where the black top was cut out. Put them into jars, divide the ginger and lemon-peel, and pour on the sirup when cold.

—— RED PEARS. Parboil a dozen of pound pears in water; peel them. Clarify the same weight of fine loaf sugar that there is of pears; add a pint of Port wine, the juice and rind of one lemon, with a little cochineal, a few cloves, and a stick of cinnamon; boil the pears in this till they become clear and red; take them out, boil up the sirup, strain, and put it over the pears.

PUDDINGS, PIES, AND TARTS. Great nicety is to be observed in preparing every material used for boiled or baked puddings.

The eggs require to be well beaten, for which purpose, if many are to be done, a whisk is used; if few, a three-pronged fork. The flour is dried and sifted. The currants are carefully cleaned, by putting them into a cullender, and pouring warm water over them; if very dirty, this is to be repeated two or three times, and after being dried in a dish before the fire, they are rubbed in a clean coarse cloth, all the stalks and stones picked out, and then a little flour dredged over them. The raisins are stoned with a small sharp-pointed knife; it is cleansed in a basin of water, which also receives the seed. The pudding cloth must be kept especially clean, or it will impart an unpleasant taste to anything that is boiled in it; and when taken off a pudding, it ought immediately to be laid in cold water, and afterwards well washed with soda or pearl-ashes in hot water. Just before being used for a rice, bread, or batter pudding, it should be dipped into hot water, wrung, shaken, and well dredged with flour; and for a plum, suet pudding, or any sort of fruit pudding in paste, it must be buttered before being floured.

The water should boil quick when the pudding is put in; and it should be moved about for a minute, for fear the ingredients should not mix.

When the pudding is done, a pan of cold water should be ready, and the pudding dipped into it as soon as it comes out of the pot, which will prevent its adhering to the cloth.

A bread pudding should be tied loose; if batter, it must be tied tight over, and a batter pudding should be strained through a coarse sieve when all is mixed. In others, the eggs only. If you boil the pudding in a basin or pan, take care that it is always well buttered.

When you make your puddings without eggs, they must have as little milk as will mix, and must boil for three or four hours. A few spoonfuls of small beer, or one of yeast, is the best substitute for eggs. Your puddings will always be much lighter if you beat the yolks and whites of the eggs long and separately. You may, if you please, use snow instead of eggs, either in puddings or pancakes. Two large spoonfuls will supply the place of one egg; the snow may be taken up from any clean spot before it is wanted, and will not lose its virtue, though the sooner it is used the better.

All puddings in paste are tied tightly, but other puddings loosely, in the cloth. When a pudding is to be boiled in a shape, a piece of buttered white paper is put upon the top of it, before the floured cloth is tied on. The pan, dish, or shape, in which the pudding is to be either boiled or baked, must always be buttered before it is filled. It is an improvement to puddings in general to let them stand some time after being prepared either for boiling or baking. When a pudding is to be boiled, it must be put on in a covered pot, in plenty of boiling water, and never for a moment be allowed to be off the boil until ready to be served. As the water wastes, more, and always boiling, must be added. A plum pudding is the better for being mixed the day before it is to be boiled. It may be useful to observe that this pudding will keep for months after it is dressed, if the cloth be allowed to remain upon it, and if, when cold, it be covered with a sheet of foolscap paper, and then hung up in a cool place. When about to be used, it must be put into a clean cloth, and again boiled for an hour; or it may be cut into slices, and broiled as wanted. If in breaking eggs a bad one should accidentally drop into the basin amongst the rest, the whole will be spoiled; and therefore they should be broken one by one into a tea-cup. When the whites only of eggs are required for a jelly, or other things, the yolks, if not broken, will keep good for three days, if the basin they are in be covered.

A slab of marble, stone, or slate, is preferable to wood for rolling out paste on. The rolling-pin, cutters, and every other implement used in these processes, must be kept particularly clean; they should always be washed immediately after being used, and then well dried. Before using butter for paste, it is laid for some time into cold water, which is changed once or twice. When salt butter is used, it is well worked in two or three waters. If it should not be convenient to make the paste immediately before it is baked, it will not suffer from standing, if made early in the morning, and the air excluded from it, by putting first a tin cover over the pie or tartlets, and above that a folded table-cloth. To ascertain if the oven be of a proper heat, a little bit of paste may be baked in it, before anything else be put in. Puff paste requires rather a brisk oven. If too hot it binds the surface and prevents the steam from rising, and if too slow it becomes sodden and flat. Raised crusts require a quick oven; puffs and tartlets, which are filled with preserved fruit, are sufficiently done when the paste is baked. When large pies have been in the oven for a few minutes, a paper is put over them to prevent their being burned.

PUDDING. Sweeten a pint and a half of cream, and boil it with the peel of a small lemon; cut the crumb of a twopenny roll, and put it into the cream, and boil it for eight minutes, stirring constantly; when thick add a quarter of a pound of fresh butter beaten to a cream, a tea-spoonful of grated nutmeg, and four well-beaten eggs; beat it all well together for some minutes. It may be baked or boiled.

—— APRICOT. Take six-and-thirty nice fine red apricots, cut them in halves, and take out the stones, and roll them in a pan with four ounces of powdered sugar. Prepare your crust, line your mould with it, put in your apricots, and finish the same as in the receipt for Apple Pudding, *a la Francaise*.

—— ALMOND, BAKED. Steep four ounces of crumbs of bread sliced in a pint and half of cream, or grate the bread; then beat half a pound of blanched almonds very fine, till they become a paste, with two tea-spoonfuls of orange-flower water; beat up the yolks of eight eggs, and the

whites of four; mix all well together; put in a quarter of a pound of loaf sugar, and stir in three or four ounces of melted butter; put it over the fire, and keep stirring until it is thick; lay a sheet of paper at the bottom of a dish, and pour in the ingredients. To bake half an hour.

—— ALMOND. Blanch and beat a pound of sweet almonds with a little rose-water, mix a pound of bread grated, a nutmeg, half a pound of butter, and the yolks of six eggs, boil a pint of cream, colored with a very little saffron, add it to the eggs and a little flour, knead it well, and then put in the almonds, beating it up till all is mixed together. Boil it for half an hour in a buttered cloth.

—— AMBER. Put a pound of butter into a saucepan, with three-quarters of a pound of powder-sugar; when melted and well mixed together, add the yolks of fifteen eggs beaten, and as much candied orange beaten to a paste as will give color and flavor to it. Line the dish with paste for turning out, and when filled with the above, lay a crust over, as you would a pie, and bake in a slow oven. It may be eaten hot or cold.

—— APPLE. (1) Weigh one pound and three-quarters of apples, pare, core, and cut them into thin bits; weigh also ten ounces of brown sugar; make a suet paste, rolled thinner towards the edges than in the middle, and sufficiently large to lay into a two-quart basin, previously buttered; put in the apple and sugar alternately, wet the edges of the paste, and fold it closely over; dredge it with flour, and tie a pudding cloth over the top of a basin; boil it for three hours. A light paste may be made with flour, half its quantity in bulk of grated bread and suet, mixing it with milk or water, and, instead of apples, currants damsons, or any other fruit, may be enclosed in it.

—— APPLE. (2) Peel and core six very large apples, stew them in six table-spoonfuls of water, with the rind of a lemon; when soft, beat them to a pulp, add six ounces of melted fresh butter, the same of good brown sugar, six well-beaten eggs, half a wine-glass of brandy, and a teaspoonful of lemon-juice; line a dish with a puff paste, and when baked, stick all over the top thin chips of candied citron and lemon-peel.

—— APPLE. (3) Make a batter with two eggs, a pint of milk, and three or four spoonfuls of flour; pour it into a deep dish, and having pared six or eight small apples, place them whole in the batter and bake it.

—— APPLE, BOILED. Chop four ounces of beef suet very fine, or two ounces of butter, lard, or dripping; but the suet makes the best and lightest crust; put it on the paste-board, with eight ounces of flour, and a salt-spoonful of salt, mix it well together with your hands, and then put it all of a heap, and make a hole in the middle; break one egg in it, stir it well together with your finger, and by degrees infuse as much water as will make it of a stiff paste: roll it out two or three times, with the rolling-pin, and then roll it large enough to receive thirteen ounces of apples. It will look neater if boiled in a basin, well buttered, than when boiled in a pudding-cloth, well floured; boil it an hour and three-quarters: but the surest way is to stew the apples first in a stewpan, with a wine-glassful of water, and then one hour will boil it. Some people like it flavored with cloves and lemon-peel, and sweeten it with two ounces of sugar. Gooseberries, currants, raspberries, and cherries, damsons, and various plums and fruits, are made into puddings with the same crust directed for apple puddings.

—— APPLE, A LA FRANCAISE. To make the *entremets* properly, it is necessary to have a mould in the form of a dome four inches deep and six in diameter; this mould and its lid should be pierced all over, the same as a skimmer. There should be a rim round the lid of the dome that it may cover it so closely that all air may be excluded.

Peel six and thirty small red apples and cut them into quarters; toss them in a stewpan with four ounces of fine sugar (over which must be grated the rind of an orange), and four ounces of butter luke-warm; then place the stewpan over the stove, with fire on the cover. When your apples are done, pour them into a dish. Whilst they are cooling mix up three-quarters of a pound of stiff paste, then roll out half of it to the thickness of the eighth of an inch. With this crust line the inside of your mould, which must be previously well buttered. Be careful that the paste lays quite flat, leaving a piece all round the edge of the mould, then put in the best quarters of the apples, and fill up the mould with the rest of the apples and their liquor, then roll out the rest of the paste very thin, into two parts, cut in rounds. Slightly moisten the paste which you have left round the edge of the mould, and place upon it one of the rounds of paste; pinching the edges carefully together, then slightly moisten, and place upon it your other round piece of paste, pinching the edge of this with the others to make it quite close, then cover them with the lid of the mould well buttered.

Now, turn your mould over into the middle of a napkin, and tie up the corners of it close over the top of the dome, and put it into a saucepan (nine inches deep and nine wide) full of boiling water; and let it be kept constantly boiling for an hour and a half; when it has boiled for this time, take it out of the saucepan, untie the napkin, take out the mould, remove the lid, place the mould on a dish, and then carefully take it off from the pudding; strew fine sugar all over your pudding, and serve it quite hot.

—— ARROW-ROOT. From a quart of new milk take a small tea-cupful, and mix it with two large spoonfuls of arrow-root. Boil the remainder of the milk, and stir it amongst the arrow-root; add, when nearly cold, four well-beaten yolks of eggs, with two ounces of pounded loaf sugar, and the same of fresh butter broken into small bits; season with grated nutmeg. Mix it well together, and bake it in a buttered dish fifteen or twenty minutes.

—— AUNT MARY'S. Of bloom raisins stoned, currants nicely cleaned, suet finely minced, bread grated, apples minced, and brown sugar, a quarter of a pound of each; four well-beaten eggs, a tea-spoonful of pounded ginger, half a one of salt, half a nutmeg grated, and one glass of brandy; mix all the ingredients well, and boil it in a cloth for two hours. Serve with a sauce of melted butter, a glass of wine, and some sugar.

—— BARLEY. Take a pound of pearl barley well washed, three quarts of new milk, one quart of cream, and half a pound of double refined sugar, a grated nutmeg, and some salt; mix them well together, then put them into a deep pan, and bake it; then take it out of the oven, and put into it six eggs well beaten, six ounces of beef marrow, and a quarter of a pound of grated bread; mix all well together, then put it into another pan, bake it again, and it will be excellent.

—— BATTER, BAKED OR BOILED. Break three eggs in a basin with as much salt as will lie on a sixpence; beat them well together, and then add four ounces of flour; beat it into a smooth batter, and by degrees add half a pint of milk: have your saucepan ready boiling, and butter an earthen mould well, put the pudding in, and tie it tight over with a pudding-cloth, and boil it one hour and a quarter. Or, put it in a dish that you have well buttered and bake it three-quarters of an hour. Currants washed and picked clean, or raisins stoned, are good in this pudding, and it is then called a black cap: or, add loaf sugar, and a little nutmeg and ginger without the fruit,—it is very good that way; serve it with wine sauce.

—— BATTER. Take six ounces of fine flour, a little salt, and three eggs; beat it well with a little milk, added by degrees till the batter become smooth; make it the thickness of cream; put into a buttered pie-dish, and bake three-quarters of an hour, or into a buttered and floured basin, tied over tight with a cloth: boil one and a half hour, or two hours.

—— BATTER, WITHOUT EGGS. Mix six spoonfuls of flour with a small portion of a quart of milk; and when smooth add the remainder of the milk, a tea-spoonful of salt, two tea-spoonfuls of grated ginger, and two of tincture of saffron; stir all together well, and boil it an hour. Fruit may be added or not.

—— BEEF-STEAK. Get rump-steaks, not too thick, beat them with a chopper, cut them into pieces about half the size of your hand, and trim off all the skin, sinews, &c.; have ready an onion peeled and chopped fine, likewise some potatoes peeled and cut into slices a quarter of an inch thick; rub the inside of a basin or an oval plain mould with butter, sheet it with paste as directed for boiled puddings, season the steaks with pepper, salt, and a little grated nutmeg; put in a layer of steak, then another of potatoes, and so on till it is full, occasionally throwing in part of the chopped onion; add to it half a gill of mushroom ketchup, a table-spoonful of lemon-pickle, and half a gill of water or veal broth; roll out a top, and close it well to prevent the water getting in; rinse a clean cloth in hot water, sprinkle a little flour over it, and tie up the pudding; have ready a large pot of water boiling, put it in, and boil it two hours and a half; take it up, remove the cloth, turn it downwards in a deep dish, and when wanted take away the basin or mould.

—— BEEF-STEAK, BAKED. Make a batter of milk, two eggs, and flour, or, which is much better, potatoes boiled and mashed through a cullender; lay a little of it at the bottom of the dish; then put in the steaks, prepared as above, and very well seasoned; pour the remainder of the batter over them, and bake it.

—— BISCUIT. Pour a pint of boiling milk over three Naples biscuits grated; cover it close; when cold add the yolks of four eggs, two whites, nutmeg, a little brandy, half a spoonful of flour, and some sugar. Boil it an hour in a basin.

—— BOSTON APPLE. Peel one dozen and a half of good apples; take out the cores, cut them small, put into a stewpan that will just hold them, with a little water, a little cinnamon, two cloves, and the peel of a lemon; stew over a slow fire till quite soft, then sweeten with moist sugar, and pass it through a hair sieve; add to it the yolks of four eggs and one white, a quarter of a pound of good butter, half a nutmeg, the peel of a lemon grated, and the juice of one lemon: beat all well together; line the inside of a pie-dish with good puff paste; put in the pudding, and bake half an hour.

—— BRANDY. Line a mould with jar-raisins stoned, or dried cherries, then lay thin slices of French roll; next put a layer of ratafias or macaroons, then the fruit, rolls, and cakes, in succession, until the mould be full, pouring in at times, two glasses of brandy. Beat four eggs, yolks and whites separately, put to them a pint of milk or cream, lightly sweetened, half a nutmeg, and the rind of half a lemon grated. Pour it into the mould, and when the solid has imbibed it all, flour a cloth, tie it tight over, and boil an hour; keep the mould the right side upwards.

—— BREAD AND BUTTER. Cut thin slices of bread and butter, without the crust, lay some in the bottom of a dish, then put a layer of well-cleaned currants, or any preserved fruit; then more bread and butter, and so on till the dish is nearly filled; mix with a quart of milk four well-beaten eggs, three table-spoonfuls of orange-flower or rose water; sweeten it well with brown sugar, and pour it over the bread and butter, and let it soak for two or three hours before being baked. It will take nearly an hour. Serve with a sauce, in a sauce-tureen, made with a tea-cupful of currant wine, a table-spoonful of brown sugar, three of water, and a bit of butter the size of a walnut, stirred till boiling hot.

—— BREAD. (1) Cut two or three slices of bread rather thin, and without the crust, put them in a dish, and pour over them half a pint of boiling milk; let it stand till cold, and then mash the bread; lay into the bottom of a pudding dish a layer of preserved gooseberries, then add the bread; sweeten well a pint of good milk, and mix with it three well-beaten eggs with two table-spoonfuls of rose water; pour it over the bread, and bake it for an hour. Before serving, nutmeg may be grated over the top.

—— BREAD. (2) Make a pint of bread-crumbs; put them in a stewpan with as much milk as will cover them, the peel of a lemon, a little nutmeg grated, and a small piece of cinnamon; boil about ten minutes; sweeten with powdered loaf sugar; take out the cinnamon, and put in four eggs; beat all well together, and bake half an hour, or boil rather more than an hour.

—— PLAIN BREAD. Make five ounces of bread-crumbs; put them in a basin; pour three-quarters of a pint of boiling milk over them; put a plate over the top to keep in the steam; let it stand twenty minutes, then beat it up quite smooth with two ounces of sugar and a salt-spoonful of nutmeg. Break four eggs on a plate, leaving out one white; beat them well, and add them to the pudding. Stir it all well together, and put it in a mould that has been well buttered and floured; tie a cloth over it, and boil it one bour.

—— BUTTER-MILK. Turn two quarts of new milk with one of butter-milk; drain off the whey, and mix with the curd the grated crumb of a twopenny roll, the grated peel of a lemon, nearly a whole nutmeg grated, half a pint of rich cream, six ounces of clarified butter, and the beaten yolks of nine, and the whites of four eggs; sweeten it well, and bake it with or without a puff paste, for three-quarters of an hour. It may be boiled.

—— CAMP. Put into a saucepan half a pint of water, a quarter of a pound of butter, a table-spoonful of brown sugar, add the peel of half a lemon or orange. Let it just come to a boil, take it off, and stir in a quarter of a pound of sifted flour; mix it perfectly smooth, and when cold, beat in four well-beaten eggs. Half fill twelve yellow tea-cups, and bake them in a quick oven. Serve them with a sauce of wine, sugar, and butter, in a sauce-tureen.

—— CARROT. Pound in a mortar the red part of two large boiled carrots; add a slice of grated bread, or pounded biscuit, two ounces of melted butter, the same quantity of sugar, a table-spoonful of marmalade, or a bit of orange-peel minced; half a tea-spoonful of grated nutmeg, and four well-beaten eggs; mix all well together; bake it in a dish lined with puff paste.

—— CALF'S FEET. Pick all the meat off three well-boiled calf's feet; chop it finely, as also half a pound of fresh beef suet; grate the crumb of a penny loaf; cut like straws an ounce of orange-peel, and the same of citron; beat well six eggs, and grate a small nutmeg; mix all these ingredients well together, with a glass of brandy or rum, and boil it in a cloth nearly three hours.

Serve with a sweet sauce.

—— CHERRY, ANGLO FRANCAIS. Pick two pounds of fine ripe cherries, and mix them with a quarter of a pound of picked red currants, (having extracted the seeds), and six ounces of powder sugar. Make your pudding as directed in the receipt for apple pudding, with Muscadel raisins. You may make use of raspberries instead of currants; or mix red or white currants and raspberries.

—— CHEESE. (1) Grate one pound of mild cheese; beat well four eggs, oil one ounce of butter; mix these ingredients together with one gill of cream, and two table-spoonfuls of grated and sifted bread, and bake it in a dish or tin lined with puff paste.

—— CHEESE. (2) Grate a quarter of a pound of good cheese, put it into a saucepan with half a pint of good milk, and nearly two ounces of grated bread, and one beaten egg; stir it till the cheese be dissolved; put it into a buttered dish, and brown it in a Dutch oven. Serve it quite hot.

—— CITRON. (1) Mix together a pint of cream and the yolks of six eggs; add to this four ounces of fine sugar, the same of citron, shred fine, two spoonfuls of flour, and a little nutmeg; place this mixture in a deep dish, bake it in a hot oven, and turn it out.

—— CITRON. (2) The yolks of three eggs beaten, half a pint of cream, one spoonful of flour, two ounces of citron cut thin; sugar to the taste; put this into large cups buttered; bake them in a tolerably quick oven; when done, turn them out of the cups, and serve.

—— COCOA-NUT. Quarter pound Cocoa-nut grated: same of powdered sugar; three and half ounces butter; whites of six eggs, half tea-spoon of rose-water, and half glass of wine and brandy mixed. Take the thin brown skin from off the meat, and wash the pieces in cold water, and wipe dry. Grate a quarter pound fine. Stir the butter and sugar to a cream, and add the liquor and rose-water to them. Beat the whites of the eggs till they stand alone, and then stir them into the butter and sugar; afterwards sprinkle in the grated nut, and stir hard all the time. Put puff paste into the bottom and sides of the dish, pour in the mixture, and bake in a moderate oven about half an hour. Grate loaf sugar over it, when cold.

—— COTTAGE POTATO OR CAKE. Peel, boil, and mash, a couple of pounds of potatoes: beat them up into a smooth batter, with about three-quarters of a pint of milk, two ounces of moist sugar, and two or three beaten eggs. Bake it about three-quarters of an hour. Three ounces of currants or raisins may be added. Leave out the milk, and add three ounces of butter,—it will make a very nice cake.

—— COTTAGE. Six ounces of currants, half a pound of minced suet, and the same quantity of grated bread, half a grated nutmeg, a table-spoonful of white wine, or rose water; mix all well together, with the beaten yolks of five eggs, to a stiff paste, and with floured hands roll it into twelve or thirteen small puddings in the form of sausages; fry them gently in butter till of a nice brown; roll them well in the frying-pan. Serve with pounded loaf sugar strewed over them, and with a sweet sauce. They may be boiled.

—— CRANBERRY. Stir into a quart of batter, made stiffer than for batter pudding, about a pint of cranberries, and boil as usual. Or, make a paste as for apple pudding, and put in the cranberries, with molasses sufficient to sweeten their acidity. Eaten with sweet sauce.

—— CURD, BOILED. Rub the curd

of two gallons of milk, well drained, through a sieve; then mix with it six eggs, a little cream, two spoonfuls of orange-flower water, half a nutmeg grated, three spoonfuls of flour, and three spoonfuls of bread-crumbs, half a pound of currants, and half a pound of raisins stoned. Let it boil for one hour, in a thick cloth well floured.

—— CURRANT. A pound of currants, a pound of suet, five eggs, four spoonfuls of flour, half a nutmeg, a tea-spoonful of ginger, a little powder sugar and a little salt; boil this for three hours.

—— CURRANT DRY. Chop a pound of suet, and mix it with a pound of flour, half a pound of currants, (well washed), a tea-spoonful of pounded ginger, half a spoonful of tincture of saffron, and a little salt; stir in a sufficient quantity of water, to make it a proper consistence; tie it in a buttered cloth, and boil it for an hour; serve it with melted butter, white wine, and sugar.

—— CUSTARD. Boil a pint of milk, and a quarter of a pint of good cream; thicken with flour and water made perfectly smooth, till it is stiff enough to bear an egg on it; break in the yolks of five eggs; sweeten with powdered loaf sugar; grate in a little nutmeg and the peel of a lemon: add half a glass of good brandy; then whip the whites of the five eggs till quite stiff, and mix gently all together: line a pie-dish with good puff paste, and bake half an hour. N. B.—Ground rice, potato flour, panada, and all puddings made from powders, are, or may be, prepared in the same way.

—— DAMSON. Make a batter with three well-beaten eggs, a pint of milk, and of flour and brown sugar four table-spoonfuls each; stone a pint of damsons, and mix them with the batter; boil it in a buttered basin for an hour and a half.

—— EGG. Melt a quarter of a pound of

butter, and when nearly cold, mix well with it the following ingredients:—ten well-beaten yolks and two whites of eggs, half a pint of rich cream, half a pound of good brown sugar, two table-spoonfuls of flour, a grated nutmeg, and a glass of brandy; bake it with or without a lining of puff paste.

—— FRUIT SUET. Of finely minced suet, flour, grated bread, and cleaned currants, a quarter of a pound each; a tea-spoonful of pounded ginger, one of salt, two ounces of brown sugar, and a tea-cupful of milk; mix all the ingredients well together, and boil it in a cloth for two hours. Serve with a sweet sauce.

—— FAMILY. Mix with a pound of flour half a pound of raisins stoned and chopped, the same quantity of minced suet, a little salt, and milk or water sufficient to make it into a stiff batter; boil it for five hours. Serve with melted butter poured over it. Two well-beaten eggs may be added.

—— GOOSEBERRY, BOILED. This pudding is made in the same manner as Apple pudding.

—— INDIAN. (1) It is a good plan to make this pudding the night before. It requires a great deal of boiling, say four or five hours. Sifted meal and warm milk stirred together pretty stiff; salt and sufficient molasses added. Boil in a stout bag, or tightly covered pan; let not the water get in, and be careful in tying to leave room for the meal to swell. Let the milk you use be warm, not scalding. You may add chopped suet, which is very much liked by some, and likewise ginger, if preferred. If you have not milk, water will answer.

—— INDIAN. (2) Boil in a quart of good milk a tea-cupful of Indian meal, stir it constantly till thick, sweeten it with treacle or brown sugar, and stir in two well-beaten eggs, and an ounce of butter; bake it in a

Dutch oven for half an hour. Half a grated nutmeg may be added, and it may be made without eggs. A boiled Indian meal pudding is made in the same way, and after being mixed with or without eggs in it, it is tied in a buttered and floured cloth, and boiled for two hours. It is eaten with cold or melted butter.

—— JELLY. Beat to a light cream ten ounces of fresh butter, then add by degrees six well-beaten yolks of eggs, and half a pound of loaf sugar pounded; stir in two or three table-spoonfuls of rose water; beat to a stiff froth the whites of six eggs, mix them in lightly; bake it five-and-twenty minutes in a dish lined with puff paste.

—— JENETON. Butter a mould, and ornament it with raisins in festoons, or in any other form; line it with sponge biscuit, and fill it up with a mixture of ratafia and sponge biscuit, then pour a rich custard over the whole, and let it stand for two hours, adding more custard as it soaks into the biscuit. The mould being quite full, tie a cloth over it, and boil it for about an hour.

—— LEMON. (1) Peel four lemons thin; boil them till they are tender; rub them through a hair sieve, and preserve the fine pulp. Take a pound of Naples biscuits, a little grated nutmeg, and two ounces of fresh butter, and pour over them some boiling milk or cream in which a stick of cinnamon has been boiled. When cold, mix with them the pulp of the lemons, and eight eggs well-beaten; sweeten according to taste, and if you choose, add brandy. Edge a dish with good puff paste, put in the mixture; garnish the top with strings of paste, as for tartlets, and bake it in a moderately heated oven.

—— LEMON. (2) Put half a pound of fresh butter with half a pound of loaf sugar, into a saucepan, and keep it stirring over the fire till it boils; put it into an earthen pan, and grate the rind of a large lemon into it, and let it stand till cold; beat eight eggs, and squeeze the juice of the lemon on them; mix the sugar and butter with them; put some rich puff paste at the bottom of a dish, then put in the preparation, and add bits of candied lemon-peel when you have put in the preparation. Bake with great care.

—— LEMON. (3) Boil in water, in a closely covered saucepan, two large lemons till quite tender; take out the seeds, and pound the lemons to a paste; add a quarter of a pound of pounded loaf sugar, the same of fresh butter beaten to a cream, and the yolks of three well-beaten eggs; mix all together, and bake it in a tin lined with puff paste; take it out, strew over the top grated loaf sugar, and serve it upon a napkin.

—— MACARONI. (1) Simmer half a pound of macaroni in plenty of water, and a table-spoonful of salt, till it is tender; but take care not to have it too soft; though tender it should be firm, and the form entirely preserved, and no part beginning to melt (this caution will serve for the preparation of all macaroni). Strain the water from it; beat up five yolks and the whites of two eggs; take half a pint of the best cream, and the breast of a fowl, and some thin slices of ham. Mince the breast of the fowl with the ham; add them with from two to three table-spoonfuls of finely-grated cheese, and season with pepper and salt. Mix all these with the macaroni, and put into a pudding-mould well buttered, and then let it steam in a stewpan of boiling water for about an hour, and serve quite hot, with rich gravy (as in Omelet).

—— MACARONI. (2) Take an ounce or two of the pipe sort of macaroni, and simmer it in a pint of milk, and a bit of lemon-peel and cinnamon, till tender; put it into a dish, with milk, three eggs, but only one white, some sugar, nutmeg, a spoonful of almond-water, and half a glass of raisin wine; lay a nice paste round the edge of the dish, and put it in the oven to bake. If you choose you may put in a layer of orange marmalade, or raspberry-jam: in this case you must not put in the almond-water or ratafia.

—— MARROW. Put into a mug the crumb of a pound loaf, and pour over it a pint and a half of boiling milk; cover it closely for an hour; cut into small bits half a pound of marrow, stone and cut a quarter of a pound of raisins, take the same quantity of nicely-cleaned currants, beat well six eggs, a tea-spoonful of grated lemon-peel, and the same of nutmeg; mix all thoroughly with the bread and milk, sweeten it well with brown sugar, and bake it, with or without a border of puff paste round the dish, three-quarters of an hour. It may be baked in a Dutch oven, and after baking it for three-quarters of an hour, put a tin cover over the top, and place the dish upon a gridiron, over a slow fire, and let it remain for fifteen minutes.

—— MILLET. Wash four table-spoonfuls of the seed, boil it in a quart of milk with grated nutmeg and lemon-peel, and stir in, when a little cooled, an ounce of fresh butter; sweeten with brown sugar and add the well-beaten yolks of four, and the whites of two eggs, and a glass of wine or spirits. Bake it in a buttered dish.

—— MY. Beat up the yolks and whites of three eggs; strain them through a sieve (to keep out the treddles), and gradually add to them about a quarter pint of milk; stir these well together. Rub together in a mortar two ounces of moist sugar and as much grated nutmeg as will lie on a shilling; stir them into the eggs and milk; then put in four ounces of flour, and beat it into a smooth batter; by degrees stir into it seven ounces of suet (minced as fine as possible) and three ounces of bread crumbs. Mix all thoroughly together at least half an hour before you put the pudding into the pot. Put it into an earthen pudding mould, that is well buttered. Tie a cloth over it very tight; put it into boiling water, and boil it three hours. Half a pound of raisins cut in half added to the above, will make a most admirable plum pudding. Grated lemon-peel is also fine.

Don't let the water cease to boil: it will spoil the pudding. And it is always best that puddings be mixed an hour or two before put into the pot, the ingredients get amalgamated, and the whole becomes richer and fuller of flavor.

The above pudding may be baked in an oven, or under meat, as Yorkshire pudding, only add half pint more milk. Should it be above an inch and quarter in thickness, it will take full two hours; and requires careful watching; for if the top gets burned, a bad flavor will pervade the whole pudding. Or, butter some tin patty-pans or saucers, fill them with pudding, and bake about an hour in a Dutch oven.

—— NASSAU. Put into a sauce-pan the whole yolks of eight, and the whites of four eggs, half a pound of pounded loaf sugar, and one pound of fresh butter; stir it over a slow fire for nearly half an hour; line a dish with thin puff paste and lay over the bottom a thick layer of orange marmalade, and then put in the pudding. Bake it for fifteen or twenty minutes.

—— NEW COLLEGE. Half a pound of fresh beef suet, finely minced, the same of currants, a quarter of a pound of grated bread, and of pounded sweet biscuit, half a tea-spoonful of salt, a small nutmeg grated, an ounce of candied orange-peel minced; mix all together with two or three well-beaten eggs, and fry them in butter till of a light brown; shake the pan, and turn them frequently till done enough. Serve with pounded loaf sugar strewed thickly over them.

—— NEWMARKET. Put on to boil a pint of good milk, with half a lemon-peel, a little cinnamon, and a bay leaf; boil gently for five or ten minutes; sweeten with loaf sugar; break the yolks of five, and the whites of three eggs, into a basin; beat them well, and add the milk: beat all well together, and strain through a fine hair sieve, or tamis: have some bread and butter cut very thin; lay a layer of it in a pie-dish, and then a layer of currants, and so on till the dish is nearly full; then pour the custard over it, and bake half an hour.

—— NEWCASTLE, OR CABINET. Butter a half melon mould, or quart basin, and stick all round with dried cherries, or fine raisins, and fill up with bread and butter, &c. as in the above; and steam it an hour and a half.

—— NOTTINGHAM. Peel six good apples; take out the core with the point of a small knife, or an apple corer, if you have one; but be sure to leave the apples whole; fill up where you took the core from with sugar; place them in a pie-dish, and pour over them a nice light batter, prepared as for batter pudding, and bake an hour in a moderate oven.

—— OATMEAL. Sift a pound of oatmeal, chop three-quarters of a pound of suet, mince some onions, and mince all together; season well with pepper and salt; half fill the skins, and boil and dress them as directed in the receipt for ox-blood puddings. Some people think a little sugar an improvement.

—— ORANGE. (1) The yolks of six and the whites of three eggs, well beaten; three table-spoonfuls of orange marmalade, a quarter of a pound of loaf sugar pounded, the same of melted butter; three table-spoonfuls of grated bread, and a quarter of a pint of cream; mix all well together, and bake them in a dish lined with puff paste.

—— ORANGE. (2) Cut in half three large Seville oranges, squeeze and strain the juice; boil the skins till quite soft in a good deal of water, pound them in a mortar, and mix them with nine beaten yolks and four whites of eggs, nearly a pound of pounded loaf suger, the juice of the oranges, and half a pound of melted butter. Bake it in a dish lined with puff paste for half an hour.

—— PEAS. Put a quart of split peas to soak for two hours into warm water; boil them in soft water, with a bit of butter, till sufficiently tender to press through a sieve; pulp them, and add the beaten yolk of one egg, a little pepper and salt, and an ounce of butter. Tie it into a buttered and floured cloth, and put it on in boiling water; boil it nearly an hour.

—— PLUM. (1)  One pound of fresh beef suet, finely minced, one pound of raisins stoned, three table-spoonfuls of flour, five of brown sugar, five well-beaten yolks, and three whites of eggs, a tea-spoonful of salt; mix all the ingredients thoroughly, and boil it in a cloth for four or five hours. Serve with grated loaf sugar, and melted butter poured over it.

—— PLUM. (2)  One pound of raisins, stoned and cut in half: one pound of currants, picked, washed, and dried: one pound beef suet chopped fine: a pound of grated bread, or half pound each of grated bread and flour: eight eggs: quarter pound of sugar: salt-spoon of salt: table-spoon of cinnamon and mace mixed: two grated nutmegs: a glass each of wine and brandy: quarter pound of sugar, and a pint of milk. Prepare all the day before, except the eggs, that you may mix them the next morning: it requires six hours boiling. Beat the eggs lightly, then put to them half the milk and beat together. Stir in the flour and bread; then the sugar by degrees; then the suet and fruit; the fruit to be well floured to keep it from sinking. Stir hard. Now add the spice and liquor, and the remainder of the milk. If it is not thick enough, add more bread or

flour; but if there be too much bread or flour the pudding will be heavy. Wet the cloth in boiling water, shake it out, and sprinkle it with flour. Lay it in a dish and pour into it the pudding. Tie it tight, allowing room to swell. Boil six hours. When you turn it out, stick over the outside blanched almonds in slips or slips of citron, or both. If you add grated lemon-peel to the other ingredients it will much improve the pudding.

—— PLUM. (3)  One pound of the best raisins stoned, half a pound of currants well cleaned, one pound of fresh beef suet finely minced, five table-spoonfuls of grated bread, three of flour, two of brown sugar, one tea-spoonful of pounded ginger, one of cinnanon, and one of salt, six well-beaten eggs, and three wine-glasses of rum, all to be mixed thoroughly together the day before it is to be boiled. Boil it in a cloth or mould for four or five hours. Serve with melted butter, or the following sauce:— Heat two or three table-spoonfuls of sweet cream, and mix it gradually with two well-beaten yolks of eggs; add three table-spoonfuls of white wine, brandy, or rum, and a table-spoonful of sugar; season with grated nutmeg, and stir it over the fire till quite hot; but do not allow it to boil.

—— PLUM. (4)  Four ounces of apples finely minced, the same quantity of currants cleaned and dried, and of grated bread, two ounces of raisins, stoned and minced, two of pounded loaf sugar, half a nutmeg grated, a little candied orange or lemon peel, four well-beaten eggs, one ounce and a half of melted butter just warm; mix all the ingredients well together, and boil it in a buttered shape for four hours. If the pudding does not fill the shape, add a slice of the crumb of bread at the bottom. Serve with a sweet sauce.

—— PLUM, WITHOUT EGGS. Half a pound of grated bread, a quarter of a pound of finely-minced suet, a table-spoonful of flour, half a pound of currants cleaned, rather more than two ounces of brown sugar, a glass of brandy; mix all together with a sufficient quantity of milk to make it into a stiff batter; boil it in a cloth for four hours. It may be baked, adding half a pound of stoned raisins, and a little candied orange and lemon-peel.

—— POTATO. (1) Boil three large mealy potatoes, mash them very smoothly, with one ounce of butter, and two or three table-spoonfuls of thick cream; add three well-beaten eggs, a little salt, grated nutmeg, and a table-spoonful of brown sugar. Beat all well together, and bake it in a buttered dish, for half an hour in an oven, and three-quarters of an hour in a Dutch oven A few currants may be added to the pudding.

—— POTATO. (2) Boil half a pint of milk, and the same quantity of cream, with a stick of cinnamon, and the peel of a lemon; strain it, and stir in gradually three table-spoonfuls of potato flour, mix it very smoothly, and add six well-beaten eggs; sweeten with pounded loaf sugar; stick all round a buttered tin mold, dried cherries, or stoned raisins, put in the pudding, and put a bit of buttered linen over the top, and then the cover of the mould; place it in a sauce-pan of boiling water, boil it for an hour and a half; take care the water does not boil over the mould. Serve with a sweet sauce.

—— POTATO-FLOUR. Boil some cinnamon, lemon-peel, and sugar, in a quart of milk; strain, and stir it with three table-spoonfuls of potato flour previously mixed smooth with a little cold milk; stir it till it be nearly cold; add four well-beaten eggs, a glass of sweet wine, or two table-spoonfuls of spirits, and a little marmalade. Bake it in a Dutch oven.

—— PRUNE. Stew a pound of prunes with half a pint of Port wine, a quarter of a pint of water, and a large table-spoonful of brown sugar; break the stones, and put the kernels with the fruit; spread it over a sheet of puff paste, wet the edges, and roll it into the form of a bolster; tie it firmly in a buttered and floured cloth, and boil it between two and three hours. Serve with sweet wine sauce.

—— QUINCE. Take a sufficient number of ripe quinces to yield a pound of pulp, to which put half a pound of powder-sugar, cinnamon, and ginger, of each two drachms, pounded; mix them well. Beat up the yolks of eight eggs in a pint of cream, add the quince, &c. stir the whole together, flour a cloth, tie the pudding in, and boil it.

—— RATAFIA. Pound, with a little rose-water, two ounces of blanched sweet almonds, and half a quarter of a pound of ratafia cakes, add the well-beaten yolks of six, and the whites of two eggs, a pint of thick cream, two glasses of white wine, and one ounce of pounded loaf sugar. Bake it in a dish, lined with puff paste, for three-quarters of an hour.

—— REGENT'S. Rub an earthenware mould with butter, and cover the bottom with bloom raisins stoned; cut thin slices of the crumb of bread, butter, and lay one or two over the raisins; upon that put a layer of ratafia cakes, then one of bread and butter, and raisins; do this till the mould is nearly full, and pour over it the following mixtures: a pint of cream well sweetened with pounded loaf sugar, and mixed with four well-beaten yolks of eggs, a glass of brandy, and two table-spoonfuls of rose-water; let it soak one or two hours; put over the top a piece of writing-paper buttered, and tie over it a cloth. Boil it for one hour and a half, and serve it with wine sauce.

—— GROUND RICE, RICH. (1) Stir into a quarter of a pound of ground rice, a pint and a half of new milk; put it into a saucepan, and keep stirring it till it boils;

then add three ounces of melted butter, the same quantity of sugar, half a grated nutmeg, and a tea-spoonful of grated lemon-peel; mix it very well, and when cold, add the well-beaten yolks of four, and the white of one egg, with a glass of ratafia, and half a one of orange-flower or rose water; bake it in a dish lined with puff paste for three-quarters of an hour. Before serving, strew over the top grated loaf sugar.

—— GROUND RICE. (2) Mix till quite smooth, with a small tea-cupful of ground rice, a quart of good milk, stir it over the fire till it boils, and let it boil for three minutes; put it into a basin, and when nearly cold, add the well-beaten yolks of six, and the whites of two eggs, with a teacupful of sweet wine, or a glass of spirits; put it into a buttered dish, and bake it for three-quarters of an hour, or for one hour in a Dutch oven, in the same way as the marrow pudding is done. Any sort of preserve may be put into the bottom of the dish, and a sweet sauce may be served with it.

—— GROUND RICE. (3) Boil in a pint of milk a quarter of a pound of flour of rice, with two table-spoonfuls of rose water, and half the peel of a lemon, stir it till thick, take it off, and mix in a quarter of a pound of butter, half a grated nutmeg, the well-beaten yolks of four, and the whites of three eggs; sweeten it with brown sugar, pick out the lemon-peel, and boil it in a buttered basin, which must be completely filled. Serve with a sauce made with a glass of white wine, boiled in melted butter, and sweetened with brown sugar.

—— RICE, BAKED OR BOILED. Wash in cold water and pick very clean six ounces of rice, put it in a quart stewpan three parts filled with cold water, set it on the fire, and let it boil five minutes; pour away the water, and put in one quart of milk, a roll of lemon-peel, and a bit of cinnamon; let it boil gently till the rice is quite tender; it will take at least one hour and a quarter; be careful to stir it every five minutes; take it off the fire, and stir in an ounce and a half of fresh butter, and beat up three eggs on a plate, a salt-spoonful of nutmeg, two ounces of sugar; put it into the pudding, and stir it till it is quite smooth; line a pie-dish big enough to hold it with puff paste, notch it round the edge, put in your pudding, and bake it three-quarters of an hour: this will be a nice firm pudding.

If you like it to eat more like custard, add one more egg, and half a pint more milk; it will be better a little thinner when boiled; one hour will boil it. If you like it in little puddings, butter small tea-cups, and either bake or boil them, half an hour will do either: you may vary the pudding by putting in candied lemon or orange peel, minced very fine, or dried cherries, or three ounces of currants, or raisins, or apples minced fine. If the puddings are baked or boiled, serve them with white wine sauce, or butter and sugar.

—— RICE. Boil a quarter of a pound of rice in water till it is soft, then drain it in a sieve, and pound it in a mortar; add five well-beaten yolks of eggs, a quarter of a pound of butter, the same proportion of sugar, a small nutmeg, and half the rind of a lemon grated; work them well together for twenty minutes, and add a pound of cleaned currants; mix it all well and boil it in a pudding cloth for an hour and a half. Serve with wine sauce.

—— RICE, WITHOUT EGGS. Weigh six ounces of rice, six of brown sugar, and three and a half of fresh butter; break the butter into small bits; wash the rice in several waters; put all into a pudding dish, and fill it up with good milk; let it soak some hours. Bake it in a moderate oven for nearly two hours, and as the milk wastes, fill up the dish with more, till the rice be swelled and soft; then let it brown.

—— RICH. Put into a saucepan four ounces of fresh butter, six ounces of pounded loaf sugar, six of marmalade, and six ounces of eggs, well beaten; stir all one way till it be thoroughly warmed; it must not be allowed to boil. Bake it in a dish lined with puff paste.

—— SAGO. (1) Boil five table-spoonfuls of sago, well picked and washed, in a quart of water, also half the peel of a lemon, and a stick of cinnamon; when it is rather thick, add half a pint of white wine, and sweeten it with good brown sugar; beat six yolks and three whites of eggs, pick out the lemon-peel and cinnamon, mix all well together, and bake it in a dish with or without puff paste.

—— SAGO. (2) Wash half a pound of sago in several waters (warm); then put it into a saucepan with a pint of good milk, and a little cinnamon; let it boil till thick, stirring frequently; pour it into a pan, and beat up with it half a pound of fresh butter, add to it the yolks of eight, and whites of four eggs, beaten separately, half a glass of white wine, sugar according to taste, and a little flour; mix all together well, and boil it. Serve with sweet sauce.

—— SALT. Take a pint of milk, four dessert-spoonfuls of flour, a little suet, shred fine, four eggs, salt, and pounded ginger; mix first the eggs and milk, then add the flour, &c.; put more flour, if necessary, to give it consistence; tie your pudding in a buttered cloth, and boil it two hours.

—— SCOTCH. Eight well-beaten yolks and three whites of eggs, half a pound of pounded loaf sugar, a quarter of a pound of melted butter, the grated peel and juice of one lemon; mix all together, and bake it in a dish lined with puff paste; turn it out to serve, and strew over the top grated loaf sugar.

—— SIPPET. Cut a small loaf into extremely thin slices, and put a layer of them at the bottom of a dish, then a layer of marrow, or beef suet, a layer of currants, and then a layer of bread again, &c., and so continue until the dish is filled; mix four eggs, well beaten, with a quart of cream, a nutmeg, a quarter of a pound of sugar, and pour over; set it in the oven, it will take half an hour baking.

—— SHROPSHIRE. Of fresh beef suet finely minced, of brown bread grated, and of brown sugar, one pound each, one nutmeg grated, a tea-cupful of brandy, eight well-beaten yolks, and four whites of eggs; mix all well together, and boil it in a cloth or mould for four hours. Serve it with a sauce of melted butter, sugar, and two table-spoonfuls of brandy.

—— SPRING FRUIT. Peel and well wash four dozen sticks of rhubarb: put into a stew-pan with the pudding a lemon, a little cinnamon, and as much moist sugar as will make it quite sweet; set it over a fire, and reduce it to a marmalade; pass through a hair sieve, and proceed as directed for the Boston pudding, leaving out the lemon-juice, as the rhubarb will be found sufficiently acid of itself.

—— SPEAKER'S. Stone and weigh three-quarters of a pound of raisins. Rub with butter a plain oval mould, and stick upon it some of the raisins, in stripes or circles. Cut some thin slices of bread without the crust, dry them awhile before the fire, butter, and cut them into strips about an inch and a quarter wide; line the mould with part of the bread, then put a layer of raisins, and strew over a table-spoonful of pounded loaf sugar; add a layer of the bread and butter; fill the shape nearly full, putting bread and butter on the top. Mix with a pint of good milk, the well-beaten yolks of four eggs, a table-spoonful of sugar, one and a half of rose-water, and a glass of brandy; pour this over the pudding, and let it soak one or two hours. Bake it three-quarters of an hour. It may be boiled by steam for an hour and a half.

—— SQUASH. One good squash stewed and well bruised; six large apples stewed tender; mix them well together; add seven spoonfuls of bread crumbs; half pint of milk; two spoonfuls of rose-water, two of wine; six eggs; one grated nutmeg; salt and sugar to taste. Beat all together till smooth, and put in a dish lined with puff paste. Bake three-quarters of an hour.

—— SUET, WIGGY'S WAY. Suet, a quarter of a pound; flour, three table-spoonfuls; eggs, two; and a little grated ginger; milk, half a pint. Mince the suet as fine as possible, roll it with the rolling-pin so as to mix it well with the flour; beat up the eggs, mix them with the milk, and then mix all together; wet your cloth well in boiling water, flour it, tie it loose, put it into boiling water, and boil it an hour and a quarter. Mrs. Glasse has it, "when you have made your water boil, then put your pudding into your pot."

—— SUET. Mix six table-spoonfuls of grated bread with a pound of finely-minced fresh beef suet, or that of a loin of mutton, one pound of flour, two tea-spoonfuls of salt, six well-beaten eggs, and nearly a pint of milk. Boil it in a cloth four or five hours. Serve it plain, or with a sweet sauce.

—— APPLE SUET. Of finely minced fresh mutton suet, grated apples, flour, and brown sugar, six ounces each, half a grated nutmeg, a tea-spoonful of salt, and four well-beaten eggs, all well mixed together; boiled for two hours, and served with a sweet sauce.

—— SUET, OR DUMPLINGS. Chop six ounces of suet very fine; put it in a basin with six ounces of flour, two ounces of bread crumbs, and a tea-spoonful of salt; stir it all well together: beat two eggs on a plate, add to them six table-spoonfuls of milk, put it by degrees into the basin, and stir it all well together; divide it into six dumplings, and tie them separate, previously dredging the cloth lightly with flour. Boil them one hour. This is very good the next day fried in a little butter. The above will make a good pudding, boiled in an earthen ware mould, with the addition of one more egg, a little more milk, and two ounces of suet. Boil it two hours.

N. B.—The most economical way of making suet dumplings, is to boil them without a cloth in a pot with beef or mutton; no eggs are then wanted, and the dumplings are quite as light without: roll them in flour before you put them into the pot; add six ounces of currants washed and picked, and you have currant pudding: or divided into six parts, currant dumplings; a little sugar will improve them.

—— SWEETMEAT. Slice thin, of orange, lemon-peel, and citron, an ounce each; lay them at the bottom of a dish, lined with a light puff paste; mix with half a pound of butter melted, the yolks of seven eggs and the whites of two, and five ounces of sugar; pour this over the sweetmeats, and set it in the oven; it will take rather more than half an hour baking.

—— TANSY. Pour over a thick slice of the crumb of bread a quart of boiling milk; cover it till cold. Beat the yolks of four and the whites of two eggs. Pound some tansy with two or three leaves of spinach; squeeze the juice, and put as much of it as will make the pudding a good green color, a glass of brandy, half a grated nutmeg, and four ounces of fresh butter; mix all the ingredients, sweeten, and put it into a saucepan, and stir it over the fire till it be hot. Bake it in a buttered dish for half an hour. Before serving, strew grated loaf sugar over the top.

—— TRANSPARENT. Put eight eggs well-beaten into a stewpan with half a pound of sugar, pounded fine, half a pound of butter, and some nutmeg grated. Set it on the fire, and keep constantly stirring till it thickens. Then set it into a basin to cool; put a rich puff paste round the edge of the dish; pour in the pudding, and bake it in a moderate oven. It will cut light and clear. Candied orange and citron may be added, if you think proper.

—— TAPIOCA. Put four table-spoonfuls of tapioca into a quart of milk, and let it remain all night, then put a spoonful of brandy, some lemon-peel, and a little spice; let them boil gently, add four eggs, and the whites well beaten, and a quarter of a pound of sugar. Bake it.

—— TREACLE. Mix together a pound of stoned raisins, three-quarters of a pound of shred suet, a pound of flour, a pint of milk, a table-spoonful of treacle, grated ginger, and pounded spice; when well stirred up, tie it in a floured cloth, and boil it four hours.

—— WEST COUNTRY. Mix, with four well-beaten eggs, half a pound of apples finely minced, the same quantity of grated bread, and of well-cleaned currants, a quarter of a pound of brown sugar, and half a tea-spoonful of grated nutmeg. This pudding may be either boiled or baked, and instead of grated bread, four ounces of whole rice may be used, which must be boiled in milk, strained, and allowed to be cold before being mixed with the other ingredients. This pudding is boiled one hour and a half, and served with a sweet sauce.

—— WHITE. Boil in a quart of milk two table-spoonfuls of rose-water; add to two well-beaten eggs, three table-spoonfuls of flour, and a little salt; stir it into the milk, and if not thick, dredge in a little more flour; just before it is taken off the fire, put in a bit of fresh butter the size of a walnut. Serve it with red currant jelly upon the top of it.

—— WHORTLEBERRY. This pudding may be made both of flour and indian meal. Use a pint of milk, some molasses, and a little salt, stirred quite stiff with meal, and a quart of berries mixed in with a spoon. Tie the bag loose, and let it boil three hours. When made of flour, prepare it like batter puddings, rather stiff to keep the berries from settling. Boil two hours. Tie the bag loose.

—— WILTSHIRE. Mix, with three well-beaten eggs and a pint of milk, as much flour as will make it a thick batter, and a little salt; beat it for some minutes, stir in gently a large tea-cupful of picked red currants; boil it in a cloth for two hours, turn it out upon the dish it is to be served in, cut it into slices about three-quarters of an inch thick, but do not separate them; put between each a thin slice of butter, and some brown sugar, and serve it hot.

—— YORKSHIRE, UNDER ROAST MEAT. This pudding is an especially excellent accompaniment to a sirloin of beef,—loin of veal,—or any fat and juicy joint. Six table-spoonfuls of flour, three eggs, a tea-spoonful of salt, and a pint of milk, so as to make a middling stiff batter, a little stiffer than you would for pancakes; beat it up well, and take care it is not lumpy; put a dish under the meat, and let the drippings drop into it till it is quite hot and well greased; then pour in the batter;—when the upper surface is brown and set, turn it, that both sides may be brown alike: if you wish it to cut firm, and the pudding an inch thick, it will take two hours at a good fire.

N. B.—The true Yorkshire pudding is about half an inch thick when done; but it is the fashion in London to make them full twice that thickness.

PUFFS. (1) Roll out puff paste nearly a

quarter of an inch thick, and, with a small saucer, or tin cutter of that size, cut it into round pieces: place upon one side raspberry or strawberry jam, or any sort of preserved fruit, or stewed apples; wet the edges, fold over the other side, and press it round with the finger and thumb. Or cut the paste into the form of a diamond, lay on the fruit, and fold over the paste, so as to give it a triangular shape. *See Paste.*

PUFFS. (2) Put into a saucepan a pint of milk, boil slowly, and stir in flour till it be very thick, like paste; when cold, mix with it six well-beaten eggs, a table-spoonful of sugar, half a nutmeg, and the peel of a small lemon grated, and a table-spoonful of brandy; beat it well together for fifteen minutes, and when quite light, drop it from a dessert-spoon into a pan of boiling clarified suet or lard. Serve with pounded loaf sugar strewed over them.

PUFFS OF PRESERVED FRUIT. Roll out, a quarter of an inch thick, good puff paste, and cut it into pieces four inches square; lay a small quantity of any kind of jam on each, double them over, and cut them into square, triangle, or, with a tin cutter, half moons; lay them with paper on a baking-plate; ice them, bake them about twenty minutes, taking care not to color the icing.

PUNCH. *See Justice's Sirup.*

## Q.

QUAILS, HUNTERS. Put the quails in a saucepan, with a little butter, a bay-leaf, sweet herbs, salt and pepper; set them on a fierce fire, and keep shaking them until they are tender, when add a dessert-spoonful of flour, half a glass of white wine, and a little stock, when this is thick, and quite hot (without boiling); take it from the fire and serve.

QUAILS, SPANISH. Mix the juice of a lemon with some butter, salt, and pepper; pick, and prepare eight quails, stuff them well with the above mixture; then fasten the legs to the body, leaving the claws free; truss them a good shape, and put them into a saucepan on slices of bacon, cover them also with slices, add a gravy, moistened with equal portions of white wine and stock; set them on the fire for half an hour; then take them out, drain and untie the birds, place each on a piece of fried bread the size of the quail, and serve with a clear spanish sauce, with the addition of a little glaze.

QUAILS, HOT PIE. Make a raised crust in the usual way, spread over the bottom of it some *farce cuite* mixed with the livers of the quails, pounded, and some sweet herbs; take eignt quails, take out the thigh bones, and half dress them in a little butter and sweet herbs; when cold, stuff each with some of the above-mentioned farce, arrange them in the pie, fill up the intestines and the centre with the remainder of the farce, season it well, lay slices of bacon over the quails; wet the edges of the paste with water, cover the pie with a very thin crust; do it over with egg, and decorate it according to fancy. Put it into the oven to bake, an hour and a quarter will suffice. When done, raise the top carefully, remove the bacon, take off all the fat, pour in some good gravy, and serve.

QUAILS, ROASTED. Truss the birds, and stuff them with beef-suet and sweet herbs, both shred very small, seasoned with salt, pepper, and nutmeg; fasten them to a spit, and put them to the fire; baste with salt and water when they first begin to get warm; then dredge them with flour, and baste with butter. Put an anchovy, two or three shallots, and the juice of a Seville orange into a little rich gravy; set it on the fire, shake it about, and when the anchovy is dissolved, serve it with the quails. Garnish the dish with fried bread crumbs. These birds are sometimes roasted, wrapped first in a slice of bacon, and then in a vine-leaf. They should be kept at a moderate distance from the fire.

QUAILS, STEWED. Put a little butter worked up with flour, and a few green onions into a stewpan; when brown, put in some quails, a glass of wine, the same of stock, parsley, some more small onions, a bay-leaf, and two or three cloves; stew these till the quails are sufficiently done. Garnish your dish with cock's-combs, artichoke bottoms, fried bread, &c.

QUEEN'S POTAGE. Draw, wash, and clean three chickens, or young fowls, put them into a stewpan, with a bunch of parsley and some well-seasoned boiling veal stock; let it stew for an hour; take out the fowls, and pound all the meat to a fine paste in a marble mortar, with the crumb of two penny loaves, previously soaked in the soup, and the yolks of three or four hard boiled eggs; rub all through a sieve, and add it to the soup stirring it well. Put a quart of rich cream on the fire, and stir it till it boils, and then mix it with the soup and serve it quite hot.

QUEEN OR HEART CAKES. One pound of sifted sugar, one pound of butter, eight eggs, one pound and a quarter of flour, two ounces of currants, and half a nutmeg grated. Cream the butter, and mix it well with the sugar and spice, then put in half the eggs, and beat it ten minutes—add the remainder of the eggs, and work it ten minutes longer—stir in the flour lightly, and the currants afterwards,—then take small tin pans of any shape (hearts the most usual), rub the inside of each with butter, fill and bake them a few minutes in a hot oven, on a sheet of matted wire, or on a baking plate—when done, remove them as early as possible from the pans.

QUEEN'S DROPS. Leave out four ounces of flour from the last receipt, and add two ounces more of currants, and two ounces of candied peel, cut small—work it the same as in the last receipt, and when ready put the mixture into a biscuit funnel, and lay them out in drops about the size of half a crown, on white paper,—bake them in a hot oven, and when *nearly cold*, take them from the paper.

QUINCE COMPOTE. Take six quinces, cut them in halves, and core them; scald and pare them neatly. Put some clear sirup into a preserving-pan, with the juice of a lemon; when hot, add the quinces, and give them a boil together; drain the fruit, arrange it in the *compotier*; leave the sirup to thicken a little, and pour it over the quinces.

QUINCE CREAM. Take four or five ripe quinces, and roast them, but not to soften them; pare, core, slice them thin, and then boil them slowly in a pint of good cream, with a little ginger; when tolerably thick, strain it, add sugar to your taste, and flavor it with rose-water.

QUINCE JELLY. Quinces for jelly ought not to be quite ripe, they should, however, be of a fine yellow color; take off the down which covers them, quarter, core, put them into a saucepan, with water enough to cover them; set them on the fire, and when soft, lay the pieces on a sieve to drain, pressing them very slightly; strain the liquor, and measure it; clarify, and boil to *casse* an equal quantity of sugar; then take it off, add the liquor to it, stirring it well; when mixed, put it on the fire, still stirring; as soon as the jelly spreads over the spoon, and falls from it like molasses; take it from the fire, and when cold, pour it into pots.

QUINCES TO KEEP. Gather the fruit quite ripe, but perfectly sound; rub each carefully with a clean cloth, to remove the down; then quarter, and put them into bottles, corked tight. Give them half an hour's boil in the *bain-marie*.

QUINCE MARMALADE. Gather the

fruit when fully ripe, and of a fine yellow; pare, quarter, and core it. Put the quinces into a saucepan, with a little water, set them on the fire until they are quite soft; then take them out, and lay them on a sieve to drain; rub them through, weigh the pulp; boil an equal quantity of sugar to *petit casse*, then add the pulp, stir them together over the fire, until it will fall from the spoon like a jelly; the marmalade is then fit to be put into pots, and when cold, cover them close.

QUINCES TO PICKLE. Pare and cut half a dozen quinces into small pieces, and put them, with a gallon of water, and two pounds of honey, into a large saucepan; mix them together well, and set them on a slow fire for half an hour: strain the liquor into a jar; when quite cold, wipe the quinces perfectly dry, and put them into it; cover them very close.

QUINCES PRESERVED IN WHITE JELLY. Take as many quinces as you may require, choose them sound; pare, quarter, and core them, strewing powder-sugar over as you do them, filling up all the holes also with sugar; throw in a small quantity of water, and when all are cut, add more water, and set them on a fierce fire to boil quickly. As soon as the quinces are tender, and the sirup clear, add some apple-jelly, give the whole one boil, and then pour it into glasses; when cold, drain off the sirup and jelly, put them into a saucepan, and let them boil as quick as you can; just before the jelly is taken off, put in a small quantity of musk, or any other ingredient you may wish to flavor the preserve with, and then pour it in the glasses again, over the quinces, and when cold cover them. This may also be colored red by adding a small quantity of prepared cochineal; in this case, the jelly should be red too.

QUINCES THE SPANISH WAY. Pare and core ten pounds of quinces, put them into a stewpan with a pint and a half of water and two pounds of fine sugar, set them on a slow fire, and when they begin to dry,

moisten them with rose-water and sack, or white wine; then press the paste through a coarse sieve, add two pounds of sugar, a little orange-flower and rose water. When sufficiently done, it will come off clean, if dropped on a plate; then set it aside to cool. Put it into shallow pots, strew perfumed comfits over, and cover them close.

QUINCES, SIRUP OF. Pare and scrape some very ripe quinces into a linen cloth, press out the juice, which put in a very warm place, or where it is exposed to the sun, until all the fecula falls to the bottom; then strain it well, and for every quarter of a pound of juice, take one pound of sugar; mix them together, and boil the whole to *perle*; take it off, and when the sirup is nearly cold, it may be bottled. Take care to keep the bottles well corked.

QUINCE TART. Take some preserved quinces, make a sirup with some sugar and water, of which, and the preserve, take an equal weight, and put it into a preserving-pan; boil, skim, and then put in the fruit; when tolerably clear, lay the quinces in a tart-dish with puff paste as usual; cover and bake it; as soon as it is done raise the top gently, pour in the sirup, ice it, and serve.

QUIN'S SAUCE. *See Sauce.*

QUINTESSENCE OF ANCHOVY. The goodness of this preparation depends almost entirely on having fine mellow fish, that have been in pickle long enough (*i e.* about twelve months) to dissolve easily, yet are not at all rusty.

Choose those that are in the state they come over in, not such as have been put into fresh pickle, mixed with red paint, which some add to improve the complexion of the fish; it has been said, that others have a trick of putting anchovy liquor on pickled sprats; you will easily discover this by washing one of them, and tasting the flesh of it, which in the fine anchovy is mellow, red, and high-flavored, and the bone moist and oily. Make only as much as will soon be used, the fresher it is the better.

Put ten or twelve anchovies into a mortar, and pound them to a pulp; put this into a very clean iron, or silver, or very well tinned saucepan; then put a large table-spoonful of cold spring-water (we prefer good vinegar) into the mortar; shake it round, and pour it to the pounded anchovies, set them by the side of a slow fire, very frequently stirring them together till they are melted, which they will be in the course of five minutes. Now stir in a quarter of a drachm of good cayenne pepper, and let it remain by the side of the fire for a few minutes longer; then, while it is warm, rub it through a hair sieve, with the back of a wooden spoon.

The essence of anchovy, is made with double the above quantity of water, as they are of opinion that it ought to be so thin as not to hang about the sides of the bottle; when it does, the large surface of it is soon acted upon by the air, and becomes rancid and spoils all the rest of it.

A roll of thin-cut lemon-peel infused with the anchovy, imparts a fine, fresh, delicate, aromatic flavor, which is very grateful; this is only recommended when you make sauce for immediate use; it will keep much better without: if you wish to acidulute it, instead of water make it with artificial lemon-juice.

wwwwww

## R.

RABBITS. (1) Truss your rabbits short, lay them in a basin of warm water for ten minutes, then put them into plenty of water, and boil them about half an hour; if large ones, three-quarters; if very old, an hour: smother them with plenty of white onion sauce, mince the liver, and lay it round the dish, or make liver sauce, and send it up in a boat.

*Obs.*—Ask those you are going to make liver sauce for, if they like plain liver sauce, or liver and parsley, or liver and lemon sauce.

*N. B.*—It will save much trouble to the carver, if the rabbit be cut up in the kitchen into pieces fit to help at table, and the head divided, one-half laid at each end, and slices of lemon and the liver, chopped very finely, laid on the sides of the dish.

At all events, cut off the head before you send it to table, we hardly remember that the thing ever lived if we don't see the head, while it may excite ugly ideas to see it cut up in an attitude imitative of life; besides, for the preservation of the head, the poor animal sometimes suffers a slower death.

RABBITS. (2) If your fire is clear and sharp, thirty minutes will roast a young, and forty a full grown rabbit. When you lay it down, baste it with butter, and dredge it lightly and carefully with flour, that you may have it frothy, and of a fine light brown. While the rabbit is roasting, boil its liver with some parsley; when tender, chop them together, and put half the mixture into some melted butter, reserving the other half for garnish, divided into little hillocks. Cut off the head, and lay half on each side of the dish.

*Obs.*—A fine, well-grown (but young) warren rabbit, kept sometime after it has been killed, and roasted with a stuffing in its belly, eats very like a hare, to the nature of which it approaches. It is nice, nourishing food when young, but hard and unwholesome when old.

RABBIT, BROILED. Take a couple of young rabbits, cut them up, and put them to steep for a few hours in a little oil, mixed with parsley, leeks, a few mushrooms, and a clove of garlic, all shred fine, salt and pepper; roll each piece of rabbit in a rasher of bacon, and put them, with a part of the seasoning, into pieces of white paper; butter the papers inside; broil upon a gridiron over a very slow fire, and serve hot in the papers.

RABBITS, IN A FRICASSEE. Take two fine white rabbits, and cut them in pieces, by cutting off the legs, shoulders, and back; blanch them in boiling water, and skim them for one minute; stir a few trimmings of mushrooms in a stewpan over the fire, with a bit of butter, till it begins to fry, then stir in a spoonful of flour; mix into the flour, a little at a time, nearly a quart of good *consomme*, which set on the fire, and when it boils, put the rabbits in, and let them boil gently till done, then put them into another stewpan, and reduce the sauce till nearly as thick as paste; mix in about half a pint of good boiling cream, and when it becomes the thickness of *bechamelle* sauce in general, squeeze it through the tammy to the rabbits; make it very hot, shake in a few mushrooms, the yolk of an egg, and a little cream, then serve it to table. Rabbits may also be preserved, white or brown, in the same manner as chickens.

RABBIT, MINCED. Take the remains of a roasted rabbit, cut off all the meat, and mince it with a little roast mutton. Then break the bones of the rabbit into small pieces, and put them into a stewpan, with a slice of butter, some shallots, half a clove of garlic, thyme, a bay-leaf, and basil; give these a few turns over the fire, then shake in a little flour; moisten with a glass of red wine, and the same quantity of stock, and let it boil over a slow fire for half an hour; strain it off, and put in the minced meat, adding salt and coarse pepper; heat the whole, without boiling, and serve hot: garnish with fried bread.

RABBITS IN A MINUTE. Cut your rabbits into pieces, wipe them perfectly dry; put a quarter of a pound of butter into a stewpan, set it on the fire, and when warm, put in the rabbit with a little pounded spice, salt, pepper, and grated nutmeg; let the fire be brisk, and as soon as the pieces are browned, add a little shred parsley and shallots, leave it three or four minutes longer on the fire, and then serve. Ten or fifteen minutes are sufficient to cook this dish.

RABBIT PIE. Cut a couple of young rabbits into quarters, and bruise a quarter of a pound of bacon in a mortar, with the livers, some pepper, salt, a little mace, parsley, cut small, and a few leaves of sweet basil; when these are all beaten fine, line your pie-dish with a nice crust, then put a layer of the seasoning at the bottom of the dish, and put in the rabbits; pound some more bacon in a mortar, mix with it some fresh butter, and cover the rabbits with it, and over that lay thin slices of bacon; put on the cover, and place it in the oven; it will be done in about two hours; when baked, take off the cover, take out the bacon and skim off the fat, and if there is not a sufficient quantity of gravy, add some rich mutton or veal gravy.

RABBIT PIE, RAISED. Cut your rabbits in pieces, and put them into a stewpan, with a bit of fresh butter, lemon-juice, pepper, salt, parsley, thyme, shallots, chopped very fine, and a little pounded mace. When the pieces of rabbit are about half done, lay them on a dish, and when cold, raise the crust; put light forcemeat at the bottom, the rabbit upon it, and more forcemeat upon the top. Cover it, and put it in a moderate oven to bake gently; when done, take off the cover, and add a ragout of sweetbreads cock's combs, &c., and serve.

RABBITS, PORTUGUESE. Cut off the heads of a couple of rabbits, turn the backs upwards, the two legs stripped to the end, and trussed with a couple of skewers in the same manner as chickens, the wings turned like the pinions of a chicken; lard and roast them with good gravy; if they are intended for boiling, they should not be larded, but be served with bacon, and greens; or celery sauce.

RABBITS, POTTED. Take two or three young, but full-grown rabbits, cut them up, and take off the leg bones at the thigh, season them well with pepper, mace, cayenne, salt, and allspice, all in very fine powder, and put them into a small pan, placing them as closely together as possble. Make the top as smooth as you can. Keep out the heads and carcasses, but take off the meat about the neck. Put plenty of butter, and let the whole bake gently. Let it remain in the pan for two days, then put it into small pots, adding butter. The livers should also be put in.

RABBIT PRESERVED. Having boned a rabbit, lard it with bacon and ham; season it well inside and out, roll it up, beginning with the legs, make it tight, and tie it. Put it into a stew-pan, with some oil, thyme, bay-leaf, and basil; set these on the fire till done enough (but without boiling). When sufficiently cooked, take out the rabbit, drain, let it cool, and then cut it into small pieces, which put into bottles; fill them with oil and cover with wet bladders. When required for table, take them out, cut them into fillets, and place on a dish with shred parsley and oil.

RABBITS PULLED. Half boil your rabbits, with an onion, a little whole pepper, a bunch of sweet herbs, a piece of lemon-peel; pull the flesh into flakes; put to it a little of the liquor, a bit of butter rolled in flour, pepper, salt, nutmeg, chopped parsley, and the liver boiled and bruised; boil this up, shaking it round, and serve.

RABBITS, ROASTED. Truss them for roasting, and stuff them with the liver minced raw, grated bread, and ham, butter or suet, and chopped parsley, seasoned with a little lemon thyme, grated nutmeg, salt, and pepper, and bound with an egg beaten. Sew them up, and roast them before a quick fire, and baste them with butter. Serve them with gravy, or melted butter with lemon pickle in it. Two will take an hour to roast. They may also be fricasseed or fried, cut into joints, with plenty of fried parsley, and served with a sauce made of the liver and some parsley chopped, and mixed in melted butter, with a little pepper and salt, or made

into a pie the same as chickens.

RABBIT SOUP. Cut an old rabbit into pieces, put them into a quart of water; boil it well, take out all the bones, and beat the meat in a marble mortar, as for potting; add a little salt, mace, and white pepper, to your taste; stir it into the liquor the rabbit was boiled in, with the addition of a very little cream.

N. B. The meat of the whole rabbit is too much for one quart; query, would it not be enough for two?

RABBITS STEWED, WITH A BROWN SAUCE, OR WITH A WHITE SAUCE: Wash and clean the rabbits well, let them lie for two or three hours in cold water, cut them into joints; wash and dry them in a cloth, dust them with flour, and fry them of a light brown with butter, and stew them in the following sauce: Brown three ounces of butter in a stewpan, with a table-spoonful of flour, a minced onion, some pepper and salt; add a pint of gravy and the rabbits, stew them till they are tender, and a little before serving, stir in a table-spoonful of ketchup. When it is wished to dress with a white sauce, the rabbits are not fried, but stewed in white stock, which is seasoned with white pepper, and salt, and thickened with a piece of butter mixed with flour. A few minutes before serving, a little cream is added, and a table-spoonful of lemon pickle.

RADISHES IN BROTH. Take some young radishes, pick and scald them, cut them into halves or quarters according to their size, and boil them with a slice of bacon in some stock. In a little time take them out, drain, and put them into another stewpan, with *consomme*, or veal gravy, and a bit of butter rolled in flour. Let them stew gently in this till they are flavored, of a good color, and the sauce pretty thick; then serve them.

RAGOUT POWDER. Two ounces of truffles, two of dried mushrooms, the peel of a lemon, and the same of a Seville orange grated, half a grated nutmeg, half an ounce of mace, the same of pepper, and one drachm of cayenne, dry them all well before the fire, pound them to a fine powder, add one ounce of salt, sift the powder through a sieve, and keep it it in a bottle for use.

RAGOUT OF SNIPES. Pick six or eight snipes very nicely, but do not wash them; take out the inside. Roast the birds, and cut off all the meat from the breasts, in thin slices; pound the bones, legs, and backs, in a mortar, and put them into a stew-pan, with the juice of a lemon, a little flour, and some well-seasoned gravy; boil it till it be thick, and well flavored with the game, then strain it. Cut half a pound of ham into thin long slices, and heat it in a little butter, with two minced shallots; put it, with the breasts of the snipes, into the strained sauce, and let it boil. Pound the inside, or trail, with a little salt, spread it over thin bits of toasted bread, and hold over it a hot salamander. Put the ragout upon this, and place the ham round it.

RAGOUT OF COLD VEAL. Either a neck, loin, or fillet of veal, will furnish this excellent ragout with a very little expense or trouble. Cut the veal into handsome cutlets; put a piece of butter or clean dripping into a frying-pan; as soon as it is hot, flour and fry the veal of a light brown: take it out and if you have no gravy ready, make some as follows: put a pint or boiling water into the frying-pan, give it a boil up for a minute, and strain it into a basin while you make some thickening in the following manner: put about an ounce of butter into a stewpan; as soon as it melts, mix with it as much flour as will dry it up; stir it over the fire for a few minutes and gradually add to it the gravy you made in the frying-pan; let them simmer together for ten minutes (till thoroughly incorporated); season it with pepper, salt, a little mace, and a wine-glassful of mushroom ketchup or wine; strain it through a tamis to the meat, and stew very gently till the meat is thoroughly warmed. If you have any ready boiled bacon, cut it in slices, and put it in to warm with the meat.

RAMEQUINS. Take a quarter of a pound of Cheshire cheese, scraped, the same quantity of Gloucester cheese, and beat them in a mortar, with a quarter of a pound of fresh butter, the yolks of four eggs, and the inside of a French roll, boiled in cream till soft; when all is beaten to a paste, mix it with the whites of the eggs, previously beaten, and put the paste into small paper cases, made rather long than square, and put them to bake in a Dutch oven, till of a fine brown. They should be served quite hot. You may, if you think proper, add a glass of white wine.

RASPBERRY CREAM. *See Cream.*

RASPBERRY DUMPLINGS. Take some good puff paste, roll it out, and spread raspberry jam over it; roll it up, and boil it rather more than an hour; cut it into five slices; pour melted butter into the dish, grate sugar round, and serve.

RASPBERRY FRITTERS. Grate two Naples biscuits, or the crumb of a French roll; put to either a pint of boiling cream. When this is cold, add to it the yolks of four eggs, well beaten; beat all well together with some raspberry juice; drop this in very small quantities, into a pan of boiling lard; stick them with blanched almonds, sliced.

RASPBERRY FLUMMERY. Mix with half a pint of white wine vinegar one pound of raspberries, or one pound of preserved raspberries, let it boil for three or four minutes, stirring it constantly; strain it through a hair sieve; dissolve one ounce of isinglass in half a pint of water; mix with it three-quarters of a pound of pounded sugar, add it to the strained raspberries stir it all well together; boil, and strain it through a bit of muslin, and put it into a shape. Turn it out when cold.

RASPBERRY JELLY *See Jelly.*

RASPBERRY ICE. Press the juice from as many raspberries as will yield a pound and a half; put it into a glazed pan, and leave it for four days. Then carefully raise the skin that has formed on the top of it, pour off the juice into another vessel; clarify a pound and a half of sugar, with a pint and a half of water, add the juice, and give them half a dozen boils; if not sufficiently red, put in a root of orkanet, which leave in till of the proper color; strain the preparation through a sieve; when cold, put it into the *sabotiere*, and freeze it.  See *Ice*.

RASPBERRY SPONGE. Dissolve in a little water three-quarters of an ounce of isinglass, add to it three-quarters of a pint of cream, and the same proportion of new milk, nearly half a pint of raspberry jelly, and the juice of a lemon. Whisk it well one way till it becomes thick, and looks like sponge, then put it into an earthenware mould, and turn it out the next day.

RASPBERRY TART. Line your dish with a nice puff paste, lay in sugar and fruit, put bars across, and bake.

RASPBERRY TART WITH CREAM. Line a patty-pan with thin puff paste, lay in some raspberries, and strew some very finely sifted sugar over them; cover them with puff paste, and bake it; when done, cut it open, and put in half a pint of cream, in which has been previously beaten the yolks of two or three eggs, and sweetened with a little sugar; when this is added to the tart, return it to the oven five or six minutes.

RED CABBAGE. Get a fine purple cabbage, take off the outside leaves, quarter it, take out the stalk, shred the leaves into a colander, sprinkle them with salt, let them remain till the morrow, drain them dry, put them into a jar, and cover them with the pickle for beet roots.

RED MULLET. Scrape and wash them,

fold them in buttered paper, lay them into a dish, and bake them gently. The liquor that comes from them, boil with a piece of butter, dusted with flour, a teaspoonful of soy, two of essence of anchovy, and a little white wine. Serve the sauce in a butter-tureen. This fish is called the sea woodcock, from being dressed with the inside.

RELISH FOR CHOPS, &c. Pound fine an ounce of black pepper, and half an ounce of allspice, with an ounce of salt, and half an ounce of scraped horseradish, and the same of eschalots, peeled and quartered; put these ingredients into a pint of mushroom ketchup, or walnut pickle, and let them steep for a fortnight, and then strain it.
*Obs.*—A tea-spoonful or two of this is generally an acceptable addition, mixed with the gravy usually sent up for chops and steaks, or added to thick melted butter.

REMOULADE, INDIAN. Pound the yolks of ten hard eggs to a paste, dilute it with eight spoonfuls of oil, put in one at a time, and continue pounding all the time, then add about a dozen allspice, a teaspoonful of saffron, four or five spoonfuls of vinegar, salt, and pepper; amalgamate the whole perfectly, strain it through a bolting-cloth, and serve it in a sauce tureen. This sauce should be rather thick.

RENNET. (1) As soon as the calf is killed, take out the stomach, and scour it inside and out with salt, after it is cleared of the curd always found in it. Let it drain for a few hours, after which sew it up with two large handfuls of salt in it, or stretch it on a stick well salted; or keep it in the salt, wet, and soak a bit, which will do over and over by fresh water.

RENNET. (2) Prepare the maw the same as in the above receipt: on the following day, put a handful of hawthorn-tops, a handful of sweet briar, a handful of rose-leaves, a stick of cinnamon, forty cloves, four blades of mace, a sprig of knotted marjoram, and two large spoonfuls of salt, into two quarts of fresh spring water; let them boil gently till the water is reduced to three pints, then strain it off, and when only milk warm, pour it on the maw. Slice a lemon, and add to it; in two days, strain it again, and put into bottles. Aromatic herbs may be put in also; take care that it is sufficiently salt. If the maw be again salted for a few days, and dried as above, it will be quite as fit for use as before; it should be kept in a cool, dry place. A small quantity of the liquid is sufficient for turning.

RHUBARB TART. Let the stalks be of a good size, take off the thin skin, and cut them into lengths of four or five inches; lay them in a dish, and put over a thin sirup of sugar and water; cover with another dish, and let it simmer slowly for an hour upon a hot hearth, or do them in a block-tin saucepan. As soon as cold, make it into a tart; when tender, the baking the crust will be sufficient; or you may cut the stalks into little bits, the size of gooseberries, and make your tart the same as gooseberry tart.

RICE BLANCMANGE. Put a teacupful of whole rice into the least water possible, till it almost bursts; then add half a pint of good milk or thin cream, and boil it till it is quite a mash, stirring it the whole time it is on the fire, that it may not burn; dip a shape in cold water, and do not dry it; put in the rice, and let it stand until quite cold, when it will come easily out of the shape. This dish is much approved of; it is eaten with cream or custard, and preserved fruits; raspberries are best. It should be made the day before it is wanted, that it may get firm. This blancmange will eat much nicer, flavored with spices, lemon-peel, &c., and sweetened with a little loaf sugar, add it with the milk, and take out the lemon-peel before you put in the mould.

RICE, TO BOIL. Wash the rice perfectly clean, and put on one pound in two quarts of cold water, let it boil twenty minutes, strain

it through a sieve, and put it before the fire; shake it up with a fork every now and then, to separate the grains, and make it quite dry. Serve it hot.

RICE CASSEROLE. Take a pound and a half of rice, wash it thoroughly in several waters (warm), and then put it into a saucepan, at least eight inches in diameter; moisten it with stock, in this proportion; if the rice lies an inch thick, let the stock come two inches above it, and four ladlefuls of fowl skimmings; place the saucepan on a hot stove; when the rice boils, set it on the side, and skim it; then put it on hot ashes, cover, and let it boil slowly for fifteen to twenty minutes; stir it, let it boil as before; in twenty or twenty-five minutes, stir it again; if by this time the rice is perfectly soft, take it off, but if not, add a little more liquid, and continue boiling until it is so; place the saucepan aslant on the side of the stove that the fat may drain away and be taken off easily. As soon as the rice is lukewarm, work it into a firm, smooth, paste, with a spatula; it can hardly be worked up too much, as every grain of rice ought to pass under pressure (if necessary, add more stock, a very little at a time). When the paste is thus thoroughly worked up, form your *casserole* of it, first laying it in a heap, four or five inches high, and seven in diameter; do it with the hand as you would a raised crust; make the ornaments of the outer surface with the point of a knife, or by carrots cut for the purpose, taking care that the decorations be detached from the mass of rice, at least an inch; attention to this particular will not only add to the beauty of the form, but to the color also, as the raised parts will be lightly colored, while the ground will be quite white. When properly formed, mask the whole surface with clarified butter, and place it in a hot oven for an hour and a half, by which time it will be of a fine clear yellow. Take off the top of your *casserole*, clear away all the rice from the inside that does not adhere to the crust (which ought to be very thin), and mix it with *bechamelle, espagnole,* or whatever other sauce may be proper, put it in again, and then fill your *casserole,* with such ragouts as your fancy may dictate; glaze the surface of the outer ornaments, and serve it. Water, with butter and salt, is frequently thought preferable to the stock, &c., as the rice is thereby rendered much whiter.

RICE CASSOLETTES. The rice prepared as above may be put into smaller moulds, those called dariole moulds, and it should be quite cold before it is turned out, the mince or whatever is put inside being also cold; it must be put in carefully, that none of it may mix with the rice, otherwise the cassolettes would break in the process of frying; for the same reason, the dripping must be very hot. Frying is the best and quickest method of doing them, but they may also be browned in the oven as the casserole of rice.

RICE CHEESE. Boil an ounce of rice, thick as hasty pudding, in rather less than half a pint of milk (new); pour it hot on an ounce and a half of butter, the same weight of sugar, mixing it well together; let it stand till cold; then add one egg, and the yolk of another, and a little white wine.

RICE CREAM. Mix some rice flour with half a glass of cold milk; then by degrees, add a pint more, also cold, and put it with a bay-leaf into a saucepan, set it on a slow fire for an hour and a half, then strain and flavor it with orange-flower water, sweeten to your taste, and serve it hot. It should be stirred frequently whilst boiling; eggs may be added if you think proper.

RICE CROQUETTES. Wash and scald a quarter of a pound of rice, put it into a saucepan, with the rind of a lemon, shred small, a quarter of a pound of powder-sugar, a pinch of salt, a little crisped orange-flowers, an ounce of butter, and half a pint of milk; set these on the fire, and when the rice is quite soft, add the yolks of four eggs,

stir them in over the fire, but do not let them boil; pour the preparation on a large tin or slab, spread it equally; let it cool, and then divide it into small equal parts; roll these into balls, dip them into an omelet, roll them in bread-crumbs, and fry them in a very hot pan. As soon as the croquettes are of a nice color, drain, sprinkle them with powder-sugar, and serve them.

RICE CUPS. Sweeten a pint of milk with pounded loaf sugar, and boil it with a stick of cinnamon; stir in sifted ground rice till thick; take it off the fire, and add the well-beaten whites of three eggs; stir it again over the fire for two or three minutes, then put it into tea-cups previously dipped in cold water; turn them out when cold, and pour round them a custard cream made with the yolks of the eggs; place upon the rice a little red currant jelly or raspberry jam. This dish may be served warm or cold; if cold, raspberry cream or custard may be poured round it.

RICE CUSTARDS WITHOUT CREAM. One tea-spoonful of rice-flour, a pint of new milk, the yolks of three eggs, a table-spoonful of ratafia (or two or three laurel leaves boiled in), sugar to your taste; mix the rice very smooth, and stir it with the eggs into the boiling milk, until thick. Arrow-root is better than rice.

RICE FLUMMERY. (1) Boil a pint of new milk, with a bit of lemon-peel and cinnamon: then mix just sufficient rice-flour, with a little cold milk as will make the whole of a good consistence, sweeten according to taste, flavor with a little pounded bitter almond; boil it, taking care not to let it burn; pour it into a shape or pint basin, taking out the spice. When the flummery is cold, turn it into a dish, and serve with cream, milk, or custard, all round, or serve with sweet sauce in a boat.

RICE FLUMMERY. (2) Boil in a quart of milk five ounces of sifted ground rice, half an ounce of bitter almonds, blanched and pounded with two table-spoonfuls of rose-water; sweeten, and stir it till very thick, so that the bottom of the saucepan is seen, and then put it into a mould; when quite cold turn it out, stick over it sweet almonds, cut into straws, and pour round it some thick cream, and a little white wine and sugar mixed with it.

RICE FRITTERS. Boil the rice in milk with some powder-sugar, orange-flower water, a pinch of cinnamon powder, and a little butter; when quite soft put to it a *liaison* of yolks of eggs, pour it into a pan to cool. Make your preparation into balls, about the size of an egg, dip them in egg, fry them, sprinkle them with sugar, and serve.

RICE, GATEAU OF. Boil a quart of cream, add to it half a pound of powder-sugar, and three-quarters of a pound of rice; when the latter is quite soft, dissolve in it a quarter of a pound of butter, and then put in the grated rind of a lemon, let it cool. When quite cold, stir in four yolks and four whole eggs, more if the rice be very thick; butter a mould lightly, put the rice into it, place the mould in hot ashes, so that it may be completely enveloped in and covered with them; in half an hour the *gateau* will be done enough; then turn it out, and serve. If you wish, you can make a *souffle,* by whipping the whites of six eggs; like other *souffles*, in this case it should be served in a silver dish. In putting the preparation into the mould, be careful not to fill it, as the rice would swell and run over the edge.

RICE MILK. Allow an ounce of rice for each person, wash it thoroughly in warm water; set some milk on the fire, and when it boils, put in the rice; continue to boil it over a slow fire, stirring often for two or three hours; add salt or sugar according to taste, and cinnamon.

RICE AND MILK. To every quart of good milk allow two ounces of rice; wash it well in several waters; put it with the milk into a closely-covered saucepan, and set it over a slow fire; when it boils take it off; let it stand till it be cold, and simmer it about an hour and a quarter before sending it to table; and serve it in a tureen.

RICE PANCAKES. Boil half a pound of rice in a small quantity of water, until quite a jelly; as soon as it is cold, mix it with a pint of cream, eight eggs, a little salt and nutmeg; make eight ounces of butter just warm, and stir in with the rest, adding to the whole as much butter as will make the batter thick enough. They must be fried in as small a quantity of lard as possible.

RICE PASTE. Rub three ounces of butter well, into half a pound of ground rice, moisten it with water, and roll it out with a little flour.

RICE, PYRAMIDS OF. Boil some whole rice, make it up into the form of pyramids about three inches high, or press it into small tin frames of that shape; take out part of the rice at the bottom, and fill the space with sausage, or rich forcemeat; place them in a dish, take off the frame, and pour round them some rich brown gravy.

RICE SAVOURY. Carefully wash and pick some rice; set it to stew very gently in a little veal or rich mutton broth, add an onion, a blade of mace, pepper, and salt. When it is swelled it should not boiled to mash; put it to dry on the shallow end of a sieve before the fire. You may serve it dry, or put it in the middle of a dish, and pour the gravy round, having first heated it.

RICE SNOW BALLS. Wash and pick half a pound of rice very clean, put it on in a saucepan with plenty of water; when it boils let it boil ten minutes, drain it on a sieve till it is quite dry, and then pare six apples, weighing two ounces and a half each. Divide the rice into six parcels, in separate cloths, put one apple in each, tie it loose, and boil it one hour; serve it with sugar and butter, or wine sauce.

RICE SOUP. (1) Carefully blanch some well picked rice, then drain it on a sieve; put about a tea-cupful in the soup-pot, with one head of celery, and a quart of *consomme*, and let it simmer by the side of the stove for three hours. If it thickens too much add more *consomme*, season with a little salt; take out the celery, and send the soup to table.

RICE SOUP. (2) Wash your rice well in warm water, changing it frequently; then put the rice into a saucepan, with some good stock; set it on the fire, and leave it to swell for half an hour, but do not let it boil; when the rice has imbibed all the stock, add a sufficient quantity to cover the rice, cover, and boil it slowly for two hours; in the meantime broil two or three slices of beef, and pepper and salt them well; when of a nice dark color, throw them into the rice soup, to which they will impart a rich flavor and a fine color.

RICE, WHOLE IN A SHAPE. Wash a large tea-cupful of rice in several waters, put it into a saucepan with cold water to cover it, and when it boils, add two cupfuls of rich milk, and boil it till it becomes dry; put it into a shape, and press it in well. When cold, turn it out, and serve with preserved black currants, raspberries, or any sort of fruit round it.

RISSOLES. (1) Cut puff paste with a round tin cutter, about three inches wide; have ready some cold fowl or veal, very finely minced, and seasoned with a little pounded garlic, grated lemon-peel, pepper, salt, and mace, the juice of half a lemon, and moistened with a little good gravy. Put some of the mince upon a bit of the paste, wet the edges, and lay over it another bit; press it gently round the rim; brush them all over with a well-beaten egg, and strew over them sifted bread crumbs; fry them a light brown in boiling clarified beef dripping, and lay them upon the back of a sieve before the fire to drain. Serve them in a napkin. The paste may be cut of the size of a large breakfast plate, then the mince put into the middle of it, the edges wet all round, and gathered up into the form of a pear, brushed over with egg, and strewed over with bread crumbs. Served in a dish garnished with fried parsley.

RISSOLES. (2) Mince very finely some cold roasted veal, and a small bit of bacon; season it with grated nutmeg and salt; moisten it with cream, and make it up into good-sized balls; dip them into the yolks of eggs beaten up, and then into finely-grated bread. Bake them in an oven, or fry them of a light brown color in fresh dripping. Before serving, drain them before the fire on the back of a sieve. Garnish with fried parsley.

ROLLS. (1) Dissolve two ounces of butter in one pint of new milk, and stir it into four pounds of flour, as also three table-spoonfuls of yeast, a tea-spoonful of salt, and the well-beaten whites of two eggs; cover the pan with a warmed towel, and set it before the fire to rise for half an hour, then work it one way for fifteen minutes; form it into rolls, place them upon tins, and let them rise for ten minutes before putting them into the oven.

ROLLS. (2) Warm an ounce of butter in half a pint of milk, then add a spoonful and a half of yeast of small beer, and a little salt. Put two pounds of flour into a pan, and put in the above. Set it to rise for an hour; knead it well; make it into seven rolls, and bake them in a quick oven.

ROLLS, FRENCH. (1) Mix rather more than an ounce of coarse salt with eight pounds of sifted flour; make a hole in the middle, and pour in about half a pint of good yeast, the well-beaten whites of four eggs, and as much new milk warmed as will mix it to a middling stiffness; clap and work it down one way for half an hour, but do not knead it; cover it with a warmed towel, and let it rise before the fire for half an hour; take off the surface, which soon becomes hard, and put it aside to be made into a roll; work and clap the dough, form it into rolls, place them upon tins, and let them rise for ten minutes; bake them in a quick oven.

ROLLS, FRENCH. (2) Rub one ounce of butter into a pound of flour; then add to it one egg beaten, a little yeast that is not bitter, and a sufficient quantity of milk, to make a dough of moderate stiffness. Beat it well, but do not knead it; let it rise, and bake on tins.

ROLLS, FRENCH. (3) Warm three spoonfuls of milk, and the same quantity of water, with a bit of butter the size of a walnut, put it to two spoonfuls of thick yeast; put this into the middle of rather more than a quart of flour, mix the whole together to the consistence of a batter-pudding, adding more flour if necessary, to make it the proper thickness; strew a little flour over it from the sides, and if the weather is cold, set it at a little distance from the fire; do this three hours before it is put into the oven; when it breaks a good deal through the flour and rises, work it into a light paste with more warm milk and water; let it lie till within a quarter of an hour of setting into the oven, then work them lightly into rolls; flour a tin, and drop them on, handle them as little as possible; set them before the fire. About twenty minutes will be sufficient time to bake them; put a little salt into the flour. Rasp the rolls.

ROLLS, SHORT, HOT. Dry before the fire a sufficient quantity of flour to make three penny-rolls, or larger if you like; add to it an egg well beaten, a little salt, two spoonfuls of yeast, and a little warm milk; make it into a light dough, let it stand by the fire all night. Bake the rolls in a quick oven.

ROSE-WATER, DOUBLE-DISTILLED. The rose generally chosen for this purpose, is the common pale (single or double) rose, but the white rose is best of all. Gather the flowers in fine weather, two hours after sunrise; take out the calix, and separate the leaves, pound them in a marble mortar to a paste, and leave them five or six hours in the mortar; then put them into a large close cloth, and let two persons wring it with all their strength. Having by this operation obtained four pounds of juice, infuse in it an equal weight of fresh rose-leaves for twenty-four hours; at the end of that time put the whole into the alembic, which place in a sand-bath, and distil it according to rule. (See *Distilling*). When you have collected about an ounce of the water, unlute the receiver, and if that which issues from the still is as odoriferous as that which proceeded first, continue the operation; but if not, collect it into another vessel, as this second water is only single, and must be kept separate from the first, which is the *Essential Water*. Should the second water have an unpleasant smell (caused by the application of too much heat), expose it to the sun for a few days, covered only by a sheet of paper. The utmost care is necessary in distilling this and all other odoriferous substances. A still more powerful essence than the above may be procured by the following method:—Gather as many roses as will afford thirty pounds of leaves, pound these with four pounds of salt; when pounded, place the paste in a vessel in layers with salt between each, press them closely, cork them tight, leave the vessel twelve days, and then distil as usual.

ROSE-WATER, SINGLE. Put four pounds of rose-leaves into a pan, with three quarts of river water, and leave it four-and-twenty hours; then put it into a metal alembic, and distil from it as much odoriferous water as you can, being sure to stop the moment you observe the phlegm. Take off the alembic, throw away its contents, and rinse it out well; after this, fill it to two-thirds with fresh-gathered rose-leaves, on which pour the above drawn rose-water; distil this, and when you have procured as much good rose-water as it will yield, let the fire go out gradually.

ROUX. Put a pound of butter into a saucepan, shake it about till dissolved, when add a sufficient quantity of sifted flour, to make it the consistence of thick *bouilli*; then set it over a fierce stove, and stir it until it begins to take color, when make a good fire of cinders, place the *roux* on it, and let it stand to increase in color; it ought to be of a clear light brown Set it by, and use it as occasion may require.

ROUX, WHITE. Prepare your butter and flour as above, place it on a moderately heated stove, stirring it constantly till very hot; be careful that it does not take color at all, for the whiter it is the more desirable.

RUSKS. To three pounds and a half of flour allow half a pound of butter, the same quantity of pounded loaf sugar, and five spoonfuls of yeast; mix the flour and sugar together; melt the butter in two pints and a half of milk, and mix it with the flour, then add the yeast and one beaten egg; work it well together; cover it, and let it stand for five or six hours; take it out of the pan, and form it into little rolls; place them upon tins, and let them rise for about an hour; bake them in a quick oven, and when they become brown, cut them through the middle or into three slices; put them again into the oven to brown and crisp.

wwwwwww

## S.

SAGE GARGLE. Boil quickly in a pint of water, a large handful of sage leaves; cover the pan closely, and when reduced to one-half, strain it; when cold, mix it with the same quantity of Port wine and of vinegar; sweeten it with honey, or with brown sugar. The decoction of sage may be used alone as a gargle, or with vinegar and honey, without the Port wine; or gargle with vinegar and water.

SAGO. Let it soak for an hour in cold water, to take off the earthy taste; pour that off, and wash it well; then add more water, and simmer gently until the berries are clear, with lemon-peel and spice. Add wine and sugar according to taste, and boil all up together.

SAGO MILK. When well cleansed, boil it slowly with new milk. A small quantity will be sufficient for a quart of milk, it swells so much, and when done, it should be reduced to about a pint. It requires neither sugar nor flavoring.

SALAD MIXTURE. Endeavor to have your salad herbs as fresh as possible; if you suspect they are not "morning gathered," they will be much refreshed by lying an hour or two in spring water; then carefully wash and pick them, and trim off all the worm-eaten, slimy, cankered, dry leaves; and, after washing, let them remain awhile in the colander to drain: lastly, swing them gently in a clean napkin: when properly picked and cut, arrange them in the salad dish, mix the sauce in a soup-plate, and put it into an ingredient bottle, or pour it down the side of the salad dish, and don't stir it up till the mouths are ready for it.

If the herbs be young, fresh gathered, trimmed neatly, and drained dry, and the sauce-maker ponders patiently over the following directions, he cannot fail obtaining the fame of being a very accomplished salad-dresser.

Boil a couple of eggs for twelve minutes, and put them in a basin of cold water for a few minutes; the yolks must be quite cold and hard, or they will not incorporate with the ingredients. Rub them through a sieve with a wooden spoon, and mix them with a table-spoonful of water, or fine double cream; then add two table-spoonfuls of oil or melted butter; when these are well mixed, add, by degrees, a tea-spoonful of salt, or powdered lump sugar, and the same of made mustard: when these are smoothly united, add very gradually three table-spoonfuls of vinegar; rub it with the other ingredients till thoroughly incorporated with them; cut up the white of the egg, and garnish the top of the salad with it. Let the sauce remain at the bottom of the bowl, and do not stir up the salad till it is to be eaten: we recommend the eaters to be mindful of the duty of mastication, without the due performance of which, all undressed vegetables are troublesome company for the principal viscera, and some are even dangerously indigestible.

SALAD, WINTER. Wash very clean one or two heads of endive, some heads of celery, some mustard and cresses; cut them all small, add a little shredded red cabbage, some slices of boiled beet-root, an onion, if the flavor is not disliked; mix them together with salad sauce. In spring, add radishes, and also garnish the dish with them.

SALINE DRAUGHT. Salt of wormwood, twenty grains; lemon-juice, a table-spoonful; water, two table-spoonfuls; magnesia, twenty grains; mix it in a tumbler, together with a little pounded sugar, and take two or three of these in the day.

SALLY LUNNS. Take three quarts of dried flour, half a cupful of yeast, a quarter of a pound of butter, melted in a sufficient quantity of milk to dissolve it, the yolks of three eggs, and a little salt: make these ingredients into a light dough, let it stand before the fire (covered), for an hour to rise, and bake in a quick oven. The above may be made into small cakes.

SALMON. When salmon is fresh and good, the gills and flesh are of a bright red, the scales clear, and the whole fish is stiff. When just killed, there is a whiteness between the flakes, which gives great firmness; by keeping, this melts down, and the fish becomes richer.

SALMON, BAKED. Clean and cut the fish into slices, put it in a dish, and make the following sauce:—Melt an ounce of butter, kneaded in flour, in a pint and a half of gravy, with two glasses of Port wine, two table-spoonfuls of ketchup, two anchovies, and a little cayenne. When the anchovies are dissolved, strain and pour the sauce over the fish, tie a sheet of buttered paper over the dish, and send it to the oven.

SALMON, BOILED. Put on a fish-kettle, with spring water enough to well cover the salmon you are going to dress, or the salmon will neither look nor taste well: (boil the liver in a separate saucepan). When the water boils, put in a handful of salt; take off the scum as soon as it rises; have the fish well washed; put it in, and if it is thick, let it boil very gently. Salmon requires almost as much boiling as meat; about a quarter of an hour to a pound of fish: but practice only can perfect the cook in dressing salmon. A quarter of a salmon will take almost as long boiling, as half a one: you must consider the thickness, not the weight: ten pounds of fine full-grown salmon will be done in an hour and a quarter. Lobster Sauce.

*Obs.*—The thinnest part of the fish is the fattest; and if you have a "grand gourmand" at table, ask him if he is for thick or thin.

N. B.—If you have any left, put it into a pie-dish, and cover it with an equal portion of vinegar and pump water, and a little salt: it will be ready in three days.

SALMON, BOILED IN WINE. Season with pepper and salt, some slices of bacon, fat and lean together, a pound of veal cut thin, and a pound and a half of beef; put these into a deep stewpan, then a fine piece of fresh salmon cut out of the middle, then pour in just as much water as will cover it, and let it simmer over a gentle fire till the salmon is almost done, then pour the water away, and put in two quarts of white wine, with an onion cut in slices, some thyme, and sweet marjoram, picked from the stalks; let them stew gently, and while they are doing, cut a sweetbread into thin slices, then cut the slices across, and stew them in a saucepan, with some rich gravy; when they are done enough, add a quarter of a pint of essence of ham; take up the salmon, lay it on a dish, and serve with the sweetbread, and its sauce poured over.

SALMON, BOILED, BERWICK RECEIPT. The tail of the salmon is first cut off near and below the last fin, the fish is then cut up the back, keeping the bone on one side, and then cut up into pieces of half a pound each, the blood well washed out of the fish in cold water, but the scales not to be removed; a pickle to be made of salt and water, strong enough to bear an egg and, when boiling, the fish to be put in, and boiled very quickly for fifteen minutes. During the boiling, the scum to be taken off carefully as soon as it rises. Sauces;—Lobster, melted butter, and anchovy sauce.
N. B.—The hardest water is preferable for boiling salmon.

SALMON, BOILED, RECEIPT BY AN ABERDEEN FISHERMAN. When the water is hot, put salt into it, and stir it well; taste it; when strong enough to force you to cast it from your mouth, it will do; when the water boils put in the fish; when it boils again, give twenty minutes for a salmon, and sixteen for a gristle. When salmon is cut in slices an inch thick, let them boil ten minutes. Serve with it a sauce tureen of the liquor the fish was boiled in.

SALMON STEAKS BROILED. Cut the steaks from the thickest parts of the fish nearly an inch thick; butter pieces of white paper; fold the steaks in them, and broil them over a slow fire for ten or twelve minutes. Take off the paper; serve and garnish with plenty of fried parsley. Dressed in

this way, they may be put round salmon boiled, in slices. Sauces;—melted butter, lobster, or shrimp sauce.

SALMON, FRESH BROILED. Clean the salmon well, and cut it into slices about an inch and a half thick; dry it thoroughly in a clean cloth; rub it over with sweet oil, or thick melted butter, and sprinkle a little salt over it: put your gridiron over a clear fire, at some distance; when it is hot, wipe it clean; rub it with sweet oil or lard; lay the salmon on, and when it is done on one side, turn it gently and broil the other. Anchovy sauce, &c.
*Obs.*—An oven does them best.

SALMON CAVEACH. Boil in two quarts of vinegar three heads of shallots, half an ounce of whole black pepper, three cloves, two blades of mace, and a little salt. Fry the fish, cut in slices, of a light brown color in fine oil, or clarified dripping; put them, when cold, into a pan, pour over the vinegar and spices, and put on the top eight or ten spoonfuls of oil. Soles may be done in this way, only lay over them sliced onions instead of shallots.

SALMON, DRIED KIPPER. Cut the fish up the back, and take out the bone; wipe it very clean with a cloth; score it, and put a handful of salt on each side, and let it lie for three days; then hang it up to dry, and it will be fit for use in two days, and eats well with a little pepper put over it, and broiled.

SALMON, DRIED, TO DRESS. Lay it in soak for two or three hours, then broil it, shaking a little pepper over it. Dried salmon is eaten broiled in paper, and only just warmed through; egg sauce and mashed potatoes are usually served with it; or it may be boiled, especially the bit next the head.

SALMON, PICKLED. (1) Cut a salmon into two or three pieces, put it in a fish-kettle, and set it on the fire with a sufficient quantity of water to cover it, and plenty of salt; as soon as it begins to boil, set it aside to simmer very gently until done; then take it off the fire, and let it stand in the liquor until cold, take it out, lay the pieces close together in a tub to pickle, and over them five anchovies, a small quantity of pounded saltpetre, and a quarter of a pint of sweet oil; being thus prepared, put the top of the salmon liquor into a stewpan, to which add the same quantity of white wine vinegar; put it on the fire to skim, and boil it for two or three minutes; take it off, and let it cool. When cold, pour it over the salmon and tie it down; in three days turn it, and in a week's time it will be fit for use; this is merely in a small way; a great quantity being done at once, requires neither oil nor anchovies. Serve garnished with fennel.

SALMON, PICKLED. (2) Cut the salmon into pieces; boil it as for eating, and lay it on a dry cloth till the following day; boil two quarts of good vinegar with one of the liquor the fish was boiled in, one ounce of whole black pepper, half an ounce of all-spice, and four blades of mace. Put the salmon into something deep, and pour over it the prepared vinegar when cold. A little sweet oil put upon the top will make it keep a twelve-month.

SALMON, PICKLED. (3) To a quart of liquor the fish has been boiled in, put rather more than half a pint of good vinegar, and half an ounce of whole black pepper; boil it, and when it is cold pour it over the fish, previously laid in a deep dish.

SALMON, PICKLED, TO DRESS. Soak a piece of pickled salmon all night in pump-water; then lay it on a fish-plate, and put it in a stewpan, with three spoonfuls of vine-gar, a little mace, some whole pepper in a bit of muslin, an onion, a nutmeg bruised, a pint of white wine, a bunch of sweet herbs, some parsley, lemon-peel, and a quarter of a pound of butter rolled in flour; cover the stewpan very close, and let it simmer over a gentle fire for a quarter of an hour; then take up the salmon, lay it in a dish, keep it hot before the fire; let the sauce boil till it is of a proper consistence; take out the spice, on-ion, and sweet herbs, and serve the sauce over the fish.

SALMON, POTTED. Take off the head; cut the salmon in thick slices; wipe it dry, but do not wash it; pound half an ounce of nutmeg, mace, and cloves, the least part of cloves, half an ounce of white pepper, and some salt; chop fine one onion, six bay-leaves, and six anchovies; season each slice; put it into a pan, with very thin slices of butter between each layer; bake it, when well done; drain off the butter, and, when cold, pour over some clarified butter.

SALMON, TO SALT. Cut the fish up the back, and cut out the bone; wipe it clean, and sprinkle it with salt; let it lay a night to drain off the liquor; wipe it dry; rub on it two or three ounces of pounded saltpetre; cut it into pieces; pack it close in a pot with a thick layer of salt between each layer of fish. If the brine does not rise in a few days, boil a strong one, and pour it, when cold, upon the salmon, which must always be covered with it.

SALMON, STEW. Clean and scrape the fish; cut it into slices, and stew it in a rich white gravy. A little before serving, add two table-spoonfuls of soy, one of essence of anchovy, and a little salt, some chopped parsley and chives.

SALMON, SPICED. Mix together, in the proportion of one third of salt-and-water to one pint of vinegar, one ounce of whole black pepper, and one ounce of cinnamon. Cut the salmon into slices, and boil it in this, when cold, pack it close in a pan, and pour over it the liquor it was boiled in, with the spices, so as to cover it completely; cover the pan closely, to exclude the air.

SALMON, MACKEREL, SPRATS, HERRINGS, &c. PICKLED. Cut the fish into proper pieces; do not take off the scales; make a brine strong enough to bear an egg, in which boil the fish; it must be boiled in only just liquor enough to cover it; do not overboil it. When the fish is boiled, lay it slantingly to drain off all the liquor; when cold, pack it close in the kits, and fill them up with equal parts of the liquor the salmon was boiled in (having first well skimmed it), and best vinegar; let them rest for a day; fill up again, striking the sides of the kit with a cooper's adz, until the kit will receive no more; then head them down as close as possible.

*Obs.*—This is in the finest condition when fresh. Some sprigs of fresh-gathered young fennel are the accompaniments.

N. B.—The three indispensable marks of the goodness of pickled salmon are, 1st, The brightness of the scales, and their sticking fast to the skin; 2dly, The firmness of the flesh, and, 3dly, Its fine, pale-red rose color. Without these it is not fit to eat, and was either stale before it was pickled, or has been kept too long after.

The above was given us as the actual practice of those who pickle it for the London market.

N. B.—Pickled salmon warmed by steam, or in its pickle liquor, is a favorite dish at Newcastle.

SALOOP. Boil a little water, wine, lemon-peel, and sugar, together; then mix with a small quantity of the powder, previously rubbed smooth, in a little cold water; stir the whole well together, and boil for a few minutes.

SALPICON. This is a mixture composed of various articles, such as sweetbreads, fat livers, tongue, ham, champignons, truffles, &c., previously dressed, cut into dice, and cooked in some rich sauce, and seasoned with pepper, salt, nutmeg, cloves, shallots, sweet herbs, and a little butter; take care that all the articles are sufficiently boiled before they are cut up. Many things, such as beef-palate, fowl, cocks'-combs, indeed almost any article you please, may be added to the above.

SALT, Is as Plutarch calls it, sauce for sauce.

Common salt is more relishing than basket salt; it should be prepared for the table by drying it in a Dutch oven before the fire; then put it on a clean paper, and roll it with a rolling pin; if you pound it in a mortar till it is quite fine, it will look as well as basket salt.

*₊* Select for table-use the lumps of salt.

*Obs.*—Your salt-box must have a close cover, and be kept in a dry place.

SALT, SPICED. Take four drachms of grated nutmeg, the same of cloves, two of white pepper, two of allspice, two of mace, two of bay-leaf, two of basil, and two of thyme (these three latter articles should be dried in an oven). Put these all into a mortar, and pound them to an impalpable powder, and sift it. Take a pound of fine white salt, dry it thoroughly in an oven, or stove, pound it as fine as possible; sift, and mix with it an ounce of the above mentioned spices; amalgamate them thoroughly, keep the spiced salt in a tin box, which will shut perfectly close. Use it in the following proportion: four drachms to a pound of boned veal.

SALTING MEAT. In the *summer* season, especially, meat is frequently spoiled by the cook forgetting to take out the kernels; one in the udder of a round of beef, in the fat in the middle of the round, those about the thick end of the flank, &c.: if these are not taken out, all the salt in the world will not keep the meat.

The art of salting meat is to rub in the salt thoroughly and evenly into every part, and to fill all the holes full of salt where the kernels were taken out, and where the butcher's skewers were.

A round of beef of 25 pounds will take a pound and a half of salt to be rubbed in all at first, and requires to be turned and rubbed every day with the brine; it will be ready for dressing in four or five days, if you do not wish it very salt.

In *summer*, the sooner meat is salted after it is killed, the better; and care must be taken to defend it from the flies.

In *winter*, it will eat the shorter and tenderer, if kept a few days (according to the temperature of the weather) until its fibre has become short and tender, as these changes do not take place after it has been acted upon by the salt.

In frosty weather, take care the meat is not frozen, and warm the salt in a frying-pan. The extremes of heat and cold are equally unfavorable for the process of salting. In the former, the meat changes before the salt can affect it; in the latter, it is so hardened, and its juices are so congealed, that the salt cannot penetrate it.

If you wish it red, rub it first with saltpetre, in the proportion of half an ounce, and the like quantity of moist sugar, to a pound of common salt.

You may impregnate meat with a very agreeable vegetable flavor, by pounding some sweet herbs, and an onion with the salt. You may make it still more relishing by addling a little ZEST or *savory spice*.

SALT PORK, BOILED. *See Bacon*

SAMPHIRE, TO DRY, OR PRESERVE. Take it in bunches as it grows; set a large deep stewpan full of water on the fire; as soon as it boils, throw in a little salt, and put in the samphire; when it looks of a fine green, remove the pan directly from the fire, and take out the samphire with a fork; lay it on sieves to drain; when cold, lay it on earthen plates, strew sugar well over it, next day turn them on a sieve, and strew it again with sugar, keep turning daily until it is dry; take care the stove is not too hot.

SAMPHIRE, TO PICKLE. Lay some samphire that is green in a pan, sprinkle over it two or three handfuls of salt, and cover it with spring water, and let it lay for twenty-four hours; then put it into a large brass saucepan; throw in a handful of salt; cover the pan close, and set it over a very slow fire; let it stand till it is quite green, and crisp; then take it off, for if it becomes soft it is spoiled; put it into a jar, cover it close, and when it is cold, tie it down.

SANDWICHES FOR TRAVELLERS. Spread butter, very thinly, upon the upper part of a stale loaf of bread cut very smooth, and then cut off the slice; now cut off another thin slice, but spread it with butter on the under side, without which precaution the two slices of bread will not fit one another. Next take some cold beef, or ham, and cut it into very minute particles. Sprinkle these thickly over the butter, and, having added a little mustard, put the slices face to face, and press them together. Lastly, cut the whole into four equal portions, each of which is to be wrapped in a separate piece of paper.

SANDWICHES. (1) Cut some bread into thin slices, pare off the crust, and spread a little butter on them; cut them nicely into oblong pieces, put between each some bits of fowl, and trim thin bits of ham, both nicely trimmed; add a little mustard and salt. Any cold roasted or potted meat may be used. Serve them for luncheon, garnished with curled parsley.

SANDWICHES, (2) Properly prepared, are an elegant and convenient luncheon or supper, but have got out of fashion, from the bad manner in which they are commonly made: to cut the bread neatly with a sharp knife seems to be considered the only essential, and the lining is composed of any offal odds and ends, that cannot be sent to table in any other form. Whatever is used must be carefully trimmed from every bit of skin, gristle, &c. and nothing introduced but what you are absolutely certain will be acceptable to the mouth.

SANDWICHES, CAKE. Cut a sponge cake, a few days old, as for bread sandwiches, and spread strawberry jam or currant jelly over them.

SAUCE. (1) Few things require more care than making sauces, as most of them should be stirred constantly, the whole attention should be directed to them; the better way therefore, is to prepare the sauces before cooking those articles which demand equal care; they may be kept hot in the *bain-marie*.

Butter, and those sauces containing eggs, ought never to boil.

The thickest stewpans should be used for making sauces, and wooden-spoons used for stirring them.

SAUCE. (2) Mix together a pint of vinegar, two shallots or heads of garlic, a tea-spoonful of cayenne, three large table-spoonfuls of Indian soy or mushroom ketchup; and two of walnut pickle. Let it stand a week, shaking it daily; strain, and bottle it for use.

—— FOR ANY SORT OF MEAT. Boil and strain three table-spoonfuls of gravy, two of vinegar, a blade of mace, a little pepper, salt, and a large sliced onion.

—— ANCHOVY. Pound three anchovies in a mortar with a little bit of butter; rub it through a double hair sieve with the back of a wooden spoon, and stir it into almost half a pint of melted butter; or stir in a table-spoonful of essence of anchovy. To the above, many cooks add lemon-juice and cayenne.

—— APPLE. (1) Pare, core, and slice some apples; boil them in water, with a bit of lemon-peel; when tender, mash them; add to them a bit of butter the size of a walnut, and some brown sugar. Heat, and serve in a sauce-tureen.

—— APPLE. (2) Pare and core three good-sized baking apples; put them into a well-tinned pint saucepan, with two table-spoonfuls of cold water; cover the saucepan close, and set it on a trivet over a slow fire a couple of hours before dinner (some apples will take a long time stewing, others will be ready in a quarter of an hour): when the apples are done enough, pour off the water, let them stand a few minutes to get dry; then beat them up with a fork, with a bit of butter about as big as a nutmeg, and a tea-spoonful of powdered sugar.

N. B.—Some add lemon-peel, grated, or minced fine, or boil a bit with the apples.

—— ATTELETS. Take of finely-minced parsley, mushrooms, and shallots, a table-spoonful each; fry them with a little butter, and then dredge in a little flour; moisten the mixture with some good stock, season it with pepper and salt, and boil it till it begins to thicken; then take it off the fire, and add the well-beaten yolks of two or three eggs. Stir it well all the time it is making.

—— BEEF-GRAVY, or *Brown Sauce for Ragout, Game, Poultry, Fish, &c.* If you want gravy immediately, see Potato Soup, or Glaze. If you have time enough, furnish a thick and well-tinned stewpan with a thin slice of salt pork, or an ounce of butter, and a middling-sized onion; on this lay a pound of nice, juicy gravy beef, (as the object in making gravy is to extract the nutritious succulence of the meat, it must be beaten to comminute the containing vessels, and scored to augment the surface to the action of the water); cover the stewpan, and set it on a slow fire; when the meat begins to brown, turn it about, and let it get slightly browned (but take care it is not at all burned): then pour in a pint and a half of boiling water; set the pan on the fire; when it boils, carefully catch the scum, and then put in a crust of bread toasted brown (don't burn it) a sprig of winter savory, or lemon thyme and parsley—a roll of thin cut lemon-peel, a dozen berries of allspice, and a dozen of black pepper. Cover the stewpan close, and let it stew very gently for about two hours, then strain it through a sieve into a basin. Now, if you wish to thicken it, set a clean stewpan over a slow fire, with about an ounce of butter in it; when it is melted, dredge to it, by degrees, as much flour as will dry it up, stirring them well together; when thoroughly mixed, pour in a little gravy—stir it well together, and add the remainder by degrees; set it over the fire, let it simmer gently for fifteen minutes longer, skim off the fat, &c. as it rises; when it is about as thick as cream, squeeze it through a tamis or fine sieve—and you will have a fine rich Brown Sauce, at a very moderate expense, and without much trouble.

—— FOR BOILED BEEF. Mince a large onion, parboil it, and drain off the water; put the onion into a saucepan, with a table-spoonful of finely-chopped parsley, some good gravy, and one ounce of butter dredged with a little flour. Let it boil nearly ten minutes, and add a spoonful of cut capers, which must be thoroughly heated before the sauce is served.

—— BROWN. Take a pound or two of steaks, two or three pounds of veal, some pickings of fowl, carrots, and onions, put all these into a saucepan with a glass of water, and set it on a brisk fire; when scarcely any moisture remains, put it on a slow fire, that the jelly may take color without burning; and as soon as it is brown, moisten it with stock (or water), add a bunch of parsley and green onions, two bay-leaves, two cloves, and some champignons, salt it well, and set it on the fire for three hours, then strain; dilute a little *roux* with your liquor, and boil it an hour over a gentle fire, take off all the fat, and run it through a bolting.

—— BONNE BOUCHE, FOR Goose, Duck, or roast Pork. Mix a tea-spoonful of made mustard, a salt-spoonful of salt, and a few grains of cayenne, in a large wine-glassful of claret or Port wine; pour it into the goose by a slit in the apron just before serving up; or, as all the company may not like it, stir it into a quarter of a pint of thick melted butter, or thickened gravy, and send it up in a boat. A favorite relish for roast pork or geese, &c. is, two ounces of leaves of green sage, an ounce of fresh lemon-peel pared thin, same of salt, minced eschalot, and half a drachm of cayenne pepper, ditto of citric acid, steeped for a fortnight in a pint of claret; shake it up well every day; let it stand a day to settle, and decant the clear liquor; bottle it, and cork it close; a table-spoonful or more in a quarter pint of gravy, or melted butter.

—— BREAD. (1) Boil, in a pint of water, the crumb of a French roll or of a slice of bread, a minced onion, and some whole pepper. When the onion is tender, drain off the water, pick out the pepper-corns, and rub the bread through a sieve; then put it into a saucepan, with a gill of cream, a bit of butter, and a little salt. Stir it till it boil, and serve it in a sauce-tureen.

—— BREAD. (2) Mix, in rather more than half a pint of milk or water, a slice of grated bread, a dessert-spoonful of potato flour, a small onion pounded, a bit of butter the size of a walnut, a few whole pepper corns, a little mace, and salt. Boil it well, pick out the spices, and mix it smooth. Serve quite hot.

—— BREAD. (3) Put a small tea-cupful of bread crumbs into a stewpan, pour on it as much milk as it will soak up, and a little more; or instead of the milk, take the giblets, head, neck, and legs, &c. of the poultry, &c. and stew them, and moisten the bread with this liquor; put it on the fire with a middling-sized onion, and a dozen berries of pepper or allspice, or a little mace; let it boil, then stir it well, and let it simmer till it is quite stiff, and then put to it about two table-spoonfuls of cream or melted butter, or a little good broth; take out the onion and pepper, and it is ready.

*Obs.*—This is an excellent accompaniment to game and poultry.

—— FOR BOILED MEAT, GAME, AND POULTRY. Bruise the yolks of two hard-boiled eggs with a little water and salt; bone one anchovy, and mince it, a small onion, two shallots, a little parsley and tarragon, and a few capers; mix them with the egg, add a table-spoonful of fine oil, a little mustard, two table-spoonfuls of lemon, and one of tarragon vinegar; mix all exceedingly well together, put it into a sauce-tureen, and serve it with the broil; or it may be served with cold veal.

—— CAPER. To make a quarter of a pint, take a table-spoonful of capers, and two tea-spoonfuls of vinegar.

The present fashion of cutting capers is to mince one-third of them very fine, and divide the others in half; put them into a quarter of a pint of melted butter, or good thickened gravy; stir them the same way as you did the melted butter, or it will oil. Some boil, and mince fine a few leaves of parsley, or chervil, or tarragon, and add these to the sauce; others the juice of half a Seville orange, or lemon.

Keep the caper bottle very closely corked, and do not use any of the caper liquor: if the capers are not well covered with it, they will immediately spoil; and it is an excellent ingredient in hashes, &c. The Dutch use it as a fish sauce, mixing it with melted butter.

—— CARRIER. Scrape a small stick of horse-radish, cut an onion or two in thin slices, put these into a sauce-tureen with a little vinegar and whole pepper; set the tureen in the dripping-pan under a shoulder of mutton whilst roasting; serve this sauce quite hot with the meat.

—— CELERY, WHITE. Pick and wash two heads of nice white celery; cut it into pieces about an inch long; stew it in a pint of water, and a tea-spoonful of salt, till the celery is tender; roll an ounce of butter with a table-spoonful of flour; add this to half a pint of cream, and give it a boil up.

—— CELERY PUREE, *for boiled Turkey, Veal, Fowls,&c.* Cut small half a dozen heads of nice white celery that is quite clean, and two onions sliced; put in a two-quart stewpan, with a small lump of butter: sweat them over a slow fire till quite tender, then put in two spoonfuls of flour, half a pint of water (or beef or veal broth), salt and pepper, and a little cream or milk; boil it a quarter of an hour, and pass through a fine hair sieve with the back of a spoon. If you wish for celery sauce when celery is not in season, a quarter of a drachm of celery seed, or a little essence of celery, will impregnate half a pint of sauce with a sufficient portion of the flavor of the vegetable.

—— CHESTNUT, FOR ROAST TURKEY. Scald a pound of good chestnuts in hot water for five minutes, skin them, and stew them slowly for two hours in white stock, seasoned and thickened with butter and flour. Cut a pound of pork sausages into bits about an inch long, dust them with flour, and fry them a light brown; lay them into the dish on which the turkey is to be served, and pour the chestnuts and sauce over them. Some people prefer the fried sausages stewed a little with the chestnuts; but this method makes the sauce of a darker color.

—— CURRANT, FOR VENISON. Boil in water for a few minutes an ounce of nicely-cleaned currants, add three table-spoonfuls of grated bread, a piece of butter the size of a walnut, four cloves, and a glass of Port wine; stir it till it boil, and serve it hot.

—— CURRY, Is made by stirring a sufficient quantity of curry powder, into gravy or melted butter, or onion sauce, or onion gravy. The compositions of curry powder, and the palates of those who eat it, vary so much, that we cannot recommend any specific quantity. The cook must add it by degrees, tasting as she proceeds, and take care not to put in too much.

—— DUTCH. (1) Beat up the yolks of six eggs, mix in a little flour, cream, salt, and lemon vinegar. Strain it through a sieve, add a small piece of fresh butter, two blades of pounded mace, and a little pepper. Put it into a saucepan, and stir it till it is almost boiling.

—— DUTCH. (2) Put into a stewpan a tea-spoonful of flour, four table-spoonfuls of elder vinegar, a quarter of a pound of fresh butter, the yolks of five eggs, and a little salt; keep stirring it over the fire, and work it well till thick. If it be not curdled, it will not require to be strained. Season with pepper.

—— DUTCH, FOR FISH OR BROILED FOWLS. Mix, with two ounces of fresh butter, one tea-spoonful of flour, two table-spoonfuls of cold water, the same quantity of vinegar, and one well-beaten egg; put it into a saucepan, and stir it over the fire till it be quite hot, but do not allow it to boil.

—— EGG. (1) This agreeable accompaniment to roasted poultry, or salted fish, is made by putting three eggs into boiling water, and boiling them for about twelve minutes, when they will be hard; put them into cold water till you want them. This will make the yolks firmer, and prevent their surface turning black, and you can cut them much neater: use only two of the whites, cut the whites into small dice, the yolks into bits about a quarter of an inch square; put them into a sauce-boat; pour to them half a pint of melted butter, and stir them together.

If you are for superlative egg sauce, pound the yolks of a couple of eggs, and rub them with the melted butter to thicken it.

N. B.—Some cooks garnish salt fish with hard-boiled eggs cut in half.

—— EGG. (2) Boil three or four eggs about a quarter of an hour, put them into cold water, take off the shells, cut three of the whites and four yolks into small pieces, mix them with melted butter, and heat it well.

—— ESCHALOT. Take four eschalots, and make it in the same manner as garlic sauce. Or, you may make this sauce more extemporaneously by putting two table-spoonfuls of eschalot wine, and a sprinkling of pepper and salt, into (almost) half a pint of thick melted butter. This is an excellent sauce for chops or steaks; many are very fond of it with roasted or boiled meat, poultry, &c.

—— ESCHALOT, FOR BOILED MUTTON. This is a very frequent and satisfactory substitute for caper sauce. Mince four eschalots very fine, and put them into a small saucepan, with almost half a pint of the liquor the mutton was boiled in: let them boil up for five minutes; then put in a table-spoonful of vinegar, a quarter tea-spoonful of pepper, a little salt, and a bit of butter (as big as a walnut) rolled in flour; shake together till it boils.

—— ESCAVEKE SAUCE, FOR COLD GAME, FOWL, OR MEAT. Beat, in a marble mortar, the following ingredients: five cloves of garlic, six cloves of shallot, as much pounded ginger as will lie upon a sixpence, and the same of cayenne, a table-spoonful of coriander seed, and a little salt. Pour upon them, boiling hot, a pint of the best white wine vinegar; add the peel of a lemon, cut very thin. When cold, put the whole into a bottle, cork it tightly, and shake it well before using.

—— FOR FISH. (1) The melted butter

for fish, should be thick enough to adhere to the fish, and, therefore, must be of the thickness of light batter, as it is to be diluted with essence of anchovy, soy, mushroom ketchup, cayenne, or Chili vinegar, lemons or lemon-juice, or artificial lemon-juice, &c. which are expected at all well-served tables. Cooks, who are jealous of the reputation of their taste, and housekeepers who value their health, will prepare these articles at home: there are quite as many reasons why they should, as there are for the preference usually given to home-baked bread, and home-brewed beer. The liver of the fish pounded and mixed with parsley and butter, with a little lemon-juice, &c. is an elegant and inoffensive relish to fish.

—— FOR FISH. (2) Two wine-glasses of Port, and two of walnut pickle, four of mushroom ketchup, half a dozen anchovies, pounded, the like number of eschalots sliced and pounded, a table-spoonful of soy, and half a drachm of cayenne pepper; let them simmer gently for ten minutes; strain it, and when cold, put it into bottles, well corked, and sealed over, it will keep for a considerable time.

*Obs.*—This is commonly called Quin's sauce.

—— FOR FISH. (3) A table-spoonful of anchovy juice, one of soy, and two of mushroom ketchup, mixed in a quarter of a pound of melted butter.

—— FOR FISH. (4) Three anchovies and an onion chopped, and a small bit of horseradish boiled in some stock, then strained, and thickened with a piece of butter rolled in flour.

—— FOR FISH. (5) Boil in half pint of water one or two anchovies, two cloves, a blade of mace, a bit of lemon-peel, a few peppercorns, and two table-spoonfuls of Port wine; strain and thicken it with a piece of butter rolled in flour.

—— FOR FISH. (6) Mix well with two ounces of melted butter, of mushroom ketchup, essence of anchovies, and lemon pickle, a table-spoonful each, a tea-spoonful of soy, and a little cayenne. Boil it before serving.

—— FOR FISH. (7) Chop two dozen of whole anchovies, mix with them half a pint of anchovy liquor, two shallots cut small, and three pints of Port wine, one of vinegar, one lemon sliced, one handful of scraped horseradish, and ten blades of mace, one nutmeg, twelve peppercorns, six cloves, all bruised, and one table-spoonful of flour of mustard. Boil these together about fifteen or twenty minutes; when cold, strain and bottle it, waxing the corks. It will keep good a year. A table-spoonful improves oyster sauce, and that quantity is sufficient for a sauce-tureen of melted butter.

—— FOR FISH. (8) A quart of Port wine, half a pint of best vinegar, one pound of bruised anchovies, one ounce of mace and one of cloves, half an ounce of pepper, one large onion, and the peel of one lemon; boil all these ingredients together, over a slow fire, till a pint is wasted; then strain, and bottle it, and keep it closely stopped.

—— FISH OR MEAT SAUCE, TO MAKE A QUART BOTTLE OF. To half a bottle of vinegar put one ounce of cayenne, two cloves of garlic, one table-spoonful of soy, two of walnut, and two of mushroom ketchup. Let it stand six days, shaking it frequently, then add the remaining half of the bottle of vinegar; let it stand another week, strain, and put it into small bottles.

—— WHITE, FOR FISH. Four anchovies chopped, two glasses of white wine, a large one of vinegar, an onion stuck with three cloves, and cut into quarters; let all these simmer till the anchovies dissolve; strain it, and add a quarter of a pound of butter kneaded in a table-spoonful of flour. When it has melted, stir in gradually, one way, half a pint of cream, taking care that it do not boil. When thoroughly heated; serve in a sauce-tureen.

—— LIVER, FOR FISH. Boil the liver of the fish, and pound it in a mortar with a little flour; stir it into some broth, or some of the liquor the fish was boiled in, or melted butter, parsley, and a few grains of cayenne, a little essence of anchovy, or soy or ketchup; give it a boil up, and rub it through a sieve: you may add a little lemon-juice, or lemon cut in dice.

—— PINK, FOR FISH. Put into a pan, or wide-mouthed jar, one quart of good vinegar, half a pint of Port wine, half an ounce of cayenne, one large table-spoonful of walnut ketchup, two ditto of anchovy liquor, a quarter of an ounce of cochineal, and six cloves of garlic. Let it remain forty hours, stirring it two or three times a-day; run it through a flannel bag, and put it into half-pint bottles.

—— FOR PIKE. Mix with a pint of cream a table-spoonful of anchovy sauce, the same of soy, and two of ketchup, a piece of butter rolled in flour; put it into a saucepan, and stir it one way till nearly boiling.

—— WHITE, FOR PIKE. Simmer till half wasted, two table-spoonfuls of white wine, one of vinegar, half a small onion, and some grated nutmeg; add a piece of butter rolled in flour, then a small tea-cupful of cream; heat it thoroughly, stirring it all the time, and taking care that it do not boil.

—— GREEN GOOSEBERRY. Boil some green gooseberries in water till soft, and sweeten them with brown sugar.

—— GOOSEBERRY. Top and tail them close with a pair of scissors, and scald half a pint of green gooseberries; drain them on a hair sieve, and put them into half a pint of melted butter. Some add grated ginger and lemon-peel, and the French, minced fennel; others send up the gooseberries whole or mashed, without any butter, &c.

—— GOOSE STUFFING. Chop very fine an ounce of onion and half an ounce of green sage leaves; put them into a stewpan with four spoonfuls of water; simmer gently for ten minutes; then put in a tea-spoonful of pepper and salt, and one ounce of fine bread crumbs; mix well together; then pour to it a quarter of a pint of broth, or gravy, or melted butter, stir well together, and simmer it a few minutes longer.

—— GRANDE. Take three or four slices from the under part of a knuckle of veal, and put them into a large stewpan with two ladlefuls of *consomme*, set it on a fierce fire, taking care to skim it as much as possible, and with a cloth wipe away all that adheres to the inside of the stewpan; when the *consomme* is reduced, prick the slices with a knife to let out the gravy; then set the stewpan on a slow fire, that the meat and glaze may adhere together, and as soon as the latter is of a clear light color, take it off, leave it covered for ten minutes, then fill it up with rich stock, in which is four or five large carrots, and three onions; let it boil slowly for two hours. In the meantime put the knuckle into a saucepan with four or five carrots, as many onions (one stuck with cloves), and two ladlefuls of *consomme*; set it on a brisk fire that the liquor may reduce to a jelly; as soon as this jelly begins to take color, pour on it the liquor from the other saucepan to dissolve the jelly gradually; then make it boil. Dilute some *roux* with the above liquor, and add it to the meat with some champignons, a bunch of parsley, scallions, and two bay-leaves, skim it when it begins to boil, and again when the *roux* is added, put in more *consomme* or *roux*, according as it is too thick or too thin.

When it has boiled an hour and a half, take off all the fat; and when the meat is quite done, strain the sauce through a bolting-cloth.

—— GRILL. To half a pint of gravy, add an ounce of fresh butter, and a tablespoonful of flour, previously well rubbed together, the same of mushroom or walnut ketchup, two tea-spoonfuls of lemon-juice, one of made mustard, one of minced capers, half a one of black pepper, a quarter of a rind of a lemon grated very thin, a teaspoonful of essence of anchovies, and a little eschalot wine, or a very small piece of minced eschalot, and a little Chili vinegar, or a few grains of cayenne; simmer together for a few minutes; pour a little of it over the grill; and send up the rest in a sauce-tureen.

—— HARVEY. Chop twelve anchovies, bones and all, very small, with one ounce of cayenne pepper, six spoonfuls of soy, six ditto of good walnut pickle, three heads of garlic, chopped not very small, a quarter of an ounce of cochineal, two heads of shallots, chopped not very small, one gallon of vinegar; let it stand fourteen days, stir it well, twice or thrice every day; then pass it through a jelly-bag, and repeat this till it is perfectly clear; then bottle it, and tie a bladder over the cork.

—— HORSERADISH, TO EAT with Hot or Cold Meat. Mix a tea-spoonful of mustard, a table-spoonful of vinegar, and three of cream; add a little salt, and as much finely-grated horseradish as will make the sauce the consistence of onion sauce.

—— FOR HASHES AND MADE DISHES. A pint of Port wine, twelve anchovies chopped, a quarter of a pint of vinegar, as much beaten pepper as will lie on half a crown, two or three cloves, a blade or two of mace, a nutmeg bruised, one small onion minced, two bay-leaves, a little lemon thyme, marjoram, and parsley, and a piece of horseradish about the length of a finger split into quarters; put all into a saucepan, and let it simmer till the anchovies are dissolved; then strain it, and, when cold, bottle it for use.

—— FOR HASHED OR MINCED VEAL. Take the bones of cold roast or boiled veal, dredge them well with flour, and put them into a stewpan with a pint and a half of broth or water, a small onion, a little grated or finely-minced lemon-peel, or the peel of a quarter of a small lemon, pared as thin as possible, half a tea-spoonful of salt, and a blade of pounded mace; to thicken it, rub a table-spoonful of flour into half an ounce of butter; stir it into the broth, and set it on the fire, and let it boil very gently for about half an hour; strain through a tamis or sieve, and it is ready to put to the veal to warm up; which is to be done by placing the stewpan by the side of the fire. Squeeze in half a lemon, and cover the bottom of the dish with toasted bread sippets cut into triangles, and garnish the dish with slices of ham or bacon.

—— FOR HASHES OF MUTTON OR BEEF. Unless you are quite sure you perfectly understand the palate of those you are working for, show those who are to eat the hash this receipt, and beg of them to direct you how they wish it seasoned.

Half the number of the ingredients enumerated will be more than enough: but as it is a receipt so often wanted we have given variety.

Chop the bones and fragments of the joint, &c., and put them into a stewpan; cover them with boiling water, six berries of black pepper, the same of allspice, a small bundle of parsley, half a head of celery cut in pieces, and a small sprig of savory, or lemon thyme, or sweet marjoram; cover up, and let it simmer gently for half an hour.

Slice half an ounce of onion, and put it into a stewpan with an ounce of butter; fry it over a sharp fire for about a couple of minutes, till it takes a little color; then stir in as much flour as will make it a stiff paste, and by degrees mix with it the gravy you have made from the bones, &c; let it boil very gently for about a quarter of an hour, till it is the consistence of cream; strain it through a tamis or sieve into a basin; put it back into the stewpan: to season it, cut in a few pickled onions, or walnuts, or a couple of gherkins, and a table-spoonful of mushroom ketchup, or walnut or other pickle liquor; or some capers, and caper liquor; or a table-spoonful of ale; or a little eschalot, or tarragon vinegar; cover the bottom of the dish with sippets of bread (that they may become savory reservoirs of gravy), which some toast and cut into triangles. You may garnish it with fried bread sippets.

N. B.—To hash meat in perfection, it should be laid in this gravy only just long enough to get properly warm through.

*Obs.*—If any of the gravy that was sent up with, or ran from the joint when it was roasted, be left, it will be a great improvement to the hash.

If you wish to make mock venison, instead of the onion, put in two or three cloves, a table-spoonful of currant jelly, and the same quantity of claret or Port wine, instead of the ketchup.

You may make a curry hash by adding some curry jam.

N. B.—A pint of Beef-gravy Sauce is an excellent gravy to warm up either meat or poultry.

—— KELLY'S, FOR BOILED Tripe, Calf-head, or Cow-heel. Garlic vinegar, a table-spoonful; of mustard, brown sugar, and black pepper, a tea-spoonful each; stirred into half a pint of oiled melted butter.

—— KELLY'S PIQUANTE. Pound a table-spoonful of capers, and one of minced parsley, as fine as possible; then add the yolks of three hard eggs, rub them well together with a table-spoonful of mustard;

bone six anchovies, and pound them, rub them through a hair sieve, and mix with two table-spoonfuls of oil, one of vinegar, one of eschalot ditto, and a few grains of cayenne pepper; rub all these well together in a mortar, till thoroughly incorporated; then stir them into half a pint of good gravy, or melted butter and put the whole through a sieve.

—— LEMON. Pare a lemon, and cut it into slices twice as thick as a half-crown piece; divide these into dice, and put them into a quarter of a pint of melted butter. Some cooks mince a bit of the lemon-peel (pared very thin) very fine, and add it to the above.

—— LEMON AND LIVER. Pare off the rind of a lemon, or of a Seville orange, as thin as possible, so as not to cut off any of the white with it; now cut off all the white, and cut the lemon into slices about as thick as a couple of half-crowns; pick out the pips, and divide the slices into small squares: add these, and a little of the peel minced very fine to the liver, prepared as directed above, and put them into the melted butter, and warm them together; but do not let them boil.

N. B.—The poulterers can always let you have fresh livers, if that of the fowl or rabbit is not good, or not large enough to make as much sauce as you wish.

*Obs.*—Some cooks, instead of pounding, mince the liver very fine (with half as much bacon), and leave out the parsley; others add the juice of half a lemon, and some of the peel grated, or a tea-spoonful of tarragon or Chili vinegar, a table-spoonful of white wine, or a little beaten mace, or nutmeg, or allspice: if you wish it a little more lively on the palate, pound an eschalot, or a few leaves of tarragon or basil, with anchovy, or ketchup, or cayenne.

—— LIVER AND PARSLEY, OR LIVER AND LEMON. Wash the liver (it must be perfectly fresh) of a fowl or rabbit, and boil it five minutes in five table-spoonfuls of water; chop it fine, or pound or bruise it in a small quantity of the liquor it was boiled in, and rub it through a sieve: wash about one-third the bulk of parsley leaves, put them on to boil in a little boiling water, with a tea-spoonful of salt in it; lay it on a hair sieve to drain, and mince it very fine; mix it with the liver, and put it into a quarter pint of melted butter, and warm it up; do not let it boil.

—— LOBSTER. (1) Bruise the body, add it to some thick melted butter; pull the flesh into small bits, and mix all together with some rich beef gravy; boil it up, and before serving add a little salt, and squeeze in a little lemon-juice.

—— LOBSTER. (2) Pound very finely the spawn of a lobster, rub it through a sieve, mix it with a quarter of a pound of melted butter, then add the meat of the lobster cut into small bits. Make it quite hot, but do not allow it to boil.

—— LOBSTER. *See Lobster.*

—— FOR LOBSTER. Bruise the yolks of two hard-boiled eggs with the back of a wooden spoon, or rather pound them in a mortar, with a tea-spoonful of water, and the soft inside and the spawn of the lobster; rub them quite smooth, with a tea-spoonful of made mustard, two table-spoonfuls of salad oil, and five of vinegar; season it with a very little cayenne pepper, and some salt.

—— LOVE-APPLE, ACCORDING TO UDE. Melt in a stewpan a dozen or two of love-apples (which, before putting in the stewpan, cut in two, and squeeze the juice and the seeds out); then put two eschalots, one onion, with a few bits of ham, a clove, a little thyme, a bay-leaf, a few leaves of mace, and when melted, rub them through a tamis. Mix a few spoonfuls of good Espag-

nole or Spanish sauce, and a little salt and pepper, with this puree. Boil it for twenty minutes, and serve up.

—— MINT. (1) Pick and wash some green mint; add, when minced, a table-spoonful of the young leaves, to four of vinegar, and put it into a sauce-tureen, with a tea-spoonful of brown sugar.

—— MINT. (2) Wash half a handful of nice, young, fresh-gathered green mint (to this some add one-third the quantity of parsley); pick the leaves from the stalks, mince them very fine, and put them into a sauce-boat, with a tea-spoonful of moist sugar, and four table-spoonfuls of vinegar.

—— MOCK CAPER. Cut some pickled green pease, French beans, gherkins, or nasturtiums, into bits the size of capers; put them into half a pint of melted butter, with two tea-spoonfuls of lemon-juice, or nice vinegar.

—— MOCK OYSTER. Put into a saucepan two or three chopped anchovies, a quarter of a pint of water, a little mace, and one or two cloves; let them simmer till the anchovies be quite dissolved. Strain it, and when cool, add a tea-cupful of cream; thicken it with a piece of butter rolled in flour, and heat it up. It may be poured over boiled fowls or veal.

—— MOCK TOMATA. The only difference between this and genuine love-apple sauce, is the substituting the pulp of apple for that of tomata, coloring it with tumeric, and communicating an acid flavor to it by vinegar.

—— MUSHROOM. Pick and peel half a pint of mushrooms (the smaller the better); wash them very clean, and put them into a saucepan, with half a pint of veal gravy or milk, a little pepper and salt, and an ounce of butter rubbed with a table-spoonful of flour; stir them together, and set them over a gentle fire, to stew slowly till tender; skim and strain it.

*Obs.*—It will be a great improvement to this, and the two following sauces, to add to them the juice of half a dozen mushrooms, prepared the day before, by sprinkling them with salt, the same as when you make ketchup; or add a large spoonful of good double mushroom ketchup.

See Quintessence of Mushrooms.

—— MUSHROOM, FOR BOILED TURKEY OR FOWL. Pick clean and wash a pint of small mushrooms, rub them with flannel, put them into a saucepan with a blade of mace, a little salt, grated nutmeg, a piece of butter rolled in flour, and a pint of cream, keep stirring them till they boil, then pour them round the turkey, fowl, or chicken.

—— WHITE ONION. The following is a more mild and delicate preparation: take half a dozen of the largest and whitest onions (the Spanish are the mildest, but these can only be had from August to December); peel them and cut them in half, and lay them in a pan of spring water for a quarter of an hour, and then boil for a quarter of an hour; and then, if you wish them to taste very mild, pour off that water, and cover them with fresh boiling water, and let them boil till they are tender, which will sometimes take three-quarters of an hour longer.

—— ONION. Boil twelve or more onions in water; when it boils, pour it off, add more hot water, and when the onions are tender, strain and mash them in a bowl, add a piece of butter, a little salt, and one or two spoonfuls of cream. Heat it before serving. An apple may be boiled with the onions.

—— ONION, OR ONION GRAVY. Peel and slice the onions (some put in an equal quantity of cucumber or celery) into a quart stewpan, with an ounce of butter; set it on a slow fire, and turn the onion about till it is very lightly browned; now gradually stir in half an ounce of flour; add a little broth, and a little pepper and salt; boil up for a few minutes; add a table-spoonful of claret, or Port wine, and same of mushroom ketchup, (you may sharpen it with a little lemon-juice or vinegar), and rub it through a tamis or fine sieve. Curry powder will convert this into excellent curry sauce.

N. B.—If this sauce is for steaks, shred an ounce of onions, fry them a nice brown, and put them to the sauce you have rubbed through a tamis; or some very small round, young silver button onions, peeled and boiled tender, and put in whole when your sauce is done, will be an acceptable addition.

*Obs.*—If you have no broth, put in half a pint of water, and just before you give it the last boil up, add to it another table-spoonful of mushroom ketchup, or the same quantity of Port wine or good ale. The flavor of this sauce may be varied by adding tarragon or burnet vinegar.

—— ONION. *See Onion.*

—— ORANGE GRAVY, FOR WILD DUCKS, WOODCOCKS, SNIPES, WIDGEON, TEAL, &c. Set on a saucepan with half a pint of veal gravy; add to it half a dozen leaves of basil, a small onion, and a roll of orange or lemon-peel, and let it boil up for a few minutes, and strain it off. Put to the clear gravy the juice of a Seville orange, or lemon, half a tea-spoonful of salt, the same of pepper, and a glass of red wine; send it up hot. Eschalot and cayenne may be added. This is an excellent sauce for all kinds of wild water-fowl.

Gravies should always be sent up in a covered boat: they keep hot longer; and it leaves it to the choice of the company to partake of them or not.

—— OYSTER. *See Oysters.*

—— PIQUANT. Put a little chopped shallot and a few spoonfuls of gravy into a saucepan; let it boil till the gravy be nearly boiled away, but not burned to the bottom of the saucepan; add as much braise as may be required for the sauce, season with pepper and salt, boil it a few minutes, then add a little lemon-juice, sugar, and a tea-spoonful of garlic vinegar.

N. B.—Braise is an onion stuck with cloves, and boiled till tender in gravy and white wine.

—— PIQUANT, *for cold Meat, Game, Poultry, Fish, &c. or Salads.* Pound in a mortar the yolks of two eggs that have been boiled hard with a mustard-spoonful of made mustard, and a little pepper and salt; add two table-spoonfuls of salad oil; mix well, and then add three table-spoonfuls of vinegar; rub it up well till it is quite smooth, and pass it through a tamis or sieve.

*Obs.*—To the above, some add an anchovy, or a table-spoonful of mushroom ketchup, or walnut pickle, some finely-chopped parsley, grated horseradish, or young onions minced, or burnet, horseradish or tarragon, or elder vinegar, &c., and cayenne or minced pickles, capers, &c. This is a *piquante* relish for lobsters, crabs, cold fish, &c.

—— SALAD OR PIQUANT, FOR COLD MEAT, FISH, &C. Pound together an ounce of scraped horseradish, half an ounce of salt, a table-spoonful of made mustard, four drachms of minced eschalots, half a drachm of celery seed, and half ditto of cayenne; adding gradually a pint of burnet, or tarragon vinegar, and let it stand in a jar a week, and then pass it through a sieve.

—— POIVRADE, FOR COLD MEAT. (1) Chop finely six shallots and a handful of picked and washed parsley; mix with it a little vinegar, mustard, cayenne some cold gravy, and salt.

—— POIVRADE, FOR COLD MEAT.

(2) Bruise the yolk of a hard-boiled egg with a little salt and mustard, oil, soy, chopped parsley, and chives, and pour it over slices of any cold meat.

—— PUDDING. Mix with half a pint of melted butter two wine-glasses of sherry, and a table-spoonful of pounded loaf sugar; make it quite hot, and serve in a sauce-tureen, with grated nutmeg on the top.

—— QUIN'S. (1) Half a pint of mushroom pickle, the same of walnut pickle, three whole and three pounded cloves of garlic, six anchovies bruised, and a tea-spoonful of cayenne. Mix all together in a large bottle, shake it daily for three weeks, then strain, and bottle it for use.

—— QUIN'S. (2) One pint of Port wine, one of mushroon ketchup, one of walnut liquor, one of essence of anchovies and a teaspoonful of cayenne; mix all together, and boil it for a quarter of an hour. If essence of anchovies, is not to be had, boil half a pound of anchovies in a quart of water till reduced to a pint. Strain, and use it.

——REVEREND. Chop up some lemon-peel, and two or three pickled cucumbers; put them into a stewpan with two spoonfuls of cullis, a little butter rolled in flour, season with salt and pepper; put it on the fire, and make it quite hot without boiling, stirring all the time, make a *liaison* with yolks of eggs, and serve.

—— RICE. Steep a quarter of a pound of rice in a pint of milk, with onion, pepper, &c. as in the last receipt; when the rice is quite tender (take out the spice), rub it through a sieve into a clean stewpan: if too thick, put a little milk or cream to it.

*Obs.*—This is a very delicate white sauce; and at elegant tables is frequently served instead of bread sauce.

—— FOR ROAST BEEF. (1) Mix well together a large table-spoonful of finely-grated horseradish, a dessert-spoonful of made mustard, and half a one of brown sugar, then add vinegar till it be as thick as made mustard. Serve in a sauce-tureen.

—— FOR ROAST BEEF. (2) Put into a stone jar one gill of soy, two of vinegar, two of water, a good-sized stick of horseradish, and two sliced onions. Cover the jar closely, and set it into a pan of cold water; when it boils, let it simmer for two or three hours.

—— ROBART, FOR BEEF STEAKS OR MUTTON CHOPS. Put into a saucepan a little gravy, two ounces of butter dredged with flour, a small slice of raw ham, and two or three minced onions; when the onions are browned, dust in a little more flour, and add nearly a pint of gravy, a little salt and pepper, a tea-spoonful of mustard, and a table-spoonful of vinegar. Boil it for some minutes, strain and serve it.

—— SALAD. (1) Bruise the yolk of a hard-boiled egg with a small tea-spoonful of salt, then add a dessert-spoonful of mustard, and stir in gradually a large table-spoonful of olive oil, oiled butter, or cream, then by degrees mix in two or three table-spoonfuls of vinegar; serve it in a sauce-tureen, or mix it with the salad. Instead of the hard egg, some persons prefer the sauce made with the yolk raw.

—— SALAD. (2) Rub smooth a hard-boiled egg, beat well a raw egg, and mix them together with a little water, a tea-spoonful of salt, one of cayenne, one of pepper, and one of mustard, a table-spoonful of vinegar, one of essence of anchovies, and five of rich cream.

The artist, as he styles himself, who invented this salad sauce drove in his carriage to his employers, and charged them ten shillings and sixpence for each visit!

SAUCES. *See also Gravy, page 116.*

—— SHALLOT. (1) Boil a few minced

shallots in a little clear gravy and nearly as much vinegar, add a few peppercorns and a little salt. Strain, and serve it in a sauce-tureen.

—— SHALLOT. (2) Take two spoonfuls of the liquor the meat was boiled in, two spoonfuls of vinegar, two or three shallots cut fine, and a little salt; put these ingredients into a saucepan, with a bit of butter rolled in flour; let it stew a little, and serve it up with your mutton or beef.

—— SHARP, FOR VENISON. Put into a silver, or very clean and well-tinned saucepan, half a pint of the best white wine vinegar, and a quarter of a pound of loaf-sugar pounded: set it over the fire, and let it simmer gently; skim it carefully; pour it through a tamis or fine sieve, and send it up in a basin.

*Obs.*— Some people like this better than the sweet wine sauces.

—— SHRIMP. (1) Pick some shrimps nicely from the shell, put them into melted butter, add a table-spoonful of lemon pickle and vinegar; heat it.

—— SHRIMP. (2) Shell a pint of shrimps; pick them clean, wash them, and put them into half a pint of good melted butter. A pint of unshelled shrimps is about enough for four persons.

*Obs.*—Some stew the heads and shells of the shrimps, (with or without a blade of bruised mace), for a quarter of an hour, and strain off the liquor to melt the butter with, and add a little lemon-juice, cayenne, and essence of anchovy, or soy, cavice, &c.; but the flavor of the shrimp is so delicate, that it will be overcome by any such additions.

MEM.—If your shrimps are not quite fresh, they will eat tough and thready, as other stale fish do.

—— SORREL. (1) Pick and wash some sorrel, put it into a stewpan with a little water, stir it, to prevent its burning, and when it is tender, drain and mince it finely; fry it for half an hour in a stewpan with a little butter, then dredge in a table-spoonful of flour, moisten it with boiling cream, and let it stew on a slow fire for an hour; add a little salt, and if too acid, a little sugar. Before serving, thicken with the beaten yolks of four eggs.

—— SORREL. (2) Pick and thoroughly wash two double handfuls of young sorrel, well drain it from water, and then put it into a stewpan, well covered with a bit of butter, and let it stew very gently over a slow fire; when done, put it to drain on a sieve for three minutes, then, with a wooden spoon, rub it through a tammy into a dish; put it into a stewpan, with a bit of butter, stirring it over the fire till thoroughly mixed; you may add, if you choose, three spoonfuls of good *consomme*, and when it has boiled for a few minutes, add to it half as much cream sauce as there is sorrel, and if necessary season with a little salt; this is proper for a *fricandeau* of veal or *entrees* of fish.

—— SUPERLATIVE. Claret, or Port wine, and mushroom ketchup, a pint of each. Half a pint of walnut or other pickle liquor. Pounded anchovies, four ounces. Fresh lemon-peel, pared very thin, an ounce. Peeled and sliced eschalots, the same. Scraped horseradish, ditto. Allspice, and black pepper powdered, half an ounce each. Cayenne, one drachm, or curry-powder, three drachms. Celery-seed bruised, one drachm. All avoirdupois weight. Put these into a wide-mouthed bottle, stop it close, shake it up every day for a fortnight, and strain it (when some think it improved by the addition of a quarter of a pint of soy, or thick browning), and you will have a "delicious double relish." Dr. Kitchiner says, this composition is one of the "chefs d'œuvre" of many experiments he has made, for the purpose of enabling the good house-wives of Great Britain to prepare their own

sauces: it is equally agreeable with fish, game, poultry, or ragouts, &c., and as a fair lady may make it herself, its relish will be not a little augmented, by the certainty that all the ingredients are good and wholesome.

*Obs.*—Under an infinity of circum-stances, a cook may be in want of the sub-stances necessary to make sauce: the above composition of the several articles from which the various gravies derive their fla-vor, will be found a very admirable extem-poraneous substitute. By mixing a large ta-ble-spoonful with a quarter of a pint of thickened melted butter, or broth, five min-utes will finish a boat of very relishing sauce, nearly equal to drawn gravy, and as likely to put your lingual nerves into good humor as any thing I know.

To make a boat of sauce for poultry, &c. put a piece of butter about as big as an egg into a stewpan, set it on the fire; when it is melted, put to it a table-spoonful of flour; stir it thoroughly together, and add to it two table-spoonfuls of sauce, and by degrees about half a pint of broth, or boiling water, let it simmer gently over a slow fire for a few minutes, skim it and strain it through a sieve, and it is ready.

—— FOR STEAKS, CHOPS, OR CUTLETS. Take your chops out of the fry-ing-pan; for a pound of meat keep a table-spoonful of the fat in the pan, or put in about an ounce of butter; put to it as much flour as will make it a paste; rub it well to-gether over the fire till they are a little brown; then add as much boiling water as will reduce it to the thickness of good cream, and a table-spoonful of mushroom or walnut ketchup, or pickle, or browning; let it boil together a few minutes, and pour it through a sieve to the steaks, &c.

*Obs.*—To the above is sometimes added a sliced onion, or a minced eschalot, with a table-spoonful of Port wine, or a little eschalot wine. Garnish with finely-scraped horseradish, or pickled walnuts, gherkins, &c. Some beef-eaters like chopped es-chalots in one saucer, and horseradish grated in vinegar, in another. Broiled mushrooms are favorite relishes to beef steaks.

—— SWEET, FOR VENISON OR HARE. Put some currant jelly into a stewpan; when it is melted, pour it into a sauceboat.

N. B.—Many send it to table without melting.

This is a more salubrious relish than either spice or salt, when the palate protests against animal food unless its flavor be masked. Currant jelly is a good accompaniment to roasted or hashed meats.

—— SWEET. Put some cinnamon into a saucepan, with as much water as will cover it; set it on the fire, and when it has boiled up once or twice, add two spoonfuls of powder sugar, a quarter of a pint of white wine, and two bay-leaves; give the whole one boil, and then strain it for table.

—— TARTARE. Pound in a mortar three hard yolks of eggs; put them into a basin, and add half a table-spoonful of made mustard, and a little pepper and salt; pour to it by degrees, stirring it fast all the while, about two wine-glassfuls of salad oil; stir it together till it comes to a good thickness.

N. B.—A little tarragon or chervil minced very fine, and a little vinegar, may be added.

——TOMATA. *See Tomata.*

——TOURNEE. To a little white thickening add some stock drawn from the trimmings of veal, poultry, and ham; do not make it too thick. Boil it slowly with a few mushrooms, a bunch of parsley, and some green onions; strain and skim it well, and use it as required. German sauce is made as the sauce tournee, adding the beaten yolks of two or more eggs, and is used for ragouts, fricassees, and any made dish which may require a rich white sauce.

—— WHITE. Thicken half a pint of cream with a little flour and butter, four shallots minced, a little mace and lemon-peel; let it boil, and a little before serving, add a spoonful of white wine, the well-beaten yolk of an egg, the squeeze of a lemon, and a tea-spoonful of anchovy liquor. This sauce will answer for boiled fowls, or for a fricassee.

—— WHITE, FOR FOWLS OR TURKEY. Put on, in a quart of water, the necks of fowls, a piece of the scrag-end of a neck of mutton, two blades of mace, twelve peppercorns, one anchovy, a small head of celery, a slice from off the end of a lemon, and a bunch of sweet herbs; cover it closely, and let it boil till reduced to nearly half a pint; strain, and put to it a quarter of a pound of butter dredged with flour; let it boil for five minutes, and then add two spoonfuls of pickled mushrooms. Mix with a tea-cupful of cream, the well-beaten yolks of two eggs, and some grated nutmeg; stir this in gradually, and shake the pan over the fire till it is all quite hot, but do not allow it to boil.

—— WHITE ITALIAN. Peel some mushrooms, and throw them into a little water and lemon-juice, to keep them white. Put into a stewpan two-thirds of sauce tournee, and one-third of good veal stock, two table-spoonfuls of finely-chopped mushrooms, and half a table-spoonful of washed and chopped shallots; let it boil till well flavored, and then serve it. The mushrooms should be as white as possible.

——WHITE SHARP. Boil with a little tarragon, or tarragon vinegar, if the tarragon is not to be had, four table-spoonfuls of white wine vinegar, and about twenty peppercorns; reduce this to one-fourth, and add it to six table-spoonfuls of sauce-tournee, and two of good stock; boil and strain it; put it again on the fire, and thicken it with the beaten yolks of two eggs, a small bit of butter, a little salt and cayenne. Just before serving, stir in a spoonful of cream.

—— WHITE, FOR BOILED FOWLS. Melt in a tea-cupful of milk a large table-spoonful of butter kneaded in flour, beat up the yolk of an egg with a tea-spoonful of cream, stir it into the butter, and heat it over the fire, stirring it constantly; chopped parsley improves this sauce. It also may be made by melting the butter with water, and mixing milk with the egg.

SAUCE, WINE, FOR VENISON OR HARE. A quarter of a pint of claret or Port wine, the same quantity of plain, unflavored mutton gravy, and a table-spoonful of currant jelly: let it just boil up, and send it to table in a sauce-boat.

SAUCE, WOW WOW, FOR STEWED OR BOUILLI BEEF. Chop some parsley-leaves very fine; quarter two or three pickled cucumbers, or walnuts, and divide them into small squares, and set them by ready: put into a saucepan a bit of butter as big as an egg; when it is melted, stir to it a table-spoonful of fine flour, and about half a pint of the broth in which the beef was boiled; add a table-spoonful of vinegar, the like quantity of mushroom ketchup, or Port wine, or both, and a tea-spoonful of made mustard; let it simmer together till it is as thick as you wish it; put in the parsley and pickles to get warm, and pour it over the beef; or rather send it up in a sauce-tureen.

*Obs.*—If you think the above not sufficiently *piquante*, add to it some capers, or a minced eschalot, or one or two tea-spoonfuls of eschalot wine, or essence of anchovy, or basil, elder, or tarragon, or horseradish, or burnet vinegar; or strew over the meat carrots and turnips cut into dice, minced capers, walnuts, red cabbage, pickled cucumbers, or French beans, &c.

SAUSAGES, (1) Are composed of various kinds of meat, chopped exceedingly small, with pounded spices, and aromatic herbs, shred fine; these ingredients are put into skins, or guts (thoroughly washed), and tied into lengths of from two to five inches.

Some persons add to the mixture a glass of Rhenish, Champagne, Madeira, or other wine.

SAUSAGES, (2) Are best when quite fresh made. Put a bit of butter, or dripping into a clean frying-pan; as soon as it is melted (before it gets hot) put in the sausages, and shake the pan for a minute, and keep turning them (be careful not to break or prick them in so doing); fry them over a very slow fire till they are nicely browned on all sides; when they are done, lay them on a hair sieve, placed before the fire for a couple of minutes to drain the fat from them. The secret of frying sausages is, to let them get hot very gradually; they then will not burst, if they are not stale. The common practice to prevent their bursting, is to prick them with a fork, but this lets the gravy out. You may froth them by rubbing them with cold fresh butter, and lightly dredge them with flour, and put them in a cheese-toaster or Dutch oven for a minute. Some over-economical cooks insist that no butter or lard, &c. is required, their own fat being sufficient to fry them: we have tried it; the sausages were partially scorched, and had that piebald appearance that all fried things have when sufficient fat is not allowed.

*Obs.*—Poached eggs, pease pudding, and mashed potatoes, are agreeable accompaniments to sausages; and sausages are as welcome boiled with roasted poultry or veal, or boiled tripe; so are ready-dressed German sausages; and a convenient, easily digestible, and invigorating food for the aged, and those whose teeth are defective.

N. B. Sausages, when finely chopped, are a delicate "*bonne bouche*;" and require very little assistance from the teeth to render them quite ready for the stomach.

SAUSAGES. (3) Take a pound of the inward fat of the pig, and half a pound of lean pork; pick them both from skin and sinews, mince them very finely, grate a large nutmeg, take its weight of pounded mace and cloves, the largest proportion mace, the weight of all of pepper, and twice the weight of the spices of salt; chop finely a few sage leaves and a little lemon thyme; mix all well together with two large table-spoonfuls of grated bread and the yolk of an egg beaten. It may be put into skins, or packed into a jar and tied closely with blad-der. When to be used, moisten it with the yolk of an egg beaten, make it up in the form of sausages, flour them, and fry them in butter.

SAUSAGES, BEEF AND OYSTER. *See Beef.*

SAUSAGES, TO MAKE. Chop together two pounds of lean pork, and one and a half of the inward fat of the pig, the crumb of a penny loaf cut into slices and soaked in cold water; season with pepper, salt, grated nut-meg, lemon thyme, and a little sage. Mix all the ingredients well, and half fill the skins; boil them half an hour.

SAUSAGES, BOLOGNA. Take the legs and shoulders of a pig, from which cut all the lean, scrape it well, remove all the sin-ews, and rub the meat well with a seasoning made of salt, pepper, coriander, cloves, cin-namon, nutmeg, and bay-leaf. When prop-erly flavored, take some bacon, lard, and leaf, and cut the whole into dice; mix the fat and lean together, and put it into ox-guts, tie up the ends, and lay the sausages in a pan of water, with salt, and saltpetre; cover the pan close, and leave it. In a week's time take out the sausages and drain them. Tie them be-tween two pieces of wood, hang them up to dry, and smoke. When dry, untie them, and rub each over with oil, and the ashes of vine-twigs, mixed together. Keep them in a dry place.

SAUSAGES, ROYAL. Mince small the meat of a partridge, a capon, or pullet, a piece of gammon, and other bacon, and a bit of leg of veal; shred also some parsley, chives, truffles, and mushrooms; mix these all together, and season with pepper, salt,

beaten spice, and garlic; bind the whole with the yolks of six, the whites of two eggs, and a little cream; when thoroughly mixed, roll the preparation into thick pieces, which wrap in very thin slices of fillet of veal, well beaten with a rolling-pin; each sausage should be about the thickness of a man's wrist, and of proportionate length. Line an oval stewpan with slices of bacon and thin beef steaks, put in the sausages, cover them with beef steaks and bacon, shut the stew-pan very close, and set it on a moderate fire, put hot embers on the lid, and let it stand ten or twelve hours; then take it off, and when cold, take out the sausages carefully, re-move the veal, and all the fat, with a sharp knife cut them into slices, and serve cold.

SAUSAGES, SPREADBURY'S. Cut from the leg or griskin one pound of nice lean pork, free from sinews and skin, mince it very finely: mince one pound of the best beef suet, mix it with the pork, and pound it as finely as possible in a marble mortar; add two large table-spoonfuls of stale bread rubbed through a sieve, also a good deal of pepper, salt, and a little finely-chopped sage, mix all together with the yolks of two eggs beaten up. It will keep for sometime, if put into an earthen jar and pressed closely down. When it is to be used, make it into rolls, and as thick as common sausages, and three or four inches long: dust them with a little flour; have ready a frying-pan made very hot, and fry them without any thing but their own fat, till they are done quite through, taking care not to make them too dry. By breaking one of them, the cook will know whether they are sufficiently done. They may be fried in lard or fresh beef dripping.

SAVORY CABBAGE. *See Cabbage*.

SAVOY BISCUITS. To be made as drop biscuits, omitting the caraways, and quarter of a pound of flour: put it into the biscuit-funnel, and lay it out about the length and size of your finger, on common shop paper;

strew sugar over, and bake them in a hot oven; when cold, wet the backs of the paper with a paste-brush and water: when they have lain sometime, take them carefully off, and place them back to back.

SAVOYS, Are boiled in the same manner as cabbages; quarter them when you send them to table.

SCOTCH BARLEY BROTH;— *a good and substantial dinner for sixpence per head.* Wash three-quarters of a pound of Scotch barley in a little cold water; put it in a soup-pot with a shin or leg of beef, of about ten pounds weight, sawed into four pieces (tell the butcher to do this for you); cover it well with cold water; set it on the fire: when it boils skim it very clean, and put in two onions of about three ounces weight each; set it by the side of the fire to simmer very gently about two hours; then skim all the fat clean off, and put in two heads of celery, and a large turnip cut into small squares; season it with salt, and let it boil an hour and a half longer, and it is ready: take out the meat (carefully with a slice, and cover it up, and set it by the fire to keep warm), and skim the broth well before you put it in the tureen.

SCOTCH BROSE. This favorite Scotch dish is generally made with the liquor meat has been boiled in. Put half a pint of oatmeal into a porringer with a little salt, if there be not enough in the broth, of which add as much as will mix it to the consistence of hasty pudding, or a little thicker; lastly, take a little of the fat that swims on the broth, and put it on the crowdie, and eat it in the same way as hasty-pudding.

*Obs.*—This Scotsman's dish is easily prepared at very little expense, and is pleasant-tasted and nutritious.

N. B.—For various methods of making and flavoring oatmeal gruel, see *Gruel.*

SCOTCH BURGOO. This humble dish forms no contemptible article of food. It possesses the grand qualities of salubrity, pleasantness, and cheapness. It is, in fact, a sort of oatmeal hasty pudding without milk; much used by those patterns of combined industry, frugality, and temperance, the Scottish peasantry; and this, among other examples of the economical Scotch, is well worthy of being occasionally adopted by all who have large families and small incomes. It is made in the following easy and expeditious manner:—To a quart of oatmeal add gradually two quarts of water, so that the whole may smoothly mix: then stirring it continually over the fire, boil it together for a quarter of an hour; after which, take it up, and stir in a little salt and butter, with or without pepper. This quantity will serve a family of five or six persons for a moderate meal.

SCOTS COLLOPS. Cut some very thin slices of beef; rub with butter the bottom of an iron stewpan that has a cover to fit quite closely; put in the meat, some pepper, and a little salt, a large onion, and an apple minced very small. Cover the stewpan, and let it simmer till the meat is very tender. Serve it hot.

SCOTCH DUMPLING. Make a paste with some oatmeal and butter, form it into a dumpling, and place a haddock's liver in the middle, well seasoned with pepper and salt; it should be boiled in a cloth.

SCOTCH HAGGIS. Make the haggis-bag perfectly clean; parboil the draught; boil the liver very well, so as it will grate; dry the meal before the fire; mince the draught and a pretty large piece of beef very small; grate about half of the liver; mince plenty of the suet and some onions small; mix all these materials very well together, with a handful or two of the dried meal; spread them on the table, and season them properly with salt and mixed spices; take any of the scraps of beef that are left from mincing, and some of the water that boiled the draught, and make about a choppin (*i. e.* a quart) of good stock of it; then put all the haggis meat into the bag, and that broth in it; then sew up the bag; but be sure to put out all the wind before you sew it quite close. If you think the bag is thin, you may put it in a cloth. If it is a large haggis, it will take at least two hours boiling.

N. B.—The above we copied *verbatim* from Mrs. MACIVER, a celebrated Caledonian professor of the culinary art, who taught, and published a book of cookery, at Edinburgh, A. D. 1787.

SCOTS KALE. Put barley on in cold water, and when it boils take off the scum, put in any piece of fresh beef, and a little salt; let it boil three hours, have ready a cullender full of kale, cut small and boil them till tender. Two or three leeks may be added with the greens, if the flavor is approved of. This broth is also made with salted beef, which must be put in water over night to soak.

SCOTCH SHORT BREAD. Take two pounds of flour, dry, and sift it well; then mix with it a pound of powder-sugar, three ounces of candied citron and orange-peel cut into dice, and half a pound of caraway comfits; put half a pound of butter into a saucepan, set it on the fire, and when quite melted, mix it with the flour, &c.; the paste being nicely made, roll it out to the thickness of half an inch, cut it into cakes, lay them on white paper, prick and bake them; they should be of a pale color.

SEA CALE, BOILED. Let it lie sometime in cold water, then clean and trim it nicely, cutting off any part that may be at all green, and parting it as little as possible. Put it on in boiling water, with a little salt. Let it boil half an hour; drain off the water. Pare the crust off a slice of toasted bread, lay it in the dish, pour over it a little melted butter, and serve the cale upon it.

SEED CAKE. Sift two and a half pounds of flour, with half a pound of good white or loaf sugar, pounded into a pan or bowl; make a cavity in the centre, and pour in half a pint of lukewarm milk, and a tablespoonful of thick yeast; mix the milk and yeast with enough flour to make it as thick as cream (this is called setting a sponge); set it by in a warm place for one hour; in the meantime, melt to an oil half a pound of fresh butter, and add it to the other ingredients, with one ounce of caraway-seeds, and enough of milk to make it of a middling stiffness; line a hoop with paper, well rubbed over with butter; put in the mixture; set it sometime to prove in a stove, or before the fire, and bake it on a plate about an hour, in rather a hot oven; when done, rub the top over wlth a paste-brush dipped in milk.

SHEEP'S KIDNEYS, BROILED. Wash and dry some nice kidneys, cut them in half and with a small skewer keep them open in imitation of two shells, season them with salt and pepper, and dip them into a little fresh melted butter. Broil first the side that is cut, and be careful not to let the gravy drop in taking them off the gridiron. Serve them in a hot dish, with finely-chopped parsley mixed with melted butter; the juice of a lemon, pepper and salt, putting a little upon each kidney. This is an excellent breakfast for a sportsman.

SHEEP'S LIVER. Cut it into slices; wash it well, and dry it in a cloth; flour and season it with pepper and salt, and fry it in butter, with a good deal of minced parsley and an onion; add a sufficient quantity of gravy or hot water to make a sauce, and let it stew a few minutes. It may be fried quite plain, and when cut into slices, should be washed in milk and water.

SHEEP'S MINCE. Wash the heart and lights very clean; boil them about half an hour; mince them finely; mix a piece of butter with flour, brown it in a stewpan, and add some of the liquor the heart and lights were boiled in. Put in the mince with some chopped onion; season with salt and pepper, cover it closely, and let it stew half an hour. Before serving, add a table-spoonful of mushroom ketchup.

SHEEP'S TONGUES, BROILED. Having parboiled the tongues in a little stock, split each, give them a few turns in some melted bacon, strewing over them salt, pepper, shred parsley, and bread crumbs; when well covered with the latter, lay them on a gridiron, and broil them slowly.

SHEEP'S TONGUES PIE. Line a dish with some good puff paste, and lay at the bottom of the dish some good forcemeat, made of roasted poultry, suet, parsley chopped, mushrooms, pepper and salt, and a few fine spices; upon this place the tongues cut in two, and upon them a good slice of ham, a little butter, and a few slices of bacon; put on the cover and bake it; when done, take out the bacon and ham, skim off all the fat, and pour on it what sauce you please.

SHEEP'S TONGUES ROASTED. Take half a dozen sheep's tongues, and having properly prepared them, lard them with small *lardons*, tie them to a skewer, wrap a buttered paper round, and fasten them on a spit, and roast them before a moderate fire; a little before they are done, take off the paper, baste the tongues with butter, and make them of a nice color. Serve with whatever sauce you may prefer.

SHEEP'S TROTTERS STUFFED. Boil the feet in good stock till the bones will come out with ease; fill the space left by them with a good fowl or chicken farce; dip them in lard, bread them well, and bake in a moderate oven. The space left by the bones is sometimes filled up with a bit of fried bread; in this case the feet are only previously boiled, and then served with cream sauce.

SHEEP'S TROTTERS FRIED. Clean some sheep's trotters nicely, scald and wash them in hot water; stew them in that sauce in which CALF'S HEAD PLAIN is boiled, and bone them. Fry, but not till brown, in a little butter, some carrots, onions, a little parsley roots, all cut small, thyme, a shallot, a small bay leaf, and a clove. When they begin to color, moisten them with water and vinegar mixed in equal parts, and let it all stew till the vegetables are quite tender; season with pepper and salt, and strain it through a silk sieve over the sheep's trotters, then fry the trotters in this batter; put nearly four table-spoonfuls of flour into an earthen pan, with a little salt, a little olive oil, and as much good beer or water as will moisten the paste; when well mixed, add the beaten whites of two eggs, dip the trotters into this, and fry them instantly. The marinade cuite, or pickle, into which the trotters are laid, and the paste in which they are fried, may be used for beef, and other meats. The same receipt may be followed exactly for calf's feet.

SHERBET. This is a delicious beverage, composed of cream, mixed with various articles, such as almonds, tea, pistachios, coffee, chocolate, &c., and sugar, and then iced. Sherbet may also be made with the juice of various fruits, sweetened to the taste. When the liquid is sufficiently limpid and cold, pour it into a silver, or tin *sorbet-iere*, and ice it as usual.

SHERBET, TURKISH. Wash a small fore quarter of veal, put it on the fire with nine pints of water; skim it well, and let it boil till reduced to two pints; run it through a sieve, and when cold, add to it a pint and a half of clear lemon-juice, and two pounds of loaf sugar which has been made into a sirup with a pint and a half of water, and cleared with the white of an egg. It is served in glass mugs for a dessert table, or offered at any other time as a refreshment.

SHRUB. (1) One measure of lemon-juice

juice is allowed to five of rum, and to every gallon of the mixture, six pounds of loaf sugar, which is to be melted in water, and the whole strained through flannel.

SHRUB. (2) To one part of lemon-juice, three of good orange are allowed, and, to every pint of juice, a pound and a half of very finely-pounded loaf sugar; these being well mixed, it is put into a cask, and one quart of the best rum added to each pint of the juice; the whole to be shaken three times a-day for a fortnight, or longer, if the cask be large. It is then allowed to stand to fine for a month, or till it be sufficiently clear to bottle. The dregs may be made into excellent milk punch, by pouring warm, but not boiling, milk on them, allowing three parts of milk to one of dregs; after being well mixed, it is fit for use.

SHRUB. (3) Put a quart of Seville orange-juice to a gallon of rum, with three pounds of lump sugar, and a handful of the peel pared extremely thin; let it stand in the cask for three months, then filter it through a cloth, and bottle it.

SHRUB. (4) Take a quart of orange-juice, strain it, put to it two pounds of lump sugar, four quarts and one pint of rum; put half the peels of the oranges into the rum, and let it stand one night. Then mix the rum with the orange-juice and sugar, put it into a vessel which has a spigot, shake it four or five times daily till the sugar be all dissolved; when it is clear, which may be in about a fortnight, bottle it off for use. If the oranges are very ripe, a pound and a half of sugar is sufficient.

SHRUB, LEMON OR ORANGE. The rind of the lemons or oranges being grated off, they are to be squeezed, and two pounds of finely-pounded loaf sugar is to be added to every pint of the strained juice; when the sugar is quite dissolved, two pints of rum are allowed to every pint of sirup; the whole is to be well mixed in a cask, and allowed to stand five or six weeks, and then drawn off.

SHRUB, WHITE CURRANT. The currants are to be bruised and put into a bag to drip; three-quarters of a pound of loaf sugar is to be dissolved in two quarts of juice; and a quart of rum being added, it is to be bottled for use.

SIRUP OF CURRANTS, RASPBERRIES, OR MULBERRIES. Pick the fruit from the stalks; squeeze the juice, and let it stand ten days or a fortnight, or till the fermentation ceases, which may be known by the scum cracking; carefully take off the scum, and pour the juice gently into a fresh vessel; let it stand twenty-four hours, and again pour it off, to one pound of pounded loaf sugar allow thirteen ounces of the juice, put it into a preserving-pan, and when it begins to boil, strain it through a jelly-bag, and bottle it when cold. Burie pears boiled, in a little of the sirup, are beautiful.

SIRUP OF ORANGE OR LEMON PEEL. Of fresh outer rind of Seville orange or lemon peel, three ounces, apothecaries' weight; boiling water a pint and a half; infuse them for a night in a close vessel; then strain the liquor: let it stand to settle; and having poured it off clear from the sediment, dissolve in it two pounds of double-refined loaf sugar, and make it into a sirup with a gentle heat.

*Obs.*—In making this sirup, if the sugar be dissolved in the infusion with as gentle a heat as possible, to prevent the exhalation of the volatile parts of the peel, this sirup will possess a great share of the fine flavor of the orange or lemon peel.

SIRUP, CLARIFIED. Break into bits two pounds (avoirdupois) of double-refined lump sugar, and put it into a clean stewpan (that is well tinned), with a pint of cold spring water; when the sugar is dissolved, set it over a moderate fire: beat about half the white of an egg, put it to the sugar before it gets warm, and stir it well together. Watch it; and when it boils take off the scum; keep it boiling till no scum rises, and it is perfectly clear; then run it through a clean napkin: put it into a close-stopped bottle; it will keep for months, and is an elegant article on the sideboard for sweetening.

*Obs.*—The proportion of sugar ordered in the above sirup is a quarter pound more than that directed in the Pharmacopœia of the London College of Physicians. The quantity of sugar must be as much as the liquor is capable of keeping dissolved when cold, or it will ferment, and quickly spoil: if kept in a temperate degree of heat, the above proportion of sugar may be considered the basis of all sirups.

SKATE, FRIED. After you have cleaned the fish, divide it into fillets; dry them on a clean cloth; beat the yolk and white of an egg thoroughly together, dip the fish in this, and then in fine bread-crumbs; fry it in hot lard or drippings till it is of a delicate brown color; lay it on a hair sieve to drain; garnish with crisp parsley, and some like caper sauce, with an anchovy in it.

SKATE, TO CRIMP. Skin the skate on both sides, cut it an inch and a half broad, and as long as the skate, roll up each piece and tie it with a thread; lay them for three hours in salt and water, and a little vinegar; boil them fifteen minutes in boiling salt and water; before serving, cut off the threads. Sauces:—shrimp, butter and anchovy. When the skate are very small, they are preferable broiled.

SKATE, LARGE, DRESSED LIKE VEAL CUTLETS. Crimp, or cut the skate in square pieces, roll them in beaten eggs, and then in grated bread mixed with chopped parsley, pepper, and salt; fry them of a nice brown color, and serve with a rich brown gravy.

SKATE, STEWED. Skin the skate, cut it into square pieces, and brown it with butter in a frying-pan; make a rich sauce with the skin and parings, to be boiled in three pints of water, with an onion, some pepper and salt; strain and thicken it with a little butter mixed with flour, add some very finely chopped parsley, and chives; of hot vinegar, mushroom ketchup, and Harvey sauce, a table-spoonful each, and a little cayenne; boil it up and put it in the skate five minutes before serving it.

SKATE, Is very good when in good season, but no fish so bad when it is otherwise: those persons that like it firm and dry, should have it crimped; but those that like it tender, should have it plain, and eat it not earlier than the second day, and if cold weather, three or four days old it is better: it cannot be kept too long, if perfectly sweet. Young skate eats very fine crimped and fried.

SKATE, SMALL, TO FRY. Clean, wash, and lay them one or two hours in vinegar, or vinegar and water, with a sliced onion, some chopped parsley, pepper, and salt; drain and dry them well, dip them into beaten eggs, dredge them with flour, and fry them of a fine brown color; garnish them with fried parsley. Sauces;—melted butter, and shrimp sauce.

SKIRRETS. Wash and scrape them, put them on in boiling water, and boil them for ten minutes; dry them in a cullender, and fry them brown in a little butter. They are sometimes plain boiled, and a little melted butter poured over them.

SMELTS, TO FRY. This delicate little fish, when perfectly fresh, must not be washed, but wiped with a clean cloth, and dredged with flour, or brushed over with a feather, dipped into the yolk of an egg beaten, and rolled in a plate of finely-grated bread-crumbs, and fried in boiling dripping, or fresh lard. They vary in size, and some will be done sooner than others. When of a clear yellow brown, take them out carefully, and lay them before the fire upon the back of a sieve to drain and keep hot. Dish them, heads and tails alternately; garnish with fried parsley. Sauce—melted butter. They may also be broiled.

SMELTS, ITALIAN. Boil your smelts with a large glass of white wine, half a glass of water, two spoonfuls of oil, two slices of lemon, a pinch of salt, and a pinch of fennel. When sufficiently done, make a *liaison* with yolks of eggs, and shred chervil, and serve your fish with its own sauce.

SNIPES. When the snipes have been picked they must be singed over a charcoal fire; in trussing them press the legs close to the side, and pierce the beak through them; tie a slice of bacon over each bird, run a long iron skewer through the sides, and tie them to the spit; in the meantime cut two or three slices of bread, according to the number of the birds, fry them of a fine brown color in butter; put the birds to roast, and put the fried bread in a dish under them, to receive the inside, which will drop after they have hung a few minutes; just before they are roasted sufficiently, cut off the bacon, that they may take color. Serve them on the dish with the bread under them, and plenty of good gravy. Some prefer eating them with butter only, considering that gravy takes off from the fine flavor of the bird. They should be carved the same as fowls or pigeons, and the head should be opened, as some are fond of the brains. Snipes are generally dressed in the same manner as woodcocks.

SNOW-BALLS, BOILED IN BUTTER. Mix with six well-beaten eggs one pint and a half of sour cream, and add by degrees as much flour as will make the batter thick enough for the spoon to stand in it; sweeten it with brown sugar, and put in a few cardamons; stir into this mixture half a pint of beer, beat it all well together, and drop it with a dessert-spoon into some boiling lard,

or butter. Drain them upon a towel before the fire, and serve them in a napkin, with sugar sifted over them.

SNOW CHEESE. Sweeten, with pounded loaf sugar, a quart of good cream; add the strained juice of three lemons, and one ounce and a half of blanched sweet almonds pounded, and two table-spoonfuls of rose-water, and one of ratafia. Beat it with a whisk till thick, and put it into a shape or sieve with a bit of muslin laid into it, and in twelve hours take it out.

SODA WATER. Tartaric acid half an ounce, arated soda, half an ounce. Have two tumblers about one-third full of water, put a tea-spoonful of the soda into one glass, and the same of the acid into the other; when dissolved, mix them together, and drink it immediately. The two sorts of salts must be kept in separate bottles, and should be bought ready powdered.

SOLES OR OTHER FISH, TO FRY. An hour before you intend to dress them, wash them thoroughly, and wrap them in clean cloth, to make them perfectly dry, or the bread-crumbs will not stick to them.

Prepare some bread-crumbs, by rubbing some stale bread through a colander; or, if you wish the fish to appear very delicate and highly finished, through a hair sieve; or use biscuit powder.

Beat the yolk and white of an egg well together, on a plate, with a fork; flour your fish, to absorb any moisture that may remain, and wipe it off with a clean cloth; dip them in the egg on both sides all over, or, what is better, egg them with a paste-brush; put the egg on in an even degree over the whole fish, or the bread crumbs will not stick to it even, and the uneven part will burn to the pan. Strew the bread crumbs all over the fish, so that they cover every part, take up the fish by the head, and shake off the loose crumbs. The fish is now ready for the frying-pan, into which put a quart or more of fresh sweet olive oil, or clarified butter, dripping, lard, or clarified drippings; be sure that they are quite sweet and perfectly clean (the fat ought to cover the fish): what we here order is for soles about ten inches long; if larger, cut them into pieces the proper size to help at table; this will save much time and trouble to the carver: when you send them to table, lay them in the same form they were before they were cut, and you may strew a little curled parsley over them: they are much easier managed in the frying-pan, and require less fat: fry the thick part a few minutes before you put in the thin, you can by this means only fry the thick part enough, without frying the thin too much. Very large soles should be boiled, or fried in fillets. Soles cut in pieces, crossways, about the size of a smelt; make a very pretty garnish for stewed fish and boiled fish.

Set the frying-pan over a sharp and clear fire; watch it, skim it with an egg-slice, and when it boils, *i. e.* when it has done bubbling, and the smoke just begins to rise from the surface, put in the fish: if the fat is not extremely hot, it is impossible to fry fish of a good color, or to keep them firm and crisp.

The best way to ascertain the heat of the fat, is to try it with a bit of bread as big as a nut; if it is quite hot enough, the bread will brown immediately. Put in the fish, and it will be crisp and brown on the side next the fire, in about four or five minutes; to turn it, stick a two-pronged fork near the head, and support the tail with a fish-slice, and fry the other side nearly the same length of time. Fry one sole at a time, except the pan is very large, and you have plenty of fat.

When the fish are fried, lay them on a soft cloth (old table-cloths are best), near enough the fire to keep them warm; turn them every two or three minutes, till they are quite dry on both sides; this common cooks commonly neglect. It will take ten or fifteen minutes, if the fat you fried them in was not hot enough; when it is, they want very little drying. When soles are fried, they will keep very good in a dry place for three or four days; warm them by hanging them on the hooks in a Dutch oven, letting them heat very gradually, by putting it some distance from the fire for about twenty minutes, or in good gravy, as eels, Wiggy's way.

*Obs.*—There are several general rules in this receipt which apply to all fried fish: we have been very particular and minute in our directions; for, although a fried sole is so frequent and favorite a dish, it is very seldom brought to table in perfection.

SOLES, TO BOIL. A fine, fresh, thick sole is almost as good eating as a turbot. Wash and clean it nicely; put it into a fish-kettle with a handful of salt, and as much cold water as will cover it; set it on the side of the fire, take off the scum as it rises, and let it boil gently; about five minutes (according to its size) will be long enough, unless it be very large. Send it up on a fish-drainer, garnished with slices of lemon and sprigs of curled parsley, or nicely-fried smelts, or oysters.

*Obs.*—Slices of lemon are a universally acceptable garnish with either fried or broiled fish: a few sprigs of crisp parsley may be added, if you wish to make it look very smart; and parsley, or fennel and butter, are excellent sauces, or chervil sauce, or anchovy.

SOLES, TO DRESS MAIGRE. Put the fish into a stewpan, with a large onion, four cloves, fifteen berries of allspice, and the same of black pepper; just cover them with boiling water, set it where they will simmer gently for ten or twenty minutes, according to the size of the fish; strain off the liquor in another stewpan, leaving the fish to keep warm till the sauce is ready. Rub together on a plate as much flour and butter as will make the sauce as thick as a double cream. Each pint of sauce season with a glass of wine, half as much mushroom ketchup, a teaspoonful of essence of anchovy, and a few grains of cayenne; let it boil a few minutes, put the fish on a deep dish, strain the gravy over it; garnish it with sippets of bread toasted or fried.

SOLE, Carp, Trout, Perch. Eel, or Flounder, to stew. When the fish has been properly washed, lay it in a stewpan, with half a pint of claret or Port wine, and a quart of good gravy, a large onion, a dozen berries of black pepper, the same of allspice, and a few cloves, or a bit of mace: cover the fish-kettle close, and let it stew gently for ten or twenty minutes, according to the thickness of the fish: take the fish up, lay on a hot dish, cover it up, and thicken the liquor it has stewed in with a little flour, and season it with pepper, salt, essence of anchovy, mushroom ketchup, and a little Chili vinegar; when it has boiled ten minutes, strain it through a tamis, and pour it over the fish: if there is more sauce than the dish will hold, send the rest up in a boat. The river trout comes into season in April, and continues till July; it is a delicious fish.

SORREL, TO STEW. Strip the leaves from the stalks, wash them well, scald them in boiling water in a silver saucepan, or in an earthen pipkin; strain and stew them in a little gravy till tender. Serve with hardboiled eggs cut in quarters.

SORREL, IN GRAVY. Mince, and put it into a saucepan, with butter, bacon, parsley, and scallions; add a glass of *consomme*; set it over a moderate fire, and when quite soft, put to it some fowl gravy, or veal *blond*. Make the sauce thick, and do not let it boil, cover the sorrel when served.

SORREL OMELET. Pick, wash, and blanch some sorrel, cut it in pieces, and fry it lightly in a little butter, with shred parsley and scallions; then put the sorrel into a saucepan, with a little cream; season, and let it boil slowly; in the meantime make an omelet in the usual way, lay it on a dish, thicken the sorrel with the yolks of two eggs, pour it on the omelet, and serve it very hot.

SOUFFLET, APPLE. Prepare apples as for baking in a pudding, put them into a deep dish, and lay upon the top, about an inch and a half thick, rice boiled in new milk with sugar; beat to a stiff froth the whites of two or three eggs, with a little sifted loaf sugar, lay it upon the rice, and bake it in an oven a light brown. Serve it instantly when done.

SOUFFLET, RICH. Soak in white wine and a little brandy, sweetened with sugar, some slices of sponge cake; put them into a deep dish, and pour over them a rich custard; beat to a stiff froth the whites of three or four eggs, and with a table-spoon lay it over the top in heaps to look rough; brown it in a Dutch oven, and serve quickly.

SOUFFLET, RICE. Soak in half a pint of milk, for an hour, one ounce of rice, and the peel of a lemon cut thin; put it into a saucepan, with a little salt, and add by degrees a pint of new milk, and a bit of butter the size of a walnut; stir it till it boil, and for five minutes after. When cool, add the yolks of six eggs, beaten with two table-spoonfuls of pounded loaf sugar, and stir in the well-beaten whites of the eggs, and dress the soufflet in the dish like a pyramid. Bake it in an oven. It may be made with two table-spoonfuls of potato flour, which mix with a little milk, and a little salt, and then thicken it over the fire with more milk; put in little orange-flower water, or any other perfume; whilst in the oven it may be glazed with sifted loaf sugar.

SOUFFLET, ORANGE. Mix with a table-spoonful of flour a pint of cream, put it into a saucepan, with two spoonfuls of rose-water, a little cinnamon and orange-peel; stir it till it boil; strain and sweeten it, and when cold, mix in two table-spoonfuls of orange marmalade; beat well six eggs with a glass of brandy; mix all together; put it in a buttered shape; place it in a saucepan of boiling water, over a stove; let it boil one hour and a quarter without a cloth or cover over it.

SOUPS. Every utensil employed in a kitchen must be kept scrupulously clean, and a cook ought to take especial care that all her saucepans be in good order. Brass pans are preferable for preserving in, and double block tin are the best sort in use for every other purpose; their covers, should be made to fit closely, and the tinning always renewed as soon as it is observed to be wearing off. While new, they may be easily kept clean by washing them regularly in hot water, and rubbing on them when quite dry, a little whiting with leather or flannel. After long use, they will require occasional scouring with fine sand; and before they are used, they ought always to be rinsed out with hot water, and wiped with a clean cloth. A landlady will find it good economy, and for her advantage in other respects, to provide plenty of stone ware and earthen vessels, and also common dishes for the kitchen, that the table set may not be used to keep cold meat on.

In boiling soup, less water is used in a digester than in a common pot, as in a digester no steam can escape.

To extract the strength from meat, long and slow boiling is necessary, but care must be taken that the pot is never off the boil. All soups are better for being made the day before they are to be used, and they should then be strained into earthen pans. When soup has jellied in the pan, it should not be removed into another, as breaking it will occasion its becoming sour sooner than it would otherwise do; when in danger of not keeping, it should be boiled up. It never keeps long with many vegetables in it. The meat used for soups or broths cannot be too fresh. When any animal food is plain boiled, the liquor, with the addition of the trimmings of meat and poultry, make good soups and gravies, as do also the bones of roasted or broiled meat. The gravies left in the dishes answer for hashes, and the liquor in which veal has been boiled, may be made into a glaze by boiling it with a ham bone till reduced to a third or fourth part, and seasoning it with the necessary herbs and spices.

In boiling weak soups, the pan should be uncovered that the watery particles may escape. Cow-heel jelly improves every sort of rich soup; and for thickening, truffles, morels, and dried mushrooms, may be used with advantage.

Directions are given with each of the following soups for thickening with flour and butter, cream and eggs; after the cream and eggs are added, the soup must not be allowed to boil.

Should brown gravy or mock turtle soup be spoiling, fresh-made charcoal, roughly pounded, tied in a little bag and boiled with either, will absorb the bad flavor and leave it sweet and good. The charcoal may be made by simply putting a bit of wood into the fire, and pounding the burnt part in a mortar.

—— ASPARAGUS. This is made with the points of asparagus, in the same manner as the green pease soup is with pease: let half the asparagus be rubbed through a sieve, and the other cut in pieces about an inch long, and boiled till done enough, and sent up in the soup: to make two quarts, there must be a pint of heads to thicken it, and half a pint cut in; take care to preserve these green and a little crisp. This soup is sometimes made by adding the asparagus heads to common pease soup.

—— BEEF, THICK. In eight quarts of water boil gently for seven hours, skimming it well, a shin, or a leg of beef, and a bunch of sweet herbs; strain it the next day, take off the fat, and cut all the gristly and sinewy parts from the bones, add them to the soup with some leeks, onions, celery, pepper, salt, and ten or twelve ounces of Scotch barley parboiled; boil it gently for two or three hours. This stock or jelly will keep good for weeks in cold weather.

—— BEEF OR MUTTON. Boil very gently in a closely covered saucepan, four quarts of water, with two table-spoonfuls of sifted bread raspings, three pounds of beef cut in small pieces, or the same quantity of mutton chops taken from the middle of the neck; season with pepper and salt, add two turnips, two carrots, two onions, and one head of celery, all cut small; let it stew with these ingredients four hours, when it will be ready to serve.

—— BEET ROOT. Boil till tender two roots of beet, and rub off the skin with a coarse towel, mince them finely, as also two or three onions; add this to five pints of rich gravy soup, so as to make it rather thick, then stir in three or four table-spoonfuls of vinegar and one of brown sugar; let it boil, and throw in some fricandellans made up in the form of corks, and rolled in flour.

—— AND BOUILLI. The best parts for this purpose, are the leg or shin, or a piece of the middle of a brisket of beef, of about seven or eight pound's weight; lay it on a fish drainer, or when you take it up, put a slice under it, which will enable you to place it on the dish entire; put it into a soup-pot or deep stewpan, with cold water enough to cover it, and a quart over, set it on a quick fire to get the scum up, which remove as it rises; then put in two carrots, two turnips, two leeks, or two large onions, two heads of celery, two or three cloves, and a faggot of parsley and sweet herbs; set the pot by the side of the fire to simmer very gently, till the meat is just tender enough to eat; this will require about four or five hours.

Put a large carrot, a turnip, a large onion, and a head or two of celery, into the soup whole,—take them out as soon as they are done enough, lay them on a dish till they are cold, then cut them into small squares:— When the BEEF is done, take it out carefully,—strain the SOUP through a hair sieve into a clean stewpan, take off the fat, and put the vegetables that are cut into the soup, the flavor of which you may heighten, by adding a table-spoonful of mushroom ketchup.

If a Thickened Soup is preferred, take four large table-spoonfuls of the clear fat from the top of the pot, and four spoonfuls of flour; mix it smooth together, then by degrees stir it well into the soup, which simmer for ten minutes longer at least,— skim it well and pass it through a tamis or fine sieve, and add the vegetables and seasoning the same as directed in the clear soup.

Keep the beef hot, and send it up (as a remove to the soup) with finely chopped parsley sprinkled on the top, and a sauce-boat of Wow Wow sauce.

—— BROWN, WITHOUT MEAT. Put three quarts or more of water, with a sufficient quantity of raspings to thicken it; two or three onions cut across, some whole pepper, and a little salt; cover it close, and let it boil an hour and a half; take it off, and strain it through a sieve; fry in butter some celery, endive, lettuce, spinach, and any other herbs cut small; then take a stewpan (sufficiently large to hold all the ingredients,) and put in a good piece of butter, stick in a little flour, and keep stirring till it is colored of a nice brown; then put in the herbs and soup; boil it till the herbs are tender, and the soup of a proper consistence, then pour the soup into a tureen, and send to table; serve with fried bread, either in the soup or in a dish.

—— BROWN GRAVY. (1) Take fifteen pounds of a leg or shin of beef, cut off the meat in bits, rub the bottom of the pot with butter, put in the meat, let it brown for nearly an hour, turning it constantly, break the bone and take out the marrow, which may be kept for a pudding, but it is considered better than butter to brown the meat with; put to it fourteen quarts of cold water, and the bones; when it boils, skim it perfectly clean, and add six good-sized red onions, one carrot cut in three, one head of celery, a good handful of whole black and Jamaica pepper mixed; let this boil very gently ten or twelve hours closely covered, if upon a fire, but if done upon a hot plate, not to be covered; strain it through a cullender, and then through a hair sieve, into a large pan, to be kept for use. Return the meat and bones into the pot with three or four quarts of hot water; let it boil nearly two hours, and strain it off. This makes good stock for gravies, stews, or any made dishes.

This gravy soup keeps perfectly good for three or four weeks. When it is to be boiled to send to table, first boil vermicelli, or macaroni, in a little salt and water, till tender; strain it, and add it to the soup just before serving, This soup is quite pure, and requires no clearing. It is a most convenient thing to have in a house in cold weather, as it is always ready for use; and, served with dry toast to eat with it, makes an acceptable luncheon.

The trimmings of meat, giblets, and bones, may be boiled with the beef for this soup.

—— BROWN GRAVY. (2) Cut down three pounds of gravy beef, and put it on in a stewpan with three onions cut small, and two ounces of butter; let it brown well, stirring it to prevent the onions from burning; then add four quarts of water, one head of celery, of carrots and turnips two each, with some whole black pepper and salt; boil it gently for four hours; strain it; and the next day take off the fat. When it is heated, add some vermicelli, previously boiled in water, and serve it after boiling ten minutes.

—— CALF'S HEAD, OR MOCK TURTLE. (1) Parboil a calf's head, take off the skin and cut it in bits about an inch and a half square, cut the fleshy part in bits, take out the black part of the eyes, and cut the rest in rings, skin the tongue, and cut it in slices, add it all to three quarts of good stock, and season it with cayenne, two or three blades of mace, salt; the peel of half a lemon, and half a pint of white wine, with about a dozen of

forcemeat balls; stew all this an hour and a half, rub down with a little cold water, two table-spoonfuls of flour, mix well amongst it half a pint of the soup, and then stir it into the pot; put in the juice of half a large lemon, and the hard-boiled yolks of eight eggs; let it simmer for ten minutes, and then put it all in the tureen.

—— CALF'S HEAD. (2) Scald and clean thoroughly a calf's head with the skin on, boil it an hour gently in three quarts of water, and parboil with it some sweetbreads. Cut off the meat, slice and fry of a light brown in butter two pounds of gravy beef, one of veal, and one of mutton, with five onions cut small; put all into the liquor, adding the bones of the head broken; rinse the frying-pan with two quarts of boiling water, and put it to the meat, and other things, with two whole onions, and a bunch of sweet herbs, and twice their quantity of parsley; the peel of one lemon, four cloves, a little allspice, salt, and black pepper, with a slice of the crumb of bread dried before the fire; let all this stew slowly for five hours, strain it, and when cold, take off all the fat. Cut the meat of the calf's head, tongue, and sweetbreads, in small square bits, add them to the soup, and when it has boiled, mix very gradually with a large table-spoonful of flour a cupful of the soup, and stir it gently into the pot; twenty minutes before serving, add a small tea-spoonful of cayenne, the yolks of eight or ten hard-boiled eggs, and the same number of forcemeat balls; a pint of white wine,—Madeira is the best,—and just before serving, add the juice of a lemon. Forcemeat balls for this soup are made as follows:—Mix the brains with five table-spoonfuls of grated bread, the same of finely minced beef suet, a tea-spoonful of salt, one of white pepper, the grated peel of a lemon, some nutmeg, and boiled parsley chopped; beat the yolks and whites of two eggs, roll the balls the size of the yolk of an egg, and fry them of a light brown in boiling dripping.

—— CALF'S HEAD. (3) Take as much as is required of not very strong veal, or beef stock, in which six onions have been boiled, brown a quarter of a pound of butter and thicken it well with flour, then add the stock by degrees; when it boils, put in the calf's head, cut in small pieces, and some fried forcemeat balls; season it with salt and pepper. The peel of half a lemon improves it. When it has boiled twenty minutes, add two table-spoonfuls of ketchup, three of essence of anchovies, and as much lemon pickle as will make it a pleasant acid. To give the soup a good color, and to enrich the flavor, may be added a large table-spoonful of flour, mixed perfectly smooth in a tea-cupful of cold water, and stirred gradually into the soup, after which let it boil a few minutes.

—— CARROT. Scrape and wash half a dozen large carrots; peel off the red outside (which is the only part used for this soup); put it into a gallon stewpan, with one head of celery, and an onion, cut into thin pieces; take two quarts of beef, veal, or mutton broth, or if you have any cold roast beef bones (or liquor, in which mutton or beef has been boiled), you may make very good broth for this soup: when you have put the broth to the roots, cover the stewpan close, and set it on a slow stove for two hours and a half, when the carrots will be soft enough (some cooks put in a tea-cupful of bread-crumbs); boil for two or three minutes; rub it through a tamis, or hair sieve, with a wooden spoon, and add as much broth as will make it a proper thickness, i. e. almost as thick as pease soup: put it into a clean stewpan; make it hot; season it with a little salt, and send it up with some toasted bread, cut into pieces half an inch square. Some put it into the soup; but the best way is to send it up on a plate, as a side dish.

—— CELERY. Split half a dozen heads of celery into slips about two inches long; wash them well; lay them on a hair sieve to drain, and put them into three quarts of clear gravy soup in a gallon soup-pot; set it by the side of the fire to stew very gently till the celery is tender (this will take about an hour). If any scum rises, take it off; season with a little salt.

*Obs.*—When celery cannot be procured, half a drachm of the seed, pounded fine, which may be considered as the essence of celery, put in a quarter of an hour before the soup is done, and a little sugar, will give as much flavor to half a gallon of soup as two heads of celery weighing seven ounces, or add a little essence of celery.

—— COCKY-LEEKY. Take a scrag of mutton, or shank of veal, three quarts of water (or liquor in which meat has been boiled), and a good sized fowl, with two or three leeks cut in pieces about an inch long, pepper and salt; boil slowly about an hour then put in as many more leeks, and give it three-quarters of an hour longer: this is very good, made of good beef stock, and leeks put in at twice.

—— CRAW FISH. This soup is sometimes made with beef, or veal broth, or with fish, in the following manner: Take flounders, eels, gudgeons, &c., and set them on to boil in cold water; when it is pretty nigh boiling, skim it well; and to three quarts put in a couple of onions, and as many carrots cut to pieces, some parsley, a dozen berries of black and Jamaica pepper, and about half a hundred craw-fish; take off the small claws and shells of the tails; pound them fine, and boil them with the broth about an hour; strain off, and break in some crusts of bread to thicken it, and, if you can get it, the spawn of a lobster; pound it, and put it to the soup; let it simmer very gently for a couple of minutes; put in your craw-fish to get hot, and the soup is ready.

—— CRESSY. (1) Wash clean, and cut small, eight carrots, eight turnips, three heads of celery, and six onions; put them in a stewpan with a quarter of a pound of butter and a slice of ham, stew them gently for an hour, stirring them constantly: when they begin to brown add as much gravy soup as will fill the tureen; let it boil till the vegetables are sufficiently tender to pulp with a spoon through a sieve, after which put it on the fire and boil it half an hour, skin, and season it with pepper and salt. This soup should be as thick as melted butter. Two pounds of beef boiled in four quarts of water till reduced to three, will answer for the soup.

——CRESSY. (2) Slice twelve large onions, and fry them pretty brown in a quarter of a pound of fresh butter; scrape and clean two dozen of good red carrots, boil them in four quarts of water till quite soft; pound them in a marble mortar, mix them with the onions and add the liquor in which the carrots were boiled, a bunch of sweet herbs, pepper, salt, a blade of mace, and two or three cloves; let them all boil about an hour, then rub them through a hair sieve; put it on again to boil rather quickly, till it be as thick as rich cream. Put a little dry boiled rice in the tureen, and pour the soup over it. If the carrots are large, one dozen will be found sufficient.

—— CUCUMBER. Make some broth with a neck of mutton, a thick slice of lean bacon, an onion stuck with three cloves, a carrot, two turnips, some salt, and a bunch of sweet herbs; strain it; brown with an ounce of butter the crumb of a French roll, to which put four large cucumbers, and two heads of lettuce cut small; let them stew a quarter of an hour, and add to them a quart of the broth; when it boils put in a pint of green pease, and as it stews, add two quarts more of the broth.

—— CURRY, OR MULLAGA-TAWNY. Cut four pounds of a breast of veal into pieces, about two inches by one; put the trimmings into a stewpan with two quarts of water, with twelve corns of black pepper, and the same of allspice; when it boils, skim it clean, and let it boil an hour

and a half, then strain it off; while it is boiling, fry of a nice brown in butter the bits of veal and four onions; when they are done, put the broth to them; put it on the fire; when it boils, skim it clean; let it simmer half an hour; then mix two spoonfuls of curry, and the same of flour, with a little cold water and a tea-spoonful of salt; add these to the soup, and simmer it gently till the veal is quite tender, and it is ready; or bone a couple of fowls or rabbits, and stew them in the manner directed above for the veal, and you may put in a bruised eschalot, and some mace and ginger, instead of black pepper and allspice.

—— CURRY. Mince small three or four onions, according to their size, put them into a saucepan with two ounces of butter, dredge in some flour, and fry them till of a light brown, taking care not to burn them; rub in by degrees a large table-spoonful and a half of curry-powder, till it be quite a paste; gradually stir in three quarts of gravy soup, mixing it well together; boil it gently till it be well flavored with the curry-powder; strain it into another saucepan, and add a fowl skinned and cut in small pieces, dividing each joint; stew it slowly an hour. In half a pint of the soup put a large table-spoonful of tamarinds, and stew them so as to separate the stalks and stones; strain and stir it into the soup with half a tea-spoonful of salt, and boil it for fifteen minutes before serving.

—— EEL. To make a tureenful, take a couple of middling-sized onions, cut them in half, and cross your knife over them two or three times; put two ounces of butter into a stewpan, when it is melted put in the onions, stir them about till they are lightly browned; cut into pieces three pounds of eels, put them into your stewpan, and shake them over the fire for five minutes; then add three quarts of boiling water, and when they come to a boil, take the scum off very clean; then put in a quarter of an ounce of the green leaves (not dried), of winter savory, the same of lemon thyme, and twice the quantity of parsley, two drachms of allspice, the same of black pepper; cover it close, and let it boil gently for two hours; then strain it off, and skim it very clean. To thicken it, put three ounces of butter into a clean stewpan; when it is melted, stir in as much flour as will make it of a stiff paste, then add the liquor by degrees; let it simmer for ten minutes, and pass it through a sieve; then put your soup on in a clean stewpan, and have ready some little square pieces of fish fried of a nice light brown, either eels, soles, plaice, or skate will do; the fried fish should be added about ten minutes before the soup is served up. Forcemeat balls are sometimes added.

—— GIBLET. Clean very nicely two sets of giblets, parboil them. Take the skin off the feet; cut the gizzards in quarters, the necks in three bits, the feet, pinions, and livers, in two, the head in two also, first taking off the bill; boil them till nearly done enough in a quart of weak gravy soup with an onion. Have ready boiling some rich highly-seasoned brown gravy soup; add the giblets and the liquor they have been boiled in, with some chopped parsley; take out the onion, and thicken the soup with a bit of butter kneaded in flour. If the giblets are not perfectly sweet and fresh, do not add the weak soup they were boiled in. Half a pint of wine may be added a little before serving, but it is very good without.

—— GOURD, Should be made of full-grown gourds, but not those that have hard skins; slice three or four, and put them in a stewpan, with two or three onions, and a good bit of butter; set them over a slow fire till quite tender (be careful not to let them burn); then add two ounces of crust of bread, and two quarts of good *consomme*; season with salt and cayenne pepper: boil ten minutes, or a quarter of an hour; skim off all the fat, and pass it through a tamis; then make it quite hot; and serve up with fried bread.

—— GRAVY, CLEAR. Cut half a pound of ham into slices, and lay them at the bottom of a large stewpan or stockpot, with two or three pounds of lean beef, and as much veal; break the bones; and lay them on the meat; take off the outer skin of two large onions and two turnips, wash, clean, and cut into pieces a couple of large carrots, and two heads of celery; and put in three cloves and a large blade of mace. Cover the stewpan close, and set over a smart fire. When the meat begins to stick to the bottom of the stewpan, turn it; and when there is a nice brown glaze at the bottom of the stewpan, cover the meat with hot water: watch it, and when it is coming to boil put in half a pint of cold water; take off the scum; then put in half a pint more cold water, and skim it again, and continue to do so till no more scum rises. Now set it on one side of the fire to boil gently for about four hours; strain it through a clean tamis or napkin (do not squeeze it, or the soup will be thick) into a clean stone pan; let it remain till it is cold, and then remove all the fat. When you decant it, be careful not to disturb the settlings at the bottom of the pan.

The broth should be of a fine amber color, and as clear as rock water. If it is not quite so bright as you wish it, put it into a stewpan; break two whites and shells of eggs into a basin; beat them well together; put them into the soup: set it on a quick fire, and stir it with a whisk till it boils; then set it on one side of the fire to settle for ten minutes; run it through a fine napkin into a basin, and it is ready.

However, if your broth is carefully skimmed, &c. according to the directions above given, it will be clear enough without clarifying; which process impairs the flavor of it in a higher proportion than it improves its appearance. This is the basis of almost all gravy soups, which are called by the name of the vegetables that are put into them. Carrots, turnips, onions, celery, and a few leaves of chervil, make what is called spring soup, or soup sante; to this a pint of green pease, or asparagus pease, or French beans cut into pieces, or a cabbage lettuce, are an improvement. With rice or Scotch barley, with macaroni or vermicelli, or celery cut into lengths, it will be the soup usually called by those names. Or turnips scooped round, or young onions, will give you a clear turnip or onion soup; and all these vegetables mixed together, soup GRESSI. The roots and vegetables you use must be boiled first, or they will impregnate the soup with too strong a flavor. The seasoning for all these soups is the same, viz. salt and a very little cayenne pepper.

—— GAME. In the game season, it is easy for a cook to give a very good soup at a very little expense, by taking all the meat off the breasts of any cold birds which have been left the preceding day, and pounding it in a mortar, and beating to pieces the legs and bones, and boiling them in some broth for an hour. Boil six turnips; mash them, and strain them through a tamis cloth with the meat that has been pounded in a mortar; strain your broth, and put a little of it at a time into the tamis to help you to strain all of it through. Put your soup-kettle near the fire, but do not let it boil: when ready to dish your dinner, have six yolks of eggs mixed with half a pint of cream; strain through a sieve; put your soup on the fire, and as it is coming to boil, put in the eggs, and stir well with a wooden spoon: do not let it boil, or it will curdle.

—— HARE. Cut the hare in joints as for a fricassee, and put it in a stewpan, with a little allspice, three blades of mace, some salt, and whole black pepper, a bunch of parsley, a sprig of lemon thyme, one of winter savory, four quarts of water, a slice of ham, and four pounds of lean beef, two carrots, and four onions cut down; let it boil till it be reduced to three quarts; separate the hare, and strain the soup over it, and add a pint of Port wine; boil it up before serving.

—— HERB. Wash and cut small twelve cabbage lettuces, a handful of chervil, one of purslane, one of parsley, eight large green onions, and three handfuls of sorrel; when pease are in season omit half the quantity of sorrel, and put a quart of young green pease; put them all into a saucepan, with half a pound of butter and three carrots cut small, some salt and pepper; let them stew closely covered for half an hour, shaking them occasionally to prevent their adhering to the pan; fry in butter six cucumbers cut longways in four pieces; add them with four quarts of hot water, half a French roll, and a crust of bread toasted upon both sides; and let the whole boil till reduced to three quarts, then strain it through a sieve; beat up the yolks of four eggs with half a pint of cream, and stir it gently into the soup just before serving.

—— HERB POWDER, OR VEGETABLE RELISH. Dried parsley, winter savory, sweet marjoram, lemon thyme, of each two ounces; lemon-peel, cut very thin, and dried, and sweet basil, an ounce of each. Some add to the above bay-leaves and celery-seed, a drachm each. Dry them in a warm, but not too hot Dutch oven: when quite dried, pound them in a mortar, and pass them through a double hair sieve; put them in a bottle closely stopped, they will retain their fragrance and flavor for several months.

*Obs.*—This composition of the fine aromatic herbs is an invaluable acquisition to the cook in those seasons or situations when fresh herbs cannot be had; and we prefer it to the ragout powder. It impregnates sauce, soup, &c. with as much relish, and renders it agreeable to the palate, and refreshes the gustatory nerves, without so much risk of offending the stomach.

—— INVALID. Cut in small pieces one pound of beef or mutton, or part of both; boil it gently in two quarts of water; take off the scum, and when reduced to a pint, strain it. Season with a little salt, and take a teacupful at a time.

—— LOBSTER. (1) Cut small a dozen

of common-sized onions, put them into a stewpan with a small bit of butter, a slice or two of lean ham, and a slice of lean beef; when the onions are quite soft, mix gradually with them some rich stock; let it boil and strain it through a fine hair sieve, pressing the pulp of the onions with a wooden spoon; then boil it well, skimming it all the time. Beat the meat of a boiled cod, the spawn and body of a large lobster, or of two small ones, in a marble mortar; add gradually to it the soup, stirring it till it is as smooth as cream; let it boil again and scum it. Cut the tail and the claws of the lobster into pieces, and add them to the soup before serving it, and also some pepper, cayenne, white pepper, and a glass of white wine. Forcemeat balls may be added to oyster soup and lobster soup, made as directed under the article " Forcemeat for fish."

—— LOBSTER. (2) You must have three fine lively young hen lobsters, split the tails; take out the fish, crack the claws, and cut the meat into mouthfuls; take out the coral, and soft part of the body, bruise part of the coral in a mortar; pick out the fish from the chines; beat part of it with the coral and with this make forcemeat balls, finely-flavored with mace or nutmeg, a little grated lemon-peel, anchovy and cayenne, pound these with the yolk of an egg.

Have three quarts of veal broth; bruise the small legs and the chine, and put them into it, to boil for twenty minutes, then strain it; and then to thicken it, take the live spawn and bruise it in a mortar with a little butter and flour; rub it through a sieve, and add it to the soup with the meat of the lobsters, and the remaining coral; let it simmer very gently for ten minutes; do not let it boil, or its fine red color will immediately fade; turn it into a tureen; add the juice of a good lemon, and a little essence of anchovy.

—— LORRAIN. Boil in four quarts of water a knuckle of veal, one pound of lean beef, and one pound of mutton, a carrot, a turnip, a bunch of parsley, and a little lemon thyme, some salt and white pepper, till reduced to three, then strain the liquor; pound very finely in a marble mortar, all the white meat of a large roasted fowl, with a quarter of a pound of blanched almonds, and the yolks of four hard-boiled eggs; boil in milk the crumb of a French roll, and pound it with the other ingredients, and stir it all well into the soup; let it boil gently for ten minutes before serving.

—— MAIGRE, OR VEGETABLE GRAVY. Put into a gallon stewpan three ounces of butter; set it over a slow fire; while it is melting, slice four ounces of onion; cut in small pieces one turnip, one carrot, and a head of celery; put them in the stewpan, cover it close, let it fry till they are lightly browned; this will take about twenty-five minutes: have ready in a saucepan, a pint of pease, with four quarts of water; when the roots in the stewpan are quite brown, and the pease come to a boil, put the pease and the water to them; put it on the fire; when it boils, skim it clean, and put in a crust of bread about as big as the top of a twopenny loaf, twenty-four berries of allspice, the same of black pepper, and two blades of mace; cover it close, and let it simmer gently for one hour and a half; then set it from the fire for ten minutes; then pour it off very gently (so as not to disturb the sediment at the bottom of the stewpan) into a large basin; let it stand (about two hours) till it is quite clear: while this is doing, shred one large turnip, the red part of a large carrot, three ounces of onion minced, and one large head of celery cut into small bits; put the turnips and carrots on the fire in cold water, let them boil five minutes, then drain them on a sieve, then pour off the soup clear into a stewpan, put in the roots, put the soup on the fire, let it simmer gently till the herbs are tender (from thirty to forty minutes), season it with salt and a little cayenne, and it is ready. You may add a table-spoonful of mushroom ketchup. You will have three quarts of soup, as well colored, and almost as well flavored, as if made with gravy meat. To make this it requires nearly five hours. To fry the herbs requires twenty-five minutes; to boil all together, one hour and a half; to settle, at the least, two hours; when clear, and put on the fire again, half an hour more.

—— MACARONI. (1) Boil for three hours very quickly, in five quarts of water, seven pounds of veal, a little salt, a dessert-spoonful of white pepper, and three or four blades of mace; strain it off, put it into a saucepan, and keep in hot upon the stove. Mix five table-spoonfuls of flour with two ounces of butter, put it into an iron-tinned saucepan, and stir it over the fire till it be melted; add half a pint of the strained stock, and then gradually mix the whole together, and keep stirring constantly till it thickens, and then add two ounces and a half of maca-roni, previously boiled in milk and water for eight minutes; stir it again till it boil. Take the pan off the stove, and stir in by degrees about three-quarters of a pint of rich sweet cream, and just let it boil before serving.

—— MACARONI. (2) Make a good stock with a knuckle of veal, a little sweet marjoram, parsley, some salt, white pepper, three blades of mace, and two or three on-ions; strain and boil it. Break in small bits a quarter of a pound of macaroni, and gently simmer it in milk and water till it be swelled and is tender; strain it, and add it to the soup, which thicken with two table-spoonfuls of flour, mixed in half a pint of cream, and stirred gradually into the soup. Boil it a few minutes before serving.

—— MOCK TURTLE. Endeavor to have the head and the broth ready for the soup, the day before it is to be eaten. It will take eight hours to prepare it properly.

| | *hours.* |
|---|---|
| Cleaning and soaking the head . . . . . . . . | 1 |
| To parboil it to cut up . . . . . . . . . . . . . . | 1 |
| Cooling, nearly . . . . . . . . . . . . . . . . . . . . . | 1 |
| Making the broth and finishing the soup . . | 5 |
| | 8 |

Get a calf's head with the skin on (the fresher the better); take out the brains, wash the head several times in cold water, let it soak for about an hour in spring water, then lay it in a stewpan, and cover it with cold water, and half a gallon over; as it becomes warm, a great deal of scum will rise, which must be immediately removed; let it boil gently for one hour, take it up, and when almost cold, cut the head into pieces about an inch and a half by an inch and a quarter, and the tongue into mouthfuls, or rather make a side-dish of the tongue and brains.

When the head is taken out, put in the stock meat, about five pounds of knuckle of veal, and as much beef; add to the stock all the trimmings and bones of the head, skim it well, and then cover it close, and let it boil five hours (reserve a couple of quarts of this to make gravy sauces); then strain it off, and let it stand till the next morning; then take off the fat, set a large stewpan on the fire with half a pound of good fresh butter, twelve ounces of onions sliced, and four ounces of green sage; chop it a little; let these fry one hour; then rub in half a pound of flour, and by degrees add your broth till it is the thickness of cream; season it with a quarter of an ounce of ground allspice and half an ounce of black pepper ground very fine, salt to your taste, and the rind of one lemon peeled very thin; let it simmer very gently for one hour and a half, then strain it through a hair sieve; do not rub your soup to get it through the sieve, or it will make it grouty; if it does not run through easily, knock your wooden spoon against the side of your sieve; put it in a clean stewpan with the head, and season it by adding to each gallon of soup half a pint of wine; this should be Madeira, or, if you wish to darken the color of your soup, claret, and two table-spoonfuls of lemon-juice; let it simmer gen-tly till the meat is tender; this may take from half an hour to an hour: take care it is not over-done; stir it frequently to prevent the meat sticking to the bottom of the stewpan, and when the meat is quite tender the soup is ready.

A head weighing twenty pounds, and ten pounds of stock meat, will make ten quarts of excellent soup, besides the two quarts of stock you have put by for made dishes.

*Obs.*—If there is more meat on the head than you wish to put in the soup, prepare it for a pie, and, with the addition of a calf's foot boiled tender, it will make an excellent ragout pie; season it with zest, and a little minced onion, put in half a tea-cupful of stock, cover it with puff paste, and bake it one hour: when the soup comes from table, if there is a deal of meat and no soup, put it into a pie-dish, season it a little, and add some little stock to it; then cover it with paste, bake it one hour, and you have a good mock turtle pie.

To season it, to each gallon of soup put two table-spoonfuls of lemon-juice, same of mushroom ketchup, and one of essence of anchovy, half a pint of wine (this should be Madeira, or, if you wish to darken the color of your soup, claret), a tea-spoonful of curry powder, or a quarter of a drachm of cayenne, and the peel of a lemon pared as thin as possible; let it simmer five minutes more, take out the lemon-peel, and the soup is ready for the tureen.

While the soup is doing, prepare for each tureen a dozen and a half of mock turtle forcemeat balls, and put them into the tureen. Brain balls, or cakes, are a very elegant addition, and are made by boiling the brains for ten minutes, then putting them in cold water, and cutting them into pieces about as big as a large nutmeg; take savory, or lemon thyme dried and finely powdered, nutmeg grated, and pepper and salt, and pound them all together; beat up an egg, dip the brains in it, and then roll them in this mixture, and make as much of it as possible stick to them; dip them in the egg again, and then in finely-grated and sifted bread-crumbs; fry them in hot fat, and send them up as a side dish.

A veal sweetbread, not too much done or it will break, cut into pieces the same size as you cut the calf's head, and put in the soup, just to get warm before it goes to table, is a superb "*bonne bouche:*" and pickled tongue, stewed till very tender, and cut into mouthfuls, is a favorite addition. We order the meat to be cut into mouthfuls, that it may be eaten with a spoon: the knife and fork have no business in a soup-plate.

N. B.—In helping this soup, the distributer of it should serve out the meat, forcemeat, and gravy, in equal parts; however trifling or needless this remark may appear, the writer has often suffered from the want of such a hint being given to the soup-server, who has sometimes sent a plate of mere gravy without meat, at others, of meat without gravy, and sometimes scarcely any thing but forcemeat balls.

*Obs.*—This is a delicious soup, within the reach of those who "eat to live;" but if it had been composed expressly for those who only "live to eat," I do not know how it could have been made more agreeable: as it is, the lover of good eating will "wish his throat a mile long, and every inch of it palate."

—— MOCK MOCK TURTLE. Line the bottom of a stewpan that will hold five pints, with an ounce of nice lean bacon or ham, a pound and a half of lean gravy beef, a cow-heel, the inner rind of a carrot, a sprig of lemon thyme, winter savory, three times the quantity of parsley, a few green leaves of sweet basil, and two eschalots; put in a large onion, with four cloves stuck in it, eighteen corns of allspice, the same of black pepper; pour on these a quarter of a pint of cold water, cover the stewpan, and set it on a slow fire, to boil gently for a quarter of an hour; then, for fear the meat should catch, take off the cover, and watch it; and when it has got a good brown color, fill up the stewpan with boiling water, and let it simmer very gently for two hours: if you wish to have the full benefit of the meat, only stew it till it is just tender, cut it into mouthfuls, and put it into the soup. To thicken it, pour two or three table-spoonfuls of flour, a ladleful of the gravy, and stir it quick till it is well mixed; pour it back into the stewpan where the gravy is, and let it simmer gently for half an hour longer; skim it, and then strain it through a tamis into the stewpan: cut the cow-heel into pieces about an inch square, squeeze through a sieve the juice of a lemon, a table-spoonful of mushroom ketchup, a tea-spoonful of salt, half a tea-spoonful of ground black pepper, as much grated nutmeg as will lie on a sixpence, and a glass of Madeira or Sherry wine; let it all simmer together for five minutes longer. Forcemeat or egg balls may be added if you please.

A pound of veal cutlets, or the belly part of pickled pork, or nice double tripe cut into pieces about an inch square, and half an inch thick, and rounded and trimmed neatly from all skin, gristle, &c. and stewed till they are tender, will be a great addition.

——MOOR-FOWL. It may be made with or without brown gravy soup; when with the former, six birds are sufficient, when with moor-fowl only, boil five in four quarts of water, pound the breasts in a mortar and rub it through a sieve, put it with the legs, backs, and three more moor-fowl, cut down in joints, into the liquor, season with a pint of Port wine, pepper, and salt, and let it boil an hour. When only six birds are used, pound the breasts of three or four.

—— MULLAGATAWNY. (1) Put half a pound of fresh butter, with six large onions sliced, three cloves of garlic, some chopped parsley, and sweet marjoram, into a stewpan, let it stew over a slow fire till of a light brown color; cut in small pieces five pounds of lean beef, and let that stew till the gravy be extracted, and then put in three quarts of boiling water, and half a pound of Scotch barley, and let it simmer four hours very slowly; mix four table-spoonfuls of curry-powder with cold water, and add it to the stock; take out the beef, and rub the barley through a sieve, to thicken the soup. Cut a fowl in joints, skin it, and put it in a stewpan with a piece of butter, and let it stew till quite tender; the stewpan must be kept closely covered: this to be added to the soup, the last thing, with a pint of boiling milk, and the juice of two lemons. Boiled rice must always be served with this soup.

—— MULLAGATAWNY. (2) Make a strong stock of the bones of roasted beef, mutton, and fowl; while it is preparing, put into a stewpan, with six ounces of butter, three quarts of sliced turnip, two quarts of carrots, and eight large onions also sliced; let them stew upon the stove till tender; then add three quarts of the prepared stock, a large slice of the crumb of bread, and two table-spoonfuls of curry-powder; let them stew four or five hours; strain it through a tammy cloth, with two wooden spoons, taking care that no bones be left amongst the vegetables; if too thick to go through, add more stock. Then cut a fowl in pieces, fry it in a frying-pan with butter, and add it to the soup; after it has boiled a little, draw it to the side of the stove, and let it simmer, that the grease may be taken off. A little good beef stock, in addition to that made of the bones will be an improvement. It is sometimes thickened with whole or ground rice, instead of bread, and ought to be made upon a stove.

—— ONION. Boil in four quarts of water six pounds of a knuckle of veal with a dessert-spoonful of whole white pepper, and a few blades of mace; when the meat is so much boiled as to leave the bone, strain off the stock. The following day boil nine or ten large Spanish onions in milk and water, till sufficiently tender to pulp through a sieve; take the fat off from the top of the stock, boil it up, and add the onions with about a quarter of a pound of fresh butter worked with two heaped table-spoonfuls of sifted flour of rice, and a little salt; boil it gently for half an hour, stirring it constantly, and a little before serving, stir in half a pint of rich cream.

—— OX-HEAD, Should be prepared the day before it is to be eaten, as you cannot cut the meat off the head into neat mouthfuls unless it is cold: therefore, the day before you want this soup, put half an ox-cheek into a tub of cold water to soak for a couple of hours; then break the bones that have not been broken at the butcher's, and wash it very well in warm water; put it into a pot, and cover it with cold water; when it boils, skim it very clean, and then put in one head of celery, a couple of carrots, a turnip, two large onions, two dozen berries of black pepper, same of allspice, and a bundle of sweet herbs, such as marjoram, lemon thyme, savory, and a handful of parsley; cover the soup-pot close, and set it on a slow fire; take off the scum, which will rise when it is coming to a boil, and set it by the fireside to stew very gently for about three hours; take out the head, lay it on a dish, pour the soup through a fine sieve into a stone-ware pan, and set it and the head by in a cool place till the next day; then cut the meat into neat mouthfuls, skim and strain off the broth, put two quarts of it and the meat into a clean stewpan, let it simmer very gently for half an hour longer, and it is ready. If you wish it thickened, put two ounces of butter into a stewpan: when it is melted, throw in as much flour as will dry it up; when they are all well mixed together, and browned by degrees, pour to this your soup, and stir it well together; let it simmer for half an hour longer; strain it through a hair sieve into a clean stewpan and put to it the meat of the head; let it stew half an hour longer, and season it with cayenne pepper, salt, and a glass of good wine, or a table-spoonful of brandy. If you serve it as soup for a dozen people, thicken one tureen, and send up the meat in that; and send up the other as a clear gravy soup, with some of the carrots and turnips shredded, or cut into shapes.

—— OX-HEEL, Must be made the day before it is to be eaten. Procure an ox-heel undressed, or only scalded, and two that have been boiled as they usually are at the tripe shops.

Cut the meat off the boiled heels into neat mouthfuls, and set it by on a plate; put the trimmings and bones in a stewpan, with three quarts of water, and the unboiled heel cut into quarters; furnish a stewpan with two onions, and two turnips pared and sliced; pare off the red part of a couple of large carrots, add a couple of eschalots cut in half, a bunch of savory or lemon thyme, and double the quantity of parsley; set this over, or by the side of a slow, steady fire, and keep it closely covered and simmering very gently (or the soup liquor will evaporate) for at least seven hours: during which, take care to remove the fat and scum that will rise to the surface of the soup, which must be kept as clean as possible.

Now strain the liquor through a sieve, and put two ounces of butter into a clean stewpan; when it is melted, stir into it as much flour as will make it a stiff paste; add to it by degrees the soup liquor; give it a boil up; strain it through a seive, and put in the peel of a lemon pared as thin as possible, and a couple of bay-leaves and the meat of the boiled heels; let it go on simmering for half an hour longer, i.e., till the meat is tender. Put in the juice of a lemon, a glass of wine, and a table-spoonful of mushroom ketchup, and the soup is ready for the tureen.

Those who are disposed to make this a more substantial dish, may introduce a couple of sets of goose or duck giblets, or ox-tails, or a pound of veal cutlets, cut into mouthfuls.

—— OX-TAIL. Three tails, costing about 2d. each, will make a tureen of soup (desire the butcher to divide them at the joints); lay them to soak in warm water, while you get ready the vegetables.

Put into a gallon stewpan eight cloves, two or three onions, half a drachm of allspice, and the same of black pepper, and the tails: cover them with cold water; skim it carefully, when and as long as you see any scum rise; then cover the pot as close as possible, and set it on the side of the fire to keep gently simmering until the meat becomes tender and will leave the bones easily, because it is to be eaten with a spoon, without the assistance of a knife or fork; this will require about two hours: mind it is not done too much: when perfectly tender, take out the meat and cut it off the bones, in neat mouthfuls; skim the broth, and strain it through a sieve; if you prefer a thickened soup, put flour and butter, as directed in the preceding receipt; or put two table-spoonfuls of the fat you have taken off the broth into a clean stewpan with as much flour as will make it into a paste; set this over the fire, and stir them well together; then pour in the broth by degrees, stirring it, and mixing it with the thickening; let it simmer for another half hour, and when you have well skimmed it, and it is quite smooth, then strain it through a tamis into a clean stewpan, put in the meat, with a table-spoonful of mushroom ketchup, a glass of wine, and season it with salt.

*Obs.*—If the meat is cut off the bones, you must have three tails for a tureen, some put an ox-cheek or tails in an earthen pan, with all the ingredients as above, and send them to a slow oven for five or six hours.

—— PEAS, GREEN. (1) A peck of peas will make you a good tureen of soup. In shelling them, put the old ones in one basin, and the young ones in another, and keep out a pint of them, and boil them separately to put into your soup when it is finished: put a large saucepan on the fire half full of water; when it boils, put the peas in, with a handful of salt; let them boil till they are done enough, *i. e.* from twenty to thirty minutes, according to their age and size; then drain them in a colander, and put them into a clean gallon stewpan, and three quarts of plain veal or mutton broth (drawn from meat without any spices or herbs, &c. which would overpower the flavor of the soup); cover the stewpan close, and set it over a slow fire to stew gently for an hour; add a tea-cupful of bread crumbs, and then rub it through a tamis into another stewpan; stir it

with a wooden spoon, and if it is too thick, add a little more broth: have ready boiled as for eating, a pint of young peas, and put them into the soup; season with a little salt and sugar.

Some cooks, while this soup is going on, slice a couple of cucumbers (as you would for eating); take out the seeds; lay them on a cloth to drain, and then flour them, and fry them a light brown in a little butter; put them into the soup the last thing before it goes to table.

If the soup is not green enough, pound a handful of pea-hulls or spinage, and squeeze the juice through a cloth into the soup: some leaves of mint may be added, if approved.

—— PEAS, GREEN. (2) Put a pint of old green peas into three quarts of water, a slice of the crumb of bread, two onions, a sprig of mint, some salt and pepper; boil them till the peas are perfectly soft, then pulp them through a sieve; have ready two lettuces stewed tender in butter, and a pint and a half of young green peas boiled; put them into the soup with a little spinach juice, and a quarter of a pint of the juice of the youngest pea pods, and boil it all together before serving.

—— PEAS, GREEN, WITHOUT MEAT. Take a quart of green peas (keep out half a pint of the youngest; boil them separately, and put them in the soup when it is finished); put them on in boiling water; boil them tender, and then pour off the water, and set it by to make the soup with: put the peas into a mortar, and pound them to a mash; then put them into two quarts of the water you boiled the peas in; stir all well together; let it boil up for about five minutes, and then rub it through a hair sieve or tamis. If the peas are good, it will be as thick and fine a vegetable soup as need be sent to table.

—— PEAS, OLD. (1) Put a pound and a half of split peas on in four quarts of water, with roast beef or mutton bones, and a ham bone, two heads of celery, and four onions, let them boil till the peas be sufficiently soft to pulp through a sieve, strain it, put it into the pot with pepper and salt, and boil it nearly an hour. Two or three handfuls of spinach, well washed and cut a little, added when the soup is strained, is a great improvement; and in the summer young green peas in place of the spinach. A tea-spoonful of celery seed, or essence of celery, if celery is not to be had.

—— PEAS, OLD. (2) Boil in five quarts of water one quart of split peas, an ounce of butter, four pounds of beef, two carrots, three turnips, four heads of celery, three onions, some salt and black pepper; boil them till the peas are dissolved and will easily pulp, put it all through a sieve, then put the soup over the fire with three ounces of butter and a table-spoonful of flour, and boil a small bit of lean ham in it, till it is time to serve; take it out before dishing, and have ready some celery stewed in butter, and fried bread cut in dice, and dried mint rubbed very fine, to send to table with it.

—— PEAS, OLD. (3) Boil in four quarts of water a shank of ham, or a piece of bacon, and about half a pound of mutton, or salt beef, and a pint of split peas; boil all together very gently till the peas are quite soft, strain them through a hair sieve, and bruise them with the back of a spoon till all is pulped through, then boil the soup gently for one hour before serving. Thin slices of bread toasted and cut in dice to be served with it, either upon a dish or in the soup; if in the soup, it should be fried in butter, and dried mint rubbed fine and sent to table in a small dish. It may be also made with fourpence worth of bones, boiled for some hours in four quarts of water, with a carrot, a head of celery, three onions, some pepper and salt, strained, and the next day the fat taken off, and the peas boiled in the liquor with a little bit of butter, till sufficiently tender to pulp through a sieve.

—— PEAS, PLAIN. To a quart of split peas, and two heads of celery (and most cooks would put a large onion), put three quarts of broth or soft water; let them simmer gently on a trivet over a slow fire for three hours, stirring up every quarter of an hour to prevent the peas burning at the bottom of the soup-kettle (if the water boils away, and the soup gets too thick, add some boiling water to it); when they are well softened, work them through a coarse sieve, and then through a fine sieve or a tamis; wash out your stewpan, and then return the soup into it, and give it a boil up; take off any scum that comes up, and it is ready. Prepare fried bread, and dried mint, as directed in Old Peas (2) and send them up with it on two side dishes.

*Obs.*—This is an excellent family soup, produced with very little trouble or expense.

—— PIGEON. (1) Have a strong beef stock, highly seasoned, and if for rich soup, take six or eight pigeons according to their size, wash them clean, cut off the necks, pinions, livers and gizzards, and put them into the stock; quarter the pigeons and brown them nicely; after having strained the stock, put in the pigeons; let them boil till nearly ready, which will be in about half an hour, then thicken it with a little flour, rubbed down in a tea-cupful of the soup, season it with half a grated nutmeg, a table-spoonful of lemon juice or of vinegar, and one of mushroom ketchup; let it boil a few minutes after all these ingredients are put in, and serve it with the pigeons in the tureen; a better thickening than flour is to boil quite tender two of the pigeons, take off all the meat and pound it in a mortar, rub it through a sieve, and put it, with the cut pigeons, into the strained soup. To make partridge soup, partridges may be substituted for pigeons, when only four birds will be required; pound the breast of one.

—— PIGEON. (2) Take eight pigeons, cut down two of the oldest, and put them, with the necks, pinions, livers, and gizzards of the others, into four quarts of water; let it boil till the substance be extracted, and strain it; season the pigeons with mixed spices and salt, and truss them as for stewing; pick and wash clean a handful of parsley, chives or young onions, and a good deal of spinach; chop them; put in a frying-pan a quarter of a pound of butter, and when it boils, mix in a handful of bread crumbs, keep stirring them with a knife till of a fine brown; boil the whole pigeons till they become tender in the stock with the herbs, and fried bread. If the soup be not sufficiently high seasoned, add more mixed spices and salt.

—— PORTABLE. Put on, in four gallons of water, ten pounds of a shin of beef, free from fat and skin, six pounds of a knuckle of veal, and two fowls, break the bones and cut the meat into small pieces, season with one ounce of whole black pepper, quarter of an ounce of Jamaica pepper, and the same of mace, cover the pot very closely, and let it simmer for twelve or fourteen hours, and then strain it. The following day, take off the fat, and clear the jelly from any sediment adhering to it; boil it gently upon a stove, without covering the saucepan, and stir it frequently till it becomes very thick and in lumps about the pan. Put it into saucers about half full, and when cold lay the cakes upon flannel to dry before the fire or in the sun; keep them in a tin box, with white paper between each cake. About an ounce weight will make a pint of rich soup; pour boiling water upon it with a little salt, and stir it till it dissolves. It also answers well for gravies and all brown sauces.

—— FOR THE POOR. Wash an ox-head very clean; break the bones, and cut the meat in pieces; put it on in thirteen gallons of water, and a peck and a half of potatoes, half a peck of turnips, the same quantity of onions, and some carrots; peel and cut them all down. A handful of pot herbs, and two quarts of oatmeal; season with pepper and salt. Cover the pot closely, and let it stew till the next morning; add as much hot water as may have wasted in boiling, and let it stew for some hours longer, when it will be fit for use. This soup will be found very good for a family dinner.

—— QUEEN. Pound in a marble mortar the white meat of three cold roasted fowls, and half a pound of sweet almonds blanched; add a little cream whilst pounding. Boil this with four quarts of well-seasoned beef stock, then strain it, and just before serving stir in a pint of cream.

—— SANTE. (1) Peel four large onions, cut them small, with four white lettuces, a handful of spinach, and a slice of grated bread. Stew all these ingredients for an hour in a quart of broth and a quarter of a pound of butter, then add three pints more of broth, skim off all the fat, and boil it a quarter of an hour, season with pepper and salt. Before serving, add half a pint of good cream. A pint of green peas, added with the other vegetables, is a great improvement.

—— SANTE. (2) Lay six or eight slices of lean ham, with some beef over them, at the bottom of a stewpan, then some veal, with some partridge-legs, or moor game, or chicken, salt, peppercorns, Jamaica pepper, three or four cloves, a bay-leaf, and one clove of garlic; let the whole stew together till it takes a fine brown color, then fill it up with half water and half good beef stock; add three heads of celery, two good turnips, parsley, lemon thyme, two carrots, three large onions, and a small bunch of winter savory; when the whole is thoroughly well done, pass it through a lawn sieve into a basin. Cut two good-sized turnips and three large leeks, into pieces, about the thickness of a quill, and an inch and a half long; fry these together of a nice brown color: next, shred two cabbage-lettuces, celery, endive, sorrel, and chervil; and stew them down on a very slow fire with a small bit of butter. When done, put them in a sieve with the turnips; then put them in a soup-pot and pour the soup from the basin over them; set it on a stove, skim it, and as soon as it boils, set it on one side, and let it simmer for two hours very gently; take the crumb of a couple of French rolls, and cut it into round pieces which brown in the oven, and put them into the tureen, and pour the soup upon them. If you think proper, it may be clarified, the same as other clear soups; but the real *Soup de Sante* ought not to be clarified.

—— SIMPLE. Cut small one pound of carrots, one pound of turnips, half a pound of onions, one lettuce, a little celery, and a handful of parsley; stew them for twenty minutes with a quarter of a pound of butter, some salt and pepper; then put them into three quarts of stock, made with two pounds of veal, and add one quart of green peas, and let it stew for three hours. Press it through a sieve, and boil it up before sending it to table.

—— SPRING. Put on in four quarts of water a knuckle of veal cut down, and a quarter of a pound of lean ham, or a gammon of bacon; a quart of green split peas; cut small three or four onions, three turnips, a little parsley, thyme, celery, and one leek; stew them all together till the peas are very soft; take out the meat and press the remainder through a fine sieve; season the soup with pepper and salt. Cut small like peas a bunch of the tops of asparagus, the hearts of two or three cabbages, cutting off the top part and the outside leaves, and a little green mint, stew them till tender, keeping them of a good green, and add them to the soup a quarter of an hour before serving. If it should not be green enough, pound some spinach, squeeze the juice through a cloth, put about a quarter of a pint into the tureen, and pour in the soup. This is the best method to make green peas soup of a good color.

—— STOVE OR SPINACH. Boil in two quarts of water three sliced onions. Pick and clean as much spinach as will make two large dishes, parboil and put it in a cullender, to let the bitter water drip from it; let cold water run upon it for a minute or two, and then press out the water. Knead two ounces of fresh butter, with a table-spoonful and a half of flour, mix it with the spinach, which boil for fifteen minutes in the water and onions, then put in half a pint of cream or good milk, some salt and pepper, boil it for fifteen minutes more. In the season of green peas, a quart added with the spinach is a great improvement. It is common to boil a lamb's head and pluck with the soup, and send them to table in the tureen. The soup is then called Lamb's Stove; but with the peas it is quite as good without.

—— VEGETABLE. Pare and cut small one dozen of common-sized onions, five large yellow turnips, two heads of celery, and the red part of three large carrots; wash and put them in a stewpan with two ounces of butter, cover it closely; and when the vegetables are a little soft, add to them four quarts of well-seasoned gravy soup made of roast beef bones, and let it stew four or five hours; rub it through a tammy, put it on the fire, boil and skim it before serving.

—— WINTER VEGETABLE. (1) Peel and slice six large onions, six potatoes and four turnips; fry them in half a pound of butter or very fresh dripping; toast a crust of bread brown and hard, put it, with two or three heads of celery cut small, some herbs, pepper, and salt, with the fried vegetables, into five pints of water, to stew gently for four hours, then strain it through a sieve, add a little carrot and celery cut small, and some chopped parsley, one anchovy or a red herring, and a little cayenne; boil it till the vegetables are tender.

—— WINTER VEGETABLE. (2) To every gallon of water allow, when cut down small, a quart of the following vegetables; equal quantities of turnips, carrots, and potatoes, three onions, two heads of celery, and a bunch of sweet herbs; fry them brown in a quarter of a pound of butter, add the water with salt and pepper, and boil it till reduced to three quarts, and serve it with fried toasted bread.

—— VENISON. Boil down in five quarts of water two pounds of a shank of veal, or fowl, and five pounds of the breast of venison cut small; two or three onions chopped, some whole white pepper and salt, with a quarter of a pound of lean ham. Let it stew till it be completely boiled down, when all the strength will be extracted; rub it through a sieve, thicken it with a little butter, kneaded in flour, and add a pint of Madeira, and boil it for a quarter of an hour or twenty minutes.

—— BROWN VENISON. Cut in small pieces six or seven pounds of the breast of venison, put it in a stewpan with two or three ounces of butter; cover it closely, stir it once or twice, and let it stew an hour. Mix four quarts of cold water with a pint and a half of the blood, put it on the fire in another stewpan, and stir it constantly till it boil; then add the stew to it with an onion minced small, and a whole carrot, some salt, black and Jamaica pepper. If the meat be young, let it boil gently for two hours; if old, two and a half will be necessary. A little before serving, take out the carrot and all the bones, leaving a little of the meat; mix in half a pint of Port wine, and let it boil a short time. It may be thickened with a little flour and butter.

—— VERMICELLI. The day before it is required make four quarts of good stock, and boil in it one carrot, one turnip, four onions, one or two parsley roots, three blades of mace, salt, and some white pepper; strain it, and, before using, take off all the fat, boil in some of the liquor the crumb of three French rolls till soft enough to mash smooth; boil the soup and stir well in the mashed rolls; boil it for a quarter of an hour, and, before serving, add the yolks of two eggs beaten with three table-spoonfuls of cream; boil in water two or three ounces of vermicelli for fifteen or twenty minutes, strain and put it into the tureen, and pour the soup upon it.

—— WHITE. (1) Boil together a knuckle of veal, a fowl, or two chickens skinned, a carrot, a turnip, an onion, some salt, and a little whole white pepper; take out the chickens when tender, cut them in joints, and add them to the soup when strained, beat up the yolks of nine eggs, mix them with a pint of cream and a table-spoonful of well-boiled rice; stir it gradually into the soup, and heat it gently before serving. A cow-heel that has been previously boiled, cut up in pieces, may be used instead of the chickens.

—— WHITE. (2) Take a good knuckle of veal, or two or three short shanks, boil it about four hours, with some whole white pepper, a little mace, salt, two onions, and a small bit of lean ham; strain it, and when cold take off all the fat and sediment; beat up six yolks of eggs and mix them with a pint of good cream, then pour the boiling soup upon it by degrees, stirring it well, and if it is liked, add the best part of the gristles.

—— WHITE. (3) Put on in four quarts of water, a knuckle of veal, six pounds weight, a quarter of a pound of lean ham or bacon, two slices of the crumb of bread, one ounce of blanched sweet almonds, put in whole; six middling-sized onions, two heads of celery, some whole white pepper, three blades of mace, a bunch of parsley, and a sprig of thyme; stew all these gently for eight hours, strain it, and when cold take off all the fat; boil it, and just before serving, take it off the fire, and stir in very gradually a pint of thick cream.

—— WHITE. (4) Boil in four quarts of water four pounds of veal, and a fowl, with some whole white pepper, a little mace, and three middling-sized onions whole, and a bunch of parsley; let it boil three hours, strain it, and put it on again to get quite hot, and just before serving, stir in gradually half a pint of cream with the yolks of three eggs well beaten. Do not let it boil, as that makes the eggs curdle.

—— WHITE. (5) Stew in three quarts of boiling water, till quite tender, a knuckle of veal, with a quarter of a pound of whole rice, three whole onions, a bunch of parsley, a little sweet marjoram, and two or three blades of mace, and some salt; a little before the soup is strained, add two anchovies; strain through a hair sieve and then through a silk one, or tammy, put it again upon the fire, and stir in half a pint of rich cream, or a pint of milk with the yolks of two eggs beat up in it; let it be hot but not boiling. If it is required to be richer, boil a fowl in the stock, with two ounces of pounded blanched sweet almonds.

—— WHITE. (6) Put on in five quarts of water, four pounds of a shank of veal, break the bone well, let it simmer till it be reduced nearly half; boil a tea-cupful of whole rice till very tender, pulp it through a cullender, strain the liquor, and add the rice, season with salt and white pepper, let it simmer for nearly an hour, and add, a little before serving, six yolks of eggs beaten extremely well.

SOUR KROUT. The best cabbage for this purpose is the drum, or white Strasburgh, and it should not be used till it has endured some severe frost; the stocks are then cut into halves, and shred down as fine as possible with a knife, or more properly with a plane made in the form of a cucumber slice. Burn a little juniper in a cask or tub which is perfectly sound and clean, and put a little leaven into the seam round the bottom,—flour and vinegar may be substituted for the leaven; then put in three or four handfuls of cabbage, a good sprinkling of salt, and a tea-spoonful of caraway seed, and press this hard with a wooden mallet; next add another layer of cabbage, with salt and caraway seed, as at first; and so on in the same manner until the cask be full, pressing down each layer firmly as you advance. A good deal of water will come to the top, of which a part may be taken off. The cask being full, put on the head so as to press upon the cabbage, and place it in a warm cellar to ferment; when it has worked well for three weeks, take off the scum which will have gathered on the top, and lay a clean cloth on the krout; replace the head, and put two or three heavy stones upon it. The juice should always stand upon the top. Thus in a good cellar it will keep for years. When to be dressed, it is boiled for five or six hours in water, or stewed with a little gravy, and may be also substituted for a crust over a beefsteak pie, when cheese is grated over it.

SOUR KROUT WITH PIKE. When the krout is boiled, clean a large pike, scrape and cut it into neat pieces, dip them into the beaten yolk of an egg, then into bread crumbs, and fry them of a nice brown; rub some butter upon a dish, and put into it a layer of krout, and some grated cheese, then a layer of pike, and a little sour cream; then krout, and so on till the dish be full. On the top put some bits of butter, and some good broth or gravy; strew crumbs of bread thickly over it, and bake it half an hour.

SPANISH PUFFS. Put into a saucepan, half a pint of water and a quarter of a pound of butter; stir it till it boils, and mix in four table-spoonfuls of flour; stir it well together, and add six yolks and four whites of eggs, two at a time; let it cool, and, with a dessert-spoon, drop it into boiling clarified dripping or lard.

To make ginger puffs, a tea-spoonful of pounded ginger may be added.

### SPARE RIB ROASTED. *See Pork.*

SPICE FOR WHITE SAUCE. Pound two ounces of pepper, a quarter of an ounce of mace, grate one nutmeg, and the peel of one lemon; mix all together in a bottle.

SPICE FOR GENERAL USE. One ounce and a half of pepper, cinnamon, nutmeg, and ginger, half an ounce each, and eight cloves; pound and mix all together in a bottle. A little of each kind of spice should be well dried, pounded, and kept separately in small bottles, which should be labelled.

SPINACH, TO DRESS. Pick the spinach with great care; strip the leaves from the stalks, and wash it in several waters, till perfectly clean; boil the spinach in salt and water; drain it well; pound it in a mortar, and put it into a stewpan with a little butter and broth, and let it stew over a slow fire for three-quarters of an hour, till it be very dry; then add a quarter of a pound of fresh butter, with salt and grated nutmeg; work the spinach well, till it is thick, but take care the butter does not turn to oil. Garnish with fried toasts of bread, which may be cut like cock's combs, or in any other form.

SPINACH, TO BOIL. (1) Pick it very carefully, and wash it thoroughly two or three times in plenty of cold water, then put it on in boiling water with a little salt; let it boil nearly twenty minutes, put it into a cullender, hold it under the water cock, and let the water run on it for a minute; put it into saucepan, beat it perfectly smooth with a beater or with a wooden spoon, add a bit of butter, and three table-spoonfuls of cream; mix it well together, and make it hot before serving. When dished, it is scored in squares with the back of a knife.

SPINACH, TO BOIL. (2) After being nicely picked and well washed, put it into a saucepan, with no more water than adheres to it; add a little salt; cover the pan closely, and boil it till tender, frequently shaking it; beat it quite smooth, adding butter and cream, and make it quite hot. Spinach may be served with poached eggs, or fried sausages laid on it.

When the spinach is bitter, it is preferable to boil it in water.

SPINACH TOAST. Boil some spinach for a quarter of an hour; then squeeze out all the water, chop it small, and put it into a mortar, with three or four spoonfuls of apple marmalade, the yolks of four hard-boiled, and three raw eggs, two biscuits soaked in cream, sugar, and a pinch of salt; pound all these together to a paste, put it into a dish, and mix with it a few dried currants, and three or four spoonfuls of melted butter. Cut some slices of bread half an inch thick, four inches long, and two broad; toast them nicely, and spread the spinach, &c. over them, to the thickness of half an inch, wash each over with white of egg; place the toasts on a baking-tin (well buttered) and bake them for half an hour. When done, grate nutmeg, and squeeze orange-juice over them, and serve.

SPRATS, TO BAKE. Clean them; take off the heads; put them into a deep dish, and cover them with vinegar and water, equal quantities of each. To a quart of liquid, put half an ounce of whole black pepper, a little allspice, two or three bay-leaves, some salt, and an onion. Tie paper over the dish, and bake them in a cool oven, or do them over a slow fire in a water bath. Herrings may be done in this way. Both will keep good some weeks.

SPRATS, STEWED. Wash and dry your sprats, and lay them as level as you can in a stewpan, and between every layer of sprats put three peppercorns, and as many allspice, with a few grains of salt; barely cover them with vinegar, and stew them one hour over a slow fire, they must not boil: a bay-leaf is sometimes added. Herrings or mackerel may be stewed the same way.

SPRATS, BROILED. If you have not a sprat gridiron, get a piece of pointed iron wire as thick as packthread, and as long as your gridiron is broad; run this through the heads of your sprats, sprinkle a little flour and salt over them, put your gridiron over a clear, quick fire, turn them in about a couple of minutes; when the other side is brown, draw out the wire, and send up the fish with melted butter in a cup.

*Obs.*—That sprats are young herrings, is evident by their anatomy, in which there is no perceptible difference. They appear very soon after the herrings are gone, and seem to be the spawn just vivified.

SPRING FRUIT—*A Mock Gooseberry Sauce for Mackerel, &c.* Make a marmalade of three dozen sticks of rhubarb, sweetened with moist sugar; pass it through a hair sieve, and serve up in a sauce-boat.

SPRING FRUIT TART. Prepare rhubarb as above: cut it into small pieces into a tart-dish; sweeten with loaf-sugar pounded; cover it with a good short crust paste; sift a little sugar over the top, and bake half an hour in a rather hot oven; serve up cold.

SPRING CREAM, *or Mock Gooseberry Fool.* Prepare a marmalade as directed for the pudding to which add a pint of good thick cream; serve up in glasses, or in a deep dish. If wanted in a shape, dissolve two ounces of isinglass in a little water; strain it through a tamis, and when nearly cold put it to the cream; pour it into a jelly mould, and when set, turn out into a dish, and serve up plain.

SPRING FRUIT SHERBET. Boil six or eight sticks of rhubarb (quite clean) ten minutes in a quart of water; strain the liquor through a tamis into a jug, with the peel of a lemon cut very thin, and two table-spoonfuls of clarified sugar; let it stand five or six hours, and it is fit to drink.

SPRUCE BEER. *See Beer.*

SPROUTS AND YOUNG GREENS. The receipt for cabbages will answer as well for sprouts, only they will be boiled enough in fifteen or twenty minutes.

STEAKS OR CHOPS. *See Chops.*

STOCK, FOR BROWN OR WHITE SOUPS. Take a pound of scate, five flounders, and two pounds of eels; cut them in pieces, put them into a stewpan, with as much water as will cover them, a little mace, an onion stuck with cloves, a head of celery, two parsley roots sliced, some pepper and salt, and a bunch of sweet herbs; cover close; strain it off for use; if it is for brown soup, fry the fish brown in butter, and then put it to stew.

STOCK, FOR GRAVY SOUP OR GRAVY. Cut a knuckle of veal into slices, slice also a pound of lean beef, and a pound of the lean of gammon of bacon; put these into a stewpan, with three scraped carrots, a couple of onions, a couple of turnips, two heads of celery, and two quarts of water. Let the meat stew till quite tender, but it must not be brown. When thus prepared it will serve either for soup, or brown or white gravy; if for brown gravy, it must be first colored in the usual manner.

STOMACHIC TINCTURE. Peruvian bark, bruised, one ounce and a half, orange-peel, do. one ounce, brandy, or proof spirit, one pint. Let these ingredients steep for ten days, shaking the bottle every day; let it remain quiet two days, and then decant the clear liquor. Dose—a tea-spoonful in a wine-glass of water, twice a day, when you feel languid, *i.e.* when the stomach is empty, about an hour before dinner, and in the evening. This agreeable aromatic tonic is an effective help to concoction; and we are under personal obligations to it, for frequently restoring our stomach to good temper, and procuring us good appetite and good digestion. In low nervous affections arising from a languid circulation, and when the stomach is in a state of debility from age, intemperance, or other causes, this is a most acceptable restorative.

N. B.—Tea made with dried and bruised orange-peel, in the same way as common tea, and drank with milk and sugar, has been taken by nervous and dyspeptic persons with great benefit. Sucking a bit of dried orange-peel about an hour before dinner, when the stomach is empty, is very grateful and strengthening to it.

STRAWBERRY CREAM. Put six ounces of strawberry jam to a pint of cream, pulp it through a sieve; add to it the juice of a lemon, whisk it fast at the edge of a dish, lay the froth on a sieve, add a little more juice of lemon, and when no more froth will rise, put the cream into a dish, or into glasses; and place the froth upon it, well drained.

STRAWBERRIES AND RASPBERRIES. From either of these fruits agreeable wine may be obtained, by following the rules given for making currant wine; but it will be found a cheaper and a better method, to add a little sirup or juice of the fruit to any flavorless currant wine; when the fermentation begins to decline, currant wine may also be flavored with odoriferous flowers, such as cowslip, elder, or mignionette. The quality of roughness is communicated by catechu and keno, chips of oak and of beech, and also the sloe; a small quantity of these, or of the flowers, is put into the cask when the first fermentation is over, and as soon as the wine has acquired the desired flavor, it is racked and fined. The flavoring articles, such as orris-root, cloves, ginger,

sweet and bitter almonds, are put into a muslin bag, and hung in the cask for a few days, during the stage of insensible fermentation, that is, after the first fermentation has ceased; care being taken to taste the liquor frequently, so that the flavoring matter may be withdrawn as soon as it has produced the desired effect.

STRAWBERRIES, POUNDED, FOR STRAWBERRY CREAM. Take equal weight of sugar and of strawberries; pound and sift the sugar, add it to the strawberries, and pound them in a marble mortar till perfectly smooth. Put it into jars, and tie them over closely with paper. It will keep good for several months.

STRAWBERRY SOUFFLE. Take a basket of very fine strawberries, pick, and crush them, and then rub them through a sieve. Whisk the whites of eighteen eggs to a firm froth, to which add a pound and a half of powder sugar, stir them together as lightly as possible; then mix them with the strawberries. Pour the whole into a *croustade,* and bake it for an hour in a moderate oven; when done, glaze it, and serve.

STRAWBERRY TART. Pick, and put into a basin two quarts of the best scarlet strawberries, then add to them half a pint of cold thick clarified sugar, and half a pint of Madeira, with the juice of two or three lemons; mix these well together, without breaking the strawberries, and put them into a puff paste, previously baked; be careful to keep them very cool.

STRING BEANS. *See French Beans.*

STUFFING WITHOUT MEAT. Season a quarter of a pound of finely-minced beef suet, and an equal quantity of grated bread, with grated nutmeg, lemon-peel, lemon thyme, and parsley, salt, and pepper; mix it well together, and bind it with a well-beaten yolk of an egg, when it may be used for stuffing veal and fowl.

STUFFING FOR TURKEY OR FOWL. Wash a quart of oysters in their own liquor, strain it, and put into it the oysters, with a little mace, whole pepper, and lemon-peel; when parboiled, chop small a dozen and a half, add an equal weight of grated bread, twice the quantity of finely-minced beef suet, the yolks of three hard-boiled eggs, one anchovy, a little salt, pepper, nutmeg, lemon-peel, and some minced parsley; bind it with the beaten yolks of two eggs. For the sauce, boil with the liquor of the oysters, a pint of white stock, half a pint of white wine, one anchovy, pepper, salt, and nutmeg; strain it, and add a quarter of a pound of butter rolled in flour, beat it up with the remainder of the oysters.

STUFFING FOR A HARE. Parboil the liver, and mince it; add an equal quantity of grated bread, double the quantity of fat bacon chopped, a bit of butter the size of a walnut. Season with pepper, salt, nutmeg, chopped lemon thyme, and parsley; bind with an egg beaten.

STUFFING FOR VEAL, ROAST TURKEY, FOWL, &c.; Mince a quarter of a pound of beef suet (beef marrow is better), the same weight of bread crumbs, two drachms of parsley leaves, a drachm and a half of sweet marjoram or lemon thyme, and the same of grated lemon-peel and onion chopped as fine as possible, a little pepper and salt; pound thoroughly together with the yolk and white of two eggs, and secure it in the veal with a skewer, or sew it in with a bit of thread. Make some of it into balls or sausages; flour them, and boil, or fry them, and send them up as a garnish, or in a side dish, with roast poultry, veal, or cutlets, &c.

N. B.—This is about the quantity for a turkey poult: a very large turkey will take nearly twice as much. To the above may be added an ounce of dressed ham; or use equal parts of the above stuffing and pork sausage meat pounded well together.

Obs.—Good stuffing has always been considered a chief thing in cookery: it has given immortality to

"Poor *Roger Fowler* who'd a generous mind,
Nor would submit to have his hand confin'd,
But aimed at all,—yet never could excel
In any thing but *stuffing* of his veal."

STUFFING FOR HARE. Two ounces of beef suet chopped fine; three ounces of fine bread crumbs; parsley, a drachm; eschalot, half a drachm; a drachm of marjoram, lemon thyme, or winter savory; a drachm of grated lemon-peel, and the same of pepper and salt: mix these with the white and yolk of an egg; do not make it thin—it must be of cohesive consistence: if your stuffing is not stiff enough, it will be good for nothing: put it in the hare, and sew it up. If the liver is quite sound, you may parboil it, and mince it very fine, and add it to the above.

STURGEON, BAKED. Clean, and take the skin from a small sturgeon; split it along the belly, without separating it. Lay it in a large baking dish, season it with salt, pepper, pounded sweet herbs; moisten with oil, lemon-juice, and a bottle of white wine. Put it in the oven, baste it frequently; make it a nice color, and serve it with its own gravy.

STURGEON, FRESH, TO BROIL. Cut it into cutlets; rub them with the yolk of an egg beat up; strew them over with some parsley, minced very fine, and mixed with grated bread crumbs, pepper, and salt; put them into pieces of white paper buttered, and broil them gently. Sauces;—oyster, melted butter, and anchovy.

STURGEON, FRESH. The best mode of dressing this, is to have it cut in thin slices like veal cutlets, and broiled, and rubbed over with a bit of butter and a little pepper, and served very hot, and eaten with a squeeze of lemon-juice. Great care, however, must be taken to cut off the skin before it is broiled, as the oil in the skin, if burned, imparts a disgusting flavor to the fish. The flesh is very fine, and comes nearer to veal, perhaps, than even turtle. Sturgeon is frequently plentiful and reasonable in the London shops. We prefer this mode of dressing it to the more savory one of stewing it in rich gravy, like carp, &c. which overpowers the peculiar flavor of the fish.

STURGEON, ROASTED. Take a large piece of sturgeon, or a whole small one, clean and skin it properly; lard it with eel and anchovies, and marinade it in a white wine marinade. Fasten it to the spit, and roast it, basting frequently with the marinade strained. Let the fish be a nice color, and serve with a pepper sauce.

SUET TO KEEP FOR A TWELVE-MONTH. Choose the firmest part, and pick it free from skin and veins. Put it into a saucepan, and set it at some distance from the fire, in order that the suet may melt without frying, or it will taste disagreeable. When it is melted, pour it into a pan of cold water. When it has caked quite hard, wipe it very dry, fold it in fine paper, and then in a linen bag, and keep it in a dry, but not in a hot place. When you wish to use it, scrape it fine, and it will make a nice crust, either with or without butter.

SUET MILK. Cut into very small shavings one ounce of fresh beef suet; dissolve it slowly over the fire in one pint of milk, together with a bit of lemon-peel and cinnamon; sweeten with pounded loaf sugar.

SUET DUMPLINGS. This batter should be made the same as for suet pudding, (second receipt), but much thicker, let your cloth be wetted, shake it all over with flour, and tie up in several parts of the cloth, as much as it will hold, two or three spoonfuls of batter. Or you may make the batter as usual, and put it in tea-cups, well buttered; tie them in cloths, and boil an hour.

SUGAR, TO CLARIFY. To every three pounds of loaf sugar, allow the beaten white of one egg, and a pint and a half of water; break the sugar small, put it into a nicely-cleaned brass pan, and pour the water over it; let it stand sometime before it be put upon the fire; then add the beaten whites of the eggs; stir it till the sugar be entirely dissolved, and when it boils up, pour in a quarter of a pint of cold water; let it boil up a second time; take it off the fire and let it settle for fifteen minutes; carefully take off all the scum; put it on the fire, and boil it till sufficiently thick, or if required, till candy high; in order to ascertain which, drop a little from a spoon into a small jar of cold water, and if it become quite hard, it is then sufficiently done; or dip the thevil into the sugar, plunge it into cold water, draw off the sugar which adheres to the stick, and if it be hard and snaps, the fruit to be preserved must be instantly put in and boiled.

SUGAR ORNAMENTS. *See Caramel.*

SUGAR RUFFS. A pound of pounded and sifted loaf sugar beaten well with the whites of three eggs, and flavored with oil of cinnamon, lemons, or orange-flower water, and baked in the same way as the meringues, served in a napkin, or used to garnish dishes of preserves.

SUGAR, TO BOIL. To every pound of sugar allow half a pint of water; stir it over the fire till the sugar be entirely dissolved; when it first boils up, pour in a little cold water, and when it boils a second time, take it off the fire; let it settle ten minutes, carefully scum it, and boil it for half an hour or a little longer, and then put in the fruit.

SWEETBREADS, Italian Attelets. Blanch some nice sweetbreads, and stew them in a well-seasoned gravy, made of meat and vegetables; when cold, cut them into pieces of nearly an inch square, put them into a sauce d'attelets, and let them cool. With silver skewers, skewer the sweetbreads, and a bit of ready-dressed calf's udder alternately; make them all as much as possible of an equal size, and of a square form. Moisten them with the sauce, and cover them with grated bread, then dip them into four well beaten eggs, strew over them some more grated bread, and level it with a knife; fry them of a fine brown, and serve with an Italian sauce, white or brown.

If the attelets are ready before they are required to be fried, strew grated bread over the cover of a stewpan, and lay them upon it.

SWEETBREAD, TO BOIL. Parboil it, rub it with butter, and broil it over a slow fire, turn it frequently, and baste it now and then, by putting it upon a plate kept warm by the fire with butter in it.

SWEETBREADS A LA DAUPHINE. If for a round dish, take four large and fine sweetbreads. If for a long dish, three will suffice. Pare off the fat and sinews, and blanch them in warm water, parboil them, and when cold, lard them. Rub a stewpan with fresh butter, and put into it a few sliced carrots and onions, then a layer of slices of fat bacon, place the sweetbreads upon the bacon, sprinkle a little salt over them, and stew them with a great deal of fire on the top, and a very slow one beneath; when they are nicely browned, cover them with a piece of buttered paper, cut round, and lessen the fire upon the top. They will require to stew for three-quarters of an hour, then drain and put them into a pan with some glaze and the bacon underneath. Leave them in the glaze till dinner time.

SWEETBREADS FULL DRESSED. Parboil them, and let them get cold; then cut them in pieces, about three-quarters of an inch thick; dip them in the yolk of an egg, then in fine bread crumbs (some add spice, lemon-peel, and sweet herbs); put some clean dripping into a frying-pan: when it boils, put in the sweetbreads, and fry them a fine brown. For garnish, crisp parsley and for sauce, mushroom ketchup and melted butter, or anchovy sauce, or bacon or ham.

SWEETBREADS, SMALL CASES OF SCOLLOPS OF. Blanch and parboil some sweetbreads, cut them into small scollops. Then chop separately, and finely, half a pint of mushrooms, a little parsley, and four or five shallots, add a little fat bacon rasped, and a piece of fresh butter; season the scollops with pepper, salt, and a little mace, stew it all together over a slow fire; when done, drain off the fat, place the scollops in small paper cases, which have been fried in olive oil, cover them with plenty of finely-chopped herbs, and strew over them fried bread crumbs; lay the paper cases for a moment into the oven, and before serving, pour into each a little rich gravy, and a little lemon-juice.

SWEET HERBS. *See Herbs.*

SWEETMEAT FRITTERS. Cut small any sort of candied fruit, and heat it with a bit of fresh butter, some good milk, and a little grated lemon-peel; when quite hot, stir in enough of flour to make it into a stiff paste, take it off the fire, and work in eight, or ten eggs, two at a time; when cold, form the fritters, and fry, and serve them with pounded loaf sugar strewed over them.

SYLLABUBS. Take the juice of a large lemon, the peel (pared very thin), a glass of brandy, two of white wine, and a quarter of a pound of powder-sugar; put these ingredients into a pan, and leave them; the next day, add a pint of thick cream, and the whites of two eggs; whip the whole well, and pour the syllabub into glasses. They are the better for keeping a day or two. If the syllabubs are not wanted quite so good as the above, raisin or mountain wine will do as well as brandy.

SYLLABUB, SOMERSETSHIRE. Put a pint of Port, and a pint of Sherry, or any other white wine, into a large bowl, sweeten it according to taste; milk the bowl full; in about twenty minutes' time, cover it tolerably high with clouted cream; grate nutmeg over it; add pounded cinnamon, and nonpareils.

SYLLABUB, STAFFORDSHIRE. Put a pint of cider, a glass of brandy, sugar, and nutmeg, into a bowl, and milk into it; or pour warm milk from a large tea-pot some height into it.

SYLLABUB. (1) One pound of ratafia cakes pounded and steeped in two bottles of Port wine, one of claret, and one of brandy, the grated peel and juice of two lemons, one large nutmeg grated, and two ounces of sweet almonds, blanched and pounded with a little rose-water, and pounded sugar sufficient to make it sweet—Put all these ingredients, well mixed, into a large China bowl, or bowls of an equal size, and let the milk of a good cow be milked upon them; add a little rich cream and sifted loaf sugar, and cover it to keep it warm. It may be served out into glasses with a silver ladle.

SYLLABUB. (2) A large glass of Madeira, one of rich sweet wine, and half a one of ratafia, half a pound of pounded loaf sugar, the grated peel of a large lemon, the juice of two, and a little pounded cinnamon; stir it all together till the sugar be dissolved, and add a quart of rich cream; whisk it well; lay some macaroons into the bottom of a dish, and pile the frothed syllabub high upon it. It may be kept nine or ten days, and is better the third and fourth than when first made.

SYLLABUB, SOLID. A quarter of a pint of mountain, the same of white wine, the grated peel of two, and juice of one lemon; sweeten, and add it to a quart of rich cream; whisk it for an hour, and put it into glasses. It will keep a week in cold weather.

SYLLABUB, COMMON. Half a pint of currant, the same of Port or white wine, half a grated nutmeg, and the peel of a lemon; sweeten well with pounded loaf or good brown sugar, and mix it together in a China bowl, and when the sugar dissolves, milk upon it three or four pints of milk. Serve it when cold.

SYLLABUB, WHIPT. (1) Mix together half a glass of brandy, a little lemon-juice, and grated peel, with sugar enough to sweeten the whole; stir it into a pint of thick cream, and add the well-beaten whites of six eggs; whisk it for an hour, and put the froth, as it rises, upon a sieve to drain; put a little Port and sweet wine into glasses, and fill them up with the froth.

SYLLABUB, WHIPT. (2) Mix with a pint of cream, half a pint of sweet wine, a glass of brandy, the juice of a lemon, grated nutmeg, six ounces of sifted loaf sugar: nearly fill the custard-glasses with the mixture, and lay on with a spoon some of the whip.

wwwwww

## T.

TAMIS, a coarse kind of cloth for straining soups and gravies.

TARTE, ROYAL BERLIN. Take half a pound of sweet almonds, and having blanched, pound them with six eggs, in a marble mortar to a very fine paste, add to it a pound of broken sugar, a pound of fresh butter and the grated rind of two lemons, beat it well as each ingredient is put in; lay about sixteen or eighteen ounces of sifted flour on the slab, place the almond paste on it, and  knead them well together. Divide this into several pieces, which roll to the eighth of an inch in thickness; from these cut from twelve to sixteen circular layers, the largest about seven inches in diameter, the rest, each somewhat smaller than the other; when all are cut, place them on white paper on tins, and bake them in a moderate oven to a clear brown, then take them out, and let them cool. As soon as cold, place the largest piece on a China dish, of a sufficient size to let it lay flat, and spread over it equally some preserved fruit; cover this with the second sized layer, on which also spread preserved fruit; then a third layer, and so on until all the paste is used, taking care to put each layer in its proper order, so that the whole may form a cone, and that between every one must be a different kind of preserve; when done, glaze, and ornament it as follows: cut some candied lemon, and orange-peel into the form of leaves, which arrange in garlands round the tart, putting here and there a small preserved fruit; when done, replace it in the oven for two or three minutes to dry, and then serve.

TARTLETS. (1) Butter some small tartlet pans; line them with a nice thin puff paste, mark it neatly round the edges; bake them; when they are cold, fill them with custard, preserve, or any sweetmeat you think proper, and if you choose, pour custard over.

TARTLETS. (2) Roll out the paste about a quarter of an inch thick, and lay upon it the top part of the patty-pan; cut it round with the paste cutter. Rub the patty-pans with a little butter, and line them with the paste, and place in the middle a little bit of bread, which take out when they are baked. They may be filled with any preserved fruit, and a star or leaf of paste placed on the top. To make ornaments of paste, roll it quite thin, and as even as possible; cut it with tin stars, leaves, or any other form, and bake them a light brown color, upon flat tins dusted with flour.

TART, APPLE, CREAMED. Use green codlings, in preference to any other apple, and proceed as in the last receipt. When the pie is done, cut out the whole of the centre, leaving the edges; when cold, pour on the apple some rich boiled custard and place round it some small leaves of puff paste of a light color.

TART, CHERRY. The cherries may be stoned, and a few red currants added; sweeten with loaf or brown sugar, and put into the bottom of the dish a small tea-cup; cover it with paste.

TART, CRANBERRY. Take cranberries, pick and wash them in several waters, put them into a dish, with the juice of half a lemon, a quarter of a pound of moist or pounded loaf sugar, to a quart of cranberries. Cover it with puff or tart paste and bake it three-quarters of an hour; if tart paste is used, draw it from the oven five minutes before it is done, and ice it, return it to the oven, and send it to table cold.

TART, CURRANT. To a quart of red currants add one pint of red raspberries, strawberries, or cherries; sweeten them well with brown sugar; before putting in the fruit, line the side of the dish with tart paste, place in it a small tea-cup, put in the fruit, and cover it with paste.

Four ounces of brown sugar are generally allowed to a quart of fruit.

TART OF PRESERVED FRUIT. Cover a flat dish, or tourte pan with tart paste, about an eighth of an inch thick; roll out puff paste, half an inch thick, and cut it out in strips an inch wide; wet the tart paste, and lay it neatly round the pan by way of a rim; fill the centre with jam or marmalade of any kind, ornament it with small leaves of puff paste, bake it half an hour, and send it to table cold.

The above may be filled before the puff paste is laid on, neatly strung with paste, and the rim put over after.

The most general way of sending tourtes to table, is with a croquante of paste, or a caramel of spun sugar put over after it is baked.

TARTS, PRESERVED FRUIT. Rub over with a little butter an oval dish, or tin shape, line it with paste, and fill it with any sort of preserved fruit. Roll out a bit of paste thin, and, with a paste cutter, cut it into narrow strips; brush with water the rim of the shape, and lay the bars of paste across and across, and then put round a border of paste, and mark it with the paste cutter.

TARTS, RIPE FRUIT. Gooseberries, damsons, morello cherries, currants mixed with raspberries, plums, green gages, white plums, &c. should be quite fresh picked, and washed: lay them in the dish with the centre highest, and about a quarter of a pound of moist or loaf sugar pounded to a quart of fruit (but if quite ripe they will not require so much); add a little water; rub the edges of the dish with yolk of egg; cover it with tart paste, about half an inch thick; press your thumb round the rim, and close it well; pare it round with a knife; make a hole in the sides below the rim; bake it in a moderate-heated oven; and ten minutes before it is done, take it out and ice it, and return it to the oven to dry.

TART, RHUBARB. Strip off the peel, and if the rhubarb is large, cut it into two or three strips, and then into bits about an inch long; sweeten well with brown sugar, and cover the dish with paste.

TART PASTE, FOR FAMILY PIES. Rub in with the hand half a pound of butter into one pound and a quarter of flour, mix it with half a pint of water, and knead it well.

TART PASTE, Sweet, or Short and Chrisped. To one pound and a quarter of fine flour add ten ounces of fresh butter, the yolks of two eggs beaten, and three ounces of sifted loaf sugar; mix up together with half a pint of new milk, and knead it well.
N. B.—This crust is frequently iced.

TEA CREAM. Infuse an ounce of the best green tea in half a pint of boiling milk, simmer it five minutes, then strain it through a tammy, pressing the leaves well. Boil a pint of rich cream, add to it the yolks of four eggs, well beaten, and a sufficient quantity of clarified sugar; pour this whilst hot to the milk, stir them together well; put in as much clarified isinglass as will set it, and pour the cream into the mould, or glasses; place them on ice; when perfectly cold, turn it out of the mould, or serve in the glasses.

TEAL, ROASTED. Shred a little lemon-peel, and mix it with a bit of butter, salt, pepper, and lemon juice; stuff your birds with this, cover them first with slices of lemon, then bacon, and lastly, buttered paper sprinkled with salt; tie them up securely, fasten them to the spit, and roast them. When done, let the butter run out, remove the wrappers, and dish them. Serve them with a sauce made as follows: put into a saucepan three ladlefuls of *espagnole,* a spoonful of *consomme*, a bit of glaze, the rind of a quarter of a lemon, and a little pepper; give them a boil up together, and strain it over the teal.

TENCH. They are a fine-flavored fresh water fish; when good, the eyes are bright, the body stiff, and the outside free from slime; tench should be dressed as soon as caught.

TENCH, FRIED. Take a couple of large tench, scale and cleanse them as for broiling. Cut off the fins, split them down the back, take out the bones; sprinkle them with flour and salt; squeeze a little lemon-juice over, and fry them in butter, and serve them dry.

TENCH, ROASTED. Take off scales, heads, and fins, of the tench, cleanse and dry them well, then put into each a little butter, mixed with sweet herbs; lay them for about five minutes in melted butter, with salt, pepper, and sweet herbs; wrap each fish in paper, fasten them to a spit, and roast them.

TEWAHDIDDLE. A pint of table beer (or ale, if you intend it for a supplement to your "night cap"), a table-spoonful of brandy, and a tea-spoonful of brown sugar, or clarified sirup; a little grated nutmeg or ginger may be added, and a roll of very thin-cut lemon-peel.

*Obs.*—Before our readers make any remarks on this composition, we beg of them to taste it: if the materials are good, and their palate vibrates in unison with our own, they will find it one of the pleasantest beverages they ever put to their lips; and, as Lord Ruthven says, "this is a right gossip's cup that far exceeds all the ale that ever Mother Bunch made in her life-time."

THICKENING. Clarified butter is best for this purpose; but if you have none ready, put some fresh butter into a stewpan over a slow, clear fire; when it is melted, add fine flour sufficient to make it the thickness of paste; stir it well together with a wooden spoon for fifteen or twenty minutes, till it is quite smooth, and the color of a guinea: this must be done very gradually and patiently; if you put it over too fierce a fire to hurry it, it will become bitter and empyreumatic: pour it into an earthen pan and keep it for use. It will keep good a fortnight in summer, and longer in winter.

A large spoonful will generally be enough to thicken a quart of gravy.

*Obs.*—This, in the French kitchen, is called *roux*. Be particularly attentive in making it; if it gets any burnt smell or taste, it will spoil every thing it is put into. When cold, it should be thick enough to cut out with a knife, like a solid paste.

It is a very essential article in the kitchen, and is the basis of consistency in most made dishes, soups, sauces, and ragouts; if the gravies, &c. are too thin, add this thickening, more or less, according to the consistence you would wish them to have.

MEM.—In making thickening, the less butter, and the more flour you use, the better; they must be thoroughly worked together, and the broth, or soup, &c. you put them to, added by degrees: take especial care to incorporate them well together, or

your sauces, &c. will taste floury, and have a disgusting, greasy appearance: therefore, after you have thickened your sauce, add to it some broth, or warm water, in the proportion of two table-spoonfuls to a pint, and set it by the side of the fire, to raise any fat, &c. that is not thoroughly incorporated with the gravy, which you must carefully remove as it comes to the top. This is called cleansing, or finishing the sauce.

Half an ounce of butter, and a table-spoonful of flour, are about the proportion for a pint of sauce to make it as thick as cream.

N. B.—The fat skimmings off the top of the broth-pot are sometimes substituted for butter; some cooks merely thicken their soups and sauces with flour.

TIMBALE. Put a pound of flour on the slab, make a hole in the middle of it, into which pour a little water, three or four spoonfuls of oil, a quarter of a pound of butter, the yolks of two eggs, and a pinch of salt; knead these ingredients thoroughly into the flour, until it becomes a tolerably firm paste; roll it out to nearly half an inch in thickness, line one large, or several small plain round moulds, with this paste; let the moulds be well buttered, and the paste come about half an inch above the top of the mould; fill your *timbale* with any *farce*, or ragout, you think proper, cover it with a layer of paste, pressing the edges together; bake it, and when done, turn the *timbale* on a dish, make a hole, pour in some rich sauce or gravy, and serve.

TINCTURE OF ALLSPICE. Of allspice bruised, three ounces, apothecaries' weight; brandy, a quart. Let it steep a fortnight, occasionally shaking it up; then pour off the clear liquor: it is a most grateful addition in all cases where allspice is used, for making a bishop, or to mulled wine extempore, or in gravies, &c. or to flavor and preserve potted meats.

TIPSY CAKE. Pour over a sponge cake,

made in the form of a porcupine, as much white wine as it will absorb, and stick it all over with blanched sweet almonds, cut like straws; or pour wine in the same manner over a thick slice of sponge cake, cover the top of it with preserved strawberries or raspberries, and stick cut almonds all round it.

TOAST AND CHEESE. *See Cheese.*

TOAST, WITH BUTTER. Spread butter over some slices of fried bread; lay on them sweet herbs, tossed up in melted butter, and serve.

TOASTS, GENOA. Lard a French roll with partly anchovies, and partly ham; cut the roll into slices, lay on each a thin slice of bacon, dip them into batter, and fry them; drain, and serve with *ravigote.*

TOASTS, GRENADA. Cut some fat and lean bacon into dice, give them a few turns over the fire with parsley, scallions, shallots, pepper, salt, and the yolks of three eggs; stir it frequently, till it forms a kind of force-meat, spread it over slices of bread, cut of an equal thickness, and fry them.

TOASTS, ITALIAN. Cut some slices of bread, about half an inch in thickness, fry them in sweet oil, let it be dry, and crisp, lay them on a dish, and spread over them any light good *farce* you may think proper; pour over them an appropriate sauce and serve them.

TOAST AND WATER. Pare the crust off a thin slice of stale bread, toast it brown upon both sides, doing it equally and slowly, that it may harden without being burnt; put it into a jug, and pour upon it boiling water; cover the jug with a saucer, and set it in a cool place.

TOASTS, SPANISH. Roll out some almond paste, nearly an inch thick, cut it into pieces, about two inches square, press them down with a square piece of wood, a little smaller than the paste, which will leave the edges higher than the rest; bake them, and when cold, pour in any prepared cream you please, as high as the borders; ice, and color them with a salamander.

TOMATA SAUCE. Bake six tomatas in an oven till quite soft; with a tea-spoon take out the pulp, add salt, cayenne, and vinegar, till of the consistence of thick cream.

TOMATA SOUP. Wash, scrape, and cut small the red part of three large carrots, three heads of celery, four large onions, and two large turnips, put them into a saucepan, with a table-spoonful of butter, and half a pound of lean new ham; let them stew very gently for an hour, then add three quarts of brown gravy soup, and some whole black pepper, with eight or ten ripe tomatas; let it boil an hour and a half, and pulp it through a sieve; serve it with fried bread cut in dice.

TOMATA SAUCE, FRENCH. Cut ten or a dozen tomatas into quarters, and put them into a saucepan, with four onions sliced, a little parsley, thyme, one clove, and a quarter of a pound of butter; set the saucepan on the fire, stirring occasionally for three-quarters of an hour; strain the sauce through a horse-hair sieve, and serve with the directed articles.

TOMATA SAUCE, ITALIAN. Take five or six onions, slice, and put them into a saucepan, with a little thyme, bay-leaf, twelve or fifteen tomatas, a bit of butter, salt, half a dozen allspice, a little India saffron, and a glass of stock; set them on the fire, taking care to stir it frequently, as it is apt to stick; when you perceive the sauce is tolerably thick, strain it like a *puree.*

TOMATA KETCHUP. (1) Take tomatas when fully ripe, bake them in a jar till tender strain them, and rub them through a sieve. To every pound of juice, add a pint of Chili vinegar, an ounce of shallots, half an ounce of garlic, both sliced, a quarter of an ounce of salt, and a quarter of an ounce of white pepper, finely powdered; boil the whole till every ingredient is soft, rub it again through the sieve. To every pound add the juice of three lemons; boil it again to the consistence of cream; when cold, bottle it, put a small quantity of sweet oil on each, tie bladders over, and keep it in a dry place.

TOMATA KETCHUP. (2) Gather a peck of tomatas, pick out the stems, and wash them; put them on the fire without water; sprinkle on a few spoonfuls of salt; let them boil steadily an hour, stirring them frequently; strain them through a colander and then through a sieve; put the liquid on the fire with half a pint of chopped onions, eighth of an ounce of mace broke into small pieces, and if not sufficiently salt, add a little more; one table-spoonful of whole black pepper; boil all together until just enough to fill two bottles; cork it tight.

[The seasoning may be varied to suit the taste. Allspice instead of mace—common red pepper instead of black pepper, and less chopped onion.]

TOMATO KETCHUP. (3) One gallon skinned tomatas, four table-spoons of salt, four do. black pepper, two do. allspice, eight pods red pepper, eight table-spoons of mustard seed. These articles to be bruised fine and simmered slowly in a pint of vinegar three hours; then strained through a hair sieve. To be stewed down to half a gallon of ketchup.

TOMATAS, METHOD OF PRESERVING. (1) A sufficient quantity of salt is dissolved in spring or river water to make it strong enough to bear an egg; select perfectly ripe tomatas, and place them well and without pressing them, in a stone or glazened earthen pot, with a deep plate in such a manner that it presses upon the fruit, and by this simple process tomatas may be preserved more than a year without attention. Before cooking them they should be soaked in fresh water for several hours.

TOMATAS, METHOD OF PRESERVING. (2) Gather them carefully without bruising; put them in a stone jar, and pour in strong brine, to the top—putting on a light weight to keep them gently pressed down below the surface of the brine. Soak them in fresh water and cook them in the usual way, seasoning to suit the taste, as when fresh from the vine.

TOMATA MARMALADE. Gather full-grown tomatas while quite green; take out the stems and stew them till soft; rub them through a sieve; put the pulp on the fire, seasoned highly with pepper, salt and powdered cloves; add some garlic, and stew all together till thick. It keeps well, and is excellent for seasoning gravies. Besides the numerous modes of preparing this delicious vegetable for the table, it may be stewed, after being peeled, with sugar, like cranberries and gooseberries, producing a tart equal to either of those fruits. *Tomatas* make good pickles, pickled green; to peel them, pour boiling water on them, when the skin will come off easily.

TONGUE. (1) A tongue which has not been dried will require very little soaking, but if dried, it should be soaked in water for three or four hours; then put it into cold water, and let it boil gently till tender.

TONGUE. (2) A tongue is so hard, whether prepared by drying or pickling, that it requires much more cooking than a ham; nothing of its weight takes so long to dress it properly.

A tongue that has been salted and dried should be put to soak (if it is old and very hard, 24 hours before it is wanted) in plenty of water; a green one fresh from the pickle requires soaking only a few hours: put your tongue into plenty of cold water; let it be an hour gradually warming; and give it from three and a half to four hours' very slow simmering, according to the size, &c.

*Obs.*—When you choose a tongue, endeavor to learn how long it has been dried or pickled, pick out the plumpest, and that which has the smoothest skin, which denotes its being young and tender.

The roots, &c. make an excellent relish potted, or peas soup.

TONGUE, TO STEW. Wash it very clean, and rub it well with common salt and a little saltpetre; let it lie two or three days, and then boil it till the skin will pull off. Put it into a saucepan, with part of the liquor it has been boiled in, and a pint of good stock. Season with black and Jamaica pepper, and two or three pounded cloves; add a glass of white wine and a table-spoonful of mushroom ketchup, and one of lemon pickle; thicken the sauce with butter rolled in flour, and pour it over the tongue.

TONGUE, PICKLED, GLAZED. Boil a large tongue till it be tender, skin and glaze it, and serve it with mashed turnips on one side, and mashed carrots, or carrots and spinach on the other.

TONGUE, POTTED. *See Ham.*

TONGUES, TO SALT. Salt two tongues, and turn them every day for four or five days; then rub them with two ounces of common salt, one of brown sugar, and half an ounce of saltpetre; turn them daily, and in a fortnight they may be used.

The best sort of vessel for salting them in is an earthen-ware pan, as wide at top as bottom, so that the tongues may lie in it long-ways.

TRIFLE. (1) Add to a pint of rich cream a tea-cupful of white wine, sweeten it with pounded loaf sugar, whisk it well, and as the froth rises lay it upon a sieve placed over a deep dish; as it drains, pour the cream into the pan in which it is whisked till all is done; dip some sponge biscuit, ratafia cakes, or Savoy biscuit, into sweet wine and a little brandy; pour over them a rich boiled custard, and when quite cold, lay on the whipt cream, piled as high as possible. Colored comfits may be strewed over the top.

TRIFLE. (2) Mix three table-spoonfuls of white wine, and one of sugar, with a pint and a half of thick cream; whisk it, and take off as much froth as will heap upon the dish, into which lay some pieces of sponge cake, or some sponge biscuit, soaked with sweet wine, and covered with preserved strawberries, or any other fruit; pile the froth upon this, and pour the remainder of the cream into the bottom of the dish; garnish with flowers.

TRIFLE. (3) Cover the bottom of the dish with Naples biscuits, and macaroons, broke in halves, wet with brandy and white wine, poured over them; cover them with patches of raspberry jam; fill the dish with a good custard, then whip up a syllabub, drain the froth on a sieve; put it on the custard, and strew comfits over all.

TRIPE. Take care to have fresh tripe; cleanse it well from the fat, and cut it into pieces about two inches broad and four long; put it into a stewpan, and cover it with milk and water, and let it boil gently till it is tender.

If the tripe has been prepared as it usually is at the tripe shops, it will be enough in about an hour, (this depends upon how long it has been previously boiled at the tripe shop); if entirely undressed, it will require two or three hours, according to the age and quality of it.

Make some onion sauce in the same manner as you do for rabbits, or boil (slowly by themselves) some Spanish or the whitest common onions you can get; peel them before you boil them; when they are tender, which a middling-sized onion will be in about three-quarters of an hour, drain them in a hair sieve, take off the top skins till they look nice and white, and put them with the tripe into a tureen or soup-dish, and take off the fat if any floats on the surface.

*Obs.*—Rashers of bacon, or fried sausages are a very good accompaniment to boiled tripe, cow-heels or calf's feet, see Kelly's sauce or parsley and butter, or caper sauce, with a little vinegar and mustard added to them, or salad mixture.

Tripe holds the same rank among solids, that water gruel does among soups, and the former is desirable at dinner, when the latter is welcome at supper.

TRIPE, TO FRY. Cut it into bits three or four inches square; make a batter thicker than for pancakes, of three eggs beaten up with flour and milk, a little salt, pepper, and nutmeg; dip in the tripe, and fry it in butter, or fresh dripping, of a light brown color. Serve it garnished with parsley. Sauce;—melted butter with lemon pickle in it.

TRIPE PIE. Lay into the bottom of a dish some thinly-sliced cold or raw ham, then put in a layer of tripe with the jelly adhering to it, season with pepper and salt, and add a bit of butter; fill the dish in this manner, and put in a few table-spoonfuls of brown stock; cover the dish with puff paste. A beef steak may be substituted for the ham, laid into the bottom, and the dish filled up with tripe.

TRIPE, TO BOIL. Clean it extremely well, and take off the fat; let it lie a night in salt-and-water, again wash it well, and let it lie in milk-and-water for the same length of time; then cut it into small pieces, roll and tie them with thread; put them, with a clean-washed marrow-bone, into a linen bag; tie it closely, and put it into a stewpan that has a cover to fit quite closely, fill it up with water, and let it boil gently for six hours. Take the tripe out of the bag, put it into a jar, and pour over it the liquor in which it was boiled. When to be dressed, boil some whole small onions in a part of the liquor, add a little salt, then put in the tripe and heat it thoroughy.

Or it may be fried in butter fricasseed, or stewed in a brown sauce.

Instead of being boiled in a bag, the tripe may be put, with some salt and whole pepper, into a stone-ware jar, which must have a piece of linen tied over it, and a plate laid upon the top. The pot should always be kept full of boiling water, taking care that it do not boil into the jar.

TRIPE, TO ROAST. Cut the tripe into two oblong pieces, make a forcemeat of bread crumbs and chopped parsley, seasoned with pepper and salt; bind it with the yolks of two eggs; spread it upon the fat side of the tripe, and lay on the other fat side; then roll it very tightly; and tie it with packthread. Roast, and baste it with butter: it will take one hour, or one hour and a half. Serve it with melted butter, into which put a table-spoonful of ketchup and one of lemon pickle.

TRIPE, BREADED. Cut your tripe into small square pieces, and give them a few turns in some butter, with parsley, salt, and pepper; roll each bit in grated bread, and broil them slowly. When done, serve them with slices of lemon.

TROUT. This fish is held in great estimation, it is a fresh water fish, and when good, of a flesh color, and the spots upon it are very bright; the female is considered the best, and is known by the head being smaller, and the body being deeper than that of the male.

TROUT, POTTED. Mix together the following quantity of finely-powdered spices: —One ounce of cloves, half an ounce of Jamaica pepper, quarter of an ounce of black pepper, quarter of an ounce of cayenne, two nutmegs, a little mace, and two tea-spoonfuls of ginger; add the weight of the spices, and half as much again of salt, and mix all thoroughly. Clean the fish, and cut off the heads, fins, and tails; put a tea-spoonful of the mixed spices into each fish, and lay them into a deep earthen jar, with the backs downwards; cover them with clarified butter, tie a paper over the mouth of the jar, and bake them slowly for eight hours. When the back bone is tender, the fish are done enough. Take them out of the jar, and put them into a milkpan with the backs upwards; cover them with a board, and place upon it a heavy weight. When perfectly cold, remove the fish into fresh jars, smooth them with a knife, and cover them with clarified butter.

TROUT, TO COLLAR. Wash them clean, split them down the back bone, and dry them well in a cloth; season them well with finely-pounded black pepper, salt, and mace; roll them tight, and lay them close into a dish; pour over an equal quantity of vinegar and beer, with two or three bay-leaves, and some whole black pepper; tie over the dish a sheet of buttered paper, and bake them an hour.

TROUT, TO BROIL. Cut off the fins, and cut the fish down the back, close to the bone, and split the head in two. Another way is, after they have been cut open, to rub a little salt over them; let them lie three or four hours, and then hang them up in the kitchen. They will be ready to broil the next morning for breakfast.

TROUT, TO BOIL. Clean and gut them; make the water as salt as for boiling salmon in, and when it boils put in the trout, and let them boil fast from fifteen to twenty minutes, according to their size. Sauce;—melted butter.

TROUT, TO FRY. Cut off the fins, clean and gut them; dust them with flour, and dip them into the yolk of an egg beaten; strew grated bread crumbs over, and fry them in fresh dripping; lay them upon the back of a sieve before the fire to drain. Sauce;—melted butter, with a table-spoonful of ketchup, and one of lemon pickle in it. When they are small, roll them in oatmeal before they are fried.

TRUFFLES. The truffle, like the mushroom, is a species of *fungus* common in France and Italy; it generally grows about eight or ten inches below the surface of the ground; as it imparts a most delicious flavor, it is much used in cookery. Being dug out of the earth, it requires a great deal of washing and brushing, before it can be applied to culinary purposes; when washed, the water should be warm, and changed frequently. It loses much of its flavor when dried.

TRUFFLE SAUCE. Mince two or three truffles very small, and toss them up lightly, in either oil or butter, according to your taste; then put to them four or five ladlefuls of *veloute* and a spoonful of *consomme*; let it boil for about a quarter of an hour over a gentle fire, skim off all the fat; keep your sauce hot in the *bain-marie.*

TRUFFLES TOURTE. Take two pounds of fine truffles, wash and pick them; put them into a stewpan, with six thin slices of ham, a very little carrot, a sliced onion, a bay-leaf, sweet herbs in powder, salt, and Champagne; lay rashers of bacon over the whole, and stew them to nearly a jelly. When cold, put the truffles into a crust with all the seasoning; bake the *tourte,* and serve as usual.

TUNBRIDGE CAKES. Rub two ounces of butter into half a pound of dried flour; add a few caraway seeds, and a quarter of a pound of pounded loaf sugar; mix it to a stiff paste with a little water, roll it out very thin, cut into round cakes with a glass or the top of a dredging box, prick them with a fork, and bake them upon floured tins.

TUNBRIDGE PUFFS. Put into a nicely-tinned saucepan a pint of milk, and when it boils, stir in as much flour as will make it a thick batter; add three well-beaten eggs, and two or three drops of oil of cinnamon, or any other seasoning; dust a large flat plate with flour, with a spoon throw on it the batter, in the form of balls or fritters, and drop them into boiling clarified dripping or lard. Serve them with pounded loaf sugar strewed over.

The batter may be made into a pudding, adding with the eggs an ounce of salt butter. Boil and serve it with a sweet sauce.

TURBOT. Turbot, when good, should be thick and full, and the belly of a yellowish white or cream color.

TURBOT, BAKED. Wash your fish in several waters, dry it well, and soak it in melted butter, with sweet herbs, parsley, pepper, salt, and nutmeg; in half an hour put the whole into a baking dish, envelope it completey in bread crumbs, and bake it.

TURBOT, BREADED. Prepare small turbot as usual, slit it across the back, and soak it for an hour in melted butter, or lemon-juice, with parsley, sweet herbs, salt, and pepper. Cover the fish with bread crumbs, and broil it; when done, squeeze lemon, or Seville orange-juice over it, and serve.

TURBOT, STUFFED AND BAKED. Your turbot being properly cleansed, turn over the skin of the under side, without cutting it off; make a *farce*, with some butter, parsley, scallions, morels, sweet herbs, all shred, and united together, with yolks of eggs, and seasoned with pepper and salt; spread this all over the under part of the fish, cover it with the skin, and sew it up. Dissolve some butter in a saucepan; add to it when melted, the yolk of an egg, sweet herbs shred, salt, and pepper; rub the fish all over with this, then bread, and bake it.

TURBOT, TO BOIL. (1) This excellent fish is in season the greatest part of the summer; when good, it is at once firm and tender, and abounds with rich gelatinous nutriment.

Being drawn, and washed clean, if it be

quite fresh, by rubbing it lightly with salt, and keeping it in a cold place, you may in moderate weather preserve it for a couple of days.

An hour or two before you dress it, soak it in spring water with some salt in it, then score the skin across the thickest part of the back, to prevent its breaking on the breast, which will happen from the fish swelling, and cracking the skin, if this precaution be not used. Put a large handful of salt into a fish-kettle with cold water, lay your fish on a fish strainer, put it in, and when it is coming to a boil, skim it well, then set the kettle on the side of the fire, to boil as gently as possible for about fifteen or twenty minutes (if it boils fast, the fish will break to pieces); supposing it a middling-sized turbot, and to weigh eight or nine pounds.

Rub a little of the inside red coral spawn of the lobster through a hair sieve, without butter; and when the turbot is dished, sprinkle the spawn over it. Garnish the dish with sprigs of curled parsley, sliced lemon, and finely-scraped horseradish.

If you like to send it to table in full dress, surround it with nicely-fried smelts, gudgeons are often used for this purpose, and may be bought very cheap when smelts are very dear; lay the largest opposite the broadest part of the turbot, so that they may form a well-proportioned fringe for it; or oysters; or cut a sole in strips, crossways, about the size of a smelt; fry them and lay them round. Send up lobster sauce, two boats of it, if it is for a large party.

*Obs.*—The thickest part is the favorite; and the carver of this fish must remember to ask his friends if they are fin-fanciers. It will save a troublesome job to the carver if the cook, when the fish is boiled, cuts the spine bone across the middle.

TURBOT, TO BOIL. (2) Put into the turbot kettle, with the water, two large handfuls of salt, and a tea-cupful of vinegar; when it boils very fast, take off the scum; put in the turbot, and when it boils again keep it boiling fast till the turbot rises from the drainer; when it is sufficiently done, dish and garnish it with a fringe of curled parsley and cut lemon. Sauces;—lobster and melted butter.

Cold boiled turbot eats well with salad sauce.

Turbot is generally considered best perfectly fresh; but some people prefer it kept for a few days, hung up by the tail in a cool place.

TURBOT, GRILLED. Split the fish down the back, and soak it for sometime, with melted butter, parsley, sweet herbs, salt, and pepper. Bread the turbot well, broil, and serve it with lemon, or Seville orange-juice.

TURBOT, WITH WHITE SAUCE. Put a sliced onion, some thyme, basil, and sweet herbs into a stewpan, place a small turbot on these, strew similar herbs, salt pepper, and a leek, cut in pieces over it; cover the fish with equal quantities of vinegar, and white wine; let it boil over a moderate fire until sufficiently done; in the meantime, melt a pound of butter, add to it a couple of boned anchovies, two spoonfuls of capers, shred small, two or three leeks, salt, pepper, nutmeg, a little vinegar, water, and a sprinkling of flour; make all these quite hot, stirring constantly till done; then dish the turbot, pour the sauce over it, and serve.

TURKEY, BOILED, Make a stuffing of bread, herbs, salt, pepper, nutmeg, lemon-peel, a few oysters, or an anchovy, a bit of butter, some suet, and an egg; put this into the crop, fasten up the skin, and boil the turkey in a floured cloth to make it very white. Have ready some oyster sauce made rich with butter, a little cream, and a spoonful of soy, and serve over the turkey, or you may serve over it a liver and lemon sauce.

TURKEY, TURKEY POULTS, AND OTHER POULTRY. A fowl and a turkey require the same management at the fire, only the latter will take longer time.

Many a Christmas dinner has been spoiled by the turkey having been hung up in a cold larder, and becoming thoroughly frozen; *Jack Frost* has ruined the reputation of many a turkey roaster.

Let them be carefully picked, &c. and break the breast bone (to make them look plump), twist up a sheet of clean writing paper, light it, and thoroughly singe the turkey all over, turning it about over the flame.

Turkeys, fowls, and capons have a much better appearance, if, instead of trussing them with the legs close together, and the feet cut off, the legs are extended on each side of the bird, and the toes only cut off, with a skewer through each foot, to keep them at a proper distance.

Be careful, when you draw it, to preserve the liver, and not to break the gall-bag, as no washing will take off the bitter taste it gives, where it once touches.

Prepare a nice, clear, brisk fire for it.

Make stuffing; stuff it under the breast, where the craw was taken out, and make some into balls, and boil or fry them, and lay them round the dish; they are handy to help, and you can then reserve some of the inside stuffing to eat with the cold turkey, or to enrich a hash.

TURKEY EN DAUBE. Take an old turkey, truss it in the usual way; roll some large *lardons* in a mixture of salt, pepper, four spices, and sweet herbs, and then lard the turkey with them; lay slices of bacon in a braising-pan, put the turkey on them, with two small knuckles of veal, the feet of the bird, four carrots, six onions, three cloves, two bay-leaves, thyme, a bunch of parsley, and young onions; cover the whole with bacon and a piece of buttered paper; dilute it with four ladlefuls of stock (or more if the turkey be very large) put in a little salt, and set the pan on the fire to boil slowly for three hours and a half; then take it off, but do not take the bird out for at least half an hour. Strain off the liquor, and then reduce it to a fourth, or more if very thin; break an egg into another saucepan, beat it up well, and then pour the liquor on it, whisk them well together, and if it wants flavor, add a few sweet herbs, parsley leaves, and a young onion or two; put it on the fire, stirring it violently until ready to boil; as soon as it has boiled up once or twice; set it by the side of a stove, put fire on the top of the saucepan, and let it simmer half an hour; then strain it carefully through a fine cloth, and let it cool to serve it with the turkey.

TURKEY, HASHED. (1) Cut up the remains of a roasted turkey, put it into a stewpan, with a glass of white wine, chopped parsley, shallots, mushrooms, truffles, salt and pepper, two spoonfuls of cullis, and a little stock; boil half an hour, and reduce to a thick sauce; when ready, add a pound of anchovy, and a squeeze of lemon; skim off all the fat from the sauce, and serve all together.

TURKEY, HASHED. (2) Stir a piece of butter rolled in flour into some cream, and a little veal gravy, till it boils up; mince some cold roasted or boiled turkey, but not too small; put it into the sauce, add grated lemon-peel, white pepper, pounded mace, a little mushroom ketchup or mushroom powder; simmer it up, and serve. Oysters may be added.

TURKEY, ROASTED. It may be either stuffed with sausage meat, or stuffing the same as for fillet of veal. As this makes a large addition to the size of the bird, take care that the heat of the fire is constantly to that part, as it frequently happens that the breast is not sufficiently done. A strip of paper should be put on the bone to prevent its scorching, while the other parts are roasting. Baste well, and froth it up. Serve with gravy in the dish, and bread sauce in a sauce tureen. A few bread crumbs, and a beaten egg should be added to the stuffing of sausage meat.

TURKEY, STUFFED WITH SAUSAGES AND CHESTNUTS. Roast what quantity of chestnuts you think necessary, peel them, and pound a part of them to make a *farce*, with the liver, chopped parsley, shallots, a little salt and pepper, a bit of butter, and the yolks of three raw eggs, put this *farce* into the crop; and stuff the body with the whole chestnuts, and small sausages, first fried in buttcr till about half done; cover the turkey with slices of bacon, and put paper over that, then roast it, and serve with a chestnut cullis.

TURNIPS, TO DRESS YOUNG WHITE. Wash, peel, and boil them till tender in water with a little salt; serve them with melted butter poured over them. Or, They may be stewed in a pint of milk thickened with a bit of butter rolled in flour, and seasoned with salt and pepper, and served with the sauce.

TURNIPS. Peel off half an inch of the stringy outside. Full-grown turnips will take about an hour and a half gentle boiling; if you slice them, which most people do, they will be done sooner; try them with a fork; when tender, take them up, and lay them on a sieve till the water is thoroughly drained from them. Send them up whole; do not slice them.

TURNIPS, TO BOIL YELLOW OR LARGE WHITE. Wash, pare, and throw them into cold water; put them on in boiling water with a little salt, and boil them from two hours to two and a half, drain them in a cullender, put them into a saucepan, and mixing in a bit of butter, with a beater mash them very smoothly, add half a pint of milk, mix it well with the turnips, and make them quite hot before serving. If they are to be served plain, dish them as soon as the watcr is drained off.

TURNIP TOPS, Are the shoots which grow out (in the spring) of the old turnip roots. Put them into cold water an hour before they are to be dressed; the more water they are boiled in, the better they will look; if boiled in a small quantity of water they will taste bitter: when the water boils, put in a small handful of salt, and then your vegetables; if fresh and young, they will be done in about twenty minutes; drain them on the back of a sieve.

TURTLE SOUP. (1) *To dress a Turtle weighing one hundred and twenty pounds.* Having cut off the head close to the shell, hang up the turtle till the next day, then open it, bearing the knife heavily on the back of the animal in cutting it off all round; turn it on its end, that all the blood and water may run out, then cut the flesh off along the spine, sloping the knife towards the bones so as to avoid touching the gall, and having also cut the flesh from the legs and other members, wash the whole well and drain it. A large vessel of boiling water being ready on the fire, put in the breast shell, and when the plates will separate easily take them out of the water; boil the back and belly in water till the softer parts can be taken off easily; but before they are sufficiently done, as they are to be again boiled in the sauce, lay them to cool singly in earthen vessels that they may not stick together, let the bones continue to stew for some time, as the liquor must be used for moistening the sauces.

All the flesh cut from the body, the four legs and head must be stewed in the following manner. Lay a few slices of ham on the bottom of a large stewpan, and over the ham two or three knuckles of veal, then above the veal, the inside flesh of the turtle, and that of the members over the whole, adding a large bunch of sweet herbs, such as sweet basil, sweet majoram, lemon thyme, a handful of parsley, and green onions, and a large onion stuck with six cloves. Then partly moisten it with the water in which the shell is boiling, and when it has stewed some time, moisten it again with the liquor in which the back and belly have been boiled. When the legs are tender, take them out, drain, and put them aside to be afterwards added to the sauce; and when the flesh is completely done, drain it through a silk sieve, and mix with the sauce some very thin white roux; then cut all the softer parts, now sufficiently cold, into pieces about an inch square, add them to the sauce, and let them simmer gently till they can be easily pierced; skim it well.

Next chop a small quantity of herbs, and boil them with a little sugar in four bottles of Madeira till reduced to two, then rub it through a tammy, mix it with the turtle sauce, and let it boil for a short time. Make some forcemeat balls as follows:—Cut off about a pound of meat from the fleshy part of a leg of veal free from sinews or fat, soak in milk about the same quantity of crumbs of bread; when quite soft, squeeze and put it into a mortar, together with the veal, a small quantity of calf's udder, a little butter, the yolks of four hard-boiled eggs, a little cayenne, salt and spices; pound the whole very finely, then thicken the mixture with two whole eggs and the yolk of a third, throw a bit into boiling water, and if not sufficiently firm, add the yolk of another egg, and for variety some chopped parsley may be mixed with half of the forcemeat. Let the whole cool so that it may be formed into balls about the size of the yolk of an egg, poach them in boiling water, and add them to the turtle. Before serving, mix a little cayenne with the juice of two or three lemons, and add it to the soup. It is generally preferable to prepare the soup the day before it is required for use, and it will be best heated in a water bath, or flat vessel containing water, which is always kept very hot, but not allowed to boil. By the same method, sauces, stews, and other made dishes may be kept hot.

When the fins of the turtle are to be served as a side dish, they must be first parboiled, then skinned, and stewed in a little turtle sauce, with some Port wine, and seasoned with cayenne, salt, and a little lemon-juice, and thickened with butter and flour.

Fricandeaux and Blanquettes may also

be made of the flesh of the turtle, in the same way as those of veal.

TURTLE SOUP. (2) The day before you dress a turtle, chop the herbs, and make the forcemeat; then, on the preceding evening, suspend the turtle by the two hind fins with a cord; and put one round the neck, with a heavy weight attached to it to draw out the neck, that the head may be cut off with more ease; let the turtle hang all night, in which time the blood will be well drained from the body. Then, early in the morning, having your stoves, and plenty of hot water in readiness, take the turtle, lay it on the table on its back, and with a strong pointed knife cut all round the under shell, (which is the callipee); there are joints at each end, which must be carefully found, gently separating it from the callipash (which is the upper shell); be careful that in cutting out the gut you do not break the gall. When the callipee and the callipash are perfectly separated, take out that part of the gut that leads from the throat; that, with the three hearts, put into a basin of water by themselves; the other interior part put away. Take the callipee, and cut off the meat which adheres to it in four quarters, laying it on a clean dish. Take twenty pounds of veal, chop it up, and set it in a large pot, as directed for *espagnole*, putting in the flesh of the turtle at the same time, with all kinds of turtle herbs, carrots, onions, one pound and a half of lean ham, pepper corns, salt, a little spice, and two bay leaves, leaving it to stew till it takes the color of *espagnole*; put the fins (the skin being scalded off) and hearts in, half an hour before you fill it, with half water, and half beef stock; then carefully skim it; put in a bunch of parsley, and let it boil gently, like *consomme*. While the turtle is stewing, carefully scald the head, the callipee, and all that is soft of the callipash, attentively observing to take off the smallest particle of skin that may remain; put them with the gut into a large pot of water to boil till tender; when so, take them out, and cut them in squares, putting them in a basin by themselves till wanted for the soup. The next thing is the thickening of the soup, which must be prepared in the same manner as sauce *tournee*. The turtle being well done, take out the fins and hearts, and lay them on a dish; the whole of the liquor must pass through a sieve into a large pan; then, with a ladle, take off all the fat, put it into a basin, then mix in the turtle liquor (a small quantity at a time) with the thickening made the same as *sauce tournee*; but it does not require to, neither must it be, one twentieth part so thick; set it over a brisk fire, and continue stirring till it boils, when it has boiled two hours, being skimmed all the while, squeeze it through the tammy into another large stewpan, put it on the fire, and stir it as before, till it boils; when it has boiled gently for one hour, put in the callipee and callipash, with the gut, hearts, and some of the best of the meat and head, all cut in squares, with the forcemeat balls and herbs, which you should have ready chopped and stewed in *espagnole*; (the herbs are parsley, lemon thyme, marjoram, basil, savory, and a few chopped mushrooms). It must be carefully attended to and skimmed, and one hour and a half before dinner, put in a bottle of Madeira wine, and nearly half a bottle of brandy, keeping it continually boiling gently, and skimming it; then take a basin, put a little cayenne pepper into it, with the juice of six lemons squeezed through a sieve. When the dinner is wanted, skim the turtle, stir it well up, and put in a little salt, if necessary; then stir in the cayenne and lemon-juice, and ladle it into the tureen. This receipt will answer for a turtle between fifty and sixty pounds.

☞ *For Mock Turtle and other Soups, See Soups.*

TWELFTH CAKE ICING. *See Icing*

V.

VEAL. The names of the joints are as follows: Loin, best end—Loin, chump end—Fillet—Hind Knuckle—Fore knuckle—Neck, best end—Neck, scrag end—Blade bone—Breast, best end—Brisket end.

Veal should be fine in the grain, firm, white, and fat; and the leg bone small. The finest calves have the smallest kidney, and its being well covered with thick white fat, indicates good veal. The fillet of a cow calf is to be preferred, on account of the udder. The prime joints are the fillet, the loin, the chump end of the loin, and the best end of the neck. To keep it, the same directions may be followed, which are given for keeping beef.

When the fillet is to be roasted, it should be washed, well dried, and the bone taken out, and the space filled with a fine stuffing, part of which should be put under the flap, then formed into a round and firmly skewered. That the fire may be clean and strong, it should be made up sometime before putting down the roast, which should at first be placed at some distance from it, and be frequently and well basted with butter. When about half roasted, a piece of white paper is tied over the fat; a little before serving, it is removed, the meat is then sprinkled with salt, dredged with flour, and well basted to froth it. When dished, finely melted butter is poured over it, with which may or may not be mixed some lemon pickle or brown gravy. It is garnished with cut lemon.

Veal is expected to come to table looking delicately clean; and it is so easily discolored, that you must be careful to have clean water, a clean vessel, and constantly catch the scum as soon and as long as it rises. Send up bacon, fried sausages, or pickled pork, greens, and parsley and butter, and onion sauce.

Veal requires particular care to roast it a nice brown. Let the fire be the same as for beef; a sound large fire for a large joint, and a brisker for a smaller; put it at some distance from the fire to soak thoroughly, and then draw it near to finish it brown.

When first laid down it is to be basted; baste it again occasionally. When the veal is on the dish, pour over it half a pint of melted butter: if you have a little brown gravy by you, add that to the butter. With those joints which are not stuffed, send up forcemeat in balls, or rolled into sausages, as garnish to the dish, or fried pork sausages; bacon and greens, are also always expected with boiled veal.

*Fillet of Veal*, Of from twelve to sixteen pounds, will require from four to five hours at a good fire; make some stuffing or force-meat, and put it in under the flap, that there may be some left to eat cold, or to season a hash; brown it, and pour good melted butter over it.

Garnish with thin slices of lemon and cakes or balls of stuffing, or duck stuffing, or fried pork sausages, curry sauce, bacon and greens, &c.

A bit of the brown outside is a favorite with the epicure in roasts. The kidney, cut out, sliced, and broiled, is a high relish, which some *bons vivants* are fond of.

*A Loin*, Is the best part of the calf, and will take about three hours roasting. Paper the kidney fat, and the back: some cooks send it up on a toast, which is eaten with the kidney and the fat of this part, which is as delicate as any marrow. If there is more of it than you think will be eaten with the veal, before you roast it cut it out; it will make an excellent suet pudding; take care to have your fire long enough to brown the ends; same accompaniments as above.

*A Shoulder*, From three hours to three hours and a half; stuff it with the force-meat ordered for the fillet of veal, in the under side.

*Neck*, *best end*, will take two hours; same accompaniments as fillet. The scrag part is best made into a pie, or broth.

*Breast*, From an hour and a half to two hours. Let the caul remain till it is almost done, then take it off to brown it; baste, flour, and froth it.

This makes a savory relish for a luncheon or supper: or, instead of roasting, boil it enough; put it in a cloth between two pewter dishes, with a weight on the upper one, and let it remain so till cold; then pare and trim, egg, and crumb it, and broil, or warm it in a Dutch oven; serve with it capers, or wow wow sauce. Breast of mutton may be dressed the same way.

VEAL ALAMODE. *See Beef Alamode.*

VEAL BREAST, STEWED WITH GREEN PEAS. Make a quart of gravy with the scrag end; strain it; cut the rest of the veal into small pieces of nearly an equal size; put it into a stewpan with the gravy, some pepper, salt, mace, half an ounce of butter, and a quart of green peas. Cover the pan closely, and let it stew nearly two hours; then put in a lettuce cut small, and let it stew half an hour longer. A little before serving, add half an ounce of browned butter, mixed with a little flour.

VEAL BREAST, BROILED. Half roast and then score it; season it with parsley, a few finely-minced sweet herbs, a little pepper and salt, and broil it. Make a sauce with some gravy seasoned with onion, grated nutmeg, mace, salt, and an anchovy; boil and strain it; thicken it with flour and butter. Add some minced capers and small mushrooms; pour it quite hot over the veal. Garnish with sliced lemon.

VEAL BREAST, COLLARED. Bone it, and lay over it a thick layer of forcemeat, made with bread crumbs, chopped oysters, parsley, and grated ham, seasoned with lemon-peel, salt, pepper, and nutmeg, mixed with an egg beaten up. Roll and bind it with tape; boil it in a cloth, and put it on in boiling water; let it boil gently for three hours. Boil the bones with an onion, a bunch of sweet herbs, salt, and pepper; strain and thicken it with three table-spoonfuls of cream, the yolks of two eggs beaten up, and

a bit of butter mixed with flour. Parboil and slice the sweetbread, dip it into an egg, and strew over it grated bread; fry it with forcemeat balls. Serve the veal with the sauce poured over it. Garnish with the sweetbread and forcemeat balls.

VEAL BREAST, STEWED. (1) Half roast the veal till of a light brown, then stew it over a stove for two hours, in a rich gravy, with a shallot, three cloves, a blade of mace, a little walnut pickle, some oyster liquor, and a few small mushrooms. Half an hour before serving, add a little anchovy liquor. Garnish with cut lemon and curled parsley.

VEAL BREAST, STEWED. (2) Cut out the blade bone, and stuff the whole with a nice forcemeat; sew it up, half roast it, and make a quart of gravy of the bones and trimmings; season it with whole pepper, two blades of mace, a bit of lemon-peel, a large onion, some salt, and a bunch of parsley. Strain and thicken it with butter rolled in flour; put in the veal, and a table-spoonful of vinegar; let it stew nearly two hours. A little before serving, add a table-spoonful of lemon pickle, and a glass of white wine. Forcemeat balls may be served with it.

VEAL BREAST, STEWED. (3) Cut off the short bones or gristles of a breast of veal; stew them in a little white stock, with a slice of ham, an onion stuck with one or two cloves, some whole pepper, a bunch of parsley, and a little salt. When tender, take out the meat, strain the stock, and put it on with a pint and a half of green peas; boil them, and add the veal, and let them stew for twenty minutes. Serve the gristles in the middle, and the peas round them.

VEAL BROTH. *See Broth.*

VEAL, BROWN ROLLKLOPS. Cut off some thin slices from a fillet of veal, and beat them. Take part of the fat from the loin and kidney: mince it finely with a small bit of veal, and six anchovies; season with salt, pounded ginger, and mace; put it over the slices of veal, and roll them up. Dip them into the beaten yolk of an egg, and then into grated bread; repeat this a second time, and fry them of a nice brown color in clarified beef dripping, then stew them in some good gravy, adding a little walnut pickle and half a pint of white wine.

VEAL CAKE. Take some nice thin slices of veal, and season them with salt, pepper, and nutmeg grated; have ready some hard-boiled eggs, sliced, and put a layer of these at the bottom of a basin or pan, then a layer of veal, then some slices of ham, over this strew marjoram, thyme, parsley, shred fine, bread crumbs and lemon-peel, chopped small; then a layer of eggs, veal, ham, &c. and so continue till the pan is filled; pour some good gravy over the whole, cover the pan with coarse brown paper, tie it closely over, and set it to bake in a slow oven; an hour will be sufficient to bake it; when cold, turn it out upon a dish, and serve; garnish with parsley.

VEAL CAKE, *to be eaten cold.* Pound in a mortar as much cold roasted lean veal as will fill a small mould, together with a slice of ham, or bacon, a piece of the crumb of bread soaked in cold milk, two beaten eggs, a small bit of butter, the same of shallot, or onion; season with pepper and salt, and mix all well together; butter the mould, fill it, and bake it in an oven for about an hour; turn it out when cold, and cut it into slices. Garnish with pickled eggs and parsley.

VEAL COLD. Cut some cold veal into thin slices, the size and thickness of a half crown, dip them into the yolk of an egg well beaten, cover them with bread crumbs, sweet herbs, lemon-peel shred fine, and grated nutmeg. Put a little fresh butter into a pan, make it quite hot, fry the veal in it, and when done, lay it on a dish by the side of the fire; make a little gravy of a bone of veal, shake a little flour into the pan, stir it round, add the gravy and a

little lemon-juice, pour it over the veal, and garnish with lemon.

VEAL CHOPS, BREADED. Take six or seven handsomely cut chops, season them well with salt and pepper, and put them into melted butter; when sufficiently soaked, put them into beaten eggs, take them out, and roll each separately in bread crumbs; make the chops as round as you can with your hand, and lay them on a dish; when all are breaded, broil them slowly over a moderate fire, that the bread may not be too highly colored. Serve with clear gravy.

VEAL, TO COLLAR. Bone a breast of veal, and beat it flat; cover the inside with a nice stuffing moistened with eggs; roll it very tightly, bind it, and bake it in an oven with some weak stock in the dish. Make a rich gravy; strain and thicken it, and pour it over the veal. Serve with or without forcemeat balls, and garnish with cut lemon. It will keep for a long time in a pickle made with bran and water, a little salt, and vinegar, poured cold over it.

VEAL CONES. Mince small one pound and a half of cold veal, two ounces of butter, and a slice of lean ham; pound them in a mortar, and mix, in five table-spoonfuls of cream, two tea-spoonfuls of pepper, one of salt, and some grated lemon-peel. Make it into cones about three inches high; rub them over with an egg beaten up, sift grated bread over them, and fry them of a light brown color; put fried bread crumbs into the dish, and place the cones upon them, or serve them with a brown gravy instead of crumbs. Cold fowl, turkey, or rabbit make good cones. Half the ingredients will be sufficient for a corner dish.

VEAL, COLD DRESSED. Mince finely the fat and lean of cold roast veal, season it with grated nutmeg, lemon-peel, pepper, and salt; moisten it with a little rich white stock, and a beaten egg; butter a pudding, shape, put in the mince, and press it firmly, cover it closely, and set into a pan of boiling water; let it boil an hour or two. Serve it with a white gravy thickened, or when turned out of the shape, rub it over the top with the beaten yolk of an egg; sift bread crumbs thickly over, and brown it in a Dutch oven; baste it with a little melted butter. Garnish with fried parsley or cut lemon.

VEAL CUTLETS. (1) Let your cutlets be about half an inch thick; trim them, and flatten them with a cleaver; you may fry them in fresh butter, or good drippings; when brown on one side, turn them and do the other; if the fire is very fierce, they must change sides oftener. The time they will take depends on the thickness of the cutlet and the heat of the fire; half an inch thick will take about fifteen minutes. Make some gravy, by putting the trimmings into a stewpan with a little soft water, an onion, a roll of lemon-peel, a blade of mace, a sprig of thyme and parsley, and a bay leaf; stew over a slow fire an hour, then strain it; put an ounce of butter into a stewpan; as soon as it is melted, mix with it as much flour as will dry it up, stir it over the fire for a few minutes, then add the gravy by degrees till it is all mixed, boil it for five minutes, and strain it through a tamis sieve, and put it to the cutlets; you may add some browning, mushroom, or walnut ketchup, or lemon pickle, &c.: Or, Cut the veal into pieces about as big as a crown-piece, beat them with a cleaver, dip them in eggs beat up with a little salt, and then in fine bread crumbs; fry them a light brown in boiling lard; serve under them some good gravy or mushroom sauce, which may be made in five minutes. Garnish with slices of ham or rashers of bacon, or pork sausages.

Veal forcemeat or stuffing, pork sausages, rashers of bacon, are very relishing accompaniments, fried and sent up in the form of balls or cakes, and laid round as a garnish.

VEAL CUTLETS. (2) Cut a neck of veal into cutlets, or take them off a leg. Season two well-beaten eggs with pounded mace, nutmeg, salt, pepper, and finely-chopped sweet marjoram , lemon thyme, and parsley; dip the cutlets into it, sift over them grated bread, and fry them in clarified butter. Serve with a white sauce, forcemeat balls, and small mushrooms. Garnish with fried parsley.

VEAL CUTLETS. (3) Cut a neck of veal into thin cutlets, and beat them; brown some butter with an onion and some parsley chopped small. Dip the cutlets into the butter, and then into finely grated bread, seasoned with pepper and salt; broil them of a brown color; mince the peel of half an orange pared very thin; add it and a grate of ginger to some good thickened gravy, and pour it hot upon the cutlets.

VEAL CUTLETS. (4) Cut them off a leg, or from the thick part of a loin of veal; beat them a little with a rolling-pin, and fry them in butter of a light brown. Take them out of the pan, pour off the butter, and strew over them grated bread, seasoned with minced parsley and lemon thyme, grated lemon-peel and nutmeg, pepper, and salt. Put them into a stewpan, with a piece of fresh butter, and let them fry slowly till of a good brown. Add a quarter of a pint of good gravy, and a small tea-cupful of thick cream; let it be made very hot, frequently shaking the pan. Serve it garnished with cut lemon or forcemeat balls, mushrooms, and false eggs. False eggs are made of the yolks of two hard-boiled eggs, which are rubbed smooth, and then made up with fresh butter into the form of small eggs.

VEAL CUTLETS, VENITIAN. Cut into neat cutlets the best part of a neck of veal; trim and flatten them. Chop separately half a pint of mushrooms, a few shallots, and a little parsley; stew these over a slow fire, with a small bit of butter and a little rasped fat bacon. When done, put in the cutlets, and season them well with pepper and salt, and let them stew over a slow fire till quite tender; skim off the fat, and add a spoonful of sauce tournee, and the yolks of three eggs beaten with a little cream, then mix in the juice of a lemon, and a little cayenne.

VEAL, FILLET, STEWED. Bone, lard, and stuff a fillet of veal; half roast, and then stew it with two quarts of white stock, a tea-spoonful of lemon pickle and one of mushroom ketchup. Before serving, strain the gravy, thicken it with butter rolled in flour, and a little cayenne, salt, and some pickled mushrooms; heat it, and pour it over the veal. Have ready two or three dozen of forcemeat balls to put round it and upon the top. Garnish with cut lemon.

VEAL, FLORENTINE. Take two veal kidneys, and mince them with their fat, very small, and mix it with a few currants, the yolks of four or five eggs, boiled hard, and chopped small, a pippin cut fine, some bread crumbs, candied lemon-peel, cut small, and season with nutmeg, cloves, salt, mace, a little mountain wine, and some orange-flower water; line the bottom of a dish with a nice puff paste, put in the above, cover it with puff paste, and set it to bake in a slow oven.

VEAL FORCEMEAT. Of undressed lean veal (after you have scraped it quite fine, and free from skin and sinews), two ounces, the same quantity of beef or veal suet, and the same of bread crumbs; chop fine two drachms of parsley, one of lemon-peel, one of sweet herbs, one of onion, and half a drachm of mace, or all-spice, beaten to fine powder; pound all together in a mortar; break into it the yolk and white of an egg; rub it all up well together, and season it with a little pepper and salt. This may be made more savory by the addition of cold boiled pickled tongue, anchovy, eschalot, cayenne or curry powder, &c.

VEAL, FRICANDEAU. (1) Cut a piece of veal from the leg, the same in width and depth, and about eight inches in length. Make a hole in the under part, and fill it with forcemeat; sew it up, lard the top and sides, cover it with slices of fat bacon, and then with white paper. Put into a saucepan some slices of undressed mutton, three onions and one carrot sliced, a bunch of sweet herbs, and a quart of good stock; put in the veal, cover the pan closely, and let it stew for three hours. Take out the veal, strain the gravy, and take off all the fat; add a ta-ble-spoonful of lemon pickle, and three of white wine; boil it quick to a glaze; keep the fricandeau over hot water and covered, then glaze it, and serve with the rest of the glaze poured round it, and sorrel sauce, in a sauce tureen.

VEAL, FRICANDEAU. (2) Cut some slices of veal, lard them all through, and put them into a saucepan with some white stock, and a bit of ham, one onion, a little mace and pepper. Stew them gently an hour and a half; take them out, strain the gravy, and take off all the fat; boil it up quickly, lay in the fricandeau, and stew them till the liquor becomes like a brown jelly; take care they do not burn. Scald in boiling water three handfuls of sorrel, chop it, take out the meat, and make the sorrel hot in the sauce, and serve the fricandeau upon it.

VEAL, FRICANDEAU. (3) Chop very finely one pound of the lean of a loin of veal, and half a pound of the kidney fat; season it with pepper, salt, grated lemon-peel, the juice of one lemon, and a finely-shred anchovy. Soak, in boiling milk, two rusks, or biscuits, and mix it all well together; make it into balls, with a little flour. Fry them of a light brown, in butter, then stew them in some highly-seasoned gravy, dish them carefully, and strain the gravy over them. Garnish with cut lemon.

VEAL, FRICANDEAU. (4) Take the round or part of the round of a fillet, fry it in butter, of a nice brown, with onions cut in slices, and a little garlic, then set it to stew in some very rich gravy or cullis: when tender, take it out, thicken the gravy with flour, add a little lemon-juice, and serve this sauce over the veal.

VEAL FRITTERS. Cut the remains of a tender piece of veal into small, thin, round pieces; dip these into a good batter, and fry them in the usual way, in oil. When done, drain, sprinkle salt over, and serve them.

VEAL, HASHED OR MINCED. To make a hash cut the meat into slices;—to prepare minced veal, mince it as fine as possible (do not chop it); put it into a stewpan with a few spoonfuls of veal or mutton broth, or make some with the bones and trimmings, as ordered for veal cutlets, a little lemon-peel minced fine, a spoonful of milk or cream; thicken with butter and flour, and season it with salt, a table-spoonful of lemon pickle, or Basil wine, or a pinch of curry powder.

If you have no cream, beat up the yolks of a couple of eggs with a little milk: line the dish with sippets of lightly toasted bread.

Minced veal makes a very pretty dish put into scollop shells, and bread crumbed over, and sprinkled with a little butter, and browned in a Dutch oven, or a cheese-toaster.

VEAL, KEBOBBED. Cut into thin bits the size of a crown-piece some lean veal; season them with tumeric, pepper, and salt. Slice onions very thinly, and some garlic: put the slices of veal and onion upon a skewer, together with thin bits of pickled pork. Fry them brown with butter, and garnish with plenty of fried parsley.

VEAL, KNUCKLE, RAGOUT. Cut a knuckle of veal into slices about half an inch thick; pepper, salt, and flour them; fry them a light brown; put the trimmings into a stewpan, with the bone broke in several places; an onion sliced, a head of celery, a bunch of sweet herbs, and two blades of bruised mace: pour in warm water enough to cover them about an inch; cover the pot close, and let it stew very gently for a couple of hours; strain it, and then thicken it with flour and butter; put in a spoonful of ketchup, a glass of wine, and juice of half a lemon; give it a boil up, and strain into a clean stewpan; put in the meat, make it hot, and serve up.

*Obs.*—If celery is not to be had, use a carrot instead or flavor it with celery seed.

VEAL KNUCKLE, STEWED WITH RICE. As boiled knuckle of veal cold is not a very favorite relish with the generality, cut off some steaks from it, which you may dress as in the foregoing receipt, and leave the knuckle no larger than will be eaten the day it is dressed. Break the shank bone, wash it clean, and put it in a large stewpan with two quarts of water, an onion, two blades of mace, and a tea-spoonful of salt: set it on a quick fire; when it boils, take off all the scum. Wash and pick a quarter of a pound of rice; put it into the stewpan with the meat, and let it stew very gently for about two hours: put the meat, &c. in a deep dish, and the rice round it. Send up bacon with it, parsnips, or greens, and finely minced parsley and butter.

VEAL, KNUCKLE, SOUP. A knuckle of veal of six pounds, weight, will make a large tureen of excellent soup, and is thus easily prepared: cut half a pound of bacon into slices about half an inch thick, lay it at the bottom of a soup-kettle, or deep stewpan, and on this place the knuckle of veal, having first chopped the bone in two or three places; furnish it with two carrots, two turnips, a head of celery, two large onions, with two or three cloves stuck in one of them, a dozen corns of black, and the same of Jamaica pepper, and a good bundle of lemon thyme, winter savory, and parsley. Just cover the meat with cold water, and set it over a quick fire till it boils; having skimmed it well, remove your soup-kettle to the side of the fire; let it stew very gently till it is quite tender, *i. e.* about four hours; then take out the bacon and veal, strain the soup, and set it by in a cool place till you want it, when you must take off the fat from the surface of your liquor, and decant it (keeping back the settlings at the bottom) into a clean pan.

If you like a thickened soup, put three table-spoonfuls of the fat you have taken off the soup into a small stewpan, and mix it with four table-spoonfuls of flour, pour a ladleful of soup to it, and mix it with the rest by degrees, and boil it up till it is smooth.

Cut the meat and gristle of the knuckle and the bacon into mouthfuls, and put them into the soup, and let them get warm.

You may make this more savory by adding ketchup, &c. Shin of beef may be dressed in the same way; see Knuckle of Veal stewed with Rice.

VEAL LEG IN SURPRISE. Lard the veal with slips of bacon, and a little lemon-peel cut very thin; make stuffing the same as for a fillet of veal, only mix with it half a pint of oysters chopped small, and stuff your veal with this, and put it to stew with just sufficient water to cover it; let it stew very gently till quite tender; then take it up; skim off the fat from the liquor, and add some lemon-juice, some mushroom ketchup, the crumb of a roll grated fine, half a pint of oysters, a pint of cream, and a bit of butter rolled in flour; let this sauce thicken over the fire, and serve it over the veal; garnish the dish with oysters, dipped in butter, and fried, and thin slices of toasted bacon.

VEAL, MINCED. Cut thin slices of lean cold veal; mince them very finely with a knife, and season with pepper, salt, grated lemon-peel and nutmeg; put it into a sauce-pan, with a little white stock or water, a ta-ble-spoonful of lemon pickle, and a little mushroom powder. Simmer, but do not let it boil; add a bit of butter rolled in flour, add a little milk or cream; put all round the dish thin sippets of bread cut into a three-cornered shape; or cover the mince thickly with grated bread, seasoned with pepper, salt, and a little butter, and brown it with a salamander; or serve with poached eggs laid upon the top.

VEAL OLIVES. Cut thin slices off a fillet, and flatten them with a roller; season them highly with pepper, mace, salt, and grated lemon-peel; put a bit of fat into each roll, and tie them with a thread. Fry them of a light brown, and stew them in some white stock with two dozen of fried oysters, a glass of white wine, a table-spoonful of lemon pickle and some small mushrooms. Stew them nearly an hour; take off the threads before serving.

Beef olives may be dressed in the same way.

VEAL PATTIES. Mince some under-done veal with a little parsley, one or two sage leaves, a very little onion; season with grated lemon-peel, nutmeg, pepper, and salt; add some grated lean ham or tongue, mois-ten it with some good gravy, heat it up, and put it into the patties.

VEAL AND HAM PATTIES. Chop about six ounces of ready-dressed lean veal, and three ounces of ham very small; put it into a stewpan with an ounce of butter rolled into flour, half a gill of cream; half a gill of veal stock; a little grated nutmeg and lemon-peel, some cayenne pepper and salt, a spoonful of essence of ham and lemon-juice, and stir it over the fire sometime, taking care it does not burn.

VEAL AND HAM PIE. Take two pounds of veal cutlets, cut them in mid-dling-sized pieces, season with pepper and a very little salt; likewise one of raw or dressed ham cut in slices, lay it alternately in the dish, and put some forced or sausage meat at the top, with some stewed button mushrooms, and the yolks of three eggs boiled hard, and a gill of water; then proceed as with rump-steak pie.

N. B.—The best end of a neck is the fine part for a pie, cut into chops, and the chine bone taken away.

VEAL PIE. (1) Cut a neck of veal into neat steaks, season them well with white pepper, salt, mace, and grated nutmeg mixed; pack them closely into a dish, and put in half a pint of white stock; five hard-boiled yolks of eggs may be added; pat puff paste on the edge of the dish, and cover with the same. Lambs' tails may be made into a pie, with lamb chops seasoned in the same manner as the above.

VEAL PIE. (2) Cut into steaks a loin or breast of veal, season them highly with pepper, salt, grated nutmeg, mace, and a little lemon-peel mixed; lay them into the bottom of a dish, and then a few slices of sweetbreads seasoned with the spices; add some oysters, forcemeat balls, and hard-boiled yolks of eggs, half a pint of white stock, a glass of white wine, and a table-spoonful of lemon pickle; put puff paste on the edge of the dish, and cover with the same; bake it for one hour.

VEAL PIE. (3) Chop; but not very small, the meat of a cold loin of veal, season it with minced parsley, pepper, salt, grated lemon-peel, and nutmeg; add rather more than half a pint of stock made with the bones, thickened with a bit of butter rolled in flour, and seasoned with a tea-spoonful of lemon pickle, and a table-spoonful of white wine; make a paste of the fat of the loin, and an equal quantity of flour, rub it together, and mix with it a little cold water, roll it out two or three times, line the sides of the dish, put in the meat, and cover it.

VEAL PIE, SOLID. Stew in veal stock, till it be perfectly tender and like a jelly, a piece of a knuckle of veal, with the gristles adhering to it; let it cool, and then pull the meat and gristles into small bits; butter a pie dish or shape, and lay at regular distances some hard-boiled yolks of eggs, and some of the white part cut into rings or strips; then put over some bits of the meat and gristle, and strew over it some pepper, salt, and grated nutmeg mixed, and a little of the gravy, and then more eggs, with small bits of beet root, green pickles, and the red part of a carrot cut to fancy; add more meat seasoning, and all the gravy; when the shape is full, put it into an oven for twenty minutes, and when quite cold turn it out. If rightly done, it will have a glazed appearance, and the variety of colors look well by candle light.

VEAL, POTTED. Cut slices off a leg of veal, and season them with pepper, pounded mace, cloves, and salt. Lay thin slices of fresh butter between each layer of meat into a potting pan or jar; cover it closely, and bake it with bread. When it is cold, pound the meat in a marble mortar, pack it closely into a jar, and pour clarified butter over it.

VEAL, COLD, AN EXCELLENT RAGOUT. Either a neck, loin, or fillet of veal, will furnish this excellent ragout with a very little expense or trouble.

Cut the veal into handsome cutlets; put a piece of butter or clean dripping into a frying-pan; as soon as it is hot, flour and fry the veal of a light brown: take it out, and if you have no gravy ready, make some as directed under sauces, or put a pint of boiling water into the frying-pan, give it a boil up for a minute, and strain it into a basin while you make some thickening in the following manner: put about an ounce of butter into a stewpan; as soon as it melts, mix with it as much flour as will dry it up; stir it over the fire for a few minutes; and gradually add to it the gravy you made in the frying-pan; let them simmer together for ten minutes (till thoroughly incorporated); season it with pepper, salt, a little mace, and a wine-glassful of mushroom ketchup or wine, strain it through a tamis to the meat, and stew very gently till the meat is thoroughly warmed. If you have any ready-boiled bacon, cut it in slices, and put it in to warm with the meat.

VEAL ROLL. Bone a small breast of veal, and spread over it a rich and highly seasoned forcemeat. Cut four hard-boiled eggs the long way into four pieces, and lay them in rows, with green pickles between each row. Roll up the veal tightly, and sew it; then put it into a cloth, and bind it with tape. Lay a slice of ham over it, and put it into a saucepan, together with some strong stock, and a little whole pepper, and stew it for three hours. Make a rich gravy, and boil it up with a little white wine and lemon-juice or lemon-pickle; pour it over the veal; add some egg and forcemeat balls, and garnish with cut green pickles. This dish is very good when cold.

VEAL SAUSAGES. Take equal quantities of lean veal and fat bacon, a handful of sage, and a few anchovies. Beat all in a mortar, and season well with pepper and salt; when wanted for use, roll and fry it, and serve either with fried sippets, or on stewed vegetables, or white collops.

VEAL SEMELLES. Cut part of a fillet of veal into slices an inch thick, season them with salt and pepper, and give them a few turns in a little butter, with a bay leaf. Lay at the bottom of a deep saucepan a very thin slice of bacon, and on it one of the slices of veal, and continue to lay them in alternately, until the whole are used, then add a glass of water and some bay leaves; close the saucepan very tight, first putting a sheet of paper over the meat; stew it on hot ashes for four or five hours; take care to keep the fire up to the same point all the time.

VEAL STOCK. Cut a leg of veal and

some lean ham into pieces, put them into a saucepan, with a quart of water, some carrots, turnips, onions, leeks, and celery; stew them down till nearly done, but do not let it color; then add a sufficient quantity of beef stock to cover the ingredients, and let it boil for an hour; skim off all the fat, and strain it; a little game stewed down with the above will greatly improve the flavor; be particularly careful that it does not burn.

VEAL SWEETBREADS ROASTED. Trim off the tough part, and blanch for three minutes in a stewpan of water, with a little salt, three heart sweetbreads, then take them out, and put them into a basin of cold water till cool; have an egg beat up in a dish, some bread crumbs, and clarified butter; run a skewer through the sweetbreads, and fasten them on the spit; egg them all over, shake some bread crumbs over, then sprinkle clarified butter over, and then bread crumbs again; put them down to roast again for a quarter of an hour, then take them off the skewer, and serve them on a dish over a little butter sauce, mixed with a spoonful of gravy, a small bit of glaze, and a squeeze of lemon-juice; let it be hot, but not boiling, and thoroughly well mixed before it is served under the sweetbreads.

VEGETABLES. There is nothing in which the difference between an elegant and an ordinary table is more seen than in the dressing of vegetables, more especially greens. They may be equally as fine at first, at one place as at another; but their look and taste are afterward very different, entirely from the careless way in which they have been cooked.

They are in greatest perfection when in greatest plenty, i. e. when in full season.

By season, I do not mean those early days, that luxury in the buyers, and avarice in the sellers, force the vegetables; but that time of the year in which by nature and common culture, and the mere operation of the sun and climate, they are in most plenty and perfection.

As to the quality of vegetables, the middle size are preferred to the largest or the smallest; they are more tender, juicy, and full of flavor, just before they are quite full-grown. Freshness is their chief value and excellence, and I should as soon think of roasting an animal alive, as of boiling a vegetable after it is dead.

The eye easily discovers if they have been kept too long; they soon lose their beauty in all respects.

Roots, greens, salads, &c. and the various productions of the garden, when first gathered, are plump and firm, and have a fragrant freshness no art can give them again, when they have lost it by long keeping; though it will refresh them a little to put them into cold spring water for sometime before they are dressed.

To boil them in soft water will preserve the color best of such as are green; if you have only hard water, put to it a tea-spoonful of *carbonate of potash.*

Take care to wash and cleanse them thoroughly from dust, dirt, and insects: this requires great attention. Pick off all the outside leaves, trim them nicely, and, if not quite fresh gathered and have become flaccid, it is absolutely necessary to restore their crispness before cooking them, or they will be tough and unpleasant: lay them in a pan of clean water, with a handful of salt in it, for an hour before you dress them.

They should always be boiled in a saucepan by themselves, and have plenty of water; if meat is boiled with them in the same pot, they will spoil the look and taste of each other.

If you wish to have vegetables delicately clean, put on your pot, make it boil, put a little salt in it, and skim it perfectly clean before you put in the greens, &c.; which should not be put in till the water boils briskly: the quicker they boil, the greener they will be. When the vegetables sink, they are generally done enough, if the water has been kept constantly boiling. Take them up immediately, or they will lose their color

and goodness. Drain the water from them thoroughly before you send them to table.

This branch of cookery requires the most vigilant attention.

If vegetables are a minute or two too long over the fire, they lose all their beauty and flavor.

If not thoroughly boiled tender, they are tremendously indigestible, and much more troublesome during their residence in the stomach, than under-done meats.

Once for all, take care your vegetables are fresh: for as the fishmonger often suffers for the sins of the cook, so the cook often gets undeservedly blamed instead of the green-grocer.

Strong-scented vegetables should be kept apart; leeks, or celery, laid among cauliflowers, &c. will quickly spoil them.

Succulent vegetables are best preserved in a cool, shady, and damp place.

Potatoes, turnips, carrots, and similar roots, intended to be stored up, should never be cleaned from the earth adhering to them, till they are to be dressed.

They must be protected from the action of the air and frost, by laying them in heaps, burying them in sand or earth, &c., or covering them with straw or mats.

When vegetables are quite fresh gathered, they will not require so much boiling, by at least a third of the time, as when they have been gathered the usual time of those that are brought to public markets.

Vegetables are always best when newly gathered, and should be brought in from the garden early in the morning; they will then have a fragrant freshness, which they lose by keeping.

They must be cleaned with the greatest care, the outside leaves of every description of greens removed, and they, and all other vegetables, more particularly when not recently gathered, should be laid for several hours in cold water and well shaken to throw out the insects. A tea-spoonful of salt should always be put into the water in which they are to be boiled, and if it is hard, a tea-spoonful of salt of tartar, or potash, may be added to preserve the green color of the vegetables.

All vegetables should be boiled quickly, and, with the exception of spinach, in an open vessel, skimming them carefully.

Kitchen greens should be kept in a cool and shady place. Potatoes, carrots, turnips, and beet root should be stored up, without being cleaned from the earth adhering to them, in layers of sand, or laid in heaps, and covered with earth and straw. Parsnips and skirrets not being injured by frost, are generally left in the ground, and taken up as wanted. Onions are stored in a warm, dry place, never in a cellar; they are sometimes strung in bunches, and suspended from the roof, and, more effectually to prevent their growing, some people select the finest bulbs, and singe the roots with a hot iron.

Herbs of all sorts should be gathered when in flower, and on a dry day, and being well cleaned from dust and dirt, they are tied up in small bunches, and dried before the fire in a Dutch oven. They may then be kept in paper bags labelled; or rubbed to a powder, sifted, and put into bottles.

VEGETABLE ESSENCES. The flavor of the various sweet and savory herbs may be obtained by combining their essential oils with rectified spirit of wine, in the proportion of one drachm of the former to two ounces of the latter, or by picking the leaves, and laying them for a couple of hours in a warm place to dry, and then filling a large-mouthed bottle with them, and pouring on them wine, brandy, proof spirit, or vinegar, and letting them steep fourteen days.

VEGETABLE MARROW, Is fit for use when about the size of a turkey's egg. After being washed clean, it is put on in boiling water, with a little salt, and when tender, it is drained from the water, cut into half, and served on toasted bread, over which some melted butter has been poured. Or, after being boiled in milk and water, they may be fricasseed as Jerusalem artichokes, or stewed like cucumbers.

VEGETABLES STEW. Pick and wash very clean as much spinach as will make a dish; mince finely three small onions, pick and chop two handfuls of parsley; put all into a saucepan, with rather more than half a pint of gravy, a bit of butter dusted with flour, a little salt and pepper. Cover the pan closely, stir it now and then, and when the spinach is tender, mash it smooth, serve it with slices of broiled ham, or with sausages.

VELOUTE. Take the cuttings and remains of any joints of veal and fowl you may have in the house, of which take four pounds, and put into a large stewpan, with some carrots, onions, parsley, scallions, three bay-leaves, three cloves, and a ladleful of stock; put your stewpan on a fierce fire, skim it well, and take care that the meat does not stick; when sufficiently reduced, add as much stock as will nearly fill the stewpan, salt it well; give it a boil, skim it, and then put it on the side of the fire to simmer for two hours; after which strain it through a tammy. Make a white *roux,* stir into it for ten minutes a few champignons, then pour on it, a little at a time, the above liquor; let it boil up once, skim it, and set it again by the side of the fire for an hour and a half: take off all the fat, strain it again, and then put it by for use. Take care that the *veloute* is not in the least colored, as, the whiter it is the better.

VENISON. The choice of venison should be regulated by the appearance of the fat, which, when the venison is young, looks thick, clear, and close; as it begins to change first towards the haunches, run a knife into that part; if tainted you will perceive a rank smell, and it will have a green or blackish appearance.

If you wish to preserve it, you may by careful management and watching, keep it for a fortnight by the following method: wash it well with milk and water very clean, and dry it perfectly with cloths until there is not the least damp remaining, then dust pounded ginger over every part; this is a good preventive against the fly. When to be dressed, wash it with a little lukewarm water, and dry it. Pepper should also be added to keep it.

VENISON COLLOPS. These are dressed in the same manner as mince collops of beef, only that, in place of the seasoning of the collops of beef, they have a little pepper, salt, and some Port wine.

VENISON, HASHED. (1) If you have enough of its own gravy left, it is preferable to any to warm it up in: if not, take some of the mutton gravy, or the bones and trimmings of the joint (after you have cut off all the handsome slices you can to make the hash); put these into some water, and stew them gently for an hour; then put some butter into a stewpan; when melted, put to it as much flour as will dry up the butter, and stir it well together; add to it by degrees the gravy you have been making of the trimmings, and some red currant jelly; give it a boil up; skim it; strain it through a sieve, and it is ready to receive the venison: put it in, and let it just get warm: if you let it boil, it will make the meat hard.

VENISON, HASHED. (2) Warm it in its own gravy; if there is no fat left, take some slices of mutton fat, set it on the fire with a little Port wine and sugar, and let it simmer till dry; then add it to the hash.

VENISON, HASHED. (3) Take some anchovies, boil them till they are dissolved, then add some oysters with their liquor, a little milk, some red wine, and a little ketchup; put in your venison, let it warm in this, but do not let it boil, and serve it with fried sippets, and the sauce &c. over it.

VENISON, MOCK. Hang up, for several days, a large fat loin of mutton; then bone it, and take off all the kidney fat, and the skin

from the upper fat; mix together two ounces of brown sugar, and one ounce of ground black pepper. Rub it well into the mutton; pour over it two or three wine-glasses of Port wine; keep it covered with the skin; rub and turn it daily for five days. When to be roasted, cover it with the skin, and paper it the same way as venison is done. Serve it with made gravy, and the same sauces as for venison.

VENISON PASTY. (1) Cut a neck or breast into small steaks, rub them over with a seasoning of sweet herbs, grated nutmeg pepper, and salt; fry them slightly in butter; line the sides and edges of a dish with puff paste, lay in the steaks, and add half a pint of rich gravy made with the trimmings of the venison; add a glass of Port wine, and the juice of half a lemon, or tea-spoonful of vinegar; cover the dish with puff paste, and bake it nearly two hours; some more gravy may be poured into the pie before serving it.

VENISON PASTY. (2) Take a neck, shoulder, or breast of venison, that has not hung too long; bone them, trim off all the skin, and cut it into pieces two inches square and put them into a stewpan, with three gills of Port wine, two onions, or a few eschalots sliced; some pepper, salt, three blades of mace, about a dozen allspice, and enough veal broth to cover it; put it over a slow fire, and let it stew till three parts done; put the trimmings into another saucepan, cover it with water, and set it on a fire. Take out the pieces you intend for the pasty, and put them into a deep dish with a little of their liquor, and set it by to cool; then add the remainder of the liquor to the bones and trimmings, and boil it till the pasty is ready; then cover the pasty with paste, ornament the top, and bake it for two hours in a slow oven; and before it is sent to table, pour in a sauce made with the gravy the venison was stewed in, strained and skimmed free from fat; some pepper, salt, half a gill of Port, the juice of half a lemon, and a little flour and butter to thicken it.

VENISON PIE OR PASTY. All kinds of meat intended for pies and pasties must be highly spiced when served hot, and still more highly spiced when served cold; but the seasoning must be regulated by judgment and taste. Take one or two breasts of venison, (according to the size you wish to make your pie or pasty), bone it thoroughly, beat it very flat, and lard it through and through with lardons, well seasoned with all sorts of spices, and sweet herbs finely chopped; roll it up as tight as possible, and tie it up with strong twine. Put into a stew-pan the bones and trimmings of the venison, with carrots, onions, parsley, one clove of garlic, thyme, bay-leaf, pepper-corns, and allspice, and let all stew till nearly dry; fill it up with equal quantities of beef or mutton braise, and water, which let boil very gently till done, then put in the roll of venison; put paper on the top, cover very close, and let it stew gently with fire over and under. When sufficiently done, take it off the fire, and let it stand in the liquor until nearly cold; then prepare a plain paste of four pounds of flour to one pound of butter, the same as for raised pie, but instead of making it stiff, mix it as soft as possible; lay part of this paste as thick as you well can round the edge of the dish; cut off the twine from the venison, skin, and lay it in the dish, and pour some of the gravy it has stewed in; put on the cover, trim it very neatly, make a hole in the top, do it over with egg, and bake it in a moderate oven for three or four hours; reduce the remainder of the liquor it was stewed in, and when the pie is baked, pour it in; serve it cold. The pasty can scarcely be made too thick.

VERMICELLI, QUEEN'S. Blanch about a quarter of a pound of vermicelli in boiling water, drain it, and throw it into some rich well-seasoned stock; when tender, take it out of the soup, and put it into the tureen; thicken the soup with eight well-beaten eggs, mixed with half a pint of cream, and pour it, when quite hot, upon the vermicelli.

VERMICELLI IN MILK. Boil the quantity of milk you may require, and put into it half a pound of vermicelli peeled, and a sufficient quantity of sugar; stir it frequently that the vermicelli may not form a paste: half an hour will be long enough to boil it.

A little almond milk may be added when ready for table.

VERMICELLI PUDDING. (1) Boil a quarter of a pound of vermicelli with a little cinnamon, in a quart of milk; in the meantime mix a quarter of a pound of melted butter with a pint of cream, and the yolks of four eggs; pour in the vermicelli when quite soft; add a little flour and beef marrow, and powder sugar to the taste; beat all up for half an hour, tie it in a floured cloth, and boil it.

VERMICELLI PUDDING. (2) Boil four ounces of vermicelli in a pint of new milk, until quite tender, with a stick or two of cinnamon. Then add half a pint of thick cream, a quarter of a pound of butter, a quarter of a pound of sugar, and the yolks of four eggs; thoroughly beaten; lay the above in a dish and bake.

VERMICELLI SOUP. Take as much good stock as you require for your tureen, strain, and set it on the fire, and when it boils, put in the vermicelli, and let it simmer for half an hour by a slow fire, that the vermicelli may not burst; the soup ought not to be very thick. Half a pound is sufficient for eight or ten persons.

VINEGAR. This is an acid liquor, prepared by a second fementation from various liquors, such as wine, cider, perry, beer, mead, skimmed milk, &c. But the most common method of making it, in England, is from malt, and the process is as follows:— infuse a quantity of malt in hot water for an hour and a half, then pour it into a cooler. As soon as the infusion is sufficiently cold, put it into deep tuns, add yeast to it, and leave it to ferment for four or five days; after which put the liquor into barrels, in a room heated with stoves, so that a moderate warmth may be kept up for six weeks, and the fermentation continue regularly. By the end of that time the whole will be completely soured, and must now be changed into other barrels; lay a tile on the bung-holes to keep out the wet, but not so close as to prevent a free circulation of air, and then place them in the open air for four or five months, according as the weather is warm or otherwise; during the whole of this period, the fermentation proceeds, and at the end, the vinegar is nearly done. The next operation is this: the vinegar is poured into large vessels, called rapetuns, to which there are false bottoms covered with rape, that is, the refuse of raisins, or other fruit, from which wine has been made; fill one of these tuns entirely with the vinegar, and another about three-fourths full, and every day take a portion of the liquor out of the fullest barrel, and put it into the other, until the vinegar is in a fit state to be drawn off; when it must be closely barrelled.

Vinegar may also be made in much smaller quantities for domestic purposes; the materials of various kinds, with the addition of sugar; raisins, currants, and ripe gooseberries, however, are the principal; sometimes it is made from brown sugar, and water alone. The proportions are the same as those necessary for strong wine; make the barrel about three-fourths full, add a toast covered with yeast, put in the bung very loosely, and place the barrel where it will be exposed to the sun, or, if it be winter, near the fire. The fermentation should be moderate and constant till the vinegar is complete; then draw it off clear, give it a boil, and when quite cold, strain and bottle it.

Vinegar is obtained from wine, by mixing with the latter its own flowers, or ferment, and its tartar reduced to powder, and put into a vinegar or any other cask; if the latter, it must be placed in a warm situation, full of the steam from vinegar; in either case the liquor should be stirred frequently; the second fermentation will speedily commence; it will become heated, and turn acid by degrees, and in a short time the vinegar will be produced.

It is commonly supposed that wine which has become acid, will produce excellent vinegar; this, however, is a mistaken idea, for the stronger and better the quality of the wine, the stronger and better will be the vinegar.

The French have several methods of making vinegar, which are subjoined.

The vinegar makers of Orleans pour the wine, of which they intend to make their vinegar, into casks, at the bottoms of which are close gratings of lime twigs; these serve to clarify the wine, as the lees adhering to the twigs, leave the liquor perfectly clear. They then procure a number of casks, each containing a hundred gallons, either new or which have previously contained vinegar; these are set upright, and in the top of every one is bored a hole, two inches in diameter, these are kept constantly open: the last mentioned casks are called *Mothers*; pour into all of them twenty-five gallons of boiling vinegar; to this, in a week's time, add three gallons of wine, drawn from the first mentioned casks; continue to add the wine, at intervals of a week, until the *Mothers* are quite full; then leave them for a fortnight, and at the end of which period they generally draw off the vinegar, taking care always to leave the *Mothers* half full, at least, and then to fill them with wine as before. The method of proving when the vinegar is fit for use, is, by plunging a stave into it; if on taking it out, a white line is perceptible on the end of it, the vinegar is quite ready. The place where the casks are kept should be very airy, and in the winter time, by means of stoves the temperature should be raised to eighteen degrees of Reaumur.

Paris vinegar varies from the above, and the process is very simple. A large quantity of wine lees is put into coarse sacks, and laid in tubs, which are placed one upon another to form a kind of press; by means of a screw, every drop of wine is gradually squeezed from the lees; this operation cannot be performed in less time than a week. The wine thus extracted is put into casks; in the headings a hole is made, as above, which holes are left constantly open; in summer time the casks so filled are placed in the sun, and, generally speaking, the vinegar is fit for use in a fortnight. In the winter, the fermentation will last double the time, and must be assisted by artificial warmth. It sometimes happens that the liquor heats to so great a degree that the hand cannot be borne in it; in this case, the progress of the fermentation must be checked by adding more wine, until it proceeds more regularly. When the vinegar is made, put it into casks, which have the beech twigs at the bottom, as above mentioned; let it remain a fortnight, by which time it will be sufficiently fermented to draw off into the casks for keeping it.

Another very simple method is also practiced in France; a few quarts are drawn from a barrel of excellent vinegar, and an equal quantity of very clear white wine is put into the barrel, close the bung lightly, and keep it in a place where the heat is moderate and regular. In a month's time draw off the same quantity as above, and pour in an equal portion of white wine. A barrel of good vinegar will thus afford a constant supply for a length of time without leaving the slightest deposit.

A cask which has not contained vinegar before, should have a quart of boiling hot vinegar poured into it, shaken till cold, and allowed to stand for some hours.

VINEGAR, BASIL. Sweet basil is in full perfection about the middle of August. Fill a wide-mouthed bottle with the fresh green leaves of basil (these give much finer and more flavor than the dried,) and cover them with vinegar, or wine, and let them steep for ten days: if you wish a very strong essence, strain the liquor, put it on some fresh leaves,

and let them steep fourteen days more.

*Obs.*—This is a very agreeable addition to sauces, soups, and to the mixture usually made for salads.

It is a secret the makers of mock turtle may thank us for telling; a table-spoonful put in when the soup is finished will impregnate a tureen of soup with the basil and acid flavors, at very small cost, when fresh basil and lemons are extravagantly dear.

The flavor of the other sweet and savory herbs, celery, &c. may be procured, and preserved in the same manner by infusing them in wine or vinegar.

VINEGAR, AMERICAN. Boil six gallons of water, and add, while it is hot, four quarts of molasses; put it into a tub to cool; when milkwarm, stir in a pint of fresh yeast; put it into the cask, and set it by the fire for twenty-four hours; then put it in the sun, with a bottle in the bung-hole. Bottle it three months afterwards.

VINEGAR, BURNET OR CUCUMBER. This is made in precisely the same manner as directed above. The flavor of burnet resembles cucumber so exactly, that when infused in vinegar, the nicest palate would pronounce it to be cucumber. This is a very favorite relish with cold meat, salads, &c.

VINEGAR, CAMP. Cayenne pepper, one drachm, avoirdupois weight. Soy, two table-spoonfuls. Walnut ketchup, four ditto. Six anchovies chopped. A small clove of garlic, minced fine. Steep all for a month in a pint of the best vinegar, frequently shaking the bottle: strain through a tamis, and keep it in small bottles, corked as tightly as possible.

VINEGAR, CHILI. This is commonly made with the foreign bird pepper; but you will obtain a much finer flavor from infusing fifty fresh red English Chilies (cut in half, or pounded) in a pint of the best vinegar for a fortnight, or a quarter of an ounce of cayenne pepper. Many people cannot eat fish without the addition of an acid and cayenne pepper: to such palates this will be an agreeable relish.

VINEGAR, CRESS. Dry and pound half an ounce of cress-seed (such as is sown in the garden with mustard,) pour upon it a quart of the best vinegar, let it steep ten days, shaking it up every day. This is very strongly flavored with cress; and for salads and cold meats, &c. it is a great favorite with many.

Celery vinegar is made in the same manner.

VINEGAR, ELDER FLOWER AND TARRAGON. Fill a quart bottle with the flowers of elder, or the leaves of tarragon, when it is in flower; pour vinegar upon them, and let them infuse for a fortnight; then strain it through a flannel bag, and put it into small bottles. By the same means, vinegar may be flavored with the fresh gathered leaves of any sweet herb.

VINEGAR, GARLIC. Cut small one ounce and a half of garlic, bruise one nutmeg and three cloves, steep them in a quart of vinegar for a week, shaking it daily; then strain and bottle it. Shallot vinegar is made in the same manner.

VINEGAR, GOOSEBERRY. Gather yellow gooseberries when quite ripe, crush and mash them well in a tub with a large wooden pestle; to every two gallons of gooseberries, after being mashed, put two of water; mix them well together; let it work for three weeks, stirring the mass two or three times each day; then strain the liquor through a hair sieve, and put to every gallon one pound of brown sugar, one pound of treacle, and a table-spoonful of fresh yeast; let it work for three or four days in the same tub, which has been well washed; then run it into iron-hooped casks. Let it stand twelve months, and bottle it for use. This is a very strong vinegar.

VINEGAR, HONEY. Half a pound of honey must be put to a pint of water, and the honey well dissolved. This mixture is then exposed to the greatest heat of the sun, without closing wholly the bung-hole of the cask, which must be merely covered with coarse linen, to prevent the admission of insects. In about six weeks, the liquor becomes acid, and changes to a very strong vinegar, and of excellent quality.

VINEGAR, HORSERADISH. Horseradish is in highest perfection about November. Pour a quart of best vinegar on three ounces of scraped horseradish, an ounce of minced eschalot, and one drachm of cayenne; let it stand a week, and you will have an excellent relish for cold beef, salads, &c. costing scarcely any thing. A portion of black pepper and mustard, celery or cress-seed, may be added to the above.

VINEGAR, RASPBERRY. The best way to make this, is to pour three pints of the best white wine vinegar on a pint and a half of fresh-gathered red raspberries in a stone jar, or china bowl (neither glazed earthenware, nor any metallic vessel, must be used;) the next day strain the liquor over a like quantity of fresh raspberries; and the day following do the same. Then drain off the liquor without pressing, and pass it through a jelly-bag (previously wetted with plain vinegar) into a stone jar, with a pound of pounded lump sugar to each pint. When the sugar is dissolved, stir it up, cover down the jar, and set it in a saucepan of water, and keep boiling for an hour, taking off the scum; add to each pint a glass of brandy, and bottle it: mixed in about eight parts of water, it is a very refreshing and delightful summer drink. An excellent cooling beverage to assuage thirst in ardent fevers, colds, and inflammatory complaints, &c. and is agreeable to most palates.

VINEGAR FOR SALADS. Take of

tarragon, savory, chives, eschalots, three ounces each; a handful of the tops of mint and balm, all dry and pounded; put into a wide-mouthed bottle, with a gallon of best vinegar; cork it close, set it in the sun, and in a fortnight strain off, and squeeze the herbs; let it stand a day to settle, and then strain it through a filtering bag.

VOL-AU-VENT. (1) Cut some cold turkey or veal into small thin slices, season it with dried lemon-peel grated, pepper, pounded mace, and salt; add one anchovy, some garlic and onion pounded, also a little good gravy, a table-spoonful of lemon pickle, one of white wine, and an ounce of butter rolled in flour; then make it quite hot, but do not allow it to boil, and serve it in the prepared vol-au-vent. The gravy may be made with the bones, or a little cream, and the beaten yolk of an egg may be substituted for the cream.

VOL-AU-VENT. (2) In opening the oysters, separate them from the liquor, which must be strained; take off the beards, and add to them the liquor, together with some white stock, a bit of butter rolled in flour, two or three blades of mace, a bit of lemon-peel, pepper, and salt; simmer them for fifteen or twerity minutes, and a little before putting them into the vol-au-vent, pick out the lemon-peel, add a table-spoonful of white wine, and three of good cream, and make it quite hot. To make oyster patties, when they are to be bearded, cut them into three or four bits, and prepare them in the same manner.

VOL-AU-VENT. (3) Roll off tart paste, till about the eighth of an inch thick: then, with a tin cutter made for that purpose (about the size of the bottom of the dish you intend sending to table,) cut out the shape, and lay it on a baking-plate with paper; rub it over with yolk of egg; roll out good puff paste an inch thick, stamp it with the same cutter, and lay it on the tart paste; then take a cutter two sizes smaller, and press it in the centre nearly through the puff paste; rub the top with yolk of egg, and bake it in a quick oven about twenty minutes, of a light brown color: when done, take out the paste inside the centre mark, preserving the top, put it on a dish in a warm place, and when wanted, fill it with a white fricasee of chicken, rabbit, ragout of sweetbread, or any other *entree* you wish.

VOLDRON. Melt eleven ounces of fresh butter in a brass pan, and when quite hot, add the same quantity of pounded loaf sugar, and eight well-beaten eggs; stir constantly for six or eight minutes, and put it into a dish; the following day, mix with it a wine glass of orange-flower water; of citron, orange, and lemon-peel, cut fine, half a pound; butter a pudding dish, and lay into the bottom a sheet of white paper buttered, then put in the voldron, and bake it for twenty minutes; turn it out, ornament it with cut citron and orange-peel, and serve it in a silver or glass dish.

## W.

WAFERS. Take a pint of good cream, half a pound of sifted flour, half a pound of powder sugar, and two drachms of orange-flower water. Beat the cream with the flour, a little at a time, until both are mixed perfectly smooth and free from lumps, then add the other articles; and as much more cream as will make the paste nearly as thin as milk; make the iron hot, dip a feather in some melted butter, and rub the iron over with it; put on the iron about a spoonful and a half of the paste, press them a little gently, and place the iron on a stove; open the iron a little frequently, to see if it be done; when one side is baked, turn the iron, and do the other. The wafers should only be lightly colored. Take them from the mould carefully with a knife.

WAFERS, GERMAN. Take seventeen ounces of sifted flour, and half a pint of good yeast, which make into a paste, with as much warm milk as will make it run from the spoon freely, without being too clear; then put it into a warm place. When it has risen well, add to it the yolks of fourteen eggs well beaten, the whites whipped to a snow, and the grated rind of two lemons. The whole being well mixed, pour over it seventeen ounces of fresh butter melted, but not too hot; stir it gently with a wooden spoon, and put the preparation again into a warm place to rise a second time; when it has risen sufficiently, and your pan quite hot, rub the latter with butter, fill it with the paste, set it over a brisk fire, and fry your wafers; make both sides equally brown; when done, sprinkle them with powder sugar (and cinnamon, if you like), and serve them hot. Be careful in taking out the paste to fill the pan, not to disturb, nor to plunge the spoon into the preparation, when not using it; the upper part of the paste should be taken off very gently, and the spoon laid across the top of the vessel; if these precautions be not attended to, the good appearance of the wafers will be destroyed.

WAFERS, ITALIAN. Take eight eggs, fourteen ounces of powder sugar, a pound of flour, six ounces of cream, the same of milk, an ounce of orange flowers, and the rind of a lemon grated. Beat the eggs with the sugar and flour first; then add the cream, milk, and other materials, by degrees; mix them well, and take care there are not the slightest lumps. Make the wafers as directed.

WALNUTS. Make a brine of salt and water, in the proportion of a quarter of a pound of salt to a quart of water; put the walnuts into this to soak for a week; or if you wish to soften them so that they may soon ready for eating, run a larding pin through them in half a dozen places—this will allow the pickle to penetrate, and they will be much softer, and of better flavor, and ready much sooner than if not perforated: put them into a stewpan with such brine, and give them a gentle simmer; put them on a sieve to drain; then lay them on a fish plate, and let them stand in the air till they turn black—this may take a couple of days; put them into glass, or unglazed stone jars; fill these about three parts with the walnuts, and fill them up with the following pickle.

To each quart of the strongest vinegar put two ounces of black pepper, one of ginger, same of eschalots, same of salt, half an ounce of allspice, and half a drachm of cayenne. Put these into a stone jar; cover it with a bladder, wetted with pickle, tie over that some leather, and set the jar on a trivet by the side of the fire for three days, shaking it up three times a day, and then pour it while hot to the walnuts, and cover them down with bladder wetted with the pickle, leather, &c.

WALNUTS AND BUTTERNUTS. Gather them for pickling when the head of a pin will pierce them easily; run a large needle through them here and there, or score them on one side with a knife; lay them into a brine of salt-and-water for twelve days, changing the brine twice in that time; strain, and put them into a jar, and sprinkle a little salt over them. Boil four quarts of vinegar for a hundred walnuts, allowing to each quart one ounce of whole pepper, and one of ginger, half an ounce each of sliced nutmeg and whole allspice, a table-spoonful of mustard seed, and one of scraped horseradish, one head of garlic, or a small onion; pour it boiling hot over the nuts, and put a plate on the jar; when cold, tie it closely down. After the nuts are used, the liquor may be boiled, strained, and bottled, to use as a pickle.

WALNUT KETCHUP. (1) Thoroughly

well bruise one hundred and twenty young walnuts; put to them three quarters of a pound of salt, and a quart of good wine vinegar; stir them every day for a fortnight; then strain and squeeze the liquor from them through a cloth, and set it aside; put to the husks half a pint of vinegar, and let it stand all night; then strain and squeeze them as before, adding the liquor which is obtained from them to what was put aside the preceding day, and add to it one ounce and a quarter of whole black pepper, forty cloves, half an ounce of nutmegs bruised, or sliced, half an ounce of ginger, and five drachms of mace, and boil it for half an hour; then strain it off from the spices, and bottle it for use.

WALNUT KETCHUP. (2) Take six half-sieves of green walnut shells, put them into a tub, mix them up well with common salt, (from two to three pounds,) let them stand for six days, frequently beating and mashing them; by this time the shells become soft and pulpy; then by banking it up on one side of the tub, and at the same time by raising the tub on that side, the liquor will drain clear off to the other; then take that liquor out: the mashing and banking-up may be repeated as often as liquor is found. The quantity will be about six quarts. When done, let it be simmered in an iron boiler as long as any scum arises; then bruise a quarter of a pound of ginger, a quarter of a pound of allspice, two ounces of long pepper, two ounces of cloves, with the above ingredients; let it slowly boil for half an hour; when bottled, let an equal quantity of the spice go into each bottle; when corked, let the bottles be filled quite up: cork them tight, seal them over, and put them into a cool and dry place for one year before they are used.

WALNUT KETCHUP, FOR FISH SAUCE. Take a quart of walnut pickle, add to it a quarter of a pound of anchovies and three-quarters of a pint of red Port, and let it boil till reduced to one-third; then strain it,

and when cold, put it into small bottles, and keep them closely corked.

WALNUT PICKLE. Put any quantity of the outside shells or green rinds of ripe walnuts into a tub in which there is a tap-hole; sprinkle them with water, raise the tub on one side, that it may stand in a sloping direction, place another vessel under it to receive the juice as it drops from the tap-hole; this it will soon begin to do; and, when a sufficient quantity has been obtained, to one gallon of this black liquor add two large table-spoonfuls of salt, one large onion, a stick of horseradish, a bunch of sweet herbs, two bay leaves, a quarter of an ounce of black pepper, the same of allspice and of bruised ginger. Boil it slowly for twenty minutes; strain it, and, when cold, stir it and bottle it for use, putting the spice into the bottles.

WALNUTS, TO PICKLE. Gather the nuts before the inside shell is hard, which may be known by trying them with a pin; lay them into salt and water nine days, changing the liquor every three days; then take them out, and dry them in the air on a sieve or mat; they should not touch each other, and they should be turned, that every side may become black alike; then put them into a jar. When half the nuts are in, put in an onion, with about thirty cloves stuck into it, and add the rest of the nuts. To one hundred walnuts allow half a pint of mustard seed, a quarter of an ounce of mace, half an ounce of peppercorns, and sixty bay leaves; boil all the spice in some good common vinegar, and pour it boiling upon the nuts, observing that they are entirely covered; stop the mouth of the jar with a cloth, and when cold, cover it with bladder or leather. In about six weeks they will be fit for use, when they should be examined, and if they have absorbed the vinegar so much as to leave any of the nuts dry, more should be added, but it need not be boiled.

WATER SOUCHY. Make a stock with

three or four flounders, boiled in three quarts of water, two onions, and a bunch of parsley, till they are soft enough to pulp through a sieve with the liquor they were boiled in; then season it with pepper, salt, and some parsley chopped, and boil in it a few flounders, with the brown skin taken off, some nicely cleaned perch or tench. Serve in a tureen, and with slices of bread and butter to eat with it.

WELSH RABBIT. Pare the crust off a slice of bread, toast it nicely, divide it in two, butter it, and lay upon each half a thin slice of cheese which has been toasted in a Dutch oven; if, when put upon the toast, it is not sufficiently browned, hold a salamander, or hot shovel, over the top. Serve it very hot.

WHEY. (1) Make a pint of milk boil; put to it a glass or two of white wine; put it on the fire till it just boils again; then set it on one side till the curd has settled, pour off the clear whey, and sweeten it as you like.

Cider is often substituted for wine, or half the quantity of vinegar that we have ordered wine. When there is no fire in the sick room, this may be put hot into a bottle, and laid between the bed and mattress; it will keep warm several hours.

WHEY. (2) Put a very small portion of rennet into a quart of milk, and let it stand by the side of the fire until turned; then serve it in a dish, with sugar and a little nutmeg, grated, and strewed over, or strain the liquor carefully from the curd, and serve quite clear.

WHEY, WHITE WINE. Boil a pint of milk, and when it rises in the pan, pour in one glass of sherry and one of currant wine; let it again boil up, take it off the fire, and, when it has stood a few minutes, remove the curd, pour off the clear whey, and sweeten it.

WHIM WHAM. Sweeten a quart of cream, and mix with it a tea-cupful of white wine, and the grated peel of a lemon; whisk it to a froth, which drain upon the back of a sieve, and put part into a deep glass dish; cut some Naples biscuit as thin as possible, and put a layer lightly over the froth, and one of red currant jelly, then a layer of the froth, and one of the biscuit and jelly; finish with the froth, and pour the remainder of the cream into the dish, and garnish with citron and candied orange-peel cut into straws.

WHITE BEET, LEAVES. Pick and wash them clean, put them on in boiling water with a little salt, cover the saucepan, and boil them longer than spinach; drain off the water, and beat them as spinach, with a bit of butter and a little salt.

WHITINGS. In choosing whitings, be careful that the skin has a silvery appearance, that the body is firm, and the fins stiff; these are sure proofs of its freshness.

WHTINGS, ENGLISH WAY. Put into a saucepan two spoonfuls of oil, half a lemon sliced (the pips and rind taken off), salt, and pepper, two glasses of white wine, the same of water, and let them boil nearly a quarter of an hour; then put the whitings, properly cleaned, cook them in the above, blanch a clove of garlic, and beat it with the back of a knife, put it with parsley, shallots, and two glasses of champagne, into a stewpan; let it boil five minutes, then add some butter, rolled in flour, salt, and pepper; stir it over the fire till smooth, then serve.

WHITINGS, FRIED. (1) Take as many whitings as you may require; cleanse, scale, and wipe them dry; then run them through the eyes with a skewer, soak them well in milk; flour, and fry them of a nice color. Serve them on a napkin.

WHITINGS, FRIED. (2) Skin them, preserve the liver, and fasten their tails to their mouths; dip them in egg, then in breadcrumbs, and fry them in hot lard, or split them, and fry them like fillets of soles. A three-quart stewpan, half full of fat, is the best utensil to fry whitings. They will be done enough in about five minutes; but it will sometimes require a quarter of an hour, to drain the fat from them and dry them (if the fat you put them into was not hot enough), turning them now and then with a fish-slice.

WHITE FISH AND SAUCE. Make a rich gravy with a bit of veal, the heads and fins of four or five haddocks, three or four onions, some parsley, a little cayenne, black pepper and salt, the juice of a lemon, half the peel, a table-spoonful of ketchup, half a pint of white wine, and two quarts of water; simmer them for an hour, strain, and put to it the meat of a lobster or crab minced, and forcemeat balls; thicken it with half a pint of cream, the yolks of three eggs beaten, and a pint of butter kneaded in flour. Have ready boiled three haddocks skinned and without their heads, pour the sauce over them in a deep dish. Make the forcemeat balls of a small boiled haddock finely minced, grated bread crumbs, butter, pepper, salt, grated nutmeg, and parsley; bind them with the whites of two eggs beaten, and fry them in fresh lard of a light brown.

WHITE POT. Beat up the yolks of eight, and the whites of four eggs, with two quarts of new milk, a little rose water, a nutmeg, grated, and a quarter of a pound of sugar; cut a small roll into very thin slices, lay them in a dish, and pour the milk, &c. over them; put a bit of butter on the top, and set it in the oven; it will take half an hour baking.

WHITE ROUX, *or White Thickening for Sauces and Made Dishes.* Melt gradually, over a slow fire, a good piece of butter, and dredge in a sufficiency of flour to make it like a thin paste; keep stirring it for a quarter of an hour, and then put into a small jar to be kept for use.

WHITE SAUCE. *See Bechamel.*

WIDGEONS AND TEAL, Are dressed exactly as the wild duck; only that less time is requisite for a widgeon, and still less for a teal.

WILD DUCKS. For roasting a wild duck, you must have a clear, brisk fire, and a hot spit; it must be browned upon the outside, without being sodden within. To have it well frothed and full of gravy is the nicety. Prepare the fire by stirring and raking it just before the bird is laid down, and fifteen or twenty minutes will do it in the fashionable way; but if you like it a little more done, allow it a few minutes longer; if it is too much, it will lose its flavor.

WINE (MADEIRA) SAUCE. Take a tea-spoonful of flour, and a preserved green lemon, cut into dice, mix them with a glass of Madeira wine, and a little *consomme,* add an ounce of butter, some salt and nutmeg; set these on a very hot stove to boil for a quarter of an hour; then take it off; put in a quarter of a pound of butter, set it again on the fire, stirring constantly till the butter is melted.

WINTER HOTCH-POTCH. Take the best end of a neck or loin of mutton; cut it into neat chops; cut four carrots, and as many turnips into slices; put on four quarts of water, with half the carrots and turnips, and a whole one of each, with a pound of dried green peas, which must be put to soak the night before; let it boil two hours, then take out the whole carrot and turnip; bruise and return them; put in the meat, and the rest of the carrot and turnips, some pepper and salt, and boil slowly three-quarters of an hour; a short time before serving, add an onion cut small and a head of celery.

WOODCOCKS. (1) The greatest possible care should be taken, in picking of these birds, to handle them as little as possible, on account of the skin being so particularly tender, that when broken it spoils  the beauty of the bird. When picked, cut off the pinions at the first joint, press the legs close to the side, through which, and the body, pierce the beak of the bird; then cross the feet, and lay a slice of bacon over the breast. Woodcocks and snipes may be dressed according to the same rules.

WOODCOCKS. (2) Take a pound of lean beef, cut it into pieces, and put it into a saucepan, with two quarts of water, an onion stuck with cloves, two blades of mace, and some whole pepper, boil all these together till reduced to half; then strain it off into another saucepan: draw the woodcocks, and lay the trail in a plate; put the woodcocks into the gravy, and let them boil in it for twelve minutes; while they are boiling, mince the trail and liver very small; put them into a small saucepan, with a little mace; add four or five spoonfuls of the gravy the woodcocks are boiled in; then take the crumb of a stale roll, rub it fine into a dish placed before the fire, and put to the trail, in the small saucepan, half a pint of red port, a bit of butter, rolled in flour, set it on the fire, and shake it round till the butter is melted; then put in the bread-crumbs, and shake the saucepan round; lay the woodcocks in the dish, pour the sauce over them, and serve.

WOODCOCKS. (3) Woodcocks should not be drawn, as the trail is by the lovers of *"haut gout"* considered a *"bonne bouche;"* truss their legs close to the body, and run an iron skewer through each thigh, close to the body, and tie them on a small bird spit; put them to roast at a clear fire; cut as many slices of bread as you have birds, toast or fry them a delicate brown, and lay them in the dripping-pan under the birds to catch the trail; baste them with butter, and froth them with flour; lay the toast on a hot dish, and the birds on the toast; pour some good beef gravy into the dish, and send some up in a boat, twenty or thirty minutes will roast them. Garnish with slices of lemon. Some epicures like this bird very much under-done, and direct that a woodcock should

be just introduced to the cook, for her to show it the fire, and then send it up to table.

WOODCOCKS IN A MINUTE. Put a brace of woodcocks into a fryingpan, with some butter, shred shallots, grated nutmeg, salt, and pepper; set the pan on a fierce fire, and fry the woodcocks lightly for seven or eight minutes; then add the juice of two lemons, half a glass of white wine, and some raspings; and leave them on the fire till the sauce has boiled up once; then serve altogether.

WOODCOCK SALMIS. Cut up the woodcock on the table, and put the pieces on a dish, which place on a stand, with a lamp under it; add pepper, salt, shred shallots, nearly a glass of white wine, the juice of three lemons, and a bit of butter; strew raspings over, and boil slowly for ten minutes, stirring occasionally. Use spirits of wine for your lamp.

WOODCOCK SAUCE. Pound the bones and livers of roasted woodcocks, and put them into a stewpan, with two spoonfuls of cullis, and two spoonfuls of red port; reduce it to the consistence of a sauce, and then strain it; when strained, add pepper, salt, and the juice of two oranges.

## Y.

YEAST. Beer yeast, which is the best for bread, should be strained through a hair sieve, and two or three quarts of cold spring water poured over it; when it has stood for twenty-four hours the water should be poured off, the yeast will then be found at the bottom of the vessel, quite thick. To preserve that which may be left over the baking, it should be put into a bottle, corked tightly, and kept in a cool place. In cold weather it will continue good for a fortnight, but fresh yeast is always preferable. When it does not appear sufficiently strong, honey or brown sugar may be mixed with it, in the proportion of a tea-spoonful to half a pint.

YEAST, BAKER'S. Boil two ounces of hops in four quarts of water one hour, adding more water as it decreases, carefully stirring it all the time, and taking care that it do not boil over; strain the liquor, and mix well with it two pounds of malt; cover it, and let it stand for eight hours, or until it be milk warm, then stir in half a pint of good yeast; when mixed well together, let it work for ten hours, and then strain it through a hair sieve.

YEAST, BRAN. Boil for ten minutes, in two quarts of water, one pint of bran, and a small handful of good hops; strain it through a sieve, and when milk warm, add three or four table-spoonfuls of beer yeast, and two of brown sugar or treacle: put it into a wooden stoup or jug; cover it, and place it before the fire to ferment. It may be bottled, tightly corked, and kept in a cool place.

YEAST DUMPLINGS. Make a very light dough with yeast, the same as for bread, but with milk instead of water, add salt; set it by the fire, covered up in a pan, for half an hour, or an hour, to rise; in the mean time, set on the fire a large saucepan of hot water, and as soon as it boils, roll up the dough into small balls, and put them into the boiling water; keep them continually boiling for ten minutes, then take them out, and serve them immediately, with wine sauce over them. To ascertain whether they are sufficiently boiled, stick a fork into one, and if it comes out clean, it is done enough. Some think the best manner of eating them is by dividing them from the top by two forks, as they become heavy by their own steam, and eat them immediately with meat, or sugar and butter, or salt.

YELLOW GLAZE. Make a glaze, with a quarter of a pound of fine sugar in powder, the white of an egg, to which add by degrees as much lemon-juice as may be necessary; when sufficiently beaten up, (and the longer it is beaten the whiter it will be), add to it a small quantity of infusion of saffron, strained, and the yellow rind of one or two lemons grated on a piece of sugar, scraped off and pounded; take care, however, not to put too much of the latter, lest the glaze should be bitter.

YEAST, TO MAKE. Boil for half an hour two quarts of water, thickened with about three spoonfuls of fine flour, and sweetened with nearly half a pound of brown sugar; when almost cold, put it into a jug, adding four spoonfuls of fresh yeast; shake it well together, let it stand uncovered near the fire for a day, to ferment. There will be a thin liquor on the top, pour this off; shake the remainder, and cork it up for use. To make a half peck loaf you should use a quarter of a pint of the above.

YEAST, POTATO. Boil some good mealy potatoes; peel and weigh them; while hot, bruise them finely, and mix them quickly with boiling water, allowing one quart to each pound; rub it through a hair sieve, then add honey or brown sugar in the proportion of one ounce to each quart of water; boil it to the consistency of batter, and when nearly cold, add a large table-spoonful of good yeast to every quart of water; cover it with a cloth to rise, and the following day it will be ready for use; keep a bottle of it, which may be used instead of beer-yeast for the next making, first pouring off the thin liquid that is on the top. It must be made with fresh beer yeast every two or three months. Double the quantity of this, as of beer yeast, is required to make bread light.

ZESTS. Zest (a term of art, used by confectioners) is the peel of oranges, lemons or citrons, cut from top to bottom, in small slips or zests, as thin as possible.

# RECEIPTS

## FOR MAKING ALL KINDS OF

## CONFECTIONERY.

# CONFECTIONERY.

---

ALMONDS, BLOWN. Scald a few almonds, and pound them to about half as fine as for biscuits, beat them with lemon-juice, whites of eggs and powder-sugar; drop them on paper, about the size of almonds and dry them in a stove or gentle oven.

ALMONDS BLOWN ROYAL. Choose four ounces of small thick almonds, and put them into an oven until they are slightly colored. Whilst they are cooling, mix four ounces of sugar with an egg; beat them up for ten minutes; add a little carmine to make it a fine rose color; dip the almonds into this: take them out; disengage them from the egg, so that they may be only just covered with it; lay them two and two on a sheet of strong paper three-quarters of an inch between each pair; they may also be placed in threes to form the tré-foil, on which may be added a fourth. Bake them in a cool oven.

ALMOND BUTTER. To a quarter of a pound of blanched almonds, well beat, put some new milk and rose water; take a quart of thick cream, and the yolks of twelve eggs beat well with a little of the cream; then add the rest of the cream; put a quarter of a pint of new milk to the almonds, and strain them into the cream till there is no strength left; strain all together into a skillet, set it over a charcoal fire, and stir it till it comes to a tender curd; put it into a strainer, and hang it up till the whey is drained out; then take six ounces of fine sifted sugar and a little rose water, and beat it all into butter with a spoon.

ALMOND BITTER CAKE. Pound three ounces (half bitter and half sweet) of almonds, put them into an earthen pan with six ounces of powder sugar; the same of sifted flour, two whole eggs, and six yolks, a spoonful of brandy and a grain or two of salt; work these up together for five minutes and then add six ounces

of fresh butter which is slightly warmed, work that in for four minutes longer. Then, having whipped the whites of two eggs, mix them into the paste. Butter a well-tinned copper mould or paper case, ten inches long, five wide, and two high; pour in your preparation, and bake it in a cool oven. While baking, whip the whites of two eggs, and mix two ounces of powder sugar with them, and cut four ounces of sweet almonds into slips (shortwise;) mix them also with two ounces of powder sugar and a spoonful of white of egg whipped. In three-quarters of an hour take out the cake, and if it be firm and well colored, cover it with the whipped egg and sugar, and on that strew the almonds equally, pressing them in, that all may be colored alike. This operation must be performed as quick as possible, and when done, turn the cake out and cut it in four slips (lengthwise,) and then divide each into six parts lozenge-shaped; this will give you twenty-four cakes, which must be arranged in stars on your dish, six to every star. They may also be cut in two lengths instead of four, and these divided into fifteen small pieces, and then, with a paste-cutter, formed into crescents. The ingredients, and the proper quantities for this cake are as follows: —six ounces of flour, the same of powder sugar, three ounces of sweet and bitter almonds, six yolks, and two whole eggs, six ounces of butter, two of sugar mixed with the whites of two eggs whipped, four ounces of cut almonds added to the sugar and eggs, a spoonful of brandy and a grain of salt.

ALMOND CANDY. Blanch a pound of the best almonds, and cut them very thin, length ways, put them into a pound of clarified sugar to crisp them, stir them over the fire till boiled to *souffle*; then take them off and keep stirring till the sugar is dry like sand: then sift it, so that the almonds may be left, divide them into four parts to color them differently, one part red, the second yellow, the third green, and the fourth left white as they come from the sugar. To color the first, soak a small quantity of carmine in clarified sugar, and lay your almonds in it; do the same with a little tincture of saffron for the yellow, and spinach juice for the green. Place the colored almonds on a sieve in a stove; when dry, mix all together, adding the white ones. Boil nearly as much sugar as your mould will require to *souffle*, put it in, and when the almonds are quite dry, garnish the surface of the sugar with them; do not, however, lay them too thick, and just press them down with a fork; put the mould into a moderate oven for five hours, then drain it well, and in another two hours it may be taken from the mould.

ALMONDS CINNAMON SPANISH. Blanch your almonds, then with a bit of butter tied in a piece of cloth, rub the pan and brown them. Have ready some clarified sugar, with powdered cinnamon stirred in it, put in the almonds, and when well covered with the sugar and cinnamon, lay them separately on tins, and dry in a slow oven.

ALMONDS TO COLOR. ALMONDS ROSE COLORED. Blanch and cut sweet almonds in small pieces, put them on a baking plate, and pour on them a little of any vegetable liquid, of an infusion of cochineal, or carmine; then rub them in your hands, to mix them well with the color; when all are so done, dry them in a stove or in the oven.

ALMONDS VIOLET. Are done in the same way, the coloring ingredients are cochineal, and a little indigo dissolved in water, put but a small quantity of the latter at a time as it is very powerful.

ALMONDS GREEN. The same proceeding: the color is made with two handfuls of fresh spinach, well washed, drained, and then pounded; when very fine, press it through a napkin; let the juice drop on a dish, which place on a hot stove; as soon as it begins to boil, take it off, stirring it constantly, till the green curdles, then pour it through a horsehair sieve, and when well drained strain it through a silk sieve or tammy;

the juice thus obtained, will give the almonds (which must be put in a few at a time) a clear and even green color.

ALMONDS BLUE. Dissolve a little indigo in water, strain it through a cloth and use it as above mentioned.

ALMONDS ORANGE COLORED. Mix a little liquid red, and a little infusion of saffron together, and proceed with the almonds as usual.

ALMONDS LEMON COLORED. Infuse a small quantity of saffron in nearly boiling water for a few minutes; strain and follow the above direction.

ALMONDS CHOCOLATE COLORED. Are dyed with chocolate dissolved in water and strained.

The almonds may be cut in slips, dice, &c. according to fancy. Observe that the color of your almonds should be light and delicate; when done, place them, either separately or mixed together, in paper cases.

ALMOND COUPEAUX. Blanch and pound half a pound of sweet almonds with the whites of three eggs into a very fine paste, add to it six ounces of powdered sugar and the rind of a lemon grated; when thoroughly mixed together, pour over it about four spoonfuls of orange-flower water: stir up the paste (which ought to be rather thin,) once more, and then lay it with a spoon on a plate of bright copper, in an oval form, about three or four inches in length. The plate being quite full, take it up by both hands, and strike it steadily upon a table, so that the paste may be extended, but not much; then bake them until they become of a deep yellow. Take them from the copper with a knife, and whilst hot put them on a wooden roller, about the thickness of an arm, and press them with your hand, that they may acquire the form of the wood, and when cool place in a box, and keep them dry. These coupeaux are very brittle.

ALMONDS CRISPED. Rub a pound of the best sweet almonds in a cloth to take off all the dust, and then put them, with a pound of sugar, half a glass of water and a little carmine, into a preserving pan; put them on the fire, and let them remain; when the almonds crackle take them off and work them about until the sugar is detached from the almonds, then take away part of the sugar, put the almonds on the fire again, and stir them lightly with a spatula, (be careful that the fire be not too quick;) and when they have taken the sugar, add that which had been removed, and continue to burn them till they have imbibed that also. Place a sheet of paper on a sieve, throw your almonds on it, separate those which adhere together, and let them cool.

ALMOND DRAGEES. Take of the best and largest almonds what quantity you please, and having washed them in cold water, let them drain and dry on a sieve for twenty-four hours. The next day weigh them, and for each pound of almonds take three pounds of sugar; clarify the latter and boil it to the degree *petit lisse*; then let it cool a little. Have your tossing pan ready; on your right hand, a chafing dish to keep your pan containing the sirup constantly warm; and on your left hand, a table with a mixture of powder and flour (of each half a pound to a pound of almonds). All being ready, put the almonds into the pan, and pour over them one or two large spoonfuls of the sirup, and shake them so that all the almonds may be wetted with sirup; then take a handful or two of the flour and powder, and strew it over the wet almonds; shake them again, that the flour may adhere all round the almonds. After this, swing the pan backwards and forwards, by which means the almonds roll about in every direction; continue this motion until they become dry; then moisten and powder them as before; swing the pan again, and when dry, repeat the process a third, fourth, and fifth time, or more, until they are of a proper size; then pour over them the sirup for the last time, without the powder, and, having swung and dried them, take them out and place them on sieves in a warm place, that they may dry perfectly before you put them by for use.

Observe, that after a few layers of the sirup, the superabundant parts of that and the powder form a white crust at the bottom of the pan; as soon as it acquires any degree of thickness, the

pan must be taken from the fire, the almonds carefully removed with an iron spatula, and the crust broken off; when the pan has been well washed and dried, replace the almonds and proceed with your work. This must be strictly attended to, not only with this, but in making all kinds of sweetmeats. The sugar thus cleared away may be made useful for many purposes.

Common Almond Dragees are made in the same manner; the only difference consists in having ingredients of an inferior quality.

ALMONDS (MILK OF) FANCHONETTES. Blanch and pound eight ounces of sweet and one of bitter almonds, and when the paste is very fine, add to it three glasses of nearly boiling milk, then press this mixture through a napkin to draw out the milk. Put into a stewpan four yolks of eggs, three ounces of powder-sugar, one of sifted flour, and a grain of salt, mix them well together, and add by degrees the almond milk, put this on a moderate fire, stirring it constantly. Line about thirty tartlet moulds with thin puff paste, and put on them a little of the above preparation, and bake them in a moderate oven. When properly done, take them out and let them cool. Mix with the whites of three hard eggs, four ounces of powder-sugar, stir it well to soften the egg, and make it work easily; put some of the remainder of your preparation on each of the *fanchon-nettes*, and cover them lightly with the egg; put some white of egg on the blade of a large knife, and with a small one as quick as possible take off seven *meringues* about the size of a filbert, and arrange them in the form of a crown on each *fanchonnette;* when you have done five or six, cover them with powder-sugar very equally, and then bake them in a cool oven. When of a reddish brown they are done and may be served.

ALMOND CHEESE, BITTER. Peel, wash, and drain, three ounces of sweet, and one ounce of bitter almonds, pound them to a paste, moistening with two spoonfuls of water. Put them into an earthen pan, with two glasses of nearly boiling milk, in which eight ounces of sugar have been dissolved; let this stand an hour, then strain it through a fine sieve, and put to it six drachms of isinglass lukewarm; place the whole in ice and when it begins to set, add some whipped cream; pour it into a mould which has been kept in ice, put it in ice again for half an hour, and then take the *fromage* from the mould.

ALMOND FLUMMERY. Boil three ounces of hartshorn in two quarts of spring water; let it simmer six or seven hours till half the water is consumed; strain it through a sieve; beat half a pound of almonds very fine, with a quantity of orange-flower water; mix a little of the jelly and some fine sugar with it; strain it with the rest of the jelly, stirring it till it is a little more than blood warm; pour it into basins or cups, and stick in almonds cut small.

ALMOND GARLANDS. Take half a pound of march-pane paste, the whites of two or three eggs, some powdered cinnamon and a little flour, knead them into a paste, and roll them into the form of sausages with your hand on the table, first strewing the table with almonds minced, but not very fine; so that they may adhere to the sausages, which ought to be about the size of your finger; then form them into rings or garlands of what size you please, fixing the ends together with water: place them on paper, and bake them in a quick oven until they are of a clear brown color.

ALMOND LITTLE CAKE, BITTER. Pound six drachms of bitter almonds, strain them through a sieve, and mix them in an earthen vessel, with nearly the white of an egg, and six ounces of sugar, stir these with a silver spoon for a few minutes. Take three-quarters of a pound of puff paste, roll it to the thickness of a quarter of an inch, and cut out of it thirty oval cakes two inches and a half long by two and a quarter wide pointed at the ends; put on each a quarter of a spoonful of the almond glaze, and with the blade of a knife spread it equally over the surface for about the eighth of an inch, and then let them stand for half an hour before you put them into the oven, which must be moderate. If you bake them immediately after putting on the glaze, it wrinkles and shrivels up, which spoils their appearance, as they ought to be quite smooth and even; the cakes also require considerable care in the baking; they should be slightly colored on the top and the lower part

reddish.

ALMOND GENOESE, BITTER. Blanch two ounces four drachms of sweet, and two ounces and a half of bitter almonds, pound them to a paste and then put them into the following preparation: blanch and pound four ounces of sweet almonds, and when perfectly smooth, mix them in an earthen pan with six ounces of flour, the same of powder-sugar, six yolks and two whole eggs, a spoonful of brandy and a grain of salt. Stir the whole for six minutes, then add six ounces of butter slightly warmed but not melted; work the butter well into the paste for four or five minutes. Butter two moulds, or paper cases, about nine or ten inches square, pour in your preparation, smooth it with the blade of a knife and then put them to bake in a moderate oven, first strewing on them four ounces of sweet almonds minced and mixed with two ounces of powder-sugar, and a little white of egg. When done, cut them into all possible forms, then replace them in the oven to dry; when brittle, take them out, let them cool, and decorate them to your fancy.

ALMOND, GRILLAGE. Blanch half a pound of almonds, cut them into four or five slips, lengthways, *pralinez* them with three-eighths of a pound of sugar, sand them when they begin to crackle; then put them on the fire again till they are well mixed together and form a mass, which put on wafer-paper lightly oiled, lay it flat, strew over it cinnamon, sugar, plain or white *nonpareils*, and then cut it in pieces.

ALMOND KNOTS. Take two pounds of almonds, and blanch them in hot water; beat them in a mortar to a very fine paste, with rose water, be careful to keep them from oiling. Take a pound of double-refined sugar, sifted through a lawn sieve, leave out some to make up the knots, put the rest in a pan upon the fire, till it is scalding hot, at the same time have the almonds scalding hot in another pan: then mix them together with the whites of three eggs beaten to froth, and let it stand until it is cold; then roll it with some of the sugar left out for that purpose, and lay them in platters of paper. They will not roll into shape, therefore lay them as well as may be, and bake them in a slow oven.

ALMOND MILK. Take six ounces of sweet almonds, and a pint of milk, four drachms of orange-flower water, and five ounces of sugar. Blanch and pound the almonds to a very smooth paste, moistening them occasionally with a few drops of milk; when your paste crumbles, put it in the milk and mix them well, and boil it till reduced to half, then let it boil up once more; let it cool and serve.

ALMOND MIRLITONS. Blanch an ounce of sweet, and the same of bitter almonds, and dry them in an oven; when cold, pound them with a little white of egg to prevent their oiling; then put them into an earthen pan with two ounces of bitter macaroons, five ounces of powder-sugar, four whole eggs, and a grain of salt; when these are well mixed together, add two ounces of butter, lukewarm. Make a proper quantity of puff paste, roll it out thin, and cut it into thirty round pieces about two inches and three-quarters in diameter, and put each of these into a tartlet mould buttered; put the *mirliton*s on this, and when all are equally full, cover them with powder sugar sifted over them through a tammy; as soon as that is dissolved strew more (but not such fine) powder sugar over, and bake them in a moderate oven. Serve either hot or cold.

ALMOND MONCEAUX. Take half a pound of sweet almonds, cut them into thin slips (lengthways) and roast them on an iron until they are of a deep yellow color, inclining to brown; beat up the whites of six or eight eggs with a spoon in an earthen pan. Pour over the almonds a pound of sugar finely powdered, four ounces of candied orange peel, the same of candied lemon-peel, also cut into thin slips, half a spoonful of powdered cinnamon, and six or eight cloves pounded; mix these ingredients well in the pan, and place it on paper in little heaps of a pyramidal form, and bake them in a well-heated oven.

ALMOND PASTE. Blanch two pounds of sweet almonds, and soak them in cold water for twelve hours, then dry them in a napkin, and pound a quarter of them to a very fine paste with a little water and lemon-juice, pass them through a sieve, and then pound the remainder

(half a pound at a time.) When all are done, mix them with a pound of sifted sugar; place them over a gentle fire, stirring it continually, until the paste will flow from the spoon; then pour it into a mortar, and when it becomes lukewarm, pound it again with an ounce of gum-dragon previously dissolved in a glass of water and strained, the juice of two lemons, and a pound of sifted sugar. As soon as your paste is of the proper consistence, take it out and lay it on the slab, sprinkled first with sugar; divide your paste into three parts, and color each part according to your fancy. The coloring or dyes are made of the same materials as are used for almonds.

ALMOND PASTE *to keep six, or even twelve months.* Blanch and pound a pound of sweet almonds, moistened occasionally with water, to prevent their oiling; when well beaten, add half a pound of fine powdered sugar, and mix the whole into a paste to use when you have occasion. When wanted, mix a piece about the size of an egg with three gills of water, and strain it through a napkin.

ALMOND PRALINES, *(dried, preserved or burnt.)* A pound of the best almonds must be washed in cold water; when thoroughly dry, put them into a preserving pan with a pound of sugar and a pint and a half of water, keep them on the fire, stirring them continually, until they crackle and fly about, and the sugar begins to color, stir them about gently to gather the sugar, and leave them in the pan to dry about two hours, in a stove or any moderate heat.

ALMONDS, RED CRISPED. Prepare them as above until they have taken the sugar and are ready to be taken off the fire, put the almonds upon a sieve with a dish under, take the sugar that drops, and put it into the same pan, adding a little fresh; refine it till it comes to the twelfth degree *au casse*, then take cochineal, color sufficient to tinge the almonds, and put them therein; give them a few turns over the fire in the sugar, and finish as at first.

ALMOND SWEETMEATS (YELLOW.) Blanch a pound of sweet almonds, wash them in cold water, and when quite dry, pound them with a sufficient quantity of yolks of eggs, into a fine but rather stiff paste: add to them a pound of powdered sugar and the rinds of two lemons grated; knead the paste well with your hands, first sprinkling the table with sugar. Form the paste into what figures you please, such as fleur-de-lis, trefoil, &c. each being about the size and weight of a macaroon. Place them on white paper and on an iron plate, fry them in a moderately hot stove. If they are of a deep yellow, they are sufficiently done.—These sweetmeats may be still further ornamented in the following manner:—Boil some sugar in orange-flower water to the degree called *grande plume*, and as soon as the sweetmeats are taken from the stove or oven, wash them over with a light brush dipped in the sirup; this will give them a delicious perfume, and they may then be called *á la glace*. When cold, take them from the paper and put them into glasses for the table.

ALMONDS, ROCK OF ALICANTE, SPANISH. Clarify honey, and stir into it as many blanched almonds as you can entangle. Leave it to cool. This makes a pretty crystaline ornament for the dessert; it is also called Rock of Gibraltar.

ALMOND WAFERS. Take a pound of sweet almonds, blanch and pound them, add a pound of powder-sugar, a pinch of orange-flowers *pralinée*, put them into a basin, and moisten them with a sufficient quantity of whites of eggs to enable you to spread the paste on wafer paper with the blade of a knife (the wafer paper must be rubbed with virgin wax and sweet oil); lay the preparation on as thin as possible; chop some sweet almonds very small, mix them with sugar, and strew them over the wafers and put them into a hot oven; when about half baked, take them out and cut them in squares; replace them a minute in the oven, take them out again, and press them on a stick to give them the proper form; as soon as they are cold, put them on a sieve. Just before they are served they should be slightly warmed.

ALMOND COMPOTE, GREEN. Take the peel very carefully from your almonds, and put them with water on the fire till they are tender; then take them off and add a little more water; when nearly cold put them on the fire again, but do not let them boil; as soon as you find the head of a pin will penetrate easily, they are then sufficiently done, and may be thrown into cold water; and when the fruit is quite cold, drain them. In the meantime put some clarified sugar on the fire, and when it boils put in the almonds; boil them in the sugar about twenty times, then remove them, and let the almonds stand to take the sugar: in about two hours' time put them on the fire again, and boil them up a dozen times; after which, take them off; skim, and let them cool. When quite cool drain and put the fruit in a *compotier*. If the sugar should not be sufficiently done, boil as much more as you may think necessary; squeeze in the juice of an orange, boil it once again, and when nearly cold strain it through a cloth into the *compotier* over the almonds.

ALMOND NONPAREILS, GREEN. Drain some green almonds that have been preserved in brandy; dip them one by one in sugar prepared *au cassé*, and roll them in white, or any other colored nonpareils, and dry them in a stove, or gentle oven.

ALMOND (GREEN) PRESERVED. Put some water into a saucepan, with two handfuls of bran, and when it has boiled up twice, throw in some green almonds; let them boil up once, then take them out with a skimmer, and rub them well in your hands to take off the down; as you do this, throw them into cold water; then boil them in water till, on pricking them, a pin easily enters and they shrink: then clarify some sugar, a pound to a pound of fruit; boil up the sirup four or five successive days, morning and evening, without the fruit, which you leave to drain upon a sieve; lastly, put the fruit into a pan, and when rather more than lukewarm, pour the sirup over it; when they look very green they are sufficiently done.

ANDAYE BRANDY. An ounce of bruised aniseed, an ounce of bruised coriander seed, two ounces of powdered Florence iris, the zestes of two oranges; put them with three quarts of distilled brandy into the alembic bain-marie; dissolve two pounds and a half of sugar in two pints and a half of clear river water, add them to the distilled liqueur, pass the whole through a strainer, and put into bottles.

ANGELICA CAKES. Take four ounces of angelica powder, and two pounds of fine sugar. Beat up the white of an egg with a little sifted sugar, until it is of the consistence of cream cheese; dissolve the sugar in a skillet and skim it; when it has boiled a little, throw in the angelica, and boil the sugar to *petit cassé*, then take it from the fire, put in half a spoonful of the beaten egg, and stir it quickly until the sugar rises, then stop, and when it has fallen again, stir till it rises a second time; it may now be poured into moulds or paper cases, well oiled and sprinkled with sifted sugar.

ANGELICA (ESSENCE OF) JELLY. Having washed and well dried two ounces of angelica-roots; cut them in pieces and throw them into boiling sirup, (three-quarters of a pound of sugar,) with an ounce of bruised angelica seeds; cover the mixture close, and when cold, add to it half a glass of *kirsch-wasser*, and pass it through a tammy; then filter, and afterwards put to it an ounce of isinglass: stir it lightly with a silver spoon; pound ten pounds of ice, and put it into a large sieve or pan, place your mould in the middle of the ice, taking care that it touches the ice in every part; pour the jelly into the mould, cover it with a saucepan lid, put ice on that, and let it stand for three hours; after that time have ready a saucepan large enough to take in the mould easily; fill it with water so warm that you can scarcely bear your hand in it; plunge the mould in so as to allow the water to pass over the whole, but as quickly as possible, and then turn the jelly into your dish for table. This last operation should be performed with great agility. Observe, in making these kind of jellies, that no tinned or pewter vessels or spoons should be used, as they impart a violet tinge to your jellies, which ought to be of the color of the ingredients employed, as for instance the above should be a clear light green color.

ANGELICA LIQUEUR. Wash, scrape, and cut in small pieces, twelve ounces of fresh, or half the quantity of Bohemian angelica roots, and infuse them for a week in six pints of brandy and one of water, with a drachm of mace, two drachms of cinnamon, and twelve cloves; at the end of that time distil it, then dissolve three pounds of sugar in three pints of water; mix it with the *liqueur*, strain it through a jelly-bag, or filter it through paper. Observe, that the best brandy for *liqueurs* is that which is made at Montpelier, as it yields more in distillation than the Cogniac. Take notice also that the first drops which fall from the alembic after it is placed on the stove, must not be mixed with the liqueur. A glass should, therefore, be placed under the mouth of the alembic to receive them, and when about a quarter of it is filled you may remove it, and place your bottles or matrass. The phlegm, as these droppings are called, are good for nothing.

ANGELICA PASTE. Take young and pithy angelica stalks, boil them till tender, drain and press all the water out; beat them in a mortar to a paste, and rub it through a sieve. Next day dry it over the fire, and to every pound of paste put a pound of powder-sugar. When the paste is hot add the sugar, stirring it till thoroughly mixed, over a gentle fire. Drop it on plates, dust a little sugar over them, and dry them in a stove.

ANGELICA PRESERVED. Take the stalks of angelica when of a good size, but before they have run to seed; clear off the leaves, and as you cut the stalks into proper lengths throw them into water, and boil them till the stalks are soft; take them from the fire, and put them into cold water; take off the skin, and again put them into cold water; then drain and put them into an earthen pan, and pour over a sufficient quantity of clarified sugar to float the angelica. In twenty-four hours boil the sugar ten or a dozen times, and when lukewarm pour it over the stalks. Proceed in the same way for four succeeding days; after which, drain the stalks, and in the meanwhile boil the sugar (adding more, if necessary) to the degree *grande perlé*; put the angelica to this, cover it close, and let it boil five or six times. Take it from the fire, scum, and put it by in pots.

ANGELICA PRESERVED DRY. Proceed as for the liquid, until you have poured the sugar *au grand perle* over the angelica; leave it for a day in the sugar, then drain and dry it on slates, or iron plates, in a stove.

ANGELICA RATAFIA. Take six pints of brandy, a pint of river water, three pounds of sugar, two ounces of fresh gathered angelica-roots, the same quantity of angelica seed; mace and clove, a drachm of each. Wash and dry the roots well, cut them in slices, and put them, with the seeds and spices bruised, into the brandy, to infuse for twenty days; then strain it, and having added to it the sugar dissolved in river water, filter and bottle your ratafia.

ANGELICA RATAFIA. Strip the angelica stalks of their leaves, and cut them into small pieces, which put into the best brandy and water, in the proportion of four litres of brandy and two of water to one pound of angelica, and four pounds of sugar to the same quantity; add cloves and cinnamon; let it stand six weeks, then filter and bottle it.

ANGELICA WATER. Wash eight handfuls of angelica leaves, cut, and lay them on a table to dry. When quite dry, put them in an earthen pot with a gallon of strong wine lees. Let it stand twenty-four hours, stir it twice in that time, then put it into a warm still or alembic; draw off into bottles, covered with paper pricked in holes, and let them stand thus two or three days. Sweeten it, and when it is settled, bottle, and stop it close.

ANISEED, OIL OF. Is made like aniseed water, the only difference is, that an additional pound of sugar is necessary to make the sirup.

ANISE PETIT PAINS. Put two glasses of water and two ounces of fresh butter into a stewpan, and when the liquid boils take it from the fire, and mix with it six ounces of sifted flour; amalgamate it thoroughly, so that it may be quite free from lumps; then dry it over the fire. Take it out of the saucepan, and add to it two eggs, and two ounces of powder-sugar; mix

them well in, and then put in two more eggs and the *zeste* of a lemon minced fine: when these are also well incorporated, add another egg or two, if the paste (which should be rather firm,) will bear them. Sprinkle your paste slab with flour, cut the paste into pieces, each the size of a walnut; roll these with as little flour as possible, to about three inches long, and as you roll them place them on a baking-tin, two inches apart; *dorez* and bake them in a tolerably warm oven till they are firm. Then cut some anise into fillets, boil a quarter of a pound of sugar to *cassé*, and the moment it reaches that degree set it by the side of the fire that the sugar may not lose its whiteness; dip the top and one side of each *petit pain* in the sugar as quick as possible, and as you take them out, strew the anise over them lightly. Red anise is also used for these *petit pains*.

ANISEED RATAFIA. To make a quart of this liqueur, boil a pound of sugar with a demisetier of water, until the sugar is quite clear; then heat another demisetier of water, and put in it three ounces of anise; take it from the fire before it boils; let it stand a quarter of an hour, and then pour it with three pints of brandy into the sugar; mix all well together, and then pour into a vessel, which must be closed tight, and placed in the sun. Let it stand three weeks, and then bottle it.

ANISEED WATER. Choose eight ounces of new green anise, sift it well to free it from the dust, and then infuse in six pints of brandy, with the zestes of three lemons, and half an ounce of cinnamon; in a week's time distil it over a moderate fire, put a pint of water into the alembic; take care to collect the phlegm before you draw off the aniseed water. Dissolve three pounds of sugar in three pints of water. As the anise contains an acid salt, which renders this liqueur milky, the following proceeding is necessary:— Reserve a pint of the water from that in which you dissolved the sugar, and mix with the white of three or four eggs, well whipped, and while the sirup is hot put to it this egg-water and the aniseed water; stir it over the fire until the whole is hot without boiling; then put it into a glass jar, cork it well, and let it stand; the next day bottle and filter it.

ANISETTE DE BORDEAUX. Take two ounces of green aniseed, half a pound of aniseed, two ounces of coriander, and the same of fennel seeds. Bruise, and put them, with sixteen pints of brandy, into an alembic bain-marie. Then dissolve thirteen pounds of sugar in two quarts of river water, which must be put to your liqueur when distilled. Filter and bottle it.

APPLE FRITTERS. Turn twelve small apples, cut them into halves, and boil them in sirup, then leave them to cool. When they are cold, make an extremely thin crust with *brioche* paste. Make a fritter for each half apple, then fry them and finish the same as Fritters *à la Dauphine*.

Pears cut into quarters are made in the same manner as the above.

APPLES AND ALMONDS LITTLE CAKES. Proceed the same as above till the marmalade is spread over the under-crust, then cover it with almonds cut in fillets, press them in lightly; mask them with powder-sugar and bake in a moderate oven. As soon as cold, cut your *gâteaux* according to your fancy, either round, oblong, lozenge, or crescent-shaped.

APPLE MARMALADE, LITTLE CAKES. Make a marmalade of twenty-four apples in the usual way, with a quarter of a pound of sugar, and a quarter of a pot of apricots, and the *zeste* of a lemon, shred fine. Make your paste, and proceed as directed for Petits Gateaux glacés of apricots. Sprinkle them (when marked) with powder-sugar. Bake them in a moderate oven and finish them.

APPLE PETIT GATEAUX WITH PISTACHIOS. Make an under-crust of the same size and thickness as directed for *petits gâteaux glacés* of apricots, and cover it with apple marmalade; when baked, mash the apples with a little apricot marmalade, and strew over a quarter of a pound of pistachio nuts cut in small pieces, and then put it in the oven again for a few minutes to dry the apricots. When cold cut them into the usual forms.

APPLES AND PISTACHIOS. Prepare and toss up a dozen apples for this gateau with apples and raisins, with the addition of two ounces of sugar, and instead of the *zeste* of an orange, grate that of a lemon, and put three ounces of pistachio nuts blanched, in the place of the raisins. Proceed in the same manner as directed in that recipe, strewing on the dome of the *gâteau* pistachio and sugar, each nut cut into six pieces; and when the crown is put round the band, place a pistachio nut in the middle of each *meringue*, bake it of a light color in a slow oven, and serve it hot.

APPLE MERINGUEES. Put some apple marmalade on a dish, in a pyramid: whip the whites of two eggs to a froth, mix with them two spoonfuls of powder-sugar and a little lemon-peel chopped extremely small; decorate your apples with this preparation, glaze them with sugar, and color them in the oven.

APPLE MERINGUE. Lay a *timbale* paste in a tart pan, egg and prick it all over, and bake it; lay in it a purée of apples, and finish with white of egg, as for à la Turque; serve it hot.

APPLES PUREE. Peel and core a dozen or more good baking apples; set them over the fire to stew with some clarified sugar and a small bit of lemon-peel; when soft, stir them well with a wooden spoon, and put in a spoonful of apricot jam; stir it at times till the jam is mixed and the apples thicken, then rub the whole through a tammy.

APPLES, SOUFFLE PARISIEN. Make a marmalade of three dozen apples, half a pound of powder-sugar, the peel of a lemon, and a glass of water; dry it as much as you possibly can, for on that the good appearance of the *soufflé parisien* chiefly depends; then put it into a large stewpan. Whip the whites of fifteen eggs to a strong froth, with a pound of powder-sugar. Mix a quarter of this at first, with the apple marmalade, then stir the whole together, pour it into a *croustade* prepared as usual. (See SOUFFLE.) Bake it for an hour in a moderate oven. Serve it as soon as possible after taking it from the oven. Glaze it with powder-sugar.

APPLE SIRUP. Take six apples, pare and cut them into small pieces; put them into a *matrass* with three-quarters of a pound of sugar and two glasses of water; stop it close and place it in a *bain marie*, and leave it about two hours, letting the water be boiling; move the *matrass* frequently  without taking it out of the water; this must be done carefully lest it should break on being exposed  to the cold air; when done put out the fire, and let the *matrass* cool before you take it out. When the sirup is nearly cold, flavor it with lemon-juice, and add a spoonful of spirits of lemon or cinnamon, orange-flower water, or whatever else you may choose. If any dregs should arise, let it stand for some hours longer, and then gently pour the sirup into bottles. Great care must be taken to prevent its being muddy.

APRICOTS BOTTLED. Press the quantity of ripe apricots you may require through a horsehair sieve; put the pulp into bottles, cork them very close, and tie them over; place these bottles upright in a large saucepan, with hay between to prevent their touching; put the saucepan on the fire, and fill it with water. When the water is near boiling, take it off and let it stand till the bottles are cold; then put them in a cellar, without touching each other, until wanted, when they will be found as good to use as fresh fruit. The apricots may also be preserved whole by the same means.

APRICOTS IN BRANDY. Choose your apricots when quite ripe, let them be free from spots, rub them carefully with a linen cloth, to take off the down. Weigh your fruit, and to each pound put a quarter of a pound of sugar. Clarify it, and boil it to the degree *grand perlé*, then put in the apricots: boil them three or four times, taking care to turn them frequently, that they may take the sugar in all parts. Take them off the fire, and put them one by one into glass bottles; the sirup being by this time nearly cold, pour the brandy (three *demisetier*s to each pound) into it by degrees, stirring constantly to mix it well with the sirup. When thoroughly incorporated, pour it into the bottles, the fruit at first will float; but when the brandy and sugar have soaked in they will sink to the bottom; they are then fit to eat.

APRICOT COMPOTE, GREEN. Green apricots are done exactly the same as green al-

monds. See ALMONDS.

APRICOT COMPOTE. Peel, cut, and take the stones from your fruit, and put them on the fire in a little water, and when they rise they are sufficiently done, and may be taken out, cooled, and drained. Then put them into a little clarified sugar and give them three or four boilings; skim them well, and then put your fruit aside; boil the sugar alone four or five times more, and pour it over the apricots. When cold place them in the *compotier*.

APRICOT CONSERVE. Take half-ripe apricots, peel and cut them into thin slices, dry them over a gentle fire; to four ounces of fruit put one pound of sugar, boiled to the degree *la plume forte*; when the sugar is nearly cold put in the fruit, taking care to stir it well with a spoon, that they may be well incorporated.

APRICOTS PARISIEN. Take five dozen very fine apricots, cut them in half, and put them, a few at a time, over the fire, with half a pound of sugar and four glasses of water; as soon as you find the peel will come off easily, take them out and drain them, and put fresh apricots into the sirup, and proceed the same until all are pealed, then reduce the sirup to the usual consistence. Put a pound of rice, half a pound of butter, the same of sugar, on which grate the zestes of four lemons, a little salt, eight or nine glasses of milk, and three-quarters of a pound of raisins, into a saucepan, and when it boils take it from the fire and put it on hot cinders, stirring it occasionally for an hour, when, if the rice be quite soft, mix the yolks of ten eggs with it.

APRICOTS IN JELLY. Pare and stone your apricots, scald them a little, lay them in a pan, and cover them with clarified sugar; next day drain the sirup, and boil it smooth, then add the apricots and boil together; the following day make a jelly with codlings, boiling some apricots among them, to give a better flavor. When the jelly is done put in the other fruit with the sirup, and boil altogether, skim it well and put it in glasses.

APRICOT MARMALADE. Peel the apricots, and take out the stones; to each pound of fruit put three-quarters of a pound of clarified sugar, boil it to the degree *gros boulet*, then put in the apricots, boil both together: when it flows readily it may be put into pots.

APRICOT RATAFIA. Peel and cut into pieces as many ripe apricots as you may require, and boil them in white wine (about a pint to four dozen;) strain and mix it with an equal quantity of brandy; put the whole into a jar, with the kernels bruised, add a quarter of a pound of sugar to each pint. Let it infuse for three weeks, then filter and bottle it.

APRICOT SWEETMEAT, WHOLE AND DRY. Choose fine firm apricots, make a little opening at the top to take out the stone, put them into cold water, then blanch them over the fire; when they begin to boil, take out those which are soft, throw them into cold water, and drain them. In the meantime, prepare some clarified sugar to *petit lissé*. When it boils put in the apricots, and boil up a few times together. The next day separate the sugar from the fruit, boil *á la nappe*, and then pour it over the apricots again; the following day boil the sugar *petit perlé*, then add the fruit, and boil together; the fourth day drain them; and, having placed them on iron plates, sprinkle them with sugar before you put them into the stove to dry; when dry, place in boxes in layers, placing a sheet of paper between each layer.

wwwwwww

# B.

BADIANE, INDIAN. Take a pound of starred anise, pound and infuse it in six quarts of good brandy for a week, when add to it a pint and a half of water, and distil it. Dissolve seven pounds and a half of sugar in seven pints of water, and add it to the distilled liqueur. Stir it well, strain and bottle it. This is also called *Badiane Cream*. Some persons color it with a little cochineal, it is then called *Oil of Badiane*.

BALM WINE. Boil twenty pounds of lump sugar in four gallons and a half of water gently for an hour, and put it in a tub to cool. Bruise two pounds of the tops of green balm, and put them into a barrel with a little new yeast, and

when the sirup is nearly cold pour it on the balm. Stir it well together, and let it stand twenty-four hours, stirring frequently; bring it up, and when it has stood for six weeks, bottle it. Put a lump of sugar into each bottle; cork it tight. The longer it is kept the better it will be.

BALSAM, SIRUP OF. Put an ounce of balsam of tolu into a quart of spring water, and boil them two hours; add a pound of white pounded sugar-candy, and boil it half an hour longer. Take out the balsam, and strain the sirup twice; when cold, bottle it.

BARBADOES CREAM. Take the zests of three fine cedrats, two drachms of cinnamon, and two of mace, and put them into three quarts of brandy; close the vessel hermetically, and let it infuse for a week, then distil it in an alembic. Dissolve over the fire three pounds of sugar in a quart of pure river water, add to it half a pound of orange-flower water, work the mixture, and filter it through a straining bag into bottles for use.

BARBADOES WATER. Take the outer rind of eight large florentine citrons, half an ounce of bruised cinnamon, and a gallon of rectified spirit; distil in the *bain marie*; dissolve two pounds of sugar in a quart of water; mix it with the distilled liquor; filter and bottle it for use.

BARBADOES WATER AMBER COLORED. Infuse the yellow rind of six bergamots, half an ounce of cinnamon, and two drachms of cloves bruised, for six days in a gallon of rectified spirit; then add a drachm of saffron, and let the whole stand six days longer. Dissolve two pounds of sugar in a quart of water, add it to the infusion, and filter for use.

BARBERRY BISCUITS. Press the juice through a sieve from two pounds of barberries, and mix with it five pounds of sifted sugar; whisk the whites of four eggs and add them to the fruit; prepare some square paper cases, fill them with the jam, make them quite smooth, lay them on sieves, and put them into a stove, and let them remain six or eight days. When perfectly dry, take away the papers: keep them in a dry place.

BARBERRIES, TO CANDY. Take the barberries out of the preserve, and wash off the sirup in warm water; then sift over them some fine sugar, and set them in an oven, often moving them, and strewing sugar upon them until they are dry.

BARBERRY DROPS. Cut off the black tops, and roast the fruit before the fire till soft enough to pulp with a silver spoon through a sieve into a china basin, then set the basin in a saucepan of water the size of the top of the basin, and stir the barberries till they become thick. When cold, put to every pint, a pound and a half of the best sugar pounded as fine as possible. Beat the fruit and sugar together for two hours and a half (or more for a large quantity), then drop it on sheets of white thick paper. If, when you drop, it runs, there is not sugar enough, and it will look rough if you put too much.

BARBERRY ICE. Put some barberries into a pan without water, set it over a gentle fire, stirring them constantly; when warm, pass them through a sieve, into a pan, add to the liquor clarified sugar; if too thick, put a little water, but no lemon-juice, as the barberries are sufficiently acid without; then put it into the *sabotiere* to congeal.

BARBERRY ICE CREAM. Put a large spoonful of barberry jam into a pint of cream; add the juice of a lemon and a little cochineal; stir it well, and finish as directed, see ICE.

BARBERRY ICE WATER. Mix one spoonful of barberry jam with the juice of a lemon, a pint of water, and a little cochineal; pass it through a sieve and freeze it; take care that it is thick and smooth before you put in moulds.

BARBERRY MARCHPANE. Take three pounds of sweet almonds, two pounds and a half of sugar, and a pound of barberries; pound the almonds to a paste, mix them with the sugar boiled to *petit boule*, and then add the juice of the barberries strained; stir them together well, and place them on hot ashes, stirring them continually until the paste is formed; then put it on a table sprinkled with sugar and let it cool; spread it out about the thickness of a crown piece, cut it into various forms, place them on sheets of paper, and bake them in a moderate oven and glaze them. You may use any other fruit you think proper.

BARBERRY PASTILE. Dissolve half an ounce of gum-dragon in a glass of water, strain it in a cloth or bag, and put it into a mortar, with a spoonful of barberry marmalade; mix it well, and add as much powder-sugar as will make it into a malleable paste; you may also put in a little cochineal dissolved; form it into what shapes you please.

BARBERRIES PRESERVED IN BUNCHES. Choose those barberries which have the largest seeds, which may be extracted carefully with the nib of a pen. Weigh your fruit, and mix it with an equal weight of sugar boiled to *petit boule*; boil them together two or three times, and skim it. Set it aside in an earthen vessel until the next day, when it may be put in pots and covered.

BARBERRY WAFERS. Press out the juice from as many barberries as you may require, and mix it with powder-sugar, and the white of one egg, and stir it up with a wooden or silver spoon, to a fine paste. Lay a sheet of wafer paper on a baking plate, and spread your paste over it very thin with a knife; cut it into twelve pieces, and put them round a stick (the paste upwards) in a hot stove to curl; when half curled, take them off carefully, and set them up endways in a sieve; let them stand for a whole day in a hot stove.

BARBERRY WATER. Put two large spoonfuls of barberry jam, the juice of two lemons and a gill of sirup in a basin, and dilute it with water; add a little cochineal, and if not rich enough, more sirup; strain it through a fine sieve.

BARLEY SUGAR. Clarify two pounds of sugar, and boil it to *caramel* height, in a deep copper vessel with a lip; pour it in straight lines about an inch thick, on a marble slab previously rubbed with butter. Whilst hot, take each end of the strips of sugar and twist it; when cold cut it into proper lengths and put them by in glasses.

They must be kept in a dry place

BARLEY SUGAR DROPS. Proceed as for barley sugar. Have ready a large sheet of white paper, covered with a smooth layer of sifted sugar. Pour out the boiled sugar in drops the size of a shilling; when cold, fold them separately in paper, a few drops of the essence of ginger or lemon will improve the flavor.

BARLEY SIRUP. Make of a pound of barley three quarts of barley water; strain out the barley, and put to the water a handful of scabious, tormentil, hyssop, agrimony, horehound, maiden hair, sanicle, betons, burage, buglose, rosemary, marigolds, sage, violets and cowslips, of each a pint, when picked; a pound of raisins stoned, half a pound of figs cut, a quarter of a pound of dates stoned; half a pound of green liquorice, caraway, fennel and aniseed, of each one ounce, hartshorn, ivy, elecampane roots, of each an ounce; the roots of fennel, asparagus, couchgrass, polipodium, and oak parsley, of each a handful: clean, bruise the seeds, slice the roots, and put all into the barley water, cover close, and boil gently for twelve hours; then strain and press out the juice, and let it stand twenty-four hours; when clear, add to it rose-water and hyssop, half a pint of each, and a pint of clarified juice of coltsfoot, a drachm of saffron, three pints of the best honey, and as many pounds of sugar as quarts of liquor, boil this an hour and a half, keeping it clean-scummed, then bottle it, cork it well and put by for use.

BARLEY WATER. Put a quarter of a pound of pearl-barley into two quarts of water, let it boil, skim it very clean, boil half away, and strain it off. Sweeten according to taste, and put in two glasses of white wine, or some lemon-juice. Drink it warm.

BERGAMOT DROPS. Mix the juice of four or five lemons, and some sifted sugar, with a wooden spoon; add to this twenty drops of essence of bergamot; mix it well in, and having stirred it over the fire three or four minutes, drop it about the size of a sixpence on writing paper, and let them stand till cold.

BERGAMOT WAFERS. Squeeze six lemons into a basin, and mix some sifted sugar, essence of bergamot, and the white of an egg, with the juice; beat them together till very white; if it becomes too thick add the juice of another lemon; spread your paste, and dry them as *barberry wafers*.

BERGAMOT WATER. To the rinds of three bergamots, put a gallon of proof spirit, and two quarts of water; draw off one gallon by the *bain marie*, and sweeten with sugar.

BERGAMOT WATER. Take three gills of sirup, the juice of six lemons, and when diluted sufficiently with water, add a tea-spoonful of essence of bergamot. Strain it through a fine sieve for use.

BERGAMOT WATER ICE. Stir together the juice of three lemons, two gills of sirup, half a pint of water, and half a tea-spoonful of essence of bergamot, strain and freeze it.

BETONY, CONSERVE OF. Take a pound of betony, three pounds of loaf sugar, beat them in a stone mortar; boil the sugar with two quarts of betony water to the thickness of a sirup, then mix them together by little and little, over a gentle fire, make it into a conserve, and keep it in glasses.

BISCUITS. Lay the rind of a lemon in boiling water, till it be tender; take half a pound of sweet almonds, and blanch them in cold water, and two ounces of gum-dragon, which soak in fair water; then pound the almonds, putting in as you pound, the whites of two eggs beaten hollow; pound the lemon in a stone mortar by itself, and put the gum and the lemon into the almonds, and mix them well together; then beat a pound of fine sugar in a mortar with the almonds, gum and lemon, and afterwards add two pounds more of fine sugar, stirring it with a spoon, then roll it up in little rolls, and lay them upon white papers, and set them in the oven.

BISCUITS IN CASES. Prepare your mixture the same as for spoon biscuits, and fill some little round or square cases with it. Then with the rolling pin crush some fine sugar, but not to a powder, and strew it over your biscuits, which place on a copper plate, and when the sugar begins to dissolve put them in a gentle oven, at the mouth of which put a shovel full of burning coals to crystallize the sugar; and when that assumes the appearance of little pearls, remove the coals and close the oven. These biscuits will require from twenty to twenty-five minutes baking.

BISCUITS ICED. Beat up the white of eight, and the yolks of six eggs, with a pound of fine powdered sugar, for two hours. Have ready fourteen ounces of well-dried sifted flour; when the oven is ready and your plates buttered, mix the flour as quick as possible with the eggs, &c., and lay the biscuits on the plates; you may add a little musk and ambergris. Bake in a quick oven.

BISCUIT, ITALIAN. Bake a biscuit, made like *Iced biscuit*, in a plain, round mould; cut it across, in slices an inch thick; pour on each slice a spoonful of true maraschino, and when they have imbibed this, place them in their proper form, and mask the whole, either with white of egg and sugar, as biscuit with sweetmeats, or with apricot marmalade, on which strew pounded macaroons.

BISCUITS OF ITALIAN WATER. Whisk up six eggs, and an equal weight of power-sugar, for half an hour. Take six more eggs and their weight of flour, and mix all together, and lay this mixture on paper, in cakes the eighth of an inch thick, and about two inches diameter; lay them quite flat, and do not let them touch. The oven should be hot; five minutes will bake them. When cold, wet the under side of the paper, and they will then remove easily.

BISCUITS, JUDGES. Break six eggs into a basin, and whisk them well for five minutes, add half a pound of powder-sugar, and whisk again for ten minutes longer; put some caraway-seeds and half a pound of dry sifted flour; mix them all together with a wooden spoon. Drop them on paper about the size of a crown-piece, and thick in the middle; sift sugar over, and bake them in a brick oven. Take them off the paper while hot.

BISCUITS, LIGHT. Take ten eggs, put the yolks of five in a pan with a few crisped orange-flowers, the peel of a green lemon, both shred fine, and three-quarters of a pound of fine sugar; beat the whole together till the sugar is dissolved and well mixed with the eggs. Beat the ten whites to a froth, and add to the sugar, stir in lightly, and by degrees, six ounces of flour, put them into buttered moulds, powdering them with fine sugar, and bake them in a moderate oven.

BISCUITS, MANQUES. Put into an earthen pan half a pound of powder-sugar, three-quarters of a pound of flour, a quarter of a pound of butter, the same of pounded almonds, a little salt, and some orange-flower water, six yolks, and two whole eggs; beat up these ingredients well; whip the six whites, and mix them gradually with the above preparation; make a paper case, butter and pour in it your biscuit paste and bake it. Meanwhile cut some almonds into either dice or slips, mix them with some powder-sugar and white of egg; when the biscuit *manques* is about three parts done, *dorez* and cover it with this latter mixture; then replace it in the oven and finish baking. As soon as it is done, take it out and cut it into whatever forms your fancy may dictate.

BISCUITS, MARBLED. Make twenty-four eggs, a pound of powder-sugar, and three-quarters of a pound of dried and sifted flour, into a biscuit paste, as directed for *Spoon Biscuits*; then beat four ounces of dissolved chocolate in an earthen pan, and add to it a third of the paste; when it is well mixed, divide it in half, and to one half mix a quarter of the biscuit-paste, which will tinge that portion a light chocolate color. After this, mix together some vegetable red and infusion of saffron to color half the remaining paste orange; then divide that again, and mix the last quarter with half the orange-color, thus your paste will be colored with two shades of chocolate and two of orange.

Make two paper cases, each eight inches square and three high, pour into one of these a large spoonful of the chocolate-paste, and when it has spread over the bottom of the case, pour in one of the orange-colored, on which another of the chocolate, and so on, alternately, until the case is half full; then sprinkle it with flour, and put it into a slow oven for three-quarters of an hour. Put the remainder of your biscuit-paste (both colors) into a pan and stir them together with a spoon till the whole is veined, or clouded with the two colors, pour it into the other case, sprinkle it with flour and bake like the former; when quite cold, cut them into slices about two inches thick, half of which should be broken, and the other half cut in pieces of an equal size, lay them on a baking-plate, and dry them in the oven. These are generally used to make the rocks in ornamental pastry, and may be colored with the usual materials, according to your fancy.

BISCUITS, MARCHPANE. Beat a pound of sweet almonds to a very fine paste, moisten them with water, then put them and a pound of powder-sugar into a saucepan, over a clear but not fierce charcoal fire, stirring constantly, till the paste leaves adhere together; put it on a floured slab, and work it well with your hands for some time, then roll small pieces of it about three inches long and half the thickness of your little finger, join the ends of each and make them into round rings, lay them on a sieve in a dry warm place for two or three days. When wanted, mix some powder-sugar with the whites of eight eggs, and beat them with a wooden spoon in each hand, add a cup of orange-flower water. Put your rings into this icing, and cover them completely; lay them on a sheet of paper and bake in a slow oven until the icing sets and they begin to change color. Do not remove them from the paper till cold.

BISCUITS, MILLEFRUIT. Take preserved orange and lemon-peel, a quarter of a pound of each, six ounces of angelica, the same of sweet, and one ounce of bitter almonds; cut all the above ingredients into pieces half an inch long and a quarter wide. Make an icing with white of eggs, sugar and orange-flower water; put the almonds, &c. into this, and having paper on your baking-tin, lay the cakes on it, of whatever size you please; then with a hair pencil touch them here and there with a little cochineal. Bake them, but not in too hot an oven.

BISCUITS, MONKEY. Take the weight of six eggs in powder-sugar, and mix it with the yolks and a little pounded cinnamon; whisk the whites to a firm froth, and stir them lightly into the yolks; add four whole eggs, and their weight of dry sifted flour, mix them well together; take this mixture in a spoon, and lay it in about the size of a half-crown piece on paper, join two together with the spoon, and when your paper is full, sprinkle powder-sugar over and bake them; a few minutes will do them. Remove them from the paper while hot and put the two undersides together.

BISCUITS, PRINCESS AMELIA. Put the whites of twelve eggs into an earthen pan, whisk them to a thick snow, and add to them eight ounces of double refined sugar, pounded and sifted; having mixed them, put in three ounces of flour, and three of powder-sugar sifted, the grated rind of one or two lemons and half a coffee cup of orange-flower water, stir them well with a wooden spoon, but take care not to spoil the snow: drop them on paper of a larger size than the sweet biscuits, and bake them to a clear brown in a moderate oven. Take them from the paper while hot.

BISCUITS, SAVOY. Whip twelve whites of eggs to a snow; beat the yolks with a pound and a quarter of powder-sugar, mix them together, with three-quarters of a pound of flour and the grated rind of a lemon, into a paste, rub your mould with melted butter, and bake it.

BISCUITS, LARGE SAVOY. Take fifty-six eggs, four pounds of sugar, the *zestes* of four oranges, a pound and three-quarters of potatoe-flour sifted; and make your biscuit as follows: grate the *zestes* of the oranges on a piece of sugar, and as soon as it becomes colored, scrape it off, and grate again until all the *zeste* is done, then dry the sugar perfectly, crush and sift it.

Break your eggs one by one, (taking care that all are perfectly fresh; ) put the yolks and whites into separate vessels; mix half your sugar with the former, stirring it in with a spatula until perfectly smooth, then add the remainder, and work it well for twenty minutes. Whip the whites till quite firm, putting in a small quantity of pounded alum; when sufficiently whipped, which may be known by little points rising when the whisk is taken out; mix a little with the yolks; still, however, keeping the whites stirring; then pour the yolks on them very gently mixing them together as you pour, with the whisk: sift over the whole a pound of pota-toe-flour, stirring the mixture all the time; when ready to put into the mould, your paste should be very smooth, and somewhat of the consis-tence of treacle. Butter the mould, and put in a few spoonfuls of your paste at first, to prevent any globules of air appearing on the top when baked; pour in the remainder carefully. Cover a baking-plate with hot ashes, lay the mould in the midst of them, and place it in a moderate oven; keep it open for an hour, that the biscuit may be watched, and if it takes color too quickly, cover it with paper. In three hours time take it from the oven, and if it be of a good color, and firm, turn it on a baking-tin, tie round it a band of double paper, and replace it in the oven for a quarter of an hour to dry.

IBID, WITH ALMONDS. The ingredients for this biscuit are the same as above, with the addition of four eggs, and half a pound of bitter almonds: blanch the almonds, then wash, drain, and dry them in a napkin; pound them with whites of eggs in the usual way, to a fine paste, pass it through a sieve, and then mix it with the additional eggs; add this to the sugar and yolks, and proceed as above.

BISCUITS, SPICE. Take three pounds of flour, three pounds of almonds, cut in half, three ounces of cinnamon and mace pounded, and one pound of powder-sugar; mix them all to-gether on your slab; boil three pounds of Lisbon sugar with some water; make the above ingredi-ents into a paste with this, and roll it to the size of a large rolling-pin; lay it on a sheet of paper, flat it down a little with your hand, keeping it higher in the middle than at the ends; put it into a very hot oven; when done, take it out, and while hot, cut it across, in slices an eighth of an inch thick, and dry them.

BISCUITS, FINE SPONGE. Break twelve eggs, separate the yolks and whites; to the for-mer put three quarters of a pound of pow-der-sugar, stir them well with a wooden spoon, till it rises in large bladders; whisk the whites to a very firm froth, and then mix them very lightly with the yolks and sugar, and when incorpo-rated, add ten ounces of fine dried and sifted flour. Stir them all together well, and pour the mixture into well-buttered tin moulds, sift sugar over, and bake them in a moderate oven. Take them from the tins while hot.

BISCUITS, SPOON. Break four eggs, put the yolks and whites into separate basins; add to the former a quarter of a pound of pow-der-sugar; having grated on it the *zeste* of a lemon, mix these together well with a spatula for ten minutes; then whip the whites to a froth, and put about half of them to the yolks, and when that is well mixed in, add the rest; stir it very lightly, and lay them with a spoon on pa-per, make them about three inches long, and the breadth of a finger. Glaze them with pow-der-sugar, and place them on baking tins, add, as the sugar dissolves, and they shine, put the biscuits into a moderate oven, which must be kept open for seven or eight minutes then close it until your biscuits are of a proper color. When cold, detach them from the paper with a thin knife-blade, and lay them by, in couples, the glazed sides outwards, till wanted

BISCUITS, SWEET. Take half a pound of fine pounded sugar, and sift it through a tammy. Put the whites of twelve eggs into a preserv-ing-pan, and the yolks into an earthenware tu-reen; whip the whites to a snow, and then care-fully pour on it the yolks and sugar; stir them gently; place your pan over a chafing-dish; con-tinue whipping the whole for a full half hour, and then, if the drop which falls from the whisk lays a little while without spreading, take it from the fire, and whisk again till it is cold; then add half a pound of fine sifted flour, stir it in gently with a wooden spoon. Drop them on paper, sift sugar over, and bake them in a warm oven until of a deep yellow; take them from the papers while warm; bake them as soon as possible after they are dropt on paper.

BISCUITS, SWEETMEAT. Cut some Naples biscuits into pieces about an inch thick, and an inch and a half square, and just crisp them in the oven. Make some icing with whites of eggs, sugar, and orange-flower water; dip one side of the biscuit into it; cut some preserved lemon and orange-peel and angelica into small pieces; strew them over the biscuits, and dry the icing in the oven.

BISCUITS, TOAD-IN-A-HOLE. Beat a pound of sweet, and an ounce and a half of bitter almonds to a fine smooth paste, moisten with water, and mix the paste, which should not be too thin, with a pound and a quarter of white sugar. Lay a sheet of writing-paper on your baking-plate, and wafer-paper on that; lay the biscuits about the size of a half-crown piece; put a dried cherry in the middle of each; sift sugar over and bake them in a moderate oven. When done, cut the wafer-paper round, but do not take it away.

BLACKBERRY WINE. Put full ripe blackberries into a large vessel with a cock in it, pour on as much boiling water as will cover them, and as soon as the heat will permit, bruise them well with the hand till all the berries are broken; cover them, and in about three or four days, when the berries rise to the top, draw off the clear part into another vessel; add to every ten quarts of the liquor one pound of sugar, stir it well in, and let it stand a week or ten days to work. Draw it off through a jelly-bag. Steep four ounces of isinglass in a pint of sweet wine for twelve hours, then boil it slowly till dissolved, put it in a gallon of the blackberry juice, boil them together and then put all together; let it stand a few days, and bottle.

BLANC-MANGE, DUTCH. Put a pint of cleared calf's-foot jelly into a stewpan; mix with it the yolks of six eggs, set it over a fire, and whisk till it begins to boil; then set the pan in cold water, and stir the mixture till nearly cold, to prevent it from curdling, and when it begins to thicken fill the moulds.

BLANC-MANGE, FRENCH. Blanch one pound of sweet, and a score of bitter almonds: drain them on a sieve, and afterwards dry them,

by rubbing them in a napkin; pound them in a mortar, continually moistening them with half a tea-spoonful of water at a time, to prevent their oiling. When they are pounded as fine as possible, take them out of the mortar, and put them into a pan; then with a silver spoon, beat up your almonds gradually, with five glasses of filtered water; after this, spread a napkin over an oval dish, and put your almonds upon it; then gather up the corners of your napkin, and wring it very tight, to press out all the milk from the almonds; then put into this milk, twelve ounces of crystallized sugar, broken into small pieces; when the sugar is dissolved, pass the whole through a napkin; and then add to it one ounce of clarified isinglass, rather warmer than lukewarm; and when the whole is well incorporated together, pour it into your mould. Your mould should be previously put into ten pounds of pounded ice; when your blanc-mange is ready to serve, (which will be in two hours after it has been put into the mould,) you must take it out of the mould according to the rule prescribed in *Violet Jelly.*

BLANC-MANGE WITH FRUIT. Boil an ounce and a half of isinglass, and when quite dissolved, strain it. Let it cool for half an hour, skim, and pour it free from sediment into another pan; then whisk with it a table-spoonful of cedrat, and half a pound of current jelly, strawberry, or raspberry jam; and when it begins to jelly, fill the moulds.

BLANC-MANGE, WITHOUT EITHER ISINGLASS OR ICING. Prepare your almonds in the same manner as in the receipt for Blanc-mange *à la Francaise*, but only using half the quantity specified in that receipt, and likewise leaving out the isinglass. Then put into a pan the whites of four eggs, and whip them till they begin to whiten, then add your blanc-mange, and place your pan over hot ashes, and continue to whip your preparation until the egg is thoroughly mixed with the almonds, and the whole begins to turn to a thick cream; and when it is of a proper consistence, pour into little cups, and serve it either hot or cold.

When you wish to serve this entremet in little cups, and of any flavor you please, you must only make use of two-thirds of the quantity of almonds, named in the receipt for *Blanc-mange French.*

BOUCHEES DE DAMES. Mix with six eggs, a quarter of a pound of sugar, three ounces of potato-flour, a little salt, and a pinch of dried orange-flowers: beat them together well, and having buttered a tin, lay your paste on it, and bake it in a gentle oven for a quarter of an hour; when done, cut it in pieces, about the size of a crown piece, and glaze them, mask them according to your pleasure, and dry them in the oven.

BOUCHEES PETITES, GLACEES. Roll some puff paste to about the eighth of an inch in thickness, and with a plain round paste-cutter, of two inches diameter, cut out as many cakes as you may require; then with a smaller cutter, take out the middle of half the number, so as to make rings of them; moisten the edges of the former, and lay the rings on them; wet them also as you lay them down, sprinkle them lightly with powder sugar, and bake them in a brisk oven. These *bouchees* require great attention in baking, as the sugar is apt to dissolve and color too quickly; when done, they should be of a reddish tinge. Fill them with sweetmeats, preserves, or whipped cream, according to fancy.

BOUCHEES DE MONSIEUR. Pound a stick of vanilla with two ounces of powder-sugar, and then sift it; mix with it seven additional ounces of dry powder-sugar, and half a pound of sifted flour; add to this the whites of four eggs, whipped firm, and work them together till the paste is very smooth and soft. Heat two copper-plates, rub them over with wax, and then wipe them; when cold, lay the paste with a knife, in pieces about the size of a filbert, shaded quite round, leave three-quarters of an inch space between each; when the plates are full, put them on stools in an oven, so that they can receive no heat from below, then put a stove with hot coals on the top of the oven, and let them remain in this state for twenty-four hours; then put them for fifteen or twenty minutes into a moderate oven. Take them from the plates whilst hot, and as soon as cold, finish them in the same way as *bouchees de dames*; glaze them with chocolate, *a la rose*, with pistachios, or-

ange, cedrat, &c. &c. They may also be masked with sugar, pistachios, currants, &c.

BOUCHEES PETITES, MERINGUES AUX PISTACHES. Make them the same as above, strew sugar over without wetting the rings, and bake them to a light color in a moderate oven. Then mix a quarter of a pound of powder-sugar with three whites of eggs, well whipped, and mask the *bouchees* lightly with it, and glaze them with sugar; having ready a quarter of a pound of pistachio-nuts blanched, and each cut across sloping; place these pieces round the edge of the *bouchees* like a crown; and each piece of the pistachios being placed on the cut side, they stand out from the edge of the *bouchee*: this process being finished, put them in the oven again a few minutes, to color the egg; and in the meantime stir up the white of egg which remains, and make with it half as many *meringuees* as you have *bouchees*, sprinkle them with sugar, and color both sides of them in a slow oven; and when the *bouchees* are ready for table, fill them with whipped cream, with pistachios, and cover each with half a *meringue.*

BOUCHEES PETITES, PERLEES. Your *bouchees* being made and baked as above, whip the whites of two eggs to a firm froth, and mix them with four spoonfuls of sifted sugar, and when very smooth, mask your *bouchees* with it: then take some white of egg, and with the point of a knife, drop them in pearls about the size of a grape-stone, round each *bouchee*, half an inch apart, sprinkle them lightly with sugar, and dry the egg in the oven, taking care they do not lose their whiteness.

When cold, place between each pearl a smaller one of red-currant jelly. Fill your *bouchees* with apricot marmalade, apple-jelly, &c.; if, however, the jelly, or whatever else you may use, be of a red color, your intermediate pearls should be composed of light-colored preserve, such as apricot marmalade, &c. These should be pearled a few at a time only.

BOUCHEES PETITES, PRALINEES. Having prepared the *bouchees* as usual, *dorez* and bake them in a moderate oven; when they are of the proper color, mask them with whites of eggs mixed with sugar, and almonds minced very small; replace them in the oven a minute or two, and then strew red, or any other colored sugar on them, but not so thick as to cover the almonds entirely. Fill the *bouchees* as usual.

BOUCHEES PETITS, A LA REINE. The same as above, only the paste must be cut thicker, and before you *dorez*, let them stand a few minutes. Bake in a brisk oven.

BUCKTHORN, SIRUP OF. (1) Gather the berries in the heat of the day, and set in an earthen vessel in the oven; squeeze out the juice, and for each peck of berries put two pounds of white sugar, and boil them together a quarter of an hour; let it cool, and then bottle it.

BUCKTHORN, SIRUP OF. (2) Take three quarts of the juice of clarified buckthorn berries, and four pounds of brown sugar; make them into a sirup over a gentle fire, and while warm, mix with it a drachm of the distilled oil of cloves, dissolved on a lump of sugar. The true buckthorn may be known by the number of its seeds, having four, the alder buckthorn has only two, and the cherry buckthorn one seed. The former is to be used.

BUTTER, BLACK. Three pounds of fruit, currants, gooseberries, raspberries, and cherries, to a pound of coarse sugar, boiled till quite thick. It must waste to half the quantity.

## C.

CAKES MADE OF FLOWERS. Boil double refined sugar to a candy height, and strew in your flowers and let them boil once up; then, with your hand, lightly strew in a little double refined sugar sifted, and put it directly into little pans made of card, and pricked full of holes at the bottom; you must set the pans on a cushion, and when they are cold, take them out.

CAKES, HONEYCOMB. Boil your sugar to a candy height; then put in your flowers, which must be cut; have little papers with four corners ready; drop some of your candy on the papers, take them off when ready, and if they are rightly done, they will look full of holes like honeycombs.

CAKES, LIQUORICE. Take hyssop and red rose water, of each half a pint; half a pound of green liquorice, the outside scraped off, and then beat with a pestle; put to it half a pound of aniseeds, and steep it all night in the water; boil it with a gentle fire till the taste is well out of the liquorice; strain it, put to it three pounds of liquorice powder, and set it on a gentle fire till it is come to the thickness of cream; take it off, and put to it half a pound of white sugar candy seered very fine; beat this well together for at least three hours, and never suffer it to stand still; as you beat it, you must strew in double-refined sugar finely seered, at least three pounds; half an hour before it is finished, put in half a spoonful of gum dragon, steeped in orange-flower water: when it is very white then it is beat enough; roll it up with white sugar, and if you want it perfumed, put in a pastil or two.

CANDYING. Fruit intended for candying must be first preserved, and dried in a stove before the fire, that none of the sirup may remain in it. Sugar intended for the use of candying must be thus prepared: put into a tossing-pan a pound of sugar, with half a pint of water, and set it over a very clear fire. Take off the scum as it rises; boil it till it looks clear and fine, and take out a little in a silver spoon. When it is cold, if it will draw a thread from your spoon, it is boiled enough for any kind of sweetmeat. Then boil your sirup, and when it begins to candy round the edge of your pan, it is candy height. It is a great mistake to put any kind of sweetmeat into too thick a sirup, especially at the first, as it withers the fruit, and both the beauty and flavor are thereby destroyed.

CANDY FLOWERS. Take the best treble-refined sugar, break it into lumps, and dip it piece by piece into water; put them into a vessel of silver, and melt them over the fire; when it just boils, strain it, and set it on the fire again, and let it boil till it draws in hairs, which you may perceive by holding up your spoon; then put in the flowers, and set them in cups or glasses. When it is of a hard candy, break it in lumps, and lay it as high as you please. Dry it in a stove, or in the sun, and it will look like sugar-candy.

CANDY, ALL SORTS OF FRUIT. When finished in the sirup, put a layer into a new sauce, and dip it suddenly into hot water, to take off the sirup that hangs about it; put it on a napkin before the fire to drain, and then do some more on the sieve. Have ready-sifted double-refined sugar, which sift over the fruit on all sides, till quite white. Set it on the shallow end of the sieves in a lightly-warm oven, and turn it two or three times. It must not be cold till dry. Watch it carefully, and it will be beautiful.

CANELLONS. Make a stiff paste, with a little melted butter, a spoonful or two of water, some rasped lemon-peel, an egg, a quarter of a pound of flour, and half that quantity of sugar; roll it very thin; make a little cane of card-paper, butter it well on the outside, and wrap it in some of the paste; bake it a few minutes; take out the card, and fill the paste with currant jelly, or any other jelly or sweetmeat you please.

CANNELLONS MERINGUES. Whip the whites of two eggs, and having mixed them with two spoonfuls of powder-sugar, then mask the cannellons; when baked, crush a quarter of a pound of fine sugar, and roll the cannellons in it; replace them a few minutes in the oven, and then finish. The masking of these cannellons may be varied according to taste, with pistachios, dried currants, &c. the former cut in pieces, the latter well washed, dried and mixed with an equal quantity of sugar.

CAPILLAIRE, SIRUP OF. The capillaire of Canada, although that of Montpelier is equally good, is a very odoriferous vegetable, light and agreeable, but so extremely volatile, that the greatest part of it is dissipated during the preparation of the sirup. To preserve then the odour of the capillaire, when your sirup is sufficiently done, pour it, whilst boiling, upon some fresh capillaire coarsely chopped up; then cover your vessel, and let it stand until it is quite cold, then pass it through a bolting-cloth to separate it from the leaves of the capillaire.

Take one ounce of the capillaire from Canada; put it into a glazed pan, pour upon it four pints of boiling water, leave it to infuse for twelve hours over some warm ashes; strain it and let it run into a vessel, it will give you a strong tincture of capillaire; melt in this tincture four pounds of sugar, put the whole into a preserving-pan, and put it on the fire, and clarify it with the white of an egg, continue the cooking; when your sirup is *perle*, put some fresh capillaire, chopped, into a pan, and pour your sirup, whilst boiling, upon it; cover your pan carefully, and let it cool; when your sirup is cold; you may flavor it if you please. Put it into bottles, and cork them hermetically.

CAPILLAIRE, SIRUP OF. (2) Take some good capillaire, chop it up, not very small, put it upon a sieve; pour upon it some boiling water, and then let it infuse for ten hours in a vessel well covered; strain this infusion, and put into it some sugar boiled *au casse*; clarify this sirup with the whites of eggs whipped; skim it till it is very clear; when it rises, take it off the fire, and leave it to cool, then put it into bottles.

Viard and Beauvilliers, whose receipts are nearly the same, boil their capillaire for a quarter of an hour in river-water; after having passed this boiling through a sieve, they put into it some powder-sugar, and clarifiy their sirup with water, or a whole egg beaten up; then skim it, and when it is very clear and has boiled *au lisse*, they take it off the fire, and put into it some orange-flower water, and strain it through a napkin or straining-bag, leaving it to cool before putting it into bottles.

For three pints and a half of sirup, you must use two good ounces of capillaire, four pints of water, and four pounds of sugar, powder-sugar is the best, as it prevents sirups from candying.

CARAMEL. Break into a small copper or brass pan one pound of refined sugar; put in a gill of spring-water; set it on a fire; when it boils skim it quite clean, and let it boil quick, till it comes to the degree called crack; which may be known by dipping a tea-spoon or skewer into the sugar, and letting it drop to the bottom of a pan of cold water; and if it remains hard, it has attained that degree: squeeze in the juice of half a lemon, and let it remain one minute longer on the fire; then set the pan into another of cold water: have ready moulds of any shape; rub them over with sweet oil; dip a spoon or fork into the sugar, and throw it over the mould in fine threads, till it is quite covered: make a small handle of caramel, or stick on two or three small gum paste rings, by way of ornament, and place it over small pastry of any description.

CARAMEL CONSERVE. Clarify the quantity of sugar you may require, and boil it to caramel; have ready some cases of double paper; pour in your sugar to the thickness of half an inch, and trace on its surface the forms you wish it to have; when cold, break it according to those marks. This conserve may be colored and flavored according to the fancy.

CARAMEL COVER FOR SWEET-MEATS. Dissolve eight ounces of double-refined sugar in three or four spoonfuls of water, and three or four drops of lemon-juice; then put it into a copper untinned skillet; when it boils to be thick, dip the handle of a spoon in it, and put that into a pint basin of water, squeeze the sugar from the spoon into it, and so on till you have all the sugar. Take a bit out of the water, and if it snaps and is brittle when cold, it is done enough; but only let it be three parts cold, then pour the water from the sugar, and having a copper mould oiled well, run the sugar on it, in the manner of a maze, and when cold you may put it on the dish it is to cover; but if, on trial, the sugar is not brittle, pour off the water, and return it into the skillet, and boil it again. It should look thick like treacle, but of a bright light gold color. It makes a most elegant cover.

CARDAMUM COMFITS. Procure your cardamums at the chemists, and they will be in a shell; put them into the oven to dry the skins, and they will break; pick all the seeds from them, put the seeds into a large comfit-pan, and have a fire under the same as for others; mix your gum, starch, and sirup, and finish them the same as caraway comfits.

CARAWAY CAKE. Dry a quarter of a peck of fine flour in an oven; rub a pound and a half of fresh butter in it, till it is crumbled so small that none of it is to be seen; then take six spoon-fuls of rose water, half a pint of canary, half a pint of cream, and three-quarters of a pint of new ale yeast, and the whites of two, and yolks of four eggs; mix all these well together, let it lie before the fire, and when you make it up put in a pound and a half of Naples biscuits, and three-quarters of a pound of caraway-comfits. Bake it.

CARAWAY COMFITS. Take some fine caraway seeds, sift all the dust from them, and have a large copper preserving-pan, about two feet wide, and with two handles and two pieces of iron made as a ring on each side; then you must have a pulley fixed to the beam, and a cord with a hook to each end, so as to fix it at each side of the pan to let it sling; then have some fine starch as white as you can get, and just soften it, boil some sirup a quarter of an hour, and mix it with the starch; take some gum arabic, put it into some water, then put that into another pan, and make it just warm; have an iron-pot with charcoal fire under the large pan, but not too hot, only just to keep the pan warm; have a large tub to put your pot of fire at bottom, and your large pan must be on the top; put the caraway seeds into your pan; add a large ladleful of gum arabic, rub them with your hands until you find they are all dry, then put a ladleful of starch and sirup, and do the same over your pan of fire, until you find they are all dry; put the gum only three or four times to them at first, then the starch and sugar, but boil your sirup more as you find they come to coat with it, and not so much starch; when you have dried them seven or eight times, put them into your sieve; put them into the stove, do them the next day, and so, successively, for six or seven days.

CARAWAY DRAGEES. Take any quantity of caraway seeds you think proper, put them into a preserving-pan, and when quite warm, put in clarified sugar, a little at a time, stirring it occasionally, till of the size you wish; then proceed as directed for *Almond Dragees*.

CASSIA CANDIED. Pound a little musk and ambergris with as much of the powder of cassia as will lie on two shillings. Having pounded them well together, take a quarter of a pound of fine sugar, and as much water as will wet it, and boil it to a candy height, then put in your powder and mix well together. Butter some pewter saucers, and when it is cold turn it out.

CASSIA RATAFIA OF. Take a pound of cassia, half a pound of bitter cherries, a quarter of a pound of cassia leaves, and half a drachm of cinnamon, bruise the two first, cut up the leaves, and pound the cinnamon, infuse these ingredients in three quarts of brandy for three weeks. Dissolve two pounds of sugar in a quart of water, and mix with the *liqueur*, and let it stand some time longer, then strain and bottle it. Cork it up close.

CEDRATS, BLANCMANGE OF. Grate the rind of a cedrat upon some sugar in the usual way, until six ounces of sugar have been used; blanch and pound a pound of sweet almonds, moistening them with water; when perfectly smooth, dilute them with five glasses of water put in by degrees; then pour them in a napkin, and squeezing it, express the milk of almonds from them; divide this into two equal parts, with one of which mix the six ounces of sugar with the cedrat, and with the other portion, mix the same quantity of plain sugar; as soon as both are dissolved, strain them, and put in each half an ounce of isinglass: your mould being placed in ice, pour into it the white blancmange to three-quarters of an inch in depth; as soon as that is set, pour in an equal quantity of the other, which ought to be of a clear yellow; when that also is set, pour in some white, and so on alternately, till the mould is full. Turn out the blancmange as directed in *Blancmange French*.

CEDRAT, CONSERVE OF. Grate the rind of a cedrat all round, until the juice is ready to ooze out; this must be done by rubbing it against a large piece of sugar, (about a pound;) remove the surface of this sugar, to which the grated rind adheres, with a knife, and squeeze to it half the juice of the cedrat. Dissolve the remainder of the sugar to the degree *grande plume*, then take it from the fire, and when it has stood a little while, put in your cedrat, stirring it with a spoon, until a sort of ice forms on the top; you may then pour your conserve into moulds. Be careful not to put it in too hot.

CEDRAT ZESTES, JELLY OF. Take three-quarters of a pound of lump sugar, grate on it the *zestes* of two cedrats, and, as the sugar becomes colored, scrape it off with a knife, and grate again, and so on until all the *zeste* is gone; dissolve the scraped sugar in two glasses of water, and with the juice of four lemons, pass it through a jelly bag. Clarify the remainder of the sugar, and then put a fourth of it into a small preserving pan; boil it to caramel height, to color the jelly; mix this, the fruit, the sirup, and an ounce of isinglass together, and finish in the usual way.

CHANTILLY BASKET. Dip some ratafia cakes into clarified sugar boiled to caramel height; place them round the inside of a dish; then cut more ratafia cakes into squares, dip them also into sugar, and pile them corner-ways on the row, and so on for two or three stories high. Line the inside with wafer-paper, and fill it with sponge biscuit, sweetmeats, blanched almonds, or some made cream; put trifle over that, and garnish the froth with rose-leaves, colored comfits, or caramel sugar thrown lightly over the top.

CHERRIES IN BRANDY. Choose the finest and ripest cherries, leave on half the stalks, and put them into very cold water. In about half an hour take them out, and drain them on a sieve; weigh them, and to every pound of fruit, allow a quarter of a pound of sugar; when you have clarified and boiled it to *grand perle*, put in the fruit, boil them up two or three times, stirring them gently with a skimmer; then take them from the fire carefully, and put the cherries into bottles or glass jars; when filled, add to each twelve cloves and half an ounce of cinnamon tied in a linen bag. Put to the sugar, when nearly cold, brandy (in the proportion of a pint and a half to a pound of fruit); mix them together well, and pour them on the cherries. In two months time taste them, and if sufficiently flavored, take out the cloves and cinnamon. Cover the jars or bottles close.

CHERRIES, TO CANDY. The fruit must be gathered before it is ripe; prick and stone them; boil clarified sugar, and pour it over them.

CHERRY ICE. Take the stones and stalks from two pounds of ripe cherries, bruise, and set them on the fire with a little water, and half a pound of sugar. When they have boiled, pass them through a hair sieve into an earthen pan. Pound a handful of the kernels, put them in a basin with the juice of two lemons. Add to the cherries a pound of sugar *au petit lisse*, and strain on them the lemon-juice and kernels; mix the whole together, and put it in a *sabotiere*, with pounded ice. Work the cherries up with it well, until it has set, then place it in glasses.

CHERRY ICE CREAM. Take half a pound of preserved cherries, pound them, stones and all; put them into a basin, with one gill of sirup, the juice of a lemon, and a pint of cream, pass it through a sieve, and freeze it according to custom.

CHERRY MARMALADE. Choose the ripest, largest, best red colored cherries, you can meet with, and take of them double the weight of the sugar you intend to use; stone and tail; and then put them on a gentle fire, and keep stirring them till reduced to half. Clarify and boil your sugar to *petit casse*, then add the fruit to it, and stir it until you can see the bottom of the pan; the marmalade is then sufficiently done, and may be put into pots.

CHERRY MARCHPANE. Take three pounds of sweet almonds, two and a half of sugar, and a pound of cherries; pound the almonds to a paste, and mix it with the sugar, boiled to *petit boule*; then having stoned, well bruised, and squeezed out the juice of the cherries, add it to the rest, stir it well, place it on hot ashes, stirring constantly until the paste is properly done; then finish it in the usual way, (See MARCHPANE.) Strawberries, raspberries, currants, or any other fruit may be used in the same way.

CHERRY RATAFIA. Crush ten pounds of cherries, and put them into a jar with a quart of brandy; cover the jar close, and infuse the cherries for five or six days; at the end of that time put the fruit into a cloth, and press the juice out through. Boil five pounds of fine currants, with three pounds of sugar, and press out the juice as you did that of the cherries; mix the two juices, measure them, and for every pint allow a pint of brandy. Add a pound of the kernels of the cherry-stones, half a pound of coriander, a little mace, some cloves and cinnamon, all well pounded, put them into a jar, and pour the liquor over them; cover it close and let it infuse for six weeks, after which, pass the whole through a jelly-bag, and bottle it; cork it carefully.

CHERRIES, SIRUP OF. The best cherries for this purpose are the black sour ones; take out the stones and express the juice into an earthen pan, where it must stand in a cool place for twenty-four hours to clear: at the end of that time pour the juice gently into a pan, and add to it, for each pound of juice, two pounds of crushed sugar, and two drachms of cinnamon, previously infused in a glass of water, wrap the cinnamon in a piece of linen, and put it with the water into your pan; boil all together for half an hour, skimming it carefully. When sufficiently done take out the cinnamon; strain the sirup till quite clear, and when cold bottle it.

CHESTNUTS IN CARAMEL. (1) Roast chestnuts as for the table; take off the skins; dip each in the whites of eggs beaten, and then roll them in powder-sugar; lay them separately on paper to dry, in a moderate oven; they may be cut into different forms if you think proper, and glazed either white or brown.

CHESTNUTS IN CARAMEL. (2) Cut some osier rods or reeds into pieces about two or three inches long, and on the point of each put a roasted and skinned chestnut. Take a piece of very fresh butter, (about the size of a nut), and rub it with the palm of the hand, on an iron plate or marble slab, taking care to rub every part well. Then having boiled some clarified sugar to *caramel* height; take a piece of the osier, with a chestnut on the end, in each hand, and dip them in the sugar, twisting them round repeatedly, that the sugar may adhere equally about the chestnut till it begins to cool, then lay them on the buttered slab, and dip in two more, proceeding as above; when all are done and cold, take out the osier twigs, and wrap each chestnut in paper, with a device if you think proper. These chestnuts make a delicious sweetmeat, but they should be eaten the day on which they are made.

CHESTNUT COMPOTE. (1) Take the outer skin from about a hundred chestnuts, and then put them into a saucepan with water, a lemon cut in pieces, and three handfuls of bran; put them on the fire and blanch them: as soon as a pin will go into them easily, they are sufficiently done; rub off the second skin, and throw them into cold water, with the juice of a lemon. Clarify and boil a pound and a half of sugar to *petit lisse*, and having drained your chestnuts, put them into the sugar with the juice of a lemon, the quarter of a glass of orange-flower water; put these on the fire for a short time, but not to let them boil: then take them off and set them by. The next day drain the chestnuts, and boil up the sirup four times; then add more sugar, and having boiled it to *souffle*, put in the chestnuts; blanch them instantly afterwards, and put them into compotiers.

CHESTNUT COMPOTE. (2) Roast your chestnuts as for the dessert, and when they are peeled and skinned, put them into a saucepan, with a quarter of a pound of sugar, and half a glass of water; let them simmer for a quarter of an hour; squeeze in a little lemon-juice, and when ready to serve, strew powder-sugar over them.

CHESTNUT CREAM. (1) Pound twenty-five roasted chestnuts in a mortar, with a little milk; then put the paste so made into a stewpan, with the yolks of two eggs, half a pint of milk, two ounces of butter, and four ounces of powder-sugar; when it has boiled a little while, strain it, put it into a dish, or glass for table, and let it cool.

CHESTNUT CREAM. (2) Roast, and then pound a quarter of a hundred of chestnuts, with a small quantity of milk; to this add the yolks of two eggs, a pint of milk, a quarter of a pound of powder-sugar, and about an ounce of butter. Boil these together for some minutes, then strain it, and set it by to cool.

CHESTNUT CUSTARD. Take three pounds of well roasted chestnuts, removing such parts as were colored by the fire, and pound them with a pound of fresh butter; when a smooth paste, add three-quarters of a pound of powder-sugar, the yolks of twelve eggs, a pinch of salt, and a few spoonfuls of whipped cream, the whites whipped firm, and finish the custard as directed.

CHESTNUT PASTE. Make a marmalade by boiling chestnuts in water, and rubbing them through a sieve, then pound them, and to three-quarters of a pound of this, add a quarter of a pound of any other fruit marmalade; mix them well up with an equal weight of sugar boiled to *grand plume*; put it into your moulds and bake it as cherry, or any other paste.

CHINESE TEMPLE. Haviing boiled an ounce of double-refined sugar, with half an ounce of butter, and a little water, set it by till cold, and then add to it an egg well beaten. With this, make four ounces of flour into a very stiff paste; roll it out as thin as possible, and lay it in a set of tins the form of a temple, and bake them in a slow oven. When cold, take the paste from the tins, and join each piece together according to the proper forms, with isinglass and water. The lower part, of course, ought to be stronger than the top, in order that it may sustain the weight of the whole. The pieces also must be cut as exact as possible to the shape of the tins.

CHOCOLATE ALMONDS. Take a pound of chocolate finely grated, and a pound and a half of the best sugar, finely sifted; soak some gum-dragon in orange-flower water, and work them into what form you please; the paste must be stiff; dry them in a stove. You may write devices on paper, roll them up, and put them in the middle.

CHOCOLATE BONBONS. Put a quarter of a pound of chocolate over a fire, to dissolve it; and having boiled two pounds of sugar to *forte perle*, put a spoonful or two into the chocolate; stir it till it forms a thin paste, and then pour it on the sugar, and boil both together to *caramel*. In the meantime melt a little butter, skim, and pour it off clear into a basin; take a spoonful of it, and rub it with your hand over a marble slab or table: on this pour the chocolate and sugar; then take two ends of a sword-blade, (one in each hand), and press lines an inch apart all down it; cross them in like manner, so as to mark the sugar in small squares all over; doing it as quick as possible, lest the sugar should cool before you have done; then pass the sword-blade between the marble and the sugar; lay under the latter sheets of paper; and when cold, break it into pieces according to the marks, and wrap each square in paper.

CHOCOLATE COMFITS. Take two ounces of chocolate, beat it small with a little warm water over the fire; when it is dissolved and reduced to a paste, pour it upon a pound of *masse pain*, or sweet paste, to which add some cinnamon or vanilla at discretion; mix the whole well together; then spread it over some wafer shapes, and bake it in a moderate oven. If the paste does not appear deep colored enough, you may color it with *bolus Armenicum*.

CHOCOLATE CONSERVE. (1) Dissolve two ounces of good chocolate in a little water, put it into a skillet with half a pound of sugar boiled to *perle*; keep the sugar stirring, and when it boils put the conserve into moulds.

CHOCOLATE CONSERVE. (2) Dissolve a quarter of a pound of grated chocolate in a small quantity of clarified sugar; boil a pound of sugar to the *premiere plume*, put your chocolate into it, stirring it well to mix it; serve it whilst it is warm.

CHOCOLATE DROPS. Take one pound and a half of chocolate, put it on a pewter sheet or plate, and put it in the oven just to warm the chocolate; then put it into a copper stewpan, with three-quarters of a pound of powdered sugar; mix it well over the fire, take it off, and roll it in pieces the size of small marbles, put them on white paper, and when they are all on, take the sheet of paper by each corner, and lift it up and down so that the paper may touch the table each time, and by that means you will see the drops come quite fat, about the size of a six-pence; put some sugar nonpareils over them, and cover all that are on the paper, then shake them off, and you will see all the chocolate

drops are covered with the sugar nonpareils; let them stand till cold, and they will come off well, and then put them in a box papered.

CHOCOLATE ICE CREAM. (1) Take any quantity of chocolate, melt it over the fire in a small pan; when melted pour it into that in which you are to make your cream; break your yolks of eggs into it, (four eggs to every pint of cream) add some pounded loaf sugar to it, keep stirring continually; then add your cream by little and little, stirring and turning it till the whole is mixed properly together; then set your pan over the fire, and keep stirring with a wooden spoon till you see your composition is near boiling, then take it off immediately, for, from the moment you set your composition over the fire till that it offers to boil, it has sufficient time to incorporate well and thicken suffi-ciently, without need of boiling; and should you let it boil, you would risk the turning your cream into whey, on account of the yolks of eggs, which would do too much. Take great care likewise your cream is fresh and sweet, for otherwise as soon as it is warm it will turn to curds and whey; therefore, be careful, stir it continually, from the time you set it on the fire till you take it off; then put it in the sabotiere to make it congeal after the usual manner.

CHOCOLATE ICE CREAM. (2) Dissolve the chocolate in a little water on a slow fire; when properly done, mix it with a pint of cream, three yolks of new laid eggs, and about half a pound of sugar.

CHOCOLATE ICE WATER. Take three ounces of chocolate, warm it, and mix with it half a gill of sirup, and half a pint of water; mix it well, and freeze it thick.

CHOCOLATE MACAROONS. Put a quarter of a pound of chocolate on a tin-plate over a coal fire, and when it is dissolved pour it on a plate; put to it a spoonful or two of sweet almond paste, made as for macaroons, stir it in well, and then pour it upon the re-mainder of the almond paste, in which you have mixed a tea-spoonful of powdered cin-namon or vanilla, or both: beat them together well in a mortar, lay them on paper, and bake them for three-quarters of an hour in a moderate oven.

CHOCOLATE PARFAIT AMOUR. For four bottles of brandy, take one pound of the best chocolate, cut in small bits; a little salt, two cloves, and a little cinnamon; you must infuse all in the brandy, with two bottles and half a pint of water, with whites of eggs, and filter it through the paper. You must be careful not to take more than two bottles from every four, except from the cinnamon, from which you are to take as much as you can get.

CHOCOLATE PASTILS. Take a little chocolate, which put in a pan over the fire to melt it; stir it with a spoon; when it is melted, take half a pound of loaf sugar, pounded in a mortar and sifted, which dissolve in a little clear water. When that is done, put in your chocolate; if you find the paste too thick, add a little water, enough to bring it to that degree of liquidity that you may take it up on a knife; then take half a sheet of paper, and cover it with little round and flat drops, which we call *pastils*, of the size of a sixpence; let them dry naturally in a cupboard; and when dry, take them off from the paper, and put them in boxes.

CHOCOLATE PASTIL PASTE. Melt half an ounce of gum-dragon in a little water till it is quite dissolved and thick; sift it through a linen cloth, pound it in a mortar with a quarter-part of whites of eggs, a chocolate cake bruised, and half a pound of fine powder-sugar, mixed by degrees, and adding either more or less sugar, according as the paste is malleable; it must be pretty firm; form it into what flowers or designs you please, as shells, lozenges, any kind of corn or beans, &c.

CHOCOLATE PETIT PAINS. These are made in the same way as *Petits Pains a la Duchesse* (see that article), but without the *dorure*. When cold fill them with a cream *patissiere*, mixed with two ounces of vanilla chocolate, and sweetened with sugar, flavored with vanilla; then put three ounces of sifted sugar, the same of chocolate, and half the white of an egg into a pan; stir these ingredients with a silver spoon until you have a smooth transparent glaze, with which mask the top and sides of the *petite pains*, spreading it equally with the blade of a knife.

CHOCOLATE SWEETMEATS. Take two ounces of chocolate, and break it into a little warm water, put it on the fire, and when quite dissolved, mix it with a pound of marchpane paste, to which may be added vanilla or cinnamon; stir it up well, and then spread it on wafer-paper in what forms you please, and bake them in a moderate oven. If the sweetmeats be not sufficiently dark colored, add a little bol-ammoniac.

CINNAMON CAKES. Whisk up half a dozen eggs with three table-spoonfuls of rose water; add to it a pound of sifted sugar, a dessert-spoonful of powdered cinnamon, and a sufficient quantity of flour to make it into a paste; roll it out thin, and cut it into whatever forms your fancy may dictate, place them on paper, and bake them. When done, remove them from the paper. Keep them dry.

CINNAMON CANDIED. (1) Soak cinnamon in water for four and twenty hours, and then cut it into pieces ahout an inch long; prepare some sugar to *grand lisse*, and give the cinnamon a boil in it; drain and dry it in a stove to the proper consistence; then put it in the moulds with sugar boiled to *soufflé*, and when half cold, dry it. Before the candy is removed from the moulds, they should be laid on one side for some time. Keep them in paper in a dry place.

CINNAMON CANDIED. (2) Cut some cinnamon into small sticks of about an inch or an inch and a half long; then put them into thin sugar, and boil them as it were in a sirup. Then take off the pan, and set it by for five or six hours to soak, take them out and lay them on a wire-grate, dry them throughly in the stove; afterwards put them in order in tin moulds upon little grates made for the purpose, and set into the moulds, so that there may be three rows set one above another, separated by those grates. In the meantime, boil sugar till it is *blown*, and pour it into your mould, so that some of it may lie upon the uppermost grate; then set them in the stove with a covered fire, and let them stand all night; the next morning take notice whether the cinnamon be well coagulated; turn the mould upside down, and set it in the stove again, with a plate underneath; and when it is thoroughly drained, take out your sticks of cinnamon, loosening them, by little and little, gently; then lay them upon a sieve, set in the stove, and dry them thoroughly.

CINNAMON, CONSERVE OF. Bruise four drachms of cinnamon, dilute it with a little clarified sugar, or sirup of mallows; boil two pounds of sugar to *petit cassé*, throw in the cinnamon, stir it well, and then take it from the fire, and when the sugar begins to whiten, pour the conserve into cases or moulds, and dry it as usual.

CINNAMON, DRAGEES OR SUGARED. Soak a quarter of a pound of the best cinnamon in sticks, for twelve hours in water to soften it, at the end of that time, cut it into slips, lay them on a sieve in a warm place for some days. When quite hard and dry, boil some fine sugar to the degree *grand perle*; have ready a quantity of fine powder, and proceed in the same manner as in doing *Almond Dragees*, until the cinnamon sticks are of the proper thickness; those which are to be twisted or curled, should not be so thick as the others. Be equally particular in removing the sugar, that cakes on the bottom of the pan, as in making *Almond Dragees*.

CINNAMON DRAGEES, COMMON. Infuse a quarter of a pound of gum-dragon, in as much water as will cover it; the next day put the infusion into a mortar, and stir it well with a pestle, and the longer it is stirred the whiter it becomes; in rather more than a quarter of an hour, add to it the caked sugar which was removed from the preserving-pan, and which must be well pounded and sifted, also a pound of powder-sugar, a spoonful of cinnamon powder, and by degrees two or three pounds of flour; moisten the whole occasionally with water; when the paste is of a proper consistence, place it on the slab or pasteboard, knead it well for a short time, roll it out in sheets, not thicker than the eighth of an inch, and then cut it into slips of

the same size as the cinnamon (see above,) put them on paper or a sieve in a warm place for some days. Then boil some common sugar to *perle*, and sugar the slips of paste as above directed; instead of the fine powder, flour is sufficient, until the last two layers, when the powder may be used to give them whiteness. When of the requisite size, lay them on sieves to dry. In a few days there may be curled and colored, which is done in the same manner as coriander seeds. Observe, fine sugared cinnamon is always white.

CINNAMON, ESSENCE OF. This is made by infusing oil of cinnamon in highly rectified spirits of wine, in the proportion of half a drachm of the former to an ounce of the latter.

CINNAMON PASTILS. Dissolve half an ounce of gum-dragon in a glass of water, and strain it through a lawn sieve into a mortar, and add to it a tea-spoonful of powdered cinnamon, and a sufficient quantity of sifted sugar to make the paste of a proper consistence; form into such figures as you may fancy, and dry them in a stove. Keep them in a dry place.

CINNAMON SWEETMEATS. Take a pound of marchpane paste, and dilute it with as many whites of eggs as will make it spread easily with a knife; add to this, a spoonful or two of prepared *bole-ammoniac*, which will give it a fine red tinge, and half an ounce of cinnamon-powder. When all these ingredients are well mixed, cut some wafer-paper into such forms as you may think proper, and lay on them the paste about the thickness of the eighth of an inch; place them on paper, and bake them in a moderate oven. When done, they may be finished in the following manner:—Boil some sugar in orange-flower water, to *la plume*, and as you take the sweetmeats from the oven; dip a hair-pencil into the sirup, and brush them over; this dries almost immediately, and considerably improves the look of them.

CINNAMON WAFERS. Pound and sift six ounces of sugar, and put it with an equal quantity of melted fresh butter, the same of flour, half an ounce of powdered cinnamon, and a small egg; stir these up in an earthenware vessel, with a sufficient quantity of milk to make it into a thin, but not too clear, paste. Make an iron plate quite hot, rub it well with butter, then lay on it a spoonful of the paste; fry it, and when brown on both sides, roll it, still over the hot iron, round a small stick; do this until all the paste is used.

CINNAMONUM. Take a quarter of a pound of cinnamon, two drachms of mace, and one ounce of stick-liquorice; bruise them well, and then put them into three quarts of the best brandy; let the infusion stand for some days before you distil it; dissolve four pounds of sugar in three pints and a half of water; mix this sirup with the liqueur, and then strain them. This is sometimes called Oil of Cinnamon.

CITRON, CANDIED. Pare the citrons very thin and narrow, and throw them into water; these are called faggots; then cut the citron into slices of any thickness you think proper; take out the inner part with great care, so as to leave only the white ring, and put them with the faggots into boiling water; when tender, drain them. Boil a sufficient quantity of clarified sugar to *souffle*; then put in the rings, and boil them together. Take it from the fire, and when a little cool, rub the sugar against the side of the preserving-pan with the back of a spoon; as soon as it becomes white, take out the rings with a fork very carefully, one by one, and lay them on a wire-grate to drain: boil and proceed with the faggots in a similar way; when taken out, cut them into proper lengths with a pair of scissors, and lay them also on the wire to drain.

CITRON PASTE. Cut off the ends of the citrons, take out the middle, with all the seeds; boil them in some water; and when quite tender, take them from the fire, and throw them into cold water a moment; then, having pressed them in a cloth to get the water out, pound and sift them. To every quarter of a pound of this marmalade put half a pound of clarified sugar; simmer them together, stirring constantly until well mixed; then put them into moulds, and place them in a stove to dry.

CITRON WHITE PRESERVED. Lay some white citrons, cut into pieces, in salt and water for four or five hours; then, having washed them in cold water, boil them; when tender, drain, and lay them into as much clarified sugar as will cover them. The next day drain off the sirup, and boil it; when quite smooth and cold, pour it on the citrons; let them stand twenty-four hours; then boil the sirup again, and put in the citrons. The third day, boil both together, and put them into moulds to candy.

CITRON PRESERVED LIQUID. Cut a slit in the sides of some small citrons, so that the inside may take the sugar as well as the outside, and put them over the fire in some water; whenever they are near boiling, put cold water to them. As soon as the citrons rise to the top, take them out, and throw them into cold water. They must then be put on the fire again, in the same water, and boiled gently until tender; then take them out, and put them in cold water. After this, boil them seven or eight times in clarified sugar; pour the whole into an earthen pan, and let it stand. The next day drain the fruit, and boil up the sirup twenty or thirty times; add a little more sugar, and pour it over the citrons; do this for three successive days, increasing the degree to which you boil the sugar daily, so that at the last boiling the degree may be *au perle*. The fruit may then be put into pots.

To preserve them dry, they must be done exactly the same; only, instead of putting the fruit into pots, they should be dried on sieves in a stove. With the remaining sugar the citrons may be glazed.

CITRON RATAFIA. Pare seven or eight citrons very thin; cut the peel into small pieces, and put them into a jar, with three pints of brandy, and let them infuse for three weeks; then add to this a pound of sugar, boiled in half a pint of water, and well skimmed; let it stand twelve or fifteen days longer, when it may be bottled.

CITRON, SIRUP OF. (1) Put into a china bowl alternate layers of fine powder-sugar, and citron, pared, and cut in very thin slices, and let them stand till the next day; then strain off the sirup, and clarify it over a gentle fire.

CITRON, SIRUP OF. (2) Put the rinds of

three citrons into an earthen vessel, and strain on them the juice; to this put a little water; pour the mixture into a basin in which is four pounds of clarified sugar, boiled to *fort boulet*. Place this basin in a large saucepan, half filled with water, over the fire; stir the contents of the basin frequently; and when the sugar is entirely dissolved, and the sirup quite clear, take the saucepan from the fire, and let it cool. As soon as it is cold it may be bottled.

CITRONNELLE RATAFIA. For two quarts of the best brandy, take the *zestes* or rinds of a dozen fine sound lemons, two drachms of bruised cinnamon, an ounce of coriander, and two pounds of sugar, dissolved in a pint and a half of water; infuse the whole for a month, then strain and bottle it.

CLOVES, OIL OF. This is made in the same manner as cinnamonum; the quantities are, an ounce of cloves to three quarts of brandy, and four pounds of sugar dissolved in four pints of water.

CLOVE PASTILS. Are made like those of cinnamon. The proportions are six cloves to half an ounce of gum-dragon.

CLOVES, SIRUP OF. Put a quarter of a pound of cloves, and a quart of boiling water into a stewpan, cover it close, and boil them gently for half an hour; drain the cloves, and to a pint of the liquor put two pounds of sugar; beat up two eggs in a little cold water, add them to the above, and simmer the whole till it becomes a strong sirup. When cold, bottle it.

COFFEE BONBONS. Take about a pint of coffee made with water; put in it a pound of loaf-sugar; set it on the fire and boil it to a high degree, then add a full pint of double cream, and let it boil again, keeping continually stirring till it comes to caramel height; to know when it is come to that point, you must have a basin of water by you; dip your finger in it, and put it quickly in your sugar, then in the water again, to remove the sugar, which will have stuck to it; take a bit of it in your teeth; if it is hard in its crackling, take it off, it is sufficiently done; pour it upon a tin plate, which must be rubbed before with a little butter, or it will stick to the plate; then spread it with a rolling pin; (observe, the rolling pin must likewise be rubbed with butter, for fear it should stick;) when it is warm, you may cut it into little squares, lozenges, or any other shaped pastilles, and draw a few strokes over them with a knife.

COFFEE CONSERVES. Clarify and boil to the first degree a pound of sugar; take the sugar off the fire, and put into it one cup of coffee; stir it about until it comes to the sixth degree, that the conserve may take the sugar and dry.

COFFEE EGGS. Make some good strong coffee; let it rest to clear as usual, and sweeten it with sugar according to discretion; beat up six yolks of eggs, with about four cups of coffee, and sift it; pour this into little moulds in the form of eggs, or of any other, (do not fill them quite,) and bake in a mild oven, or a Dutch one, or with a brazing-pan; cover between two fires. They are made after this manner, in the shape of any fruits or birds, if you have proper moulds, either of copper or china, &c.

COLTSFOOT, SIRUP OF. Take of coltsfoot six ounces, maidenhair two ounces, hyssop one ounce, liquorice-root one ounce; boil them in two quarts of spring water till one fourth is consumed; then strain it, and put to the liquor two pounds of fine powder-sugar; clarify it with the whites of eggs, and boil it till it is nearly as thick as honey.

CONSERVES, DRIED. For all sorts of conserves, the sugar should be prepared to the ninth degree, according to the quantity wanted; they are all made much after the same manner, the only difference being in the quantity of fruits proposed. Conserves are made with all sorts of sweetmeat marmalade, sifted in a sieve, and soaked pretty dry over a slow fire; use about half a pound of the sugar thus prepared, to a quarter of a pound of sweetmeat marmalade; take the sugar off the fire to work them well together; warm the whole for a moment, and pour it into paper cases made for the purpose; when it is cool it may be cut into cakes of what size you please.

CONSERVE OF FOUR FRUITS. Take strawberries, currants, cherries, and raspberries, of each a quarter of a pound, and three pounds of sugar. Bruise your fruit, and having strained off the juice, put it in a saucepan over a gentle fire, strring it till reduced to half. Dissolve the sugar, skim, and boil it to *casse;* take it from the fire while you put in the juice, then put it on again, and give it one boil, take it off, and keep stirring till the sugar bubbles, when the conserve may be poured into moulds.

CONSERVES, HARD IN MOULDS. These are made in the same manner as other conserves, except that they are composed of sugar, and distilled aromatic water; and may be colored like pastils.

CORIANDER DRAGEES. Take any quantity of coriander seeds, put them in the tossing-pan over the fire, and let them warm; when they are warm throw in about half a glass of vinegar, stir them well till they are dry; have clarified sugar, which boil in another pan; then when the corianders are dry, add a little gum to them, and do the same again till they are dry, and continue so doing till you see the corianders are covered to the size you want to have them; when that is done, take the corianders out from the pan, wash them well, and put them in again, and stir them well till they are all warm; then take your clarified sugar, which you have previously boiled to the first degree; when this is done, put it in an instrument of copper, made on purpose for the operation, and at the bottom of which there is a little hole; hang it up by a packthread string, that the sugar may fall from about a yard height into the pan where the corianders are; while the sugar falls into your pan keep stirring well your dragees till you see they are well pearled over, or rough and grainy; when they are sufficiently so, take them out, and place them in the stove to finish drying.

CORIANDER SUGARED. These seeds are sugared in the same manner as sugared almonds.

CREAM, BAIN-MARIE. Mix up whatever ingredient of which the cream is to be made, with eggs and sugar; for the proportions, see the respective articles; strain them through a fine sieve, and pour the preparation into a mould lightly buttered within side. Put this mould into a large saucepan, with a sufficient quantity of boiling water to reach within an inch of the mould; place the saucepan on hot ashes, cover it, and place hot coals on the lid; renew the fire underneath occasionally, so as to keep the water at the same temperature, that is, nearly, but never quite, boiling for an hour and a half; then, if the cream is properly set, which may be known by touching it with your finger, and observing whether it may be easily detached from the mould, take it from the *bain-marie* and let it stand; when no more than lukewarm, turn it out on your dish.

It sometimes happens, unavoidably, that bubbles arise on the surface of the cream; in such a case, boil a glass of cream, and add to it, by degrees, three yolks of eggs; stir it constantly with a wooden spoon; mix three ounces of fine sugar with it, and continue stirring it over the fire, till of a proper consistence, and on the point of boiling, then take it off and strain it. When the cream is ready for table, cover it completely with the last made cream, which will hide its defects.

CREAM BISCUITS. Break six eggs, separate the yolks and whites, beat the former with six ounces of powder-sugar, and the same of flour; whisk the whites, and then mix them together; add to it whipped cream, in proportion to the sugar and flour, stir it carefully, pour this into moulds or paper cases, and bake.

CREAM CARAMEL. Put a pint of milk and half a pint of cream, with a bit of cinnamon, some coriander-seeds, and the peel of a young lemon, into a saucepan, and boil them for a quarter of an hour; then take it off the fire; and boil a quarter of a pound of sugar with half a glass of water, until it becomes of a nice dark color; take it off the fire, and mix with the cream; then put it on the fire again, until the sugar and cream are well mixed together; then place a saucepan, with some hot water in it, over hot ashes; take a dish, in which you intend serving, and pour into it your cream, then place it in the saucepan; put on the lid of the saucepan, with fire above, and let it boil till the cream is set. Serve hot.

CREAM, SNOW. Put to a quart of cream the whites of three eggs well beaten, four spoonfuls of sweet wine, sugar to your taste, and a bit of lemon-peel; whip it to a froth; remove the peel, and serve in a dish.

CREAM OF ANY PRESERVED FRUIT. Take half a pound of the pulp of any preserved fruit, put it in a large pan, put to it the whites of two or three eggs, beat together well for an hour; take it off with a spoon, and lay it heaped on a dish, or glass salver, with other creams, or put it in the middle of a basin. Raspberries will not do this way.

CREAM RHENISH. Put over the fire a pint of Rhenish wine, a stick of cinnamon, and half a pound of sugar; while this is boiling, take seven yolks and whites of eggs, beat them well together with a whisk, till your wine is half driven in them, and your eggs to a sirup; strike it very fast with the whisk, till it comes to such thickness that you may lift it on the point of a knife, but be sure not to let it curdle; add to it the juice of a lemon, and orange-flower water; pour it into your dish; garnish it with citron, sugar, or biscuit, and serve.

CREAM, ROYAL ICES. Take any quantity of cream, add to it yolks of eggs in proportion (that is, four yolks of eggs to every pint of cream) put a little half pounded coriander, cinnamon, orange or lemon-peel; add some pounded lump sugar, and set it on the fire till it nearly boils; then pass it through a sieve, and put it to ice.

CREAM, WHITE SHERBET. Put the yolks of six eggs, and a dessert spoonful of orange-flower water or crisped orange flowers in powder, into two quarts of cream, and boil it up once in a covered saucepan; then pass it through a sieve, add to it three-quarters of a pound of powder-sugar, and as soon as it is perfectly dissolved, pour the whole into a *sorbetiere*, which place in an ice pail, and proceed to cool it as di-

rected. See *Sherbet*.

CREAM SNOW. Mix a quart of cream with the whites of six eggs, sweeten it with sugar and rose water, and strain them; then beat up the cream with a bundle of reeds tied together, or with a whisk; and as the snow rises take it up with a spoon in the cullender, that the liquid part may run out: when you have taken off as much of the snow as you please, boil the rest of the cream, with a stick of cinnamon, some cloves, and a little bruised ginger; boil it till it is thick; strain it, and when it is cold, put it into a dish, and lay your snow upon it.

CREAM, CARAMEL WHIPPED. Boil six ounces of sugar to caramel, and when it has acquired the proper reddish, yellow tinge, dissolve it in half a glass of boiling water, over hot ashes; after which, it must be reduced to a rather thick sirup. When cold, mix it with the whipped cream in the usual way. See *Whipped Cream*.

CROQUETTES OF DESTREES. Use the best puff paste; roll it pretty thin, and cut it into different shapes, as fancy leads; bake it, and dress each piece upon a dish, in a handsome manner; rub them with a little caramel, to make them stick as you place them; then put some currant jelly all over the top, and make what flower or design you please, with nonpareils of different colors, round it.

CROQUETTES OF PARIS. Take a stick of vanilla, pound it with two ounces of sugar, and sift both through a silk sieve; mix it with seven ounces of sugar, well dried and pounded, and half a pound of fine sifted flour; then stir in the whites of four eggs, whipped firm, and work the whole together for some minutes.

Heat two large baking-plates of copper, rub them over lightly with virgin wax; when they are cold, take a spoonful of the preparation, and lay it on the plate the same as the spoon-biscuits, taking care to lay them three-quarters of an inch apart; when both plates are full, place them on stools, in the oven or stove; close the top, and lay embers over it, so that the croquettes may be as far removed from the fire as possible; let them remain in this state all night;

all night; the next morning put them into a moderate oven, and bake them fifteen or twenty minutes; they should then quit the plate easily, and be of a clear reddish color; remove them from the plates while hot. The *croquettes* may be flavored according to your fancy.

CURACAO. This is a species of bitter or wild orange, of which the rind is dried, and may be had at the druggists. To make the liqueur called by this name, wash a pound of curacao several times in warm water; then, having well drained, put them into a vessel with four quarts of brandy, and one of water; let it stand closely covered for a fortnight, shaking it frequently; distil it after that in the usual way, and drain the curacao on a sieve. Sweeten it with five pounds and a half of sugar, dissolved in three pints of water, mix it with the spirit and then filter it.

CURDS AND WHEY. Take a number of the rough coats that line the gizzards of turkeys and fowls; clean them from the pebbles they contain, rub them well with salt, and hang them to dry. This makes a more tender and delicate curd than common rennet. When to be used, break off some bits of the skin, and put on it some boiling water; in eight or nine hours use the liquor as you do other rennet.

CURRANT CAKES. Pick and wash the currants, either white or red; to two quarts of currants, put one pint of water; when boiled, run the juice through a jelly bag, do not press the bag; to one quart of juice put three pounds of sugar; boil up the juice, and strew in the sugar; pour it into glasses, dry it in a stove till it will turn out, then dry the cakes on plates.

CURRANTS, CONSERVE OF. Take the seeds from two pounds of red currants, and put them on the fire in a silver pan, to dry them; then press them through a sieve, and put them again on the fire, stirring constantly until you can see the bottom of the pan; then, having dissolved and boiled three pounds of sugar to *casse,* pour it on the fruit, stirring continually; in a short time take it off, stirring

it as before until it bubbles; then pour it into moulds.

CURRANT ICES. (1) Boil two pounds of red currants a moment with a quarter of a pound of raspberries; rub them through a sieve, adding a pint of water, and then the sugar, which must be very well dissolved before icing.

CURRANT ICES. (2) Pick some currants from their stalks, and squeeze them through a sieve; then take clarified sugar, boil it to a very high degree, add it to your currant juice, and, if you choose, squeeze in the juice of four lemons, it will make it more mellow; strain them through the sieve a second time, put them in the icing pot, and finish the same as all other ices.

CURRANT ICE CREAM. Take one large spoonful and a half of currant jelly, put it into a basin, with half a gill of sirup, squeeze in one lemon and a half; add a pint of cream and a little cochineal, then pass it through a sieve, and freeze it according to custom.

CURRANT WATER ICE. Take a large spoonful and a half of currant jelly, put it into a basin, and add to it the juice of two lemons, half a gill of sirup, and a pint of water: then freeze it rich.

CURRANT JELLY FRAMBOISEE. Take seven pounds of fine ripe red currants, three of white, and two of white raspberries, press them through a very close horse-hair sieve; pour the juice on nine pounds of double-refined sugar, broken in small pieces, place the whole on a brisk fire, taking care to remove the scum as soon as it appears. When the boilings follow each other very quickly, take out the skimmer (which should be of copper) stir it, and let the jelly fall from it; on quitting the skimmer it ought to fall like treacle. If it does so, it is sufficiently done. This jelly should be rose-colored; by making it entirely of red currants and red raspberries, the color of the jelly will be red.

CURRANT PASTE. Pick and take the seeds from ten pounds of fine red currants, crush them, and having pressed out the juice, strain it through a silk sieve. Clarify and boil to *casse* an equal quantity of sugar, pour the currant juice on it, set the whole over a gentle fire, stirring constantly until it becomes of a proper consistence, which may be known by observing when the bottom of the pan can be seen clearly; take it off from the fire as soon as that is the case, and pour the paste into tin moulds, which must be placed on slates, or copper plates: smooth the tops with the blade of a knife, sprinkle sifted sugar over, and place them in a stove, where they must remain till next day; when the paste should be turned in the moulds; sprinkle sifted sugar over them again, and set them in the stove a second night; on the following day remove them from the moulds, lay it in boxes, with white paper between each layer, and keep them in a dry place. A sixth part of the quantity of raspberries added to the currants, would greatly improve the flavor of this paste.

CURRANT PASTILS. Take half a pound of pounded loaf sugar on a plate, then a quantity of currants, which squeeze through a sieve; when that is done, add the juice to the sugar, till it makes a paste as clear and thick as you think proper.

CURRANT SHRUB. To five pints of currant juice, either red or white, one pound and a half of loaf sugar; when dissolved, put to it one gallon of rum or brandy; clear it through a flannel bag.

CURRANT SIRUP. Put five or six pounds of red, two of white currants, and two bottles of raspberries, into a sieve; crush them, and press the juice through it into a pan, and place it in a cellar to ferment; in a week's time, pass the juice through a straining bag, and having clarified, and boiled to *fort souffle* four pounds of sugar, put the juice to it, and boil them together once; skim, and take it from the fire. It is necessary that the currant juice should ferment, to prevent its becoming a jelly in the bottles.

D.

DRAGEES, COMMON. The paste for these *dragees* is made in the same manner as for the better sort, but the materials differ a little: thus to a quarter of a pound of the gum, take either equal quantities of sugar and powder, or one-third of the former to two-thirds of the latter. When these and the gum are well mixed, roll out the paste until it is as thin as the back of a knife-blade; then take a paste-cutter, shaped like a sugar-loaf, with the top taken off, with the largest end of which, cut as many pieces of the paste as will about two-thirds fill the cutter; press these through the smaller end into paper cases; set them in a warm place for several days. These kind of *dragees* may, if liked, be sugared in the same manner as almonds.

DRAGEES EN PASTILLAGE. These *dragees* are made of the same materials as the superfine *dragees*; the only difference consists in their forms, which resemble the *bonbons*: to make them, it is necessary to have a number of wooden moulds, (pear-tree wood is the best), on which must be stamped small squares, with various devices engraved on them. Cut your paste into small pieces; press each piece on a mould; take off all the super-abundant paste; then dip your finger in water, and with it remove the paste from the mould; dry them in cases like the other *dragees*.

DRAGEES, SUPERFINE. Put quarter of a pound of the best gum-dragon into a pan, with a pint of cold water, cover and let it stand for twenty-four hours; then take a strong close cloth, about two feet long, and put a part of your gum into it; fold it three times, so as to envelope the gum; then wring the cloth, by which means the purest gum will be forced through; scrape it off carefully with a knife, and then proceed in the same way, until all the gum be strained; put it into a marble mortar, and stir it about with a pestle for half an hour; then add to it a pound of double-refined sifted sugar; mix them together well, until it becomes a stiff paste; divide this into five parts, four of which must be tinged as follows: red, blue, yellow, and green, (the fifth left white), with the usual coloring materials. Before, however, they are colored, add to each piece, a pound and a half of double-refined sugar, sifted, dipping the paste in water occasionally, to enable it to receive the additional quantity of sugar. When you mix in the coloring materials, add also a corresponding perfume: as, to the red, rose water, and a few drops of essence of roses; to the blue, oil of violets; to the yellow, essence of cedar; to the green, essence of bergamot; and with the white, mix a little orange-flower water, and some drops of essence of *Neroli.*

Your paste being thus prepared, form it of whatever little ornaments you please, such as eggs, balls, turnips, (adding green leaves to these), &c. of the white; of the yellow, apricots, pears, carrots, &c.; plums, &c, of the blue; and so on; rolling them in your hands to smooth them, and make them all quite small; to those which imitate fruits, add tails and tops, cut from cherry-stalks and stuck on whilst the paste is damp; and with a hair-pencil, dipped in powdered cinnabar, tinge the pears, apples, and apricots, slightly breathing on them to moisten the surface. When all are done, put them into paper cases, and set them in a warm place for several days, to dry.

### E.

EGGS CARAMEL. Take the yolks of a dozen hard eggs, bruise them in a saucepan, with some powder-sugar, three almond biscuits, and half a glass of cream; make these into a paste, of which form little eggs, dip them in caramel sugar, and brown them.

EGGS DUCHESSE. Boil a pint and a half of cream with some sugar, orange-flower, candied lemon-peel, marchpane, and burnt almonds, all chopped small or bruised; whip up the whites of eight eggs well, and then take two or three spoonfuls of them at a time, and poach them in the cream; drain, and lay them on a dish, so as to resemble eggs poached without the yolks. When all the whites are thus used, put the cream on the fire, and reduce it, and as the dish is sent to table, add the yolks to the cream, and pour the sauce gently over the eggs.

EGGS FILAGRAMME. Take a pint of white wine, half a pound of fine powder-sugar, and make it into a clear sirup with the white of an egg; beat up well eight eggs, and pour them through a colander into the sirup; a very short time is sufficient to cook them. Serve either hot or cold.

EGGS OF SNOW. Break ten eggs, and having separated the yolks and whites, whip the latter as for biscuits; then add two spoonfuls of powder-sugar, and a little dried orange-flower in powder. Pour a quart of milk, six ounces of powder-sugar, and a little orange-flower, into a saucepan, and when it boils put into it, a dessert-spoonful at a time, of the white of egg; poach the latter, and then set them on a sieve to drain. Then beat up the yolks, and mix them with half the milk, put it on the fire, and stir it with a wooden-spoon till it begins to thicken; then take it off, lay the poached eggs in a dish, and cover them with the yolks and milk.

EGGS, WHITE OF. To make a dish of these, take the whites of twelve eggs, beat them up with four spoonfuls of rose-water, some lemon-peel grated, and a little nutmeg; sweeten them with sugar, mix them well, and boil them in four bladders; tie them in the shape of an egg, and boil them hard; they will take half an hour; lay them in a dish; when cold, mix half a pint of thick cream, a gill of mountain, and the juice of half an orange all together; sweeten it with fine sugar, and serve it over the eggs.

### F.

FILBERT BISCUITS. Take some Barcelona filbert nuts, and put them in a mortar to break their shells; pick all the shells from them clean, pound them in a mortar very fine, and mix whites of eggs with them; take care they do not oil; mix three pounds of powdered-sugar, with the nuts and whites of eggs, to a proper thickness; let your oven be of a moderate heat, then with the spaddle and knife, drop small pieces, about half as big as a nutmeg; put two or three sheets of paper under them, let them bake of a fine brown, and all alike; and let them be cold before you take them off the paper.

FILBERT CANNELLONS. Burn and pound

six ounces of filberts, moistening them with white of egg; when well pounded, add a quarter of a pound of fine pounded sugar, and half the white of an egg; dry this paste a little, and then press it through a syringe, cutting the *cannellons* about four inches in length; make the *friture* quite hot, dip the *cannellons* in batter, and fry them. Sprinkle them with sugar, and glaze them with a salamander. Take particular care to keep the *cannellons* perfectly straight.

FILBERT BURNT, ICE CREAM. Roast some Barcelona nuts well in the oven; and pound them a little with some cream; put four eggs into a stewpan, with one pint of cream and two gills of sirup; boil it till it becomes thick, pass it through a sieve, and freeze it; then mix the filberts with it before you put it into your moulds.

FILBERT MACAROONS. Take a pound of filberts, and put a quarter of them into a preserving-pan (immediately after you have taken them from the shells,) over a moderate fire; stir them continually with a silver spoon, until they are colored, and the skin begins to peel off; then take them out; rub off the skin entirely, and when quite cold, pound them with a little white of egg: proceed in the same manner with the remaining three-quarters; and when all are thus pounded separately, put the whole together into the mortar, with a pound of sugar, and the whites of two eggs, and beat them for ten minutes; after which, add two pounds more of sifted sugar, previously beaten up with six whites of eggs; stir all these together well for five or six minutes, when the preparation should be sufficiently firm, to prevent its spreading when laid; if, however, it be too firm, add to it more white of egg. When you have proceeded so far, wet the palms of your hands, and roll a spoonful of the preparation to the size and form of a nutmeg; when all done, dip your hands in water, and pass them gently over the macaroons, which will make their surface smooth and shining; put them into a nearly cold oven; close it tight, and let them remain in it for three-quarters of an hour. Lay the macaroons at least an inch apart, and as round as possible.

FLOWERS IN SUGAR. Clarify sugar to a caramel height, which may be known by dip-

ping in a fork, and if it throws the sugar as fine as threads, put in the flowers. Have ready some tea-cups, with the insides rubbed with sweet oil; put into each cup four table-spoonfuls of the sugar and flowers, and when cold turn them out of the cups, and serve them to table piled one upon another.

FRUIT BISCUITS. To the pulp of any scalded fruit, put an equal quantity of sugar sifted, beat it two hours; then put it into little white paper forms; dry them in a cool oven, turn them the next day, and in two or three days box them.

FRUIT, PRESERVED, BISCUITS OF. Take dried preserved fruits, such as apricots, verjuice, grapes, plums, oranges, and a little orange-flower marmalade; pound them together, and sift in a sieve; then mix it with yolks of new laid eggs, and fine powder-sugar, until it comes to a supple paste, not too liquid; then bake them on paper in a moderate oven.

~~~~~

### G.

GINGER, CANDIED. Put an ounce of ginger, grated fine, and a pound of sifted sugar into a preserving-pan with as much water as will dissolve it. Stir them well together over a slow fire, till the sugar begins to boil; then add another pound, stirring constantly till it thickens. Take it from the fire, drop it on earthen dishes, set them in a warm place to dry, and they will be hard and brittle and look white.

GOOSEBERRY CAKES. Break the gooseberries, press out the juice, and strain it through a muslin; to one pint of juice a pound of sugar; boil up the juice; strew in the sugar: stir it well; simmer it well till the sugar is melted; pour it into glasses: dry it in a stove till it will turn out, then dry the cakes on plates.

GOOSEBERRIES, GREEN, COMPOTE OF. Give them a little cut on one side to squeeze out the seeds, and put them in hot water to scald, till they rise to the top; then put cold water to them, adding a little salt, to bring them to their natural green; simmer them in clarified sugar, and let them remain in sometime to imbibe the sweet; take them out, and put them in the compotier; reduce the sirup to a good consistence, and pour it over the fruit. This is for green gooseberries; but if you make use of preserved ones, warm them in their own sirup and a little water, and serve it either hot or cold. These will not keep long, particularly if they have been warmed again: if exposed to the air any time, they will lose their color.

GRAPE ICE. Take ripe grapes, pick them from their stalks, pass them through a sieve; mix some sugar with the juice of four lemons squeezed upon it; pass the whole together a second time through a sieve, then freeze it.

GRAPES RATAFIA. Take some fine muscadine grapes, pick them from the stalks; bruise and press them so as to extract all their juice; then dissolve some sugar in the grape juice, adding to it brandy and cinnamon; let the whole infuse for a fortnight; then strain it through a filtering bag, and bottle it off. The proper proportions are one pint of brandy, and ten ounces of sugar to one pint of grape juice.

GREEN-GAGES TO CANDY. When finished in the sirup, *(see green-gages to preserve,)* put a layer into a new sieve, and dip it suddenly into hot water, to take off the sirup that hangs about it; then put it on a napkin before the fire to drain, and then do some more on the sieve. Have ready some sifted double-refined sugar, sift this all over every part of the fruit, till it is perfectly white. Set it on the shallow end of sieves in a lightly warm oven, and turn it two or three times. It must not be cold till dry. Watch it carefully.

GREEN GAGES TO PRESERVE. You must choose the largest, when they begin to soften; split without paring them, and having previously weighed an equal quantity of sugar, strew a part of it over them; blanch the kernels with a small sharp knife; next day, pour the sirup from the fruit, and boil it with the other sugar, very gently, for six or eight minutes, skim, and add the plums and kernels. Simmer till clear, taking off any scum that rises; put the fruit single into small pots, and pour the sirup and kernels upon it.

GUM PASTE. Put a pound of gum-dragon in a basin, with warm water enough to cover one inch above the gum; set this in a warm closet for four and twenty hours; have a new tammy ready laid over a dish; spread it on it, and squeeze through as much as you can at first; then open the tammy, spread the gum out again, and then squeeze it; repeat this till the whole is through; then lay it on the slab, work it well with your hand, put in nearly all the juice of one lemon, and a pound of the best double refined powder-sugar, by degrees, as you work it; but before you have put in the whole of the sugar, begin to add some of the best starch powder; blend them thoroughly together, till the paste begins to take an impression; then roll it in a cloth, and let it stand in a damp place for a week or ten days, (it is the better for keeping), work it with powder, and it will cut and mould to any shape you please, and when you want it to harden, set it in a dry place; If you wish to color it, to make it red, use cochineal or carmine; for blue or violet color, use indigo; for yellow, saffron; for green, the juice of beet leaves, scalded over the fire, the thick part mix with the paste. When you put in colors, be careful to blend them well, and be particular that the color is good.

wwwwwww

## H.

HARTSHORN CREAM. Boil a quarter of a pound of hartshorn-shavings in three pints of water; when reduced to half a pint, strain it through a jelly-bag; put it to a pint of cream and a quarter of a pound of powder-sugar, and give them one boil together; then put it into cups or glasses, and let them stand till cold, when turn them out on a dish; stick some sliced blanched almonds on the top of each. White wine and sugar is usually eaten with them.

### J.

JUNIPER BERRIES, ICES OF. Infuse some juniper berries in warm water, or take about a handful of the berries, and boil them a moment with a pint of water, half a pound of sugar, and a bit of cinnamon, and sift them through a sieve with expression, and finish the same as all others.

JUNIPER RATAFIA. Take three ounces of juniper berries, anise, coriander, cinnamon, and cloves, of each eighteen grains; bruise all these ingredients, and infuse them, for a month, in three pints of brandy; then strain it, add three-quarters of a pound of sugar dissolved in half a pint of water, stir them together, pass the whole through a jelly-bag, and bottle it; keep it well corked.

### L.

LEMON BRANDY. Put the peel of two lemons into a bottle of brandy, let it stand for four and twenty hours, then strain it; boil two ounces of loaf sugar in a quarter of a pint of water; then skim, and let it stand till cold; when cold, mix it with the brandy.

LEMON CAKES. Quarter as many lemons as you think proper, they must have good rinds, and boil them in two or three waters, till they are tender, and have lost their bitterness; then skin them, and put them in a napkin to fry; with a knife take all the skins and seeds out of the pulp, shred the peels fine, put them to the pulp, weigh them, and put rather more than their weight of fine sugar into a tossing-pan, with just sufficient water to dissolve the sugar; boil it till it becomes perfectly dissolved, and then by degrees put in the peel and pulps; stir them well before you set them on the fire, boil it very gently till it looks clear and thick, and then put it into flat-bottomed glasses; set them in a stove, and keep them in a continual and moderate heat, and turn them out upon glasses, as soon as they are candied.

LEMON COMPOTE. Cut them in small pieces, and boil them in water till they are tender, then change them into cold water; then make a sirup with a glass of water, and a quarter of a pound of sugar, and put in the fruit; let it simmer gently over a slow fire for half an hour, and serve cold.

LEMON CONSERVE. Grate the rind of a lemon on a piece of sugar (about a pound,) scrape off the surface of the sugar as the lemon adheres to it, until you have rasped the whole of the rind; squeeze half the juice on the scraped sugar, and then boil the rest to *la grande plume*; take it from the fire when at this degree, and let it stand a little; stir in the lemon gently, and when it forms a sort of *glace* on the top of the sugar, pour the conserve into moulds; being careful, however, that it is not too hot.

LEMON DROPS. Grate three large lemons, with a large piece of double refined sugar; then scrape the sugar into a plate, add half a teaspoonful of flour; mix well together, and beat it into a light paste, with the white of an egg. Drop it upon white paper, put them on a tin-plate, and set them in moderate oven.

LEMON ICE CREAM. Take the juice of three or four lemons, and grate the peel of one lemon; add two gills of sirup, and one pint of cream; mix it all together, pass it through a sieve, and freeze it.

LEMONS TO KEEP FOR PUDDINGS. When you squeeze the fruit, throw the outside in water, without the pulp; let them remain in the same a fortnight, adding no more; boil them in the same till tender; strain it from them, and when they are nearly dry, throw them into any jar of candy you may have remaining from old sweetmeats; or, if you have none, boil a small quantity of sirup, of common loaf sugar and water, and pour over them; in a week or ten days, boil them gently in it till they look clear; and that they may be covered with it in the jar, you may cut each half of the fruit in two, and they will occupy a smaller space.

LEMON PASTILS. Take half a pound of pounded loaf sugar, sifted as fine as possible;

put it in a plate, take three or four lemons, and squeeze their juice over the sugar; mix it well with a spoon, till you make it rather a thickish paste, so that you can take it upon a knife; then take half a sheet of paper, and cover it with little round and flat drops, about the size of a sixpence, place them in a stove with a slow fire till they are quite dry, then take them off from the paper; you may use, if you please, some of the peel grated, but not chipped; for, as it is a melting pastil, some of the bits would remain in the mouth.

LEMON PEEL CANDIED. Take some thick-rinded lemons, pare off the yellow peel, and throw it into boiling water till soft, when it must be put into cold water. Clarify some fine sugar, and boil it *au petit lisse*, and having drained the lemon-peel, pour on it the sirup (whilst hot); the next day boil the sirup again, and return it to the peel; the third and fourth days proceed in the same manner, adding a small quantity of clarifed sugar; the last time the sirup is boiled, as soon as it rises to *perle*, put in the peel, cover and boil the whole together once, and when cold, drain and dry them in a stove.

LEMON PEEL, TO CANDY. Take some lemon-peels, and clean them well from the pulp, and let them lay two days in salt and water; then scald and drain them dry, then boil them in a thin sirup till they look quite clear. After which, take them out, and have ready a thick sirup made with fine loaf sugar; put them into it, and simmer them till the sugar-candies about the pan and peels. Then lay them separately on a hair sieve to drain, strew sifted sugar over them, and set them to dry in a slow oven.

LEMON PEEL, CARAMEL. Take some very dry preserved lemon-peel, and cut it into several small square pieces; put these pieces each on the point of little sticks for this purpose, and dip them into *caramel* sugar as directed. See *chestnuts au caramel*.

LEMON PEEL SIRUP OF. Take five ounces of fresh lemon-peel, put it into a glass cucurbite, which has been gradually heated; pour on them two pounds of nearly boiling water; close the vessel very tight, and place it on hot ashes for twelve hours; after which, let the infusion run out gently without pressing the peel; add two pounds of powder-sugar, and then boil the whole to *grand perle*, when about half cold, put in a few drops of spirit of lemon.

LEMON SWEETMEATS. Take a pound of marchpane paste, and mix it with as many yolks of eggs as will enable you to spread the paste with a knife; add to it a sufficient quantity of grated lemon-peel to impart the flavor required. The whole being well mixed, cut some sheets of wafer paper into such figures as your fancy may dictate, and spread the paste over them, about a quarter of an inch in thickness; place them on paper, and bake them in a moderate oven. If you wish to glaze your sweetmeats, boil some sugar with orange-flower water to *la plume*, and when they are taken out of the oven, wash them over with the sirup, which dries almost immediately.

LEMONS, SIRUP OF. Squeeze as many lemons as will yield about three-quarters of a pound of juice, taking particular care that the peel of every lemon is perfectly sound, and that they are none of them in the least degree bitter. Set your juice in the cellar for four days, and then filter it through blotting-paper. Break a pound and a half of double-refined sugar into pieces about an inch square; put them into a gallon matrass, pour the lemon-juice over it, close the matrass with paper, and place it in a *bain marie* until the sugar is entirely dissolved; then extinguish your fire, and let the matrass cool gradually; when cold, add two spoonfuls of spirit of lemons, then bottle it, keep it well corked.

LEMON WAFERS. Squeeze the juice of six lemons into a basin; pound and sift some double-refined sugar, and mix it with the lemon-juice; put the white of one egg with it, and mix the whole well together with a wooden spoon, to make it of a good consistence; take some sheets of wafer-paper, and put one sheet of it on a pewter sheet or tin plate; put on it a spoonful of the preparation, and spread it all over the paper with a knife; cut it into twelve pieces, and put them across a stick in a hot stove, with that side the paste is on uppermost, and you will find they will curl; when they are half curled, take them off very carefully and put them up, endways, in a sieve, that they may stand up; let them be in the hot stove one day, and you will find they will be all curled, and then they are done.

LIQUORICE PASTE. Scrape and bruise a quarter of a pound of liquorice-root, and boil it in a little water till it is much reduced; let it stand to settle, and pour it clear off, and dissolve in it half an ounce of gum-dragon: when thoroughly dissolved, sift it in a linen bag, and mix sugar with it till it is brought to the consistence of a paste; then cut it into what flowers or designs you think proper.

wwwwwwww

## M.

MACAROONS, SPICED. Take a pound of sweet almonds, and two pounds of sifted sugar; make your paste as usual, to which add a spoonful of powdered cinnamon, six or eight cloves, also pounded, same preserved lemon and orange-peel (of each a spoonful,) chopped small, and the grated rind of two lemons; mix them all together in the mortar, and then lay your macaroons as usual, and bake them with equal care.

MACEDOINE OF FRUIT. The *macedoine* is an ornamental dish, composed of transparent jelly, with various fruits enclosed in it; for this purpose it should be done as follows: Have a dome-shaped mould six inches and a half in diameter, and four in height, the sides fluted; the smaller mould must be of a similar form, but only four inches and a half in diameter, and two and three-quarters high; to this latter have four handles, bent at the end, to hang it exactly in the centre of the larger mould. Prepare a strawberry transparent jelly, place the larger mould as straight as possible in pounded ice, hang the small one in it, and pour the jelly into the former; whilst it is congealing, pick about twenty fine white strawberries, the same number of very red ones, the same of white raspberries, a dozen bunches of red, and the same of white currants; wash all these well, but touch them as little as possible, that they may not lose their freshness; when the jelly in perfectly set, pour some hot water into the small mould which will enable you to remove it with ease; raise it with great care, so that the space may be found without the slightest flaw; then place on the jelly (in the centre of this space) two bunches of white currants, surround these with a ring of white strawberries, and the latter with a crown or ring of white raspberries; pour over very carefully two or three spoonfuls of the jelly, and when that is congealed, proceed in the same way with the red currants, strawberries, and raspberries, then the jelly, and so on alternately, until all the fruit is used; fill the mould with jelly; as soon as the whole is congealed, dip your mould into a large saucepan of hot water, and then turn it into a dish instantly. The *macedoine* may be garnished in this manner with any kind of fruit you think proper. It may also be filled with two jellies as follows: white lemon jelly in the large mould, and finished with the same jelly, tinged with either rose color or yellow; indeed the moulds may be varied in any way your fancy may dictate.

MALLOWS, SIRUP OF. Take half a pound of mallows root, and having scraped and washed it well, cut it into small pieces, which set on the fire with three pints of water; when sufficiently boiled, the water will be glutinous, strain off the decoction, and pour into it four pounds of sugar; clarify it in the same manner as capillaire; boil it to *lisse*, run it through a jelly-bag, and when cold, bottle it.

MARASCHINO. Take sixteen pounds of fine sharp cherries, stone and take off the stalks; put them into five quarts of brandy to infuse, covered close for three days, then distil the infusion; distil also a pound of cherry-leaves in six quarts of filtered river water, from which you will obtain about a gallon; dissolve in this four pounds and a half of fine sugar; add it to the liqueur, with two pints and a half of kirschen-wasser, an ounce and four drachms of spirits of rose, the same of orange-flowers, and three drachms of spirits of jessamine; mix them altogether, run it through a jelly-bag, and bottle it; cork them well.

MARASCHINO, CONSERVE OF. Pound and sift some of the best lump sugar, mix it in a china basin with spirit of maraschino, until it is of the consistence of pastil paste; then put it into a skillet over the fire, and heat it gently, stirring it constantly (but without letting it boil,) till very liquid, when it may be poured into funnel-shaped tin moulds; put these moulds on iron plates, and dry the conserve in a stove.

MARASCHINO ICE CREAM. Take two quarts of cream, twelve eggs, a pound of double-refined sugar, and three glasses of true maraschino; put the cream on to boil, and in the meantime whisk the whites of the eggs to a firm snow, then pour in eight yolks, and the sugar pounded and sifted, stir them together lightly, and then add by degrees the boiling cream, whipping continually; set it on the fire, and do not cease whipping until it has boiled up three or four times; pour it through a sieve into a basin, stirring a little to enable it to run more freely; when cold put it into the *sorbetiere* with the maraschino; cover it instantly, and ice it as usual.

MARCHPANE. Take four pounds of sweet almonds, throw them into boiling water. Let them lay till the skin loosens, then put them into cold water, after a few minutes blanch and throw them again into cold water to wash them thoroughly. When dry, pound them (a handful at a time) to a very fine paste, moistening each handful with two spoonfuls of water; the whole quantity of almonds being pounded, put the paste into a large preserving pan, with four pounds of the best lump sugar finely pounded and sifted; set the pan on a coal fire, stir and work them up together with a large wooden spatula, rather sharp at the bottom: be very careful that none of the paste adheres to the pan; the consequence of such neglect would be, that the marchpane would be spotted with yellow, and would smell unpleasantly. Whilst working it up, the paste, which when put in was tolerably firm, will become rather liquid, and a great deal of vapor may be observed; the first is caused by the sugar dissolved by the heat and moisture, the second by the evaporation of the water. Continue to stir and work it up in this manner without ceasing for two hours, and if at the end of that time, you can touch the paste without its adhering to your fingers, it is sufficiently dried; in which case remove it all to one side of the pan, clean the bottom and side of the other, sprinkle it well with flour, then put the paste to that part, clean and sprinkle that side also; then take the pan by both ears and move it round and round, so that the paste may all unite together; as soon as it has done so, put it into a sheet of paper, or, if you want to use it immediately, on a well floured table. This paste, if the almonds be well pounded and then thoroughly dried, will keep good for six months; if these two precautions are not properly attended to, it will become sour in ten days.

MARIGOLDS, CONSERVE OF. Take four ounces of marigold flowers, conserve of hyacinth and hermes, of each four drachms, the powder of pearl two ounces, and as much sirup of citron as will make them into a conserve, mixing and bruising them together with refined sugar.

MARJORAM CONSERVE. Take the tops and tenderest part of sweet marjoram, bruise it well in a wooden mortar or bowl; take double its weight of fine sugar, boil it with marjoram-water till it is as thick as sirup, then put in your beaten marjoram.

MARSEILLES, OR GINGER. Take a pound and a half of double-refined sugar, and boil it to *fort souffle*, add to it an ounce of ginger in powder, remove the pan from the fire, and with a round stick (like a plain round rule) stir the sugar, inclining the stick towards the sides of the pan, then with a spoon take the sugar that sticks to the edges and put it amongst the liquid, then work it up again with the stick, remove the solid sugar as before, and repeat this operation four times, when it will have become tolerably thick and firm; pour it into paper cases, about half an inch thick, and with a fork trace on its surface, whilst warm, lozenges of what size you please; afterwards, with the point of a knife, mark some of these deeper than the others; when quite cold, take them out of the papers, and separate them, where the lines are deepest. The Marseilles, if preserved in a warm or dry place, will keep good for a long time.

MARSEILLES SPICED. Take a pound and a half of fine sugar, boil it to *casse*; take a quarter of preserved orange-peel, the same of candied lemon-peel, (or, if you like it better, two ounces of blanched pistachio nuts), cut them into dice, and put them with half an ounce of cloves, the same of cinnamon (both pounded) into the sugar, stir them in gently, continue to boil your sirup to *forte plume*; then beat it up, pour it into cases, and finish as the *Marseilles*.

MELONS, TO PRESERVE LIKE GINGER. Half a pound of ginger to one pound of melon; scrape the ginger, and save the scrapings: pour a quart of boiling water on the ginger, let it stand two days: scald the melon (with the scrapings of the ginger in the water), taking care not to make it too soft: cut it into small pieces resembling ginger; then prepare a sirup, half a pound of sugar to a pint of water; boil the ginger in it; when cold, put in the melon, and set it over the fire for a short time, but not to boil; let the sirup, with the ginger, be boiled every day for a fortnight, but not poured upon the melon till nearly cold; then boil a rich sirup to keep it in.

N.B. Carrot is equally good with melon.

MERINGUES. (1) Whisk the whites of nine eggs to a solid froth; then add the rind of six lemons, grated extremely fine, and a spoonful of sifted sugar; after which, lay a sheet of wet paper on a tin, and with a spoon drop the mixture in little lumps, separately upon it, sift sugar over, and put them to bake in a moderately heated oven, taking care that

they are done of a nice color. Then put raspberry, apricot, or any other kind of jam between two of these bottoms, add them together, and lay them in a warm place, or before the fire to dry.

MERINGUES. (2) Take the whites of twelve eggs, six ounces of the best lump sugar, pounded and sifted, and half a pound of pistachios; blanch and beat the latter in a mortar, with a little white of egg, to a very fine paste. Whisk the whites of eggs to a snow, then add the sugar, and pistachio paste, mix them well, but very lightly, and when they are thoroughly incorporated, put some sheets of paper on tin plates, lay your preparation on the paper, with a spoon, lay the *meringues*, at least an inch apart; sprinkle sifted sugar over them, and put them into a moderate oven or stove; when done, detach them gently from the paper with a knife, and place them on a sieve in a dry place. Just before they are sent to table, fill each with a little whipped cream, to which add a small quantity of either orange-flower, rose, or vanilla water.

MILK PUNCH. Pare six oranges, and six lemons, as thin as you possibly can, grate them after with sugar to obtain the flavor. Steep the peels in a bottle of rum or brandy, stopped close for four and twenty hours. Squeeze the fruit on two pounds of sugar, add four quarts of water to it, and one quart of new milk, boiling hot; stir the rum into the above, and run it through a jelly-bag until it is quite clear: bottle and cork it close immediately.

MINT, DISTILLED LIQUEUR OF. Take two handfuls of fresh gathered garden mint, and infuse it for some days in a gallon and a half of brandy, and a quart of water; then distil it as usual. Dissolve three pounds and a half of sugar in seven pints of water, mix the sirup with the *liqueur*, and run the whole through a jelly bag.

MINT WATER. Take four pounds of dried

mint, two gallons and a half of proof spirits, and three gallons of water; distil them, and sweeten the water with a pound and a half of sugar.

MIRLITONS. Put into a pan two yolks, and two whole eggs, four ounces of powder-sugar, three ounces of sweet macaroons crushed, half an ounce of crisped orange-flowers in powder, and a grain of salt; stir these together a minute, then add two ounces of melted butter; whip the two whites very firm, and put them also to the preparation. Line thirty tartlet moulds with puff-paste, into each of which pour an equal quantity of the above; cover them with sifted sugar, and when that is dissolved, strew over a little sugar, *a la grele*; and put them into a moderate oven: serve either hot or cold.

MULBERRIES, SIRUP OF. Take as many mulberries as will yield three pints of juice, which put into a preserving pan with three pints of water; boil until this quantity is reduced to one pint; then lay the fruit on a sieve to drain. Clarify three pounds of sugar, boil it to *bouille*; then add the mulberry-juice; give them one boil, and skim them. Pour the sirup into a pan, and let it stand; when cold, bottle it.

MUSK, TO PREPARE FOR LIQUEURS. Take two grains of musk and a quarter of a pound of sugar, pound them in a mortar and mix them well; keep it in a closely stopped bottle. The quantity required of this is one pinch to four or five quarts of liqueur. Ambergris is prepared in a similar manner, but being less powerful than the musk, four grains is the proportion to a quarter of a pound of sugar.

MYRTLE, OIL OF. Put two ounces of peach leaves, and the half of a nutmeg, bruised, into six quarts of brandy; distil from this in a *bain marie* alembic your liqueur, in which, infuse half a pound of myrtle flowers for four days. Dissolve five pounds of sugar in three quarts of pure river water; the mo-

ment it begins to boil, take it from the fire, and let it cool; take the myrtle flowers from the liqueur, and put in the sugar; mix them well, color it with tincture of saffron, strain and bottle it.

N.

NONPAREIL. Poppy seeds sugared in the manner directed under the articles *Sugared Seeds*, are called *Nonpareils*; they are tinged of different colors, by the introduction of the various coloring materials into the sugar with which they are covered.

NOUGAT. Blanch and wash a pound of sweet almonds, and having drained them well, cut each into five slips, which place in a gentle oven to dry; let them be all equally colored of a clear yellow; in the meantime, put three-quarters of a pound of fine sugar into a preserving pan, set it on a stove, stirring with a wooden spoon until completely dissolved; then take the almonds out of the oven, and whilst hot throw them into the liquid sugar; mix them together well. Have ready a mould well oiled, of any shape you think proper, in the interior of which place the slips of almonds, by means of lemon-juice, when the whole is covered, remove the mould carefully, and serve the *Nougat*.

NOYAU, ENGLISH. Two gallons of gin, two pounds of bitter almonds, one pound of sweet almonds, both beaten to a fine paste; six pounds of lump sugar, pounded (some of it with the almonds.) Let these stand ten days in the gin, then filter it through blotting paper, and bottle it.

NUT BONBONS. Boil a pound of Spanish nuts; when they are well boiled, rub off their skin with a napkin, if some stick too hard, pare it off with a knife; grate your nuts very fine on a sheet of paper; then take a pound of powdered sugar to a pound of nuts, put it in a pan over a slow fire; when your sugar is all melted (you must stir it constantly with a wooden spoon) put your nuts in, and work them well till all is well mixed, and pour it upon a tin plate; then spread it with a rolling pin, this must be done very quickly, as it cools very fast; when it is cold, cut it into what form you please; you must take care the sugar is not too much melted, for it is very apt to soften when the nuts are added to it.

NUTS PRALINED. Take a pound of Spanish nuts, take them out of their shells, and put them into a pan, with a pound of loaf sugar, and a little water; let them boil till they begin to sparkle; then take them off the fire, and stir them well with a wooden spoon, till you perceive the sugar turns gravelly; then set them again over a slow fire, to dissolve the sugar; keep stirring, that the sugar may stick to the nuts, and when you see them turn reddish, and are well covered with sugar, take them off, pour them into a sieve, cover them with a clean cloth, and put them into a stove; this will preserve their gloss.

NUTMEGS TO CANDY. Take a pound and a half of double refined sugar, half a quarter of a pint of damask rose-water, and a very little gum arabic; boil these to a candy height; let your nutmegs be first soaked in water; then put them into an earthen pan, pour your candy to them, keep them very close covered, set them in a warm place for about three weeks, and they will be of a rock candy.

## O.

OIL OF JUPITER. Take three quarts of spirits of wine, flavored with essential oil of lemon, the same quantity flavored with spirit of cedrat; make a sirup with seven pounds of sugar, a gallon of water, and two bottles of Scubac; mix the whole together, and by stirring, it will become thick; to clarify it, take the whites of two eggs in about a pint of the liqueur, and afterwards put it to the whole; stir it; then put it into a still in the *bain marie*

moderately heated; let it remain for twelve hours; filter the produce of your distillation, and bottle it.

OIL OF VENUS. Reduce the following articles to an impalpable powder:—an ounce of skirret seeds, an ounce of caraway seeds, an ounce of anise seeds, a drachm and a half of mace, and the rind of an orange; infuse these for five days in a gallon of brandy, then distil from it in a *bain marie*, two quarts of *liqueur*; dissolve over the fire four pounds of sugar in two quarts of pure water; when cold, mix it with the distilled *liqueur*, and color it of a clear yellow, with a little tincture of saffron; filter and bottle it; seal the corks.

ORANGES IN BRANDY. Choose the oranges very round and smooth, pare, prick them in the middle, and put them into cold water; then blanch them in boiling water; when they are tender, throw them again into cold water; in a short time give them seven or eight boils in sugar, *a la petite nappe*, skim, and let them stand till next day, when the same process must be gone through; skim them again, then put them into bottles, pour over them equal quantities of sirup and water; take care to cork them well.

ORANGE, COMPOTE. Cut them in small pieces, and boil them in water until they are tender, then change them into cold water; next make a sirup with one glass of water and four ounces of sugar, and put in the fruit; let it simmer gently over a slow fire for half an hour; serve cold.

ORANGE, CROQUE EN BOUCHES OF. Pare a dozen fine oranges, and divide each into twelve pieces, all of the same size; scrape off every particle of the white, without breaking the thin skin which contains the juice; when all are done, dip each piece into some sugar boiled to *casse* (and lightly colored,) and place them in a plain mould of six inches diameter, and five in height; the first row inclined one way, the second the reverse way, and so on; lay them at the bottom in a star. As soon as the mould is full, turn it out, and serve it with all possible expedition, as the moisture of the fruit dissolves the sugar so rapidly, that the *croque en bouche* is liable to fall to pieces.

ORANGE CAKES. Divide the oranges in half, take out the seeds, and put the pulp and juice into a basin; boil the rinds in a saucepan of water, closely covered; when very tender take them out, and dry them upon a cloth; allow to a pound of orange rinds, two of pounded loaf sugar; pound the rinds in a mortar; add by degrees the sugar, and then the juice and pulp; mix it thoroughly till thick and yellow; drop it upon tins in small cakes, and dry them under garden glasses, or in a cool oven. If it be too thick to drop, let it stand a night.

ORANGE SHERBET. Dissolve a pound and half of sugar in a quart of very pure water; take nine fine oranges and two lemons; wipe them well with a napkin, and having grated the most fragrant rinds, squeeze on them the juice of these fruits; sweeten this juice with the above sirup, run the whole through a close hair sieve, and finish in the usual way. (See *Sherbet*.)

ORANGE SHRUB. Put ten pounds of crushed sugar to two gallons of water, and boil it until the sugar be dissolved; skim it well, and put it into a tub; when quite cold, pour it into a barrel; add three quarts of Jamaica rum, and six quarts of orange-juice (take care there are no pips.) Beat up the white of an egg, mix it with the shrub, and let it stand for a week; then draw it off and bottle it.

ORANGE SUGAR. Rasp on a piece of sugar the rinds of the best oranges, but so lightly that not a particle of the white is mixed with it; scrape off the surface of the sugar as it becomes colored, and continue this operation until you have as much sugar as you require; then lay it in a stove, or at the mouth of the oven to dry; when it is perfectly

so, pass it through a very fine sieve. Lemons and cedrats may be grated, and the sugar dried in the same manner.

ORANGES, GREEN. Scrape out the insides of the oranges quite clean, then let them lie for three days in cold water, changing the water daily, then boil them very slowly till the water is bitter; then put them into other boiling water, set them by; repeating this daily till all the bitterness is extracted: make a rich sirup of the last water they are boiled in, with Lisbon sugar; when cold, put them in; the next day boil them in the sirup; repeat this till they are green and tender; cover with brandy-paper.

ORANGE, WATER ICE. Take off the rind of two Seville oranges, very fine and thin; squeeze the juice into a basin with one lemon; add half a pint of sirup, and half a pint of water; pass them through a sieve, and freeze them rich.

ORANGE-FLOWER CONSERVE. Boil half a pound of clarified sugar to *grande plume*, take it from the fire, and pour into it a dessert spoonful of orange-flower water; stir them together well, set the mixture on the fire, and when warm, pour it into shallow paper-cases; let it cool, and then cut it into cakes of any form you please.

ORANGE-FLOWER PASTILS. Pulverise a good pinch of dried orange-flowers; pound them with gum-dragon, previously dissolved in one glass of plain, and the same quantity of orange-flower water; add a sufficient proportion of powder-sugar, to make the paste of the requisite consistence, which form according to your taste into cones, lozenges, &c.

ORANGE-FLOWER PRALINES. Take a pound of very fresh white orange-flowers, pick, and throw them into cold water; clarify, and boil two pounds of sugar to *souffle*, then put in the flowers; stir them with a spatula, until your sugar regains the degree of *souffle*; take the pan from the fire, and continue stirring till the sugar is separated from the flowers, and becomes a powder; set it in a stove to dry, then set the whole on a sieve, that the sugar may run through and leave the flowers, which put into bottles. If preserved in a dry place they will keep for twelve months.

ORANGE-FLOWERS SIRUP. Clarify and boil four pounds of sugar to *perle*, then add three-quarters of a pound of fresh orange-flowers picked, and boil them once; then take the pan from the fire, and let it stand for two hours, after which, replace it on the fire; when it has had about a dozen boilings, pour it through a sieve into another saucepan, boil the sirup to *lisse*, and put it aside; when it is quite cold, bottle it. The flowers may be used as follows: put them into powder-sugar, with which rub them well with your hands, till quite dry, then sift and put them in a stove.

ORANGE-FLOWER WATER. Put into a still ten pounds of fresh gathered orange-flowers, and six quarts of pure river water; take particular care to close up all the apertures of the still perfectly, and set it on a moderate fire, that the ebullition may not be too strong; be particular in cooling it frequently, or, at least, whenever the water in the boiler becomes too warm, change it, and put in fresh; much depends on the attention paid to this part of the operation. From the above quantity, three quarts of orange-flower water may be drawn.

ORANGE-FLOWER DOUBLE WATER. Draw four quarts of orange-flower water from six quarts distilled as above; put to this water the same quantity of fresh flowers, distil it in the same manner, and it will yield five pints.

ORANGE PEEL TO CANDY. Take some orange peel, and let it soak in several waters till it has lost its bitterness, then boil it in a solution of double-refined sugar in water, till it becomes tender and transparent.

ORANGE PEEL TO PRESERVE. Cut the oranges in halves, take out the pulp, put the peel in strong salt and spring water, to soak for three days, repeat this three times, then put them on a sieve to dry; take one pound of loaf sugar, add to it one quart of spring water, boil it, skim it until quite clear; let the peels simmer until they are quite transparent; dry them before the fire; take loaf-sugar, with just sufficient water to dissolve it; whilst the sugar is boiling, put in the peels, stirring continually until all the sugar is candied round them, then put them to dry either before the fire or in an oven, and when perfectly dried, put them by for use.

ORGEAT. Blanch a pound of sweet, and twenty-four bitter almonds; pound them to an exceedingly fine paste, adding water occasionally to prevent their oiling; mix a gallon of water, two pounds of sugar and orange-flower water, with this paste; beat them together for some time; then strain it two or three times through a jelly-bag, stirring it with a spatula, and serve it in decanters.

ORGEAT PASTE. Pound the almonds with a little orange-flower water to a fine paste, and then work up with it an equal weight of powder-sugar.This paste will keep a long while, and by dissolving a small portion of it in water, and straining it, orgeat may be prepared very quickly. An ounce of the paste is sufficient for half a pint of water.

ORGEAT SIRUP. Take a pound and a half of sweet, and half a pound of bitter almonds, throw them into boiling water, and leave then till the skins can be removed with ease, then throw them into cold water for a minute before you blanch them, after which, they must again be put into cold water; then pound them, a few at a time, in a marble mortar, adding occasionally some water to prevent their oiling; when all are beaten to a very fine paste, dilute this with the greater part of a quart of water, (of which reserve six ounces); put the paste into a strong cloth; squeeze and wring out all the milk from the almonds, put the latter into the mortar, and pound them again, adding by degrees the remainder of the water, and then squeeze these also in a cloth; pour the whole of this milk into a matrass, large enough to contain, at least, one-third more liquid, add to it two pounds of lump-sugar, and a pint of orange-flower water; cork the matrass tight, and set it on a *bain marie*; when the sugar is completely dissolved, (which should be accelerated by shaking the matrass occasionally), lessen the fire by degrees, and as soon as the vessel is quite cold, put the sirup into bottles.

If you should have no matrass, you may make your sirup in the following manner: boil the above mentioned quantity of sugar to *forte plume*, then add the milk of almonds, and as soon as it has boiled up twice, take it from the fire; when cold, flavor it with a pint of orange-flower water.

Or this sirup may be made in a still more simple way, as thus: put the milk of almonds into some pounded sugar, without being clarified or boiled previously; when the sirup begins to boil, add about a coffee-cupful of orange-flower water and after it has boiled up two or three times, take it from the fire; let it get quite cold before you bottle it. Keep it well corked.

## P.

PARFAIT AMOUR. Take four very fine fresh cedrats, pare them very thin, and infuse them with half an ounce of fine cinnamon, and four ounces of coriander, in three gallons of strong brandy, and a quart of water, for a week or ten days, when distil it in the *bain marie;* this quantity of brandy, if good, will yield two gallons and half a pint of spirit. Dissolve three pounds and a half of sugar in seven pints of river water, color it with cochineal, then add it to the spirit, filter, and bottle it.

PASTILLES. To make these articles, it is necessary to have a small copper stewpan that will hold about a pint, rather deep than wide, with a pointed lip on the right side, and a tol-

erably long handle, also two pieces of wood, one about eighteen inches long, and four in diameter, called the *bois a tabeller*, the other about half the length, one inch in diameter, and the lower end, pointed so that it will exactly fit the lip of the pan; this is called the *bois a egoutter*; six or eight tin plates about the size of a sheet of letter-paper.

For the best *pastilles*, take a pound of double-refined sugar reduced to an impalpable powder; sift it through a tammy on a sheet of white paper, put four or five spoonfuls of this sugar into your pan, pour on it a little orange-flower water, and beat it well with the larger stick, until the preparation is sufficiently thin to run from the stick without being clear; if it be so, more sugar must be added. Put the pan over a chafing-dish filled with live coals; and let it stand (stirring constantly) till it boils; then take it off the chafing-dish, add two more spoonfuls of sugar, work it up well, scrape away whatever sugar adheres to the stick, set it aside, and take the smaller stick in your right hand, hold the pan in your left (slanting) over one of the tin-plates; the sugar will, by these means, flow to the lip, then strike the point of the stick into the lip of the pan, which action will separate the liquid; so that each time the stick strikes the lip a single drop of the preparation will fall on the tin; a little practice will be necessary before this operation can be performed neatly. As soon as all your sugar, &c. is used, replenish the pan and proceed as above directed, until you have as many *pastilles* as you may require. When cold and hard, remove them from the tins with your hand, and keep them in boxes in a dry place. You may, if you please, color the *pastilles*, taking care to perfume them with a corresponding odour.

PASTILLES, COMMON. These are made in the same manner as the best sort, the difference consists in the materials, (which are a quarter of a pound of powder to three-quarters of a pound of sugar) and the perfumes are omitted.

PASTILLAGES. Put two ounces of well-washed gum dragon into an earthen pan, with as much clear hot water as will cover it, lay a sheet of paper to keep out the dust, and let it stand twenty-four hours; then squeeze it through a coarse cloth into a marble mortar, and add to it as much starch and sugar (both in powder) as the gum water will contain; pound these ingredients well, and strain them through a tammy into a pan which keep covered with a damp cloth. This pastillage is used to form the ornamental parts of pastry and confectionary, such as temples, baskets, &c., and may be tinged of the requisite shades, by mixing with it any of the coloring materials.

PEACHES IN A COMPOTE. Cut your peaches in half, take out the stones, peel them, then set them on the fire in a sugar-pan, with a sufficient quantity of thick clarified sugar to cover them, and let them simmer in this gently till done; then take them out in a basin, put in the kernels to the sugar, and let it boil until tolerably thick; put in the juice of two or three lemons, and pour the sirup over the peaches; serve them in a deep hot dish.

PEARS IN BRANDY. Take some *beurre* pears, not too ripe, put them into a saucepan with a sufficient quantity of water to cover them, set them on the fire, and let them simmer, but not boil, until the pears will yield to the pressure of your finger; then change them into cold water; pare them with the greatest care, so that not a single spot may remain; prick, and put them again on the fire in fresh water and the juice of a lemon; let them boil very fast. As soon as the pears are soft enough for the head of a pin to penetrate them easily, take them out carefully with a skimmer, and lay them in cold water. In the meantime, having boiled your sugar to *lisse*, pour the boiling sirup on the pears, (previously drained from the water,) and leave them. The next day drain off the sirup, boil it to *la nappe*, then put in the pears, give them a boil also; proceed in the same manner on the third day, after which,

drain the fruit, and put it into bottles. Boil up the sirup a few more times, let it cool, and then pour on it some brandy, (three-fourths of the quantity of the sirup;) run the mixture through a bag, put it to the pears, and cork the bottles well.

PEARS CANDIED. Are done like apricots.

PEARS, COMPOTE OF. Take some good sized pears, cut them in halves, and put them into boiling water; when soft, change them into cold water, in which squeeze a little lemon-juice. Boil some clarified sugar, drain the fruit well from the water, and then put them into the sirup; boil together until the pears are sufficiently done; skim, and place them in the *compotier*. A little Burgundy wine and prepared cochineal will give the *compote* a red color.

PEAR MARMALADE. Take six pounds of small pears and four pounds of sugar; put the pears into a saucepan with a little water, set it on the fire; when the fruit is soft, take them out, pare, quarter, and core them; as you do this, throw each piece into cold water, in another saucepan, and when all are done, set them on the fire. As soon as they are sufficiently soft, rub them through a sieve, and having in the meantime clarified and boiled the sugar to *petit lisee*, pour the sirup to the pulp, set it on the fire, and stir them together until the marmalade is of the proper consistence; then take it off, put it into pots, and when cold, tie them down.

PERSICA. Cut about one hundred peach leaves, put them into a wide-mouthed bottle, pour on them a quart of the best brandy, cork it close; in three weeks strain it off, and put to it an equal quantity of capillaire. It is good in custards, puddings, and as a *liqueur*.

PINE APPLE CHIPS. Pare and trim a pine-apple, divide, and slice each half into pieces a quarter of an inch thick; take half the weight of the fruit in powder-sugar: lay the slices in a basin, with sugar strewed between; let it stand till the sugar be dissolved, then set it on a moderate fire to simmer till the chips be quite clear, when set it by. The next day remove all the sirup from the slices, place them on glasses, and dry them in a gentle oven.

PINE APPLE IN A COMPOTE. Turn off the rind of a pine, cut it in slices, but not too thin; have some sugar on the fire in a sugar-pan, into which put the slices of pine, and let them boil gently till the sirup is tolerably thick, then take out the pine, and lay it on a dish; mix with the sugar, the juice of a couple of lemons, and pour it over the pine.

PISTACHIO MARCHPANE. Put a pound and a half of pistachios into a mortar, pound them, moistening with white of egg, to a very fine paste; in the meantime clarify the same quantity of sugar, boil it to *petit boule*; then take the pan from the fire, put in the pistachios, stir them together well, replace the pan on hot ashes, continually stirring, till the paste is of a proper consistence, then pour it on a slab well sprinkled with sugar; as soon as it is cold, cut it into whatever forms your fancy may dictate.

PLUMS, IN BRANDY. Take twelve pounds of fine *magnum bonum* plums, and three pounds of sugar; the fruit should be turned in color, but not ripe; prick, and put them into a saucepan with cold water; set them on the fire; when the water boils and the plums rise, take them out carefully with a skimmer and put them into a pan of cold water; clarify and boil the sugar to *petit lisse*, put the plums to it, and give them a boil; the two succeeding days, drain off and boil the sirup, first alone; and afterwards with the fruit; the third day drain the plums, and put them into bottles; then boil the sirup to *la nappe*, and when cold, add to it three-fourths of its quantity of the best brandy, stir it well, strain and pour the mixture over the plums. Cork the bottles tight. Green-gage plums are done like apricots. (See *Apricots in Brandy*.)

PLUMS CANDIED. Choose your fruit of a nice shape and good size; cut them in halves, lay them on a large shallow dish, strew powder-sugar over, and put them into a moderate oven, tightly closed; in half an hour's time, take them out, and place the plums one by one on glass plates to dry.

PLUMS, CLEAR CAKES OF. Fill a jar with the white pear plums, set it in a saucepan of boiling water on the fire; when sufficiently done, let the clear juice run from it, and to every pint of it, add an equal quantity of sugar, boiled to candy height; put the juice to the sirup, set it on the fire, and keep stirring it till the whole is quite hot, but not boiling; then pour it into glasses, and dry the cakes in a stove.

PLUMS, MARMALADE OF. Take six pounds of plums, and four pounds of sugar; stone, and put the fruit into a cullender, beat it through with a wooden pestle into a preserving-pan, which set on the fire, to dry the pulp, stirring it constantly. In the meantime, clarify and boil the sugar to *petit casse*, then mix it with the fruit (still on the fire,) stir it till the whole is of the consistence of jelly, then take it off, and pour the marmalade into pots.

If the plums are not quite ripe, they must be boiled once or twice before they are pressed through the cullender. Some of the kernels may be added, if approved; they should be pounded before putting in the mamalade.

PLUMS PRESERVED, DRY. Gather the plums when full grown and just turning color; prick and put them into a saucepan of cold water, set them on the fire until the water is on the point of boiling; then take them out, drain and boil them well in some clarified sugar, let them settle, and then boil them again; if they shrink and will not take the sugar, prick them as they lay in the pan, and then give them another boil, skim and set them by: the next day, add some more sugar, boiled to *souffle*, to the fruit, and sirup, then do them together; place them in a stove till next day, when drain the plums from the sirup, sprinkle a little powder-sugar over, and dry them in a stove.

PLUMS, PRESERVED LIQUID. Gather the plums green, firm, and when the stone may be extracted with ease, cut the stalks close, and prick the fruit in several places, especially round the stalk; then place them in a saucepan of water over the fire, and as soon as the water is ready to boil, take the saucepan from the fire; in four-and-twenty hours, replace the plums in the same water on a gentle fire, with a small quantity of verjuice to preserve their color. Keep the water hot, without allowing it to boil, for three hours, stirring it occasionally; when the fruit is perfectly green, increase the heat till the plums rise to the surface, when they must be taken out and thrown into cold water, which change frequently till the plums are perfectly cold, then drain them. Put the fruit in some sugar boiled to *la nappe*, boil them up a few times; adding a little water; skim, and then pour the whole into a pan; the next two days, drain off the sirup, and increase the degree of boiling each day; the third and fourth days, boil the fruit with the sirup, keeping them covered, and increasing the degree, until the last time, it reaches to *perle*. Put the preserve into pots, and place them for two days in a stove.

The same fruit may be preserved dry also. The operation is the same, but the sirup is drained off, and the plums laid on tin plates before they are put into the stove.

POMEGRANATE CLEAR CAKES. Pare some good boiling apples, and put them into a saucepan with as much water as will cover them, set them on the fire, and when perfectly soft, press the pulp through a sieve, and then strain it. Boil this jelly with the juice of two or three pomegranates, that of one orange, and one lemon, and the rind of each grated; strain it again, and to every pound of jelly add a pound and a quarter of fine sugar, boiled till it cracks, color it with

cochineal; pour it into glasses (taking off the scum before it becomes cold). Set them in a stove, and when the top is dry, turn them out, and put them to dry again, then cut them into whatever forms you please, put them into the stove or oven to harden, then lay them on sieves, and when thoroughly dry, place them in boxes with paper between. As they are apt to become moist, they should be looked at frequently.

POMEGRANATE JELLY, TRANSPARENT. Take the seeds from five very fine pomegranates, from which extract the juice by pressing it hard through a horse-hair sieve; filter this juice and mix it with some sirup tinged of a rose color, with a little cochineal; add the isinglass to this, and finish as usual. (See *Jelly Fruit*.)

POMEGRANATE SIRUP. Take five very ripe large pomegranates, extract the seeds (which must be very red); crush, and put them into a skillet, with half a pint of water; set them on the fire till soft, and then squeeze the juice through a new coarse cloth; clarify a pound and half of sugar, and boil it to *souffle*, then add the juice, boil them together to the usual consistence of sirups. It must not be bottled until quite cold. This number of pomegranates will yield a quart of sirup.

POUPELIN. Put into a saucepan four glasses of water, a quarter of a pound of butter, the *zeste* of a lemon, and a pinch of fine salt; set it on the fire, and as soon as it begins to boil, take it off, and put in as much sifted flour as will make a paste the consistence of *choux*, then replace it on the fire, and keep stirring till it dries; make a similar mixture, and when that also is dry, put both into a mortar, with half a pound of powder sugar, an ounce of orange-flowers, and two eggs at a time, until five and twenty or thirty are used, by which time the paste will be of the proper consistence, then pour it into a lightly buttered tin; put it into a moderate oven, and leave it. In three hours' time, if the *poupelin* is of a nice gold color, take it out, cut off the top, and with a spoon remove all the inside, then set it in the oven to dry. When cold, spread all over the interior apricot marmalade, on which strew sweet macaroons crushed, then turn it on a dish, and serve.

wwwwwww

## Q.

QUINCE CAKES. Pare and core half a dozen quinces, boil them till quite soft; then rub the pulp through a sieve, and strain it; mix this with half a pint of sirup of quinces, and the same of sirup of barberries, and a quarter of a pound of fine sugar; boil the whole to *casse*, and then pour it into small shallow moulds, of any shape you please; let them cool a little, and then dry them in a stove.

QUINCE CAKES TRANSPARENT. Take a quart of sirup of quinces, and half a pint of the sirup of barberries; set them on a gentle fire, boil and skim them well; then add two pounds and a half of fine sugar, keep stirring until it reaches candy height; then take it off, and when nearly cold, lay it, in any form you please, on tin plates. Dry them in a stove.

wwwwwww

## R.

RASPBERRY CAKES. Gather some raspberries before they are quite ripe, pick, and lay them in a stove to dry; then beat them in a mortar. Take a pound and quarter of fine sugar, clarify and boil it to *casse*; then weigh half a pound of raspberries, dried as above; throw them into the sirup, with half a spoonful of white of egg, beaten in cream; stir it carefully, give it a boil, and pour it in moulds or paper cases.

RASPBERRIES OF MARCHPANE. Take a pound of marchpane, the juice of four lemons, a quarter of a pound of raspberry jelly, and a little cochineal; mix these together with a strong wooden spatula; then add two handfuls of flour, and some powder sugar; when well worked up, roll them into pieces about the size of a finger, cut these into dice, roll each into a ball, pinch the top into a point, so as to resemble the form of a raspberry: then put them one by one into paper cases, which place in a dry warm place, for eight or ten days. At the end of that time, put a portion of sirup of raspberries, a little cochineal, and a small quantity of powder-sugar into a pan; mix them together with a spoon, and then throw into it a couple of handfuls of the raspberries; take the pan in both hands, and shake it about, so that the raspberries may be equally covered with the red sirup; then put sugar *a la grele* on a large sheet of paper, spread it out a little, and while the raspberries are wet with the sirup, throw them into the sugar; then take the four corners of the paper, shake it about well, by which means the sugar will adhere to the raspberries in all parts, and give them a perfect resemblance to the real fruit; take them out carefully one by one, lay them on paper, and put them in a warm place for some days. These artificial raspberries are of a pleasant flavor, and will keep several years.

RASPBERRY MARMALADE. Take double the weight of raspberries to that of sugar. Rub the fruit through a sieve, and put the pulp into a saucepan; set it on the fire, and stir till it is reduced to half; then pour on the sugar, previously clarified and boiled to *petit boule*, stir it well in, put it on the fire, give it a few boils, and then pour it into pots.

RASPBERRIES PRESERVED. Take five or six pounds of red, but not too ripe raspberries, pick, and put them into a preserving pan, with an equal weight of clarified sugar, boiled to *petit boule*; when they have boiled up about a dozen times, skim, and pour the whole into a pan till the next day, then drain the fruit, and put it into jars; put to the sirup about two glasses of cherry juice, previously strained; boil the sugar to *la nappe*, and then pour it over the raspberries; add afterwards, about a spoonful of currant jelly to each pot, and when cold, lay on brandy papers, and tie them down.

RATAFIA OF FOUR FRUITS. Take ten pounds of very ripe cherries, two pounds and a half of raspberries, five pounds and a half of red and two pounds of black currants; pick, and mix these fruits together, press the juice from them, measure it, and for every quart of juice, take half a pound of sugar, and an equal quantity of brandy; dissolve the sugar in the juice, then put in the brandy, a drachm of mace, and two drachms of cloves. Let the whole stand some time, filter, and bottle it. Keep them well corked.

ROSES, CANDIED. Crisp two handfuls of rose-leaves in some clarified sugar, boil them to *fort souffle*, then take the pan from the fire, pour it on a sieve, let the sirup run from the leaves, rubbing the latter in your hands, then dry them in a stove. Boil your sugar again to *souffle*, adding a little carmine to color it, have a proper mould ready, pour the sugar into it, and put the flowers on it, push them down lightly with a fork, that they may be completely covered with the sugar; place the mould in a moderate stove or oven for five days, then drain off the sirup; lay a sheet of paper on the table, and turn the candy quickly out of the mould.

ROSES, CONSERVE OF. Boil half a pound of sugar to *fort souffle*, pour into this sirup the best double-distilled rose water; boil it again to *fort perle*, mix with it a little prepared cochineal or carmine to color it, and pour your conserve into moulds.

ROSE RED DROPS. Take a small quantity of red bastard saffron, and a little calcined alum, boil these in some water until it is sufficiently tinged for your purpose; then filter or strain it through a very close linen cloth; put five or six spoonfuls of sifted sugar into the pan, dilute it with the colored water, work it well with the *bois a tabeller*, and set it over a chafing-dish; when it begins to boil, add two more spoonfuls of sugar, and having

worked it well, perfume it with some drops of essence of roses, and finish as directed. (See *Orange-flower Drops*.)

ROSSOLS. Take three-quarters of a pound of picked orange-flowers, a pound of musk roses, six drachms of cinnamon, and two of cloves (both bruised); put them into a cucurbite with three gallons of pure water; on distilling this, it will yield a gallon and a half, in which dissolve twelve pounds of fine sugar broken up; add to it an equal quantity of spirit of jessamine, color it crimson with cochineal, filter and bottle it.

## S.

SEEDS, SUGARED. These are done in the same manner as sugared almonds. The seeds most generally used for this purpose are anise, cummin, and fennel.

The best method of proceeding is as follows: place a small preserving-pan over a charcoal fire, on the side of which have a chafing dish, on which keep a pan with a quantity of sugar boiled to *lisse*; (this sugar should be kept quite hot, but not boiling); on the other side have some fine powder. When so far prepared, put your seeds into the pan, and as soon as they begin to heat, pour over them a large spoonful or two of the sirup; stir them about, that all may be thoroughly saturated with it; then sprinkle over it a handful or two of powder, still shaking the pan to make the seeds equally white. When dry, pour on some more sirup, then the powder, and continue this alternately until your seeds are sufficiently large; then lay them on a sieve, keep them in a warm place for some days, after which put them into glass bottles.

SOUFFLE FRANCAIS. Make a *croustade* eleven inches in diameter, and three and three-quarters in height; put round it three sheets of buttered paper, and bake it.

Take twelve glasses of boiling milk, in which infuse whatever ingredients you may think proper, such as vanilla, coffee, orange-flowers, &c. (the proportions will be found under the different articles). In the meantime, wash a pound of rice thoroughly in warm water, then put it into a saucepan of cold water, and when it has boiled a few minutes, strain the rice, and put it with your infusion into another saucepan, and set it again on the fire; as soon as it boils, place the saucepan on hot ashes, that the rice may burst gradually; in three-quarters of an hour, add a pound of powder-sugar, three-quarters of a pound of fresh butter, and a pinch of salt, stir them well in; put fresh hot ashes under the saucepan, that the rice may be kept constantly simmering for an hour, by which time it ought to be perfectly soft, and should be rubbed through a bolting-cloth quickly, like a *puree*; put this into another saucepan over hot ashes, to keep it warm. Take sixteen eggs, separate the yolks and whites, beat the former well, and whisk the latter till nearly firm; then mix the yolks with the rice (taking off the ashes); the preparation ought to be of the same consistence as a cream *palissiere*; add, at first, a quarter, and afterwards the whole of the whites; stir them in as lightly as for biscuit paste; the whole being thoroughly amalgamated, pour it into the *croustade*, and place it in a moderate oven for two hours and a half; when done, cover a baking tin with red cinders, on which place the *souffle* the moment it is taken out of the oven; this prevents its falling, whilst you mask it with powder-sugar, and glaze with the salamander; carry it into the dining-room on a tin, have a dish ready with a napkin folded on it; place the *souffle* on the dish, and let it be served immediately. Remember that a *souffle* cannot be served too quickly.

STRAWBERRY, COMPOTE OF. This is made in the same manner as Raspberries, only that the strawberries do not require being mixed with any other fruit.

STRAWBERRY CONSERVE. Take some very ripe fresh strawberries, pick, and crush them through a tammy. For every dessert spoonful of juice, allow six ounces of sugar; boil this to *fort perle*, take it off the fire, and pour in the juice; stir them together with a silver spoon, until the conserve begins to whiten and dry, then put it into moulds or paper cases. If the conserve be too white, add a little carmine to the sirup.

STRAWBERRY MARCHPANE. Take two pounds of sweet almonds, two pounds and a half of sugar, and a pound of picked strawberries. Beat the almonds to a fine paste. and mix them with the sugar (boiled to *petit boule*;) crush, and strain the juice of the fruit, which add to the almond paste and sirup; stir the mixture well, set it on hot ashes, and continue stirring until the paste is sufficiently done; this may be proved by laying a piece on the back of your hand; if it may be removed without its sticking, it is enough; when cold, spread it over a slab, and cut it of any size and shape you think proper.

SUGAR, TO CLARIFY. Take four pounds of sugar, and break it into pieces; put into a preserving-pan the white of an egg, and a glass of pure spring water; mix them well with a whisk, add another glass, still whipping, until two quarts of water have been put in; when the pan is full of froth, throw in the sugar, and set it on the fire, being careful to skim it every time the scum rises, which will be the case as the sugar boils up. After a few boilings, the sugar will rise so high as to run over the edges of the pan, to prevent which, throw on it a little cold water; this will lower it instantly, and give time for the skimming, for the scum should never be taken off whilst the sugar is bubbling; the cold water stills it, and that is the moment to skim it. Repeat this operation carefully three or four times, when a whitish light scum only will rise, then take the pan off, lay a napkin, slightly wetted, over a basin, and pour the sugar through it.

The scum thus taken off, put into a china basin; and when the sugar is clarified, wash the pan and the skimmer with a glass of water, which put to the scum, and set it aside for more common purposes.

SUGAR, *Different Degrees of Preparing*.

The various purposes to which sugar is applied, require it to be in different states; these are called *degrees*, and are thirteen in number, called as follows:

*Petit Lisse,* or *First Degree.* Replace the clarified sugar in the preserving-pan, to boil gently, take a drop of it on the thumb, touch it with the fore-finger; if, on opening them, it draws to a fine thread, and in breaking, forms two drops on each finger, it is at the right point.

*Lisse, Second Degree.* A little more boiling brings it to this point; when the thread will draw further before it breaks.

*Petit Perle, Third Degree.* At this point the thread may be drawn as far as the span will open, without breaking.

*Grand Perle, Fourth Degree.* On still increasing the boiling, little raised balls are formed on the surface of the sugar.

*Petit Queue de Cochon, Fifth Degree.* Take up some of the sugar on a skimmer, and drop it on the rest, when it should form a slanting streak on the surface. Boil it a little longer, and it will reach the

*Grande Queue de Cochon, or Sixth Degree.* The streak or tail is now larger.

*Souffle, Seventh Degree.* Take out a skimmerful of the sugar, blow through it, and small sparks of sugar will fly from it.

*Petit-Plume, Eighth Degree.* The same proof as above; the sparks should be larger and stronger.

*Grande Plume, Ninth Degree.* Take the sugar in the skimmer, as before, give it a shake, and if the sparks are large, and adhere together on rising, it is at the right point.

*Petit Boulet, Tenth Degree.* Dip your fingers in cold water, and then into the sugar instantly, and again into the water, when the sugar will roll into a ball, which will be supple when cold.

*Gros Boulet, Eleventh Degree.* At this point, the ball or bullet will be harder when cold than at the last.

*Casse, Twelfth Degree.* Prove as above; the bullet should crumble between the fingers, and on biting, will stick to the teeth; at the next point,

*Caramel, Thirteenth Degree,* It should snap clean. This point is very difficult to attain, for in increasing the height, the sugar is apt to burn; it is better therefore to try the proof very frequently.

Another caramel is frequently used by the confectioner, and is of a deep color; it is made by putting a little water to the sugar, and boiling it without skimming, or otherwise touching the sugar, till of the right color, then take it off and use immediately.

If, on preparing the sugar, you happen to miss the right point, add a little cold water, and boil once more.

*Observations.*—The skimmer should never be left in the preserving-pan after the sugar is clarified, nor after the scum is removed.

Be very careful not to stir or disturb the sugar, as that would cause its diminution.

In boiling the sugar (particularly the two last degrees), the sugar is continually rising and falling; and on falling, leaves marks on the sides of the pan, which the heat of the fire would soon burn, and thereby spoil the whole of the sugar; to avoid this, have by the side of you a pan of cold water, and a sponge, with which wipe the sides of the pan carefully, the instant after the sugar has fallen.

SUGAR LIKE SNOW. Blanch a quarter of a pound of bitter almonds, pound them to a very fine paste in a marble mortar, with the whites of four eggs; when perfectly smooth, add a pound of the best lump sugar (in powder), and five or six more whites of eggs; stir all together well, until of such consistence that it may be kneaded without adhering to the hands. Divide this preparation into two parts, one of which, tinge of a red color, either with *bolus armena*, or cochineal, and perfume it with essential oil of roses or bergamot; leave the other portion of paste white, but flavor it as follows:—grate the rind of two fine sound lemons on a small piece of sugar, scrape off the surface, and when pounded in a small mortar, work it into the uncolored portion of sugar-paste, then roll it out to about half an inch in thickness (having previously sprinkled the slab with powder-sugar,) cut it with a tin-paste cutter about two inches diameter; arrange them on white paper, which place on a baking tin, and put them into a moderate oven for about three-quarters of an hour; proceed in the same manner with the colored paste. When cold, detach them from the paper.

SUGAR PASTE. Take a pound of flour, a quarter of a pound of sugar, a quarter of a pound of butter, a little salt, one egg; mix all together with a little water. This paste may be used for any second-course dish.

wwwww

## T.

TABLET OF PATIENCE. Take eight eggs, and whip the whites to a firm snow; in the meantime have the yolks beaten up with six ounces of powder-sugar; (both these operations should be performed for at least half an hour); then mix the two together, add six ounces of sifted flour, and when well incorporated, pour in half a pint of rose or orange-flower water; stir the whole together for some time. Have ready some tin plates, well rubbed with butter; take a funnel that has three or four tubes, fill it with the paste, and push out your *tablets*; when the tin plates are full, put them into a pretty warm oven. When done, take them from the tins while hot.

TRIFLE. (1) Sweeten three pints of cream; add to it half a pint of mountain wine, grate in the rind of a lemon, squeeze in the juice, and grate in half a nutmeg; whisk this up, lay the froth on a large sieve, and the sieve over a dish that has ratafia cakes, macaroons, sweet almonds, blanched and pounded, citron, and candied orange-peel, cut into small pieces, some currant jelly, and raspberry jam in it, that the liquor may run upon them; when they are soaked, lay them in the dish you intend to serve in, put on the froth as high as possible, well drained; strew over nonpareils, and stick

on little slices of citron, orange, or lemon-peel.

TRIFLE. (2) Lay some macaroons and ratafia drops over the bottom of your dish, and soak them well with raisin wine, when soaked, pour on them a very rich cold custard. It must stand two or three inches thick; on that put a layer of raspberry jam, and cover the whole with a very high whip made the preceding day, of rich cream, the whites of two eggs, well beaten, sugar, lemon-peel, and raisin wine, well beat with a whisk. It is best to make it the day before it is wanted, being more solid and better tasted.

TRIFLE. (3) Put half a pound of macaroons into a dish, pour over them some white wine, and a pint of custard over that, make a whip, and put on it; garnish according to your fancy.

wwwww

## V.

VANILLA CREAM. Take two drachms of vanilla, a quart of milk, the yolks of three eggs, five ounces of sugar, and a pint of cream; beat up the eggs well with the milk, and then add the other ingredients; set the whole on a moderate fire, and stir it constantly with a wooden spoon, till the cream will adhere to it; then strain, and serve it cold.

VANILLA CREAM, BOLTED. Take as much cream as will fill the mould you intend to use, and boil it up a few times, with the proportionate quantities of vanilla and sugar; then let it cool, and if the mould will contain a quart, mix twelve yolks and three whole eggs with the cream, and run it five times through a bolting cloth. Butter the mould, pour the cream into it, and place it in the *bain marie*, but not too hot; when the cream is set, which you may know by touching it gently with your finger, turn it on a dish; take the remainder of the cream, stir it over the fire like white sauce, and as soon as it sticks to the spoon (which must be of wood), take it off, stir it an instant, and then pour it over the other cream, and serve cold.

VANILLA CREAM WHIPPED. Put a pinch of gum-dragon into a pint of cream, add a small quantity of orange-flower water, powder-sugar to the taste, and a little milk, in which some vanilla has been boiled, and the milk strained; whip these ingredients with a whisk, until the whole is sufficiently frothed; then lay it carefully on a dish, in a pyramidal form, and serve it.

VANILLA CREAM ICE. Whisk the whites of twelve eggs to a firm froth in a preserving pan, pour on them the yolks of eight, and a pound of sifted sugar, whip the whole well with a whisk, and pour in by degrees two quarts of boiling cream; continue to whip it for some little time, and then put it on the fire, with half an ounce of vanilla bruised; still whipping, when it has boiled up three or four times, strain it, and freeze as usual. (See *Ice*.)

VANILLA CREAM LIQUEUR. Dissolve over the fire two pounds ten ounces of broken sugar, in three pints of purified river water; when it has boiled up once, pour it into a jar, on three drachms of vanilla, cut in pieces, and half a grain of amber. When quite cold, add three pints of good brandy, cover the vessel, and when it has infused six days, color it with a little prepared cochineal; filter, and bottle the *liqueur*. Cork the bottles tight, and seal the corks.

VANILLA STICKS. Take some marchpane paste, a quarter of a pound of chocolate, and the same of vanilla; mix these well into the paste, and then form it into sticks, like the vanilla in its original form; lay them on a sheet of paper, and bake in a slow oven.

VERDE. Infuse the rind of three lemons and four oranges in two quarts of rum or brandy, for four-and-twenty hours, closely stopped; then squeeze the juice through a strainer; if the fruit is good, there will be half a pint, and if there is not so much, make it that; add to it a pound and a quarter of sugar, pour to it three quarts of water, and keep stirring till all the sugar is dissolved; when it is dissolved, stir in the peel and spirits, and then one pint of cold new milk; pass it through a bag till clear; bottle it. It will keep good for twelve months.

VERJUICE. (1) Verjuice is the young, unripe, and sour grape; it is frequently used in French cookery, but very rarely put into English dishes.

VERJUICE. (2) Take some crab apples when the kernels turn black, lay them in a heap to sweat; then pick them from the stalks and rottenness, beat them to a mash, and press the juice through a bag of coarse hair cloth into a clean vessel; it will be fit for use in a month's time. If intended for white pickles, distil it in a cold still. It may be put into sauces when lemon is wanting.

VESPETRO. Take half a pound of each of the following seeds: angelica, coriander, fennel, and caraway, the rinds of four lemons, and as many oranges, infuse all these in two gallons and a half of the best brandy, close the vessel hermetically. In five days time, distil it in the *bain marie* alembic, and draw from the above quantity five quarts of *liqueur*. Dissolve seven pounds of sugar in a gallon of pure river water; add this sirup to the *liqueur*, filter, and bottle it.

VIOLETS CANDIED. Pick off the green stalks from some double violets; boil some sugar to *souffle*; put in the violets, and keep them in till the sugar again boils to *souffle*; then rub the sugar against the sides of the pan until it is white; stir all together till the sugar leaves the violets, and then sift and dry them.

VIOLETS TO ROCK CANDY. Pick the leaves off the violets; then boil some of the best, and finest sugar to *souffle*, pour it into a candying-pan made of tin, in the form of a dripping-pan, about three inches deep; then strew the violet leaves as thick as possible on the top, and put it into a hot stove, in which let it remain for ten days; when it is hard candied, break a hole in one corner of it, and drain off all the sirup; break it out, and place it in heaps upon a tin to dry in a stove.

VIOLETS, CONSERVE OF. Take a quarter of a pound of early violets, picked; bruise them in a mortar; boil two pounds of sugar to *casse*, take it off, put in the pulp, and mix them together over the fire, and when the sugar bubbles up, pour the conserve into the moulds.

VIOLET DROPS. (1) Take a certain quantity of sirup of violets, which mix with an equal portion of water; use this mixture, and make your drop precisely as directed. You may, if you please, perfume it with oil of violets, but that is not necessary, as the sirup, imparts sufficient odour.

VIOLET DROPS. (2) Take the juice of six lemons, mix with it some finely sifted powdered sugar, and two spoonfuls of essence of violets, and color it of a fine blue color; mix the whole well together, and dry it over the fire, the same as all others, and drop them off a knife on paper, the usual size of drops; let them stand till cold, be careful that your mixture is not too thin; when the drops are cold, put them into papered boxes.

VIOLETS, MARMALADE OF. Take three pounds of violets, and four pounds of sugar, put the former into a mortar and bruise them to a pulp; in the meantime boil the sugar to *souffle*, then add the flowers; stir them together, add two pounds of apple marmalade, and when it has boiled up a few times, put the marmalade into pots.

VIOLETS, SIRUP OF. Pound very lightly in a marble mortar, and with a wooden pestle, one pound of picked violets; warm gradually a glass, or earthenware vessel with a small opening, into which put the pounded flowers, and pour over them two pounds of boiling water; close the vessel hermetically, and place it on hot ashes, renewing them when necessary, to keep up an equal temperature for twelve hours; after that time pass the whole through a close cloth, squeezing it well; let it stand for half an hour; then pour it off very carefully, that all the sediment may remain at the bottom; weigh it, and the above quantities will have yielded seventeen ounces; put into a matrass two pounds of crushed sugar with the infusion, close the matrass tight, and set it in the *bain marie*, over a moderate fire; shake it occasionally to accelerate the dissolution of the sugar, and when perfectly dissolved, let the fire go out and the matrass cool gradually. When cold, pour the sirup into bottles.

## W.

WORMWOOD CREME LIQUEUR. Distil in the *bain-marie* the zests of two oranges, and half a pound of fresh gathered wormwood tops, in a gallon of brandy, which will produce nearly half the quantity of *liqueur*. Dissolve four pounds of sugar in as many pints of filtered river water; mix this sirup with the *liqueur*; run it through a jelly-bag, and bottle it.

☞ Many receipts for Confectionary may be found in the first part of this Book.

# EXPLANATION

*Of some of the Terms made use of in the foregoing Pages.*

*Atelets*—Small silver skewers.

*Baba*— French sweet yeast cake.

*Bain-Marie*—See the word in its place.

*Bouquet*—A bunch of parsley and scallions tied up to put in soups, &c.

*Bouquet garni, or Assaisonne*—The same, with the addition of cloves and aromatic herbs.

*Bourguignote*—A ragout of truffles.

*Braise*—See word in its place.

*Brioche*—A French yeast cake.

*Buisson*—A whimsical method of dressing up pastry, &c.

*Capilotade*—A common hash of poultry.

*Caramel,* see page 376.

*Casse,* see page 376.

*Civet*—A hash of game or wild fowl.

*Compiegne*—A French sweet yeast cake with fruit, &c. &c.

*Compote*—A fine mixed ragout to garnish white poultry, &c.; also a method of stewing fruit with sirup for desserts.

*Compotier*—A dish amongst the dessert service appropriated to the use of the compote.

*Couronne*—To serve any prescribed articles on a dish in the form of a crown.

*Court or short (to stew)*— To reduce a sauce very thick.

*Croustade*— Bread baked in a mould, and scooped out to contain minces, &c.

*Croutons*— Bread cut in various shapes, and fried lightly in butter or oil.

*Dorez*— To wash pastry, &c. with yolk of egg well beaten.

*Dorure*—Yolks of eggs beaten well.

*Entrees*— Are dishes served at the commencement, or during the first course of the dinner.

*Entremets*— Small ornamental dishes, served in the second and third courses.

*Farce*— stuffing.

*Financiere*—An expensive, highly-flavored, mixed ragout.

*Flan*—A French custard.

*Glaze, (to fall to a)*—To reduce sauces till they become a jelly, and adhere to the meat.

*Glaze*—Is usually made from reduced *consomme*, or juices from the bottoms of braised white meats; it should be preserved in jelly-pots.

*Glaze, Glace, or Ice*—Is composed of white of egg beaten with powder-sugar.

*Godiveau*—A common veal forcemeat.

*Grand Plume,* see page 376.

*Grand Perle,* see page 376.

*Grand Queue de Cochon,* see page 376.

*Gros Boulet,* see page 376.

*Gras (au)*—This signifies that the article specified is dressed with meat gravy.

*Gratin*—A layer of some particular article is spread over a silver, or any other dish that will bear the fire, and placed on a stove or hot ashes until it burns to it.

*Hors d'œuvre*—A small dish, served during the first course.

# COOKERY TERMS EXPLAINED

*Hatelets*—The same as Atelets.

*Lard*—To stick bacon, or other specified articles, into poultry, meat, &c.; it is done by means of a larding-pin, one end of which is pointed, the other square, and hollow; the lardon is put into this hollow, the point is then inserted into the meat, and on being drawn out, leaves the lardon standing up in its proper place.

*Lardons*—The pieces into which bacon and other things are cut, for the purpose of larding meat &c. &c.

*Larding-pan*—an utensil by means of which meat, &c. is larded.

*Liaison*— A finish with yokes of eggs and cream, for ragouts and sauces.

*Lisse*, see page 376.

*Madeleines*— Cakes made of the same composition as pound-cakes.

*Maigre*— Soups, &c. dressed without meat.

*Marinade*— A prepared pickle for meat, fish, &c.

*Mask*— To cover completely.

*Nouilles*— An Italian paste, resembling macaroni; it is flat, instead of being in pipes.

*Panada*— Bread soaked in milk, used principally for *quenelles* and fine farces.

*Passer*—To fry lightly.

*Pate*— A raised crust pie.

*Petit Boulet*, see page 376.

*Petit Lisse*, see page 376.

*Petit Perle*, see page 376.

*Petit Plume*, see page 376.

*Petit Queue de Cochon*, see page 376.

*Poele*— A light braise for white meats. The difference between this and the braise is, that in the former the meat, or whatever it may be, need not be so much done as in the latter.

*Potage*— Another term for soup.

*Puree*— Any meat, fish, or other article, boiled to a pulp, and rubbed through a sieve.

*Quenelles*— A fine farce, it is generally poached when used.

*Salmi*— A highly seasoned hash.

*Sauter*—To fry very lightly.

*Sabotiere, or Sorbetiere*— A pewter or tin vessel, in which are placed the moulds containing the substance to be frozen.

*Souffle*, see page 376.

*Tammy*—A silk sieve.

*Tourner, or Turn*--- To stir a sauce; also to pare and cut roots, vegetables, and fruits, neatly.

*Tourte*--- A puff-paste pie.

*Vanner*--- To take up sauce, or other liquid, in a spoon, and turn it over quickly.

# THE COOK'S OWN BOOK

## Publisher's Supplementary Glossary

**Note:** *Refer to receipt content when more than one definition is given. Many terms used have variable spellings but are similar in meaning.*

*Advoirdupois weight*— The system in common use in English-speaking countries, i.e., 1 lb. = 16 oz.

*Alembic*— Apparatus formerly used in distillation.

*Angelica powder*— Angelica; any of the genus of herbs of the carrot family. A biennial whose roots and fruit furnish a flavoring oil.

*Apothecaries' weight*—The system used for compounding medical prescriptions, i.e., 1 lb. = 12 oz.

*Arrow-root*— A West Indian plant yielding an easily digestible starch.

*Bain-marie*— Also known as a water bath; a large pan filled with water in which saucepans are set. Used to keep prepared foods hot and moist and for cooking delicate foods such as custards and sauces.

*Bitter Almonds*— More strongly flavored then sweet almonds, they contain traces of lethal prussic acid when raw— the toxicity is destroyed when the nuts are heated. (Currently their sale is illegal in the United States.) Used to flavor extracts, liqueurs, and orgeat syrup.

*Bergamot*— A kind of orange having pear-shaped fruit, or any one of several kinds of mint.

*Biscuit*— English term for a small, flat, usually sweetened cake; a cookie.

*Blancmange*— (See also Blanc Mange) A dessert made from gelatinous or starchy substances and milk, usually sweetened, flavored and shaped in a mold.

*Bolus Armenicum*— (See also bolus armena) Armenian bole; a soft clayey, bright-red earth used as a coloring material and, formerly, in medicine.

*Bonne bouche*—(Fr.) a pleasant taste; hence, a tidbit.

*Brimstone*— Sulphur.

*Bullace*— A small wild or half-domesticated European plum related to the damson, but of inferior quality.

*Cappillaire*— Any simple sirup flavored with orange flowers; or the maidenhair fern, or a sirup prepared from the maidenhair.

*Cardoon*— Large perennial plant related to the artichoke.

*Carmine*— Rich scarlet pigment made from cochineal.

*Catechu*— Extract of acacia heartwood; a resinous astringent substance.

*Caul*— Thin fatty membrane that lines the abdominal cavity, usually taken from pigs or sheep; pork caul is considered superior. It resembles a lacy net used to wrap and contain pâtés and forcemeats and melts during the baking or cooking process.

*Cedret*— Cedrat; fruit similar to a lemon; citron.

*Cochineal*— A red dye made of dried female cochineal insects.

*Codling*— A small immature apple (Eng.: cooking apple); a young cod or hake.

*Collops*—Slices of meat.

*Coltsfoot*— A perennial European herb.

*Comfits*— Fruits or vegetables preserved in sugar, often with brandy added. Also meat or poultry preserved in its own fat.

*Cucurbite*— A gourd or similar plant product, often used for distillation.

*Cullis*— A sauce or gravy, sometimes with meat added.

*Device*—Anything fancifully and ingeniously designed, as a trinket; an artistic motif.

*Digester*— An autoclave, a vessel used to extract soluble elements by cooking.

*Drachm*— A dram; from the Greek, Drachma. 1/16 oz. advoirdupois weight.

*Eschalot*— Shallot; a small onion.

*Espagnole sauce*— Made by boiling meat, flavoring vegetables and spices, in beef broth to a glaze, and thickening.

*Faggot*— A bundle of sticks or other items.

*Foolscap paper*— Writing paper.

*Forcemeat*— A mixture of finely chopped and highly seasoned meat or fish, vegetables, or bread, either served alone or used as a stuffing.

*Frangipane*— A species of pastry cream flavored with almonds; also the cream-filled tart.

*Galange* — Rhizome of the sedge family.

*Gateau*—A cake (Fr.).

*Gill*— Four fluid ounces.

*Gum Arabic*—A water-soluble gum from acacia trees used in confectionary and pharmacy.

*Gum-benjamin*— Benzoin. A fragrant balsamic resin obtained from the Styrax tree.

*Gum-dragon*—Tragacanth— a gum obtained from various trees used as an emulsifying agent.

*Haggis Bag*— Sheep or calf stomach.

*Hartshorn*— Deer horn shavings, used as a form of gelatin.

*Horehound*— A bitter mint with hoary, downy leaves; extract or confection made from this plant.

*Hyssop*— A European mint with highly aromatic and pungent leaves; (Local U.S.: any of several species of artemisia).

*Isinglass*— A semi-transparent very pure gelatin prepared from the air bladders of fishes (such as sturgeons).

*Jamaican Pepper*— Allspice.

*Lake*— Purplish red pigment prepared from lac or cochineal.

*Lambstones*— Testicles of lambs.

*Lights*— The lungs, esp. of a slaughtered animal.

*Love-apples*— Tomato (trans. from French: *pomme d'amour.*)

*Lozenges*— Shapes which have four equal sides and two obtuse angles; diamond.

*Mace*— A membrane covering the nutmeg seed. Sold ground; when whole, it is called a "blade."

*Malmsey*— Greek sweet wine.

*Mallows root*— Mallow is a plant similar to okra.

*Masse pain*— Marzipan. (See also Marchpane).

*Matrass*— A glass flask with a long neck.

*Mazarine*— A kind of deep dish or plate.

*Medlar*— A small Eurasian tree; the fruit resembles crabapples and is widely used for preserves.

*Naples biscuit*— Ladyfingers.

*Neat*— The common domestic bovine.

*Negus*— A beverage of wine, hot water, sugar, lemon juice, and spices.

*Noyeau rouge*— Noyau. A liqueur made from brandy and walnuts.

*Orris-root*— Fragrant root stock of iris; the powdered root is used in sachets.

*Packthread*— Strong thread or small twine.

*Pastils*— Drops of low-melting food substances prepared in small portions; e.g. chocolate drops.

*Pearl-ashes*— See Perlash.

*Perlash*— Pearlash (potassium carbonate) is a purified form of potash, which is the residue which remains from evaporating liquid lye. Pearlash, or pearl-ash, was used as a leavening agent in baking, as we now use baking soda or powder.

*Pipkin*— Small earthenware or metal pot usually with a horizontal handle.

*Pippin*— Cooking apple, usually yellow-skinned, flushed with red.

*Porter*—A weak stout, rich in saccharine matter and containing about four per cent alcohol; originally a mixture of ale and stout.

*Poult*— Young fowl, esp. a young turkey (pullet).

*Powder sugar*—(See also powder-sugar.) Fine granulated sugar, not modern confectioner's sugar. Granulated sugar was sold in a loaf or cone.

*Quartern loaf*— A quartern loaf weighed 4 lbs. 5-1/2 oz. (the weight of a loaf baked from a quarter peck of flour). Quartern means a quarter, or 1/4 of a measure.

*Ratafia*— Sweet alcoholic beverage made from the infusion of flavoring and a spirit; also called cordial or liqueur.

*Rattleran*— The upper back section of the plate piece in beef, often corned.

*Rectified spirit*— Purified alcohol, esp. by repeated distillation.

*Sack*— Sherry.

*Salamander*— A cast-iron dish at the end of a long rod, heated and passed closely over the top of food to brown it; it can still be purchased.

*Samphire*— Old world seashore plant of the parsley family; same as glasswort.

*Sago*— Starch from the sago palm, usually in pellet form.

*Saponaceous*— Resembling or having the qualities of soap.

*Scorzonera*— A European herb; black salsify.

*Scrag of mutton*—The neck or back of a sheep's neck.

*Sloe*— Small astringent fruit of the blackthorn.

*Sippit*—A small piece of toasted or fried bread for garnishing.

*Sprat*— Small herring.

*Succedaneum*— Substitute.

*Sweetbreads*— The thymus of a young animal (calf or lamb).

*Sweet herbs*— Parsley, thyme, shallots, mushrooms, pepper, and salt.

*Teneriffe*— A white wine.

*Trail*— Entrail; the intestines of game birds.

*Treacle*— Molasses (chiefly Brit.).

*Treddle*— (See also treadle). The incipient embryo in an egg, generally newly-laid.

*Veal blond* — Concentrated meat juice or stock added to a sauce to strengthen or color it; veal juice.

*Vol-au-vent*— A large baked patty shell filled with a ragout of meat, fowl, game or fish in a sauce.

*Wine lees*— The dregs or sediment of wine.

# Rare Book Republishers

P.O. Box 3202
Merrifield, VA., 22116-3202
Tel. 703-573-5116
FAX 703-573-5897

Please send _____ copies of The Cook's Own Book, (1832) @$28.95 each $_____

*Less discount if applicable* [1]  $_____

Postage and Handling [2]  $_____

For Virginia residents, add 4.5% sales tax, or $1.30 each  $_____

Total Enclosed  $_____

[1] **20% discount for 3 or more copies**

[2] **Postage and Handling:**

No. Of Copies
1. . . . . . . . . . .$2.50      4. . . . . . . . . .$8.50
2. . . . . . . . . . .$4.75      5. . . . . . . . . .$10.00
3. . . . . . . . . . .$6.75      6 or more, add $1.00 per copy.

SHIP TO:   Name_____

Address _____

City_____ State_____ ZIP_____

Daytime telephone number _____
(We appreciate having your phone number in case there is a question concerning your order.)

Please let us know if you would like to receive announcements of forthcoming publications from RBR.    ☐ Yes  ☐ No

# Thank you for your Order.